RETAILING
Principles and Methods

RETAILING

Principles and Methods

DELBERT J. DUNCAN, Ph.D.
Professor of Marketing, Emeritus
Schools of Business Administration
University of California

CHARLES F. PHILLIPS, Ph.D., LL.D., L.H.D., Litt.D.
President Emeritus
Bates College

Seventh Edition · 1967
RICHARD D. IRWIN, INC.
Homewood, Illinois

SEVENTH EDITION

First Printing, April, 1967
Second Printing, November, 1967
Third Printing, May, 1968
Fourth Printing, November, 1968

Library of Congress Catalog Card No. 66–29976
PRINTED IN THE UNITED STATES OF AMERICA

To
MARY H. DUNCAN
and
FRANK G. PHILLIPS

Preface

Retailing continues in a state of ferment, accentuated by the technological developments of recent years, as well as by changes in the environment within which retail stores must operate. New management methods are being devised and new tools are being utilized as executives become increasingly aware of their responsibilities and opportunities in the highly dynamic conditions of today. In this seventh edition of *Retailing: Principles and Methods,* the authors have attempted to review and to evaluate the many elements of ferment in the retail field and to discuss the responses of retailing institutions, including management policies and operating methods.

In the process of revision, the entire volume has been subjected to close scrutiny to improve its effectiveness as a teaching instrument. Suggestions from students, teachers, and businessmen have been welcomed and incorporated in the treatment. And, as the comprehensive documentation and the supplementary readings at the close of each chapter indicate, each chapter has been brought up-to-date in terms of current thought on the subject, including recent and prospective changes in policies and methods. In addition, some changes in chapter titles and in the organization of material within chapters should prove helpful both to student and teacher.

Although the present volume has been extensively revised throughout, certain major changes suggested mainly by our colleagues should be mentioned.

First, to provide a setting or background for a study of retail store management, the first chapter is devoted to "Retailing: Its Structure and Environment." This approach provides the reader with an understanding of the various types of retailing establishments in our economy and the significant developments taking place in the major environments within which retailers must operate today—social, economic, technological, legal, and governmental. Responses of retailers to these developments also are considered briefly.

Second, automation in its various forms—particularly Electronic Data

Processing (EDP)—is discussed in appropriate chapters. This subject is so broad that it is difficult to do it justice and still confine our textbook within reasonable teaching limits. Chief emphasis, therefore, is given to its application as a control device in the chapters on "Merchandise Management," "Control of Sales Transactions," and in the handling of "Retail Credit." In the final chapter, devoted to broad aspects of managerial control, the contributions of automation to the improvement of management effectiveness is given attention.

Third, the chapters on "Retail Management Requirements" and "Retailing and the College Graduate" now place even greater emphasis on the role of the retail executive, especially in such areas as giving direction to the entire enterprise, motivating change, and long-range planning. The executive's part in developing the proper organizational structure and in planning the store's personnel activities are stressed in the chapters dealing with these aspects of retailing.

Fourth, in view of the rapid shifts currently occurring in the location of retail stores, it is inevitable that additional attention be devoted to this subject. In the chapter on "Store Location," the reader will find an up-to-date discussion of the evolution from the city to the metropolis to megalopolis, as well as shopping centers, free-standing stores, and the future of downtown areas.

Finally, in the chapter on "Managing Incoming Merchandise," we give greater emphasis to various aspects of the physical distribution of merchandise. In view of the rising cost of receiving, marking, and storing merchandise, this additional attention seems justified.

The listing of "Selected Cases from Current Case Books" has been omitted from this edition because no recent editions of any of those listed previously, or of similar new ones, are available. Teachers desiring to use case materials will find a variety of them in the *Teacher's Manual* provided without charge to adopters of this textbook.

In the Preface of the preceding edition it was stated that "We are fully aware of the trend toward emphasizing 'Management,' both in titles of textbooks and in courses covering all phases of marketing. In our judgment, however, effective retailing management is based on a broad knowledge of current practices and essential principles governing courses of action in the retail field. Consequently, no change has been made in the title of the book, which has proved to be satisfactory for many years." Experience has served to confirm that judgment. We have also, as in that preceding edition, retained as a distinctive feature of the book the chapter on opportunities and careers in retailing but under a new title, "Retailing and the College Graduate."

As in previous editions, it is not feasible to name all of our former students, teachers, and businessmen who have contributed ideas and suggestions for improving this volume. They are primarily responsible for its widespread adoption through six previous editions. The authors are deeply grateful for this assistance and hope that the present edition will continue to meet the needs of both (1) college and business school students, and (2) employees and executives of retail stores interested in understanding the place of retailing in our economy, and in the effective performance of the retailing function.

DELBERT J. DUNCAN
CHARLES F. PHILLIPS

March, 1967

Table of Contents

PART VII.   RETAIL CONTROL

INDEX

PART I

The Retail Revolution

1

CHAPTER

Retailing: Its Structure and Environment

The dynamic nature of *retailing*—a term which covers the activities involved in selling consumers' goods to ultimate consumers—has never been demonstrated better than during the 1960s. Tremendous changes in the broad environment within which retailers of all kinds must operate—including social, economic, technological, and competitive aspects—have forced adjustments in policies, methods, and in managerial strategy that justify the term "fantastic." And the end is not yet in sight!

Since current developments may make retailing tomorrow significantly different from retailing today, it is important that the nature and implications of these changes be appreciated by the student early in his study of this field. The development of such an appreciation is the goal of this chapter. To this end, we shall, first, note certain basic facts about the present status of retailing in the United States. Second, we will examine some of the current major environmental changes affecting retailing operations. Finally, our attention will be directed to retailing's responses to these changes.

In view of the reader's background from the basic marketing course[1] and because of the discussion in succeeding chapters, relatively few statistics will be included in this chapter. The reader seeking statistical support for the trends cited can find it by referring to the subject index at the end of this volume. The index can also be used to locate definitions of any terms with which the reader may not be familiar.

---

[1] Where this background is lacking, the chapters dealing with retailing institutions in a marketing text should be read. Cf. C. F. Phillips and D. J. Duncan, *Marketing: Principles and Methods* (5th ed.; Homewood, Ill.: Richard D. Irwin, Inc., 1964), chaps vi–xi.

RETAILERS IN THE UNITED STATES TODAY

The Nature of Retailing

Retailing: A Study in Contrasts. In the United States there are about 1,708,000 business establishments engaged in retailing.[2] Some of these retail units are very small, with daily sales of as little as $20; others have sales of $100,000 or more each business day. Some carry small assortments of very limited lines of goods—for example, the tobacco shop and the small newsstand; the department stores, in contrast, carry broad assortments of many kinds of goods. Some stores extend a large number of services along with the goods they sell—credit, delivery, sale on approval, music while you shop, and air conditioning; others offer their goods for sale in establishments where the service is so limited that the customer has to serve herself. Certain stores are well managed and operated; others show obvious signs of poor management. Some stores are organized as proprietorships, others as partnerships and cooperatives; still others have taken the corporate form of business organization. Alongside of the independently owned and operated store, we find the store controlled by an organization with a thousand or more units. Truly, a study of the retail establishments of this country is a study in contrasts.

Yet if we look beneath some of the contrasting features of the 1,708,000 retail establishments in the United States, we find that the operators of these stores have more in common than is apparent at first glance. As already indicated, practically all of them are engaged in the final stage of the marketing of consumers' goods: They obtain goods from various sources of supply and resell to ultimate consumers. More specifically, retailers exist to serve their customers and prospective customers through providing wanted goods and services at the proper times, places, and prices. In the performance of these tasks there are certain basic activities or functions to be performed. Generally speaking, these are the same as the marketing functions and are classified in the same manner. For example, buying and selling are known as functions involving transfer of title; transporting, storage, and plant maintenance are functions involving physical supply; and financing, risk raking, market information, and personnel management are termed "facilitating functions."[3]

---

[2] Cf. Table 1–1, p. 5, below.

[3] For detailed discussions of the marketing functions see any of the "standard" textbooks on marketing.

Methods of Retailing. The retail functions are performed by organizations that reach customers in one or more of four ways: through stores, the mail, house-to-house salesmen, and automatic vending machines. Of these ways—commonly termed "methods of retailing"—stores are most important, accounting for about 97 percent of all retail sales. Mail-order retailing and house-to-house selling are each responsible for nearly 1 percent. Although census data show sales through vending machines of $1.45 billion or about 0.6 percent of all retail sales, these figures considerably understate the importance of this method of retailing. Many vending machines are located in stores and their sales are reported in the figures for these establishments. Actually, vending machines probably dispense merchandise valued from $3 to $4 billion annually, and the total may well reach the $4 or $5 billion level in the next few years.[4]

Our Retailing Structure

Number and Sales of Retailers. Table 1–1 shows the number of retailers, total retail sales, and average sales per store for selected years

TABLE 1–1

RETAILERS AND SALES, SELECTED YEARS, 1929–1966

Year	Number of Retailers (000 Omitted)	Total Sales (000,000 Omitted)	Average Sales per Store
1929	1,476	$ 48,330	$ 33,000
1933	1,526	25,037	16,000
1935	1,588	32,791	21,000
1939	1,770	42,042	24,000
1948	1,770	130,521	74,000
1954	1,722	169,968	99,000
1958	1,788	199,646	112,000
1963	1,708	244,202	143,000
1964	n.a.	261,630	n.a.
1965	n.a.	283,950	n.a.
1966	n.a.	303,686	n.a.

SOURCE: The 1929–63 data are from the *Census of Business*. The sales estimated for 1964–66 are from the U.S. Department of Commerce as reported in the *Wall Street Journal*, January 11, 1967, p. 2. These data are not strictly comparable for all the years covered by this table. Not included in the 1963 sales figures are the $1.8 billion made by commissaries, exchanges, and eating places operated for military personnel by the Department of Defense. Moreover, sales in Alaska and Hawaii are included for 1963 and later years.

---

[4] *1963 Census of Business, Retail Trade, United States Summary*, BC63-RA1 (Washington, D.C.: U.S. Government Printing Office, 1965), pp. 1-7 and 1-8. Vending machine sales are from the National Automatic Merchandising Association.

beginning in 1929. In examining these figures, however, we must bear in mind the substantial decline in the price level between 1929 and 1933 and the increase following the latter year, especially since 1939. It was this decline in the price level which was largely responsible for the 48 percent decrease in retail sales between 1929 and 1933; likewise, rising prices played an important role in the more than twelvefold gain since 1933. By no means has the physical volume of goods sold at retail fluctuated as much as the dollar figures might lead one to believe.

TABLE 1–2

RETAIL SALES BY TYPE OF OUTLET, 1948, 1954, 1958, 1963
(In Billions of Dollars)

Type of Outlet	1948	1954	1958	1963	% change 1958 to 1963
Food...............................	$ 29.2	$ 39.8	$ 49.3	$ 57.1	16.0
Automotive group.................	20.1	29.9	31.9	45.4	42.2
Filling stations....................	6.5	10.7	14.2	17.8	24.8
Eating and drinking places..........	10.6	13.1	15.3	18.4	20.4
Apparel and accessory stores........	9.7	11.1	12.6	14.0	11.7
Department stores.................	9.4	10.6	13.4	20.5	53.7
Lumber-building materials group....	11.1	13.1	14.3	14.6	2.0
Furniture and appliance stores.......	6.6	9.0	10.1	10.9	8.1
Variety stores (limited prices).......	2.5	3.1	3.6	4.5	25.3
General and general merchandise stores......................	3.9	4.2	4.9	4.9	0.6
Drug and proprietary stores........	4.0	5.3	6.8	8.5	24.7
All others......................	15.2	20.1	24.0	27.6	15.0
Totals...................	$128.8	$170.0	$200.4	$244.2	21.9

SOURCE: Same as Table 1–1, except that the figures have been adjusted to the more recent census definitions for each type of outlet.

Although total dollar sales have increased from a low of $25 billion in 1933 to a high of nearly $304 in 1966, the total number of retail stores has remained surprisingly steady during the period covered by Table 1–1. Consequently, the average sales per store have risen rapidly from a low of $16,000 in 1933 to $143,000 in 1963 and have likely increased further since that time.

Sales by Type of Retail Outlet. In Table 1–2, retail sales have been classified by the type of retail outlet. The importance of retailers who deal mainly in food is evident from the fact that in 1963 they accounted for 23.4 percent of all sales, this figure increasing to 30.9 percent if eating and drinking places are also included. The automotive group transacted 18.6 percent of all sales, and department stores accounted for 8.4 percent.

Independent and Chain Stores. Census data make it clear that the great predominance of our stores—87 percent of all—are operated by firms which have only one store in the same general kind of business and that such stores account for 63 percent of all retail sales. Firms operating more than one store in the same general kind of business control about 13 percent of all stores, with 37 percent of all retail sales.

So far as chain stores are concerned, their importance in the retail field varies by kind of business. In contrast to their average of 37 percent of the retail business in all fields, the chains did 83 percent of all business in variety stores, 61 percent in shoe stores, 57 percent in food stores, 33 percent in drugstores, and 25 percent in furniture stores.[5]

Surveying trends in the retail field as a whole, it is noteworthy that the chains accounted for 30 percent of all retail business in 1929 and 37 percent in 1963—an insignificant change in view of the many shifts which have taken place in retailing during more than three decades. It is evident, therefore, that despite the growth of chain-store organizations, the predominant retail institution is still the small single-unit store. This fact is made increasingly apparent in the following two paragraphs.

Retailers by Size of Establishment and Firm. The small size of the typical retail establishment often astonishes the person who is not well acquainted with retailing conditions. Using annual sales as the measure of size and relying upon 1963 data, 23 percent of all stores had sales of less than $20,000 for the year; and they transacted only 2.3 percent of all retail

TABLE 1-3

RELATIVE DISTRIBUTION OF RETAIL ESTABLISHMENTS IN OPERATION NOVEMBER 15, 1963, BY NUMBER OF PAID EMPLOYEES

Number of Employees	Percentage of Establishments
0–5	79.9
6–9	9.5
10–19	6.1
20–49	3.6
50–99	0.6
100 or more	0.3
Total	100.0

SOURCE: *1963 Census of Business, Retail Trade —Employment Size,* BC63–RS3 (Washington, D.C.: U.S. Government Printing Office, 1965), p. 3-1. Figures are for establishments operated during the entire year.

[5] *1963 Census of Business, Retail Trade—Single Units and Multiunits,* BC63-RS4 (Washington, D.C.: U.S. Government Printing Office, 1965), pp. 4-2 to 4-8.

TABLE 1-4

SALES AND EARNINGS OF THE 25 LARGEST RETAILERS, 1964 AND 1965

Company	Sales (Thousands of Dollars)			Earnings After Taxes (Thousands of Dollars)			Profit Margin	
	1964	1965	Percent Change	1964	1965	Percent Change	1964	1965
Sears	5,740,035	6,390,000	11.3	304,094	323,348	6.3	5.3	5.1
A & P	5,079,564	5,118,978	0.8	52,133	52,339	0.4	1.0	1.0
Safeway	2,817,569	2,939,043	4.3	49,980	48,185	− 3.6	1.8	1.6
Kroger	2,327,563	2,555,109	9.8	27,923	31,302	12.1	1.2	1.2
Penney	2,079,426	2,289,209	10.1	68,271	78,898	15.6	3.3	3.4
Montgomery Ward	1,697,391	1,748,360	3.0	21,865	23,963	9.6	1.3	1.4
Woolworth	1,338,366	1,443,322	7.8	57,793	73,001	26.3	4.3	5.1
Federated	1,257,035	1,330,737	5.9	64,469	70,518	9.4	5.1	5.3
Food Fair	1,119,640	1,204,520	7.6	8,847*	10,957*	35.4	0.8	0.8
Acme	1,161,198	1,200,750	3.4	12,884	10,450	−18.9	1.1	0.9
National Tea	1,122,516	1,161,948	3.5	10,640	11,316	6.4	1.0	1.0
Allied Stores	893,373	955,490	7.0	17,735	22,255	25.5	2.0	2.3
Winn-Dixie	894,648	951,273	6.3	21,622	23,372	8.1	2.4	2.5
Jewel	790,980	874,007	10.5	13,550	14,971	10.5	1.7	1.7
May	843,500	869,169	3.0	43,195	45,860	6.2	5.1	5.3
Kresge	688,776	851,443	23.6	17,374	22,154	27.5	2.5	2.6
Grant	769,921	839,715	9.1	22,526	31,248	38.7	2.9	3.7
Korvette	719,941	800,000†	11.1	9,978	—‡	—	1.4	—
Grand Union	740,040	779,683	5.4	9,572	10,852	13.4	1.3	1.4
Macy	663,983	704,449§	6.1	15,256	17,630§	15.6	2.3	2.5
First National	706,670	684,492	− 3.1	5,560	2,385	−57.1	0.8	0.3
Gamble-Skogmo	555,463	608,243	9.5	11,270	12,539	11.3	2.0	2.1
Gimbel	536,008	560,941	4.7	14,913	18,215	22.1	2.8	3.2
Associated Dry Goods	496,545	526,056	5.9	17,496	22,292	27.4	3.5	4.2
McCrory	547,433	513,229	− 6.2	8,666	10,063	16.1	1.6	2.0

* Excludes special credits.
† Estimated sales, year ending July 31, 1966.
‡ Earnings 39 weeks ending May 1, 1966 were $9,425,000 vs. $15,510,000 for 39 weeks ending May 2, 1965.
§ 52 weeks ended April 30, 1966 vs. 52 weeks ended May 1, 1965.
SOURCE: *Business Week*, July 23, 1966, p. 73.

business.[6] These stores, together with those in the $20,000–$49,999 class, which accounted for 26.5 percent of all stores and 5.4 percent of all sales, may be considered as small stores. Hence small stores accounted for 49.5 percent of all stores and 7.7 percent of all sales. At the other extreme, 5.2 percent of all stores each had sales of $500,000 or over; and these stores together did slightly over one half (51.1 percent) of all retail business. In between these two extreme groups, we find 45.3 percent of all the stores (stores with sales from $50,000 to $499,999 per year) doing 41.2 percent of the business. These establishments may be designated as medium-sized stores.

When another measure of size is used—the number of employees—the small size of our typical retail firm becomes even more apparent. An examination of Table 1–3 reveals that 79.9 percent of the retail establishments employed 5 persons or less, and that 95.5 percent employed 19 or less. Despite the fact that sales of retail stores of all sizes have increased substantially in recent years, the retail structure is still composed of a very large number of small stores, a fairly large number of medium-sized establishments, and a very small number of gigantic stores.

Some Large Retail Organizations. In view of the sales importance of some of our major retail companies, Table 1–4 reports 1964 and 1965 sales and earnings for twenty-five of the largest retailers. Of particular interest are (1) the sharp increases in sales by S. S. Kresge, Sears, Roebuck and Company, Korvette, Jewel, and J. C. Penney; (2) substantial advances in earnings by Food Fair Stores, W. T. Grant, S. S. Kresge, F. W. Woolworth, Associated Dry Goods, and Allied Stores; and (3) declines in profit margins for Sears and three food chains—First National Stores, Acme, and Safeway.

THE CHANGING ENVIRONMENT OF RETAILING[7]

With the foregoing brief background on the structure of retailing, let us turn to the tremendous changes taking place in the environment within which retailers must operate. In reality, this environment consists of several significant forces or elements such as social, economic, technological, and competitive, each of which for practical purposes may be considered an

[6] These data are from *1963 Census of Business, Retail Trade—Sales Size,* BC63–RS2 (Washington, D.C.: U.S. Government Printing Office, 1965), p. 2-2. They cover only those establishments which operated the entire year.

[7] Although many readers will have covered similar material to that in this section in the basic marketing course, numerous others will not have done so. In any event, both groups should benefit from a review of the environmental factors currently affecting retailing.

environment by itself. The retailer should be familiar with these forces because they have a vital impact on his policies, practices, and ultimate success.

Social Forces Affecting Retailing

Multitudes of social forces have influenced the conduct of retail enterprises over the years and these forces have been particularly strong since World War II. Only a few of them may be mentioned here, but those discussed indicate the broad spectrum of developments with which retailers must cope in our growing, dynamic economy.

Overall Population Growth. In the fifty-year period between 1910 and 1960 the population of continental United States grew from 92 to 178 million persons. If we include the newly admitted states of Alaska and Hawaii, the latter figure exceeds 179 million, an increase of almost 28 million or more than 18 percent in the last census decade alone. More recent years have witnessed a continuation of this "population explosion." On March 1, 1966 it is estimated that our total resident population reached 195 million, an advance in six years of about 16 million or 8.9 percent.[8] Projections for the next two decades indicate still further growth—over 223 million by 1975 and 268 million by 1985[9]—although there has been a slowdown in the rate in recent years and these projections may require revision downward if present trends continue.

Also of interest to the retailer is the formation of households and families, since these constitute buying units from his point of view. The number of households in the United States has been increasing recently at a rate of about 900,000 a year and it is probable that before the 1960s are over the rate will be one million. By 1975 the total number may reach 70 million or more.

Population Growth in Certain Age Groups. The teenage and young adult segments of our population especially are showing tremendous growth. Between 1960 and 1964 the 14–17 age group in our country increased 27.3 percent, while the 18–24 age group gained 17.2 percent. By 1970 it is expected that there will be 99 million persons under 25 years of age out of a projected total of 208 million.[10] Taking another segment of our population—the 20 to 34 age group—one close student of this subject

---

[8] *Population Estimates,* Current Population Reports, Series P–25, No. 334 (Washington, D.C.: U.S. Department of Commerce, Bureau of the Census, April 14, 1966), p. 1.

[9] *Population Estimates,* Current Population Reports, Series P–25, No. 329, March 10, 1966, p. 1.

[10] "Will Markets Develop as Hoped?" *Business Week,* May 15, 1965, p. 32.

estimates that it will increase 40 percent in the next decade, more than twice that of any other age group.[11] Our youth-oriented economy and the prospect that we may well be in it for some time, has important implications for the retailer.[12]

The "over 65" segment of our population also continues to grow rapidly, and will probably gain about 50 percent between 1960 and 1985. By the latter year there may well be over 25 million of these "oldsters."[13]

Mobility of Our People. Retailing is also affected by the mobility of our residents, a phenomenon which has long prevailed. Since Colonial days our people have shifted from the East to the new agricultural lands of the West, from rural to urban areas, from major cities to suburbs, and, more recently, some of them have abandoned suburbia in favor of city living—not to mention the movements from one region or state to another in our large country.[14]

Significantly, also, our farm population has declined steadily since the 1930s. During the decade of the 1950s alone, the net migration from farms to metropolitan areas averaged one million persons per year.

Suburban Living. The movement of people into metropolitan areas, and particularly into the suburbs, has brought about important changes in their modes of living, in their buying behavior, and in their future expectations as members of our affluent society.

Our great middle class has, as one informed observer expresses it, "suddenly experienced a widening horizon of the economic good life: [these people want] a better house, . . . better education for their children, improved health and medical care, opportunity to develop all kinds of personal interests and hobbies, vacations, travel, sports, a second car, and all the expensive household conveniences of the modern age."[15] These desires for casual living, for more and better quality merchandise, and in general for a better standard of living, have generated demands which have exceeded current income in many instances. One result has been a tremendous surge

---

[11] Arno Johnson in *Advertising Age*, August 9, 1965, p. 72.

[12] States George Katona, [This group is] "not savings oriented." And Burleigh Gardner agrees—"This is the great age for self-indulgence." Cf. "Young Single Spenders Pour It on the Market," *Business Week*, January 1, 1966, p. 52.

[13] "Will Markets Develop as Hoped?" *op. cit.*, p. 32. Also cf. M. S. Pitzele, "Spending and Consumption in Retirement: The Dimensions of the Over-65 Market Today and Tomorrow," *University of Houston Business Review*, Fall, 1965, pp. 24–31.

[14] One source notes that over 100,000 people change their addresses every day, 38 million a year, representing about 20 percent of our population. Cf. "The Movers," *Progressive Grocer*, November, 1965, pp. K35–58, Part II of a series on "Consumer Dynamics in the Market Place."

[15] M. P. McNair, in an address entitled "Change and Challenges in the Department Store Industry," New York City, October 5, 1964.

in "buying on time." Today the amount of consumer credit outstanding is at the highest level in our history.[16] Although this "widening horizon" is not confined to residents of our suburbs, it is probably most pronounced in these areas.

Other Social Forces. Examples of other changes in the social environment of retailing include the following: (1) Better-educated and better-informed buyers, notably reflected in the so-called "culture explosion," with the consequent accelerated demand for better quality merchandise and a higher standard of living;[17] (2) growing leisure,[18] resulting in the marked growth of such recreational activities as boating, bowling, and swimming, and in the utilization of leisure time through travel, search for art objects and antiques, attendance at concerts and similar affairs, and self-education in cultural subjects; (3) a sharpened "fashion consciousness" among all segments of our population, but especially among teenagers and the under-25-year-old group—and, although to a lesser degree, among adult men, evident not only in wearing apparel but also in cosmetics;[19] (4) changes in the composition of our working population, reflected in a higher proportion of better-educated and skilled men and in the number of married women employed;[20] (5) the continued expansion of services of various kinds; (6) the growth of our suburbs which has contributed to the deterioration of the downtown areas of the larger cities; and (7) the possible rebirth of some downtown areas as a result of urban renewal and other programs.[21]

The Economic Forces Affecting Retailing

Personal Income. Personal income, providing spending capacity for consumers and strongly affecting total retail sales, has shown a sharp rise in the United States. For the country as a whole, individual incomes rose

[16] For details, cf. pp. 13–14 and Chapter 22, "Retail Credit."

[17] One astute observer, however, remarks wryly: "We are continuously told that nearly 8 percent of our adult population now are college graduates, but we are not told that nearly 9 percent of the same adult population are so illiterate that they have difficulty reading a newspaper." E. A. Jones, *Printers' Ink*, July 9, 1965, p. 3.

[18] A recent investigation by the Stanford Research Institute led to the estimate that by 1975 Americans will be spending 30 percent of their waking hours involved in some form of leisure. Cf. William Royce and John Baumeister, *Home Furnishing Trends to 1975*, (Chicago, Illinois: National Retail Furniture Association, 1965).

[19] Cf. "Men's Toiletry Market: How Lusty Is It Really?" *Printers' Ink*, November 12, 1965, pp. 15–24. It is predicted that sales will double to $1 billion by 1970.

[20] In 1964 there were 25 million women workers in the United States. About 9.5 million were mothers with children under 18 years of age, and over 20 million had husbands living at home. Cf. "Who Are the Working Mothers?" a leaflet issued by the U.S. Department of Labor, 1965.

[21] Cf. the statement by the then Secretary of Commerce, J. T. Connor, "Looking Ahead to 1970," *Sales Management*, November 10, 1965, p. 23.

from $401 billion in 1960 to an estimated $528 billion in 1966, a gain in six years of $127 billion or over 31 percent.[22] Per capita income increased also, reaching a record $2,724. Viewed in the light of the sharp gain in civilian employment—from 66.7 million persons in 1960 to an estimated 74 million in 1966, an advance of 11 percent—the spending power generated is noteworthy indeed.[23] Although it is not possible at this time to judge accurately the effects on personal expenditures of the changes made in Social Security benefits in 1965, or those of the legislation increasing minimum wages, one authority estimates that by 1975 "discretionary income will grow to 66 percent of all disposable income after taxes."[24]

Distribution of Income. The growing affluence of our society is readily apparent if we examine the redistribution of income that has taken place in comparatively recent years. Families with annual incomes of $5,000 and over increased from 19 percent of the total in 1947 to 65 percent in 1964. In the latter year 10.8 million families, or about 22 percent of all, had incomes of $10,000 or more.[25] Arno Johnson is of the opinion that by 1975 the average income per household will exceed $11,300 and that the number of families of two or more persons with real purchasing power of more than $10,000 should grow to 28 million, or ten times the number existing in 1950.[26]

Consumer Credit. Still another significant factor in the economic environment affecting retailing is credit. Since 1945 private debt in this country has increased more than 500 percent and continues to advance 10 percent annually.[27] Personal debt now exceeds $264 billion—70 percent accounted for by mortgages—or $4,700 for the average American family. Revolving credit in department stores alone is about $2.5 billion, more than double that of 1961, while credit cards account for $633 million. Consumer installment credit reached an all-time high of $68 billion in 1966.[28] To pay off this enormous load takes 14.3 percent of disposable income.[29]

Still another way to look at the significance of credit is afforded by the

---

[22] "Total and Per Capita Personal Income, 1965—Record High in All States and Regions," *Survey of Current Business*, April, 1966, p. 7.

[23] Private spending in the United States (personal and business) was $404.2 billion in 1960 and is expected to reach $575 billion in 1966, a gain of some 42 percent. "A Measure of the Boom LBJ Sees Ahead," *U.S. News and World Report*, February 7, 1966, pp. 32–34.

[24] Arno Johnson, *op. cit.*, p. 72.

[25] U.S. Bureau of the Census material given in *Advertising Age*, June 21, 1965, p. 91. Also cf. "Tender, Loving Care for the Masses," *Business Week*, March 5, 1966, p. 84.

[26] Arno Johnson, *op. cit.*, p. 72.

[27] *Time*, June 18, 1965, p. 82.

[28] *Statistical Abstract of the United States* (Washington, D.C.: U.S. Bureau of the Census, 1966), p. 466.

[29] "Installment Credit Soars to a Record," *Business Week*, January 8, 1966, p. 46.

1965 annual "Survey of Consumer Finances" by the Survey Research Center of the University of Michigan which revealed that about 47 percent of all families are making time payments. Approximately one family out of four in debt is paying off a car, one out of five owes money on durable goods, and one out of twenty is financing additions and repairs to a home.[30]

It is clear that we are in a credit economy, one providing great opportunities and challenges to the retailer. But obligations are equally great. There is a vital, growing need for more careful appraisal of credit risks, closer scrutiny of the regularity of payments, and prompt follow-up on past-due accounts. The personal bankruptcy rate has increased recently in some areas.

Technological Developments Affecting Retailing

Very recent years have witnessed a real revolution in technology and the concomitant development of management science. Electronic technology, for example, has created a number of information-handling tools that are altering the processes of retail management.[31] With all business operations, including retailing, becoming more complicated in our dynamic economy, these changes are welcomed by all progressive retailers.[32]

Despite these developments, however, a gap of some magnitude continues to exist between the capabilities of the equipment and systems available and their use by retailers and others. Today there is an obvious need to equate management functions and electronic system capabilities. One student of this subject suggests we need to push ahead in two main areas: (1) ". . . the quest for new and improved devices and techniques to increase further the speed, capacity, reliability, and operating economy of computing and data processing systems;" and (2) ". . . a conceptual approach which seeks to develop new programs and new thinking that will take greater advantage of what the systems already offer as a direct aid to management."[33]

Developments in business electronics are but one significant factor in the technological environment affecting retailing. Among food retailers, for example, where chain stores and voluntary and cooperative groups predom-

---

[30] Reported in "Marketing Pictograph," *Sales Management,* October 1, 1965, p. 28.

[31] "The initial impact of computer science on business forces managers to rethink their basic business goals, to study their own aims and responsibilities, and to question their traditional patterns of operation." O. W. Tuthill, "The Thrust of Information Technology on Management," *Financial Executive,* January, 1966, p. 18.

[32] Also cf. the discussion of computers in Chapter 13, "Merchandise Management."

[33] E. W. Engstrom, "New Concepts in Business Electronics," *Retail Control,* October, 1963, Part II, p. 45.

inate, the impact of automation is of considerable magnitude.[34] It is evident in automatic merchandising, in office procedures, and in the various physical handling activities of store, warehouse, and distribution center operations.[35]

The Changing Competitive Environment

From our earlier discussion of retailing structure it is clear that the competitive environment of retailing is characterized by many types and sizes of stores, located in all kinds of areas, offering various assortments of merchandise, and providing a wide range of services to their customers. A brief examination of some of the competitive forces and developments now prevailing will demonstrate how retailers are responding to their changing environment, that retailing is an ever-changing field, that constant vigilance on the part of the retailer is necessary to strengthen or even maintain his competitive position, and that continuous innovation is a prime requisite of success under the turbulent conditions of today. This exploration takes place in the next section of this chapter.

RETAILING'S RESPONSE TO ENVIRONMENTAL CHANGES

The responses of retailing institutions to the changes taking place in their environment have varied sharply both in nature and in timing. Some progressive organizations are quick to recognize the opportunities and accept the challenges afforded by the changing environment surrounding them and respond with constructive action in various directions. Other firms are reluctant—even lethargic—in departing from existing operational patterns until changes are practically forced upon them by the activities of their competitors. To cite but one illustration, it was the lethargy and reluctance of many department stores during the 1950s that opened the door for more alert entrepreneurs, such as the discounters, convenience store operators, and others to enter the field and compete actively for consumer patronage.

The Discount House

This institution in its "primitive" form has existed for more than three decades, but its emergence as a going, highly-competitive retailer has come since 1950. Its nature and significance, in response to the changes taking

---

[34] Cf. J. W. Ewing and James Murphy, "Impact of Automation on United States Retail Food Distribution," *Journal of Retailing*, Vol. XLI, No. 1 (Spring, 1965), pp. 38–47.

[35] Cf. Chapter 15, "Handling Incoming Merchandise."

place in our economy, can best be understood by examining its characteristics.[36]

Characteristics of Full-Line Discount House. What this text refers to as a discount house has all or most of these features:

1. A broad merchandise assortment, including both "hard" and "soft" goods and frequently food as well.
2. Price lines aimed at low- and middle-income families.
3. Emphasis on rapid turnover of merchandise. Through relatively low prices and a rigid limitation of merchandise to the fast-moving items, the typical discount house turns its inventory about six times a year. However, such firms as King's Department Stores and Zayre's achieve from 12 to 15 stock turns annually.
4. Price as main sales appeal, even to the point of a willingness to bargain over prices where necessary. To this end, every effort is exerted to reduce operating cost.
5. Relatively inexpensive buildings, equipment, and fixtures. In contrast to a construction cost of $15–$20 per square foot for a department store, the discount house building may cost from $6 to $12.
6. Low-rent locations.
7. An emphasis on self-service operation with a minimum of salespeople where self-service is not applicable. Whereas payroll in a department store may equal 18 percent of sales, in the discount house this cost may be between 6 and 7 percent.
8. Limited customer services such as credit and delivery, or the offering of these services at a special charge to the customer.
9. Less use of merchandise and accounting controls than in the typical chain or department store.
10. Low profit as a percentage of sales (1 to 2 percent is quite common). However, the return on investment is very satisfactory (10 to 20 percent is not unusual).
11. Long hours, frequently from 10:00 A.M. to 10:00 P.M. and often including Sunday.
12. Large stores, with 50,000 to 100,000 square feet on one floor being common and 200,000 square feet or more not being too exceptional.
13. Large parking area.
14. A carnival atmosphere based on extensive sales promotional activities, including advertising, in-store display and promotions, and major special events.

Importance of Full-Line Discount Houses. The authors estimate that at the beginning of 1967 there were more than 2,900 retail institutions with the characteristics outlined in the previous section. Of these about 400 were opened in each of 1965 and 1966. Their sales in 1966 were between $11–$12 billion, up from $9–$10 billion the previous year and less than

---

[36] On the difficulties of formulating a satisfactory definition of a discount house cf. "Name-Game—Pin Tag on Discounters," *Women's Wear Daily,* July 28, 1966, pp. 1, 28.

$3 billion in 1960.[37] Looking ahead, their sales may reach $20–$25 billion before 1975.[38]

Other Low-Margin Retailers. There are many other retailers with some of the features of the full-time discount house, and some of these frequently add the word "discount" to their name. The food supermarket which has added a limited number of nonfood lines sometimes tries to capitalize on the current popularity of the discount house. Other food supermarkets have adopted the designation "discount food stores" for some of their units after (1) giving up trading stamps, (2) limiting their stocks to the more rapidly moving items, (3) eliminating their carry-out service, and (4) reducing their markups. Some women's apparel retailers have placed their dresses on pipe racks, adopted self-service selling, and entered upon an aggressive promotional program under the designation of discount house, instead of the more accurate term apparel supermarket. Appliance retailers and operators of hardware stores have likewise switched to the new name. Some of the older bargain-type stores—John's Bargain Stores, for example—which operate without a basic inventory, depending heavily on out-of-season, closed-out, and discontinued items, are termed discount houses by some retail students. In this text all these retailers are excluded from the discount house classification.

Future of the Discount House. It is evident that the discount house has assumed a role of importance among our retailing institutions. In this process it has had a strong impact on other retailers in two directions mainly. First, in a relatively few years discount houses have achieved annual sales of more than $11 billion that otherwise might have gone to other retail institutions. Second, they have forced many of the more conventional retailers to adopt some of the discounters' policies and methods to guard against the loss of additional sales volume. For example, some department stores such as Macy's in New York and Abraham & Straus of Brooklyn have reduced prices to meet all competition. Others have attempted to "trade-up" their merchandise[39] and service to attract a different clientele. Still others have turned to self-service basement stores, longer store hours with more night openings, and more extensive promotions.

Among the variety and junior department store chains, which have probably been hurt by the discount house more seriously than any other

[37] Cf. the annual census of discount stores in the late August issue of *Discount Store News*, August 22, 1966, pp. 17–119.

[38] "Discounters Sales Racing to New Highs," *Women's Wear Daily*, August 11, 1966, p. 1.

[39] Cf. Stanley Slom, "Haute Discount: Working up to the Joneses," *Women's Wear Daily*, December 28, 1965, pp. 1, 29.

retailer, Woolworth and Kresge have developed their own discount house chains—the former operating 27 Woolco Department Stores early in 1966 with 30 additional units scheduled for opening before January 1, 1967; and the latter with 122 K-Marts at the end of 1965.[40] W. T. Grant is also opening large retail units, as well as converting some of its smaller units to a junior-type discount operation.[41] Aldens, a division of Gamble-Skogmo, Inc., which operates mainly on a mail-order basis, has a number of discount houses under the name of Shoppers World and more are in the planning stage. Walgreen Company, a drug chain, is expanding a discount house chain through purchases and opening of new units. Melville Shoe Corporation, operator of Thom McAn shoe stores, is leasing shoe departments in discount stores. Women's apparel chains, such as Diana Stores and Franklin Stores, are buying discount stores, opening their own, and operating leased departments.

In an affluent society such as presently exists in this country it would seem that the appeal of the discount house to potential customers would decline. But this has not been the case! Despite some failures—characteristic of all retailing—well-managed discount firms have manifested an awareness of the changing status of their customers and potential customers by "trading up" their stores, their merchandise, their services, and their public relations. As a result their growth has continued and, if such alertness is demonstrated in the years ahead, the future of this retailing institution is assured.

Growth of Small, Convenience-Type Stores

These establishments, often called "bantam stores," are another recent development.[42] They offer a limited selection of brand-name merchandise but usually compensate for this by convenient locations and typically long hours—frequently 7 A.M. to 11 P.M.—on a seven-day a week basis. Sunday is their busiest day. These "vest-pocket" supermarkets cater to workers whose odd hours prevent their shopping regularly elsewhere and to customers who desire fast service. They operate with a minimum of personnel and usually are slightly higher on prices than their larger namesakes. Although the average sale may be between 50¢ and $1, their careful inventory control and low labor costs often enable them to earn more per dollar of sales than the conventional supermarkets.

---

[40] *Annual Report,* F. W. Woolworth Co., year ended December 31, 1965, p. 14; *Annual Report,* S. S. Kresge Co., year ended December 31, 1965, p. 6.

[41] E. B. Weiss, "Grant and Kresge Set Promising Plans for the Future of Variety Chains," *Advertising Age,* May 23, 1966, pp. 98, 100.

[42] For details cf. "Snaring Sales While Others Sleep," *Business Week,* November 6, 1965, p. 128 ff.

Most of these convenience stores are chain-operated by organizations such as the 7-Eleven of Dallas, Texas, with more than 1,700 stores; Li'l General Stores, Inc., with about 250 stores in the South; Utotem, Inc., with 235 stores in the Southwest; and the Lawson Milk Company, operating more than 500 stores in the Midwest. That stores of this type are fulfilling a genuine need is shown by the fact that their number increased from an estimated 5,000 in 1964 to 6,000 in 1965. During this period their sales gained over 13 percent to exceed $1 billion.[43]

Branch Stores[44]

The rapid growth of our suburbs following World War II, the deterioration of downtown areas, and the widespread ownership of the private automobile convinced many department stores of the need ". . . to sally forth from [their] protective downtown walls and join the battle in the open plains. . . ." through the opening of branch stores.[45] Yet some of the oldest and best known stores in all sections of the country failed to recognize the need for branches with the result that several paid the ultimate price— failure—for their oversight. Established in their "ivory towers," they considered themselves impregnable to the great social and economic changes swirling around them. But they were in the minority and today branch stores are "a way of life" among successful department stores throughout the United States.

Present indications are that branch stores will continue to increase in importance and will soon surpass—in some cases they have already done so —the sales volume of downtown stores.[46] One observer predicts that "by 1975 the leading stores will derive 70 to 80 percent of their annual volume from branch units; the branch units, in many instances, will be larger than the downtown units; they will be more truly modern department stores; [and] they will have a large measure of autonomy . . ."[47]

[43] R. D. Hershey, Jr., "Convenience Stores Filling Their Role," *New York Times,* January 23, 1966, pp. Fl, 12. Also cf. "The Bantam Store Looks Promising," *Super Market Merchandising,* October, 1965, pp. 28–33.

[44] Also cf. the discussions of this subject in Chapter 4, "Store Location," and Chapter 7, "Structure of the Retail Firm."

[45] McNair, *op. cit.*

[46] One large operator of such stores—May Department Stores Company—reports that in 1964 its 11 downtown stores did 45 percent of the business and that "shortly we will be doing two-thirds of our business in the suburbs." Cf. Wight Martindale, "May Co. Back from Huddle, Shop Concept a Key Goal," *Women's Wear Daily,* October 20, 1965, p. 12.

[47] E. B. Weiss, "Department Store Marketing Shifting Toward Bigger Chains, Bigger Units," *Advertising Age,* November 29, 1965, p. 76. Also cf. E. A. Miller, "Can Independent Stores Survive in Tomorrow's Mass Merchandising Era?", *Journal of Retailing,* Vol. XXXIX, No. 4 (Winter 1963–64), pp. 26–35 ff; and "Branch Stores—Is the Tail Wagging the Dog?" *Department Store Economist,* August, 1965, pp. 19–21.

Leased Departments

Extent of Leasing.   The practice of leasing departments is far from a new idea. For many years some department stores have used leased departments for millinery, beauty parlors, optical goods, jewelry, furs, books, groceries, shoes, candy, soda fountains, and restaurants. In other words, leasing arrangements are prevalent among both merchandise and service departments. That the number of leased departments is still growing is evident from a survey of some 200 department stores by the National Retail Merchants Association. On the average, one of every twelve merchandise departments and one of every two and one-half service departments were leased and, compared with two years before, 20 percent more stores were leasing merchandise departments and 14 percent more were leasing service departments. Leased departments typically produced 9 percent of sales.[48]

Leased departments have also long been used by supermarkets to expand their offerings in such areas as drugs, liquors, flowers, and other nonfood items. In some cases even the meat and produce departments have been leased. Yet the most significant growth of these departments in recent years has been among discount houses. Even the Woolco stores of the F. W. Woolworth Company and the K-Mart units of the S. S. Kresge Company rely upon leasing for some of their departments.

Chain organizations continue to increase in importance as operators of leased departments. One of the better known of these organizations is the Consolidated Millinery Company, which operates leased departments in large stores throughout the country. Some of the shoe chains—Melville Shoe Corporation and Crown Shoe are examples—are also important operators of leased departments. In recent years at least one large chain selling men's and women's clothing has begun to operate leased departments in department stores, while another chain specializing in men's and boys' clothing (Rockower Brothers, Inc.) is rapidly opening departments in discount houses. As to other fields, leased departments are operated by such chains as Kroger (foods), Diana (women's apparel), Katz Drug Company, Kay Jewelry Stores, Inc., and Reliable Furniture Corporation.

Leasing Arrangements.   While lease terms vary widely, in the department store field the lessor (the store) usually provides the necessary space, fixtures, heat, and light and, in addition, such services as bookkeeping,

---

[48] "Leased Departments," *Stores,* July-August, 1964, p. 31. On the managerial problems involved in leasing departments cf. H. C. Goldsmith, "The Art of Managing Leased Departments," *ibid.,* October, 1964, pp. 54–58.

credit extension and collection, plus delivery. The lessee assumes responsibility for merchandise handled and for management of the department. While the lessee may pay a flat monthly rental charge, a fixed percentage of his sales is also a very common arrangement. Among discount houses, the lessee's rent is frequently stated in terms of so many dollars per square foot of space occupied (such as $4.50 per year per square foot) or a percentage of sales (10 percent on women's apparel is the figure in some leases), whichever is larger. So far as the customer is concerned, she would not know whether her purchases are made in a store-operated or a leased department.

Advantages and Disadvantages of Leasing.   There has always been disagreement among store owners as to the desirability of leased departments. Although some retailers express satisfaction with the cooperation they receive from lessees in maintaining overall store policies, others believe that the effective coordination required to maximize profits is possible only under centralized ownership. The reason for these contrasting opinions lies in the different weights given to the factors which follow:

Advantages for Store:

1. Permits more rapid expansion, that is, leased departments minimize the lessor's investment.
2. Provides expert management in leased departments.
3. Method of experimenting with new departments at minimum cost and risk.
4. If lease is with a chain organization, lessor gets the advantages of chain operation.

Disadvantages to Store:

1. Coordination problems are increased.
2. Pricing flexibility is reduced. For example, a leased food department cannot be used as a loss leader to attract customers for other departments.
3. A single poorly operated leased department harms the store's "image."
4. Possible disagreements between lessor and lessee on policies and procedures may develop.
5. Ceiling is placed on income the lessor may obtain from a department.

Advantages for Leasing Organization:

1. Many sales to customers attracted to store by other departments.
2. Benefits from customers attracted by overall promotions of the store.
3. Use of customer services provided by the store.
4. Can concentrate on limited breadth of merchandise.
5. Minimum or no expenditures for fixtures.
6. If department provides unprofitable, usually easier to close business than when separate establishment is involved.

Disadvantages for Leasing Organization:

1. Basic operating policies determined by the store may conflict with desires of lessee.
2. Good will developed for store, rather than for lessee.
3. May lose lease after developing a good business.
4. In some cases, high rentals and advertising charges.

Leased Departments in the Future. Despite the "taking-over" of leased departments[49] by many landlords (lessors), one authority concludes there is growing evidence that the leased department operator, "through acquisition, diversification, and the aggressive pursuit of new landlords . . . represents a solid financial portrait with a realistic expansion program."[50] But he foresees certain developments which will test the leasing organization's mettle and determine its success, as follows:

1. Longer leases will be arranged.
2. As lessees grow in strength, the probability of a "take-over" by landlords will diminish.
3. Lessees will probably assume ownership of more stores and be able to do more experimenting in them than is possible under the traditional arrangement.
4. Greater emphasis will be placed on "middle-market" merchandise by operators of leased departments.
5. Automated inventory controls will be widely adopted to obtain better-balanced stocks and to reduce costs.
6. Sales and earnings will likely continue to grow.

By no means are all observers so optimistic about the future of leased departments.

Government Restrictions on Mergers and Acquisitions

Recent years have witnessed many mergers and acquisitions among retail organizations. While the small and medium-sized firms have been involved, the merger trend has also added to the size of some of the large retail companies.[51] In response, the Federal Trade Commission has taken steps to curtail the *external* growth of the very large organizations through restricting

---

[49] For an illustration, cf. "Bradlees Expands Lease Takeover. . . ." *Discount Store News,* August 22, 1966, p. 115.

[50] S. L. Davis, "The Leased Department Paradox—Bigger in Size and Sales, They are Shrinking in Number," *Modern Retailer,* May, 1966, p. 15.

[51] Some of the resulting large firms are included in E. B. Weiss, "Who's Who Among the 50 Retail Billionaires," *Advertising Age,* June 6, 1966, pp. 128, 130. This valuable summary includes "The 100 Largest Retailers Compiled by First National City Bank"; 22 "Food Chains Selling over $20 Million," compiled by *Super Market Merchandising;* "Weiss' List of the 100 Major Department Stores"; and the 45 firms constituting the "Billionaires Club of 1975."

their acquisition of other firms and by forcing them to dispose of some of the stores already acquired.

Only a few of the Commission's restrictive actions can be cited here. In the department store field, the Commission reached an agreement with the Federated Department Stores, Inc., in August, 1965, "by which the chain agreed to table its merger thinking for five years;" a similar agreement was expected to be worked out with Allied Stores; and four other companies— May Department Stores, R. H. Macy and Company, Associated Dry Goods, and City Stores—were "given an unmistakable warning that future acquisitions will be viewed with suspicion."[52] The Commission reported these six groups had made 45 acquisitions since 1951. An example of Commission action against food chains is afforded by the ten-year consent agreement signed in June, 1965, by the Grand Union Company. The Company agreed to sell ten supermarkets in New York State which it acquired in 1958 and to obtain prior approval on sizable supermarket acquisitions in localized areas where it already has stores, unless the merger would leave the company's share of local sales below 5 percent.

Of even greater significance than Commission action, however, was a decision of the United States Supreme Court in May, 1966, *un*merging Von's Grocery Company and Shopping Bag Food Stores, both of Los Angeles. The merger took place in 1960 and the combined sales of the two firms constituted 7.5 percent of the area's retail grocery sales. Breaking new ground, the Court in effect ruled that "mergers of substantial, healthy competitors must be blocked in a market that is still highly competitive but tending toward an oligopoly—where a few giants operate."[53]

National versus Private Brands

For many years retailers with adequate resources and sufficient prestige to consider the problem have had to decide what sort of balance should be maintained in their merchandise offerings and sales promotional efforts between national brands and private brands.[54] The degree of emphasis given each type of brand has varied from company to company and even from time to time within a firm; but, in general, many retailers favor national

---

[52] "Halting Department Store Mergers," *Business Week*, August 21, 1965, p. 36. Also cf. Fred Eichelbaum, "No Red Light Is Reflected in FTC Order—R. Lazarus," *Women's Wear Daily*, January 17, 1966, pp. 1, 10; and I. M. Millstein, "Retail Expansion and the Antitrust Laws," *Stores*, February 6, 1966, pp. 53–58.

[53] Cf. "High Court Bars Merger of Rivals," *Business Week*, June 4, 1966, p. 36. For the actual decision cf. *United States* v. *Von's Grocery Company et al* (S. Ct., May, 1966).

[54] As the terms are used here a "national brand" is a manufacturer's brand whereas a "private brand" is a middleman's or reseller's brand. Cf. the discussion in Chapter 19.

brands because of the substantial advertising expenditures and aggressive merchandising tactics of their manufacturers.

In 1965 the A. C. Nielsen Company, a leading marketing research organization, conducted a survey of consumer brand preferences in the food field. This study revealed that manufacturers' advertised brands, although accounting for only 18 percent of the total of some 2,250 grocery brands on the market, represented some 74 percent of sales.[55] It also concluded that the

FIGURE 1–1
PRIVATE BRAND ADVERTISEMENT

SAFEWAY ⑤ BRANDS
What are they? Why do they sell for less?

Our Safeway ad usually includes a lot of brands which are sold in almost every food store. But this week, our biggest specials are on brands you can buy *only* at Safeway. We call them Safeway ⑤ Brands and each carries the famous ⑤ mark right on its label.

It's a family of top quality products. Several of them may be old friends to you: Lucerne, Bel-air, Mrs. Wright's and Town House. And there are many others we want you to meet. (That's the reason for this big sale!)

Some Safeway ⑤ Brands we manufacture ourselves; others are made for us by the most responsible manufacturers in the country. All are made under rigid quality specifications. All carry Safeway's Money Back Guarantee. We sell them for less because they cost us less. It's as simple as that!

SOURCE: *San Francisco Chronicle*, May 11, 1966.

stockturn of these brands was "34 percent faster than competing minor brands, private labels, and wholesalers' brands." Despite these findings, "prestige" retail organizations continue to promote their own brands heav-

---

[55] "Advertised Brands Up Market Share Over Private Labels, Nielsen Finds," *Advertising Age,* November 15, 1965, pp. 1, 135. Cf., however, E. B. Weiss, "Weiss vs. Nielsen," *Advertising Age,* January 24, 1966, pp. 82–86. Also cf. H. W. Boyd, Jr., and R. E. Frank, "The Importance of Private Labels in Food Marketing," *Business Horizons,* Summer, 1966, pp. 81–90.

ily, as is indicated by the excerpt from a recent advertisement of Safeway Stores, Inc. in Figure 1–1. The "battle of the brands" is far from over.

Other Forms of Response

In addition to the responses already mentioned, retailers have adopted numerous other measures to meet their changing environment. The number is so great, in fact, that only a sampling of them can be mentioned here and even these must be presented in summary form. Many of these developments, however, are discussed in some detail in later chapters.

1. Stores are being relocated in suburban areas and outlying shopping centers because of the deterioration of many downtown sections and the movement of population to the suburbs.[56] Scientific methods are being employed in the choice of these relocation sites to insure attraction of sufficient patronage to realize a profit.

2. Recent emphasis seems to be on the establishment of larger outlying stores with more departments featuring wider selections of merchandise.

3. Modernization of existing stores has continued at a high rate with many improvements in materials, fixtures and equipment.[57]

4. Changes are being made in the organizational structure of department stores and other multi-unit retailers to strengthen controls over merchandise stocks and operating activities.[58]

5. Shifts in store hours are being made to accommodate the needs of customers; several night openings plus Sundays—particularly for food stores—are becoming increasingly common.[59]

6. In the area of sales promotion techniques, the use of trading stamps continues at a high level, although such games as "Bonus Bingo" and "Win-a-check" have lost some popularity among supermarkets and other stores because of unfavorable customer reaction.[60]

7. Growing recognition is being given to imported merchandise in regular merchandise inventories and for special sales events. In some areas "Import Stores" have been established to meet the demand.

8. More store space is being given to "leisure-time" merchandise offerings and to art objects, antiques, and similar items demanded by a growing culture-conscious population.

9. The tendency for retailers to broaden and extend their lines—"scrambled merchandising"—continues, with the result that competition in the retail field is intensified. No longer does the small-appliance dealer compete only with similar specialty stores. He is also in keen competition with the discount house, super-

[56] Cf. Chapter 4, "Store Location."
[57] Cf. Chapter 5, "Store Building, Fixtures, and Equipment."
[58] Cf. Chapter 7, "Structure of the Retail Firm."
[59] Cf. discussion of "Retail Working Conditions" in Chapter 9.
[60] Cf. Chapter 19.

market, drugstore, variety retailer, department store—and frequently the filling station and auto-supply outlet as well.

10. A constant alertness is being manifested by retailers in changing their "mix" of merchandise and operating policies and methods. Some seek a more profitable mix through store modernization programs, self-service operation, and the promotion of private brands; others place their emphasis on widespread promotional activities for bargain-price merchandise; and still others prefer to maintain "regular" prices with greater attention to improved personal salesmanship. Change in the retailing mix is still another factor intensifying competition among retailers.

11. In response to technological developments, increasingly retailers are using data-capturing and data-processing equipment for such activities as merchandise planning and control, pricing, checking credits, accounting for receivables and payables, improving turnover, payroll, and sales audit and analysis.[61]

REVIEW AND DISCUSSION QUESTIONS

1. Formulate your own definition of the term "retailing," being sure to include all of its forms.

2. Note and explain the major changes in the number of retail stores and in total retail sales during the period 1929 to 1966.

3. How do you account for the variations in growth of sales among the various types of retail outlets between 1958 and 1963?

4. What factors, in your judgment, are responsible for the continuing growth of giant retailers?

5. As the proprietor of a small, independent store what measures would you adopt to meet the growing competition of the large retailers?

6. Why is it so important for all retailers to keep informed regarding changes in the environment in which they must operate?

7. Prepare a short paper analyzing the retail impact of the so-called "cultural explosion."

8. Summarize significant developments in the following environmental areas during recent years: (a) social; (b) economic; and (c) technological.

9. Prepare a paper of some 1,500 words on one of the following subjects: (a) "The Teenagers—What Retail Stores Should Do about Them"; (b) "The Oldsters (65 and over)—Retailers' Opportunities for Service and Profit"; (c) "Implications for the Retailer in the Growing Affluence of our Society."

10. How do you explain the continuing growth of the "discount house" in our affluent society?

11. With personal income and personal savings at record levels, how do you account for the tremendous amount of buying on credit—also at an all-time high?

12. Are you in sympathy with the federal government's efforts to curtail the external growth of large-scale retailers? State your reasons.

---

[61] Cf. the discussion of "The Retailer and Electronic Equipment" in Chapter 5.

13. Name and explain briefly five significant recent changes in the competitive environment of retailing.
14. Argue both sides of the question—"Resolved: The traditional department store's future is very uncertain in retail trade."
15. Evaluate the pros and cons of private branding by retail stores as compared with the handling of nationally advertised brands exclusively.

SUPPLEMENTARY READINGS

"Annual Discount Store Census," *Discount Store News,* August 22, 1966, pp. 17–119. Statistics covering 2,684 discount houses in the United States; their distribution among states and selected areas; and the expansion plans of discount chains, are some of the subjects covered in this annual study.

BROWN, F. E., AND FISK, GEORGE. "Department Stores and Discount Houses: Who Dies Next?" *Journal of Retailing,* Vol. XLI, No. 3 (Fall, 1965), pp. 15–27. This "minimum-risk, maximum-benefit" theory of patronage throws interesting light on the future of these two institutions.

BROOKS, JOHN. *The Great Leap,* New York: Harper & Row, 1966. Changes in the United States since 1939 are detailed and, to some degree, appraised in this volume.

CUNDIFF, E. W. "Concepts in Comparative Retailing," *Journal of Marketing,* Vol. XXIX, No. 1 (January, 1965), pp. 59–63. Presenting a framework for generalizing about retailing in different countries, the author's hypothesis and its testing are of considerable interest.

"Data Processing in U.S. Retailing," *Retail Business,* Special Report No. 3, November, 1965, pp. 37–43. This article discusses the benefits derived from the use of EDP systems.

DUBBS, ED. "The Private-Label Duel in Housewares: Where Does the Retailer Stand?" *Merchandising Week,* May 24, 1965, pp. 23–25. The effects on the retailer of the keen competition among brands are treated in this article.

FISK, GEORGE. *Leisure Spending-Behavior* (Philadelphia: University of Pennsylvania Press, 1965). The author's careful study refutes the belief that leisure spending is growing faster than other spending.

"Giants Plan to Get Bigger: Retailers Hone their Tools to Combine Growth with Fragmented Selling," *Business Week,* June 6, 1964, pp. 100–102 ff. This discussion of the expansion plans of large retailers is of particular interest in view of the government's efforts to limit their external growth.

GOELDNER, C. R. (ed.). *Automatic Merchandising* (Chicago: American Marketing Association, 1965). In this excellent listing, the author summarizes the literature available on automatic merchandising in books, reports, bulletins, articles, dissertations, directories, and other sources.

GOLDSMITH, H. C. "The Art of Managing Leased Departments," *Stores,* October, 1964, pp. 54–8; and "The Ameron Study," *Discount Merchandiser,* September, 1965, pp. 45–76, provide two valuable discussions of leased departments.

HOLLANDER, S. C. *Restraints Upon Retail Competition* (East Lansing, Mich.: Bureau of Business and Economic Research, Michigan State University, 1965). This excellent monograph examines the factors influencing the retailer's choice of price, service, merchandising, and promotion responses to conditions in the market place.

————. "The Wheel of Retailing," *Journal of Marketing,* Vol. XXV, No. 1 (July, 1960), pp. 37–42. The "trading-up theory" of retail institutions is examined by Professor Hollander.

————. "Social Pressures and Retail Competition," *Business Topics,* Winter, 1965, pp. 7–14. Pointing out that "The relationship between retailing and its environment is complex . . . [and] . . . difficult for us to perceive . . . ," this careful student discusses the factors limiting the independence of the retailer.

————. "Notes on the Retail Accordion," *Journal of Retailing,* Vol. XXXXII, No. 2 (Summer, 1966), pp. 29–40, 54. The trend toward scrambled merchandising and the counter-movement toward specialization are the subjects of this discussion.

HOUTHAKKER, H. S., and TAYLOR, L. D. *Consumer Demand in the United States, 1929–1970* (Cambridge: Harvard University Press, 1966). Making extensive use of a dynamic model of demand, the authors view consumers' expenditures for over 80 commodities in the period 1929 to 1961 and project the demand for each through 1970.

KEAR, E. A. "Shifting Patterns in Retail Trade," *Survey of Current Business,* May, 1964, pp. 19–23. Some of the changes taking place in retailing are outlined in this analysis.

LEVITT, THEODORE. "Branding on Trial," *Harvard Business Review,* Vol. XLIV, No. 2 (March–April, 1966), pp. 20–38 ff. In this "thinking ahead" article, the author discusses the implications of current government attacks on brand-name marketing.

"The Management of Branch Stores; Organization and Communication," *Stores,* May, 1965, pp. 10–14. This summary of opinions and problems of branch store managers is based on a seminar of the National Retail Merchants Association held in April, 1965.

NELSON, W. H. *The Great Discount Delusion.* (New York: David McKay Co., Inc., 1965). In this critique the author points out many alleged undesirable practices by discount houses. One answer to this criticism is available in DICK GROBERG, "The Big Smear," *Discount Store News,* July 26, 1965, p. 2.

NEW YORK UNIVERSITY INSTITUTE OF RETAIL MANAGEMENT. *The Challenge of Discount Houses.* Rev. ed. New York, 1965. Reprints of articles on discounting from the *Journal of Retailing* during the period 1958–1965 are available in this revised edition.

NEWMAN, J. W. (ed.). *On Knowing the Consumer* (New York: John Wiley & Sons, Inc., 1966). The editor has assembled a collection of brief essays about the behavior of people as buyers and users of goods and services.

SILBERMAN, C. E. "The Revolutionists of Retailing," *Fortune,* Vol. LXV, No. 4 (April, 1962), pp. 99–102 ff. and "The Discounters Choose Their Weapons," *ibid.,* No. 5 (May, 1962), pp. 118–20 ff. These two excellent articles, although somewhat old, cover important aspects of the discount house, its characteristics, and its strategies.

STERN, L. W. "The New World of Private Brands," *California Management Review,* Vol. VIII, No. 3 (Spring, 1966), pp. 43–50. The historical alternatives involved in private brands, the bargaining configurations, and the rationale for brand segmentation are the sub-subjects of this analysis.

TAYLOR, J. L., JR. "Revolution in Retailing," *Credit and Financial Management,* December, 1964, pp. 32–33. The author reviews some of the significant trends in the ever-changing field of retailing.

TOFFLER, ALVIN. *The Culture Consumers: A Study of Art and Affluence in America* (New York: St. Martin's Press, 1964). A former associate editor of *Fortune* analyzes the effects of our sharp increase in income on the various segments of contemporary American culture.

WEISS, E. B. *Marketing Through Tomorrow's 100 Top Department Stores* (New York: Doyle Dane Bernbach, Inc., 1966). In this challenging discussion the author names his choice of the 100 leading firms which account for 60 percent of the total sales of all traditional department stores. He predicts that by 1970 their sales will exceed $16 billion and that they will operate 800–1,000 units.

————. *A Reappraisal of New Retail Trends* (New York: Doyle Dane Bernbach, Inc., 1964). Devoted mainly to department stores, chain stores, and discount houses, this booklet summarizes and appraises recent developments.

SELECTED RETAILING PERIODICALS

The student of retailing should become familiar with the leading trade papers and periodicals in the field. They provide an excellent source of supplementary readings on all the subjects covered in this text. Some of the leading periodicals are the following:

American Druggist, Hearst Magazines, Inc., 1790 Broadway, New York, New York 10019. Biweekly.

Chain Store Age, Lebhar-Friedman Publications, Inc., 2 Park Ave., New York, New York 10016. Various editions, monthly.

Department Store Economist, Chilton Co., Inc., Chestnut and 56th Sts., Philadelphia, Pennsylvania 19139. Monthly.

Discount Merchandiser, Super Market Publishing Co., Inc., 205 East 42nd St. New York, New York 10017. Monthly.

Discount Store News, Lebhar-Friedman Publications, Inc., 2 Park Ave., New York, New York 10016. Biweekly.

Display World, The Display Publishing Company, 407 Gilbert Ave., Cincinnati, Ohio. Monthly.

Drug Topics and *Food Topics,* Topics Publishing Co., Inc., 155 West 44th St., New York, New York 10017. Biweeklies.

Electrical Merchandising, McGraw-Hill Book Co., Inc., 330 West 42nd St., New York, New York 10036. Monthly.

Hardware Age, Chilton Co., Inc., Chestnut and 56th Sts., Philadelphia, Pennsylvania 19139. Biweekly.

Hardware Retailer, National Retail Hardware Association, 964 N. Pennsylvania St., Indianapolis, Ind. 46204. Monthly.

Home Furnishings Daily, Fairchild Publications, Inc., 7 East 12th St., New York, New York 10003. Daily, except Saturday, Sunday, and holidays.

Journal of Retailing, Institute of Retail Management, New York University, 100 Washington Square, New York, New York 10003. Quarterly.

Men's Wear, Fairchild Publications, Inc., 7 East 12th St., New York, New York 10003. Bimonthly.

Modern Retailer, Larkin Publications, 99 Chauncy St., Boston, Mass. 02111. Monthly.

N.A.R.D. Journal, National Association of Retail Druggists, 1 East Wacker Dr., Chicago, Ill. 60601. Semimonthly.

Nargus Bulletin, National Association of Retail Grocers, 360 N. Michigan Ave., Chicago, Ill. 60601. Monthly.

National Furniture Review, National Retail Furniture Association, Merchandise Mart, Chicago, Ill. 60611. Monthly.

National Jeweler and National Watchmaker, Schwartz Publications, 6 West 57th St., New York, New York.

Progressive Grocer, Butterick Company, Inc., 420 Lexington Ave., New York, New York 10017. Monthly.

Stores, National Retail Merchants Association, 100 W. 31st St., New York, New York 10001. Monthly.

Super Market Merchandising, Super Market Publishing Co., Inc., 205 East 42nd St., New York, New York 10017. Monthly.

Women's Wear Daily, Daily News Record (men's wear), and *Retailing Daily* (home furnishings), Fairchild Publications, Inc., 7 E. 12th St., New York, New York 10003. Daily, except Saturday, Sunday, and holidays.

RETAILING BIBLIOGRAPHY

For further readings on subjects covered in this text, the student is referred to:

BARDEN, J. M. *Retailing Bibliography, 1950–1964* (Rochester, N.Y.: School of Retailing, Rochester Institute of Technology, 1964).

CHUTE, A. H. *Selected and Annotated Bibliography of Retailing* (Rev. ed., Austin, Texas: University of Texas Bureau of Business Research 1964).

EDWARDS, C. M., JR.; McCARTHY, C. E.; McNAIR, M. P.; and WINGATE, J. W. *A Bibliography for Students of Retailing* (New York: B. Earl Puckett Fund for Retail Education, Inc., 1966).

PART II

Retailing as a Career

2

CHAPTER

Retail Management Requirements

The previous chapter analyzed the general structure and dynamic nature of retailing in the United States. The tremendous changes now taking place, often described by such terms as "Revolution in Retailing," "Retailing in Turmoil," and "The Retailing Ferment," suggest that the successful operation of a retail business is not an easy task. In the present chapter, therefore, we shall examine some of the main requirements of effective retail management viewed within the broad framework discussed previously and keeping in mind the political, social, and economic environments in which the businessman must operate. For convenience, these requirements have been classified into five broad groups, as follows: (1) Personal qualifications of the proprietor or of top management; (2) adequate financial structure; (3) physical facilities necessary to the conduct of the business; (4) effective policies and procedures for operating the store; and (5) competence, loyalty, and productiveness on the part of the personnel engaged in selling and sales-supporting activities. The effective combination and correlation of these factors will result in continued patronage from satisfied customers and profit for the retailer.

PERSONAL REQUIREMENTS OF MANAGEMENT

Most young men and women who enter retailing eventually hope to become store owners or managers of a department, a division, a store as a whole, or a group of stores. Consequently, it is advisable, at the very beginning of our study of retailing, to turn our attention to their ultimate goal: the retail executive. What is the role of the executive? What makes a retail executive; that is, what personal qualities are necessary for success? What is his social contribution?

Role of the Executive

If one had to select a single ingredient as the main factor in the success of a retail business, clearly it would be the key executives or, in other words, management.[1] Yet, to many individuals, the word "executive" conjures up the rising young man portrayed in *How to Succeed in Business Without Really Trying.* In their mind's eye a retail executive is a person who sits calmly in a comfortable swivel chair in an air-conditioned office, and whose (short) day consists of a few visits from subordinates who need words of advice on their problems. Such a picture is a far cry from the truth![2] While it is true that visits from associates are part of an executive's daily program, they are a small part of his work. Moreover, the busy executive is just as likely to find himself running to his associate's office for a quick conference as he is to find the associate coming to him. The protocol of "always going to one's superior" has long since lost its standing in the rapidly evolving world of retailing.

As a general rule, successful retail executives are hard working, self-disciplined men and women who are willing to accept significant responsibilities and to give unstintingly of themselves to their organizations. Without these qualities they simply could not perform their essential functions, which one writer suggests are threefold: (1) *Giving direction* to the firm (establishing goals, developing operating programs, initiating action, and coordinating activities to achieve the goals), (2) *representing the company* to the public ("the most underrated of management's multiple responsibilities"), and (3) *evaluating results,* that is, taking the necessary steps "to examine the consequences of what has been done, to analyze the causes of deviations (from goals), and to determine what steps must be taken to put operations back on course."[3]

Another way to look at the functions of a retail executive is to think of him as a teacher or a coach. Individually and in groups he should mold his associates into an effective team by teaching them how to work together and by training them for greater responsibilities. At the same time, he should

[1] On this point, cf. the Columbia-McKinsey Foundation lectures given by Charles G. Mortimer as summarized in "Its the Men Up Front that Count," *Business Week,* May 1, 1965, pp. 73–74; and fully reported in *The Purposeful Pursuit of Profits and Growth in Business* (New York: McGraw-Hill Book Co., Inc., 1965).

[2] For a survey of executive hours cf. "How Much Executive Overtime?" *Business Management,* Vol. XXVIII (June, 1965), pp. 22–23 ff. How retail executives actually use their time is suggested by a study of thirty-five retailers. Cf. P. J. Reilly, *Old Masters of Retailing* (New York: Fairchild Publications, 1966).

[3] W. N. Mitchell, *The Business Executive in a Changing World* (New York: American Management Association, 1965), pp. 48, 58, 60, 75.

provide the drive necessary to stimulate the group to greater accomplishments. By establishing goals and leading the group toward them he builds morale in the organization. He should keep himself informed about developments in his own firm, in the entire retail field, and in the overall environment in which the store operates. Unless he keeps abreast in all these areas, he will fail to institute the changes necessary to adjust his firm to shifting conditions—and to make the adjustments at the proper time.[4] Not only should he play a significant role in long-range planning[5] and policy formation; he should also institute procedures to be sure the plans and policies are put into effect. If, in addition to the foregoing functions, we again emphasize his role as the representative of his company in the community—at public functions and in community betterment activities, the breadth and time-consuming aspects of his many tasks are obvious.

The Retail Executive's Personal Qualities

As already suggested, advancement to positions of responsibility at commensurate salaries in retail stores and satisfactory performance at the management level require the possession of certain personal characteristics. Although generalizations in this area are dangerous, the authors believe that these characteristics are, in general, the same as those required by good managers in most lines of business.[6] The importance of certain characteristics, however, should be stressed. These include, among others, knowledge, experience, drive, friendliness, leadership, judgment, decision making, vision, effective expression, and character. Overlapping these characteristics is the need for overall administrative ability.[7]

Knowledge. There is an old adage that "anyone can operate a retail store because all that is necessary for success is to buy cheap and sell dear." It is evident that under the highly competitive conditions of today nothing

---

[4] For an analysis of the failure of many managements to "keep up with the times" (managerial obsolescence) cf. W. R. Mahler, "Every Company's Problem," *Personnel*, Vol. XLII (July, 1965), pp. 8–16.

[5] "If the (long-range) planning is to prove successful, top management must give continuing and active attention to the work being done." B. W. Scott, *Long-Range Planning in American Industry* (New York: American Management Association, Inc., 1965), p. 193. Also cf. the excellent statement by M. L. Mace, "President and Corporate Planning," *Harvard Business Review*, Volume XLIII, No. 1 (January–February, 1965), pp. 49–62.

[6] Some social psychologists would likely disagree with this statement and assert that retail executives are especially sensitive to short-term changes in business activity and probably possessed of less analytical ability than executives in other organizations.

[7] For another grouping of the characteristics of successful executives cf. G. E. Spaulding, Jr., "Effective Executive: What Qualities Make the Difference," *Management Review*, Vol. LIII (November, 1964), pp. 4–15.

could be farther from the truth. There is no substitute for knowledge, and without it failure is a certainty. But what is the nature of this "knowledge"? So far as retailing is concerned, it encompasses, for example, knowledge of (1) merchandise and sources of supply, (2) consumer buying motives and habits, (3) retail operating methods and procedures, and (4) human relations in retailing, including the effective supervision and direction of employees and satisfactory customer relations. As noted previously, the successful retailer of today should also understand the nature and structure of retailing, its place in our economy, and keep aware of current developments and trends.

1. *The Consumer is King.* One of the most important facts for the retailer to recognize is that his success depends on satisfied customers because, without continued patronage, profits are impossible. Consequently, he must offer the goods and services the customer wants, when, how, and where she wants them, and at the prices she is willing to pay. As Daniel Defoe wrote in *The Complete English Tradesman* in 1726: "The sum of the matter is this, it is necessary for the tradesman to subject himself, by all the ways possible, to his business; his customers are to be his idols; so far as he may worship idols by allowance, he is to bow down to them, and worship them. . . ." To use a more recent statement, the operator of a small grocery store put Defoe's thought in these words: A retailer must so please his customers that they will never "go to another store. They might like it better there, and not come back."[8] And the author of a study of the J. C. Penney Company explains much of the success of this firm by the fact that its executives "never lost sight of the elementary fact that without customers they could not remain in business. They looked upon their customers as their *real* board of directors. They realized that the success of their stores and the security of their own jobs were decisions completely within the keeping of the public."[9] No retailer—small or large—should ever forget that "the customer is king."

2. *The Marketing Concept.* In recent years retailers and marketers in general who accept and practice this "consumer is king" philosophy are said to be using the marketing concept. Specifically, they accept "customer needs and wants . . . (as) . . . the starting points for all their efforts."[10] Consequently, they plan their merchandise assortments, the services they render,

---

[8] "The Agile Man Who Built Third Avenue," *Fortune,* Vol. XXI, No. 5 (May, 1965), p. 146.

[9] Norman Beasley, *Main Street Merchant: The Story of the J. C. Penney Company* (New York: Whittlesey House, McGraw-Hill Book Co., Inc., 1948), p. 80.

[10] E. H. Fram, "Application of the Marketing Concept to Retailing," *Journal of Retailing,* Vol. XLI, No. 2 (Summer, 1965), p. 19.

their physical facilities, and their personnel policies so as to meet these needs and wants. Everyone in the firm takes his "marching orders from the market."[11]

Experience. Truly, "there is no substitute for experience" as a fundamental determinant of accomplishment. As a matter of fact, unless the retailer has had some years of experience performing or dealing with the major retailing activities and unless that experience has involved several major phases of store operation and included the establishment of effective operating methods and procedures, his chances of "reaching the top" are slim.

The following activities or functions, common to all progressive operators of retail stores, are those in which experience is particularly valuable to the retailer:

1. Effective buying
2. Judicious pricing
3. Sound merchandise control methods
4. Creative advertising and sales promotion
5. Constructive salesmanship
6. An adequate store system
7. Enlightened personnel administration
8. Customer-attracting customer services
9. Effective expense control

There is no intention of implying that experience in or with all the activities or functions listed is essential to success in retailing, but experience in *some* of them, and an appreciation of the relationships involved in *all* of them, will prove of great benefit to the retailer and contribute importantly to his future success. The need for such experience and appreciation will become increasingly evident as we discuss these topics in later chapters. The point to be stressed at this time is this: The young man or woman who seeks a top position in retailing should attain experience in a wide variety of retail activities or functions.

Experience of and by itself, of course, does not insure profitable operation: it is perfectly possible for a retailer to have one year's experience twenty times while another has twenty years of experience. One will learn much from trial and error provided he reviews carefully the causes of his mistakes and does not repeat them. Moreover, if he learns to appraise situations systematically and deliberately, to recognize the value of assembling all relevant and pertinent data, to evaluate alternative courses of action, and to think objectively and logically, his chances of success will be

---

[11] Wroe Alderson and P. E. Green, *Planning and Problem Solving in Marketing* (Homewood, Ill.: Richard D. Irwin, Inc., 1964), p. 5.

considerably enhanced. Mature judgment is aided by experience, and without such judgment invalid decisions may result.

Drive. The word *drive* is perhaps a modern word for old-fashioned ambition and hard work. In his *Republic,* Plato observed that ". . . retailers are commonly those who are weakest in bodily strength, and therefore of little use for any other purpose." Untrue even in Plato's day, today's retail executive merely smiles at such a naïve statement. He knows that success in retailing usually comes at a high price—paid for in physical energy and the sacrifice of many personal comforts, especially in the United States where competition among retailers is so keen.[12] All too often he—by seeming to work without obvious effort—is envied by some who, unlike his family and immediate associates, fail to recognize the long hours and hard work which are responsible for his apparently easy achievements. As one successful retailer has put it: the way to a top management post is to "forget the glamour, accept the responsibilities, and work like hell." Drive—not the kind typified by the man who works hard for a few days and then loses his enthusiasm, but the type which perseveres year after year—is a key ingredient to success for the modern retailer.[13]

In the hours which he gives to his job, the successful retail executive must think constantly about a wide range of problems, meet a steady demand for new ideas, and face everlasting competition both from inside and from outside his company. He must attend numerous conferences and meetings, travel to distant places when necessary, and take an active part in the life of the community. This latter obligation includes participation in such activities as Community Chest campaigns, church work, youth movements, leadership of clubs, and speaking engagements. Someone has said that "success consists not only of doing extraordinary things but of doing ordinary things extraordinarily well." The successful executive gets keen satisfaction from doing the best possible job in every assigned task. Moreover, he is one who builds a reputation for doing the job right the *first* time.

Friendliness. The retail executive should sincerely try to get along well with people: his employees, his superiors, and his business associates. To win the friendship and the respect of the employees under his supervi-

---

[12] For an opinion that retail competition is "much less aggressive" in Europe as contrasted with the United States cf. Reavis Cox, Wroe Alderson, and S. J. Shapiro, *Theory in Marketing* (Homewood, Ill.: Richard D. Irwin, Inc., 1964), p. 5. However, the intensity of competition in Europe is certainly increasing each year.

[13] To no small degree the amount of drive demonstrated depends upon conditions within the firm. On this point cf. M. S. Myers, "Conditions for Manager Motivation," *Harvard Business Review,* Vol. XLIV, No. 1 (January–February, 1966), pp. 58–71.

sion is no easy task.[14] A successful supervisor leads rather than drives his employees, but he loses their respect when he fails to enforce company rules and regulations. When criticism is made, it should be based upon careful study of the circumstances involved, expressed to the employee privately, and should be constructive. Unjust criticism, or even justified criticism made under improper conditions, can do considerable harm to the individual criticized as well as to the executive.

A liking for people, which is probably best considered as one element of friendliness, is an important asset to the retail executive who is constantly in association with others. Solutions to important retailing problems are frequently found through conferences of executives. Moreover, the integrated nature of retail store activities necessitates frequent consultation among executives to minimize the friction that develops among the various operations. Standing between top management and employees, the retail executive must think in terms of both. The board chairman of E. I. du Pont de Nemours & Company, C. H. Greenewalt, is of the opinion that the executive's "most important function is to reconcile, to coordinate, to compromise, and to appraise the various viewpoints and talents under his direction to the end that each individual contributes his full measure to the business at hand."[15] Because of the humanized nature of the business, the success of the retail executive who does not like to work with people will be definitely limited. In fact, he would find his talents could be used better elsewhere.

Leadership. A good manager inspires the confidence of others in his ability as a leader. Even when in his own mind he has some doubts about the wisdom of a particular decision, he acts with such self-assurance that any doubts are minimized in the thoughts of those around him. He used his authority to guide his organization, not to compel obedience.[16] As he delegates tasks to his associates,[17] he demands much of them: "His role is never

---

[14] There is a valuable discussion of this task in R. N. McMurry, "Are You the Kind of Boss People Want to Work For?" *Business Management,* Vol. XXVIII (August, 1965), pp. 59–61.

[15] Various theories of participative leadership are developed by R. E. Miles, "Human Relations or Human Resources?" *Harvard Business Review,* Vol. XLIII, No. 4 (July–August, 1965), pp. 148–49. Also cf. the guidelines for leadership in the resolving of conflicts among individuals as set forth in A. Zaleznik, "Dynamics of Subordinacy," *Harvard Business Review,* Vol. XLIII, No. 3 (May–June, 1965), pp. 119–31.

[16] However, there are all kinds of leaders and some successful ones do rely substantially on autocratic methods. For an excellent analysis of this phase of leadership cf. E. E. Jennings, *The Executive: Autocrat, Bureaucrat, Democrat* (New York: Harper & Brothers, 1962).

[17] A substantial volume of literature is in existence concerning the "whys" and "wherefores" of delegation. As an example, cf. N. D. Gardner and J. N. Davis, *The Art of Delegating* (New York: Doubleday & Company, 1965).

to be satisfied, never to believe that outstanding performance was quite good enough."[18] To this end, he must arouse the enthusiasm of those in his organization as to the firm's goals, policies, and procedures. "I consider my ability to arouse enthusiasm among men the greatest asset I possess," said Charles Schwab, famed steel executive of a generation ago. "The way to develop the best that is in man is by appreciation and encouragement."

By no means should the retail executive assume that authority and leadership will automatically be his because of the title of his office. He must earn it through the confidence, respect, and support of the people with whom he works. He gains authority when he demonstrates his ability to assume it.[19]

Judgment. The successful executive must be able to judge the probable outcome of his own decisions. Also, he must gauge the effect of outside events on his own business. The ability to reason, to draw valid conclusions from facts, to withstand some pressures and give way to others, and to sift good advice from bad—all these call for judgment on his part. Frequently he is called upon to exercise judgment on merchandise; in such cases his aesthetic taste, his sense of style, and his appreciation of merchandise may be important in reaching valid decisions. Of course his judgment will not be infallible, but his wise decisions must outweigh his faulty ones.

Decision Making. The ability to make decisions—which one successful executive has remarked "is an art, not a science"[20]—is an absolute "must" for the able executive. Without it, his business will lack true "management." So important is this personal qualification of management that Clarence B. Randall once said: "The outstanding characteristic of the good executive is his capacity for reaching decisions—for making up his mind and then translating thought into action."[21]

Especially is the executive's ability to reach a decision tested when he has to decide an urgent matter upon which all the facts he would like are not available; and this is probably the typical situation, despite the great flow

---

[18] Alderson and Green, *op. cit.,* p. 11. Also cf. the statements attributed to P. F. Drucker by Samuel Feinberg in his column, "From Where I Sit," *Women's Wear Daily,* June 14, 1966, p. 12.

[19] For a report of a series of interviews with executives widely recognized as having the quality of leadership, cf. "Lessons of Leadership," *Nations Business,* Vol. LIII (June, 1965), pp. 34–35 ff. and succeeding issues.

[20] Mortimer, "It's the Men up Front that Count," *op. cit.,* p. 73. As a matter of fact, a high degree of artistry is required in the field of management, a point of view which is developed in L. A. Appley, "Art in Management," *Supervisory Management,* Vol. X (June, 1965), pp. 24–25; and in J. B. Weiner, "Fine Art of High-Yield Management," *Dun's Review and Modern Industry,* Vol. LXXXVI (October, 1965), pp. 38–41 ff.

[21] Mr. Randall is the retired chairman of Inland Steel Corporation. Also cf. F. J. Valiente, "Guide to Decision Making," *Advanced Management Journal,* Vol. XXX (April, 1965), pp. 74–81.

of data from modern day computers.[22] Will he then procrastinate, or will he recognize that there are many times when it is better for an executive to reach a decision, even if he decides incorrectly, than it is to wait for more facts? Stated another way, will he recognize, to quote the late Alfred P. Sloan, that "the final act of business judgment is intuitive?"[23] Or, again, will he be able to reach a decision when the answer must be an unpopular "no"?

In making decisions the alert executive needs to keep the overall well-being of the company before him. All too often one hears the expression "we'll take care of our own department; let the others solve their own problems." Such a point of view is far too narrow. Top retail positions should be filled by individuals who keep the purpose and aim of the institution uppermost in their mind.

Vision. The outstanding executive has the ability to thrust his imagination beyond the immediate problems and goals and to grasp a vivid picture of his final achievement. Accepting the philosophy that "change is inevitable; and that the old way is not necessarily the right way," his vision develops new products, invents new methods, opens new markets. He plans a broad future while he builds soundly for the present. Wrote one successful executive: "The constant responsibility of the head of a business is to do today those things that will build strength for the future . . . leadership that devotes itself wholly to operating successfully in the here and now—essential as this is—will not measure up to its total responsibility."[24]

The executive's vision of the future must go far beyond the confines of his business and embrace the entire environment in which his firm operates. Thus, along with the need to achieve effective internal operations, he must give his "best to help preserve a vigorous and free market economy. . . . Free enterprise is a concept with which nearly everyone in our particular society agrees in principle but which . . . seems continually in danger of being gradually whittled away by ill-considered public and selfish private actions."[25]

Effective Expression. Having a vision of desirable changes is only half the battle: The retail executive must also be able to "sell" the vision to his associates, his customers, and the public. Consequently, effective commu-

---

[22] On the aid given by computers in decision making, cf. H. I. Ansoff, "Firm of the Future," *Harvard Business Review,* Vol. XLIII, No. 5 (September–October, 1965), pp. 162–63 ff.

[23] Quoted by J. T. Kimball, "The Age of the Intuitive Manager," *Management Review,* March, 1966, p. 19.

[24] F. R. Kappel (Chairman of the Executive Committee, American Telephone and Telegraph Company), *Vitality in a Business Enterprise* (New York: McGraw-Hill Book Co., Inc., 1960), p. 3.

[25] Mitchell, *op. cit.,* p. 13.

nication—the ability to use the English language convincingly and persuasively, both orally and in writing—is important to his success.[26]

Character. A good retail executive is both reliable and courageous. He never forgets his obligations to his firm's customers, employees, stockholders, and sources of supply. He knows that his reputation for keeping promises is his business livelihood, that his character is reflected in the actions of his company, in the quality of the products it handles and the services it renders. He is aware that honesty in dealing with his customers and employees is not just the *best* policy but that it is the *only* policy upon which continued patronage and employee loyalty can be founded.[27]

Administrative Ability. Another approach to many of the characteristics already discussed is to say that the executive must have a high degree of administrative ability. One authority believes that successful administration rests upon three basic and related skills—technical, human, and conceptual—which he defines as follows:

Technical skill [which] implies an understanding of, and proficiency in, a specific kind of activity, particularly one involving methods, processes, procedures or techniques. . . . It involves specialized knowledge, analytical ability within that specialty, and facility in the use of the tools and techniques of a specific discipline.

Human skill is . . . the executive's ability to work effectively as a group member and to build co-operative effort within the team he leads. As *technical skill* is primarily concerned with working with "things" (processes or physical objects) so *human skill* is primarily concerned with working with people.

Conceptual skill . . . involves the ability to see the enterprise as a whole; it includes recognizing how the various functions of the organization depend on one another, and how changes in any one part affect all the others; and it extends to visualizing the relationship of the individual business to the industry, the community, and the political, social and economic forces of the nation as a whole. Recognizing these relationships, and perceiving the significant elements in any situation, the administrator should then be able to act in a way which advances the overall welfare of the organization.[28]

In the retail field the executive who possesses such skills and utilizes them with discretion and judgment is likely to be a *good* administrator. Exercising the leadership which such skills imply and remaining in close touch with the

---

[26] For helpful suggestions on this subject cf. R. N. McMurry, "Clear Communications for Chief Executives," *Harvard Business Review,* Vol. XLIII, No. 2 (March–April, 1965), pp. 131–2 ff.

[27] This point is developed more fully in L. M. Gilbreth, "Integrity; The Touchstone of Good Management," *Advanced Management Journal,* Vol. XXIX (October, 1964), pp. 13–18.

[28] R. L. Katz, *Executive Skills* (Hanover, N.H.: Amos Tuck School of Business Administration, 1954), pp. 4–6. For another approach to this problem cf. Roger Bellows, T. Q. Gilson, and G. S. Odiorne, *Executive Skills: Their Dynamics and Development* (Englewood Cliffs, N.J.: Prentice-Hall, Inc., 1962).

major activities of his business should give satisfactory results both in the short and the long run.

Summary: The Retail Executive's Social Contribution

It is evident from the foregoing that the successful retail executive is a composite of many qualities. Adequate knowledge, practical experience, and certain personal attributes are all essential. The knowledge necessary for advancement in retailing comes from a variety of sources—formal academic training, careful observation, reading and study on one's own initiative, and experience. Again, it should be emphasized that there is no substitute for experience in the learning process. The actual doing of jobs, the perform-ance of specialized tasks, personal observation of customer buying habits, and intimate contact with day-to-day problems as they arise are an important part of the retail executive's training.

As will be suggested again in the next chapter, for the individual who has the necessary personal qualifications, retailing offers not only a financially rewarding career; it also provides one in which the individual can make a significant social contribution. Certainly the retailer plays a major role in raising our standard of living and expanding our economy. Careful students of this subject, in a report on *Dynamic Retailing in the Modern Economy,* comment as follows:

It is retailing that is most closely in touch with the consumer and able to inter-pret the consumer's desires and needs. It is retailing that is best able to serve as the purchasing agent for the consumer. It is retailing that has the best oppor-tunity to make it easier and more attractive for consumers to buy. It is retailing that can best coordinate the product development, merchandising, and promo-tional activities of manufacturers with the requirements and aspirations of the consumer market.[29]

FINANCIAL STRUCTURE

The second basic requirement of successful retail management is adequate capital. Regardless of one's personal qualifications and interest in the field, continuous, profitable operation of a retail store is impossible without suffi-cient funds. This need for funds permeates all phases of the business from the exploratory and planning stages to the final payment for goods pur-chased, and services rendered by employees.

---

[29] Quoted in M. P. McNair, E. A. Burnham, and A. C. Hersum, *Cases in Retail Management* (New York: McGraw-Hill Book Co., Inc., 1957), p. 14. For a review of some thirty books, many of which stress the social contribution of business, cf. W. G. Broehl, Jr., "Insights Into Business and Society," *Harvard Business Review,* Vol. XLIV, No. 3 (May–June, 1966), pp. 6–16.

Prior to the establishment of a new store or the purchase of a "going concern," careful estimates should be made of the capital needed to insure accomplishment of one's goal. The experience of "new" retailers indicates that all too often estimates of expenses to be met during the initial stage of operation are much too low and estimates of sales and profits to be realized during this period are too high. Consequently, these estimates of expenditures and income should be checked and rechecked prior to starting a business. Sources from which the needed funds are to come should then be determined.[30] The retailer should also be prepared to meet unexpected demands for funds not covered in his estimates. Once his business passes through the difficult period covered by his opening and the first few months of operation, it is possible to formulate reasonably accurate budgets, including the merchandise budget, the expense budget, and the over-all financial budget.[31]

PHYSICAL FACILITIES

Adequate physical facilities, the third broad group of factors underlying the successful operation of a retail store, include a satisfactory building— properly located and arranged, suitable fixtures and equipment, and other devices and mechanisms necessary to provide customers with needed merchandise and services in a pleasant environment. Recent years have witnessed important advances and improvements in site selection, store arrangement, merchandise handling and storage, and electronic equipment for accounting purposes—to mention but a few of the major areas. These matters are discussed in considerable detail in Chapters 4, 5, and 6.

EFFECTIVE RETAILING POLICIES

A fourth major requirement of profitable store management is the establishment and maintenance of effective policies under which the business is to operate. In addition, top management must effectively coordinate all the activities of the business, established in conformance with such policies, to the end that the business will provide needed merchandise and satisfactory customer services and thus become a profit-making entity. Too often, businessmen and beginning students in retailing alike tend to think of a retail establishment as consisting of a number of parts, each of which operates in its own interest. As a result, insufficient attention is given to the necessity of integrating these parts effectively.

---

[30] These points are developed more fully later in "Financing the Store," pp. 67–70.

[31] The merchandise budget is discussed in Chapter 14 and the expense and financial budgets in Chapter 25.

Nature of Policies

Business policies are the rules of conduct, either written or implied, under which the firm operates. Put another way, a policy establishes a definite and uniform course of action to be followed, both over time and by all members of the organization, under substantially similar and recurrent circumstances.

In small businesses these "rules of conduct" generally exist merely in the mind of the proprietor and represent his ideas of the way in which he desires to conduct his store. When he decides to sell on account rather than for cash only, and when he decides to pay his salespeople bonuses in addition to their regular salary, he is adopting policies. In the case of larger retailers, however, policies are usually written, because they must be communicated to many people, frequently at several locations. In stores of all sizes it is important that the policies established be clear and definite, that they be stable and consistent as long as circumstances are similar, that they be workable, and that they be adjusted promptly when fundamental conditions change. If these requirements are met, each business policy can serve as a very useful "management tool" for the retail store proprietor or executive.

Need for Retailing Policies

It is evident from our discussion in the previous chapter that retail stores of today operate under trying conditions. The intensity of competition among retailers is increasing daily: the "product mix" in supermarkets and other stores continues to broaden, discount houses are growing rapidly, and additional services are being added by traditional retailers. Population shifts, particularly the growth of suburban areas, complicate the problems of downtown stores. High taxes make it difficult to generate funds for expansion purposes, and the high cost of construction and modernization gives cause for considerable thought before decisions for physical changes are made. The potential growth of unions in the retail field and the increase in governmental regulations place restrictions on some of the retailer's former freedoms. Shorter hours, higher wage rates, and night openings have raised his "break-even" point and made profitable operation more difficult.

Changing and trying conditions, such as those mentioned in the preceding paragraph, call for some carefully established policies. Without the stabilizing influence of such sign posts, the retailer may be swept along with the tide—merely trying one opportunistic adjustment after another without carefully thinking through their long run implications. Stated positively, the retailer who goes through the mental process of determining policies finds that he has a set of standards to guide his actions and those of his associates; that he does not drift off the main road because of the superficial attractiveness of some bypath.

At the same time, changing conditions may well call for policy adjustments. In fact, as has already been emphasized, a policy is valid only so long as the circumstances which brought it into existence remain substantially the same. But the retailer who has carefully established his policies for a certain set of conditions, will usually be the one who is willing to make adjustments in them *after investigation* indicates changes are necessary.

The existence of well-established policies reduces the number of decisions that key executives are called upon to make. Comparable cases can be settled on a routine basis according to predetermined and well-understood rules. Thus, the time of major executives is conserved by allowing others in the organization to make decisions based on the policies in effect.

Establishing Retailing Policies

Policy formation begins with a careful study of the problems to be met; that is, a determination of the areas in which policy decisions must be made. Concerning each area, accurate and complete information should be secured rather than relying upon hunches or guesswork. To obtain such information, careful analyses should be made of the objectives of the business, the conditions under which it is proposed to operate, the possible alternative policies, and the potential results. With this knowledge available in proper form, actual formulation of policies may proceed.

Factors Influencing Choice of Policies. While the judgment of the proprietor, management, or the board of directors is the final determinant in each policy decision, it is essential to recognize at the outset that the business policies of any firm will depend upon what is desired and what is possible. What is desired, of course, is not always possible. Like most businessmen, the retailer must constantly make compromises to meet the situations that confront him and especially to meet the restrictions placed upon his freedom of action. These include, among other factors, laws of the land, public opinion, profitability of operation, activities of competitors, vested interests of individuals in his own organization, his personal prejudices, usual services provided to customers of his own and similar stores, and the resources at his command.

Responsibility for Policy Formation. Responsibility for establishing proper policies in retail stores varies with the size and the kind of business and with the type of ownership organization under which the store operates. Most small stores and some rather large ones operate as individual proprietorships or as partnerships. In such concerns the proprietor or the partners, frequently with the assistance of members of their families, set up the rules under which their businesses will be conducted. In those small stores which are incorporated, the board of directors should play a major role in policy formation. Unfortunately, in many cases the board of directors of the small corporation meets the legal requirements by having several persons designated to serve on it, but does not participate in policy formation.

In the larger retail firms, such as corporate department stores and chains, responsibility for major policies usually resides in the boards of directors, with the authority to approve other policies delegated to the chief executive officer or perhaps to a management committee. Regardless of where responsibility lies in the retail organization and also regardless of the fact that the actual drafting of policies may be in the hands of one individual or a small group, insofar as possible those who will be expected to carry out a policy should play some part in its development. In no other way can they become so convinced of its necessity.

Many retailers become so busy with daily routine affairs that they fail to devote enough time to policy formation. Despite the pressure resulting from a constant stream of matters demanding his attention, each retailer should so organize his time and distribute his energy that he can give consideration to questions of policy. The proprietor or chief executive should never forget that, in cooperation with his board of directors, if one exists, setting up suitable policies is one of his major tasks.

Areas of Policy Decisions

There are numerous areas in which policy decisions must be made by the retailer, including, for example, kind and quality of merchandise to be handled, forms of customer service to be rendered, types of sales promotional efforts to be carried out, and problems related to personnel administration. Policies concerning each of these and other matters are discussed in subsequent chapters and need not be treated at this point. In passing, however, let us consider briefly two other areas in which policies should be established—participation in community activities and membership in trade associations.

Participation in Community Activities. Many retailers—small and large—belong to service clubs such as the Kiwanis, Lions, or Rotary. Membership is considered a mark of distinction because of the interest such organizations take in community affairs and because of the exchange of ideas on business problems. Other retailers are members of chambers of commerce, local school boards, Community Fund committees, hospital boards, and parent-teacher associations. Still others serve as Boy Scout leaders, aldermen, city officials, and church officers. In deciding how active a part he will play in the life of the community, the retailer will be governed by his desire to serve, the time involved, and his judgment of the long-run effect such participation will have on his sales and profits.[32]

Membership in Trade Associations.   Sooner or later the retailer is confronted with the question of whether he should join an association of stores in his field. His decision will be based largely upon the services the association can render him, the cost involved, and the time he will have to devote to it. Recent years have witnessed a continued growth in the membership of such associations because of the increase in services provided to members. Today there exist strong associations—local, state, and national —in almost every field of retail enterprise; and their membership lists include most of the successful retailers in the country.[33]

Policy Enforcement and Revision

Policies and Procedures.   Once policies have been established, operating procedures must be developed to carry them out. Such procedures must be simple enough so that they may be understood and applied by the persons who are responsible for their performance. Otherwise the time spent in developing them is wasted, and the business cannot function according to the plans that have been made.

A simple illustration will clarify the relationship between policies and procedures. When the owner of a supermarket decides he will offer delivery service to his customers he is adopting a policy. In choosing a method of handling the goods sold so that they will be delivered to customers as promptly and as economically as possible he is establishing operating procedures.

Importance of Policy Enforcement.   No policy, however well conceived, can be of value to a retail store unless it is adhered to closely and consistently throughout the organization. Continual follow-up and enforcement are necessary to assure such adherence, especially in regard to the rank and file of employees.

---

[32] For the community-must-be-served philosophy of an outstanding merchant, cf. the address of the late Gottlieb Duttweiler published under the title of *Business Leadership and Social Responsibility* (East Lansing, Michigan: Bureau of Business and Economic Research, Michigan State University, 1960).

[33] For an analysis of trade associations, including both the individual and the overall social points of view, cf. J. F. Bradley, *The Role of Trade Associations and Professional Business Societies in America* (University Park, Pa.: The Pennsylvania State University Press, 1965).

Many employees of retail stores tend to disregard rules and regulations, not because of disagreement with the rules but because of unwillingness to spend the time and effort to become familiar with them. Others are particularly averse to making changes, to being forced to learn "something new." It is necessary, therefore, that provision be made for education in the purposes of the new rules as well as in the advantages that accrue to the employees personally through conformance to them. If employees can be shown that the new procedure is simple in operation, that it saves time, that it achieves the objective substantially better than the old procedure, or that it results in overcoming customer dissatisfaction, they accept the situation more readily and adjust themselves to it.

Despite the apparent advantages which accrue from following the suggestions made in the previous paragraphs, many retail executives fail to adopt them. They become so engrossed in major decisions affecting immediate profits that they neglect the continual re-emphasis of established policies and procedures which is so essential. Their own negligence is an important contributing factor to the carelessness of their employees.

Adjusting Policies to Changing Conditions. Since the dynamic nature of retailing necessitates the continuous development and adjustment of policies, this task becomes one of the major responsibilities of top management. Policies, like retail prices, are constantly on trial. They must be examined closely in the light of experience, and adjustments must be made whenever conditions change substantially.

However, a word of caution is called for in the adjustment of policies. Occasionally, management or a board of directors discards a policy after a short period of trial because it has apparently failed to yield the results expected; when further investigation would have revealed that it was not the policy itself, but rather the program to implement it, which was responsible for the failure. All of which suggests again that the successful operation of a retail store depends to an important degree upon how closely the proprietor or chief executive officer remains in contact with the essential activities of his business. Systematic and thorough follow-up of policies and procedures substantially influences profits.

COMPETENCY AND LOYALTY OF RETAIL PERSONNEL

The importance of the human factor in retailing, the fifth basic requirement of success in this field, has already been stressed in previous pages. It should be emphasized further, however, that unless an adequate staff of employees in both sales and sales-supporting activities is selected carefully, trained effectively, compensated adequately, and supervised properly, successful store operation is impossible. Competency in the particular activities in which they are engaged, loyalty to top management and their immediate supervisors through close adherence to established policies and practices, and performance of duties and responsibilities efficiently and at reasonable cost are major obligations of every employee. Likewise, it is the obligation of the proprietor or of top management to be so objective, logical, and progressive in policies and practices that loyalty and respect on the part of employees is engendered. Chapters 8 and 9 are devoted to personnel management in the retail store.

REVIEW AND DISCUSSION QUESTIONS

1. How is the "Revolution in Retailing" related to retail management requirements? Be specific.
2. Why is it important for the retailer to understand the social, economic, and legal environments in which he does business? Which aspects of these environments do you consider most significant to the retailer? Why?
3. According to W. N. Mitchell what are the three essential functions of the executive?
4. Do you agree or disagree with the opinion of some social psychologists that retail executives are particularly sensitive to short-term changes in business activity and probably possess less analytical ability than executives in other kinds of business?
5. Explain the "marketing concept," discuss its applicability to retailing, and indicate how widely it is employed in the retail field.
6. What do you consider the essential personal qualification of an effective retail executive? Defend your answer.
7. Discuss: "Retail Management is more Art than Science."
8. Distinguish among "technical skill," "human skill," and "conceptual skill." Of what value are these concepts in connection with good administration?
9. Define "retailing policy" in your own words and point out the characteristics of a *good* policy.
10. Explain why effective policies are essential to success in retailing and illustrate three areas in which they are required.
11. "Responsibility for policy formation in retail stores varies with the size and kind of the business and with the type of ownership under which the business operates." Discuss, with emphasis on current practices regarding policy formation.
12. Based on your observation in retail stores or your recent reading, give examples of policy changes by specific retail firms. Explain, where possible, the circumstances which brought about the changes.
13. As a retailer, precisely how would you keep acquainted with current developments and improvements in merchandising methods?
14. Assume that your first job following graduation is in a retail store and that the controller asks you to suggest ways through which better adherence to

established rules and regulations can be obtained. Prepare a brief report covering this assignment.

15. Discuss: "Adjusting Retail Policies to Changing Conditions."

SUPPLEMENTARY READINGS

ALBERS, H. H. *Principles of Organization and Management* (2nd. ed; New York: John Wiley & Sons, Inc., 1965). In this general text dealing with management, emphasis is placed on the need for policies.

ALDERSON, WROE, AND GREEN, P. E. *Planning and Problem Solving in Marketing* (Homewood, Ill.: Richard D. Irwin, Inc., 1964). Chapter I of this volume offers an excellent discussion of the nature of leadership under the title "System and Leadership."

BELLOWS, ROGER; GILSON, T. Q.; AND ODIORNE, G. S. *Executive Skills: Their Dynamics and Development* (Englewood Cliffs, N.J.: Prentice-Hall, Inc., 1962). Based on the assumption that the executive is "made, not born," the authors suggest how the executive may be developed.

CARSON, DAVID. "Guide for Constructing a Merchandising Policy," *Journal of Retailing,* Vol. XXXIII, No. 4 (Winter, 1962), pp. 24–31. The author covers basic decision making in all major phases of store operation in this valuable treatment.

FEINBERG, SAMUEL. *How Do You Manage?* (New York: Fairchild Publications, 1965). With emphasis on retailing, the author analyzes the transition from family-type management to the professional executive.

FRAM, E. H. "Application of the Marketing Concept to Retailing." *Journal of Retailing,* Vol. XLI, No. 2 (Summer, 1965), pp. 19–26. the author argues that, in practice, too few retailers really apply the marketing concept to their operations.

GOLDENTHAL, IRVING. *How to Be a Successful Executive* (Philadelphia: Chilton Co., 1960). Referring specifically to the retail executive, this small brochure offers many helpful leads.

JENNINGS, E. E. *The Executive: Autocrat, Bureaucrat, Democrat* (New York: Harper & Brothers, 1962). The author supports this thesis: the best executive is a combination of all three elements.

KAPLAN, R. M. (ed.). *The Marketing Concept in Action* (Chicago, Ill.: American Marketing Association, 1964). The papers read at the 47th National Conference of the American Marketing Association are presented in this publication.

KAPPEL, F. R. *Vitality in a Business Enterprise* (New York: McGraw-Hill Book Co., Inc., 1960). This volume is based on the author's McKinsey Foundation lectures given at Columbia University in 1960. He emphasizes the need for vigor and vision in business and suggests pertinent questions the executive should ask himself.

KILLIAN, R. A. *Effective Leadership* (New York: American Management Association, 1966). How a leader gets results through other people, motivation, and human attitudes are covered in this common-sense guide on leadership.

KIMBALL, J. T. "The Age of the Intuitive Manager," *Management Review,*

March, 1966, pp. 17–20. The author states the case for the "intuitive manager"—who "does not necessarily follow standard formulas or long-standing procedures . . . (but) is an activist, equipped to move fast . . . to find unique solutions to different problems."

MARCH, J. G. (ed.). *Handbook of Organizations* (Chicago, Ill.: Rand McNally & Company, 1965). This 1247 page symposium, which seeks "to summarize and report the present state of knowledge about human organizations," has three sections of value in connection with the present chapter: Chapter I, "Influence, Leadership, Control;" Chapter II, "Decision Making and Problem Solving;" and Chapter 14, "Organizational Decision Making."

MITCHELL, W. N. *The Business Executive in a Changing World* (New York: American Management Association, 1965). Beginning with the assumption that the top problems of today's business are "executive manpower and how to organize available human effort," a partner of the management consulting firm of A. T. Kearney & Company discusses (among other subjects) the executive functions, motivation, and development.

MORTIMER, C. G. *The Purposeful Pursuit of Profits and Growth in Business* (New York: McGraw-Hill Book Co., Inc., 1965). For many years Mr. Mortimer played a major role in the General Foods Corporation. Based on his experience, he uses this volume to state his belief in the key role played by the chief executive in the success of any business.

Profitable Community Relations for Small Business (Washington, D.C.: Small Business Administration, Small Business Management Series No. 27, 1961). Information on how the small firm can build respect on the part of the various publics with which it comes into contact is presented in this booklet.

REILLY, P. J. *Old Masters of Retailing* (New York: Fairchild Publications, 1966). This fascinating and revealing account of the innovations and contributions of thirty-five retailers was written by the late long-time active head of the Associated Merchandising Corp.

SCOTT, B. W. *Long-Range Planning in American Industry* (New York: American Management Association, Inc., 1965). This "contribution toward an understanding of corporate long-range planning" focuses attention on a significant area of management responsibility. The study covers the nature, historical evaluation, mission, organization, and implications of long-range planning.

STRONG, E. P. *The Management of Business* (New York: Harper & Row, 1965). The author presents an introductory analysis of the management function which evaluates the manager's role and suggests how it may be performed.

VANCE, S. C. *Boards of Directors: Structure and Performance* (Eugene, Oregon: University of Oregon Press, 1965). Because of their function as policymakers, this study of corporate directors has significance in relation to the present chapter.

WARREN, E. K. *Long-Range Planning: The Executive Viewpoint* (Englewood Cliffs, N.J.: Prentice-Hall, Inc., 1966). In a brief volume of 108 pages, Professor Warren of the Graduate School of Business at Columbia University identifies and analyzes five major problems facing the planner.

3

Retailing and the College Graduate

There are numerous and rewarding opportunities for college students in the field of retailing.[1] In view of such factors as our rapidly expanding population, the growth of shopping centers and suburban stores, the large number and different types of retail stores, and the variety of positions in such stores, it is not surprising that retailing furnishes a livelihood for more people in this country than any other field except manufacturing and farming. Moreover, there is sufficient diversity in retailing so that it provides opportunities for almost every kind of ability, training, ambition, need, and desire. Finally, top management is increasingly aware of the advantages of college training for success in this field.

SCOPE OF THE CHAPTER

Many employees of retail stores in this country are unskilled and poorly trained. Often employed on a part-time basis, they bear little or no important responsibility, and yet they seem to be well satisfied with their status. This discussion, however, is restricted primarily to the opportunities in retailing available for college students on a full-time basis. More particularly, attention is centered upon students who desire to get ahead in retailing and who wish to qualify for positions of responsibility calling for full use of their abilities, with commensurate salaries. Unfortunately, some students are unwilling to accept the responsibilities that accompany advancement. As the personnel manager of one large firm once stated: "It is astounding to note

---

[1] This discussion is restricted to *retail stores,* although opportunities exist in other forms of retailing, such as house-to-house selling, mail-order houses, and vending-machine ownership or lease.

the number of employees who will deliberately side-step responsibility, in many cases actually refusing promotion where this involves supervision of other people's work." For such persons, of course, the opportunities in retailing—and in other fields as well—are definitely limited.

Employment opportunities for college students are available in retail institutions with varying sales—large, medium, and small, so that stores of all sizes will be considered. It is impossible to generalize safely, however, upon whether opportunities are greatest in large organizations, middle-sized institutions, or small stores. The same is true as far as the size of the city is concerned. Opportunities depend upon the needs which exist in the community, the satisfactoriness of the merchandise and service provided, the circumstances that prevail within the company and in its competitive situation, the attitude of the management of the particular concern, the movement of the business cycle, the applicant himself, and the "breaks" he receives.

For convenience the discussion in this chapter is divided into six parts: (1) General employment aspects of retailing; (2) prospects in small and medium-sized stores; (3) opportunities in department and specialty stores; (4) careers in chain stores; (5) advancement possibilities in discount houses; and (6) attitudes of college graduates toward retailing careers.

GENERAL EMPLOYMENT ASPECTS OF RETAILING

The significant characteristics of retailing as a field of employment for college graduates are ten in number, as follows:

Large Number Employed

In 1965, retail stores of all sizes and types in the United States employed 9.8 million people.[2] This figure represents an increase of about 1.6 million since 1950 and 0.6 million over 1960. Looking ahead, the United States Labor Department estimates that by 1975 an additional four million people will be absorbed by the retail and wholesale fields, with most of them in retailing.[3]

Stable Employment for Full-Time Employees

The retail field offers more stable employment than many other industries. For some types of retail businesses, such as food stores, there is

---

[2] *Statistical Abstract of the United States,* 1966, p. 811.
[3] *Women's Wear Daily,* February 4, 1966, p. 9.

relatively little seasonal fluctuation in sales. In other fields, although seasonal variations in sales are significant, these variations are not so great as those in the rates of production of many manufacturing industries. The increasing use of part-time employees in retailing permits adjustments in the size of the total force with the maintenance of the regular staff at about its usual size.

Shifting Employment Opportunities

Although retailing is a stable industry, it is not a static one. Total retail volume and employment fluctuate with, and are dependent upon, national income. Moreover, certain groups of retail stores are increasing in importance, whereas others are decreasing. Evidence of some of the changes that took place in the years between 1958 and 1963 are shown in Table 3–1. The first six types of businesses listed are examples of "growing industries" in which there may be greater opportunities for young men and women than in the declining types of stores shown in the third division of the table. It is significant to note, however, that although the *number* of stores declined in some of the categories listed, the *average volume of sales* per store did not necessarily follow the same trend. This latter fact reflects both the inflation which occurred during the years covered by Table 3–1 and the increase in square footage per store.

Employment possibilities are also found in the newer retailing developments. Consider just two examples. While the total number of food stores has been declining in recent years, a new type of small food unit, sometimes referred to as a bantam store—with limited stocks, long hours, frequently open seven days each week, has become "the fastest-growing segment of the retail food business."[4] Again, recent years have witnessed the expansion of stores which rent, rather than sell, merchandise—furniture, rugs, lamps, paintings, home tools, television sets, air conditioning units. Already at least one rental organization has more than 400 affiliated dealer-outlets.[5]

A Decentralized Industry

Retailing is a decentralized industry offering opportunities either as an employee or a proprietor in every city, town, and village in the country. With some 1,708,000 stores scattered over every section of the nation, few

---

[4] "Snaring Sales While Others Sleep," *Business Week,* November 6, 1965, p. 130. Also cf. the section on "Growth of Small, Convenience-Type Stores," pp. 18–19, above.

[5] F. A. Babione, "Retailer Adjustment to a Rental Economy," *Journal of Retailing,* Vol. XL, No. 3 (Fall, 1964), p. 48.

TABLE 3–1

Changes in the Number of Establishments by
Type of Retail Store, 1958 and 1963

From 1958 to 1963 more establishments appeared in these retail businesses:

	Number of Establishments	
Type of Business	1958	1963
Men's and boys' apparel.....	18,116	22,451
Women's ready-to-wear......	26,559	29,696
Family clothing............	13,551	18,139
Drugstores.................	47,032	50,318
Department stores..........	3,157	4,251
Gasoline stations...........	206,755	211,473

. . . in these businesses, the number remained nearly constant:

	Number of Establishments	
Type of Business	1958	1963
Variety stores..............	21,017	22,378
Tire, battery, and accessory...	20,912	20,913
Furniture, home furnishings..	54,458	54,889
Shoe stores................	24,437	24,568

. . . while the number declined in these businesses:

	Number of Establishments	
Type of Business	1958	1963
Hardware.................	34,670	29,595
Food.....................	356,754	319,433
Household appliances, radio, T.V.....................	48,959	38,760
Jewelry stores..............	23,751	20,935
New automobile dealers......	38,555	33,349
Drinking places............	114,925	110,605

Source: *1963 Census of Business, Retail Trade: United States Summary*, BC63-RAI, pp. 1–6 to 1–10. Once again the reader should be reminded that census data for all years are not strictly comparable.

persons seeking employment have to go far to reach a possible employer. Although opportunities for promotion may be strictly limited in the smaller stores and in the smaller towns, even the most talented and ambitious person can receive highly useful experience near his own home. There is a very strong belief among large retailers that both promotional training and experience are necessary before an individual is ready for promotion. Students seeking employment and career opportunities in such stores can often obtain valuable experience in their home-town stores.

Variety of Occupations

Ordinarily employment in retailing is thought of as selling. Actually, however, in the larger organizations only about 55 percent of those employed are directly engaged in meeting the customer on the sales floor. Where self-service predominates the proportion is considerably less. Many retail stores need buyers, fashion experts, accountants, advertising men and women, traffic and delivery experts, research directors, and employees trained for personnel work, as well as salespeople.

Many Kinds of Stores

Another characteristic of retailing as a field of employment is the wide variety of stores. The 1963 *Census of Business* shows 89 separate classifications of stores and 79,792 "nonstore retailers." The different interests and backgrounds of experience, knowledge, abilities, and desires required by these varied stores provide an opportunity for the individual to find an interesting career in retailing.

Many Women Employed

Retailing has traditionally been a field offering employment to a large number of women. According to the latest information available there are more women employed in retailing than in any other single field, and the ratio of women to all those engaged in retailing is probably around 30 percent.[6] And the total number of women in retailing is increasing rapidly. Naturally, the ratio of women to total employees varies widely with the kind of business; it is low in such fields as tire and automotive accessory stores and high in millinery stores.

Retailing is especially attractive to women interested in a career rather than a mere job. Although in most industries only the very exceptional woman can hope to reach an executive position, in retailing women compete with men more nearly on a basis of ability. In fact, many, if not most, department stores demand that those training as managers and buyers of at

---

[6] This estimate is calculated from data on occupations by sex for managers and proprietors *in general* and for the self-employed and sales workers in retail trade in 1960. Cf. *U.S. Census of Population, United States Summary,* General Social and Economic Characteristics, pp. 1–216.

least some departments—such as lingerie, corsets and brassieres, millinery, dresses, and sportswear—be women. For department stores as a whole, almost half of the executive jobs are filled by women: At J. L. Hudson Company (Detroit) one third of the buyers are women, while at Neiman-Marcus Company (Dallas and Houston) the ratio rises to 50 percent.[7] In some of the high-fashioned specialty shops all buyers may be women, except possibly the shoe buyer, the fur buyer, and occasionally the coat buyer. Opportunities for women above the rank of buyer are more limited, but some women have become publicity directors, fashion directors, divisional or general merchandise managers, and a few, store presidents.[8] Women managers in apparel chains are also on the increase.

During the past two decades and more, the offering of comprehensive training programs by a number of universities, many of them on the work-study plan, and the active interest and support supplied by leading department and specialty stores and chain-store companies have done much to acquaint women college students with the opportunities in retailing.

Training Essential for Key Positions

Although retailing employs a large number of the unskilled, training is highly important for many types of positions, especially in the larger stores. "Training" may refer to academic background, trade or business school education, in-store training, or practical experience.

Many of the larger retail organizations, despite adoption of a policy known as "promotion from within," have found that the potential executive material originating within their stores is insufficient for their executive requirements. Therefore, an increasing number of department, chain, and mail-order companies have been sending personnel managers to various colleges to secure graduating seniors for executive training programs. Some firms have even made financial grants to certain colleges to encourage the establishment of courses, departments, or schools to develop college graduates with the kinds of knowledge and skills in which they are particularly interested.[9] It is probable that a higher percentage of college men and

---

[7] "How Top Retailers Build Executives," *Business Week,* June 5, 1965, p. 96.

[8] For a woman in the field of advertising cf. "Woman's Colorful Ads Sells Korvette Stores," *Editor & Publisher,* September 26, 1964, pp. 58 ff. For women in the world of fashion, cf. those contributing to *Profitable Fashion Merchandise Coordination* (rev. ed.; New York: National Retail Merchants Association, 1965). Both Henri Bendel, Inc. (Geraldine Stutz) and Bonwit Teller (Mildred Custin) have women as presidents. Cf. "Store President Retains Femininity," *New York Times,* January 15, 1965, p. 25.

[9] An example: The Academy of Food Marketing at Philadelphia's St. Joseph's College. Cf. *Chain Store Age* (Supermarket Executives Edition), May, 1965, pp. 130, 132.

women are employed by retail stores today than ever before. In addition, leading firms have organized training classes consisting of college graduates and other "promotional" individuals already working in their own organizations. In some cases these training programs consist of no more than a series of lectures by store executives, or a rotating work experience in every major store division, or, in the chain stores, experience in a number of different stores. The more complete executive training programs, however, include not only organized lectures, discussions, and store tours, carried on by qualified outside men and store executives, but rotating work experience as well.[10] These steps taken by the larger, more progressive stores, of course, indicate the desirability of self-training for anyone really ambitious for a career in retailing.

Retailing Salaries

Salespeople and Nonselling Employees. Table 3–2 provides hourly earnings and workweek figures from the *Monthly Labor Review,* based upon reports from cooperating establishments covering both full- and part-time employees. In examining these figures, the reader is cautioned to note that they are for nonsupervisory employees and working supervisors only.

TABLE 3–2

AVERAGE GROSS EARNINGS AND HOURS OF NONSUPERVISORY EMPLOYEES IN SELECTED RETAIL TRADES, 1965

Type of Store	Average Hourly Earnings	Average Weekly Hours
Retail trade (except eating and drinking places)	$1.85	36.9
General merchandise stores	1.63	34.0
Department stores	1.75	33.6
Grocery, meat, vegetable stores	1.91	34.3
Apparel and accessories stores	1.70	33.8
Shoe stores	1.84	33.8
Men's and boys' apparel stores	1.92	36.7

SOURCE: *Monthly Labor Review,* August, 1966, pp. 878–89.

The figures in Table 3–2 have more significance when supplemented by data indicating the usual range within which wages fall for persons engaged in performing various jobs in the retail field. Beginning salaries for salespeople in the stores of small communities commonly range from $50 to $70 per week. In supermarkets, department, and variety stores located in

---

[10] Also cf. the discussion of executive training programs on pp. 72–73 and 78–81 below.

large cities this range is from $70 to $95. However, capable specialty salespeople in men's suits, rugs, furniture, and sporting goods frequently have weekly earnings averaging as much as $80 to $125 or more. The typical nonselling employee also falls in the low-wage bracket, with weekly earnings of from $65 to $90, although employees in the more responsible positions, usually department managers, may receive from $80 to $120 or more.

Beginning Salaries.   When one considers the beginning salaries offered college graduates, the picture is somewhat brighter. During recent years these salaries have moved upward as retailers increasingly have recog-

TABLE 3–3

NATIONAL AVERAGE MONTHLY SALARY OFFERS TO MALE, BACHELOR'S-DEGREE CANDIDATES, 1965–66

By Type of Employer for All Curricula	No. Offers 1965–66 1–2 Period Cumulative	1965–66 1–2 Period Cumulative	1964–65 Year's Total
Accounting-Public.............................	545	$575	$556
Aircraft, Space Vehicles, & Components........	2140	661	641
Automotive & Mechanical Equipment..........	524	644	608
Banking, Finance, & Insurance................	162	499	483
Chemicals, Drugs, & Allied Products...........	1210	662	627
Construction & Building Materials Mfrs........	210	638	603
Electrical Machinery & Equipment............	802	655	625
Electronics & Instruments....................	941	656	632
Food & Beverage Processing..................	108	571	552
Glass, Paper, Packaging, & Products...........	324	632	597
Merchandising & Related Services.............	182	513	483
Metal & Metal Products......................	809	647	618
Petroleum & Products (inc. Nat. Gas).........	748	648	608
Research/Consulting Organizations............	128	646	602
Tire & Rubber..............................	186	641	609
Utilities-Public (inc. Transportation)..........	622	634	604

Source: Salary Survey, 1965–66 Recruiting Year, Report No. 2 (Bethlehem, Pa.: The College Placement Council, 1966).

nized the necessity of offering higher salaries to interest qualified candidates in such work. In Table 3–3, which presents data on salaries offered in 1965–66, figures for students entering retailing are included under "Merchandising and Related Services." Yet these data make it clear that retail organizations must do considerably more to meet the inducements of other industries. Still higher beginning salaries must be offered and, equally important, qualified trainees must be advanced more rapidly than in the past.[11]

---

[11] These points of view are well expressed by J. L. Goldstucker, "Competent Retail Trainees—Where Are They?," *Journal of Marketing.* Vol. XXVII, No. 2 (April, 1963), pp. 38–41, especially p. 41; and by Professor Harold Shaffer in an address reported in *Women's Wear Daily,* February 4, 1966, p. 3.

Top Executive Salaries. The salaries of top retail executives in large firms provide an interesting contrast with the figures in Table 3–3 and demonstrate the income opportunities available to qualified young men and women. In a recent year, the chief executive officer of Montgomery Ward & Company received $100,000; Kroger Company, $160,000; Safeway Stores, Inc., $175,000; and Sears, Roebuck and Co., $250,000.[12] These annual salaries are frequently supplemented by deferred compensation and profit-sharing plans.

Notwithstanding these facts, many college graduates are kept from entering retailing by salary offers below those provided by other types of businesses competing for them. Perhaps even more are reluctant to enter retailing because of the prospect of some Saturday, Sunday, and evening work, especially during the first few years in business. Yet is is evident from the executive salaries given in the preceding paragraph that those who can "stick out" the first hard years and who have the particular personality and types of abilities required may eventually make large earnings. Moreover, many persons earn very good salaries in the intermediate executive positions in retailing, as will be indicated later in this chapter.

Nonfinancial Rewards for Success in Retailing. All too frequently college students think of the rewards for success in retail store management in terms of salaries alone. Obviously, it is true that "executive motivation in business enterprise is invariably contingent in some part upon financial inducement . . ."[13] Yet "man does not live by bread alone" and other factors are equally or even more significant. The late Harvey S. Firestone once said: "I have never found that pay and pay alone would either bring together or hold good men."

Young men and women may look forward to many nonmonetary satisfactions as retail executives. There is the personal satisfaction of achievement, of being at the top in the field, and of having others in the company and the community recognize one's success. The retailer makes a significant contribution to today's high standard of living, a fact which is an important motivating force for many people. He is in a position to extend job opportunities to others, to try new ways of operating his store, and to assume a leadership role in community betterment programs. As in other fields of business, executive positions in retailing offer an intellectual challenge which should appeal to many of today's young people.[14] Add to these satisfac-

---

[12] *Business Week,* May 21, 1966, pp. 184–86.

[13] W. N. Mitchell, *The Business Executive in a Changing World* (New York: American Management Association, 1965), p. 135.

[14] R. M. Blough, "Business Can Satisfy the Young Intellectual," *Harvard Business Review,* Vol. XLIV, No. 1 (January–February, 1966), pp. 49–57.

tions the stimulation that comes from meeting new problems and making new contacts, and it is difficult to understand why more college students are not interested in retailing careers.

Working Conditions in the Retail Field

Working conditions in retailing vary greatly among different concerns in the same field, firms in different fields, different types of work in the same company, and different sections of the country. In view of these variations, the following discussion must be in general terms.

Hours. Working hours per week in the retail field as in other fields of employment have been sharply reduced in recent years. Although many small stores, particularly those staffed by the proprietor and his family, work their employees 48, 54, and even more hours per week, more and more retail organizations are adopting a 40-hour week. Moreover, although stores remain open six days or even seven per week, and increasingly are open evenings, the five-day work-week has become common. As a practical matter, work schedules in retailing are frequently far more regular than they are for those who seek careers with airlines, newspapers, television or in such professions as medicine and law. And the fact remains that those who are willing to "pay the price" of hard work during their first years in retailing will find ample rewards in later years to compensate for this time and effort.

Surroundings. The surroundings of the retail employee vary greatly with the kind of work, the particular store, and the community. Nonselling employees often work in unattractive surroundings, although "modernization" of nonselling areas has increased in recent years. Most stores, however, give precedence to painting and improvements on the selling floors where customers will see the results: These areas have been greatly improved in the past decade, both through the construction of new stores and the upgrading of existing ones. So far as executives are concerned, the dignified private office and the secretary, which constitute two of the emoluments of many positions in other industries, are becoming common.

Probably as important as the physical surroundings are the mental and social conditions of work. Fortunately, retailers are recognizing the need for improvements in these areas and are doing something about it. Libraries, house organs, concerts, athletic contests, and similar activities all contribute to the development of an *esprit de corps* among employees which is conductive to their happiness and contentment. In addition, retailing offers many social contacts and opportunities to talk with customers and fellow employees alike, which are very stimulating to some types of people.

Vacations. Vacations in retailing are comparable with those in the majority of other business fields. The larger retailers offer their employees a vacation of at least a week with pay, usually extending it to two, three, or even four weeks with added years of service.[15] Most vacation periods are confined to the summer months, when business is slow and the employee need not be replaced, but increasingly arrangements for winter vacations are being made. At the executive level, there is great flexibility as to when vacations can be taken.

Job Security. As indicated previously, retailing is a stable business and consequently provides a high degree of job security. To date, retail employees have also been spared from any large amount of technological unemployment. Whereas the introduction of machines in manufacturing has resulted in the displacement of men in the performance of many jobs, retailing is still largely a hand industry, especially in its selling aspects. Despite (1) the present rapid development of mechanical equipment for warehouses and other operating activities; (2) the employment of computers for tasks formerly assigned to individuals; (3) the growth of the self-service store; and (4) the possible expansion of automation to the selling function, the weight of opinion is that retailing will remain dominantly a hand industry for some time to come.

Closely connected with job security is the security that larger retailers are increasingly providing for their employees in the form of group insurance, pensions, health insurance, and the like, as well as governmental provisions such as medicare, old-age pensions, and unemployment benefits.[16]

Unions. In many industries labor unions have had a very considerable influence on working conditions; the retail field has proved no exception, although the relative growth of unions in retailing has been far less than elsewhere. Beginning rather slowly but progressing more rapidly since 1933, labor unions have secured a number of agreements with large retail organizations involving important concessions. Most of these contracts have resulted in improved working conditions and higher wages for the employees covered.[17]

Future Prospects. Despite the trend toward night and Sunday openings, overall working conditions in the retail field will undoubtedly continue to improve in the coming years. This improvement, however, will probably affect neither the small-store owner who can successfully compete only on a basis of customer convenience—such as remaining open evenings and

---

[15] S. S. Kresge Company offers a vacation of four weeks after fifteen years of service. *Discount Store News,* June 13, 1966, p. 2. Also cf. A. A. Sloane, "Trends Toward More Liberalized Vacations," *Personnel,* Vol. XLIII, No. 1 (January–February, 1966), pp. 56–61.

[16] These benefits are discussed in Chapter 9, "Retail Personnel Management."

[17] Cf. Chapter 9.

Sundays when most other stores are closed—nor the ambitious junior executive who is seeking to get ahead. Promotion or success in any business is seldom achieved by short hours and easy work, although many of the long hours may not be spent directly on the job but in studying in the evening. It should also be remembered that in any field promotion usually means not an easier life but a harder one, since additional responsibilities must be assumed.

PROSPECTS IN SMALL AND MEDIUM-SIZED STORES

Opportunities for college men and women in small and medium-sized stores are of two broad types. First, family and personal interests may well dictate that the graduate enter a business to assist a relative or a friend with its operation, with a long-run view of becoming manager and, possibly, owner. Second, the graduate may desire to enter business for himself, either through the purchase of an established store or the opening of a new one. In this instance, of course, it must be assumed that he has had sufficient experience to insure a reasonable chance of success and that adequate funds are available to establish the store and "see it through" the first months of operation.

All too often the college student finds himself unable to take immediate advantage of either of the types of situations described. Therefore, he must first take a beginner's job with someone else hoping thereby to gain the experience and training that will enable him to obtain a better position elsewhere or perhaps to open a store of his own at some future date. Let us examine some of his opportunities in this direction.

Limited Opportunities as an Employee

Despite important progress made in recent years, far too many small- and medium-sized independent retailers still conduct their businesses by methods so outmoded that even the employee who works hard will not receive the training he should get. Such stores should be avoided. Stated positively, the college graduate should seek employment in a progressive independent store where he can get a variety of experiences in all aspects of retailing, including, among others, knowledge of merchandise, operating problems, sales promotion, relations with customers, and store records and control. He should supplement such in-store experiences by reading trade magazines and textbooks on all phases of store operations, by consulting governmental and other reports on subjects related to his business, and by observing and studying carefully the policies and practices of competitors and other stores.

Ownership Possibilities

Impressed with the earnings of the chief executives in large retail organizations, and also possibly suffering from a case of "payroll paralysis" brought on by a college education often overemphasizing "big business," most college students overlook the opportunities available in owning their own retail store.

Profitability of Independent Store Ownership. Too often retailing is thought of as an unprofitable business. This idea has been encouraged by various expense studies showing retail profits of only 1 percent to 4 percent *of sales.* The fact is sometimes overlooked that such small profit ratios frequently represent 10 percent to 20 percent or more *on net worth* and that they are *in addition* to the proprietor's salary or drawing account for services rendered to the business. To cite a specific example of income possibilities, a study of a typical group of owners of single-store supermarkets in a voluntary chain disclosed their average salary plus net profit was over $17,000.[18]

Future of Independent Store. There is also increasing optimism concerning future profits for the smaller retailers. Two students of this subject put the matter this way: ". . . despite many prevailing prophecies of doom, there is underway growing strength in small retailing . . . This strength could reverse, or at least hold in check, the gradual trend toward consolidation in retailing."[19] Specifically they point to (1) the small retailer's current ability to practice quasi-integration through franchise and voluntary chain arrangements, (2) the limitations of large-scale retailing (such as burdensome union contracts and difficulties in providing meaningful incentives),[20] and (3) the developing diversity of consumer markets which calls for the flexibility of independent operation (special services, breadth of assortments). And they conclude: "The extent to which the small retailer will once again become a major competitive force will depend on the vigor and aggressiveness with which he accepts the challenge and develops programs appropriate to his given line of business. This will require a philosophy of innovation rather than of imitation and the full cooperation of all organizations that stand to gain from this development. Obviously, not all

[18] Seymour Freedgood, "Uncle to 1,700 Grocers," *Fortune,* Vol. LXXI, No. 3 (March, 1965), p. 133.

[19] A. F. Doody and W. R. Davidson," Growing Strength in Small Retailing," *Harvard Business Review,* Vol. XLII, No. 4 (July–August, 1964), p. 69.

[20] Supporting this point is an analysis of Internal Revenue data developed from income tax returns which suggests that the economies of size in retailing are limited, with the most efficient size frequently far less than the largest firms in the field. Cf. Edna Douglas, "Size of the Firm and the Structure of Costs in Retailing," *Journal of Business,* April, 1962, pp. 158–90.

small retailers will participate in this opportunity, but for those who do, a bright future lies ahead."[21]

In view of the foregoing, it is not going too far to suggest that ownership of a well-managed store can mean a "good" living for the owner-manager. If the owner is ambitious enough to plan and work toward this end, store ownership provides an opportunity to build a large and successful business on a very limited investment. Right through the depression of the thirties many profitable stores were established and expanded into sizable business enterprises. Trade magazines regularly carry articles describing the growth of merchants from shoestring beginnings, and the more spectacular are sometimes reported in the general business magazines.[22]

In brief, there will always be ample opportunity in the retail field for those owners with the proper qualifications and for those who are not too concerned with rapid progress and immediate high income. In the final analysis, success in the retail business is based upon knowledge and application of merchandising principles and the intelligent handling of customer and employee relationships.

Many Opportunities for Store Ownership.   Few fields of employment still offer as great an opportunity of being one's own "boss" as the retail field. There are a tremendous number of opportunities. Of the 1,708,000 retail stores in this country, 87 percent are independent stores. Every newspaper carries classified advertisements of stores for sale, many for legitimate reasons, and salesmen calling on the trade, jobbers and wholesalers, officers of trade associations, and editors and staffs of trade papers usually known of others, although the owners may not be actively soliciting a buyer.

Manufacturers, wholesalers, store designers and builders, and equipment houses are also eager for outlets and sales; and these people may be of considerable assistance in finding an existing store to buy or in opening a new one, both through advice and extension of credit. Thus a manufacturer of women's dresses will help the new owner plan a revised layout for the store he has purchased, train sales personnel, and organize fashion shows.[23] Automobile manufacturers serve as the "complete management consultant" to their new (and old) dealers, as do other franchise-granting firms for such

---

[21] *Ibid.,* p. 79. That the able, small businessman has a future in nonretailing areas is the conclusion of an independent study financed by the Small Business Administration. Cf. "A Future for Small Business," *Business Week,* July 31, 1965, pp. 35–36, 38.

[22] As an example of a trade magazine article, cf. the 54 page report on *What's Behind the Rise of Two Guys,* in Section Two of *Discount Store News,* November 1, 1965.

[23] Cf. "Bobbie Brooks," in *How They Sell* (New York: Dow Jones & Co., 1965), pp. 137–40.

products as ice cream, doughnuts, and hamburgers.[24] Some voluntary chain wholesalers, especially in the food field, will even find the location, put up the store building, and stock it for the owner.[25] Even large department stores and the rapidly expanding chain discount houses create opportunities for many smaller retailers in that they lease out some of their departments.[26] All in all, those who wish to own stores can find many opportunities to do so.

Failures in Retailing. Despite the profit possibilities of retail store ownership and the great number of opportunities for such ownership, it is evident to the observer of the retail scene that ownership also involves dangers. The most serious of these is the danger of failure, especially in the early years of a new venture.

Although there are no universally accepted figures and although the failure rate varies from field to field and from year to year depending upon general economic conditions, it is not uncommon to find that from 10 to 20 percent of those who open their own stores fail within the first year. Within the first five years of operation perhaps as many as 30 to 40 percent have failed.[27]

When retail failures are analyzed carefully, some interesting facts are revealed. First, while the rate of failure seems high, it is certainly no higher than for those who begin their own wholesaling or manufacturing businesses. Second, by far the most important reasons for retail failures are found in two factors: (1) lack of capital, and (2) incompetence, much of which is caused by inexperience and the absence of managerial ability.[28] These facts suggest that, if the college graduate who opens his own retail store has secured proper financial backing and has adequate retail experience and managerial ability, he may well succeed in his retailing venture.

Financing the Store. As we have just noted, lack of capital is a major cause of failure in retailing. In 1960 Dun & Bradstreet estimated the starting capital for certain types of stores as follows: men's and boys' clothing, $14,000; dry goods, $24,000; women's shoes, $8,900; men's and boys' furnishings, $11,000; children's and infants' wear, $10,100; and women's

---

[24] "Surest Shortcut to Being Your Own Boss," *Reader's Digest,* June, 1965, pp. 209–14.

[25] Cf. "Wetterau Foods, St. Louis: Its Formula for Retailer Profits," *Super Market Merchandising,* September, 1965, especially pp. 29–30.

[26] "Leased Departments: A 1½ Billion Baby is Growing," *Department Store Economist,* March, 1965, pp. 34–37.

[27] For some specific studies of retail failures cf. C. F. Phillips and D. J. Duncan, *Marketing: Principles and Methods* (5th ed.; Homewood, Ill.: Richard D. Irwin, Inc., 1964) pp. 144–46.

[28] Cf. the reasons for retail failures during the twelve months ended June 30, 1966 in *Dun's Review and Modern Industry,* September, 1966, Part I, p. 15.

ready-to-wear, $9,300.[29] The National Retail Hardware Association estimates that $17,500 is needed to start a store expecting $50,000 sales in the first year of operation.[30] These figures do not include the store building, which is usually rented. In contrast to these investments is that required for a modern supermarket which, including the building, may involve $500,000 or more.[31] As is emphasized in a later paragraph, however, the owner need not be called upon to provide cash to meet all of the necessary financing.

1. *Determining Financial Needs.* When the purchase of an *established business* is contemplated, it is fairly easy for the buyer to arrive at an approximation of his total financial requirements: he uses the purchase price plus rough estimates of an additional amount for any layout changes, inventory adjustments, any additional working capital required, and contingencies.

When a *new business* is being considered, a threefold approach is recommended. First, the prospective buyer should visit a friendly and somewhat comparable retailer in another community and get information from him as to his investment in fixtures and equipment, merchandise inventory, accounts receivable (if credit sales are contemplated), and other working capital items. To this figure should be added an amount for unforeseen contingencies and for expenses incurred while he is getting the store ready for its opening day.

Second, the buyer should compare the figures referred to in the previous paragraph with all relevant and available data from his trade association—if he belongs to one, a university bureau of business research, or the Small Business Administration.

Third, the prospective retailer should check carefully the information obtained in the previous two steps against his own estimates for each major expense. For example, he can prepare his own estimate of the amount to be invested in fixtures and equipment by submitting a list of these items to two or three firms selling them.

2. *Securing Financial Backing.* For purposes of discussion, let us assume that the foregoing steps result in an estimate of $20,000 as the total financial requirements of the proposed retail business. What are the sources from which such funds may be secured?

Probably the most important source is the capital possessed by the new owner himself. As a general rule, but one to which in practice many

---

[29] Quoted in *New York Retailer,* December, 1960, p. 13.

[30] Cf. *Managing a Retail Hardware Store* (Indianapolis: The Association, 1961), p. 28.

[31] *Facts About New Super Markets Opened in 1965* (Chicago, Ill.: Super Market Institute, Inc., 1966), p. 13.

exceptions are made, he should provide at least 50 percent of the total investment—in this case, at least $10,000. Without a personal investment of this amount he may find it difficult to secure additional funds from other sources. Moreover, if he depends too heavily on borrowed capital, his interest payments may be so high that he cannot meet them if he runs into a period of unfavorable economic conditions.

For the remaining $10,000 required, several sources are available. His resources (the wholesalers and manufacturers from whom he buys) will usually finance a substantial part of his inventory on 30-, 60-, or 90-day credit. Furthermore, his needed fixtures and equipment may be financed on an installment basis with the seller. Commercial banks are also available to provide short-term loans, if the prospective retailer can show that the loan will be liquidated within what the banker considers to be a reasonable period of time.

In many cases loans may be secured from friends or, if a corporation is being formed, friends may purchase some of the stock. If the latter happens, the retailer must be careful that he does not lose control of his business. If a going business is being purchased, perhaps the seller will accept a well-secured note of the buyer for a substantial part of the purchase price. Currently the federal government—through the Small Business Administration—is a source of loans to retailers who may find the more usual sources of funds closed to them.[32]

In a few retail fields, special situations exist with regard to financing. Wholesalers and others sponsoring voluntary chains (variety stores, food stores, hardware stores, drugstores) are sometimes willing to equip and stock a store and accept a note from the buyer for a substantial part of the investment. To illustrate, McKesson & Robbins, a wholesale drug firm, offers such a service to prospective retailers of its products: during a five-year period this wholesaler aided retailers "to design or modernize 10,000 drugstores."[33] Manufacturers of automobiles are usually willing to extend aid to their new dealers, a typical arrangement being that the dealer provide at least one quarter of the total investment in the business. Other franchise-granting organizations—Dipper Dan Ice Cream (Swift & Company), Stuckey's (Pet Milk Company), and Dunkin' Donuts—either extend some financial aid or use their "know how" to produce it.[34] The marketing divisions of major oil companies often give new dealers very substantial

---

[32] Susan Artigiani, "SBA Plays Good Neighbor Role, Issues New Loan Plan Checks," *Women's Wear Daily,* August 19, 1964, p. 9.

[33] Seymour Freedgood, "The Reluctant Dragon of the Drug Industry," *Fortune,* Vol. LXVI, No. 5 (November, 1962), p. 143.

[34] "Franchising Finds It's An Industry," *Business Week,* June 19, 1965, pp. 72–76.

assistance in equipping and stocking filling stations, with the result that all the dealer needs to supply is the working capital—and this may be as little as $10,000.

Buying or Starting a Business? There is no single answer to the question: Should I buy a going business or start a new one? The best answer is, "It all depends!" Consideration must be given to such factors as the availability of a going business, the price the seller will accept, whether or not there is a good location available for a new store, whether or not the community can support an additional establishment, and which of the two propositions is easier to finance.

Of course, there are some positive advantages in starting an entirely new business. It enables the retailer to begin with a "clean" stock. New fixtures and equipment provide an attractive shopping atmosphere, and a modern layout may contribute to low operating expenses. No payment for good will is involved, and the store does not have to "live down" any ill will which the former owner might have created.

Yet the purchase of a going business frequently offers compensating advantages. The assembly of new fixtures and equipment as well as inventory and personnel is time consuming. A going business has a system of record keeping already established. It may also have at least a nucleus of "steady customers." By taking over a going business, the purchaser is not adding to the total number of stores in the area and thereby spreading the business among more retailers.

In the majority of cases the question of "whether to buy an established store or to start a new one" comes down to the price which the proposed seller will accept for his business. If this is low enough, even a poorly equipped and stocked store may be a "good buy." The buyer should keep firmly in mind that the actual price to be paid is usually the subject of a great deal of bargaining. Consequently, an appraisal of the store's assets is but the point of departure. Sometimes the location of a store and its well-developed clientele are such that the payment of a premium over "book value" is both necessary and profitable; in other cases the reverse is true. Before the bargaining begins the buyer will do well to have the store's assets appraised carefully and its profit possibilities estimated, so that he will have a sound basis for judging the maximum amount he will pay.

Proprietorship, Partnership, or Corporation? Another decision faced by the individual establishing his own retail store is the legal form of organization to employ. Since most readers of this text will have studied these legal forms—including the relative advantages and disadvantages of each—in such earlier courses as principles of economics, business organization, accounting, or corporation finance, it is unnecessary to analyze them here except to make a few comments concerning their use in the retail field.

The overwhelming majority of small retailers in this country are proprietorships. In fact, about two thirds of our retail stores employ this form of business organization. The size of these stores is indicated by the fact that their yearly sales, as reported to the most recent *Census of Business,* averaged $58,000 as contrasted with $113,000 for partnerships and $421,000 for corporation owned outlets.

Two main factors have encouraged such widespread reliance on the proprietorship in the retail field: (1) the relative ease with which it can be adopted, including lack of legal problems; and (2) the tax saving which it makes possible. To the individual who is investing a substantial part of his savings or who is borrowing heavily to begin a new venture, however, these advantages may be more than offset by the limited liability and not-terminated-by-death aspects of the corporation. Although the new retailer may wish to begin with a proprietorship or partnership form, he may find it advisable to convert to a corporation as soon as his business has shown some growth.

PROSPECTS IN DEPARTMENT AND SPECIALTY STORES

The number of department stores increased from 3,157 to 4,251 between 1958 and 1963 and their sales gained 54 percent as compared with the average for all retail stores of 22 percent.[35] Department stores have also rapidly opened branch and suburban stores, thus expanding their demand for qualified managerial personnel. However, it still is true that rapidity of promotion in the department store field depends to a great extent upon the particular store. If a store is growing rapidly and has a policy of promotion-from-within, or if a new management has just taken over a poorly managed or unprofitable store, or if an individual just happens to "get the breaks" when vacancies occur through resignation, retirement, or otherwise, promotion may be very rapid. In contrast, if the store has "gone to seed," if the management finds it easier to fill most good executive positions from outside, or if it is a well-organized store with a seasoned and established executive staff but with no real growth prospects, promotion will undoubtedly be very slow. Everything considered, the authors are convinced that many attractive opportunities are available to college graduates in department and specialty stores.

Need for Department Store Executives

During the past decade and more department stores and many large specialty stores have sought to improve their competitive position through

---

[35] *1963 Census of Business, Retail Trade: United States Summary,* BC 63–RA1, p. 1–6.

more alert merchandising efforts, the development of units in shopping centers, and the opening of free-standing suburban stores. These developments, as noted in the previous paragraph, have created numerous opportunities for college graduates and have resulted in stronger recruiting programs by leading institutions to meet their needs. Thus the demand for executives by Allied Stores Corporation is such that each year it places about 500 young men and women in its executive training program.[36] Federated Department Stores, Inc., estimates that its current ten year expansion program of 45 units will require 3,200 additional executives, and it expects to get a "large percentage" of them from college campuses.[37]

As for salaries, while more details will be included in later sections on opportunities available in the various divisions of department stores, it may be noted here that junior retailing executives generally earn from $6,500 to $8,500 yearly. Many buyers receive between $10,000 and $30,000 annually, and division heads in large stores draw $18,000 to $50,000.

Training Programs for Junior Executives

A favorable aspect for the college graduate in the department store field is the existence of a number of executive training programs. Once admitted to such a program, the college graduate—although not assured of success—is certainly guaranteed an opportunity to learn all aspects of the business within a relatively short period. Moreover, he can be quite sure that his progress (or lack of progress) will be brought to the attention of top management.

The Macy Program. Although training programs naturally differ from store to store, since they are designed to meet particular requirements, a brief glance at one of them will serve to illustrate their general nature. For this purpose we have selected the executive training program currently in operation at R. H. Macy & Co., with six major stores and numerous "branches" located from coast to coast.

In a brochure prepared for distribution to college graduates, the company describes the opportunities it provides as follows:

In 1919 Macy's started the first organized program for training executives: The Macy Executive Training Squad. The careers of many of the country's leading retail executives began with this program and the Macy system is the forerunner for all other department store executive training programs.

[36] Edward Coyle, "Allied Doesn't Spare Staff in Executive Training Setup," *Women's Wear Daily,* February 21, 1963, p. 40.

[37] James O'Connor and Doris Searcy, "Federated Department Stores' Needs," *ibid.,* p. 40.

The Executive Training Squad is, in essence, a post-graduate program in business, but a post-graduate program in which you learn by doing as well as studying . . . and get paid at the same time. The program lasts from 6 to 8 months and includes classroom instruction, seminars, lectures, and work assignments in almost all divisions of your store.

As openings occur for which you are suited, you will move into them. You'll be carefully guided and counseled, moved upward from job-to-job.

Your development will be planned, the opportunities will be there . . . and the future will be all yours.

Once on the Training Squad you, of course, become a member of the Macy organization, with all its privileges and benefits. These include sick benefits, pension and profit-sharing plan, group insurance, paid vacations and discounts.

Admission to this program is highly competitive and is granted to college graduates who successfully complete a series of interviews with the store's executives. Qualifications considered are not only the college academic record but also extracurricular activities, work experience, outstanding personal qualities, skills, and ambition. Typical career progress in the Macy organization is illustrated in Figure 3–1.

TYPICAL CAREER PROGRESS

CONTROL
OPERATIONS
PERSONNEL

MERCHANDISING

Junior Assistant Buyer

Sales Manager
(Branch Store)

Senior Assistant Buyer

Group Manager
(Branch Store)

Department Manager

Administrator

Vice President

Junior Assistant
(Accountant, Employment Interviewer, Floor Supervisor, etc.)

Senior Assistant
(Wage Analyst, Receiving Supervisor, Purchasing Assistant, etc.)

Assist. Department Manager
(Merchandise Control, Labor Relations, Comparison shopping, etc.)

Department Manager
(Adjustment Service, Merchandise Statistics, Training, etc.)

Administrator

Vice President

SALES PROMOTION

Junior Assistant
(Copywriter, Stylist, etc.)

Senior Assistant
(Art, Production, etc.)

Assist. Department Manager
(Interior Display, Photography, etc.)

Department Manager
(Advertising, Public Relations, etc.)

Administrator

Vice President

FIG. 3–1. Typical career progress in R. H. Macy & Company.

Opportunities in the Merchandising Division

As suggested in the Macy training squad program described above, opportunities are available to college graduates in a variety of activities in department and specialty stores. These may best be discussed for each of the main divisions of such stores—merchandising, publicity, operating, accounting or control, and personnel.

Promotion from a selling position in a department store is usually fairly slow, unless the person has been hired by the management with the thought that he is good material for an executive position. When advancement comes, the salesperson usually moves to the position of head of stock, to assistant buyer, to buyer, and finally to merchandise manager, the latter two being very important to the success of a department store.

The work of the head of stock is usually to supervise the stock of one section in a department, keeping it clean and orderly, notifying the buyer of needed merchandise, and instructing and helping new sales-people. He may also assist in departmental administrative work, such as aiding in the preparation of advertising copy (in the smaller stores); planning departmental and window displays; and helping with some clerical work, especially that connected with merchandise records and stock counts prior to the buyer's placing of orders. Sometimes the head of stock is authorized to make out the reorders on basic stock, subject to the buyer's approval. He will normally earn $10 or $20 a week more than a salesperson in the department.

The assistant buyer, as his title implies, aids the buyer in performing his duties. His activities may vary from those of head of stock to those of buyer, depending upon the buyer, the size of the department, experience, and whether or not the buyer is in town. Salaries normally range from $90 to $120 a week but may go to $150 or more in exceptional cases.

The traditional buyer takes charge of his department just as if it were his own small store. He selects and purchases merchandise; supervises stock and record keeping; in cooperation with the advertising department, supervises advertising; is responsible for planning departmental and window displays; and supervises actual sales to customers. Currently, there is a trend for department stores to separate the buying from the selling function, so that buyers in many stores no longer supervise sales. Because of the importance of the buyer's activities, it takes a minimum of two or three years before an able young man or woman is prepared to assume the responsibilities involved; usually it requires a longer period to obtain such a position. Earnings depend on sales volume and profit; but they frequently run between $125 and $200 a week and sometimes reach $30,000 a year.

The merchandise manager is the next step up the promotional ladder for the buyer. In smaller stores there may be only one merchandise manager, and the position may be assumed by the president or owner. In larger stores a number of divisional merchandise managers, each supervising the work of possibly five to twenty buyers, are responsible to the senior, or general, merchandise manager. Although the duties of the merchandise manager will vary among different stores, the usual situation is for him to supervise and advise the buyers; guide their thinking, planning, and performance; and exercise general financial and merchandising control over his departments.

The merchandise manager's earnings vary with volume and frequently include a bonus or profit-sharing arrangement, so that his income is even more dependent than that of the buyers upon ability to get results. His remuneration usually ranges from $10,000 or $12,000 to $30,000 a year, or more.

Opportunities in the Publicity Division

College men and women who have ability in writing and planning, who have imagination and originality, and who understand human nature are often drawn into advertising. Unless such persons have had sales experience, however, their beginning position will probably be in the merchandising division, so as to provide practical experience with the public's reaction to merchandise. Applicants with some advertising experience may begin as copy writers, or as window trimmers and display men. Good copy writers and display men earn from $100 to $125 per week, and often more.

For the person who makes a success of his work in advertising, advancement to the position of publicity director or manager is possible. In this position, yearly earnings range from $8,000 to $25,000 a year or more, depending upon the size of the organization. Work in the advertising department is very closely allied to that in the merchandising division; and in some organizations good copy writers may also be promoted to buying positions, especially in fashion departments.

Opportunities in the Service or Operating Division

Because of the large number and variety of functions performed by the service or operating division, much of the work is performed by unskilled and uneducated workers, although skilled employees are required for carpentry, plumbing, and electrical work. Other jobs require different types of training; and college men and women may find work adapted to their abilities and interests in connection with the supervision of receiving, marking, and delivery of merchandise, special service activities, complaints and adjustments, purchasing store supplies, and systems research. Some experience in these and related tasks is essential before promotion to a supervisory job.

Salaries and, ordinarily, opportunities for promotion are considerably less in the service division than in the merchandising division. It should be remembered, however, that many of the successful "operating types" are not interested in—and would not be particularly successful in—merchandising.

The store superintendent or operating manager heads the division. He should be a man of considerable ability and experience, usually rising from the ranks. His salary will range from $15,000 to $30,000 a year or more, which is less than the successful merchandise manager ordinarily receives.

Opportunities in the Accounting and Control Division

The controller heads the accounting and control division and is responsible for administering the store's finances, collections, credits, and accounting records.[38] Beginning positions for trained men and women include: cashier, bookkeeper, auditor, correspondent, credit clerk, and payroll clerk. Promotion requires a thorough knowledge of accounting and leads to the position of office manager, credit manager or assistant controller and, eventually, to controller. Opportunities in this division have increased substantially during the past three decades because of numerous federal and state regulations with which the retailer must comply and because of new developments in systems and electronic data processing.

Qualifications for success in this division are somewhat different from those in other divisions of the firm. One must like figures and must be exact —a stickler for detail and accuracy—and should have analytical ability to interpret figures in the light of broad store policy. One needs an orderly type of mind, adapted to the creation of systems for recording voluminous data and summarizing these data for easy interpretation by other executives.

Beginners in this division may earn from $85 to $100 per week. Eventual rewards are not so large as in the merchandising division. Head cashiers, head bookkeepers, head billers, paymasters, head correspondents, and assistant credit managers may earn from $5,000 to $8,000 per year as junior executives, seldom more. Over these men are the credit manager, the office manager, and the manager of the statistical office, with earnings from $8,000 to $13,000. The position of controller carries a substantial

---

[38] The functions of the controller are fully explored in E. A. Helfert, E. G. May, and M. P. McNair, *Controllership in Department Stores* (Boston, Mass.: Harvard University, Division of Research, Graduate School of Business Administration, 1965).

income, ranging from $15,000 to $20,000 and up to possibly $40,000 in the largest firms.

Opportunities in the Personnel Division

There are growing opportunities in personnel work both for young men and for young women. The large majority of retail training directors are women and centralized training staffs in department stores are composed almost entirely of women. Yet the personnel function also includes numerous other responsibilities where men predominate, for example, in the top jobs in employment compensation—including wage standards and incentives, governmental rules and regulations affecting retail employees, and personnel research.

A college man or woman may begin work in the personnel division as personnel clerk, as assistant employment manager, or in the training department, although some experience on the selling floor is considered essential before good work can be done in these departments. Promotion from these departments may be eventually to personnel, employment, or training manager. Training supervisors and other junior executives in the employment and personnel offices may receive from $100 to $125 per week and more. The personnel manager, as head of the division, receives an annual income of from $10,000 to $25,000 or more.

PROSPECTS IN CHAIN STORES

Marked successes of chain-store organizations have opened vast employment possibilities for college graduates. The F. W. Woolworth Company needs from 300 to 400 new managers each year, and many of them come up from the firm's four year executive training program—which currently includes some 3000 trainees.[39] In a recent year, Sears, Roebuck and Co. interviewed 5,000 college men on 200 campuses and employed 1,120 of them.[40] Nearly three quarters of those in the Company's management program are college men, and the percentage is still rising.

In contrast to the variety, junior department store, and department store chains, the majority of chains in other fields do little recruiting on college campus. Consequently, the college man or woman who wishes chain store employment in such lines as food, drug, women's apparel, and men's clothing must usually seek the personnel officer of the chain involved. Yet these chains frequently offer fine employment opportunities, in part simply be-

[39] "How Top Retailers Build Executives," *op. cit.*, p. 88.
[40] *Ibid.*, p. 90.

cause the number of college men and women competing for the top executive post is decidedly limited.

Chain store managerships and store supervisory assignments, as well as executive positions in regional and home offices, often provide substantial incomes. Even relatively new managers often earn up to $10,000 a year with experienced managers going up to $25,000 and more. In the larger food chains regional or branch managers may earn $25,000 or more and major executives over $50,000.

Naturally the opportunities in chain stores vary widely from company to company. Some chains are growing rapidly, some expanding slowly, others just holding their own, and a few are actually contracting in size. Therefore, the college student will want to make a careful analysis of the various firms offering employment opportunities which, in general, will be much greater with the growing organization—provided, of course, that such growth is soundly financed.

One way to illustrate the opportunities available in chain stores for college graduates is to review the promotion ladder in a general merchandise chain—the W. T. Grant Company.

Promotion Ladder to Store Managership[41]

Type of Men Needed. This company is continually seeking young men with character, better-than-average mental ability, leadership qualities, ambition, and practical ideas. Previous retail experience is not required. Practically every man who joins the firm starts as a store-management trainee. The intensive training requires hard work—and long hours. Stores are generally open one or more evenings a week. During holiday seasons and special sales events the work is particularly strenuous. Consequently, the positions available are only for men with determination. They must be willing to work hard at a moderate income during the training period in order successfully to establish their careers.

Promotion Steps. The main steps in the store-management promotion ladder are management trainee, division merchandiser, assistant manager, manager, district manager, regional operating or merchandise manager, and regional manager; for some men there are opportunities at headquarters as buyers, real estate men, advertising managers, merchandise executives, personnel managers, and controllers. Promotion is on a strictly competitive basis. It is based not upon experience or length of service but upon merit.

---

[41] The following discussion is adapted from W. T. Grant Company, *Training for Retail Merchants* (New York, n.d.) and *A Career with the W. T. Grant Company* (New York, n.d.).

Through district and regional managers and the personnel department the company keeps in close touch with the progress of all trainees. This contact is made more effective through the use of reports, ratings, and tests. Twice a year a personnel review is made of each man in training, and the resultant rating is discussed with him. This affords each trainee a chance to determine the kind of job his superiors believe he is doing, to discover and eliminate any weaknesses he may have, and to review once again his future prospects.

Management Trainee. A man in training for store management usually starts working as a management trainee in one of the stores. His first four weeks, known as the introductory training phase, give him a general view of many phases of store operation. He sells, and also learns some of the basic facts of store work: the sizes of counters, names and uses of counter fixtures, store regulations, and customer service. Part of this time he also works in the stock room, where he learns about the protection of stock, marking, and the handling of supplies. His learning progress is checked periodically through a series of tests.

Following his introductory training, the management trainee becomes responsible for the operations of one or two departments. Now he learns more about counter and window display, discovers which items sell best, finds out how to figure markup, markdown, and turnover, and how to use the inventory control records that are necessary to maintain the proper sales volume in his department or departments. Almost every day he is in the stock room for a while learning more about receiving, shipping, and stock-room procedures. He works directly with the salespeople in his department, who give him considerable help in learning the details of his job.

In addition to learning by doing, the management trainee adds to his knowledge through a management training course which he begins as soon as his introductory training has been completed. This course, which is based on a store manual, covers subjects such as sales and stock-room procedure, inventory control, office procedure, merchandising, and sales promotion. As each section of the manual is completed, the trainee prepares a report which goes to the regional office, where it is graded and recorded.

Division Merchandiser. After a total of about six months, the management trainee is ready to become a division merchandiser. Now his responsibilities are broadened to include supervision of six to twelve departments and to assume, under the store manager's direction, some of the store's overall problems. This period usually lasts about one and a half years. By the time it ends, the trainee has completed the entire management training course. The district manager gives an oral examination to test his knowledge of the various phases of store operation, and discusses informally his progress and future prospects.

Assistant Manager. With a total of about two years of training behind him, plus a favorable recommendation from the store manager and a satisfactory performance on his oral examination, the trainee who has become a successful division merchandiser is eligible for promotion to an assistant managership. In this position he is in charge of the store when the manager is away, may represent the manager in district meetings and in community affairs, and helps the manager with his plans and sees that they are followed through. He is now starting to "manage" in the full sense of the word. But he is still training, still learning—to practice the principles of good public relations and personnel work; to promote good will among his store employees, his competitors, and in the community; to select and train store personnel; to work with people and delegate responsibilities. The ability to develop a loyal, efficient organization is the outstanding characteristic of successful store managers.

Naturally, while he is an assistant manager, further study of operating methods, merchandise assortments, fast-selling items, and inventory control will continue to be part of his daily routine. He must become completely familiar with the merchandise sold in all departments of the store.

Length of Training Period and Salary. The complete period to qualify a trainee to become a store manager generally takes from three to five years.[42] It depends, of course, upon the trainee's adaptability and rapidity of learning during the training period. During this period a man will usually be transferred several times from one store to another since experience in a variety of stores is very desirable in obtaining a well-rounded background.

Trainees are paid from $105 to $125 a week at the start. Although the company has no schedule of automatic increases for a man in training, advances are made according to his ability and adaptability to his work.

Store Manager. Except for the functions of financing, real estate, and accounting, the manager has the same responsibilities for his store as the proprietor of any retail store. Consequently, he is vested with all necessary authority and is held strictly accountable for the success of his store. To succeed in this role, he must be a merchant capable of handling, displaying, and selling merchandise; a leader capable of inspiring enthusiasm and loyalty; and an executive capable of planning and directing the work of others.

Every store manager receives a weekly salary, and in addition is given a bonus on the net profits of his store. Total earnings of managers range from

---

[42] During 1965, 118 assistant store managers were promoted to store managerships. In addition, 262 store managers were moved to larger stores. At the close of 1965, men-in-training numbered 1,203. Data from personnel department of the W. T. Grant Company.

a minimum of $8,000 a year in the smaller stores to over $50,000 in the larger stores.

Although there is considerable variation in detail, the foregoing promotional ladder ending in a managership is fairly typical of chains in general. In chains with smaller stores, such as chains operating small drug and food units, promotion may be more rapid; but the income of the manager is smaller, usually ranging from $85 to $100 a week in grocery chains and from $80 to $175 a week in drug units. Chains operating larger units, such as Sears, Roebuck and Co., Montgomery Ward & Company, and the J. C. Penney Company, may require a somewhat longer premanager training period.

Advancement above Managerships

Chains fill the majority of their headquarter and top executive positions from the men who have made a success of operating a retail store. These positions include, among others, work in personnel, financing, real estate, buying, advertising and display, and accounting. However, for the man who wants to stay in the store-management end of the business, one step above the manager is the supervisor, who is directly responsible for the managers of several stores. In addition to his general supervisory tasks, instructions from headquarters go through him; and he is responsible for seeing that the managers put the instructions into effect. At the same time he carries to headquarters managers' problems which he cannot settle.

Income from a position as supervisor varies greatly. In food chains it is not uncommon for supervisors to receive incomes as low as $8,000 plus a small bonus, although incomes in excess of $10,000 are more typical. In those chains in which the supervisor is allowed to share in the profits produced by the stores under his control there is a chance for a very good income, especially in chains operating large stores.

If the chain is large enough, a district manager may stand between the supervisor and headquarters; this man is responsible for a number of supervisors. Such a position carries great responsibility and hence the opportunity of a large financial reward. Even in food chains, where salaries tend to be lower than in some fields in which chains operate, some district managers earn in excess of $25,000 per year.

PROSPECTS IN DISCOUNT HOUSES

Although it is still too early to appraise thoroughly the job and career opportunities which the discount house will afford college graduates, some students are being attracted to it. They believe that this retail institution offers greater freedom to experiment with new merchandising ideas and operating methods, and maintains less rigid control over their activities than does the conventional retail establishment. Consequently, they insist, if their ideas prove successful, they progress faster and thus reap greater rewards more quickly. To justify their opinion they point to the rapid growth of some discount houses and to the important positions occupied by some of their friends after relatively few years of experience.

There is considerable validity in the argument of the preceding paragraph. Yet rapid advancement in retailing is not limited to discount houses. Numerous instances could be cited of college graduates entering various kinds of retail stores who have advanced quickly to positions of responsibility with commensurate salaries. But, as a new and rapidly expending field, the discount house does offer career opportunities. In studying them, the college graduate should carefully appraise the financial stability of the specific company, its past record and growth prospects, its standing in the business community, and the opportunities it provides him to advance as he demonstrates his abilities.[43] So long as the discount house offers beginning salaries competitive with other industries and so long as it adopts policies and methods designed to serve the needs of the community, it will continue to attract its share of college graduates.

ATTITUDES TOWARD RETAILING CAREERS

One of the paradoxes of the present day is this: As business leaders are increasingly recognizing that a shortage of able executives is perhaps their most important problem, "the prospect of an executive career is progressively less appealing (to college graduates). Placement officers in good universities . . . (are) asserting that their best graduates are tending more and more to seek careers in law, in science, in the 'creative' arts, in public service, and in teaching instead of in business, which hitherto has had a steady appeal for college graduates."[44]

Despite the career opportunities which retailing offers to college men and women, there is ample evidence that the trend suggested by the preceding paragraph is also found in this field. A study by Professor Luck reports a

---

[43] The importance of a sufficient number of well-trained executives for any company embarking on a rapid expansion program is illustrated by the growing pains suffered by E. J. Korvette, one of the early discount houses. Cf. L. A. Mayer, "How Confusion Caught up with Korvette," *Fortune*, Vol. LXXIII, No. 2 (February, 1966), pp. 153–54 ff.

[44] Mitchell, *op. cit.*, p. 10. Also cf. the discussion of college student attitudes toward business careers in Duncan Norton-Taylor "The Private World of the Class of '66," *Fortune*, Vol. LXXIII, No. 2 (February, 1966), pp. 128–32 ff.

decrease in the number registered for retailing courses.[45] Professor Wingate found that, in a recent year, but five alumni of a leading graduate school of business began careers in the retail field.[46] Writing of the entire field of marketing, Professor Cowan finds himself "impressed with the progress made in marketing (during the past fifty years), but dismayed by (marketing's) unfavorable image in the eyes of prospective marketing students."[47] Still another study, this one limited just to retailing, concludes that this "unfavorable image" is equally applicable to student attitudes concerning this career area.[48] No wonder that *Women's Wear Daily*, after surveying both colleges and retailers in June, 1966, headlined a story, "June Grads Are Not Buying Retail Jobs to Great Degree."[49]

In view of the foregoing, it seems advisable to conclude this discussion of the opportunities for college graduates in the field of retailing by summarizing the merits and limitations which this broad and varied area provides. In the final analysis only the student himself can make the decision whether or not to enter this field. But his decision should be based upon a careful evaluation of all relevant facts, his own preferences and experiences, and the knowledge that the rewards for high-quality work and accomplishment in retailing—as in other trades and professions—go far beyond monetary income.

Pro Side of Retailing Careers. Among the major advantages which careers in retailing provide for the college graduate are the following:

1. A wide range of opportunities is afforded both for men and women of various talents and interests and in all geographical areas.
2. The size and growth of retailing to meet the needs of our rapidly expanding population provides an increasing number of executive positions for qualified personnel.
3. Advancement to positions of responsibility with commensurate salaries is probably more rapid for men and women of demonstrated abilities than in most other fields of employment.
4. Knowledge and experience are gained which may be easily transferred from one business to another including the establishment of one's own store.
5. Unique opportunities are afforded for wide personal contacts and stimulat-

---

[45] D. J. Luck, *Marketing Education in the United States* (Philadelphia, Pa.: Marketing Science Institute, 1965).

[46] J. W. Wingate, "The End of an Era in Collegiate Education for Retailing," *New York Retailer,* April, 1964, p. 5.

[47] Cf. the review of D. R. G. Cowan, "The Making of a Marketing Man," *Michigan Business Review,* March, 1965, pp. 5–9, in *Journal of Marketing,* Vol. XXIX, No. 3 (July, 1965), p. 87.

[48] Cf. Dwight Gentry, "Attitude of College Students Toward Retailing as a Career," *Journal of Retailing,* Vol. XXXVII, No. 4 (Winter, 1961–62), pp. 44–48, 56.

[49] Issue of June 9, 1966, p. 1.

ing travel thus broadening one's perspective and improving his judgment and decisions.

6. Reasonable security is provided because retailing is less subject to wide fluctuations in annual sales than most other industries and trades. Inefficiency in retailing, however, is just as unacceptable as in any other field.

7. Interested and qualified personnel in retailing find considerable personal satisfaction through the significant contributions they make to the welfare of the community in which they are located.

Con Aspects of Careers in Retailing. Despite its advantages, retailing possesses certain limitations for the college graduate.

1. Beginning salaries are frequently lower in retailing than in other fields and have increased less in the past two decades than in other areas of employment. Fortunately, many retailers have recognized this fact and adjusted salaries upward.

2. Long hours of work, frequently requiring being on the job on Saturdays, Sundays, and evenings, are unattractive to many interested in retailing.

3. Some stores do not have organized training programs for college graduates and discouragement often results when the graduate is assigned to a selling job when he begins work.

4. The competitive pressures, physical strain, and nervous tension which exist in retailing are probably felt more strongly by men and women than in other industries, thus tending to provide an uncongenial atmosphere in which to work.

5. The frequent travel, and the change of location sometimes required of chain-store personnel, is disagreeable to many persons who prefer "to get their roots established" as soon as possible.

6. The impersonal nature of most large and medium-sized retail stores, where major executives are not known and seldom seen by employees, often results in a low *esprit de corps* which college graduates dislike.

7. Some people assert that retailing lacks social prestige as compared with banking and finance, for example; that it does not offer a sufficient "intellectual challenge," particularly to those with "creative talents"; and that it gives but a limited opportunity to serve others.[50]

REVIEW AND DISCUSSION QUESTIONS

1. Prepare a five minute talk outlining and evaluating the major factors considered by college students as they seek a career.

2. Talk with owners and managers of various retail stores in your community and summarize their opinions regarding the opportunities which retailing affords the college graduate. What do they consider to be the chief limitations?

3. What are some of the more recent developments in retailing which encourage (discourage) college students to seek careers in this field?

---

[50] The objections summarized in item 7 are reported more fully in Cowan, *op. cit.*

4. From your observations of retail stores, how great are the opportunities they offer to college women?

5. Based on a talk with your college personnel officer, discuss the number and kinds of retailers visiting your campus in search of college men and women.

6. To what extent do you believe that night, Saturday, and Sunday openings by some retail stores have lessened the interest of college graduates in careers in retailing? Present evidence to support your opinion.

7. Evaluate the relative weight which college students assign to financial and nonfinancial incentives as they seek a career.

8. Prepare a brief essay on the subject "Probable Changes in Working Conditions in Retail Stores during the Next Decade."

9. Assuming that you expect to own and operate your own small independent store in the future and desire to obtain the best experience possible to prepare you for this task, would you prefer to obtain that experience in a small store, a department store, or a chain store? Why?

10. How would you proceed, and what factors would you take into account, in determining whether or not you would open a retail store of your own?

11. Assume that you have an interview with a recruiter for a department store concerning possible employment with the firm upon your graduation. Explain briefly (a) how you would prepare for such an interview and (b) the questions you would want answered before accepting a position if one were offered.

12. Talk with two college graduates who have been through the junior executive training programs of a large retailer. Report to the class on their evaluation of the program.

13. Outline the "promotional ladder" of a general merchandise chain.

14. Compare and contrast the opportunities existing for college graduates in "conventional" retail stores and discount houses.

15. Prepare a paper of about 2,000 words on the subject: "A Constructive Program for Attracting Qualified College Graduates into Retailing."

SUPPLEMENTARY READINGS

Some of the readings suggested for Chapter 2 are also applicable to the present chapter.

BABIONE, F. A. "Retailer Adjustment to a Rental Economy," *Journal of Retailing*, Vol. XL, No. 3 (Fall, 1964) pp. 1–5, 48. Opportunities for retailing careers in the leasing field are suggested by the author's analysis.

BOWMAN, G. W. *et al.* "Are Women Executives People?" *Harvard Business Review*, Vol. XLIII, No. 4 (July–August, 1965), pp. 14–16 ff. A survey of attitudes toward women executives is provided by this article.

BRENNER, BARBARA. *Careers and Opportunities in Fashion* (New York: E. P. Dutton, 1964). The best available analysis of this subject will be found in this volume, making it a "must" for one seeking a career in the fashion world.

DOODY, A. F., AND DAVIDSON, W. R. "Growing Strength in Small Retailing,"

Harvard Business Review, Vol. XLII, No. 4 (July–August, 1964), pp. 69–79. The student seeking to begin a career in a relatively small store can take comfort in the thesis of these two authors—the small retailer can succeed if he is aggressive and has a "philosophy of innovation."

Fairchild Publications, Inc. *Fairchild's Financial Manual of Retail Stores— 1966.* New York, 1966. An annual compilation of data concerning nearly 300 publically-owned retail organizations, this volume is a valuable source of information for the career-searching student.

FREEDGOOD, SEYMOUR. "Uncle to 1,700 Grocers," *Fortune,* Vol. LXXI, No. 3 (March, 1965), pp. 130–33. The role of the voluntary chain as an aid to the independent food store owner is the subject of this *Fortune* report.

GERSTNER, L. V., JR. "College Recruiting: Why the Good Ones Get Away," *Management Review,* March, 1966, pp. 4–12. The reactions of a recent college graduate to the college recruiting methods of corporations are reported in this illuminating article. His conclusion: Few companies "take account of the subjective nature of the student's selection decisions." Also cf. FIELDEN, J. S. "The Right Young People for Business," *Harvard Business Review,* Vol. XLIV, No. 2 (March–April, 1966), pp. 76–83.

GILLESPIE, K. R. "What Education Do Retailers Recommend for Potential Merchants?" *Journal of Retailing,* Vol. XXXVIII, No. 1 (Spring, 1962), pp. 1–15. A summary of retailer opinion is offered in this article.

GREEN, H. L. "Choosing and Using Retailing Consultants," *Journal of Retailing,* Vol. XXXVIII, No. 4 (Winter, 1962–63), pp. 7–16. Another possible career in retailing is that of the consultant.

HAMPE, E. C., JR., AND WITTENBERG, MERLE. *The Lifeline of America* (New York: McGraw-Hill Book Co., Inc., 1964). Well-described by its sub-title, *Development of the Food Industry,* this historical volume covers the production, processing, and marketing of food in the United States. Those seeking careers in food retailing will benefit from this book.

HELFERT, E. A.; MAY, E. G.; AND McNAIR, M. P. *Controllership in Department Stores* (Boston, Mass.: Harvard University, Division of Research, Graduate School of Business Administration, 1965). The functions of the controller in the department and specialty store fields, together with his relations to other executives, are covered in this valuable analysis.

INGRAM, E. W., SR. *All This from a 5-cent Hamburger!* (New York: Newcomen Society in North America, 1964). How a major chain can grow from small beginnings is well illustrated by this portrayal of the trials, tribulations, and success of the White Castle System.

KURSH, HARRY. *The Franchise Boom* (Englewood Cliffs, N.J.: Prentice-Hall, Inc., 1962). The franchise type of retail store is growing in significance. The pros and cons of franchising are analyzed in this volume.

LEBHAR, G. M. *Chain Stores in America, 1859–1962* (3rd ed.; New York: Chain Store Publishing Co., 1963). A history of the chain store.

LUCK, D. J. *Marketing Education in the United States* (Philadelphia, Pa.: Marketing Science Institute, 1964). Curricula and registration trends in retailing (and other marketing courses) are included in this 56 page study.

NORTON-TAYLOR, DUNCAN. "The Private World of the Class of '66," *Fortune,* Vol. LXXIII, No. 2 (February, 1966), pp. 128–132 ff. A former editor of *Fortune,* after visiting several campuses, uses this article to report his findings on current attitudes of college students toward business careers.

ROBINSON, O. P., AND HAAS, K. B. *How to Establish and Operate a Retail Store* (2d ed.; Englewood Cliffs, N.J.: Prentice-Hall, Inc., 1952). Although rather old this book offers valuable suggestions to the prospective small retailer in setting up and operating his store.

SCOTT, GEORGE. *Your Future in Retailing* (New York: Richards Rosen Associates, 1961). In this brief readable volume the author enables the reader to weigh his own interests and abilities in the light of the requirements of a retailing career.

SIMON, J. L. *How to Start and Operate a Mail-Order Business* (New York: McGraw-Hill Book Co., Inc., 1965). A how-to-do-it book, the author's treatment should minimize some of the "rough spots" for the careerist in this type of retailing.

What's Behind the Rise of Two Guys, a special report in Section Two of *Discount Store News,* November 1, 1965. This 54 page study covers the history, policies, and operating methods of a pioneer discount house. It well illustrates the potentials of a career in the discount area.

WINGATE, J. W. "The End of an Era in Collegiate Education for Retailing," *New York Retailer,* April, 1964, pp. 2–5. In outlining the reasons for the disappearance of the School of Retailing as a separate school at New York University, Professor Wingate also touches on some of the factors which bear on current student attitudes toward retailing.

PART III

The Retail Store

4
CHAPTER

Store Location

The location of a retail store, since it determines to a large degree the sales made and the profits realized, plays a vital part in the store's success. Some retailers, such as those selling variety store merchandise and women's apparel, consider location such an important factor in their success that they prefer to pay a larger-than-usual rental to obtain desirable sites, even if this means that they must restrict other expenses. Although good locations frequently offset deficiencies in management, poor locations seriously handicap the most skillful merchandisers.

LOCATION: A CONTINUING PROBLEM

Although most discussions of retailing place emphasis upon the choice of a location for a *new* store, location problems are by no means restricted to situations of this nature. Because of population shifts, the movement (in or out) of other retailers, the improvement or deterioration of buildings, and the establishment of shopping centers, suburban and roadside stores, and discount houses, good locations of one period may gradually become poorer (or better) ones. As one expert in store location writes: "In our dynamic urban economy the life-span of most retail facilities is comparatively short. Even successful chain stores are faced with the problem of store mortality due to obsolescence and other factors. . . . Typically a store has a life cycle of three successive stages: ascent, peak, and decline. The ascent and decline stages may be very steep or gradual, and the peak stage may be of long or short duration."[1]

In view of the foregoing, the retail store proprietor is always faced with a

---

[1] William Applebaum, "Store Performance in Relation to Location and Other Characteristics," *Chain Store Age* (Executives Edition), November, 1965, p. E14.

location problem. He must be on the alert to detect shifts and changes and to interpret their probable effects upon his business. Lack of alertness and delay in making adjustments to new situations usually result in declining sales and reduced profit or even a loss.

That progressive retailers recognize the continuing nature of the location problem is evident both from their statements and their actions. The president of the F. W. Woolworth Company told those attending the firm's 1965 annual meeting that "our market research people are constantly reappraising the older stores. . . . Many stores in decaying neighborhoods have been relocated or closed down."[2] Reported a food retailer: "We actually research our own store locations again just as we would do preparatory to opening a store."[3] The fact that 38 percent of a large sample of supermarkets are less than five years old, while 73 percent have existed less than ten years, is eloquent testimony to management's actions based on continuous study of existing locations.[4]

Location and the Landlord. A location suitable to the successful conduct of business is important to the owner of the land and building occupied by the store as well as to the retail merchant. The value of a lease is dependent upon the ability of a tenant to realize a profit under it, and only through careful selection of tenants can a reasonable and regular return upon property investment be assured. Moreover, it is axiomatic that property values are maximized only when a site is used so as to extract the greatest economic utility from it. The best locations tend to be held by the better store managers because these managers are able to obtain greater productiveness from such locations that are less capable competitors.

Insufficient Attention to the Location Problem

Despite the significance of location, too many retailers still decide upon locations without proper analysis. Frequently shopping center developers, chain stores, and voluntary chain organizations are singled out as among those who plan locations on a scientific basis. To a degree, of course, this conclusion is valid, since some developers and large-scale retailers conduct careful studies of locations before final decisions are made. For example, before Eastern Shopping Centers approves a site for a proposed shopping center, that location is subjected to a searching analysis covering, among

---

[2] *Woolworth's Report of Annual Meeting of Stockholders, May 19, 1965* (New York: The Company, 1965), p. 7.

[3] *Super Market Merchandising,* November, 1965, p. 22.

[4] *The Super Market Industry Speaks: 1965* (Chicago, Ill.: Super Market Institute, 1965), p. 15.

many other points, current population in the trading area, population trends, current and potential per capita income of the area, competing centers or retailers, shopping loyalty of potential customers, road patterns, and expected sales by major classes of merchandise. Frequently, outside consultants on locations are used to conduct the study.[5] Similar investigations are conducted by Sears, Roebuck and Co., J. C. Penney Company, W. T. Grant Company and other leading chains before they authorize a contract for a new store.[6] Leading voluntary and cooperative food chain organizations increasingly offer their retailer members a carefully devised location analysis service.[7]

In contrast to the foregoing procedures, however, is the practice of a local drug chain which relies largely on the judgement of one of its chief executives who usually appraises a site "just by taking a ride around a particular area, talking to some of the people living there, and getting a general feel of the site's expansion possibilities." Even among large chain organizations the amount spent on "current store location effort compared with the magnitude of the investment (and risk) in new stores is very modest," the research cost averaging $4,075 for an average location investment of $373,000.[8] And thousands of small stores are opened each year in particular sites largely because locations are available, and with little or no scientific analyses. No wonder that many stores and shopping centers fail to achieve sufficient profits to make them viable enterprises!

Some Reasons for Neglect of Location Problem. Many retailers neglect to study the location problem simply because they are inexperienced and fail to appreciate its significance for successful operation. Moreover, most prospective retailers have the confident expectation of doing better in a particular location than their predecessors and hence consider it unnecessary to study the past history of a site. Some of those who would like a pre-site-selection study or continuing analysis of a location simply consider that the cost is too great. Still others are so eager to start "tending the store" that they do not want to take the time essential for a worthwhile site-selection investigation; whereas the researcher "is innately cautious and slow-mov-

---

[5] For a listing of such consultants cf. *Directory of Consultant Members* (New York: American Management Association, Inc., 1964), p. 94.

[6] The store location program of the F. W. Woolworth Company is described in the firm's *Annual Report,* February 14, 1966, p. 7.

[7] For illustrations of this service, cf. "Thriftway: 'We Stole the Play'," *Super Market Merchandising,* September, 1964, p. 60; "Wetterau Foods, St. Louis: Its Formula for Retailer Profits," *ibid.,* September, 1965, p. 33; R. O. Harb, "New Horizons for Retailer-Owned Cooperatives," *Progressive Grocer,* April, 1966, pp. 310–22; and Jerry Peck, "The Voluntary Group Concept of Food Distribution," *ibid.,* pp. 300–309.

[8] William Applebaum, "Store Location Research—A Survey of Retailing Chains," *Journal of Retailing,* Vol. XL, No. 2 (Summer, 1964), pp. 53 and 55.

ing," the rapidly-moving executive may lack the necessary "patience" to wait for the results.[9]

Even some retailers who recognize the importance of location research and are willing to spend money and time on it consider it too complex a problem for them to approach entirely on a scientific basis. They point out that research techniques in this area have made little progress in recent years, a statement with which the location experts are forced to agree.[10] Furthermore, while these retailers may gather and analyze statistical data on a site, they believe that the validity of the decision rests with the man making the final judgment—and that his judgment cannot be replaced with a computer. To quote the real estate vice president of a leading variety-discount house chain: "People with experience in looking at sites are better 'computers' than any computer can be—because we cannot yet feed accurate information, reduced to definite numbers, into a location-evaluating machine."[11]

Although the foregoing factors *explain* why the location problem is not studied sufficiently by some retailers, they do not *justify* this neglect. Even the criticism that research cannot "produce all the answers" is beside the point, since no one claims that it does. At best research is but an aid to judgment, never a substitute for it. In brief, location plays such an important part in determining sales and profits that the retailer should assemble and evaluate carefully all available information in choosing a location for his store.

BASIC FACTORS IN LOCATION

Factors governing the choice of a location for a retail store may be divided logically into two groups: (1) those that influence the choice of a city or trading area in which to locate and (2) those that determine the particular site within the chosen city or trading area.[12] These groups of factors are closely related. For example, the availability of desirable sites in a certain city or shopping center obviously affects the decision to locate or not

---

[9] This point (also the quotations) is well developed in S. B. Cohen, "Facing Today's Store Location Challenges," *Chain Store Age* (Supermarket Executives Edition), November, 1963, pp. E23–E28.

[10] However, after agreeing with this point, one expert proceeds to outline five possible steps to improve location research. Cf. William Applebaum, "Five Frontiers for Store Location Research," *Super Market Merchandising,* April, 1964, pp. 74–76.

[11] "Nailing Down Locations is the Key to Kresge's Expansion," *Chain Store Age* (Executives Edition), December, 1965, p. E16.

[12] Many of the factors included in this analysis are also applicable (1) to the location of shopping centers and (2) to the selection of sites within such centers. Also cf. the discussion of shopping centers on pp. 111–15, below.

to locate in that area. Yet, for purposes of analysis, the distinction between the two groups is helpful.

Although this discussion is in terms of a *new* store, the factors involved are equally applicable—as already indicated—to the appraisal of an established store. Moreover, the number of factors mentioned must not cause one to forget the basic determinants in any location, that is, the sales and profit potentials which can reasonably be expected assuming suitable store facilities are provided.

Selecting a City or Trading Area

At the outset of our discussion it should be noted that the small retailer is at a serious competitive disadvantage when it comes to the careful selection of a town in which to locate. In contrast to the large operator, especially the chain store and the shopping center developer, he has neither the financial resources nor the manpower to conduct a systematic review of cities, suburban areas, or even shopping centers. His decision is often based on considerations of health, climate, or nearness of relatives and friends. It is evident, however, that his chances of success will be much greater if he assembles and evaluates all pertinent information. In this process he should take maximum advantage of aid offered by the manufacturers and wholesalers from whom he makes or expects to make purchases, his banker, the Chamber of Commerce in the area considered, and any studies available from shopping center developers.[13]

Type and Character of Industries. The number, type, and character of the industries within the confines of a city and its surrounding trading area are important because they influence (1) the amount and the stability of potential customer income and (2) the kind of goods customers will want. The alert retailer will attempt to locate, as far as possible, within an area where income is regular, assured, and substantial in amount. Generally speaking, income is more stable and assured in cities with diversified industries than in areas where one single industry dominates the picture. In the former situation, not all the firms will be affected by seasonal factors or by fluctuations in general business conditions in the same manner or at the same time. Only in a comparatively few instances, such as major depressions, will income for the area as a whole be sharply reduced and severe declines in sales experienced.

---

[13] For an analysis of a specific trading area, cf. Iowa State University, Bureau of Business Research, *A Retail Trading Area Analysis of Rock Rapids, Iowa* (Ames, Iowa, 1965). For another list of factors influencing the choice of a trading area cf. William Applebaum, "Guidelines for a Store-Location Strategy Study," *Journal of Marketing*, Vol. XXX, No. 4 (October, 1966), pp. 42–45.

One factor in the stability of income from local industries is the labor-management relationship. Investigation of this factor is important, since the existence of a poor relationship may mean constant labor strife and periodic strikes. The effects of such strikes on retail sales may be significant: for the cash store, they may result in violent fluctuations in volume; for the credit store, they may encourage an overextension of credit.

The retailers will also be interested in the growth of local industries. Obviously, an area in which industry is progressive and expansion is likely has advantages over an area in which maximum development has already been attained. Towns and cities from which industries are moving have serious limitations as retail locations.

Population of the Trading Area. The population of the city and the surrounding trading area determines the number of potential customers of the retail store. But knowledge of those currently living in the area is not sufficient; equally important is information on the rate of growth (or decline).[14]

Even the casual reader is aware of the tremendous growth of our population and of the fact that this expansion is unevenly distributed among regions, states, cities, and their environs. Between 1950 and 1960, for example, the urban dwellers increased from 64 to 70 percent of our total population.[15] During this same period the Western states led other regions with a 38.9 percent population gain. Among states the highest rates of population increase occurred in Florida (78.7 percent), Nevada (78.2 percent), Alaska (75.8 percent), and Arizona (73.7 percent). Among cities the following areas experienced large growth in part through annexations: Phoenix, Arizona (311 percent); Parma, Ohio (187 percent); Odessa, Texas (172 percent); San Leandro, California (139 percent); Tampa, Florida (120 percent); Santa Ana, California (120 percent); El Paso, Texas (112 percent); and Albuquerque, New Mexico (108 percent).[16]

Some cities, of course, remain almost stationary as regards population; and this fact alone does not mean, necessarily, that they are undesirable as areas in which to locate stores. But in such cases the need is apparent for a

---

[14] *Current Population Reports, Population Estimates,* published frequently but irregularly by the Bureau of the Census of the U.S. Department of Commerce, contains a variety of information concerning population such as growth, shifts, and age groupings by regions and states. Special censuses covering numerous cities and areas are also available from the Bureau.

[15] *1960 Census of Population,* Vol. I, *Characteristics of the Population,* Part A, Number of Inhabitants (Washington, D.C.: U.S. Government Printing Office, 1961), p. xiii.

[16] *Ibid.,* pp. xv, xxiii.

careful investigation of the reasons for lack of growth and the impact of this factor on the retailers of the area.

Some attention should also be given to seasonal shifts in population. Many trading areas gain people during the summer and lose them during the winter months. Thus communities in Maine, Vermont, Michigan, and Colorado have a large influx of summer residents who substantially increase the potential customers in these states for several months each year. In contrast, Florida, California, and Arizona experience population gains during the winter months.

Progressiveness of the City. Closely related to the type and character of industries, to population trend, and to factors discussed in the following paragraphs is the progressiveness of an area. Is it an area in which there is an active Chamber of Commerce or industrial development group which is attempting to attract new industries? Is there an urban renewal program? Is the local school system adequate, so that people are encouraged to move into the area? Do local hospitals attract patients from a considerable distance and thus bring in friends and relatives who may make purchases? Is an effort made to attract conventions that bring to the area another group of customers? Are local service clubs active in community betterment? Is there a local area-sponsored recreation program, indicating a community interest in promoting better citizenship? Do the local merchants work together in the sponsorship of periodic events—dollar days, festivals, and fairs—to expand the trading area? Are the local theaters, churches, and bowling centers such that they serve to attract people from a wide and growing area? Do the streets allow for a free flow of traffic? What about the availability of off-street parking areas? Is there adequate public transportation? All of these factors and others must be given careful consideration in forecasting the city's future.

Buying Habits of Potential Customers. The selection of an area in which to locate is also influenced by the buying habits or practices of the populace, such as the extent to which potential customers do their buying at the most convenient and accessible locations; the degree to which they customarily rely on mail-order catalogs; the importance they attach to large assortments of merchandise offering a wider range of choice; their willingness to drive 25, 50, or more miles to do their shopping because they can combine the shopping expedition with a pleasure trip;[17] the kinds of stores

---

[17] To determine distances which shoppers are willing to drive, Montgomery Ward & Company checks license plates of shoppers in a community, obtaining home addresses from the automobile registration officials. Cf. "Area Research Gives Wards Detailed Basis for Growth," *Chain Store Age* (Executives Edition), December, 1964, p. E28.

they prefer to patronize for particular types of merchandise and the extent to which they divide their purchases among such stores; the services, such as credit and delivery, which they customarily require and expect; and the influence of age distribution on their purchases. Consideration should be given also to the differences in buying practices among various nationalities and races residing in the trading district. The more familiar the prospective store owner is with the customary buying habits, preferences, and prejudices of the people in the area, the greater the assurance that his location will meet with their approval.

Purchasing Power of the Population. Since total retail sales in an area are closely correlated with the purchasing ability of the nearby population, purchasing power is another important determinant in the choice of a city or area. The number of people employed, the total payrolls of the industries located in the district and the average wage, the regularity and frequency of payment of wages and salaries, and the amount of and trend in bank deposits are among the significant factors indicative of the purchasing power of the area under consideration.[18] As a matter of fact, skilled retailers can frequently use these factors as the basis of a reasonably accurate estimate of the sales that a proposed store can achieve. Once again, any seasonal fluctuations in the area's purchasing power should be noted.

Dispersion of Wealth. The dispersion of wealth in an area has an important bearing on the sales and profit opportunities which exist for any particular store. A retailer who proposes to open a store dealing in fancy groceries, high-priced dresses, or custom-made men's clothes should not seek an area populated largely by persons with low incomes. In this connection, it is important to note that the rise in earnings during the 1950's and 1960's, widely distributed among the population, brought about considerable "trading up," with people buying better-quality merchandise and patronizing higher-class stores.

Some specific evidence of the relationship between (1) family income, and (2) the sales and profits of the retailer is given in Table 4–1. This table classifies the sales and profits achieved by each unit of a chain according to the annual income of the families which it served. It will be noted that the units in areas having the highest annual incomes achieved over three times the sales and nearly twice the profits as compared with the units in the lowest annual income areas.

In an effort to determine the dispersion of income in a trading area, the

---

[18] Some retailers have developed their own special ways of judging the purchasing power of an area. To illustrate: Sears, Roebuck and Co. makes use of its mail order sales. Experience has demonstrated that an area producing $1 million in mail order business can support a Sears store. *Time,* January 21, 1966, p. 69B.

prospective store owner finds the following information of value: the types or kinds of homes, the proportion of home owners, the educational level of the community, the number of telephones, the number and makes of automobiles, per capita retail sales, and the number of credit accounts. The publications of the population census also contain much information which enables the retailer to judge more effectively the extent of his potential market and to arrive more accurately at anticipated or planned sales figures against which actual results may be checked.

TABLE 4–1

SALES AND PROFITS OF STORES IN A CHAIN
CLASSIFIED BY ANNUAL INCOME OF
FAMILIES SERVED

Annual Income of Families Served	Index of Store	
	Sales	Profits
Under $3,000................100		100
$3,000–$4,999..............160		112
$5,000–$7,999..............240		125
$8,000 and over............320		188

SOURCE: William Applebaum, "Store Performance in Relation to Location and other Characteristics," *op. cit.*, p. E15.

Nature and Strength of Competition. The number, type, floor space, and location of competing retail stores, viewed in the light of the economic need of the community for a store of the type being considered, also influence the choice of a city or of a shopping center in which to locate. Competing stores must be analyzed carefully to determine the services they offer, the extent to which they are alert to the present and prospective demands of consumers, and their merchandising methods in general.

In analyzing the nature and strength of competition, the retailer must be aware of the implications of the trend toward "scrambled merchandising." Today much of the competition for an electric appliance store may come from auto supply stores, department stores, or hardware stores, while drugstores are feeling the effects of the expanding lines of supermarkets. The women's wear shop is in competition with many items sold by the variety store, the mail-order house, and the discount store. In other words, the study of competitors must be made on a realistic basis and not just on the basis of the name given to a particular kind of retail establishment.

1. *Index of Retail Saturation.* Some retailers, in their attempt to select those cities or trading areas which are most attractive for new stores, have been aided by the construction of an index of retail saturation. Specifically,

they seek some number which summarizes an area's population, per capita sales for the type of merchandise which they sell, and the competitive retail facilities already in the area. Figure 4–1 suggests how such an index can be computed.

For those retailers who find it difficult to include in the index per capita sales for their type of merchandise, the index of retail saturation merely relates population to retail facilities for the type of merchandise. Thus Montgomery Ward & Company has concluded that "about 2½ square feet of retail sales space per person pretty well takes care of the general merchandise space needs of an area."[19] Consequently, this firm looks for areas where the index of retail saturation is less than 2½ square feet. By studying an area's index over a period of years, significant trends can quickly be noted.[20]

State and Local Legislation.   The nature of existing legislation within the state and the city under consideration is important. The number and types of taxes that must be paid, together with the trend in tax rates, and the various licenses which must be obtained in the city often influence the decision on location. Variations in sales tax rates among nearby cities and across state lines are particularly troublesome elements in the location decision. Fair-trade laws and unfair-trade-practice acts must be taken into account. Local or state regulations concerning hours of business are significant in view of recent trends toward additional night and Sunday openings for many stores.

Other Factors Influencing Choice of a City.   Brief mention should also be made of several other factors which influence the choice of a city or trading area in which to locate a store. On occasion, practically all retailers find it necessary to secure bank loans to finance expansion plans, seasonal inventories, or larger-than-usual credit accounts. Hence, the existence in the community of bankers who have some understanding of the retailer's financial problems is much to be desired. Likewise, the attractiveness of a community is increased if adequate and reasonable advertising media are available; if police and fire protection are satisfactory; if trade-union regulations are not so restrictive that profitable operation is difficult; if adequate merchandise resources are conveniently located; and if the area is served satisfactorily by the highways and public transportation facilities leading into it.

---

[19] "Area Research Gives Ward Detailed Basis for Growth," *op. cit.,* p. E28.

[20] For an excellent study of retail market penetration cf. William Applebaum, "Measuring Retail Market Penetration for a Discount Food Supermarket—A Case Study," *Journal of Retailing,* Vol. XLI, No. 2 (Summer, 1965), pp. 1–14, 47. Also cf. his "Methods for Determining Store Trade Areas, Market Penetration, and Potential Sales," *Journal of Marketing Research,* Vol. III, No. 2 (May, 1966), pp. 127–41.

It is possible to calculate the amount of food sales available in any geographic area with reasonable accuracy. It is also possible to quantify certain characteristics of supermarket facilities in any geographic area. These two factors can be combined to form an index of supermarket saturation. This index could be defined as: an index number providing a relative measure of supermarket saturation in any given trading area. Expressed as a functional relationship:

Formula for Index of Supermarket Saturation

$$IRS_1 = \frac{C_1 \times RE_1}{RF_1}$$

Where: IRS_1 = Index of Super Market Saturation for area one
  C_1 = Number of Consumers in area one
  RE_1 = Food Expenditure per consumer in area one
  RF_1 = Retail Facilities in area one

Consider the following example in analyzing supermarket potential in Market A:

The one hundred thousand consumers in Market A spend an average of $5.50 per week in food stores. There are 15 supermarkets serving Market A with a total of 144,000 square feet of selling area.

$$IRS_A = \frac{100,000 \times 5.50}{144,000} = \frac{550,000}{144,000} = \$3.82$$

The $3.82 per square foot of selling area measured against the dollars per square feet necessary to break even would provide the measure of saturation in Market A. The $3.82 figure would also be useful in evaluating relative opportunity in different market areas.

If an operator was considering entering four different market areas and the IRS for each market was calculated as follows: Market area A = $3.82; Market area B = $1.76; Market area C = $2.12; and Market area D = $2.94, his course of action would be reasonably clear.

The index of supermarket saturation provides valuable insights for the supermarket operator into the evaluation of available potential in any market. It provides a superior measurement to the simple analysis of market potential, since it would take into account both the demand side (potential) and the supply side (retail facilities) in evaluating a market.

SOURCE: B. J. LaLonde, "New Frontiers in Store Location," *Super Market Merchandising*, February, 1963, p. 110.

FIG. 4–1. How to compute an index of retail saturation for supermarkets.

Selecting a Specific Site

The selection of a particular location within the chosen city or trading area is determined by the following major considerations.[21]

Estimated Volume of Business. Early in the appraisal of a possible store site the retailer should estimate the potential annual sales that can be obtained, because volume is an important factor in determining whether a store in the location will be profitable.

For a chain store organization, the sales estimate is sometimes based on the per capita annual sales of company stores of comparable size located in cities of about the same population, type of industries, and number of persons employed; in other cases, annual sales per counter-foot in company stores approximately equal in size are relied upon for the estimate. Such inside-the-company forecasts are commonly supplemented by estimates of sales of competitors in the city. These "educated guesses" are obtained by measurements of the counter-feet space in directly competing stores, by customer counts in such stores at various times of the day, and by ascertaining the number of salespeople in these stores at specific hours and on certain days. Finally, outside experts may be used in the sales forecasting for a specific location: In locating gasoline stations, one major oil company uses an independent market research firm which has developed a formula based on "numerical estimates of registration of automobiles garaged in the vicinity of the station, traffic count, highway characteristics, and appearance of the station in relation to other stations in the vicinity."[22]

For independent stores, volume forecasts are also frequently based on estimates of sales of nearby competitors. In addition, wholesalers and manufacturers' salesmen who are well acquainted with the area can be helpful with well-informed guesses. Sometimes the independent may have prepared for him an estimate based on family incomes in the area. This approach is not always reliable, however, because many cities attract a large amount of trade from outside the immediate area. In other words, they serve as trading centers for the surrounding area or they attract many tourists or business visitors.

1. *Long-Run Considerations.* In estimating the volume of business for a

---

[21] A great amount of data helpful to an analysis of some of these site factors is becoming available from the nationwide urban transportation planning study covering 225 different urban areas. Among the facts being assembled are these: land use, residential population distribution, employment, retail sales, car ownership, and family income. For a report on these data cf. H. K. Evans, "A Vast New Storehouse of Transportation and Marketing Date," *Journal of Marketing,* Vol. XXX, No. 1 (January, 1966), pp. 33–40.

[22] R. A. Miller, "Sales Variability in Service Stations," *Journal of Marketing,* Vol. XXIX, No. 2 (April, 1965), p. 31.

particular site, long-run considerations should be taken into account. That is, the past history and the probable future of the district should be studied; and any shifts or movements in the business sections should be weighed carefully to ascertain their probable effects on the traffic stream. No business site stands still in value. The main shopping block in a city today may be several blocks removed from the significant block of three decades ago. What is an undeveloped and outlying piece of land today may be a flourishing shopping center five years from now.

2. *Accuracy of Sales Estimates.* Some idea of management's ability to forecast sales in a specific store is given by the supermarket data of Table 4–2. If we call anything within ten percent of the estimate as being "on

TABLE 4–2

ACTUAL SALES VERSUS ESTIMATED SALES.

Difference Between Actual and Estimated Sales	Percentage of Supermarkets
26% to 118% above estimate.........14	
11% to 25% above estimate.........15	
Up to 10% above estimate..........13	
Total above estimate........	42
Sales as estimated..........	8
Up to 10% below estimate..........18	
11% to 25% below estimate.........26	
26% to 48% below estimate......... 6	
Total below estimate........	50
All supermarkets...........	100

SOURCE: *Facts about New Super Markets Opened in 1965* (Chicago, Ill.: Super Market Institute, 1966), p. 4.

target," then in 39 percent of the cases the forecast was accurate. However, 29 percent of the stores produced sales substantially above the estimate and 32 percent fell appreciably below. These data make it clear that far better techniques of sales forecasting for the individual store are needed.

Customer Buying Habits in Relation to Types of Goods Sold. The importance of customer buying habits was pointed out in the discussion of factors affecting the choice of a city or town. They are equally important in the selection of a site. A store handling convenience goods—staple groceries, for example—ordinarily will be located (1) close to the homes of the customers it hopes to serve or (2) in shopping centers or areas where parking facilities are available and which can easily be patronized when the customer is also after other merchandise. If shopping goods constitute the main lines handled, then the store should be situated within an area where other stores of the same type are located. For instance, it has long been recognized that department stores, the best example of a shopping institution, thrive best in groups: this fact is being increasingly acted upon by shopping center developers through their efforts to bring two or three department stores into a single center. When specialty goods are sold and customers are attracted on bases other than convenience and opportunity for shopping, the store proprietor has a greater degree of freedom in choosing a location. Accessibility remains important, however, with the result that stores handling goods of this type are commonly located in the chief shopping districts, either on the main thoroughfare or on a better-class side street, or in shopping centers.

Good roads, increased use of automobiles, urban decentralization, shopping centers, and discount houses, are all bringing changes or reflecting shifts in buying habits. Consequently, revisions in plans and in methods on the part of retail store executives responsible for locations have been necessary.[23]

Customer Traffic: The Traffic Count. The amount, kind, and distribution of potential customer traffic by hours of the day and days of the week influence the choice of a location. In this connection there is an old "rule of thumb" which says: "The heavier the pedestrian traffic, the greater the volume of business, other things being equal." But other things are never equal and, during recent years, retailers have given increased attention to qualitative analyses of such traffic as opposed to the previous emphasis upon quantity alone.

The fundamental purpose of traffic analysis, of course, is to estimate the proportion of pedestrians who constitute potential customers and who would probably be attracted into a store of the type proposed. The usual method employed to analyze traffic is the traffic count. Prior to making the actual count, however, it is necessary (1) to determine who shall be counted—such as all pedestrians, those of one sex, or just those within certain ages; and (2) to decide the days of the week and the length of the times when counts are to be made. Streams of pedestrian traffic are now being analyzed to ascertain reasons for passing a particular site at a given time. In other words, attention is given to the state of mind of the individuals in the traffic stream, to their purchasing power, and to other factors of a similar nature. Customer counts are also frequently made in the stores of chief competitors.

In passing, it should be noted that the significance of a flow of potential customers past a store varies widely from one retailer to another. To illustrate: A high traffic count may be essential for a cash-and-carry variety

---

[23] Cf. "Decentralization of Retailing," pp. 109–10, below.

store which depends mainly upon small purchases from a large number of customers. In contrast, the retailer of fancy groceries who appeals largely to the "carriage trade" through a telephone sale-credit-delivery type of service will be less interested in a high-traffic-count location. Likewise, the household appliance retailer who makes a substantial part of his sales through house-to-house salesmen has less concern for the traffic passing his store.

Location in Relation to Competitors and Other Stores. The prospective retailer should study the proximity of his store to his chief competitors and to other types of retail establishments. For some types of stores, location in the central shopping district or in a large shopping center is almost essential to success; for others, successful operations may be conducted outside such areas. A retailer of automobiles, for example, may find it highly desirable to locate near his competitors on "automobile row;" in a few instances, competing dealers have even joined together to purchase or lease an outlying site and built their establishments upon it.[24] A women's wear store may also seek a site near other similar shops or near a department store to make it more possible to sell to customers who desire to shop from one store to another. Other retailers, perhaps those selling drugs and groceries, may seek neighborhood locations which are removed from direct competitors.

For many retailers the reputation and merchandising methods of the other stores in the immediate area are important considerations. An exclusive dress-shop operator will not seek to locate beside a "cut-rate" drugstore or near a retailer of low-priced women's wear. A children's shop will not rent a building contiguous to a liquor store. Some areas have obtained reputations as locations for "good" merchants, and this fact is significant to the retailer who seeks to acquire a comparable designation.

Accessibility. Despite its obvious importance, accessibility is all too often neglected by the retailer who is eager to find a site and "get in business." Especially are employees' needs neglected or given inadequate attention. Among the numerous considerations relating to accessibility which warrant detailed investigation and study are the following:

1. Public transportation facilities to the proposed store, such as streetcars, buses, and subways.
2. Distance of the proposed store from residences of potential customers and employees.
3. Amount of traffic congestion prevailing in the district and the variations in this congestion during hours of the day and days of the week.
4. Parking facilities available within convenient walking distance of the proposed store and the charges therefor.

---

[24] For an illustration, cf. "One-Stop Center for Buying Cars," *Business Week,* October 16, 1965, pp. 92–94.

5. Side of the street upon which the site is located (in many towns and cities, one side is more popular than the other).
6. Width of the street, so that potential customers are not discouraged from visiting the store because of being jostled or by a slow flow of street traffic. Streets with marked inclines and dead ends are also less desirable.
7. The part of the block in which the site is located, i.e., whether it is a corner location or an "inside" location and, in the case of a large store, whether entrances may be made available on two, three, or four streets.

It should be emphasized that some retailers may successfully overcome part of the inaccessibility of a particular location by means of a low-price appeal. This possibility is well illustrated by a chain of men's clothing stores which makes use of second-floor locations. Similarly, other retailers attempting to "build up" locations frequently sell at low prices for a time.

Return on Capital Investment. Of major concern to the retailer, of course, is the return on his capital investment in a specific site. This determination would involve such considerations as the equipment and fixtures he plans to use, the size and turnover of his merchandise inventory, and the amount of rent he must pay or the cost of the site and building.[25] Although he may be willing to accept a small return in the short run, over a longer period he needs to obtain a satisfactory return on his investment.

Site Characteristics Detrimental to Retail Outlets. The prospective retailer should be fully aware of those site characteristics which decrease his ability to attract customers. Among these are the following: (1) smoke, dust, disagreeable odors, and noise; (2) proximity to garages, hospitals, taverns, and similar places; (3) poor sidewalks; and (4) old and worn-out neighboring structures.

Availability of the Site. Other considerations may be favorable, but the desired site may not be available under terms and conditions satisfactory to the retailer. Although the type and construction of the building may be suitable either with or without remodeling, it may be impossible to work out a favorable leasing arrangement covering the period desired, the amount of rental, privilege of renewal, and similar matters. If mutually satisfactory leasing arrangements for a given structure cannot be completed, one alternative is to investigate the possibilities of obtaining land and constructing a building. In such an instance, zoning regulations, land cost, building-construction costs, and taxes must be carefully weighed.

Some Other Factors Affecting Choice of Site. In the case of the chain organization, or the parent store considering the establishment of a

---

[25] Professor Webb argues that, under present day conditions, it is often more profitable to buy stores than to rent them. Cf. D. R. Webb, "Is Leaseback Better Financing than Long-Term Debt?" *Journal of Retailing,* Vol. XL, No. 4 (Winter, 1964–65), pp. 42–46, 59.

branch, certain operating factors are of considerable importance in the selection of a specific site. The distance of the proposed unit from headquarters, the parent store, or from a warehouse for effective supervision and servicing; the incremental advertising expense required; and the availability of qualified personnel at the firm's existing pay rates are of major concern.

FROM CITY TO METROPOLIS TO MEGALOPOLIS

Already we have noted that in the decade of the fifties the number of people living in our urban areas increased from 64 to 70 percent of the total population.[26] This trend, which has existed throughout our entire history, has continued during the sixties so that the percentage of our people now classified by the census as urban dwellers is at an all-time high.

"Explosion" in Suburbia

From a retailer point of view, it is extremely important to interpret correctly this trend toward urban areas. Particularly should it be emphasized that in recent decades the relative gain in urban population has taken place largely in the *suburban* areas. As a matter of fact, and subject to important exceptions, the central areas of our larger cities are now growing very slowly or not at all. To be specific, in the 1950–60 decade, the population in older central city areas gained less than 10 percent, whereas their suburbs jumped over 54 percent.[27]

The relative shift of population to the suburbs may be partially explained by a desire for improved living conditions and for a more open type of housing with larger lots, trees, flowers, and grass. The shorter workweek, longer vacation periods, and more paid holidays—estimated to give the average American 125 days a year away from his job—encourage people to live some distance from their work.[28] Many persons have sought to escape from the high taxes prevalent in large cities. In addition, private housing developments as well as the housing activities of the federal government have made possible the ownership of property at lower interest rates and

---

[26] Cf. p. 96, above.

[27] Some students of the rapid shift to suburbia believe that, in the absence of a greater amount of long range planning, we will end up with another "slum problem" on our hands. Cf. S. E. Wood, "Spreading Slurbs," *National Civic Review,* June, 1965, pp. 304–8 ff. For some positive suggestions for dealing with this problem cf. E. K. Faltermayer, "We Can Cope with the Coming Suburban Explosion," *Fortune,* Vol. LXXIV, No. 4 (September, 1966), pp. 147–151 ff.

[28] The impact of the shorter workweek on the move to the suburbs is explored in M. C. Faught, "Split-Week Living a Threat to the City," *Banking,* April, 1965, pp. 41–42.

with relatively larger mortgages than were heretofore considered practicable.

Regardless of the reasons for the population shift, in the outlying areas a way of life has gradually developed that is quite different from that of the typical city dweller. With a higher per capita income, the suburbanite is more apt to own a home and to buy more furniture, appliances, garden tools, records and books, and sportswear than his city contemporary. He also engages in a different variety of leisure-time activities.[29]

The Metropolitan Area

What the foregoing trends mean is this: During the last 25 to 35 years a new metropolis or metropolitan area has emerged as a social and economic unit.[30] Defined by the census as a "county or group of contiguous counties . . . which contains at least one city of 50,000 inhabitants or more or 'twin cities' with a combined population of at least 50,000,"[31] in practice it consists of a declining or slowly growing central city and an exploding suburban area. The 1963 Census of Business lists 217 such areas with 64.6 percent of our total population and 69.5 percent of all retail sales.[32] And a leading student of these "large conglomerations" refers to them as "the most efficient producing-consuming unit that mankind has ever devised."[33]

Trend toward Megalopolis

Today the conglomeration is becoming even larger! As metropolitan areas expand, some of them begin to overlap to produce what we refer to as a "megalopolis": Witness the coming-together of the Boston, New York, Philadelphia, Baltimore, and Washington metropolitan areas so that they—in effect—form a single stretch of urban and suburban areas.[34] Similar megalopolises are gradually taking shape in other parts of the country,

---

[29] For details, cf. S. D. Clark, *The Suburban Society* (Toronto, Canada: The University of Toronto Press, 1966).

[30] An analysis of this relatively new development will be found in J. C. Bollens and H. J. Schmandt, *The Metropolis* (New York: Harper & Row, 1965). As to possible future developments, cf. P. M. Hauser, "Future Population Trends," *Dun's Review and Modern Industry*, March, 1966, pp. 23–24.

[31] For a careful evaluation of this concept, cf. A. G. Feldt, "Metropolitan Area Concept," *Journal of the American Statistical Association*, June, 1965, pp. 617–36.

[32] *1963 Census of Business, Retail Trade: United States Summary*, BC 63–RA1, p. 1–74.

[33] P. M. Hauser, "Is the Market Moving Away from You?" *A View to 1970* (Chicago, Ill.: Super Market Institute, 1965), p. 11.

[34] By far the best treatment of megalopolis is found in Jean Gottman, *Megalopolis* (New York: Twentieth Century Fund, 1961).

especially along the California coast, along Puget Sound in the Northwest, and in the lower Lake Michigan area.[35]

Decentralization of Retailing

Anyone who has observed retailing trends in recent decades is well aware that the "explosion in Suburbia" has been accompanied by a relatively large gain in the retail sales of such areas. Although retail sales in many of the older downtown central shopping districts of our metropolitan areas have declined, the total retail sales of these same areas have advanced. It is quite clear that retailing has been decentralizing. Why?

Some Reasons for Decentralization. It is axiomatic that the retailer must follow his customers. Consequently, we may say that:

1. The pronounced shift of population to the suburbs is clearly the first reason for the rapid development of retail facilities in the outlying areas. But there are other factors as well.

2. Changes in shopping habits of women during the last twenty years and more. The desire to compare merchandise and prices in more than one store is no longer so great, with the result that one-stop shopping has become increasingly common. Women are continually broadening their interests outside their homes; consequently they have less time for shopping. Moreover, the rapid and widespread dissemination of fashion information through motion pictures, radio, television, newspapers, and magazines probably has brought about an increased willingness and desire on the part of women to rely on their own judgment in selecting styles. As a result, they patronize to an increasing extent the women's specialty stores located near their homes, visit nearby shopping centers, or make their selections from advertisements of stores in the central shopping district and place their orders by telephone or mail.

3. The increased use of the automobile. This factor is closely related to, or even a part of, the changes that have taken place in buying habits. Use of their cars for shopping has a wide appeal among women, especially in the better-class suburbs; and it is likely that this appeal will continue to grow. Incidentally, it is this greater use of the automobile which has made possible a substantial growth of roadside retailing. Today such retailing goes far beyond gasoline stations and farmers' stands; it includes men's and women's clothing, furniture, and other shopping goods.

4. The rapid rise in the cost of public transportation facilities used to reach the downtown areas and the traffic congestion which exists there. For example, residents of East Bay sections in the San Francisco metropolitan area must pay a minimum of $1.00 round-trip bus fare to the downtown area, plus as much as 30 cents for additional transportation by bus or streetcar to reach the major downtown stores.

5. The lack of economical and convenient parking lots in the central shop-

---

[35] For a map showing these developments, cf. First National City Bank, *Monthly Economic Letter*, June, 1965, p. 64.

ping districts. Even though the customer willingly confronts the traffic congestion in downtown areas, she is faced with the problem of finding a conveniently
accessible parking space at a reasonable cost.

6. The excellent retail facilities which have been developed in the suburbs.
Since many of our best retail buildings—containing the most modern equipment
and fixtures and stocked with both broad and deep assortments of merchandise—
are now found in the newer shopping centers and as free-standing units scattered
about metropolitan areas, the customer no longer finds the "pull" of downtown
what it was twenty years ago.

RETAIL STRUCTURE OF THE METROPOLITAN AREA

While there are significant differences in the retail structures of our 217
metropolitan areas, it is possible to present a structure analysis which is
applicable in a general way to all of them. Each area seems to contain an
older central shopping district, one or more older secondary shopping districts, one or more of the newer shopping centers, several scattered but large
free standing stores, some neighborhood business stands, and many scattered
areas with single units or clusters of small stores.

The Older Central Shopping District

The central shopping district is the heart of the retail structure of the city
which, in turn, is an integral part of each metropolitan area. All means of
intracity communication converge on this shopping district. Here are concentrated many of the area's leading shopping and specialty-goods stores—department stores, departmentized specialty stores, and limited-line independent and chain stores engaged in selling such merchandise as apparel, furniture, shoes, and jewelry. These stores are typically much larger in both floor
space and sales than the average store in the city, and they draw a far greater
part of their total business from nonresidents than do the other city retailers.
In addition, there are a number of convenience-goods retailers—drugstores,
cigar stores, and grocery stores. Although the area covered by this district is
small, it draws customers from the entire metropolitan area, so that its total
sales form an appreciable although declining part of the total sales of the
whole metropolitan area.

The Older Secondary Shopping Districts

The older secondary shopping districts of the metropolitan area came into
existence mainly as the city increased in population and spread over a
broader area. Gradually it became more convenient for some of the people

to buy at least part of their shopping and specialty goods outside the older central shopping district. Consequently, the stores located on a neighborhood business street expanded to supply more of the wants of the people living in the vicinity. Several centers which have developed in this manner may be found in practically every large city, each well located on the main traffic arteries leading from residential districts to the older central shopping district. In addition, some of these secondary shopping districts developed within the smaller towns which have gradually been absorbed by the metropolitan area. But, regardless of their origin, to a considerable degree the kinds of goods sold here are similar to those sold in the main shopping district; but the stores are smaller, selection may be more limited, people are not attracted from such wide areas, and the sale of convenience goods is relatively more important.

The Newer Shopping Centers

Nature and Growth of Shopping Centers. One major response to (and also a factor encouraging) the decentralization of shopping areas is the rapid growth of outlying shopping centers on a planned or controlled basis. Usually the entire center is an integrated development, under single ownership, with coordinated and complete shopping facilities, and with adequate parking space. The stores in the center are leased to various retailers. Sometimes all of the stores in the center engage in joint advertising, stage a common fashion show or cooking school, and adopt a unified public relations program. Often such joint activities are required by or are actually carried out by the central organization which owns the center.

Although a few of these newer shopping centers date from thirty or more years ago, the overwhelming majority have been built since the end of World War II. From 1,000 centers at the end of 1955, the number advanced spectacularly to 4,500 at the close of 1960, and to an estimated 9,500 by January 1, 1967.[36] The authors estimate that they now account for 25 to 30 percent of *all* retail sales; by 1975 their share may approach 40 to 50 percent.[37]

Shopping Center Developers. So far as sponsorship is concerned, there are two main types of shopping centers. By far the most numerous are those centers which have been built by real estate organizations, that is,

---

[36] S. O. Kaylin, "27th Annual *Chain Store Age* Survey of Construction & Modernization," *Chain Store Age* (Supermarket Executives Edition), January, 1966, P. E8. Of the 9,700 chain stores planned for 1966, 60 percent were scheduled for shopping centers.

[37] Max Shapiro, "Mass Market Getting Classier," *Women's Wear Daily*, April 19, 1966, p. 1.

firms which expect to make a profit on their investment by leasing all the units of the center to others. However, many centers have been developed by large retailers. In some cases, a large chain has organized what is, in effect, a subsidiary corporation to develop centers. Examples are Food Fair Properties, Inc., sponsored by Food Fair Stores, and Eastern Shopping Centers organized by the Grand Union Company. In other instances the developer is a large department store which operates the department store in the center and leases the remaining buildings to others. Centers developed by May Department Stores (through its subsidiary, May Realty & Investment Company) and the Broadway Department Store in southern California, and Allied Stores Corporation in Seattle through its affiliate, Bon Marche, are examples of this type. The Southdale Shopping Center, near Minneapolis, Minnesota, developed by Dayton's, provides still another illustration.

Trends and Problems. The dynamic nature of retailing is no better demonstrated than in the case of shopping center development. Continuous improvements are being made to attract customers, to make it more convenient for them to park and shop, and to provide merchandise and services comparable to those "downtown" or in the older central shopping districts. Some of the other major current trends and problems of this development are as follows:

1. Currently there is a strong trend toward the fully-enclosed-mall-air-conditioned type of shopping center. Although the first of this type dates just from 1956 (Southdale near Minneapolis), it has accounted for more than 80 percent of all the regional (large) centers built since 1964.[38] Moreover, many existing centers are including these features in their modernization and expansion programs.[39]

2. In contrast to the early large centers which included just one major department store, today's large centers attempt to attract at least two full-line department stores and a few centers with three or four stores of this type are in existence.

3. Along with the development of new centers, successful established centers are also expanding: Of the 180 million square feet added to shopping center space in 1965, probably one half was accounted for by additions to existing facilities.[40] These expansion programs are giving many retailers an opportunity to enlarge their stores. During lease negotiations, some retailers now seek a clause which guarantees them an area for later expansion if it proves desirable.

4. In locations with limited acreage or very high land costs, a few multi-

[38] "Shopping Centers Pace Retail Sales," *American Invester,* May, 1965, p. 3.

[39] For evidence of this trend, cf. C. D. Mericle, "Air Conditioned Mall," *Air Conditioning, Heating & Refrigeration News,* May 17, 1965, p. 16; "When an Open-Mall Center Is Enclosed," *Chain Store Age* (Executives Edition), January, 1965, pp. 20–23; and "Expansion & Remodeling: A Major Trend in Centers," *ibid.,* April, 1966, pp. E38–E39.

[40] "Shopping Centers Pace Retail Sales," *op. cit.,* p. 3.

level centers are being built. Likewise, a limited number of centers are providing vertical parking facilities.

5. There is growing recognition of the fact that more careful planning and research is necessary, both for the center developer and the lessees of the space occupied. Far too many centers have been built without a sufficient number of "lead in" roads; or they have generated more traffic than the nearby road system can handle, with the result that customers have difficulty entering or leaving the center. Additional marketing research data are also needed regarding customer preferences, wants, buying motives, and buying habits.

6. Improved methods and devices for projecting sales volume in new shopping centers are required. A variety chain found that its methods of forecasting volume for new stores in established central shopping districts and smaller communities were inaccurate for shopping center units.

7. As more centers are built in a single metropolitan area so that the small retailer has a choice of centers, he needs outside aid in reaching a decision. Some of the factors which he should consider are included in Figure 4–2.

8. Both many retailers and shopping center landlords are uncertain about the entry of the discount house into shopping centers. It is the opinion of some retailers that the newer, low-margin operators draw traffic to the center and, thus, represent a favorable development. Others either fear the competition afforded by the discount firms or believe that their presence cheapens the center and object to their entry.

9. As real estate taxes rise, the insertion of tax escalation clauses in shopping center leases is gaining despite opposition by many center tenants. Landlords and tenants are joining together in an effort to fight the proposed increases which they believe are excessive.

10. Location of regional shopping centers adjacent to major freeways is a development of some significance.

11. A few planned shopping centers have found locations in downtown business districts as a part of the urban renewal activities.

12. Determining uniform and profitable hours of operation, including Sunday openings, constitutes a problem for operators of shopping centers. It is made more difficult because of disagreement among tenants on the number of nights (and which nights) they wish to remain open. The trend seems to be toward as many as three to five nights per week plus Sunday.

13. Merchants' associations are being discussed more frequently, with emphasis on whether membership should be a condition of the lease. Although it is recognized that the success of such an association depends on the cooperation and participation of the tenants, the consensus among them is that active leadership by the developer of the center is the basic factor in success.

14. Greater attention is being given to the establishment of medical centers within shopping centers. Usually, however, the building is physically separated from the main center buildings and has its own parking lot.

Future. Despite a long-persisting worry that the country will become "over-stored", there seems no question but that the development of shopping centers will continue. It is important to note, however, that the trend toward shopping centers does not insure the success of each center. As has

1. Who is the shopping center developer?
2. How long has he been in the business of developing real estate?
3. What are his financial resources?
4. With whom has he arranged for the financing of the center?
5. What is his reputation for integrity?
6. Who performed the economic analysis? Does the report cover both favorable and unfavorable factors?
7. What experience has the economic consultant had?
8. Has an architectural firm been retained to plan the center?
9. Has the architect designed other centers? Have they been successful from a retailing standpoint?
10. Who will build the center? The developer? An experienced contractor? An inexperienced contractor?
11. Has the developer had experience with other centers?
12. What is, or will be, the quality of management for the center?
13. Will the management have merchandising and promotion experience? (Some developers are large retailers rather than real estate operators.)
14. What percent of the leases have been signed? Are they on a contingent basis?
15. Has every facet of the lease been carefully studied?
16. Is the ratio of parking area to selling area 3-to-1 or more?
17. Has sufficient space (400 feet) been assigned to each car?
18. Is the parking space designed so that the shopper does not walk more than 300 to 350 feet from the farthest spot to the store?
19. What is the angle of parking space? (Ninety degrees provides the best expacity and circulation.)
20. What is the planned or actual car turnover? (3.3 cars per parking space per day is the average.)
21. Is the number of total spaces adequate for the planned business volume? (Too many spaces make the center look dead; too few openly invite competition around the center.)
22. Does the parking scheme distribute the cars so as to favor no one area?
23. Is there an adequate number of ingress/egress roads in proper relationship with the arrangement of parking spaces?
24. For the larger centers, a ring road is preferable. Is this the case?
25. Is the site large enough for the type of center?
26. Is the size sufficiently dominant to forestall the construction of similar shopping centers nearby?
27. Is the center of regular shape? If not, does the location of the buildings minimize the disadvantage of the site's shape?
28. Is the site sufficiently deep? (A depth of at least 400 feet is preferred; if less, the center may look like a strip development.)
29. Is the site level? Is it on well-drained land?
30. Does the center face north and/or east?
31. Can the center be seen from a distance?
32. Are any structures, such as a service station, located in the parking area? (If so, do they impede the site's visibility?)
33. Is the site a complete unit? (A road should not pass through the site.)
34. Are the buildings set far enough back on the site that the entire area may be seen?
35. Are all the stores readily accessible to each other, with none having an advantage?

SOURCE: J. E. Mertes, "Site Opportunities for the Small Retailer," *Journal of Retailing*, Vol. XXXIX, No. 3 (Fall, 1963), p. 44.

FIG. 4–2. Check points for evaluating shopping center locations.

been indicated in previous paragraphs, great care is necessary in choosing locations, studying competition, designing buildings, providing adequate parking space, selecting tenants, preparing leases, and arranging proper promotion. Probably the major failing of many shopping centers being built today is lack of careful economic appraisal prior to their development.

Some criticism has also been directed toward the roles large stores play in shopping center developments. It is sometimes alleged that department and chain stores too often assume the "self-appointed position of Prime Minister," without giving adequate consideration to the needs and preferences of smaller, independent tenants. Some smaller independent merchants have even moved out of shopping centers because of high rentals and limited profits. But, despite these problems and others, the future of the shopping center seems assured.

Large Free-Standing Stores

Another fairly recent retailing development is the large free-standing store. Normally located in the suburban parts of the metropolitan areas, this store is usually: (1) a discount store, (2) a department store, or (3) a departmentized specialty store. If it is one of the latter two types, it is typically a unit of a chain or a branch of a downtown store.

The Free-Standing Discount House. It has already been mentioned that discount houses are not always welcomed into the newer shopping centers.[41] As a result, some discount house retailers have turned to the free-standing store as an alternative to the center. But many others make this decision as a matter of choice: To quote the real estate vice president of S. S. Kresge Company, "(For our K-Marts) we favor free-standing units . . ."[42] The result: All but eight of the present more-than-122 K-Marts are outside of shopping centers.[43] Back of this policy is the belief of many discount retailers that the free-standing store gives them a lower rental, complete freedom of choice on merchandise lines (in centers, merchandise restrictions are typically included in leases), better parking facilities (usually around a great part of the store building), and a greater flow of traffic for the types and quality of merchandise they offer for sale. By "ringing a city" with units (for example, E. J. Korvette, Inc., has used the

[41] Cf. p. 113, above.

[42] "Nailing Down Locations is the Key to Kresge's Expansion," *op. cit.*, p. E15. In contrast, practically all of the Woolco units of the F. W. Woolworth Company are in shopping centers.

[43] "Kresge's Triple-Threat Retailing," *Business Week,* January 29, 1966, p. 130.

"cluster" approach around New York, St. Louis, Chicago, and Baltimore[44]), a substantial promotional program is possible at a relatively low cost per store.

The Department Store and the Departmentized Specialty Store. During the late 1920s and the 1930s, as Sears, Roebuck and Co. began to develop its chain of department stores, the firm's management correctly interpreted the trend to the suburbs and began to open free-standing units in such areas. At the same time, a few downtown department and departmentized specialty stores started to serve these areas through branches, that is, stores usually smaller than (and dominated by) the parent stores.

It was not until after World War II, however, that the number of these stores, both chain and branch, became of great significance. Today their importance is well illustrated by what has happened in the greater Los Angeles area: The six department and departmentized specialty stores located in that city have opened more than 40 branches, some of which are located as far away as Palm Springs—90 miles from the Los Angeles central shopping district. And the trend is nationwide, with branches now operated by such well-known organizations as Marshall Field & Company and Carson, Pirie, Scott & Co. of Chicago; William Filene's Sons Company of Boston; R. H. Macy & Company and Lord & Taylor of New York City; Woodward & Lothrop of Washington, D. C.; Bullock's, Inc., of Los Angeles; and Emporium-Capwell of San Francisco. Moreover, the branches have continued to gain in size, although the majority of them still make no pretense of carrying as complete a stock as does the parent store.

1. *Benefits and Problems of Branch Stores.* Through branches, downtown stores have found a way to follow their customers to the suburbs. They discovered that branches attract business because of the downtown store's prestige and also acquainted people with the firm, so that even the parent store acquired new customers. Experience also indicated that the nonmerchandising departments of the parent store could handle some added work, such as accounting and advertising, without a substantial increase in total overhead cost. The net result is that the branch store has added substantially to the total profit of the organization.

Although the trend is still strongly toward a substantial further increase in number, branch stores are not without their problems. In some instances the opening of a branch has cut substantially into the sales of the parent store or has at least reduced the rate of sales increase. Others have been placed in such poor locations that they have resulted in losses rather than

---

[44] "For Korvette: More Unified Merchandising," *Discount Store News,* August 23, 1965, p. 51; and L. A. Mayer, "How Confusion Caught up with Korvette," *Fortune,* Vol. LXXIII, No. 2 (February, 1966), p. 154.

additional profits. Just how they can be managed to the greatest advantage is still another problem. Some organizations attempt to solve this problem by assigning the merchandising function, for example, to the parent store with the branch responsible mainly for selling; others allow the branch to select merchandise from parent-store stocks; still others authorize the branch to buy directly in wholesale markets; but, increasingly, chain-store principles of organization are being adopted.[45] None of these solutions nor the others which have been tried, has eliminated all the friction and overlapping of responsibility between branch and parent stores.

Neighborhood Business Streets

Far more numerous than any of the foregoing types of locations in the metropolitan area are neighborhood business streets, made up mainly of convenience-goods stores located one next to the other or with only reasonably small distances between them. Here are the grocery stores, superettes, meat markets, small bakery shops, fruit and vegetable stores, small variety stores, and drugstores, although a few of the smaller shopping- and specialty-goods stores are located on these streets. In the majority of cases these streets follow the main arteries of traffic throughout both the city and its satellite towns and villages. The stores are relatively small and attract business from the immediately surrounding area.

In recent years a development somewhat comparable to the controlled shopping center has taken place in regard to neighborhood business streets. Instead of developing gradually as in the past, in some areas a large building —sometimes known as a "shopping plaza"—has been constructed and its various sections rented out to several retailers. Ample parking space is usually provided.

In spite of competition from stores in other parts of the metropolitan area, those located on the neighborhood business streets (as well as those situated in small clusters and scattered, discussed below) have demonstrated a remarkable vitality. One close student of retailing trends attributed their continued success to the fact that "people do not always act rationally. They follow the easiest course of behavior. They don't always select the best buys at the lowest prices. They don't anticipate their needs, and consequently are always patronizing some neighborhood store to fill in what they forgot on an orderly shopping trip."[46]

---

[45] Cf. the discussion of organizational "Structure for Branch Operation," pp. 194–97, below.

[46] P. D. Martineau, "Customers' Shopping Center Habits Change Retailing," *Editor & Publisher,* October 26, 1964, pp. 16, 56.

Small Clusters and Scattered Stores

The clusters or scattered individual small stores of the metropolitan area are distinguished from the neighborhood business streets largely by the number of stores. Typically, the stores are complementary; that is, a cluster may be made up of a grocery store, a drugstore, and one or two other noncompetitive stores. For a cluster of these stores to be located in a centrally owned plaza or retail development is also a current trend. Instead of a cluster of stores, however, there may be only a single grocery store or drugstore in the area. Such stores are small, and they deal mainly in convenience-type goods. Although they attract most of their customers from the adjacent area, dealers handling such products as automobiles and gasoline may attract trade from a substantial part of the metropolitan area.

The Future of the Central Shopping District

The decentralization of shopping areas has proceeded so rapidly that it gives rise to the question: Does it eventually mean the end of the central shopping district? Victor Gruen, head of the well-known firm of architects, engineers, and planners, believes that the city will end up "like a doughnut —all the dough on the outside, and a hole in the middle" unless downtown is adapted "to new business sources and forces, and (is set free) from strangulation by (the) automobile. . . ."[47] Both retailers and customers agree that today's downtown presents great problems for them: Customer access difficulties, limited parking, high land cost, substantial property taxes, high building cost, difficulties in moving merchandise into the store and in delivering it to the customer, split ownership of land and buildings, old retail structures. No wonder Montgomery Ward & Company's corporate manager of real estate has said: ". . . Time is running out for most downtowns that do not have realistic plans in process."[48] The late Frank Lloyd Wright even proclaimed that the downtown shopping center will disappear.

However, the authors believe that the center shopping district, while relatively less important than in past decades, will remain of great significance to the retailer. Although growing at much slower rates than the

---

[47] Quoted by Walter Guzzardi, Jr., "An Architect of Environments," *Fortune,* Vol. LXV, No. 1 (January, 1962), p. 136.

[48] Quoted by S. O. Kaylin, "Research and Development Program: Key to Ward's Dynamic Leap," *Chain Store Age* (Supermarket Executives Edition), December, 1964, p. E16.

suburban areas, most of our cities are still gaining population within their old boundaries. Some observers are of the opinion that, as urban renewal programs are completed and downtown high-rise residential buildings are constructed, many of the middle-income families who have moved to the suburbs may return to the cities.[49] In addition, there is the possibility that low-cost housing subsidized by the government will continue to expand and thus induce many families to remain in the cities.

In the larger cities the great congregation of stores in the downtown area offers a breadth of merchandise assortment not matched by the largest of the planned shopping centers. The desire to "make a day" of a shopping trip still brings many from the outlying areas to the central shopping area while the thousands who work in that area or who come to the city as out-of-town visitors find it convenient to buy there.

Moreover, in many cities the downtown merchants in cooperation with transit authorities and city-federal governments are making efforts to increase the attractiveness of downtown shopping. Express highways leading directly to the heart of the city are being built. Public transportation systems are being modernized and unified to give better schedules.[50] More downtown parking facilities are becoming available, some through additional parking lots, some by underground developments, and still others by creating ramps or mechanical devices to provide above-the-ground parking. A combination of fringe parking lots plus public transportation (in a few instances, without charge) to the center of the city is being used in some cities. Downtown retailers are modernizing their stores, establishing shopping malls, adopting night hours, and joining together on promotional programs similar to those of the shopping center.[51] It is in the light of such developments that there is far greater optimism among many merchants about the future of downtown than has prevailed for many years.

---

[49] Edward Coyle, "Barr of Ward's Cites Swing to Downtown Area," *Women's Wear Daily*, May 22, 1964, p. 1.

[50] But much remains to be done: cf. J. R. Meyer, *et al.*, *The Urban Transportation Problem* (Boston, Mass: Harvard University Press, 1965). For an attempt to look ahead on this problem, cf. E. B. Weiss, "Downtown Retailing and the Coming Revolution in Mass Transit," *Advertising Age*, July 19, 1965, pp. 80 ff.

[51] For details on these trends, cf. S. O. Kaylin and Martin Ezra, "Recapturing the Downtown Marketplace," *Chain Store Age* (Supermarket Executives Edition), September, 1964, pp. E20–E36; "The Shopping Center Moves Back to Midtown," *Fortune*, Vol. LXXXI, No. 1 (January, 1965), p. 190; R. K. Moffett, "Downtown's Comeback," *Merchandising Week*, July 26, 1965, pp. 10–14; Victor Gruen and Associates, "Upgrading Downtown," *Architectural Record*, June, 1965, pp. 186–87; Trudy Prokop, "Philadelphia Stores Study Urban Mall Scratch Sheet," *Women's Wear Daily*, February 17, 1966, p. 32; and "The Merchants' High Hopes in Minneapolis," *Fortune*, Vol. LXXIII, No. 6 (June, 1966), pp. 161–62.

REVIEW AND DISCUSSION QUESTIONS

1. Discuss: "An effective retailer can be successful in a poor location."
2. "Location problems are not confined to *new* stores; they are also faced by established stores." Explain why this statement is true, and illustrate your point of view by reference to the situation in your local community.
3. "The best locations go to the best retailers." Discuss.
4. How do you account for the fact that even among large-scale retailers the amount of money spent on store location research is relatively very modest?
5. Assume you have decided to open a store in your local community or a nearby one. From a location point of view, analyze the possibilities of your success as a retailer.
6. Survey the sources of information on store location available to a prospective retailer in your community from the local Chamber of Commerce, Merchants Service Bureau, and similar organizations. In other words, where would an "outsider" find helpful information in evaluating the desirability of opening a store in your city? Evaluate this information.
7. Compute the index of retail saturation for a trading area of 30,000 people spending an average of $6.00 per week in five supermarkets having a total of 75,000 square feet of selling space. What is the significance of this index in site selection?
8. What steps would you take in arriving at an estimate of the volume of business which you might achieve in a given location? Apply your steps to a nearby site.
9. Visit a leading retailer in your city and determine from him the considerations which dictated the choice of his particular location. Contrast these considerations with those given in the text relative to the choice of a site.
10. Define "suburbia," "metropolis" and "megalopolis." From the point of view of retail location, discuss current population trends in relation to each of these terms.
11. Discuss the major factors responsible for the decentralization of retail trade.
12. Outline and describe briefly the major elements in the retail structure of the metropolitan area.
13. Prepare a ten minute talk on "Current Trends in Shopping Center Development." Support each trend with specific evidence drawn from your reading or observations.
14. How do you account for the development of large free-standing stores in the suburban parts of metropolitan areas?
15. Assume that you have been employed by the retail trade board of a city of 400,000 people to make recommendations for revitalizing the downtown area and prevent further loss of sales to suburban stores. What steps would you recommend to meet this problem? Why?

SUPPLEMENTARY READINGS

APPLEBAUM, WILLIAM. "Guidelines for a Store-Location Strategy Study," *Journal of Marketing,* Vol. XXX, No. 4 (October, 1966), pp. 42–45. In this article, sixteen fundamental steps for planning and executing store-location studies are presented.

————. *Patterns of Food Distribution in a Metropolis* (Chicago, Ill.: Super Market Institute, Inc., 1966). This careful study of the Boston metropolitan area suggests how other areas may be analyzed for store locations. A valuable technical note on location analysis is offered by the same author's "Methods for Determining Store Trade Areas, Market Penetration, and Potential Sales," *Journal of Marketing Research,* Vol. III, No. 2 (May, 1966), pp. 127–141. Also cf. APPLEBAUM, WILLIAM, AND SCHELL, EILEEN, *Marketing Maps for Store Location Studies* (Chicago: Super Market Institute, 1965).

————. "Store Location Research—A Survey of Retailing Chains," *Journal of Retailing,* Vol. XL, No. 2 (Summer, 1964), pp. 53–6. The author "reports the results of an exploratory survey of store location research currently being done by retailing chains in the United States."

————. "Store Performance in Relation to Location and Other Characteristics," *Chain Store Age* (Executives Edition), November, 1965, pp. E14–E16. The relation of sales and profits to various types of locations are among the subjects of this article.

BOLLENS, J. C., AND SCHMANDT, H. J. *The Metropolis* (New York: Harper & Row, 1965). The development and problems of the metropolis explain much of the current shifting of retail locations. For another analysis of this subject cf. MURPHY, R. E. *The American City* (New York: McGraw-Hill Book Co., Inc., 1966).

CHINITZ, B. (ed.) *City and Suburb* (Englewood Cliffs, N.J.: Prentice-Hall, Inc., 1965). The problems arising from the explosion in suburbia are explored in this volume.

DANIELSON, M. N. *Federal-Metropolitan Politics and The Commuter Crisis* (New York: Columbia University Press, 1965). With a substantial part of his sales going to commuters, the downtown retailer has a personal interest in efforts to ease the commuter crisis.

FELDT, A. G. "Metropolitan Area Concept," *Journal of The American Statistical Association,* June, 1965, pp. 617–36. The student searching for a careful evaluation of the metropolitan area concept will find it in this article.

GOTTMANN, JEAN. *Megalopolis: The Urbanized Northeastern Seaboard of the United States* (New York: The Twentieth Century Fund, 1961). This major study of the urbanized northeastern seaboard of the United States discusses the "greatest urban concentration on the globe."

HUFF, D. L., AND BLUE, LARRY. *A Programmed Solution for Estimating Retail Sales Potentials* (Lawrence, Kansas: University of Kansas, Center for Regional Studies, 1966). Based on a computer program, the authors present a probability model for estimating retail sales.

IOWA STATE UNIVERSITY, BUREAU OF BUSINESS RESEARCH. *A Retail Trading Area Analysis of Rock Rapids, Iowa* (Ames, Iowa, 1965). This case study presents an analysis which can be applied to other retail trading areas.

KANE, B. J. *A Systematic Guide to Supermarket Location Analysis* (New York: Fairchild Publications, 1966). Techniques and sources of information concerning location analysis are offered by the author.

MERTES, J. E. "Site Opportunities for the Small Retailer," *Journal of Retailing,* Vol. XXXIX, No. 3 (Fall, 1963), pp. 36–45. Professor Mertes places special emphasis on the selection of drive-in sites and shopping centers.

MEYER, J. R., *et al. The Urban Transportation Problem* (Boston, Mass.: Harvard University Press, 1965). Since much of the hope for "saving downtown" lies in solving the urban transportation problem, the student of retailing will find of value this analysis by a group of experts in this field. Also cf. OWEN, WILFRED. *The Metropolitan Transportation Problem* (rev. ed.; Washington, D.C.: The Brookings Institution, 1966).

MEYERS, PERRY. *The Planning of Branch Stores* (New York: National Retail Merchants Association, 1960). Among other aspects of branch stores, the author deals with the problem of site selection.

"Shopping Center Trends," *Chain Store Age* (Supermarket Executives Edition), May, 1965, pp. E22–E44. The value of this analysis is increased by the inclusion of a five-year study of leasing trends. Also cf. "Shopping Centers are Still Booming," *ibid,* April, 1966, pp. E30–E40.

SIMMONS, J. W. *The Changing Pattern of Retail Location* (Chicago, Ill.: University of Chicago Department of Geography, 1964). The factors giving rise to shopping centers and other current developments in retail location are discussed by the author.

WATTENBERG, BEN, AND SCAMMON, R. M. *This U.S.A.* (New York: Doubleday, 1965). Many of the trends developed in this analysis of census data are important from the point of view of store location.

URBAN LAND INSTITUTE, *Parking Requirements for Shopping Centers* (Washington, D.C., 1965). In view of the still-growing importance of the automobile to the shopper, this extensive study of parking needs is important. Its major conclusion: the typical center should plan on 5.5 spaces per 1,000 square feet of gross leasable area.

WEBB, D. R. "Is Leaseback Better Financing Than Long-Term Debt?" *Journal of Retailing,* Vol. XL, No. 4 (Winter, 1964–1965), pp. 42–46, 59. Conclusion: under present conditions, many retailers should purchase store sites and buildings rather than lease them.

WOOD, S. E. "Spreading Slurbs," *National Civic Review,* June, 1965, pp. 304–8 ff. The author presents the case for long range planning of land use in the suburbs.

5

CHAPTER

Store Building, Fixtures, and Equipment

After a suitable location has been chosen, a building must be prepared for occupancy. This preparation involves the following: (1) constructing a new building or making whatever structural changes are necessary in an existing one to provide space and facilities for the performance of the selling and nonselling activities planned; (2) providing adequate lighting equipment, properly colored walls and ceilings, and suitable floor coverings; (3) procuring the fixtures and equipment essential to the conduct of the business; and (4) arranging and locating the merchandise, fixtures, and equipment in such a manner that customers may be served promptly and satisfactorily at the lowest cost to the store. The successful operation of the store will depend to an important degree upon the care with which plans for these steps are made, appraised, and carried out.

The present chapter discusses the first three of these steps, and Chapter 6 is concerned with the fourth, that is, an effective store layout.

GREATER EMPHASIS ON WELL-DESIGNED BUILDINGS

A well-designed store may be described as one embodying features that attract customers and facilitates their movement inside the store, provides a pleasant environment in which they may shop, makes possible economical operations and maintenance, is well lighted and ventilated, and provides adequate space for selling and sales-supporting activities currently and in the foreseeable future.

The Store Building as a Selling Instrument

To an increasing degree during the last three decades, retailers have recognized that well-designed stores are as essential to profitable operation as good assortments of merchandise at reasonable prices. Likewise, contemporary architects have come to realize not only that "form follows function" but also that the buildings they design must be effective selling instruments. Experience demonstrates that effective store planning may result in sales 10 to 100 percent higher than in the poorly planned unit. Consequently, interest in better design has permeated the whole field of retailing, from the large city to the small town; from the large store to the small one; and from the small shopping plaza to the huge regional shopping center. Through the cooperation of store executives, building architects, lighting and ventilating engineers, and specialists in store equipment, marked progress in retail facilities has resulted. As a result, some of the newest units of Sears, Roebuck and Co. and Montgomery Ward & Company "are more beautiful [and more effective retailing plants] than the 'carriage trade' stores of fifteen years ago."[1] In no field perhaps has the triumph of the architect been more complete.

Land, Building, and Equipment Expenditures.   Retailers are also aware that buildings and land cost a great deal of money. To purchase land and then to build and equip a large supermarket may involve an expenditure of nearly $500,000, a modern full-line drugstore handling a broad assortment of nondrug merchandise may cost $100,000 to $250,000, a large discount house may require an investment of $1–2 million, and a free-standing full-line department store may range between $3 and $10 million.[2] Moreover, as the price level continues to advance and as the size of the store increases,[3] these cost figures are showing a strong upward trend.

In view of these large and ever-growing sums, retailers are becoming increasingly cost conscious in their store building programs. Many of the larger retailers have assigned to their architects and engineers the task of achieving equally efficient and impressive facilities at lower costs. Put another way, while they have sought architects who are "young enough to hope for a world . . . where the ugly will no longer be tolerated," they also want them "old enough to know that the words economy and profit in architecture are not ugly words . . ."[4]

Some firms have achieved their economy goal by reducing the construction period through more careful integration of all phases of the job,

---

[1] P. D. Martineau, "Customers' Shopping Center Habits Change Retailing," *Editor & Publisher,* October 26, 1964, p. 56.

[2] These figures are based on retailers' statements to the authors. Also cf. the store cost data in *Facts about New Super Markets Opened in 1965* (Chicago, Ill.: Super Market Institute, 1966), pp. 12–13.

[3] "The average Woolworth store opened in 1964 had 25,000 square feet compared with 15,000 square feet for those opened in 1960." Remarks of the chairman, *Woolworth's Report of Annual Meeting of Stockholders,* May 19, 1965, p. 5.

[4] Architect Tasso Katselas, quoted in Walter McQuade, "The Architects: A Chance for Greatness," *Fortune,* Vol. LXXIII, No. 1 (January, 1966), p. 151.

including use of the Program Evaluation and Review Technique—commonly known as PERT.[5] Others have discovered that a newer, and less costly, material may be substituted. In some instances, less expensive fixtures may be installed. Perhaps a prefabricated structure or section of a building may be used.[6] By careful planning, the same sales potential may be achieved in a somewhat smaller building. Chain and voluntary chain organizations frequently develop a prototype or pattern store which reflects all these savings and which can then be approximately duplicated many times, with just those changes essential to each specific site.[7]

Some Common Features of the Newer-Store Buildings. Although it is impossible to describe any particular store building as the "typical building" of today, it is possible to indicate common features of the newer buildings. Reinforced concrete and concrete and cinderblock tile, as well as brick and highly finished tile, are being widely used, often forming a plain, functional, and windowless building—although display windows are typically constructed on the ground-floor level. The roofs are often flat, pitch and gravel being used for the surface. For floors, terrazzo and vinyl tile are common in basements, the heavy traffic-bearing first floor, and washrooms; asphalt or vinyl tiles are generally used on the other selling floors, although carpeting placed over concrete is appearing in more and more departments; and concrete in the receiving areas. Glass block is often used for at least part of the outside walls to admit natural light. Entrances and exits, as well as interior aisles, are planned for maximum movement of customers.

THE STORE FRONT AND EXTERIOR

Since "the front often sells the store," increasing attention is now being devoted to this part of the building. The exterior of the store should give the impression of a going concern and reflect neither stagnation nor decline; it should typify the spirit of the organization and the nature of the activity within. By suggesting stability and permanence, the front and exterior create confidence and good will. The massive stone columns in front of Marshall Field & Company in Chicago and Selfridge's in London give this impression. Since identification is another function of the store front and exterior, symbols and distinctive store fronts—as well as large signs—have long

---

[5] J. D. Herrick, "How PERT Builds Markets Faster and More Efficiently," *Chain Store Age* (Executives Edition), July, 1966, pp. E35–E39.

[6] For examples, cf. T. A. Durbin, "Basic Evaluation of the Pre-Engineered Building," *Chain Store Age* (Executives Edition), July, 1965, pp. E28–E29.

[7] For a Sears, Roebuck and Co. prototype store, cf. "New Prototype for Sears," *Chain Store Age,* p. E17. A supermarket-pharmacy prototype developed by Giant Food, Inc. is illustrated in "Prototype Stores Smooth Giant's Expansion," *Chain Store Age* (Supermarket Executives Edition), October, 1965, pp. 130–39.

Courtesy: Montgomery Ward & Company

FIG. 5–1.   The Montgomery Ward & Company unit, Wonderland Shopping Center, San Antonio, Texas.

Courtesy: Safeway Stores, Inc.

FIG. 5–2.   A New Safeway Store with extensive parking area.

Courtesy: W. T. Grant Co.

FIG. 5–3.   A W. T. Grant Company 120,000 square foot free-standing store with front and exterior which emphasize company identification.

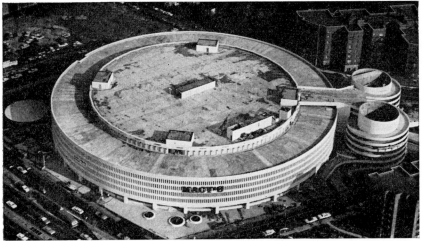

Source: R. H. Macy & Co., Inc.

FIG. 5-4.   The R. H. Macy & Company, Inc.'s department store, Queens Boulevard, Queens, New York. Opened in 1965 with over 330,000 square feet of area, this unusual structure parks 1,500 cars on its roof and ramps.

Source: J. W. Robinson Co.

FIG. 5-5.   An unusual Spanish type department store scheduled for completion in 1967 at Santa Barbara, California, by the J. W. Robinson Company.

been used. Finally, a minimum maintenance cost and protection of the store's windows and interior from sun damage are two other attributes of the exterior.

Figures 5-1, 5-2, and 5-3 provide quite typical examples of the exterior appearance of present-day store buildings, while Figures 5-4 and 5-5 present somewhat unusual structures.[8]

---

[8] Additional illustrations of retail stores and restaurants are given in "Stores: Elements of Change in Location and Design," *Architectural Record*, May, 1965, pp. 187–210; "Shopping Centers and Stores," *ibid.*, April, 1966, pp. 149–59; Macy's Rego Park branch is described, with illustrations, in "Multi-Level Store with Wrap-Around Parking," *ibid.*, April, 1966, pp. 168–70; and "Restaurants," *Interior Design*, October, 1964, pp. 165–80.

Customer Entrances

Because of the "blind spots," or unproductive areas which often develop just inside store entrances in some stores, careful attention should be devoted to planning all customer entrances to the building. Entrances should be wide and inviting,[9] with doorsills preferably at the street level. To avoid congestion and concentration of customer traffic, two entrances are advisable for stores with a frontage of 75 feet or more. When corner locations are occupied, entrances on two streets are preferable to a single corner entrance.

Doors should be of a type that permit ease of access; in fact, some retailers have replaced them with "curtains of air" (warm or cold, depending on the weather), thus eliminating them as a deterrent to entrance by the customer. Whether or not revolving doors are used depends on the size of the store, the willingness of the proprietor to assume the expense, and the climate. In sections of the country where winters are rather severe, many large stores use both swing doors and revolving doors in the same entrance, with a heated vestibule in between.

Show Windows

The use of windows to display merchandise offered for sale is an almost universal practice, with supermarkets and some discount houses the most notable exceptions. Known as the "eyes" of the store, they are the most important feature of the store exterior from the sales point of view. In a study of the window displays of 15 major department and specialty stores in New York City, 32 percent of the women passing by looked at the windows and 40 percent of these actually stopped for closer study of the merchandise.[10] Frequently the impressions received from the windows and the merchandise displayed therein largely determine whether or not customers will enter the store. Consequently, even the so-called "windowless" stores have windows at the ground level to "show their wares." Moreover, although formal windows are lacking in the more recently constructed "open-front" or "visual-front" stores (all glass), the area immediately inside the glass front is frequently used for display purposes just as if it were a window.

[9] The main entrance of F. R. Lazarus and Co., Columbus, Ohio, department store, is over 33 feet wide. Open winter and summer, merchandise displays are brought close to customers. When the store is closed, folding doors protect the entrance.

[10] M. J. Unger, "A Study of the Relative Attraction of Window Displays of Women's Fashion Outerwear," *New York Retailer,* June, 1964, p. 2.

While "window displays attract customers," how successfully they attract them varies widely from window to window. In the New York City study referred to in the preceding paragraph, the "fashion window of one store only attracted the attention of 19 women out of each 100 who passed whereas another store attracted 45 . . . almost 2½ times as great! . . . Large windows with dramatic display had the greatest attraction."[11] In view of such facts, the retailer should take full advantage of the "pulling power" of his windows.[12]

Variations in Show Windows. The size and type of windows used in a particular establishment are determined by the kind of store and the goods displayed. Department stores, with items varying in size from furniture suites to notions, have large and deep windows to accommodate many different types of merchandise. Variety stores frequently use large, shallow windows with no backgrounds above eye level, thus affording an unobstructed view of the store's interior. Bookstores likewise find that shallow windows are sufficient, although there is much disagreement among retailers in this field as to the desirability of closing off the window from the rest of the store.[13] Some jewelry stores favor the so-called "invisible" window, which consists of a curved sheet of glass so formed as to cast reflections downward and away from the observer's eye, thus giving the effect of an open window.

Show Window Backgrounds. Three general types of backgrounds are used: (1) The open background, which permits the passer-by to see into the store, commonly found in grocery stores, candy stores, and florists' shops; (2) the semiclosed background, with a partition extending to a height below the line of vision, sometimes found in drugstores and hardware stores; and (3) the closed background, which shuts off the window completely, found in the large majority of department stores and in specialty stores handling men's and women's wearing apparel. Without a specific background to the window, much of the store's interior is visible to the passer-by, thus acquainting him with the entire offerings of the establishment. Retailers preferring the closed or semiclosed background claim that they focus attention upon displays, provide attractive settings for the merchandise shown, and permit more effective illumination.

---

[11] *Ibid.*

[12] For some valuable suggestions on window displays, cf. J. A. Head and N. M. Cartmell, *Making the Most of Your Store Windows,* Small Marketers Aids, No. 63 (Washington, D.C., Small Business Administration, 1961).

[13] The extent of this disagreement is evident from the illustrations of bookstore windows given in "Window Displays in Small and Medium-Sized Stores," *Publishers' Weekly,* March 15, 1965, pp. 50–51; and "Window Display Roundup," *ibid.,* October 4, 1965, pp. 60–61.

Visual Fronts. One step away from the window with an open background is the open or visual store front, as illustrated in Figure 5–6.[14] Increasing popular in recent years, this type of front has no formal window; instead, the customer looks through glass directly to the store's interior displays.

Even more so than the window with an open background, the visual front increases the customer's ability to see into the store and to grasp more

Courtesy: Libbey-Owens-Ford Glass Company

FIG. 5–6. Sliding glass doors and "visual walls" permit maximum customer visibility of the interior of a women's apparel shop located in a shopping center.

quickly the scope of merchandise offered for sale. Frequently the store also gains selling space. The time necessary to trim windows is reduced, although this saving may not be substantial in view of the additional time necessary to maintain the entire front of the store in "window-display" condition. Also, the store may be made to appear more open and attractive since the amount of natural light is greater than that from the closed type of window.

THE STORE INTERIOR

Regardless of the reasons why the customer enters the store, her impression of the interior must be favorable. If she finds narrow, crowded aisles that confuse her or if the ceiling is so low and the lighting so bad that she is

---

[14] Additional illustrations will be found in "Enclosed Mall with Open Store Fronts," *Architectural Record,* May, 1965, pp. 191–93.

ill at ease, all the promotional activities used to induce her to enter the store have been wasted. But if she finds an open area inside the entrance, aisles wide enough to accommodate customer traffic readily, good light, ceilings of the proper height, and colorful displays, she immediately feels "at home" and proceeds with her shopping in the proper frame of mind.

To create the proper "atmosphere," retailers are going to considerable expense. They are giving particular attention to floor, wall, and ceiling finishes; to store equipment and fixtures, including lighting, elevators and escalators, and air conditioning; and to proper harmonizing of these factors.

Floor, Wall, and Ceiling of the Store

There are more than fifty floor finishes from which the retailer of today may choose, made of such materials as wood, marble, tile, linoleum, rubber, and cork. Different types, of course, are required for different purposes; the finish in the receiving or marking room, for example, would be unlike that required on the second floor of a department store. Likewise, exclusive specialty shops, where wall-to-wall carpeting is growing in popularity, require a floor different from that of a neighborhood grocery store.[15] In general, however, there is a definite trend toward the newer types of vinyl and other resilient tiles as replacements for the older masonry and wood floors. These tiles have practical value because of their durability and they also add to the attractiveness of the store through various combinations of color and design.

Wall and ceiling finishes are dictated by considerations of attractiveness, economy, and preference of store executives. While many economy-type stores rely heavily on paint spread directly on cinder or concrete blocks for much of their wall area, even these establishments usually finish off some areas with wood panels, reclaimed brick, or some of the plastic laminates. In other stores, plastered walls finished with paint or decorative wall paper are common. The newer vinyl fabrics, while involving a larger original cost, are preferred by many retailers because they "can supply texture and color effects very difficult to get with paint, and much of the increased cost is recoverable in reduced maintenance costs and the greatly-extended life of the wallcovering material."[16]

---

[15] Even a few supermarkets are trying out wall-to-wall carpeting. For an example, cf. "Chicago Super Is Latest to Install All-Carpeted Floor," *Modern Retailer,* April, 1966, p. 49. This particular store has also added Pop art, vivid merchandise display, and color coordination to create a new shopping atmosphere.

[16] Arthur Southwood, "Versatility in Interior Materials," *Chain Store Age* (Executives Edition), July, 1965, p. E21.

The factor of color in the store's interior is receiving increased attention from retailers. By making the store more attractive, color encourages people —just walking by—to walk in. Frequently it can aid in the sale of specific merchandise. Color combinations can also be employed to emphasize the individuality and character of a store and to reduce lighting costs. In fact, in all his color planning, the retailer should keep in mind what he plans to do with his lighting. Since the colors used are usually perceived by the customer under artificial light, the two factors must be carefully coordinated to produce the best results.

Store Fixtures and Equipment

Not only the appearance of the store's interior, but also its effectiveness as a retail facility is determined in large measure by the fixtures and equipment which are installed. As is true with the store's exterior, recent years have witnessed many changes in these items. Reports a leading trade paper: "It would be sheer folly to (compare) today's streamlined, functional fixtures with the wooden counters and tables of ten years back."[17]

The terms "store fixtures" and "store equipment" are often used interchangeably by students of retailing: some retailers speak of the lights they install as "light fixtures" while others refer to their "lighting equipment." Despite such loose usage, however, the term "fixtures" is properly reserved for those durable goods which the retailer uses directly in the sale, display, storage, and protection of merchandise, such as display cabinets and cases, shelves, counters, and tables; whereas the term "equipment" refers to such other durable goods as elevators, escalators, air-conditioning units, sales registers, and delivery trucks, which are used throughout the store to facilitate both selling and nonselling activities.

Selecting Fixtures and Equipment. In choosing these items for his store, several factors are decisive. First, the clientele or class of trade to which the store intends to cater should be considered. The fixtures and equipment must reflect the character, or the basic appeal, of the store to its customers. Second, they should not divert customers' attention from the merchandise: a display cabinet which is so constructed and finished that the customer's "Ohs" and "Ahs" are focused on it, rather than on the merchandise which it displays, is not a good sales instrument. Third, fixtures and equipment must be adjusted to the type of merchandise handled, including such closely related factors as the size of the merchandise, its value, need for protection from theft and deterioration or spoilage, and the methods em-

---

[17] "Fixturing & Layout Strategy," *Chain Store Age* (Variety Store-General Merchandise Managers Edition), December, 1964, p. 158.

ployed to display and sell it. Toilet articles and expensive jewelry, for example, require widely different treatment than medium-priced dresses and fur coats. It is evident, also, that refrigeration must be provided for dairy products, whereas bintop counters will suffice for many hardware items. Likewise, the delivery truck for a druggist will be quite different from that suitable for a dealer in large electrical appliances.

A fourth factor to be considered in choosing fixtures and equipment is the type of service rendered in connection with the merchandise. In a store or a department conducted on a self-service basis, or nearly so, the amount of fixtures required will be relatively large. If various kinds of services are afforded and customers rely chiefly upon salespeople for merchandise presentation, however, the importance of fixtures will be decreased. Fifth, the original cost and maintenance expense involved for competing fixture and equipment items are significant factors in the purchase decision. Finally, the types and kinds of items available for use in the particular kind of store under consideration influence the choice. The retailer should examine the offerings of fixtures and equipment manufacturers and consider the advantages of (say) standardized display cases as contrasted with those designed especially for his needs.

Lighting the Modern Store

In the modern store effective lighting is required for the conduct of both selling and nonselling activities. While cost of equipment and economy in operation are factors for consideration, the retailer is also interested in how his lighting—among other things—improves the appearance of the store's interior, adds to the customer's shopping pleasure, steps up sales personnel productivity, makes self-selection easier, increases merchandise turnover, decreases shoplifting, ties in with the kind of merchandise he sells, and adds to the effectiveness of his displays.[18] Especially does he think of lighting as a sales tool.[19] To quote one leading architect, "Good lighting first of all focuses attention on the merchandise, so that the customer's eye is drawn to it. The merchandise is the 'actor' in a store—lighting should dramatize and put it squarely in the center of the stage."[20]

[18] Some of these points are developed by text and illustrations in "How Chains Can Upgrade with Light," *Chain Store Age* (Executives Edition), April, 1965, pp. 24–25 ff; Bert Berger, "New Lighting Weapons for Chain Selling Arsenals," *ibid.*, October, 1966, pp. 28–33; and "Programed Lighting for Staging Merchandising Display," *Illuminating Engineering*, April, 1966, Sec. 2, pp. 295–98.

[19] That it is an effective sales tool is supported by "Extra Investment in Lighting Builds Extra Sales for Tops," *Progressive Grocer*, December, 1964, pp. 90–91.

[20] Morris Ketchum, Jr., quoted by Martin Ezra, "Chains Take A New Look at Store Lighting," *Chain Store Age* (Executive Edition), November, 1963, p. E17.

Some Questions Leading to Effective Lighting. Typical of the questions which the retailer must answer as he attempts to meet his lighting requirements are the following:

1. Does the lighting arrangement make it easy for customers to find and identify the store during evening hours through effective use of electric signs, luminous façades, and well-lighted parking lots?
2. Do customers find it difficult to see through window reflections in the daytime?
3. Does the lighting plan cause the customer to look where it is desired that she look?

Courtesy: Bond Stores, Inc.

FIG. 5-7. The boys' department of this chain clothing store uses a Hollophane fixture to permit careful inspection by customers.

4. Are the lighting conditions most effective for buying decisions through providing for the best rendition of color on all types of merchandise and avoiding distracting brightness that competes with the merchandise for attention?
5. Does the lighting add emphasis to merchandise and yield maximum results from display space?
6. Is lighting used effectively to identify departments and direct customers?
7. Is proper lighting used at check-out counters and sales registers to permit easy reading of prices and the writing of sales slips, yet avoid glare shining from surfaces on merchandise and sales registers?
8. Does the lighting plan speed stocking and order filling in the storage areas of the store thus improving production?

9. Does the lighting arrangement minimize the maintenance of cleaning light fixtures, replacing lamps, and similar work?
10. Does the complete lighting program provide an atmosphere where the customer can shop pleasantly and cause her to return to the store to make additional purchases?

Because of the technical nature of lighting, it is highly desirable for the retailer to consult a qualified lighting engineer to insure satisfactory solutions to these problems. Figure 5–7 shows how one retailer solved these problems insofar as they relate to the sales area.

Equipment for Handling Vertical Customer Traffic

The problem of handling vertical customer traffic, especially during peak periods, has long perplexed retailers who operate on more than one level. Although stationary stairways are adequate for many stores with just a basement or perhaps only one floor above the street level, other stores find they must install elevators and escalators or moving stairways. R. H. Macy & Company, New York City, to cite an extreme example, found that 70 escalators and 29 passenger elevators were needed to provide vertical transportation for its 150,000 daily customers.

The marked improvement in elevator types has increased their usefulness because large numbers of customers can be handled more rapidly and more comfortably than formerly. Automatic stopping, microleveling, and power-operated doors have all contributed to greater speed. Currently, "America's retailers are embarking on a headlong rush to convert from manually operated to self-service elevators."[21] While this "rush" is partly stimulated by rising wages for elevator operators, experience has demonstrated that better customer service also results.

Escalators have been used in retail stores since 1901, although their rapid growth has taken place since 1930. For years executives of many stores objected to escalators as unsightly, impractical equipment but today they are a "must" in the larger stores. Improved design resulting in greater harmony with surroundings, "streamlined" effects, and inlaid lighting have contributed to this growth. Moreover, the advantages of escalators as compared with elevators are increasingly being recognized. The electric moving stairway eliminates the necessity of waiting for elevators and reduces congestion and crowding, thus saving the customer's time and energy; it provides fast and comfortable transportation between floors and affords a good view of adjacent merchandise offerings; finally, in the large store which needs to

[21] Richard Rosenthal, "Stores Looking for Lift from Automatic Elevators," *Women's Wear Daily,* October 6, 1964, p. 7.

provide for a great amount of vertical transportation, it occupies far less space than elevators, requires no operators and only a few attendants during rush periods, and provides continuity of motion with low power cost.

In the smaller store with a limited amount of vertical transportation, the elevator is usually more advantageous than moving stairways. If a single elevator will meet the store's needs, it will require but one third as much space as an escalator. Moreover, its original installation cost is lower. An observer of the heavy loads carried by escalators during the peak Christmas business in the larger stores, however, wonders how they operated without escalators for so many years. But even in these stores some elevators are needed, especially to provide rapid movement for customers wishing to move vertically several floors at one time, for those who are aged or infirm, and for those who prefer to ride in them.

Trend Toward Air Conditioning in Retail Stores

The trend toward air conditioning in retail stores was one of the most interesting developments of the depression period beginning in 1930. Since then, many stores—both large and small—as a means of stimulating business during the slack summer months, and for competitive reasons, have installed air-conditioning equipment. Currently, practically all major department and departmentized specialty stores are air conditioned, at least in part. Among chain stores air conditioning is so common that an informed source reports some 13,950 new and remodeled stores planned to install air conditioning in 1966 at a cost of $162 million compared with expenditures of $154 million in 1965.[22] We have already noted that the fully air-conditioned mall is increasingly popular in shopping centers.[23]

The most obvious advantage of air conditioning is its attractiveness to the customer. It encourages shopping on warm days, and it increases impulse sales to people drawn into stores just "to cool off": the net result is additional sales. But air conditioning is also a factor in improving employee morale; and better morale results in more efficient performance of both selling and nonselling activities. Air conditioning also contributes to a cleaner store and cleaner merchandise. Finally, if a retailer's main competitors adopt air conditioning, he may well be forced into taking a similar step merely to maintain his competitive position.

---

[22] S. O. Kaylin, "New High for Air Conditioning," *Chain Store Age* (Executives Edition), January, 1966, p. E29. Also cf. "Chain Store Air Conditioning Will Hit High in 1966," *Air Conditioning, Heating & Refrigeration News,* January 31, 1966, p. 58.

[23] Cf. pp. 112, above; and R. J. Abramson, "Modern Shopping Center," *Air Conditioning, Heating and Ventilating,* August, 1965, pp. 59–62.

Some Limitations. Despite the growing popularity of air conditioning and the satisfaction it affords customers particularly during the summer months, the trend to install the necessary equipment is not a universal one. In fact, only a low percentage of the smaller independent stores have followed the trend and, as we have already noted, some of the larger stores have restricted installations to a few floors or departments. It is not difficult to understand why many retailers have proceeded with caution. Initial costs and operating costs of various types of equipment need to be examined and evaluated as well as the amount of sales or storage space which may be lost. Air-conditioning equipment designed primarily to provide cool, clean air during periods of hot weather represents a considerable investment, which is magnified when viewed in the light of the number of days in the year it is required. Even the fact that a competitor has installed such equipment should not cause undue alarm, unless that competitor also practices effective retailing methods. Air conditioning a store will not overcome unsound merchandising practices.

The foregoing is not intended to minimize the many substantial advantages of air conditioning in retail stores; rather, it is to caution against the substitution of air conditioning for acceptable merchandising methods.

Other Kinds of Equipment

Equipment For Selling Activities. Exclusive of service equipment,[24] various other kinds of equipment are required to facilitate the handling of sales transactions. In grocery stores, weighing machines or scales are essential in selling bulk goods, fruits, and vegetables. In department stores, certain departments—candy, for example—also require scales. For stores that sell yard goods or piece goods and therefore need linear measurements, there have been developed machines that measure such merchandise accurately, provided care is exercised in operating them. The types and amounts of these kinds of equipment used in particular stores and departments will depend upon existing needs and conditions.

Equipment for Sales-Supporting Activities. A wide variety of equipment has been developed to carry out the sales-supporting functions in retail stores. This equipment, which has contributed to improved performance and to reduced costs, may be classified as follows: (1) mechanical equipment used in receiving, marking, checking, and delivery rooms, including small floor trucks, movable marking tables, price-ticket machines, marking machines, time-stamp machines, belt conveyor systems, and wastepaper

---

[24] Service equipment, such as sales registers, is discussed in Chapter 26, "Control of Sales Transactions."

baling machines; (2) labor-saving devices used in the general offices for
handling correspondence and other clerical work necessary to the conduct of
the business, for example, typewriters and machines used for calculating,
duplicating, bookkeeping, addressing, and stamping; (3) store communication devices, such as call systems—bells, lights, or electronic—for store
executives, private telephone systems, dictagraphs, and telautographs; and
(4) miscellaneous equipment, including time clocks, signature-recording
machines for timekeeping purposes, and sewing and textile-repair machines
in workrooms. Relatively few stores, of course, use all of these types of

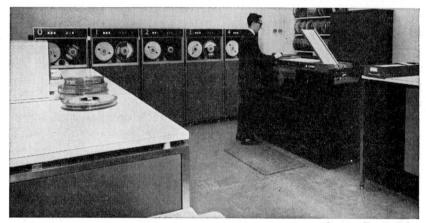

Courtesy: Honeywell, Inc.

FIG. 5–8.   An electronic data-processing system at Donaldson's Golden Rule Department Store in Minneapolis: RAMAC 305.

equipment; but retail executives should be aware of the fact that such
equipment is available when, as, and if it may be used advantageously.[25]

The Retailer and Electronic Equipment.   Increasingly, the retailer
must give careful consideration to the use of an electronic data-processing
system, frequently referred to as EDP. Such a system provides a means of
(1) assembling and storing a great amount of data, (2) processing these
data according to the wishes of the retailer, and (3) printing the results. In
performing these three main steps several different machines may be involved (see Figure 5–8), perhaps connected by cables or perhaps activated
by tapes or cards produced by some previous machine in the sequence.[26]

---

[25] For the food store operator, a very helpful listing of equipment for selling and
non-selling activities will be found in "Checklist of Store Equipment," *Progressive Grocer,*
December, 1964, pp. 52 ff.

[26] A careful survey of currently available EDP equipment will be found in "Electronic
Data Processing," *Dun's Review & Modern Industry,* September, 1966, pp. 140–42 ff.

Already so complicated that no one man knows a large computer's wiring diagram in full detail, many new electronic machines with even greater complexity are under development. In fact, it may prove true that the machines assisting us now are Neanderthal models compared to what is coming in the new "third generation" of computers.[27]

1. *Current Uses of EDP in Retailing.* In the hands of an able operator, usually referred to as the programmer, EDP can do many things for the retailer.[28] It affords a steady flow of data on such matters as (1) sales by departments or stores and by individual items broken down by price lines, sizes, colors, or other factors, (2) inventories, (3) expenses, (4) purchases, (5) accounts payable, (6) accounts receivable, (7) gross margin, and (8) returned goods. Clerical work can be minimized, and speed and accuracy maximized, by using EDP to prepare payrolls, to reorder certain items automatically, to supply open-to-buy reports, and to prepare checks for merchandise and other purchases. Eventually, some retailers expect that—by "feeding" into the machines certain basic data—the desirability of a store location may be analyzed, the most efficient truck routing determined, and a judgment on the advisability of adding a new product may be secured.

Although "retailing firms have lagged behind firms in other industry categories in the use of computers,"[29] EDP is being used in the retail field to perform many of the services indicated in the previous paragraph. Within the Associated Dry Goods Corporation, which operates over 40 department and departmentized specialty stores, uses of such equipment "range from the huge task of preparing customers' monthly statements of account through the accounting functions of paying vendors' invoices, payroll, statistical and specialized applications to merchandising and stock keeping records."[30] Stop & Shop, Inc., with over 140 supermarkets and 30 discount houses, has a data processing information center which provides for "warehouse inventory control and store billing procedure coupled with direct store to warehouse transmission of ordering data . . . Our computers (also) handle payrolls and accounts payable."[31] Woodward & Lothrop, Washington department and branch stores, has over 300 computer programs, including "accounts payable, billing, payroll, sales audit, sales analyses, and merchandise control . . . (and is) testing an automated system for reordering staple mer-

[27] For a look at the potentials of these forthcoming computers, cf. "The Cybernated Generation," *Time,* April 2, 1965, pp. 84–91.

[28] In later chapters, including our discussions of merchandise management and accounting, some of these uses of EDP are developed at greater length.

[29] D. H. Sanders, "Experiences of Small Retailers with Electronic Data Processing," *Journal of Retailing,* Vol. XLII, No. 1 (Spring, 1966), p. 13.

[30] *Annual Report: 1964,* p. 4.

[31] *Annual Report: 1965,* p. 9.

chandise."[32] At the headquarters of a major shoe chain, Edison Brothers Stores, Inc., "data processing is continuing to expand . . . Particular emphasis at this time concerns the more detailed computer applications to shoe merchandising of individual stores."[33]

2. *Limitations and Future of EDP in Retailing.* EDP systems are very costly. While some of the small and medium-sized computers (the processing unit) are in the $25,000 to $500,000 range, the larger ones are priced at $7 to $10 million. Although about 90 percent of such equipment is rented, the monthly rentals may range from $695 to $75,000, with $1,200 to $3,500 about the normal monthly rent for the smaller Univac models and $13,000 for the much larger and faster General Electric 265 model.[34] Moreover, considerable expense is involved in the year or two of study leading to the selection of the equipment and in the comparable "breaking-in" period after the equipment has been installed. Consequently, the purchase or full-time lease of EDP systems is open just to the large retail organizations. Yet the medium-size retailer can still secure some of the advantages of these systems by renting their use for a few hours at a time. Both the equipment manufacturers and independent firms now offer a rental service, including the aid of programmers and other skilled personnel, throughout the country.[35]

In view of the cost involved, even among large-scale retailers there is a wide range of opinion as to how rapidly they should adopt electronic equipment. Certainly the retailer should precede his purchase or "time sharing" of electronic equipment with a careful study of his needs, exercise great care in retraining his people to think in terms of the new machines, and not expect his new equipment to serve as a panacea for all his problems. He must keep firmly in mind the facts "that these new devices are only tools" to aid his judgments and that some "data refinements of the precision which these devices make possible may not be needed at all by many astute executives in making many business decisions."[36] As a matter of fact, some

---

[32] Betty Morse, "EDP Benefits Follow Trying Years," *Women's Wear Daily,* June 28, 1965, p. 17; C. R. McBrier, "Management Uses EDP in Retailing," *Office,* January, 1965, pp. 143–44 ff; and "Where the Computers Care, too," *Business Week,* March 12, 1966, pp. 140–46.

[33] *Annual Report: 1964,* p. 5. Examples of other firms using EDP will be found in "Data Processing," *Women's Wear Daily,* June 20, 1966, pp. 14–23; and Bert Berger, "Accelerating Retail Velocity with EDP," *Chain Store Age* (Executives Edition), May, 1966, pp. E28–E32.

[34] "Sharing the Computer's Time," *Time,* November 12, 1965, p. 104; *Business Week,* March 6, 1965, p. 154; and "Univac Thinks Small—But Fast," *ibid.,* June 25, 1966, pp. 173–74.

[35] For examples, cf. "Computer Time Sharing Goes on the Market," *Business Week,* December 4, 1965, p. 116.

[36] W. N. Mitchell, *The Business Executive in a Changing World* (New York: American Management Association, 1965), p. 77.

very successful retailers operate with a minimum of reports. One large English retailer, for example, abolished many of his reports, thereby eliminating 8,000 out of 28,000 jobs, reduced his prices, and added to his sales and profits.[37] Some discount houses also operate with a minimum of records. How to balance the gains from added information against the cost of obtaining it is not one of the retailer's easy decisions. It seems clear, however, that during the next decade he will seek more aid from the newer electronic equipment.

Leasing Fixtures and Equipment. The foregoing statement that retailers lease most of the electronic equipment which they use is illustrative of a trend toward the leasing of fixtures and equipment in general. Many retailers, faced with a growing need for capital as a result of rising inventories, greater credit sales, and other factors practice leasing to ease this problem. To illustrate, some large retailers lease a complete fleet of trucks, many of their store fixtures, and their headquarters' bookkeeping and billing equipment. But before this step is taken by any retailer all aspects of the question should be weighed carefully.[38]

MODERNIZING EXISTING STORES

Store modernization may be defined as bringing and keeping up to date the physical appearance, the fixtures, and the equipment of a store to increase its attractiveness to customers and to aid in obtaining continuous patronage. Moreover, it is designed to minimize operating costs and improve profit possibilities by such means as increasing the flow of traffic through the store, stepping up employee productivity in both selling and nonselling activities, and cutting maintenance expenses. As a continuing responsibility of the retailer, modernization involves the utilization of improved construction materials and techniques as well as the most modern equipment and fixtures which are adapted to his requirements.

Modernization Expenditures

During the past decade and more the United States has experienced its greatest modernization program in retail history. Progressive retailers of all types are well aware of the necessity to keep their stores up to date whether they be located in central business districts, neighborhood streets, shopping

---

[37] Christina Fulop, *Competition for Consumers* (London: Institute for Economic Affairs, 1964), p. 186. Also cf. "The English Unorthodoxy of Marks & Spencer," *Dun's Review and Modern Industry,* October, 1966, p. 128.

[38] For excellent analyses of leasing cf. the 40 page bulletin, *Taking Stock of Leasing: A Practical Appraisal* (New York: American Management Association, 1965), and "Leasing: All Systems Go," *Dun's Review and Modern Industry,* May, 1966, Part II, pp. 136–38 ff.

centers, or elsewhere. They know modernization is essential for satisfactory service to customers and for the maintenance of ones' competitive position. And they spend large sums in the process: for 1966 alone chain organizations in various fields and their landlords budgeted $420 million to remodel 14,400 stores, an average of over $29,000 per job.[39] As a matter of fact, they modernized more old stores than they opened as new units (9,700). Among the department store organizations, Marshall Field & Company reports an annual total capital expenditure of $4.9 million, of which $3.2 million was for modernization; and the annual report of the Associated Dry Goods Corporation indicates that modernization accounted for the bulk of the $6.2 million capital expenditure.[40]

The continuing nature of store modernization is well illustrated by the supermarket field. During the 1962–1964 period major remodeling took place in 25 percent of a large sample of supermarkets opened in 1955–1959.[41] That such major remodeling programs are expensive is suggested by a study among independent supermarkets: The average modernization job cost $10,550 for structural changes and $11,570 for new fixtures and equipment, a total of $22,120.[42]

Modernization Programs

As retailers have moved to modernize their stores, some of them, for financial reasons, have limited their expenditures to new store fronts, or perhaps just to improved windows. Even such relatively simple changes often result in a substantial sales increase; a window modernization program in one drugstore, for example, expanded sales as much as they had previously been increased by an entire store interior modernization program.[43] Other retailers have undertaken more extensive programs; some even constructing new facades for old stores and tearing out entire store interiors and replacing them with modern designs and materials.[44] Large stores have

---

[39] S. O. Kaylin, "1966 to be Record-Breaking Year for Chain Construction, Remodeling," *Chain Store Age* (Executives Edition), January, 1966, p. E27.

[40] *Annual Report of Marshall Field & Company,* year ended January 31, 1965, p. 4; *Associated Dry Goods Corporation Annual Report,* year ended January 30, 1965, pp. 3–4.

[41] *The Super Market Industry Speaks: 1965* (Chicago, Ill.: Super Market Institute, 1965), p. 15.

[42] *Grocery Business Annual Report* (New York: Progressive Grocer, 1965), p. F23.

[43] For somewhat similar results in a bookstore cf. "Facelifting Increases Sales in Pittsburgh Cokesbury Store," *Publishers' Weekly,* May 3, 1965, pp. 58–59.

[44] For some examples (food store, gasoline station, and bookstore) cf. "Big Bear Remodeling Dramatizes Departments," *Progressive Grocer,* March, 1965, pp. 170–71; "Remodeling Boom! A Coast to Coast Facelifting for Food Retailing," *ibid.,* May, 1966, pp. 143–214; "Major Gives a New Look to Dated Design," *National Petroleum News,* September, 1965, pp. 124–27; and "Santa Fe Book and Stationery Company: An Old Shop in Modern Dress," *Publishers' Weekly,* June 7, 1965, pp. 180–82.

centered major attention upon elevators, escalators, air conditioning, improved illumination, and additional selling and nonselling space; and smaller retailers have emphasized better illumination, more attractive windows, and—to a substantially lesser degree—air conditioning.

Retailer Aids on Modernization. Although large-scale retailers can retain experts in layout, lighting, and other aspects of modernization, smaller retailers often find these services too expensive. Fortunately many of the smaller retailers are members of trade associations which stand ready to be of great service in this matter. The National Retail Hardware Association can serve as an illustration. Not only does it advise all its members to "Consult Your Association First on All Store Modernizations," but it also actually encourages modernization by the preparation and dissemination of printed material.

In addition to his trade association, the retailer may seek aid on modernization from a local architect. In fact, he will probably wish to employ an architect regardless of the amount of aid he receives from other sources. If he is a member of a voluntary chain or buying group, the headquarters staff of this organization may be of value. Some wholesalers work closely with their retailer outlets on modernization programs.[45] Manufacturers of fixtures and equipment as well as of paint and glass also offer valuable assistance.

FUTURE PROSPECTS

The projected increase in our population during the years ahead, the urban renewal program, and the trend toward shopping centers and large free-standing stores, among other factors, suggest that the present new store building boom will continue. In turn, the competition offered by these new units will further stimulate the trend toward store modernization. Despite high break-even points, narrowing profit margins, and the high cost of modernization—which will cause stress to be placed increasingly upon careful control of such costs—many of today's merchants are convinced that improved buildings and better equipment are essential to the preservation of their profit margins, however small. Furthermore, remodeling and renovation are encouraged by the development of new materials, equipment, and devices which tend to make those in use obsolete.

In view of the foregoing, it is not surprising that by 1966 chain store annual expenditures on new construction and modernization had exceeded $2.5 billion, up from $2.0 billion in 1964, and that further rises were

[45] One wholesaler firm goes so far as to offer its retailer accounts a free engineering service, and even carries the financial paper on equipment involved in the resulting modernization program. "Springfield Sugar," *Super Market Merchandising,* March, 1965, p. 38.

predicted for the future.[46] As for smaller retailers, some of them will undoubtedly continue to operate as they have in the past, rationalizing their actions on the ground that they cannot afford to make extensive structural and equipment changes. But the progressive ones—both large and small—will seek to develop stores that are both more attractive to customers and more efficient as selling instruments.

REVIEW AND DISCUSSION QUESTIONS

1. Explain in detail why the present-day retailer places so much emphasis on the physical facilities in which his business is conducted.
2. In a general way, describe the "typical" new store of the 1960's.
3. What are prototype stores? Why are they developed?
4. From a retailing point of view, what are the main functions of the store's front and exterior?
5. "The size and type of windows used in a particular establishment are determined by the kind of store and the goods displayed." Illustrate, using specific examples of local stores.
6. Visit some local establishments handling floor, wall, and ceiling finishes and determine the newest developments with respect to such finishes for use in retail stores. What recommendations do these dealers make and what reasons do they offer in support of them?
7. Discuss and illustrate the factors that are significant to the retailer in choosing store fixtures and equipment.
8. A local merchant has asked your advice as to how he should proceed to improve the lighting of his store. What advice would you give him?
9. What are the relative advantages of elevators and escalators (a) in the moderate-sized store operating with three floors and a basement and (b) in the large department store?
10. "Air conditioning is the most important single factor in the success of a store in those areas of the United States subject to hot summer weather." Do you agree? Why or why not?
11. Discuss the benefits which electronic data-processing equipment offers the large retailer (the small retailer) and describe the probable extent of its use in the foreseeable future.
12. Based on library reading, prepare a five minute talk on the subject: The advantages (disadvantages) to the retailer from the leasing of his delivery trucks (the fixtures in his store).
13. Make a survey of chain and independent stores in your community, and prepare a concise report on the need for modernization. (A good way to handle this project is to assign each student a particular store or a particular kind of store—for example, independent drugstores.)

---

[46] Kaylin, "1966 to be Record-Breaking Year for Chain Construction, Remodeling," *op. cit.,* p. E27.

14. How do you account for the tremendous expenditures for store modernization in recent years? Be specific.
15. Have each student obtain data on the recent and projected population growth of a nearby metropolitan center and estimate the number of retail stores of various types that will be required to meet consumers' needs in 1970. Projections and estimates should be fully supported.

SUPPLEMENTARY READINGS

ABRAMSON, R. J. "Modern Shopping Center," *Air Conditioning, Heating and Ventilating,* August, 1965, pp. 59–62. Focusing on one of the major trends in individual stores and shopping centers, the author discusses air conditioning in the shopping center. Attention is also given to heating and to ventilation.

AMERICAN MANAGEMENT ASSOCIATION. *Taking Stock of Leasing* (New York, 1965). Among other subjects, this 40 page pamphlet covers tax implications of leasing, how to analyze the lease-or-buy question, and the relationship of leasing to other financing methods. Also cf. "Leasing: All Systems Go," *Dun's Review and Modern Industry,* May, 1966, Part II, pp. 136–38 ff.

Architectural Record is an excellent source for current ideas on store buildings. To illustrate: Cf. the review (with illustrations) of several stores and shopping centers in "Stores: Elements of Change in Location and Design," May, 1965, pp. 187–210; "Upgrading Downtown," June, 1965, pp. 186–7; and "Shopping Centers and Stores," April, 1966, pp. 149–59.

Chain Store Age, Staff of. *1966 Equipment & Construction Guide* (New York: Lebhar-Friedman Publications, Inc., March 15, 1966). Published annually, this guide also includes a classified directory of fixture and equipment manufacturers.

Illuminating Engineering offers many articles on store lighting, such as "Programmed Lighting for Staging Merchandise Display," April, 1966, Section 2, pp. 295–98.

Interior Design is a helpful source of material on store interiors. As an example, cf. the review (with illustrations) of several restaurants in "Restaurants," October, 1964, pp. 165–80.

MARTIN, E. W., JR. *Electronic Data Processing* (rev. ed.; Homewood, Ill.: Richard D. Irwin, Inc., 1965). For the nonmathematical and nontechnical reader, this basic textbook offers an up-to-date and understandable introduction to EDP.

"New Macy's: Park 'Round Store Core," *Women's Wear Daily,* February 13, 1964, pp. 1 and 14; "The Well-Rounded Shopping Center," *Fortune,* Vol. LXXII, No. 6 (December, 1965), pp. 189–90; "Drive-Up Shopping Brings Cars to Circular Store's Doors," *Chain Store Age* (Executives Ed.), January, 1966, p. E21; and "Multi-Level Store with Wrap-Around Parking," *Architectural Record,* April, 1966, pp. 168–70. Both by text and pictures, these articles present many details concerning some of today's modern retailing facilities operated by R. H. Macy & Co.

RESEARCH DIVISION OF SUPER MARKET INSTITUTE. *Facts About New Super Markets Opened in 1965* (Chicago, Ill., 1966). Published annually, this study contains a great deal of information which is of interest in connection with this chapter, including store size, parking facilities, building cost and overall investment, and distinctive features of the stores.

SANDERS, D. H. "Experiences of Small Retailers with Electronic Data Processing," *Journal of Retailing*, Vol. XLII, No. 1 (Spring, 1966), pp. 13–17, 61. Some of the problems of adjusting to EDP are set forth in this investigation of the experiences of 100 firms, including 8 in the retail field.

"Store Modernization." *Chain Store Age* (Executives Edition), September, 1965, pp. E16–E29. Among other subjects, these are included: "When Does Remodeling Pay?" pp. E16–E17; "Remodeling with Minimum Loss of Sales," pp. E19–E21; and "Ground Rules to Renovate 95 Stores in a Limited Time," pp. E28–E29. A series of six articles on modernization will be found under the title "Remodeling Boom! A Coast-to-Coast Facelifting for Food Retailers," *Progressive Grocer,* May, 1966, pp. 143–214.

"Store Modernization Guide." *Department Store Economist,* June, 1965, pp. 47–70. A special report on major aspects of store modernization, this material was developed in a seminar of leading architects.

UNGER, M. J. "A Study of the Relative Attraction of Window Displays of Women's Fashion Outerwear," *New York Retailer,* June, 1964, pp. 2–6. Since the main purpose of the window is to attract the attention of those passing by, this study of how effective windows are in achieving their goal has significance for the retailer.

Women's Wear Daily, Staff of. "Retailers Boldly Enter EDP Wonderland," June 28, 1965, pp. 1, 15–22. The 1965 status of EDP in retailing, relation of EDP to buying and buyers, potential benefits, and the future are among the topics of this report.

6
CHAPTER

Planning the Store's Layout

In the previous chapter, some of the factors involved in preparing the store building for use were developed. The present chapter continues that discussion by taking us inside the store building for an analysis of its arrangement. Specifically, we shall now concern ourselves with arranging and locating the merchandise, fixtures, and equipment so as to provide the desired standard of customer service at the lowest cost to the retailer.

DEFINITION AND SIGNIFICANCE OF LAYOUT

The layout of a retail store refers to the arrangement of equipment and fixtures, merchandise, selling and sales-supporting departments, displays, aisles, and check-out stands where needed in proper relationship to each other and in accordance with a *definite plan*. According to this concept, stores that have "just grown" on a haphazard basis are not actually "laid out" despite the fact that, broadly speaking, they are arranged in a particular manner.

Factors Influencing Layout

As the following paragraphs of this chapter will suggest, the layout of any retail store is affected by such factors as (1) the size and shape of the space to be occupied, including the number of floors; (2) the location of the unloading dock or area, elevators, escalators, and other permanent installations; (3) the kinds and amounts of merchandise to be handled; (4) the type of operation to be employed, such as self-service; (5) the characteristics and buying habits of the clientele to be served; (6) the nature and

147

quantity of the fixtures and equipment to be installed; and (7) the personal preferences of the retailer.

In giving consideration to the foregoing factors, the retailer will be seeking a layout: (1) to make the store as attractive, inviting, and convenient as possible to the customer; and (2) to provide the most effective and efficient utilization of the space. He will especially emphasize the sales promotion aspect of layout, including maximum exposure of goods to sale. Perhaps the only important exception to this rule is afforded by certain exclusive specialty shops where the layout is deliberately planned to hide merchandise from the customer's view. In Bonwit Teller's store in Boston, for example, the only ready-to-wear shown is that displayed on a few mannequins; the merchandise is brought by sales personnel to customers who sit at small tables. Although such personal service may be possible in a few retail stores, most retailers cannot resort to such an expensive way of selling.

Increased Attention to Layout

The trend toward larger stores, the desire to gain more sales space at the expense of nonselling area, the development of stores on shopping center malls, new kinds of fixtures and equipment, and the tremendous growth of simplified selling, self-selection, and self-service have outmoded old store arrangement patterns and resulted in more attention to and far-reaching changes in the layouts of stores of all types. To a degree not witnessed previously, layouts are being designed to permit easy access to merchandise by customers; to facilitate selection through grouping of related items, which permits comparison of brands and prices; to allow for future expansion of the store; and to provide sufficient check-out stands and trained cashiers to insure fast service to the customer.

Without doubt, the large retail organizations, such as department stores, discount houses, and chain stores, have devoted the greatest amount of attention to store layout. Many small retailers have believed other considerations to be more important or they were unaware of the benefits to be gained through improved layouts. Recently, however, even small retailers have given increased emphasis to layout; and retailing literature has continued to stress its importance. Retail trade journals, trade association literature and meetings, the obvious success of other stores which have shifted their layouts, and the efforts of equipment and fixture manufacturers—all these, and others, have made both large and small retailers more conscious of the need to study layout problems.

LAYOUT PROCEDURE

To accomplish the main purposes of layout referred to previously, it is advisable to follow a logical procedure. The appropriate steps include a survey of space requirements; a review of the characteristics of adequate layouts; visits to other stores; the securing of recommendations from equipment and fixture manufacturers, merchandise resources, store engineers, and architects; and the location of selling and sales-supporting departments. In addition, the layout should remain sufficiently flexible to allow for adaptations to the changing needs of both the customers and the retailer.

In going through these steps, it is usually desirable that the retailer be guided by a competent store architect and, in some instances, by an engineer. The large retailer may have well qualified architects and engineers on his staff, although on many occasions even these need to be supplemented by outside experts who can bring in a "fresh" point of view. The small retailer usually hesitates to engage an architect because of the added cost, but he may end up with a less satisfactory layout. As a matter of fact, a competent architect can often recommend cost savings which more than offset his fee.

Survey Space Requirements

Sales Forecast. Fundamental to a decision on the space requirements for a particular store is the expected sales, both immediately and in the future.[1] Once the immediate sales forecast is at hand, the minimum square footage of the store can be determined by dividing into it what experience has indicated as a reasonable projection of sales per square foot.[2] Such projections are available from the merchant's previous experience (if any), trade associations, and studies reported in trade papers. If a substantial future sales increase seems possible, provision should be made to enlarge the area at a later date—perhaps by a new wing to the building or by adding a floor or floors. To make practical such a step, the Macy store illustrated in Figure 5–4 (page 127) has been constructed strongly enough to carry one additional floor.[3]

In deciding on his total space requirements the retailer should avoid one

---

[1] Cf. "Estimated Volume of Business," pp. 102–03, above.

[2] An illustration of this approach by a food-drug retailer is given in "Prototype Stores Smooth Giant's Expansion," *Chain Store Age* (Supermarket Executives Edition), October, 1965, p. 134.

[3] "The Well-Rounded Shopping Center," *Fortune,* Vol. LXXII, No. 6 (December, 1965), p. 189.

error which is all too common in the present-day thinking of some retailers
—the idea that a high figure for sales per square foot can be attained merely
by constructing a large store without worrying too much about its layout.
The fact of the matter seems to be that large stores frequently waste space
simply because they have so much of it.

Check List of Space Needs. Along with his analysis of overall space
requirements the retailer should prepare a detailed check list of all the
merchandise, functions, and facilities for which space must be provided
within the store. This list, naturally, will reflect store policy and procedure.
It is apparent, furthermore, that the kinds and amounts of merchandise
stocked and the services rendered will depend on the type of store. But,
regardless of variations from store to store, each retailer should ask if, to
illustrate, he has provided space for the following:

1. Merchandise departments, including the necessary space for storing, displaying and selling goods in appropriate fixtures and on shelves.
2. Sales-supporting departments of all types—receiving and marking goods,
   reserve stock storage space, deliveries, returns and adjustments, storage of
   supplies, and similar activities.
3. Comforts and conveniences for customers and employees.
4. Office space, including areas for purchase of merchandise.
5. Workroom space.
6. Heating, lighting, air conditioning, and ventilating equipment and fixtures.
7. Stairways, elevators, and escalators.
8. Aisles wide enough to permit free flow of customer traffic.
9. Window space adequate to display kinds of merchandise carried.

The prospective store proprietor should give full consideration to his
check-list items, viewing them in relationship to each other in the light of
his tentative plans. As he analyzes each item, he will discover that the
experiences of other retailers are very helpful. For example, the prospective
supermarket retailer can take advantage of the judgment of a number of
food retailers that the "ideal" one-floor supermarket requires 72 percent of
its space for sales and 28 percent for "back up" activities. These same
operators suggest that the sales space needs for merchandise lines are as
follows: groceries, 49 percent (of sales space only); meat, 14 percent;
produce, 11 percent; nonfoods, 7 percent; dairy products, 6 percent; with
the remaining 13 percent required for such customer services as checkout,
check cashing, and kiddie corner.[4] Similar space requirements are available
for drug, hardware, and other retail fields.

---

[4] *The Super Market Industry Speaks: 1965* (Chicago, Ill.: Super Market Institute,
1965) p. 19.

Review Characteristics of Good Layouts

Customer Point of View. The desirable characteristics of a good layout from the point of view of the customer should be reviewed carefully, since "the logical basis for (layout) decisions should be consumer preferences."[5] Generally speaking, customers want an attractive place in which to shop, convenient access to merchandise throughout the store, aisles wide enough to prevent crowding during normal business days, freedom from obstructions that prevent a general view of the floor, related merchandise together, similar arrangement of merchandise in the stores in which they concentrate their purchases, privacy for the fitting of garments and other items of a similar nature, daylight rather than artificial light for judging color of certain merchandise, and infrequent changes in the location of departments. In addition, stores that cater primarily to women but desire to attract men to certain departments may need to plan their layouts so that men can enter these departments without going through other areas of the store.

Developing a layout to meet customer wishes is not always easy, a point which is illustrated by the problems encountered by department stores in bringing together related merchandise. At first thought it may seem easy to set up a bath shop (with "everything for the bathroom," from towels and bath mats to marbletopped lavatories) and a ski shop (including men's and women's ski clothing as well as ski equipment). But such arrangements immediately raise such questions as: Who buys the men's clothing in the ski shop—the shop personnel or the buyer in the men's clothing department? Can a seller in the ski shop be trained to sell both men's and women's clothing as well as ski equipment? Will garments on sale in the ski shop be duplicated in the women's apparel departments?

In practice, there is no single answer to any of these questions. For example, some stores let the ski shop personnel do all their buying while other retailers spread the buying function among regular department buyers. But each store must find its own answers since "selling by category is the newest wrinkle in big store merchandising and is going to spread."[6]

Retailer Point of View. The store proprietor, of course, should give serious consideration to the preferences of his potential customers; more

---

[5] M. S. Sommers and J. B. Kernan, "A Behavioral Approach to Planning, Layout, and Display," *Journal of Retailing,* Vol. XLI, No. 4 (Winter, 1965–66), p. 21. For several layout plans employing the customer point of view, cf. "Customer Traffic Patterns Key to Selling Efficiency," *Progressive Grocer,* January, 1966, pp. 47–59.

[6] " 'Category' Selling New Magic Carpet, Goes Wall-to-Wall," *Women's Wear Daily,* April 26, 1963, p. 9. Also cf. Macy's attempt to group merchandise as reported in "Stores Scanning Macy Recipe for Sales Mix," *ibid.,* November 2, 1965, pp. 1 and 44.

than any other factor, their needs and expectations should dictate the arrangement of the store's interior. But other considerations are also important to the retailer. Because of the increase in night and Sunday openings, shorter hours, and the higher rates of pay that have been established in retail stores during recent years, he needs a layout which will increase employee productivity. Consequently he seeks a store plan which will reduce both the time required to complete sales transactions and the amount of walking necessary both for customers and for salespeople.

To encourage self-selection and impulse buying, the retailer wishes a layout that will facilitate the movement of traffic throughout the store, a goal which is especially important if more than one floor is occupied.[7] To this end, many recently modernized stores have adopted the so-called "wandering aisle," which replaces the more or less straight aisles with a series of circular, octagonal, or oval counters around which traffic moves so that more merchandise is brought into the customer's view. Still others have moved in the opposite direction, to a mall-type or wide central aisle which encourages the flow of traffic in a predetermined pattern. Under such an arrangement, as is illustrated in Figure 6–7 (page 162), each department in the store fronts on this main aisle, with two advantages: (1) the department is easily located by the customer, and (2) the department can use this front as a promotional spot.

Layout's relation to the retailer's profit is suggested by the efforts of a growing number of retailers to place high margin merchandise where it gets the maximum customer exposure. One self-service retailer found that the first two aisles near the entrance carried more traffic than any others, so he moved his better margin-yielding departments to these areas with a resulting gain in profits.[8] Other retailers have discovered that the amount of merchandise of a particular kind displayed on a shelf, as well as the location of the shelf in the store, is important from a sales point of view and have rearranged their stocks to take advantage of this fact.[9]

Figures 6–1, 6–2, and 6–3 illustrate layouts in various stores which seek

---

[7] Mr. E. B. Weiss forecasts that traffic flow will eventually be facilitated by the installation of moving aisles. Cf. his "What Will Retailing Be Like in 1975?" *Advertising Age,* March 7, 1966, pp. 119–20 ff.

[8] "Store Layout Breakthrough," *Chain Store Age* (Supermarket Executives Edition), December, 1965, p. 48.

[9] K. K. Cox, *The Relationship Between Shelf Space and Product Sales in Supermarkets* (Austin, Texas: University of Texas Bureau of Business Research, 1964); "Responsiveness of Food Sales to Supermarket Shelf-Space Changes," *Journal of Marketing Research,* Vol. I, No. 2 (May, 1964), pp. 63 ff.; and "Grocery Shelf Arrangements: Key to More Efficient Operations," *Progressive Grocer,* December, 1964, pp. 120–22.

FIG. 6–1. A china and gift department.

to meet the wishes of customers and, at the same time, take into account those considerations which are important to the retailer.

A Checklist of Good Layout Characteristics. To make certain that the characteristics of good layouts are carefully considerd for each new store, many retailers have developed their own checklists. Some of the questions appearing in one of these guides are as follows:

( ) Has space been allocated to meet the needs of major departments?
( ) Are major departments located logically with relation to one another?
( ) Does the floor plan show sufficient detail for exact placement of the fixtures?
( ) Where practicable, are stock areas located near the departments they serve?
( ) Is stockroom in best location for receiving? for stocking the store?
( ) Have stockroom bin openings been sized to eliminate waste space?
( ) How would you, as a customer, like to have shopping arranged?
( ) Are pickup items exposed to heaviest traffic movement?
( ) Are the departments in the sequence in which people might logically be expected to buy?
( ) Does the layout provide for drawing traffic to rear of store through: (1) location of aisles; (2) provision for dramatic and well-lighted displays; and (3) location of wanted items at rear?

Courtesy: The Bulman Corporation

FIG. 6–2. Automotive supplies, with sporting goods and appliances in the background.

( ) Do adjacent departments suggest additional purchases? For instance, the hardware department in some stores is logically adjacent to building supplies, paint supplies, and small electrical appliances. One food chain arranges its stores so that to reach the three departments most housewives shop (produce, meat, dairy) the customer must pass all other parts of the store.

( ) Does the layout provide for such needs as:
    ( ) Special display areas requiring special lighting needs?
    ( ) Special demonstration areas requiring special electrical outlets?
    ( ) Spot lighting for visual front windows?
    ( ) Employees' restaurant?
    ( ) Model kitchen setup?
    ( ) Conveyors in stockroom?
    ( ) Phone outlets; intercom connections, speakers?
    ( ) Heating and air conditioning for fitting rooms?

( ) Has flexibility for future expansion been assured by careful consideration of such questions as:
    ( ) Is there space for additional future checkouts?
    ( ) Has refrigeration been placed for permanence so that expansion can be accomplished around it?
    ( ) Are wall fixtures of the type that can be moved easily?

Courtesy: Bond Stores, Inc.

FIG. 6–3. A well-arranged men's furnishings department.

( ) If the present building provides 50,000 square feet, and future expansion is indicated, has a second set of plans incorporating possible expansion to, say, 75,000 square feet been drawn over the original plans?

( ) Are the fixtures in departments adjoining areas of possible expansion of such a nature that they can be moved?[10]

Sources of Information on Effective Layouts. A study of available literature on store arrangement is invaluable to the retail merchant, whether he already operates a store or contemplates opening one. Through such study he familarizes himself not only with the opinions of authorities

---

[10] Another check list for "Interior Planning and Expansion" will be found in *1965 Equipment & Construction Guide* (New York: Lebhar-Friedman Publications, Inc., 1965), p. 17.

on the subject with respect to the desirable characteristics of good store layouts but also with current developments in this field. Such sources as the United States Department of Commerce, including the Small Business Administration, trade associations and trade magazines in the retail field, equipment manufacturers, and periodicals such as *Architectural Record* provide numerous services designed to help retailers in this direction.

Visit New Stores of Same Type

Although most written material on store arrangement includes diagrams and illustrations to facilitate understanding, many retailers find it difficult to visualize actual operation under the conditions described. Consequently, it is advisable for such merchants to visit new and recently remodeled stores similar to their own and to observe the layouts and the flow of traffic during business hours. Retailers are then in a better position to judge the wisdom of arranging their stores along similar lines.

Secure Recommendations from Outside Sources

Already reference has been made to the architect as an outside source of aid on layout problems.[11] Recommendations of manufacturers from whom equipment, fixtures, materials, and merchandise have been or may be purchased are also valuable guides in deciding upon the arrangement of the store's interior. These firms are well qualified to make suggestions based upon their experience in solving such problems and upon their researches in this field. Some of them, voluntary chain wholesalers and equipment manufacturers, for instance, have developed prototype layouts for stores of different sizes, which are available to the retailer. A few of them have constructed small scale model fixtures and equipment so that the retailer can more easily visualize exactly how his store will look. Because of their interest in selling store equipment adapted to the needs of the retailer or in having a store well planned from the point of view of the merchandise handled, no charge is ordinarily made for these services.

Locate Selling and Sales-Supporting Departments

The next step is to locate each particular selling and sales-supporting department. In this connection the major considerations include: (1) providing the best possible service to customers based on their known buying habits, (2) establishing the most effective coordination of selling and sales-

---

[11] Cf. p. 149, above.

supporting activities, and (3) maximizing the selling area in relation to that given to other functions. The immediate objective of these considerations, of course, is to increase sales and minimize expenses.

Locating particular departments is commonly done through the preparation of diagrams or blueprints, because of the convenience afforded in visualizing relationships of departments and because of the ease with which changes in plans may be made if considered advisable. It should be recognized, however, that regardless of the care exercised in planning a layout on paper, unless that plan is the result of a well-thought-out selling policy based upon one's own experience or the experience of others, it may be doomed to failure. It is helpful also, both in planning the layout and in judging its effectiveness, for the store proprietor to obtain the ideas and opinions of associates in whose judgment he has confidence. In the large majority of cases it will be found that full agreement on all points is impossible and that compromises are necessary.

A Specific Example. How selling and sales-supporting departments in a department store may be placed in close proximity to each other is well illustrated in Figure 6–4. Designed to provide the maximum in economy and efficiency, the main feature of this arrangement is a "magic core" occupying 36,000 of the store's 297,000 square feet of floor space. Despite its size, customers are almost unaware of the core because it is partially hidden by display counters. Yet all the facilities for handling merchandise and customer traffic are present. Each of the three main shopping floors has two levels in the "magic core" and the upper one (the mezzanine) is connected with the floor on which the goods will be sold. Goods are carried by elevators to the mezzanine where they are checked and marked. Then they are sent to the appropriate stockroom on the same floor or delivered by chute to the level below.

Variations in Space Value within a Store. In locating selling and sales-supporting departments, it is important to note that there are wide variations in the value of space in different parts of the store with respect both to sections of a single floor and to floors, when more than one floor is occupied. In large stores particularly, the assignment of values to specific areas or sections on an equitable basis continues to plague management.[12] These values, of course, are based upon the management's estimate of the sales and profit possibilities of the various parts of the store and thus are chiefly arbitrary in nature. Generally speaking, space charges become lower as one goes from the front to the rear of a one-story building and as one moves away from the traffic lanes. In a multiple-story structure, the

---

[12] The allocation of rental charges to specific departments is discussed in Chapter 25.

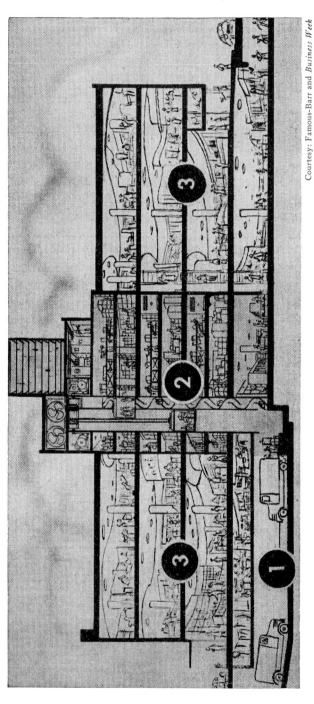

FIG. 6–4. An illustration of the "magic core" of Famous-Barr's Southtown store in St. Louis, Missouri. A truck ramp leads to the basement platform (1), where goods are unloaded and later stored on various levels of the operating core (2), then fed to the various sales floors (3).

charges assigned to each floor decrease as the height of the floor increases; that is, space on the second floor is less valuable than space on the first, on the third less valuable than on the second, and so on.

Layout Flexibility

Once the layout of the store has been decided, the problem is by no means permanently solved. As already indicated, even the original layout should aim at giving the retailer the maximum degree of flexibility to make future changes. From time to time he will find it necessary to make adjustments because of shifting seasonal demands, changes in buying habits and in tastes of customers, and new policies and practices of competitors. He may wish to expand the area given to those kinds of merchandise growing in popularity and to shrink that devoted to items losing in customer acceptance, and to convert certain departments or areas to self-service.[13] "Change is the order of the day" in retailing, and store layout is not exempted from this rule.

SOME ILLUSTRATIONS OF STORE LAYOUT

A suggested layout of a hardware store, reflecting consideration of the steps discussed, and intended primarily to stimulate the thinking of the retailer in arranging his store, is shown in Figure 6–5. The layout in Figure 6–6 is that of a 94,000 square foot discount house in which foods play an important role. Figure 6–7 shows an effective layout used in a one-floor unit of Montgomery Ward & Company. Especially noteworthy is this layout's broad aisles which funnel store traffic in a pre-determined pattern for maximum merchandise exposure. Finally, Figure 6–8 (p. 163) provides a sample layout for a supermarket which also sells many items in its pharmacy section.

A comparison of the layouts in Figures 6–5 to 6–8 with those of other retailers will suggest that there is no ideal layout which will meet the needs of all stores handling the same kinds of merchandise. Local circumstances and individual preferences markedly influence the particular arrangement adopted. Some chain-store organizations, however, have adopted a few standard layouts with the result that they achieve considerable economy in the cost of opening new stores. To illustrate, Colonial Stores has carefully developed standardized layouts for food stores of five different sizes. In the course of developing these layouts, all the steps suggested in the previous section of this chapter were taken with the final decisions made by a store-planning committee. Of course, these standardized arrangements are

---

[13] Cf. the discussion of self-service on pp. 166–72, below.

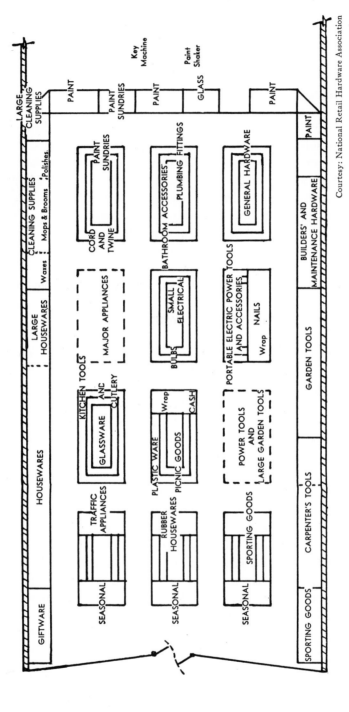

FIG. 6–5. A suggested layout for a hardware store.

Courtesy: National Retail Hardware Association

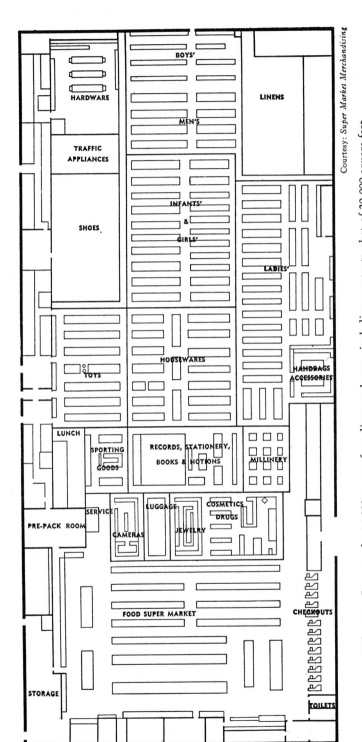

Courtesy: *Super Market Merchandising*

FIG. 6-6. Layout of a 94,000 square foot discount house, including a supermarket of 20,000 square feet.

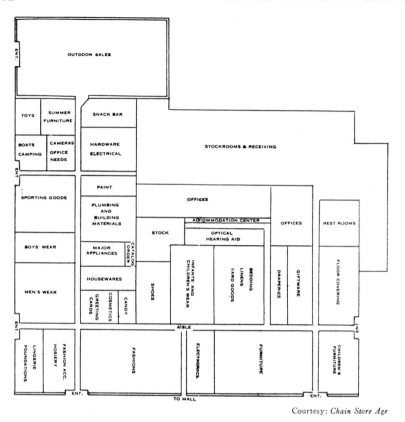

FIG. 6–7. A one-level Montgomery Ward & Company store located on a shopping center mall.

changed periodically so as to take advantage of new developments and suggestions from store personnel.

DISPLAY: A MAJOR FACTOR IN LAYOUT[14]

Previous mention has been made of the fact that, broadly considered, layout is a form of sales promotion. An effective layout facilitates sales from the point of view of both the customer and the store proprietor and display considerations are inseparable from layout. Display means simply that goods are exposed to customers to facilitate observation, examination, and selection —and the way a store displays its merchandise has much to do with its sales volume. A study of over 300 shoppers in New York City department and specialty stores a few years ago revealed that about one third of them

---

[14] Also cf. the discussion of "Interior Displays" on pp. 540–42, below.

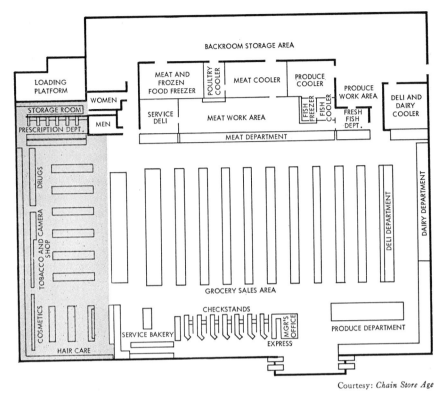

FIG. 6–8. Layout of a modern supermarket-pharmacy with 27,000 square feet of which 5,000 is in the pharmacy section (shaded area).

entered these stores without any intention to buy. Attractive merchandise displays, however, induced over half of this group to make purchases.

Since most types of retail stores carry large assortments of merchandise, proprietors are faced with the problems of deciding upon the amount of display and the kind of display to give certain items. These problems are not easy ones to solve, since at some point the variety of merchandise becomes confusing to the customer. In addition, retailers are concerned with the best time and the length of time to display merchandise. These are problems that must be solved by individual merchants in the light of their particular situations. Certain general rules are available, however, for guidance.

Types of Interior Display

Merchandise Characteristics. In addition to an overall emphasis on the profitability of the merchandise given special display facilities in the retail store, the type of display for any specific item depends upon such characteristics as its perishability, bulk, value, breakage, packaging, danger to customers, attractiveness, and salability. The significance of these factors can be demonstrated with a few examples from various kinds of merchandise, as follows:

While cured meats can be openly displayed without special equipment, fresh meats demand refrigeration; passenger-car tires, which are bulky, may be displayed with little thought of the danger of theft, but pilferage is a consideration for small items which can be slipped into a pocket or handbag; valuable jewelry usually requires closed display cases; mechanical toys may be damaged if they are available for everyone to handle; packaging encourages open display in that it makes the merchandise more attractive and reduces the possibility of deterioration. Special precautions should be taken for items which create hazards: Poisons should be out of the reach of customers and heavy items may be dangerous if hung on display over store aisles. Unattractive items, such as bulk vinegar in a food store, may not even be placed on display. As for salability, items which rely heavily on impulse buying are especially good candidates for open display.

Display Variations by Type of Store. Wide differences exist among retail stores in the planning of their interior displays and in the frequency with which they are used to promote the sale of specific merchandise. Discount houses as well as food, drug, and auto accessory stores, for example, make extensive use of "merchandise islands" in their layouts—that is, tables, counters, cases, or a small group of any or all of these—upon which merchandise is displayed and which are surrounded by adequate aisle space. Many of the display materials (racks, stands, signs) placed on these aisle tables are provided by merchandise resources, and some of these are less than satisfactory from the retailer's point of view.[15] These retailers also use shelves and racks to a considerable extent for display purposes; but they seldom use closed display fixtures, such as cabinets or cases, which are so commonly employed by department store and specialty shops. Furthermore, jewelry stores, camera stores, and others handling expensive merchandise enclose their displays to provide necessary protection.

Food stores place considerable emphasis upon displays as "silent salesmen"; upon the merits of "talking signs" which give convincing reason for purchase; upon "mass displays" for the purpose of impressing the customer with the quantity of items sold at a particular price; upon "dining-room" displays for delicatessen and dairy products; and upon the arrangement of merchandise items in a manner designed to induce customers to pick them

---

[15] A recent study reports: "Up to 50 percent of the point-of-purchase display stands received by retailers (from manufacturer resources) are considered inferior by store managers . . ." *Printers' Ink,* November 26, 1965, p. 3.

up, as opposed to balanced symmetrical arrangements designed chiefly for decorative purposes.

Other types of retail stores have merchandise display problems peculiar in many respects to themselves, as is also true of individual departments in department and specialty stores. In such cases the guiding considerations should be the following: (1) the type of product, its value, size, and appeal to the buyer; (2) the purpose of the display, i.e., the actual sale of the article or the creation of prestige or "atmosphere"; (3) suitable location; (4) attractiveness; (5) timeliness as related to seasonableness; and (6) desired frequency of change.[16] Each store must solve its own display problems in the light of the existing situation. In doing so, originality and distinctiveness should continually be sought so that the store may be set apart from its competitors.

Exterior Displays

Although food retailers have long made use of out-of-door displays—such as the display of fruits and vegetables on sidewalks in front of the store—today there is also a strong trend for many other kinds of retailers to employ exterior displays. Branch department stores, many discount houses, the so-called home and garden stores, and supermarkets typically have their own parking areas and these serve as locations for displays of lawn and garden supplies and tools; plants, shrubbery, grass, seeds, and weed killers; automobile tires and tubes; Christmas trees and other seasonal items. In general, such displays are rather crude, boxes of the merchandise being placed on the parking area surface or on plain tables. Frequently the display is unprotected from the weather, although canopies—either canvas or permanent—are also being used. Figure 6–7 shows the location of the "outdoor sales" area of a Montgomery Ward & Company store.

Outside display offers such advantages as (1) relatively inexpensive selling space, (2) opportunity to show additional merchandise, and in a more natural setting, (3) a place for bulky and untidy goods which otherwise detract from the appearance of a store, (4) visibility to a greater number of potential customers, and (5) customer convenience in that much of this merchandise is not suited to shopping cart transportation.

AISLE TABLES

Mention has been made of the fact that many retailers rely in part on "merchandise islands" in promoting the sale of certain articles. When tables

---

[16] These considerations and others are developed and illustrated in E. M. Mauger, *Modern Display Techniques* (New York: Fairchild Publications, Inc., 1965).

located in the aisles of the store are used as islands, as is frequently the case in department and specialty stores, they are referred to as "aisle tables."

An aisle table is usually located on a main traffic artery, and is used to display either regular or special merchandise. In a service store, the aisle table—or several adjacent tables—usually has a salesperson regularly assigned to it and a cash register is placed on or near the table. When tables are arranged in units of four in the form of squares and when merchandise is offered at reduced prices or at featured prices as a regular practice, they are known as "bargain squares." Some stores prefer the "Y" arrangement.[17]

Whether or not a store uses aisle tables will depend largely upon the type or types of merchandise handled, upon the clientele to which the store caters, and upon the desire of the store management to avoid congestion in customer traffic, particularly during busy periods such as the holiday season.

SELF-SELECTION AND SELF-SERVICE

A major problem associated with store arrangement concerns the proprietors' decision regarding the extent to which he will allow access to merchandise by customers and permit them to serve themselves, with aid being provided by sales help if needed. This decision obviously influences the entire layout of his store as well as the kind and amount of store equipment he purchases. Consequently, it is essential that all the factors involved be weighed carefully before a decision is made.

Definition of Terms

When a store is operated on a *self-selection* basis, merchandise is so displayed and arranged that the customer can make her selection without the aid of a salesperson. Typically, open display shelves and tables are used, frequently supplemented by racks, stands, and islands. Once the selection is made, the merchandise is usually handed to a nearby salesperson, who takes the further steps necessary to complete the sale. This type of operation has long been characteristic of variety stores such as those operated by F. W. Woolworth, S. H. Kress, and many independent retailers.

Under *self-service* operation the customer not only makes her selection, but she also is responsible for bringing the goods she proposes to buy to a check-out stand, where she makes payment and her purchases are bundled or "sacked." Credit, delivery, and other special customer services commonly found in service stores ordinarily are not offered by the self-service store,

---

[17] Cf. "How Y-Shaped Produce Racks 'Capture' Customers," *Chain Store Age* (Supermarket Executives Edition), December, 1965, pp. 70 and 73.

since a low operating cost is one of its major goals. Although, technically speaking, the term "self-service store" should refer to one with all of its sales on this basis, many stores described by this name handle a substantial amount of business on a service basis. To illustrate: Many self-service discount stores provide salesperson service for jewelry, cameras and supplies, major appliances, and for bakery products, meats, and fruits and vegetables in their supermarket areas.

For some years it has become customary, especially among department and specialty store retailers, to speak of *simplified selling*. Within the scope of this term they include both self-selection and self-service—and much more, such as better fixtures, improved layouts, more effective packaging, displays which lead to increased sales, and techniques and devices to speed up sales transactions. So broad is this usage that, for purposes of this chapter, we shall limit the discussion to self-selection and self-service as defined above; however, we must recognize that where self-selection and self-service techniques are used, many of the other aspects of simplified selling are also involved.[18]

Historical Development

Contrary to much current opinion, neither self-selection nor self-service operations are particularly new. This statement is especially true of self-selection. As has already been mentioned, this operating method has long been used in variety stores. Moreover, for years the trend in stores of many types has been toward open displays which encourage self-selection. Yet self-selection has experienced widespread adoption during the past three decades: Today it is practiced in varying degrees by stores of practically all types.

In Food Stores. The self-service plan of operation was employed by a few grocery stores in southern California at least as early as 1912. Immediately after World War I the Piggly-Wiggly grocery stores began to expand on this basis. Moreover, there were some early successes in the ready-to-wear and drug fields; the S. Klein store in New York City and the Pay-Less Drug Stores on the Pacific Coast are good illustrations.

Despite this earlier development, as late as 1927 only two of the major food chains in the Los Angeles market—the area in which self-service first developed to any significant degree—used the self-service method. Consequently, we may conclude that it was during the depression of the early thirties, which also saw the development of the supermarket, that self-

---

[18] Cf. the discussion of "Requirements for Self-Selection and Self-Service," pp. 169–70, below.

service became popular in the food field. As retailers sought ways to reduce their costs, they were naturally attracted by any method which would lower their payments for wages—the greatest single item in the cost of operating a store. The trend was further encouraged by the manpower shortage of World War II and by the "profit squeeze" of the early 1960s. Today 84 percent of the retail food business (up from 61 percent in 1952) takes place in self-service supermarkets and superettes, and much of the remaining 16

Courtesy: *The Bulman Corporation*

FIG. 6–9.   A drug store providing self-service.

percent is handled by smaller stores which rely on some degree of self-service operation.[19] Figure 6–8, on page 163, gives the layout of one of these modern self-service supermarkets, this particular store also including a pharmacy section.

In Other Stores.   Following the success of self-service in food stores, and recognizing that "service" provided by the salespeople in many stores leaves much to be desired, self-service has been adopted by many kinds of stores handling a wide variety of merchandise and operating independently or as chains. Among those now offering self-service in some or all their departments are department stores, discount houses, and stores selling drugs, variety merchandise, shoes, stationery, and home furnishings.

---

[19] *Grocery Industry's Annual Report* (New York: Progressive Grocer, April, 1966), p. 58.

To take a few specific illustrations, during 1965 S. S. Kresge Company opened 64 new or remodeled self-service stores: all of its new stores are of this type and 75 percent of all the stores in the chain now operate on this principle.[20] In the drug field, Walgreen added 32 units during the year—all of which were self-service.[21] In the stores operated by R. H. Macy & Company the basements have been almost completely converted to self-service and self-selection operations. Moreover, while retaining personal selling for major home appliances and higher priced fashion merchandise, the trend is still in the direction of additional stores and departments on the self-service principle. Figure 6–9 shows part of a drug store operating on this basis.

Requirements for Self-Selection and Self-Service

Experience with self-selection and self-service reveals that among the factors essential to success are the following:

1. Sound merchandising decisions made in advance regarding the following: a.) the basic stocks to be carried with particular reference to styles, types, price lines, sizes, and colors; b.) the amount of space that will be required for each style, size, and price line; and c.) the extent to which feature items will be used and the importance that will be given to them.

2. Good fixturing. The merchandise to be stocked will govern the types of fixtures to be used. Sometimes good fixtures prove unsatisfactory because of improper use.

3. A layout which allows for, and encourages, the flow of customer traffic.

4. Adequate checkout facilities.

5. Well-filled stocks and appropriate signs. Unbalanced stocks, poorly designed signs, and incorrect prices irritate customers and lose sales.

6. Attractive packages. Because competition for the customer's attention is strong under self-selection and self-service arrangements, attractive packages are essential.

7. Cooperation of personnel. When a shift to a self-service plan is contemplated, resentment within the department or store will be minimized if the personnel involved are kept fully informed.

8. Training of personnel in new duties. Particular emphasis should be placed on the need for proper coverage of the floor to provide satisfactory service to customers and to prevent pilferage.

In general, arrangement of a store for self-selection or self-service operation is motivated by the same considerations which determine the layout of any store—that is, attractiveness and convenience from the customer point of view, exposure of merchandise for sale, and satisfactory sales volume and

[20] *Annual Report*, 1965, p. 3.
[21] *Annual Report*, 1965, p. 8.

economical operation from the point of view of the proprietor. But attainment of these goals is no easy matter and, whether a new store is being opened or the conversion of a service store into one providing less service is being weighed, the favorable and unfavorable elements of the self-selection and self-service plans should be studied carefully. These elements will now be summarized as far as self-service is concerned; and many of these statements, with only slight modification, are also applicable to self-selection.

Advantages of Self-Service Operation

1. Generally speaking, stores arranged on the self-service plan have wider aisles with fewer obstructions, and thus encourage circulation of customers and minimize congestion in customer traffic.

2. Many customers prefer self-service because it enables them a.) to examine merchandise in a leisurely and minute manner and to make selections upon the basis of their own judgment, and b.) to minimize their dependency upon a salesperson who may not exhibit the courtesy and helpfulness the customer has the right to expect.

3. When customers serve themselves (a step which is also frequently accompanied by a reduction in other customer services), fewer salespeople and other personnel are required; selling expenses are therefore reduced and personnel problems are minimized.[22]

4. Because of economies in operation, self-service stores are able to sell at lower prices than others and to appeal to customers on this basis.

5. Self-service arrangements make possible larger and better displays of merchandise which, in turn, contribute to greater sales.

6. Customers of self-service stores purchase more at one time, both in amount and in variety, than patrons of other stores. The important considerations here are that customers shop in a more leisurely manner and examine more merchandise. A considerable proportion of sales in many stores result from impulse buying; and self-service encourages such purchasing.

7. Arrangement of a store on the self-service plan brings recognition on the part of customers that the management is alert and is familiar with new developments in merchandising. This recognition, although it is difficult to measure, manifests itself in satisfied old customers and in the attraction of new ones.

Disadvantages of Self-Service Operation

The widespread publicity given to successful stores and departments using the self-service plan frequently has resulted in failure to consider the shortcomings of this type of operation, such as the following:

---

[22] For evidence, cf. Christina Fulop, *Competition for Consumers* (London: Institute of Economic Affairs, 1964), p. 25.

1. The physical makeup of the store—its size, shape, and location—may not be adaptable to self-service. Generally speaking, the self-service arrangement requires more floor space for a given volume of business than the counter-service type of store.

2. Many customers, because of established buying habits, prefer to be served by salespeople and resent being forced to locate specific merchandise and to bring it to the cashier's desk for checking, wrapping, and payment.

3. Some stores have such a large volume of business that long lines develop at check-out points, especially during rush periods. The result is both inconvenience for the customer and more errors by the check-out operators.[23]

4. Since experience reveals that self-service arrangement and operation are most successful in stores catering to middle- and low-income groups and offering well-known brands of packaged merchandise, retailers appealing to upper-income groups and selling unadvertised goods which are not customarily packaged find it difficult to operate profitably on the self-service plan.

5. In the case of self-service food markets, at least, customers expect adequate parking space for cars either at the curb or in a nearby parking lot. Providing curb-parking space in urban areas is difficult because of traffic congestion and the enforcement of time limits. Space in parking lots is expensive except in outlying areas.

6. Shoplifting and common thievery are easier and more prevalent in self-service stores, and consequently losses are greater.[24]

7. Certain types of products require service by salespeople. For high-priced merchandise of nearly every description such as mechanical durable goods, drug prescriptions, women's hats, and many other items, the customer frequently needs and expects the aid and advice of a salesperson.[25] Nevertheless, as is indicated by the experience of the discount house, many customers like to serve themselves even when buying such items as shoes, dresses, and millinery.

8. An impersonal atmosphere is common in the large, self-service store, so that the shopper fails to develop any emotional attachment or loyalty to a specific establishment.[26]

Future of Self-Selection and Self-Service Operation

Recent years have witnessed a tremendous increase in self-selection and self-service and this growth seems likely to continue in the foreseeable future. Currently even gasoline stations seem on the verge of adopting self-

---

[23] One study disclosed that errors were made on 11.3 percent of all the items "rung up" by the check-out operators of food stores, the final result being an undercharge equal to .7 percent of sales. Cf. E. M. Harwell, *Checkout Management* (New York: Chain Store Age Publishing Co., 1963), p. 7.

[24] Cf. "Stock Shortages Stick, Stores Slap Shoplifters," *Women's Wear Daily*, August 11, 1965, p. 1.

[25] A case in point is the meat market: One chain found that 58 percent of its customers favored the service market. "Service Markets on the Comeback Trail," *Chain Store Age* (Supermarket Executives Edition), November, 1964, p. 5.

[26] This point is developed in "The Store Image in an Age of Self-Serve 'Look-A-Likes'," *Modern Retailer*, April, 1966, p. 54.

service.[27] Moreover, further improvements in techniques will undoubtedly be developed. To illustrate, one of the present serious problems of self-service operations is that the shopper must bring purchases to the checkout point. In this process, pilferage takes place, merchandise is damaged, customer fatigue results and customer time is involved. However, one authority is convinced that mechanization will eventually make it unnecessary for the shopper to bring purchases to a checkout point.[28] Already a Stockholm store is operating on this principle: the customer picks up a data-punch card from a tray beneath each item she wishes, takes these cards to a check-out point, and her order is automatically assembled in the stockroom.[29]

All conversions to self-selection and self-service, however, are not—and will not be—successful. Despite the care with which they are planned, conditions in every case may not be suited to such methods of operation. A case in point is the experience of Famous-Barr Company in St. Louis. A few years ago check-out merchandising operations were instituted on an experimental basis in the basements of three stores. Discontinued two months later, management reported the check-out failed because (1) it could not handle efficiently the large number of transactions on peak days, (2) the high fashion level of much of the merchandise, and (3) the large share of "big ticket" items.

The future of self-selection and self-service will depend mainly upon (1) the continued willingness of customers to serve themselves in return for the savings they realize on their purchases; (2) improvements in fixtures, displays, and package design; and (3) the conviction of retail store management that these methods afford excellent opportunities to increase sales, reduce expenses, and alleviate some of their problems in the existing profit squeeze.

REVIEW AND DISCUSSION QUESTIONS

1. List and illustrate six factors which influence the layout of a specific store.
2. How do you account for the increased emphasis placed upon layout by retail store executives in recent years?
3. Discuss: "The architect's role in planning the layout of the store being modernized."

[27] "Self-Service Moves in on the Pump," *Business Week*, October 1, 1966, pp. 129–30; and E. B. Weiss, "Self-Service Gas Gasses Up," *Advertising Age*, September 27, 1965, pp. 110 ff.

[28] Automation in retailing is discussed in E. B. Weiss, "Robot Retailing Inches Along," *Advertising Age*, April 5, 1965, pp. 131–32.

[29] "Swedish Computerized Store A View of Things to Come?" *Chain Store Age* (Supermarket Executives Ed.), May, 1966, p. 8.

4. You are planning to construct a new store. Outline how you would proceed to determine your space requirements for layout purposes.

5. From your reading or based upon conversations with a voluntary chain retailer or wholesaler, outline and appraise the layout services offered the voluntary chain retailer by his wholesaler.

6. What do you consider to be the major problems regarding layout facing department stores today? Compare and contrast these problems with another type of retailer of your own choosing and preferably in your own community.

7. Visit a branch store in or near your local community and compare its layout with the main or parent store of the company which owns it. Give special attention to location of specific departments, size of space devoted to particular merchandise, width of aisles, and use of displays.

8. In some stores related merchandise is placed together, whereas in other stores less emphasis is placed on this factor. For example, in certain men's haberdashery shops, shirts, ties, socks, and handkerchiefs are shown in combination; in other shops, each of these items is shown in its separate area. Evaluate the merits of each of these types of arrangement.

9. Evaluate the layout of Figure 6–5 (6–6, 6–7, 6–8).

10. Explain carefully how the type of display employed by a store depends upon each of the following: value of the item, bulk of the item, perishability, staple or impulse character of the item, hazards, packaging, and profitability.

11. Compare and contrast the interior displays typical of self-service food stores with those of jewelry (shoe) stores.

12. Distinguish among self-selection, self-service, and simplified selling. Explain the factors responsible for the growth of these methods in recent years.

13. Prepare a list of basic requirements for self-service operation; and use your list to appraise a local self-service store.

14. Assume that you are the operator of a drugstore (a discount house or a hardware store). Evaluate the possibilities of successful operation of your store on a self-service basis.

15. Discuss the future of the self-service principle in department stores.

SUPPLEMENTARY READINGS

Another Look at Self-Selection is the title of a special issue of the *Journal of Retailing*, Vol. XXXVI, No. 2 (Summer, 1960). Especially recommended is the article by HOLLANDER, S. C. "How Self-Selection Affects Vendor Relations," pp. 58–60.

Architectural Record and *Chain Store Age*. Periodically these excellent publications present valuable material useful to the retailer in planning his store. For example, cf. "Store Layout Breakthrough," pp. 48–54, and "How Y-Shaped Produce Racks 'Capture' Customers," pp. 70 and 73, in the December, 1965, issue of the latter publication.

Cox, K. K. *The Relationship Between Shelf Space and Product Sales in Supermarkets* (Austin, Texas: University of Texas Bureau of Business Research, 1964). That this relationship is an important one from the retailer's profit point of view is clearly demonstrated by this analysis. Also cf. "Grocery Shelf Arrangements: Key to More Efficient Operations," *Progressive Grocer,* December, 1964, pp. 120–22.

Discount Merchandiser. "Layout and Equipment Guide," issue of September, 1964, pp. 48–62. The layouts and space allocation by departments for seven discount houses are covered in these pages.

Fulop, Christina. *Competition for Consumers* (London: Institute of Economic Affairs, 1964). Self-service retailing in Great Britain is covered in this discussion. Cf. especially pp. 19–21, 24–27, and 93–94.

Harwell, E. M. *Checkout Management* (New York: Chain Store Publishing Corporation, 1963). This authoratative guide to the subject includes, among others, chapters on checker accuracy, training checkers, checkout supervision, determining the number of checkstands, and checkout equipment.

Mauger, E. M. *Modern Display Techniques* (New York: Fairchild Publications, Inc., 1965). An up-to-date study which is "must" reading for the retailer.

National Cash Register Co. *Display Selling* (n.d.), and *Suggestions for Check-Out Market Planning* (n.d.) (Dayton, Ohio: The Company). These pamphlets contain valuable illustrations and suggestions covering several phases of store arrangement.

National Retail Hardware Association. *Basic Store Layout* (Indianapolis, Ind.: The Association, Bulletin No. 27, n.d.). This bulletin, which provides an excellent discussion of the basic principles of layout as applied to a hardware store, is a good example of the aid which a retailer can obtain from his trade association.

New York State Department of Commerce. *Store Arrangement and Display* (Albany, New York: The Department, n.d.). The small store point of view is emphasized in this pamphlet.

Payne, G. K. *Creative Display* (New York: National Retail Merchants Association, 1965). Both window and interior displays are considered in this excellent volume by the display director of Woodward and Lothrop, Washington, D.C.

Progressive Grocer. "Customer Traffic Patterns Key to Selling Efficiency," issue of January, 1966, pp. 47–59. The plans, illustrations, and diagrams included in this issue emphasize the need to lay out the store from the customer point of view.

Regan, W. J. "Full Cycle for Self-Service?" *Journal of Marketing,* Vol. XXV, No. 4 (April, 1961), pp. 15–21. The pros and cons of self-service are considered by the author.

Sommers, M. S., and Kernan, J. B. "A Behavioral Approach to Planning, Layout, and Display," *Journal of Retailing,* Vol. XLI, No. 4 (Winter, 1965–66), pp. 21–26, 62. "This article explains the basis for behaviorally-oriented layout and display, indicates how it can be applied, and considers the obstacles involved."

"Store Planning," *Stores,* October, 1964, p. 13–65. Important aspects of store construction and layout are considered in these pages.

"Stores Scanning Macy Recipe for Sales Mix," *Women's Wear Daily,* November 2, 1965, pp. 1 and 44. Merchandise grouping according to customer buying habits is discussed.

WEISS, E. B. "Self-Service Gas Gasses Up," *Advertising Age,* September 27, 1965, pp. 110 ff. The author foresees a trend for gasoline to be retailed on a self-service basis. Also cf. the prediction of moving aisles, robot service, and drive-in stores in the author's "What Will Retailing Be Like in 1975?", *ibid.,* March 7, 1966, pp. 119–20 ff.

PART IV

Retail Organization

7

CHAPTER

Structure of the Retail Firm

In any business, there must be some structure or organization to carry out the firm's policies. In retailing, as we shall see in some detail, this structure or organization will vary with such factors as size, kinds of merchandise sold, services rendered, and preferences and desires of the executives. In other words, the structure of a particular retail firm—whether it is a three-man company with little division of labor or whether it employs thousands of people on a specialized basis—must be founded securely upon its specific needs and requirements. We shall also discover that what was "good organization" at one time in a firm's history may be quite unsatisfactory at a later period; that a structure must be flexible enough to meet changes in fundamental conditions when they occur.

The aims of this chapter, therefore, are three-fold: (1) to define exactly what is meant by the term "organization"; (2) to explore the structures that different kinds of retailers have developed to meet their specific needs; and (3) to note the major current trends in retail organization.

NATURE OF "ORGANIZATION"

Organization has been defined in various ways.[1] Some students of this subject refer to it as "the functional structure through which the force of management flows to accomplish the objectives, goals, and purposes of a business."[2] Another writer says that it "consists of breaking operations into

---

[1] Two important types or forms of organization, classified according to purpose, may be distinguished: (1) organization for *ownership,* or *legal,* purposes; and (2) organization for *operation,* or *administrative,* purposes. The present discussion is restricted to the latter. For detailed discussions of legal forms of organization, consult any standard textbook on business organization or business finance.

[2] O. P. Robinson, J. G. Robinson, and M. P. Matthews, *Store Organization and Operation* (2d ed.; Englewood Cliffs, N.J.: Prentice-Hall, Inc., 1957), p. 18.

their constituent elements and skills, assigning manpower, devising an acceptable formula of cooperation, opening up avenues for internal communication, establishing discipline, and steering performance toward intended goals."[3] Still other authorities, and the present authors agree with them, extend the term to include the selection of personnel.

Perhaps the most understandable approach from the student's point of view is the definition of "organization" which is based on its component parts. Using this approach, we may say that organization involves four aspects, as follows:

1. Arranging the activities that the retailer has decided to perform in convenient groups for assignment to specific individuals[4]
2. Providing for the selection of the personnel to whom the activities will be assigned
3. Making the assignment of responsibility for each group of activities and determining the authority that is to go with the responsibility
4. Providing for control of and harmonious adjustment among the individuals to whom responsibilities are assigned

Three of these four aspects of organizational structure are treated in this chapter, with the selection of personnel included in the discussion of the two following chapters.

Organization Charts

There is no better way to indicate the grouping of the functions of a business and the lines of authority and responsibility than by means of an organization chart or diagram, especially if supplemented by carefully prepared executive job descriptions. Just as in the case of store layout, drawing plans on paper is an aid to clear thinking and proper coordination of activities in the building of the organization; moreover, it is indispensable in visualizing the company as a whole, in defining the responsibilities and authority of individuals, and in indicating to whom these individuals report.

Yet it must not be forgotten that there is danger in an organization chart being mistaken for an organization. A firm may have a fine-appearing chart and still fail to function effectively. Also business organizations should be thought of in terms of the human beings of which they consist; at times, concentration on an organization chart has resulted in the neglect of the personalities involved. Moreover, in a fast-changing business such as retail-

---

[3] W. N. Mitchell, *The Business Executive in a Changing World* (New York: American Management Association, Inc., 1965), p. 89.

[4] The present authors believe that the *selection* of the particular activities which a specific retailer will undertake—for example, credit extension, comparison shopping, and delivery service—is a matter of *policy,* not of organization.

ing, an organization chart may become obsolete almost as soon as it is placed on paper: frequent revision of the chart is a "must." Giving full recognition to these facts, retailers of all types, particularly the larger ones, will find organization charts of much value for the reasons indicated.[5]

Some Introductory Comments

As an introduction to the detailed discussion of the structure of the retail firm which follows, three points need emphasis. First, since "organization is squarely based upon a systematic and clearly understood division of labor"[6] the organizational task differs greatly between the small and the large retailer. In the one-man store, all aspects of organization center around the question: How can the small retailer best plan *his own time* to serve as "purchasing agent" for his customers? In contrast, the large retailer is required to assign responsibilities to different persons, to determine the authority to be granted to each, and to provide for harmonious adjustment among these many individuals.

Second, the organizational task is never completed; or, as two authorities have written, "it is only a slight exaggeration to say that the best organization plan starts to become obsolete the day it is installed."[7] Retailers frequently find it necessary to expand or contract their activities; and as their activities change, a different structural pattern may be required. A better way of grouping the present activities may be discovered, or perhaps study may convince top management that its business will function better if the lines of authority are shifted. Just a few years ago, for example, who would have thought of a "plural" chief executive? Yet, today a number of firms have divided the chief executive's functions among two or three individuals who operate as a "team."[8]

Third, it should be re-emphasized that "good organization in itself does have a very definite value" to the retailer. "It defines the function and the authority of the various units that comprise the whole; it defines the relationship of one department to another; it definitely places responsibility for the accomplishment of certain objectives; it tends toward a specialization of effort and the development of skills in particular phases of the company's

---

[5] For a more detailed analysis of organization charts cf. A. R. Janger, "Charting Authority Relationships," *Conference Board Record,* December, 1964, pp. 8–13.

[6] Mitchell, *op. cit.,* p. 37.

[7] Wroe Alderson and P. E. Green, *Planning and Problem Solving in Marketing* (Homewood, Ill.: Richard D. Irwin, Inc., 1964), p. 547. How a firm keeps its organization up-to-date is discussed in J. K. Bailey, "Organization Planning—Whose Responsibility?" *Stores,* September, 1964, pp. 49–53.

[8] Cf. D. R. Daniel, "Team at the Top," *Harvard Business Review,* Vol. XLIII, No. 2 (March–April, 1965), pp. 74–82.

work; it facilitates better planning and less waste effort; and, in general, it results in greater overall effectiveness."[9]

ORGANIZATION OF SMALL STORES

The structure of small businesses, particularly retail stores, and the problems they encounter from day to day have been sadly neglected in retailing literature. Usually, the small store is dismissed with the statement that the "fundamental principles of organization" are comparable for both small and large stores; and then only large stores are discussed. However, the matter is not so simple. Despite the fact that certain activities or functions must be performed in all stores, there are—as we have already suggested—basic points of difference between the small store and the large one from the point of view of structural requirements. These differences will become clear as we examine the structures of both small and large retailers.

The Small Independent Store

In the small store the proprietor, in addition to acting as general manager, must perform personally a variety of buying, selling, and allied activities which in the large store are divided among several individuals who specialize in the performance of certain tasks. Moreover, employees of small stores must also perform a greater number of duties than employees of large stores. This difference in specialization is one of the two chief distinguishing features between small and large stores insofar as structure is concerned. The second relates to the number of activities carried on by the store. The large retailer performs a broader list of functions than his smaller competitor; he often provides more services, frequently he stocks a wider variety of merchandise, and prepares merchandise budgets.

The activities performed by small stores and their degree of specialization are well illustrated in Figure 7–1. Here is shown the organization of a store employing four persons in addition to the proprietor. If Figure 7–1 is compared with Figure 7–2, the lesser number of activities in the small store and its limited degree of specialization will become clear. The student should note particularly that, although it is very simple in structure, the organization set forth in Figure 7–1 provides for all three aspects of organization discussed in this chapter: It groups the firm's activities for assignment; it assigns authority to employees and fixes responsibility for carrying out activities; and it provides—in the person of the proprietor

---

[9] W. B. England, *Procurement: Principles and Cases* (4th ed.; Homewood, Ill.: Richard D. Irwin, Inc., 1962), p. 50.

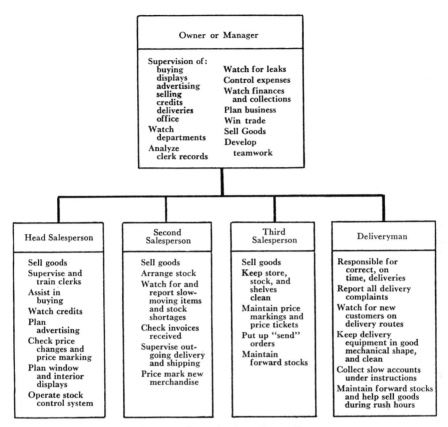

FIG. 7–1. Organization of a small store.

himself—a means of control and of making any necessary adjustments among the store's personnel.

The Small Department Store

As stores increase in size and greater specialization becomes necessary, such operating activities as store maintenance, adjustments, and deliveries are usually separated from the merchandising activities associated with buying and selling. A two-function structure for a small department store is shown in Figure 7–2. In practice the general manager of a store of the size shown in this chart is usually in active charge of either merchandising or operating activities.

This plan also provides for the creation of two staff officers, a combination treasurer-controller and a personnel director, both of whom report directly to the general manager or proprietor. It is clear that the duties of these two officers must be store-wide in scope: placing them in staff capaci-

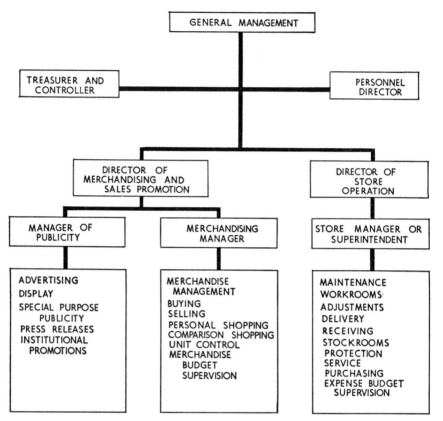

FIG. 7–2.   Two-function organization chart for a small department store.

ties means that they can carry out these store-wide activities without interfering with the day-by-day operating problems of line executives.[10]

Since the responsibilities of the directors of merchandising and sales promotion and of store operations are shown in Figure 7–2 and since these and other responsibilities are discussed in connection with the structure of large stores in a following section, they will not be considered in detail at this point. Some of the advantages of this relatively simple structural plan for small department stores, however, should be mentioned. It is simple, establishing a degree of specialization but not providing a complicated structure; it separates the personnel job from operations, thus enabling personnel to function on a store-wide basis; it centralizes responsibility for control activities in the treasurer-controller; and it unifies buying and selling activities. The specialized nature of publicity is recognized by establishing a

---

[10] Some interesting observations on the relationship of staff to line personnel will be found in J. K. Bailey and A. H. Savage, "How Pure Should the Staff Role Be?" *Personnel Administration,* September, 1965, pp. 3–5 ff.

manager for this work, who reports directly to the director of merchandising and sales promotion, so that there is a close integration of publicity work with the whole merchandising process.

DEPARTMENTIZING THE STORE

An important aspect of retail store structure is departmentizing. As small stores become larger, it is increasingly difficult for proprietors to maintain close contact with each line of merchandise; consequently, they are less able to locate (and eliminate) the weak spots in their merchandising activities. To effect improvement, therefore, they departmentize; that is, they divide their various lines of merchandise into a number of groups, with each group known as a department and operated more or less as a separate unit.

Benefits of Departmentizing

The advantages of departmentizing a store may be summarized as follows:

Profitable lines are revealed.
Unprofitable lines are brought to management's attention.
Profitable average margin can be maintained.
Margins can be easily adjusted on each kind of merchandise.
Necessary markup can be computed for each line.
Inventory is more easily controlled.
Stockturn is increased.
Responsibility is more easily assigned among personnel.
Salespeople can be assigned by departments and specialize on selling a line of merchandise.
Specific assignment of responsibility to salespeople gives them a greater incentive to work and to take a greater interest in the business.
"Leaks" and losses are more easily located and checked.
Customers are aided to find what they want to buy.
Management is simplified.
Checkup can be made of any part of the business at any time.
Better control is possible over each part of the business.
Larger profits are obtained.

Steps in Departmentizing

Once the retailer is convinced that he will benefit from departmentizing and desires to operate his store under such a plan, he ordinarily proceeds as follows:

1. He takes a physical inventory of his stock and proceeds to separate it into well-defined and related groups of merchandise. The extent of this separation

depends upon the kinds and the quantities of the merchandise carried, as well as upon the type of store.

2. He decides upon the departments. In this process, it is customary to place in one department a complete line, or two or more related smaller lines. He should guard against creating too many departments.

3. He assigns to each department a definite location within the store and assembles there the necessary merchandise. In this connection the retailer should pay particular attention to the buying habits of his customers, to the types and kinds of merchandise involved, to the size and shape of the space available, and to his past experience in selling the types of goods concerned.[11]

4. He determines the expenses chargeable against each department and the bases upon which they will be prorated. This step involves the charging of direct expenses—such as salaries and wages of the sales force and advertising—and the allocating of indirect expenses—such as rent, heat, light, and power—on some reasonable and equitable basis.[12]

5. He computes gross margins attainable for each department. This task is difficult, since the gross margin realized on some items of merchandise within a given department is greater than on other items. A satisfactory sales relationship between high-margin and low-margin merchandise should be maintained so that the department may realize a profit or minimize any loss.

6. He provides for the recording of purchases, returns to vendors, sales, returns by and allowances to customers, and markdowns by departments.

When done properly and carried on systematically, departmentizing enables a retailer to become better acquainted with the detailed merchandising activities of his business, improves his operations, and results in better profits. The retailer, however, should make constant use of the facts available to him, interpret these facts properly, and adjust his methods whenever conditions warrant such changes.

ORGANIZATION OF LARGE STORES

Although there are several types of large retail firms, the organizational problems and practices of all of them can be illustrated by a discussion of department stores and chain stores.

Department Store Structure

Four-Function or Mazur Plan. As has already been suggested, the greater degree of specialization and the wider variety of activities in large stores make necessary a more complicated structure than is found in small stores. Whereas the typical organization among smaller department stores is a two-functional setup which separates merchandising and operating activi-

---

[11] Cf. the discussion of "Regrouping of Merchandise Lines," pp. 208–9, below.

[12] Methods of allocating expenses to departments are discussed in Chapter 25.

ties (see Fig. 7–2), in medium- and large-size department stores the four-function or four-pyramid plan is most widely accepted today. Frequently this plan is referred to as the Mazur Plan, since it was set forth in Paul Mazur's report made on behalf of a Committee of the National Retail Merchants Association.[13] It is illustrated in Figure 7–3, in which department store activities are classified into the following four groups: merchandising, publicity, store management or operation, and accounting and control.

1. *Some Weaknesses.* Studies made by the Retail Research Institute of the National Retail Merchants Association have indicated four basic weaknesses in the traditional four-function setup of the previous paragraph.[14]

a) Responsibilities for profit performance can not be delegated below the level of general manager.
b) The general manager is overburdened, and lacks time for long-range planning, community activity, and policy development.
c) The selling function is spread over many areas, including merchandising, sales promotion, personnel, operations and finance-control, instead of being located under one key functional executive.
d) Buyers are over-burdened with parts of the selling function along with their merchandising responsibilities.

2. *Some Recommendations.* To overcome these weaknesses the Institute has recommended:

a) A general manager and the planning research and public relations staff reporting directly to the president.
b) Assigning to an executive below the general manager level the responsibility of directing and coordinating merchandising and selling.
c) Delegating to this executive—to be known as general merchandising manager—primary responsibility for sales, gross margin, and controllable expense performance of all store units.
d) The general merchandise manager and managers of central finance-control, personnel and operations staff reporting to the general manager.
e) Store managers and a supporting staff of managers of merchandise, sales promotion, selling services, and merchandise control reporting to the general merchandise manager.

Later in this chapter we shall return to some of the implications and current trends resulting from the Institute's recommendations on organiza-

---

[13] P. M. Mazur, *Principles of Organization Applied to Modern Retailing* (New York: Harper & Bros., 1927). Also cf. the excellent discussion of the Mazur Plan and modifications of it by R. C. Bond, 'Department Store Organization," in National Retail Merchants Association, *The Buyer's Manual* (4th ed.; New York: The Association, 1965), pp. 11–22.

[14] *Survey of Organization of Single Unit Department and Specialty Stores* (New York: The Association, 1959) and *Organization in Multi-Unit Department and Specialty Stores* (1961).

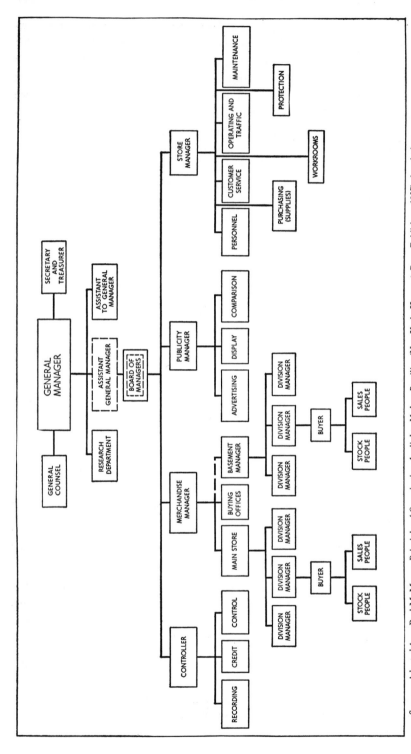

FIG. 7–3. The four-functional organization chart of a department store.

tion.[15] At this point, our goal is to provide a greater understanding of the specific duties performed in each of the four traditional divisions of the department store.

Merchandising Division. The responsibilities of this division are centered in buying and selling activities. Because these functions are considered the "heart" of the retail business and because other functions performed are designed to supplement them and render them more effective, they usually receive the greatest amount of executive attention.

1. *Functions and Key Personnel.* More specifically, the major functions and responsibilities of the merchandising division are as follows:

a) Interpret and execute the merchandising policies of the company
b) Unify the efforts of all buyers or department managers so as to present a single "image" to the buying public
c) Aid buyers to get and use current information regarding business trends and market conditions
d) Provide the buyer with an objective point of view regarding his department's operation
e) Establish and administer a merchandise control system
f) Assist each department in planning and carrying out its individual buying plans
g) In cooperation with the publicity or sales promotion division, plan sales promotions
h) Supervise departmental activities of buyers
i) Assist buyers in locating and developing new resources
j) Plan and supervise comparison shopping (unless assigned to the publicity division)[16]

The merchandising division, as previously indicated in Figure 7–3, is under the direction of the general merchandise manager, who supervises merchandising activities in all locations, including the main store, the basement store, and buying offices.[17] Under him are several divisional merchandise managers, the number depending on the size of the store and the number of departments operated. The chief responsibilities of division managers are to supervise the operation of groups of related and adjacent merchandise departments and to coordinate effectively their activities, to assist buyers (department managers) in the performance of their regular

---

[15] Cf. "Major Trends in Store Organization," pp. 202–12, below.

[16] This list is based on that developed by E. J. Brown in his chapter on "The Merchandising Division," in *The Buyer's Manual, op. cit.,* pp. 29–30.

[17] The basement store typically operates as a separate unit with its own merchandise manager and buying staff. For an exception to this rule cf. "Bloomingdale's Basement Goes Up the Staircase," *Women's Wear Daily,* November 15, 1966, pp. 1, 6. Some stores refer to the basement store as the "Budget Floor," while others designate it as the "Downstairs Store" or "The Store of Lower Prices." Increasingly basements are being used for self-selection, check-out operations.

duties, and to relieve the general merchandise manager of some of his more detailed responsibilities associated with departmental merchandising activities. Especially can the division manager assist the buyer in preparing his preliminary merchandise plan or budget at periodic intervals, and in analyzing and interpreting merchandise statistics and reports prepared by the general merchandising office and by the control office.

2. *Buyers or Department Managers.*   The buyers are very important individuals in the merchandising operation. They have major responsibility for buying and selling activities within their departments and consequently influence more than anyone else the results obtained.[18] With respect to buying, their duties generally include preparing preliminary merchandise plans or budgets with the assistance of the division manager; making contacts with manufacturers, wholesalers, and other sources of merchandise; studying fashion trends and price movements; through inspection, tests, and other means, obtaining proper qualities and grades of merchandise in the styles suited to the demands of customers; securing deliveries of merchandise at the proper time; and making purchases at prices which permit selling prices to be set at levels that yield the desired markup. As an aid in buying, complete information on the merchandise offerings of competitors, including fashions, materials, and prices, is often obtained. This information may come through comparison shoppers, who systematically and regularly examine the merchandise offered for sale in competing stores and obtain full details about it.

In connection with his responsibility for selling activities, the buyer plans in advance the number of salespeople who will be required in his department; determines their qualifications; and, in cooperation with the personnel department, maintains the proper size selling force at all times. Because of his detailed knowledge of the merchandise he has purchased and because of his familiarity with fashion trends in his particular field, he instructs salespeople on these points and insures conformance to his instructions through close supervision.[19] He cooperates in the preparation of merchandise displays in his department and does everything possible to insure customer satisfaction and the profitableness of departmental operations.

It should be noted that even under the four-functional plan of organization sole responsibility for sales efforts does not rest on the buyer. As a matter of fact, the selling function is divided among three major divisions:

---

[18] Cf., however, the discussion on pp. 206–8, below. As an example of a firm (Bullock's of Los Angeles, a division of Federated Department Stores, Inc.) which continues to combine buying and selling responsibilities in its buyers cf. "Prestige Store Grows Without Losing Gloss," *Business Week,* April 9, 1966, pp. 58–62.

[19] Cf. the excellent discussion of "The Buyer As Manager of People," by David Bluthenthal in *The Buyer's Manual, op. cit.,* pp. 37–45.

the merchandising division, as indicated; the publicity division, with its advertising and display efforts; and the store management division, with its responsibility for recruiting and maintaining a satisfactory sales force. Moreover, partly in response to the growth of branch or suburban stores, significant changes are taking place with respect to the buyer's responsibilities for selling activities. In fact, as already noted, the entire merchandising organization is being re-evaluated. These changes are considered in some detail in a subsequent section of this chapter.[20]

Publicity Division. The publicity division, which is often referred to as the sales promotion and advertising division and which is under the direction of the publicity or advertising manager, is responsible for all selling efforts not classified as personal selling. In the words of Mazur, it "presents the store and its merchandise so that the public will be constantly attracted to purchase from the store."[21] Specifically, the responsibilities of the publicity division include the following:

1. All forms of advertising
2. Window displays
3. Interior displays, usually excluding counter displays
4. The planning and executing of sales-promotion events, in cooperation with the merchandising division
5. Special forms of sales promotion, such as fashion shows and educational exhibits
6. Advertising research
7. Public relations
8. Comparison shopping (unless assigned to the merchandising division)[22]

In carrying out the responsibilities mentioned, the publicity manager has a number of important duties. All forms of publicity must conform to general store policy; consequently, plans should be discussed with top management, and present and probable future policies should be reviewed. Store policy will govern, for example, the size of the advertising budget and the extent to which purely institutional advertising will be used. Working with

---

[20] Cf. pp. 206–8.

[21] Mazur, *op. cit.,* p. 203.

[22] Disagreement exists among store executives and students of retailing regarding the proper place of the comparison department in the store organization. Some believe that comparisons of merchandise offerings of competitors are essential to effective buying and that it is therefore natural and logical for the department to be under the merchandise manager. Others are of the opinion that, since the major function of the comparison department is to provide a check upon the merchandising function, it is impracticable and unsound to permit the check to be made by those responsible for it; consequently, the comparison job is often made a responsibility of the publicity division (cf. Fig. 7–3). This assignment is defended on the ground, also, that shoppers report on the advertisements of both their own stores and competitors.

the personnel department, the publicity manager must also recruit and maintain an advertising staff and a display staff ample to meet the store's requirements. In connection with special forms of sales promotion, he should supervise existing methods, and be constantly on the alert to meet or to beat the efforts of his chief competitors. Finally, close cooperation with the merchandising division is necessary. In fact, this cooperation is so close in many stores that the publicity division is virtually subordinate to the key merchandising executive.

Store Management or Operating Division. This division, headed by the store manager or store superintendent, covers a greater variety of activities than any other. In fact, the operating division is usually charged with responsibility for the performance of all activities not directly associated with buying and selling, with the exception of accounting and financial control. Despite the multiplicity of responsibilities charged to this division, the number of its duties has tended to increase over the years because the heads of other divisions have refused to assume them.

The activities for which the store manager is usually responsible include the following, grouped according to their natural relationships:

A. Store maintenance
    1. Construction
    2. Repairs and renovations
    3. Maintenance of mechanical equipment
    4. Ventilation, including air conditioning
    5. Heat, light, and power
    6. Janitor service
B. Customer service
    1. Adjustment bureaus
    2. Service superintendents
    3. Floor service supervisors
    4. Personal service bureaus
C. Operating activities
    1. Receiving, checking, and marking
    2. Stock rooms
    3. Warehouses
    4. Shipping rooms
    5. Deliveries
    6. Returned goods
D. Purchasing of store supplies, equipment, and other property
    1. Supplies needed for store use
    2. Fixtures and equipment of all kinds
    3. Fuel
E. Store and merchandise protection
    1. Special service operators
    2. Night watchmen

3. Service shopping
4. Outside protective agencies
5. Insurance (in cooperation with control division or treasurer)
F. Personnel[23]
1. Employment[24]
2. Training
3. Compensation
4. Welfare
5. Employment stabilization
G. Workrooms
1. Cost departments, such as restaurants, soda fountains, beauty shops, and drapery workrooms
2. Manufacturing departments, such as candy and ice-cream making, and bakeries
3. Expense workrooms, such as laundries and employee cafeterias

Control Division. This division, the fourth in the organizational structure of a typical department store, is headed by the controller or, occasionally, by the treasurer. The chief tasks of the head of this division, known as the "watchdog of the treasury," are to protect the company's assets and to provide adequate working capital to meet the needs of the business. He contributes the "show-me" attitude, taking very little for granted until the results reflect accomplishment.

The detailed responsibilities of the controller usually include the following:

1. Devising and maintaining adequate accounting records
2. Planning, taking, and calculating the physical inventory
3. Credits and collections
4. Merchandise budgeting and control (in cooperation with the merchandising division)
5. Expense budgeting and control
6. Development of procedures to provide the desired control
7. Preparing reports for general management
8. Insurance (often the responsibility of the treasurer)
9. Safekeeping of all records prepared by or furnished to him
10. Familiarity and compliance with governmental rules and regulations, state and federal
11. Preparing reports for governmental and other agencies[25]

---

[23] There has been a definite trend in recent years toward removing the director of personnel from under the jurisdiction of the store manager and making the personnel officer a major executive reporting directly to the general manager. This trend is discussed at some length in the latter part of this chapter in the section entitled "Major Trends in Store Organization."

[24] With the employment function growing rapidly in size and complexity some students believe it may be advisable to give it a place of its own in the organization structure.

[25] Also cf. the discussion of the growing responsibilities of the controller, p. 209, below.

General Management.[26]   The prime functions of the general management of the department store are to direct, to correlate and coordinate, and to control the activities of the four divisions through their respective heads, so that the business will operate effectively and yield a profit. Unless policies are formulated carefully and unless sound principles of retailing are followed in handling both merchandise and customer relationships, chances of success are small. Because of the need for additional accurate information upon which management may formulate its policies, the past decade has witnessed the development and growth of research departments in many large stores. These departments, which serve in a staff capacity, commonly report directly to the general management because their investigations cover all divisions of the business, as well as outside conditions.

Structure of Ownership Groups.   The previous paragraphs of this section have referred mainly to the organization or structure of individual department stores. We must now recognize the fact that many of today's department stores are controlled by the so-called "ownership group." By this term we do not refer to the large department stores operated by Sears and Ward's: such stores are really chain stores and their organization will be discussed later in this chapter.[27] Rather, we mean department stores which have usually been in existence for a long time and which were gradually brought together under common ownership.

While management responsibilities in some ownership groups have been centralized much as is true of chain-store operation, in most of them—Federated Department Stores, Inc., for example—the stores have retained many of the management functions they had when they were individual units. Each store typically has its own merchandising, publicity, operations, and control divisions. What the group's central management does is to establish basic policies and to provide certain services for the benefit of its units—such as financing, research, central market-buying facilities, exchange of operating statistics. In addition, it aids each store to set overall goals, thereby stimulating local management to improve its operating results. Finally, it provides a small staff of experts to aid each store in the solution of problems.

Structure for Branch Operation.   With the development of branch stores, which now account for about one half of the total sales of department stores,[28] store executives were faced with the difficult organizational problem

---

[26] For a more extended discussion of the general manager's responsibility for coordination, cf. Chapter 28 "Coordination and Retailing Management."

[27] Cf. "Chain-Store Organization," pp. 197–202, below.

[28] Sam Flanel, *Department Merchandising and Operating Results of Department and Specialty Stores in 1965* (New York: National Retail Merchants Association, 1966), p. 2. Among stores with annual sales over $50 million, branches contributed 56.2 percent of the

of how best to coordinate parent and branch-store management. To date, no single answer has emerged, but three general patterns are now quite clear.[29]

1. *"Brood Hen and Chick" Organization.*   When a department store opens its first few branches, and especially when they are considerably smaller than the parent store, the "brood hen and chick" concept of organization is usually followed. Specifically this concept means that the parent store organization operates the branch: the parent publicity director advertises for the branch, the controller and store superintendent perform their functions for both parent and branch store, and parent store buyers or department managers are responsible for all buying. Under this plan, while employees in the branch have a line responsibility to the branch manager, the branch department sales supervisors and maintenance supervisor, for example, must work closely with parent store buyers and store superintendent.

2. *"Separate Store" Plan.*   As the number of branches increases or as the branches grow in size, however, the obvious limitation of the "brood hen and chick" structure is soon reached: the parent store, especially its buyers, cannot continue indefinitely to absorb the additional work load. At this point, some firms—especially those with large branch units—have decided to treat each branch as a separate store with its own management and buying staffs organized on the same basis as the parent unit. Bullock's, Inc., of California, follows this principle, and has every intention of maintaining this plan of organization.[30]

3. *"Equal-Store" Structure.*   In contrast with the separate store concept of Bullock's, other firms—specialty-store firms such as Best and Company and department store organizations such as Burdine's of Miami, Florida—have moved in the opposite direction and reorganized their branches according to chain-store principles, concentrating major management functions including buying at a single headquarters.[31] An organizational model embodying this concept is presented in Figure 7–4.

As the parent store expands its number of branches, it seems likely that

---

volume. For New York's major retail firms, branch store sales advanced 61 percent between 1961 and 1965 while downtown sales were up but 15 percent. H. G. Elam, "The Performance of New York's Great Stores," *New York Retailer,* May, 1966, p. 4.

[29] The opinions of several retailers on these three general patterns of management and others will be found in "The Management of Branch Stores," *Stores,* May, 1965, pp. 10–14 ff. Also cf. A. J. O'Brien, "Working with the Branch Store," *The Buyer's Manual, op. cit.,* pp. 305–15.

[30] J. W. Wingate and J. S. Friedlander, *The Management of Buying* (Englewood Cliffs, N.J.: Prentice-Hall, Inc., 1963), p. 57.

[31] Of considerable importance in this organizational development is the separation of buying and selling functions. Cf. the discussion of trends in store organization, pp. 206–8, below.

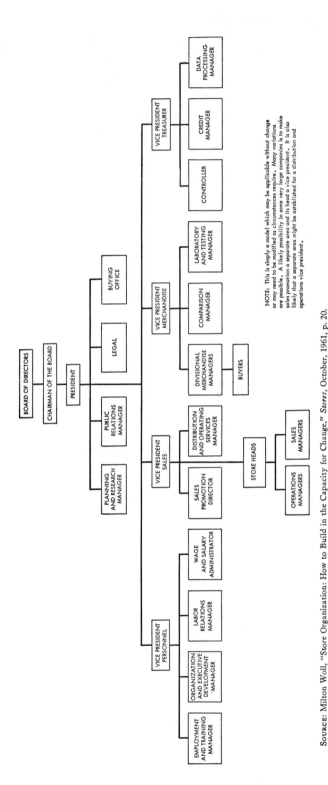

NOTE: This is simply a model which may be applicable without change or may need to be modified as circumstances require. Many variations are possible. A likely possibility in some very large companies is to make sales promotion a separate area and its head a vice president. It is also likely that a separate area might be established for a distribution and operations vice president.

SOURCE: Milton Woll, "Store Organization: How to Build in the Capacity for Change," *Stores*, October, 1961, p. 20.

FIG. 7–4. An organization model for department or specialty stores with four or more selling units.

even greater attention will be given to the chain-store form of organization with the parent or main store considered as just another unit in the system. The major objective of this equal-store or central organization concept, of course, is to achieve the efficiencies and the economies of a chain-store system.

Chain-Store Organization

Some Common Characteristics. Although chain-store companies vary in organization because of differences in types of merchandise handled, in services performed, in size of individual retail units, and in territory covered, they usually have certain common characteristics, as follows:

1. Centralization of major responsibilities in the headquarters or home office, whether organized on a national, regional, or local basis. The chief exception to this rule is responsibility for selling, which is decentralized.

2. Breakdown of the organization into a greater number of main divisions than is typical of department stores, such as real estate and maintenance, merchandising (including buying), sales promotion, retail operation, personnel, control, and, perhaps, warehouse operation, traffic and transportation, and others.

3. Recognition of the great importance of the personnel division, and the appointment of a personnel director or manager as a major executive. This action is in contrast to that taken in many department stores, where personnel is a subordinate function of the management division.

4. Employment of trained and capable executives to direct each of the divisions into which the company's activities are grouped.

5. Careful provision for the supervision and follow-up of activities carried on in individual stores.

6. An elaborate system of reports designed to keep the headquarters office currently informed on results of operations and to enable the executives involved to maintain effective control over all activities for which they are responsible.

The importance of these factors in any given chain-store company is dependent upon company policy, past experience, and the preferences and personalities of executives.

Organization of an Apparel Chain. Some of the foregoing major characteristics of chain-store organizations may be illustrated by describing the setup of an apparel chain with over 100 stores. These stores are divided into districts of approximately 10 units each, with a manager for each store and a field manager or supervisor for each district.

The division of responsibilities between the store manager and the field manager is well defined. The store manager's main function is the sale of merchandise, with its selection and purchase largely centralized at the chain's headquarters. To carry out the selling function, the store manager actually makes sales himself, hires and trains a sales staff which varies from 4 to 20 persons, arranges store displays, and reports daily sales to headquarters. The field manager acts as the connecting link between headquarters and the store. Specifically, he hires store managers, takes physical inventories, checks displays, and passes on to buyers at headquarters the suggestions of store managers for merchandise to meet local demand.

At headquarters a merchandise manager, aided by 5 buyers and 8 divisional distribution managers, supervises buying and merchandise control. Each buyer is responsible for the purchase of a specific type of merchandise, such as dresses or hosiery; but the shipment of this merchandise to the stores is controlled by the divisional distribution managers, with each manager responsible for from 10 to 20 stores. Shipments are based upon information provided by stubs of tickets from merchandise sold, the daily reports of store managers, and the knowledge of the divisional distribution managers as to style, price, and consumer buying trends.

Chain-Store Organization Charts. Figures 7–5 and 7–6 afford a comparison between the organization of a regional food chain of 450 stores and that of a national food chain with more than 4,500 outlets. In both of these firms, each store is visited at least once a week by a district manager (store supervisor, is the term used by A & P) who, in turn, reports to a higher ranking executive. A former successful store manager, the district manager's main task is to help each store manager operate his store more effectively.[32]

Figure 7–7 is especially interesting since it shows how Montgomery Ward & Company has faced the problem of integrating chain-store and mail-order activities. In commenting upon this chart, a former president of Ward's has written:

The chairman and president, in conjunction with the Board of Directors, directs the management of the business. The president receives advice and counsel from his staff in the formulation and development of the general policies and programs of the Company and in the appraisal of their effectiveness.

There is a direct line of responsibility from the chairman and president through the executive vice president to the field organization and the individual managers of stores, mail order houses, and warehouses. This shows up in the center of the chart as the line organization, the backbone of the management structure. Commensurate authority has been delegated to each management level.

Essential staff functions support the line organization at each management level. For example, the executive vice president is supported by a merchandising

---

[32] A "typical day" in the life of a district manager or store supervisor is set forth in "The Store Supervisor: Key Communicator in a Complicated Business," *Progressive Grocer*, July, 1964, p. 32.

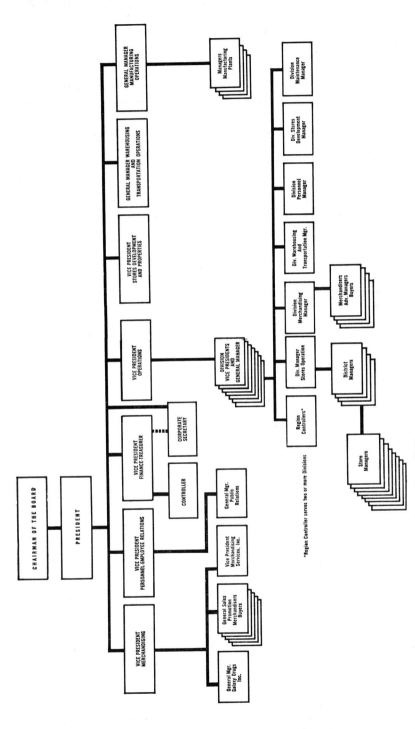

SOURCE: *Super Market Merchandising*, February, 1965, pp. 28-29.

FIG. 7-5. Organization chart of Colonial Stores, Inc., a regional food chain of 450 stores.

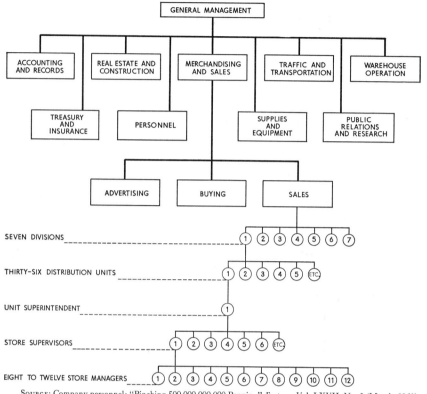

Source: Company personnel; "Pinching 500,000,000,000 Pennies," *Fortune*, Vol. LXVII, No. 3 (March, 1963), p. 177; and "New Crowd Minds Store for the Tea Company," *Business Week*, June 13, 1964, p. 90.

FIG. 7–6.　Organization chart of the Great Atlantic & Pacific Tea Company.

vice president responsible for all merchandising functions and an operating vice president responsible for all operating and service functions.

The executive vice president, through four regional managers and one area manager, directs the merchandising and operating functions of the managers of Ward's 1,029 stores and 9 mail order houses. These regional and area managers, with their staffs, are responsible and accountable for the growth of Ward's sales and the achievement of profit objectives in their respective geographic areas within the framework of the Company's policies and programs.[33]

Responsibilities of Major Executives in Large Companies.　In view of the extended discussion of department store organization, it does not seem necessary to analyze the functions of each department or officer mentioned in the charts of Figures 7–5 through 7–7. Instead, we shall summarize the responsibilities of the chief executives of a national variety store chain and let the student provide his own analysis for the others.

---

[33] Montgomery Ward *Annual Report* for the fiscal year ended January 31, 1958, p. 9. On February 2, 1966, the company was operating 502 retail stores and 864 catalog stores. *Annual Report* for the fiscal year ended February 2, 1966, p. 6.

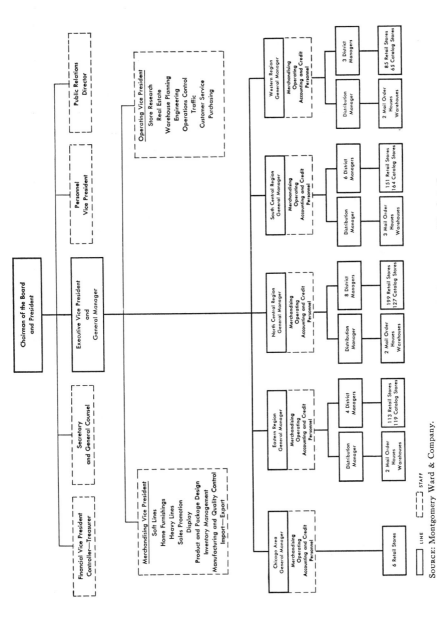

SOURCE: Montgomery Ward & Company.

FIG. 7-7. Organization chart of Montgomery Ward & Company.

The president of this particular firm is charged with the overall administration and coordination of the company. He relies heavily on studies made by the research manager for the policy decisions which come from his office and upon the general counsel for legal advice. The treasurer is responsible for handling company funds, arrangements for financing, and the purchase and management of insurance.

Turning to the operating divisions of the firm, six officers report directly to the president. The controller has responsibilities similar to those of his counterpart in the department store,[34] except that (1) his firm sells for cash so there are no credit and collection problems, (2) insurance problems are handled by the treasurer, and (3) the taking of the physical inventory is a function of the director of retail operations. The advertising director plans and initiates sales and promotional campaigns, prepares the basic material for the advertising budget and has the responsibility of "living" with it.

The merchandise manager is concerned with the buying of merchandise and supplies and with related activities. He establishes retail prices and prepares merchandise bulletins for store managers. In this particular firm he also is in charge of company-operated warehouses and supervises shipments, although in some large chains these duties fall to other executives.

The actual operation of this chain's retail units falls to the director of retail operations, although the director of real estate and maintenance is responsible for obtaining the stores, planning layouts, installing fixtures, and maintenance. All district managers report to the retail operations director, and each store manager to the district manager of his district. Finally, the personnel director performs duties comparable to those already outlined on page 193 for the department store.

MAJOR TRENDS IN STORE ORGANIZATION

Organization in the retail field is currently in a state of flux, although evidence is plentiful to indicate that improvement is quite limited. Some authorities believe that department stores, as an illustration, are encumbered with outdated organization concepts and are operating with "patched-up" structures that fail to meet the requirements of present-day merchandising. Despite such opinions, certain significant structural developments are taking place, particularly in multiunit companies, and these require some discussion in this chapter. Other organizational developments, having particular application to specific functions of retailing, are examined in connection with

---

[34] Cf. p. 193, above.

such functions. The "Buying Committee," for example, is analyzed in Chapter 10.

Some Decentralization Steps in Chain Organizations

Many years ago the direct control exercised by the headquarters of a chain over its stores was so great that it gave rise to the saying: "When a chain-store manager sneezed, the president—seated in his office hundreds of miles away—said, 'Gesundheit.'" Such close control still exists in many chains; in fact, with the newer electronic equipment providing headquarters with more data than ever before, some chains are becoming even more centralized.[35] Despite the foregoing, one of the current major trends in chain-store organization—and this trend extends far beyond the retail field[36]—is that toward decentralization of buying, selling, and sales promotion activities. In some cases—as is true of the Kroger and Safeway firms—divisional headquarters have been established to carry out these activities for a group of stores. In other instances, especially in regard to chains that have been opening a larger type of store, the store (district or zone) manager has been given more authority.

Some Illustrations of Decentralization. The trend toward decentralization can be illustrated by company after company. Sears, Roebuck and Co. has divided its stores into five territorial groups, with each group under a regional vice president. Each of these executives has a considerable degree of autonomy within his geographic area and, as a director of the company, also plays an important role in overall policy determination.[37] While much of the buying function at Sears is still centralized, store managers have freedom to select many of their merchandise items from lists prepared at headquarters.[38] At Montgomery Ward & Company both retail stores and catalog offices have been regrouped as "another step in carrying forward the Company's basic philosophy of decentralization of operations, providing the manager of each district with the local flexibility and authority needed to

---

[35] One of the best analyses of the computer's impact on central control is in Gilbert Burck and the Editors of *Fortune, The Computer Age and Its Potential for Management* (New York: Harper & Row, 1965).

[36] After a careful analysis of centralization *vs* decentralization of management, Max Ways concludes: "The probability increases that decentralization will in the coming decades be carried to lengths undreamed of ten years ago." Cf. his "Tomorrow's Management," *Fortune,* Vol. LXXIV, No. 1 (July, 1966), p. 84.

[37] "Inside Sears, Roebuck," *Printers' Ink,* October 22, 1965, p. 20.

[38] Wingate and Friedlander, *op. cit.,* p. 52; and John McDonald, "Sears Makes It Look Easy," *Fortune,* Vol. LXIX, No. 5 (May, 1964), pp. 218–19.

develop his own strategy and tactics for increasing the Company's competitive position in his particular geographic marketing area."[39]

The decentralization trend has even influenced the organization of food chains which have probably been (and perhaps still remain) the most highly centralized of all types of chains. Safeway Stores, Inc. offers an illustration of the trend, with its chairmen reporting that division managers are now responsible for the "profits of their divisions. Within a broad company policy they are responsible for prices and buy those products they think they can sell best. Safeway managers, too, are given enormous latitude in developing the personalities of their stores with almost complete control over in-store display and merchandising. Our growth pattern would indicate that decentralization has paid off."[40] Although the chain store may still be described as having a centralized organization, it is probably less centralized today than ever before.

Balancing Decentralization and Centralization. The tendency of chains to practice a greater degree of decentralization is in keeping with management trends in many fields of activity. Increasingly it is recognized that "the complexity of modern knowledge, reflected in the complexity of organized action, demands that much of the decision making be decentralized . . . [In fact] the art of modern management consists largely in discovering what to centralize and what to decentralize, and in constructing the channels through which information and decision, generated at many levels, flow."[41]

Some Centralization Moves by Other Multiunit Firms

Department Stores. While chain stores are moving somewhat toward organizational decentralization, the formerly highly decentralized multiunit retail firms—especially in the department store field—are instituting centralization programs to obtain the greater efficiencies and economies of chain-store operation.[42] In some instances, as we have already noted, this move has resulted from growth in the number of branch stores and from the formation of ownership groups.[43] In other cases, the trend is an effort to achieve a company-wide image, as illustrated by R. H. Macy & Company. To

---

[39] *Annual Report,* year ended January 29, 1964, p. 6.

[40] Quoted in "Decentralization Has Paid," *Chain Store Age* (Grocery Executives Edition), July, 1961, p. 15. The Jewel Companies, Inc. offers another example of the decentralization trend. For details, cf. "When People are the Heart of a Business," *Progressive Grocer,* April, 1966, pp. 327–40.

[41] Max Ways, " 'Creative Federalism' and the Great Society," *Fortune,* Vol. LXXIII, No. 1 (January, 1966), p. 222.

[42] For a listing of some of these firms cf. E. B. Weiss, "Meet Our Newest Mass Retailers," *Advertising Age,* June 7, 1965, pp. 124 ff.

[43] Cf. pp. 194–97, above.

provide a single company identity for its 50 department stores from New York to California, each unit must stock (and promote) a certain amount of Macy private brand merchandise, and carry in its advertising a slug identifying it as a part of R. H. Macy & Company.[44] Increasingly company-wide policies are being enforced. Yet, despite these developments, each of the six geographic operating divisions of the company retains far more freedom of action than is common in the usual chain store system.[45]

Departmentized Specialty Stores.   Among the smaller firms, Cherry and Webb Company, Providence, Rhode Island, a women's and children's clothing chain with five stores and two branches, has moved from the separate store concept to centralized operations. The Cherry and Webb reorganization yielded these benefits:

1. Greater efficiency as a centralized merchandising, advertising, and accounting organization
2. Greater flexibility in distribution of stocks and transfer of inventories
3. More use of the New York buying office for enhanced purchasing power and market prestige
4. Trend away from price-emphasis in certain units and toward fashion
5. One company image instead of varying local images
6. Immediate economies of more than $100,000 annually
7. Gross profit increase of at least two percentage points

Discount Houses.   The trend toward centralization among discount stores is probably best illustrated by the current effort of some retailers to decrease the number of leased departments.[46] Originally used to give merchandise breadth, especially in lines with which the discount retailer lacked experience, by the early 1960s as much as 40 percent of discount house sales came from leased areas in the store.[47] Since then, to achieve greater organizational control, a number of major operators have taken over many of their lessees—and with improved financial results.[48] Two Guys had reduced its leased department sales from nearly 50 percent of all in 1959 to 5 percent in 1965.[49] Similar figures for Zayre Corporation show 70 percent in 1957, 30 percent in 1964, and by 1966 the firm's leased departments were

[44] "Macy's Puts Its Stamp on Every Store It Owns," *Business Week,* October 2, 1965, p. 70.

[45] For another attempt (Belk's) to achieve a "balance" between centralization and decentralization, cf. "Holdout in a World of Chains," *ibid.,* October 23, 1965, pp. 113–16.

[46] Cf. the earlier discussion of this subject, p. 22, above.

[47] "Is Success Spoiling Discount Stores?" *Business Week,* June 26, 1965, p. 100.

[48] "Find Discounters Picked Up Sales After Dropping Lessees," *Women's Wear Daily,* April 28, 1966, p. 6.

[49] *Ibid.,* p. 102; and "Two Guys Thrives on Big Store Diet," *Discount Store News,* August 23, 1965, p. 59.

limited to shoes, yarn and fabrics, and snack bars.[50] The K-Marts of the S. S. Kresge Company have taken over many lessees from women's apparel to sporting goods.[51] While leasing remains important in the discount house, a larger-than-ever area of such stores is today subject to the central direction of the key retailer.

Voluntary and Cooperative Chains. In an important sense, a substantial degree of centralized control has gradually been built up in these types of organizations. As former independent retailers have increased their reliance upon the wholesaler's services (store planning, financing, accounting, supervision[52]), they also have acted less independently than formerly was the case. Put another way, greater control has been centralized in the wholesaler.

Separation of Buying and Selling Activities

Closely related to the centralization programs of multiunit organizations —indeed even one of the main stimulants to this development—is the increasing desire to separate buying and selling activities. As noted in our previous discussion, chain-store organizations have long separated these activities, with each of these functions placed in the hands of a major executive. Mail-order houses have followed a comparable plan of organization. Departmentized specialty stores and department stores, however, have typically centralized responsibility for both buying and selling activities in the buyer or department manager. The major arguments for this arrangement are as follows:

1. Separation of buying and selling will result in lack of responsibility for department profits.
2. The person who buys the merchandise should be responsible for selling it.
3. The buyer needs direct consumer contact so that he can interpret correctly the consumer's wants.
4. Only the person who buys the merchandise can convey the necessary information and enthusiasm to the salespeople.
5. Too much expense is involved in developing section managers as the selling heads of departments, since in any event buyers will still be necessary.

---

[50] "Retailing Ruckus," *Wall Street Journal*, July 7, 1964, p. 1; and *ibid.*, April 7, 1966, p. 19.

[51] "Lessees Link with Store Chains," *Discount Store News*, December 27, 1965, p. 2.

[52] For a description of these services in two specific voluntary chains cf. "Foodland's Big Bid," *Food Topics*, July, 1964, p. 7; and "Wetterau Foods, Inc.," *Progressive Grocer*, April, 1966, pp. 302–9.

Reasons for Separation. Despite these arguments, there is today a definite trend for department stores to separate buying and selling responsibilities. Just to illustrate the point: A few years ago R. H. Macy & Company, Inc., was organized with both buying and selling responsibilities centered in department managers; today these activities rest in different hands.[53] Basic to this trend are two factors: (1) the growth in size and number of branch or suburban stores and (2) the impossibility of the main store buyer supervising selling activities in a number of locations and still performing his buying duties. But there are also other pertinent arguments, as follows:

1. Buying and selling are different jobs, which require different types of ability, personality, and training.
2. Combining buying and selling has resulted in buying becoming predominant and overshadowing selling.
3. Suitable emphasis on selling can be obtained only by setting up a sales organization which is divorced from buying.
4. Separation of buying and selling works well in chain stores, even those handling fashion merchandise.
5. Merchandise control records have now been developed to a point where it is no longer necessary for the same person to be responsible for both buying and selling to achieve proper coordination.
6. The tendency in departmentizing is to group merchandise for selling purposes into such combinations as those represented by cruise shops, sport shops, gun shops, and ski shops. This trend sugests that the combinations of goods most strategically suited to sales promotion are not necessarily those best suited to buying.[54]
7. Separation of buying and selling makes it easier to shift salespeople among departments according to need.
8. To obtain efficiency in buying, frequently one man should buy for several departments; if he does, he has little time to handle the selling function.

Organization for Separation. When buying and selling are separated, various organizational plans have been employed. In some instances the separation is as complete as it is in the typical chain-store organization, with buying and selling coordinated at top management level only. Under this plan a merchandise director who heads all buying and a sales director who is responsible for all personal selling and publicity may each report directly to the general manager.[55] Other retailers have separated buying and selling at lower levels of the organization by leaving both responsibilities in the

---

[53] The transition at Macy's is reported by two of the firm's key executives in W. H. Bingham and D. L. Yunich, "Retail Organization," *Harvard Business Review,* Vol. XLIII, No. 4 (July–August, 1965), pp. 129–46.

[54] Cf. the further discussion of this trend on p. 208, below.

[55] For an organization chart showing this arrangement cf. Robinson, Robinson, and Matthews, *op. cit.,* p. 39.

merchandise manager, who then delegates buying to a specialized group of buyers under one executive and selling to division and department sales managers who report to another executive. As is true with all organization plans, the structure followed by any specific retailer will depend on such factors as personal preferences of the key executives, size of the firm, and willingness of the management to experiment in an effort to find the "best" plan for its own purposes.[56]

Regrouping of Merchandise Lines

In keeping with the marketing concept's emphasis on service to the customer, departmentized stores are rethinking their merchandise groupings.[57] Specifically, they seek to regroup and relocate merchandise lines so they conform to the way present day customers wish to buy.[58] The ski enthusiast has little interest in trudging from department to department to purchase a pair of skis (sporting goods), stretch ski pants (men's sportswear or women's sportswear), and ski hose (hosiery); and, to meet his (or her) wishes, all these items and many others have been brought together in the ski shop. In similar fashion stores have developed cruise shops, sports shops, gun shops, bath shops, and junior miss shops; and, according to an executive of May Department Store Company, in the future "there will be even more emphasis on shops."[59]

Not all regrouping has resulted in specialty shops within the store; some of it merely brings together broad merchandise categories.[60] Instead of having various items of children's wear scattered throughout the store, they may be concentrated in a single area; while all women's outerwear may be placed on (say) the second floor.

Although this trend to regroup merchandise may enable the store better to serve the customer, it creates organizational problems. Will the ski shop

---

[56] For some specific illustrations of how different firms have separated buying and selling functions cf. proposals of the Retail Research Institute of the National Retail Merchants Association, *Survey of Organization of Single Unit Department and Specialty Stores,* and *Organization in Multi-Unit Department and Specialty Stores, op. cit.*

[57] On the marketing concept cf. pp. 36–37, above; and E. H. Fram, "Application of the Marketing Concept to Retailing," *Journal of Retailing,* Vol. XLI, No. 2 (Summer, 1965), pp. 19–26.

[58] Frank Burnside refers to this development as "customer-oriented merchandising by classification." Cf. his discussion of "Merchandising by Classification," in *The Buyer's Manual, op. cit.,* pp. 181–92.

[59] Quoted by Wight Martindale, Jr., "May Co. Back from Huddle, Shop Concept a Key Goal," *Women's Wear Daily,* October 20, 1965, p. 12.

[60] E. B. Weiss, "Classification Merchandising Topples Departmental Barriers," *Advertising Age,* August 9, 1965, pp. 75–76; and August 16, 1965, p. 76 ff.

personnel purchase skis, stretch pants, and ski hose; or will the buying be handled by the sporting goods, men's wear, and hosiery buyers? No standard answer to this question has yet emerged: both plans are in use in different stores.

Growing Responsibilities of Personnel Director and Controller

Because of additional problems in connection with personnel—brought about by the necessity for improving productivity of employees, the move to unionize retail store employees, shorter hours and increased wage rates, night and Sunday openings, branch stores, competition from discount houses, and social security legislation—the importance of personnel has been increasingly recognized by both small and large retailers. Consequently, for some years, in chain stores, mail-order houses, department stores, and the larger independent specialty stores, there has been a trend toward making the director of personnel a major executive responsible directly to the proprietor, general manager, or president.[61]

Recent years also have brought additional responsibilities and prestige to the controller. Frequent changes in the social security laws, wide-spread use of the sales tax, an increase in credit selling, the application of electronic data processing to retailing, and periodic revisions of federal income tax requirements have widened the controller's obligations to general management and have made necessary the addition of specialized assistants to his staff.[62] As an illustration of the personnel which he now needs, handling credit alone has become so important that his credit manager now frequently has a staff as large as the entire personnel of the controller's office just a few years ago.

Expansion of Staff Services

Among large scale retailers, various staff services continue to expand in usefulness and in personnel. Merchandise testing, which results in better buying on the store's part, more satisfied customers, and reduced merchandise returns, is being adopted by additional retail firms.[63] Comparison shop-

[61] The director of personnel, of course, should be prepared to assume his responsibilities successfully. On this topic cf. "What a President Should Expect from His Personnel Officer," *Personnel Journal,* April, 1965, p. 208 ff.; and S. K. Datta, "Education and Training of Personnel Managers," *Personnel Management,* March, 1966, pp. 7–8.

[62] The expanding responsibilities of the controller are explored in E. A. Helfert, E. G. May, and M. P. McNair, *Controllership in Department Stores* (Boston, Mass.: Harvard University, Graduate School of Business Administration, 1965); and in W. B. Murphy, "Enlarged Role of the Financial Executive," *Financial Executive,* February, 1966, pp. 32 ff.

[63] On this subject, also cf. pp. 331–32, below.

ping plays a growing role as retailers find themselves faced with an ever-more-competitive market.[64] Recognition of the benefits from applying industrial engineering principles to work simplification and work standards has encouraged some retailers to establish standards bureaus. A public relations staff has been created by many firms. As in other fields, top management in retailing is sponsoring more research as a basis for policy decisions. To implement a policy of offering for sale merchandise of comparable fashion and quality in all departments of the firm, fashion coordinators have been appointed.[65] In some instances two such coordinators are employed: one to provide coordination for wearing apparel and the other to correlate offerings of home furnishings, although apparel continues to receive the greater fashion emphasis.

Staff Services on the Organization Chart. There is no widespread agreement among retailers as to where these various staff services appear in the organization structure. In some instances, a number of them are grouped together and placed under a staff vice president. In contrast, the activities may be distributed throughout the organization to those chiefly concerned. Under the latter arrangement, for example, the heads of merchandise testing and comparison shopping might report to the general merchandise manager, the fashion coordinator to the advertising and sales-promotion manager or to the general merchandise manager, with the research and public relations directors responsible to the general manager. As is true with so many aspects of organization, existing personnel and management preferences play leading roles in determining within each company exactly where these staff services will report.

Long-Range Planning. As yet, few retailers have developed special staffs to aid top management with long-range planning activities. The trend toward this staff service in other fields, however, is so strong that it will likely make itself felt soon in the retail field.

In varying degrees, every chief executive is aware that an important part of his task is to answer two questions:

1. What should be the position of this firm five (ten, twenty) years from now?
2. What must we do in terms of policies and actions to reach that position?

As a practical matter, however, few chief executives find that they can set aside sufficient time to engage in all the detail study and careful analysis

---

[64] Also cf. the discussion on p. 292, below.

[65] The work of the fashion bureau is summarized in Wingate and Friedlander, *op. cit.,* pp. 37–39. For details, cf. K. A. Casey *et al, Profitable Fashion Merchandise Coordination* (rev. ed.; New York: National Retail Merchants Association, 1965). The impact of the fashion coordinator in a specific firm (Montgomery Ward & Company) is related in "Fashion Strategy," *Chain-Store Age* (Executives Edition), December, 1964, pp. 88–96.

essential for valid answers to these questions. So they are turning to a long-range planning staff for help—and the word "help" is chosen deliberately: they, and their boards of directors, must still make the final decisions.

Typically, the director of long-range planning reports directly to the chief executive. But some boards of directors wish to play a direct role in these activities. To this end, they establish long range planning committees composed of board members and the chief executive, supplemented perhaps by one or two other executives and an outside consultant. In such instances, the director of long-range planning may report to this committee, either directly or indirectly through the chief executive.[66]

Changes in the Orthodox Four-Function Structure in Department Stores

The trends discussed above are bringing about many changes in the traditional four-function organization in the department store. In some firms a five-function structure has been created by having the personnel director report directly to the president. Marshall Field & Company, for instance, adopted such a plan as early as 1944. When buying and selling are separated, the former merchandising division is replaced by buying and selling divisions, and thus still another change is created in the traditional pattern.

The late Edward A. Filene proposed a seven-function structure. In his judgment, "selling and personnel must be emphasized as the two major functions of a department store. . . . The prevailing organization [four-function] . . . fails to recognize the vital importance of these two functions . . . , and does not give them proper importance in the organization."[67] To overcome these defects, Mr. Filene proposed the following division of functions: finance, control, operating, personnel, selling (including buying), public relations, and research and planning.

But not all changes in the traditional four-function plan have resulted in more major divisions. Some department stores have simplified their organization by concentrating responsibility in just three or even in two divisions. When the number is reduced to three, publicity and sales promotion are frequently made subordinate to merchandising; and when two divisions are eliminated, the remaining ones are merchandising and store operation.

A High-Level Policy Committee

A policy committee, established to help top management and the board of directors reach major policy decisions, is usually composed of a firm's key

---

[66] The entire subject of long-range planning is explored in B. W. Scott, *Long-Range Planning in American Industry* (New York: American Management Association, Inc., 1965).

[67] Cf. E. A. Filene, W. K. Gabler, and P. S. Brown, *Next Steps Forward in Retailing* (New York: Harper & Bros., 1937), pp. 98–99.

executives plus perhaps an outside consultant and one or two board members. While such committees are not new in the retail field, in recent years they have come to play a more important role and to occupy a now well-established niche in the large organization. Their growing significance may be attributed to the greater emphasis which firms in all fields are placing upon the need for bringing all points of view to bear upon all major decisions.

REVIEW AND DISCUSSION QUESTIONS

1. Discuss and illustrate: "Organization is squarely based upon a systematic and clearly understood division of labor."

2. Do you agree or disagree with the statement that "the firm's organizational task is never completed?" Give the reasons for your opinion.

3. What is meant by a "plural" chief executive? Analyze the pros and cons of such an arrangement.

4. Compare and contrast the organization needs of each of the following: a small food store and a large food chain; a general store and a department store; a mail-order company and a chain selling similar goods.

5. "An important aspect of retail store structure is departmentizing." What is meant by "departmentizing" and what steps would be involved in departmentizing a women's clothing store?

6. Explain the traditional or orthodox organization of a department store in sufficient detail to make clear the major duties and responsibilities of each division.

7. What are the weaknesses of the traditional structure of the department store and what steps have been taken to minimize them?

8. How may one rationalize the conditions and circumstances responsible for the wide range of activities and functions supervised by the operating or store manager?

9. Visit a department store which is part of an ownership group and report to the class the division of labor between store personnel and the group's central office personnel.

10. "Chain-store companies vary in organization because of differences in types of merchandise handled, in services performed, in size of individual stores, and in territory covered." Explain how each of these factors has an influence on the organization structure.

11. Compare and contrast the general characteristics of chain-store organization with the four-function department-store organization.

12. How do you account for the trend among chain stores toward decentralization as some other multiunit retailers are moving toward centralization? Give examples of these trends.

13. Through a study of library materials and visits to a nearby discount house, outline the differences and similarities between the structure of this organization and the more conventional type of retailer.

14. Discuss the reasons giving rise to the present regrouping of merchandise lines and the relation of such regrouping to organization.
15. What is meant by the term "staff services"? Why are they being expanded in retail stores? Give examples of their expansion.

SUPPLEMENTARY READINGS

ALBERS, H. H. *Principles of Organization and Management* (2d ed.; New York: John Wiley & Sons, 1965). The student without a basic background in organization will find this volume a helpful one.

ALDERSON, WROE, AND GREEN, P. E. *Planning and Problem Solving in Marketing* (Homewood, Ill.: Richard D. Irwin, Inc., 1964), Chapter 19, "Designing Marketing Organizations." In this chapter the authors deal with certain principles of organization which have immediate applicability to retailing.

BAILEY, J. K. "Organization Planning—Whose Responsibility?" *Stores,* September, 1964, pp. 49–53. The duties of the organization planning manager are detailed in this article.

BINGHAM, W. H., and YUNICH, D. L. "Retail Organization," *Harvard Business Review,* Vol. XLIII, No. 4 (July–August, 1965), pp. 129–46. The evolution of R. H. Macy & Co., Inc., (1) from the traditional organization with both buying and selling responsibilities centered in department managers (2) to its present structure in which buying and selling responsibilities rest in different hands, is told by two key Macy executives. For a successful firm pursuing the opposite policy, cf. "Prestige Store Grows Without Losing Gloss," *Business Week,* April 9, 1966, pp. 58–62.

CASEY, K. A., *et al. Profitable Fashion Merchandise Coordination* (rev. ed.; New York: National Retail Merchants Association, 1965). The work of the fashion coordinator is detailed in this volume. Also cf. "Fashion Strategy," *Chain Store Age* (Variety Store-General Merchandise Managers Ed.), December, 1964, pp. 88–96.

DANIEL, D. R. "Team at the Top," *Harvard Business Review,* Vol. XLIII, No. 2 (March–April, 1965), pp. 74–82. One of the newer concepts in organization, the "plural" executive, is illustrated and examined in this article.

DILL, W. R. "Business Organizations," in MARCH, J. G. (ed.), *Handbook of Organization* (Chicago, Ill.: Rand McNally & Company, 1965), pp. 1071–1106. The author presents a review of (1) "the essential characteristics of business organizations" and (2) "the theory and empirical knowledge that have been built up around them."

HELFERT, E. A., MAY, E. G., AND MCNAIR, M. P. *Controllership in Department Stores* (Boston, Mass.: Harvard University Graduate School of Business Administration, 1965). Current trends in the controller's responsibilities and organizational status are covered in this analysis. Also cf. MURPHY, W. B. "Enlarged Role of the Financial Executive," *Financial Executive,* February, 1966, p. 32 ff.

Jewel Companies, Inc. "Where People are the Heart of a Business," *Progressive Grocer,* April, 1966, pp. 327–40. The management philosophy and decentralized organization of this successful firm are set forth in this helpful article.

McDonald, John. "Sears Makes It Look Easy," *Fortune,* Vol. LXIX, No. 5 (May, 1964), pp. 120–27 ff. The interplay of centralization and decentralization in the organization of this leading retailer is portrayed in this article. On this subject also cf. "Macy's Puts Its Stamp on Every Store It Owns," *Business Week,* October 2, 1965, pp. 64–70; and "Holdout in a World of Chains," *ibid.,* October 23, 1965, pp. 113–16.

Miller, R. L. "The Quality of Selling and Organization Structure," *Journal of Retailing,* Vol. XXXVII, No. 2 (Summer, 1961), pp. 28–32. The author believes that buying and selling are so closely related that they should not be separated in the retailing organization.

National Retail Merchants Association. *The Buyer's Manual* (4th ed.; New York, 1965). In connection with the present chapter cf. Bond, R. C., "Department Store Organization," chapter 2; Brown, E. J., "The Merchandising Division," chapter 3; Bluthenthal, David, "The Buyer as Manager of People," chapter 4; Burnside, Frank, "Merchandising by Classification," chapter 17; and O'Brien, A. J., "Working with the Branch Store," chapter 31.

———. *Survey of Organization of Single Unit Department and Specialty Stores* (New York: The Association, 1959), and *Organization in Multi-Unit Department and Specialty Stores* (1961). The Retail Research Institute of the Association summarizes in these two publications the results of its extensive organizational studies.

Scott, B. W. *Long-Range Planning in American Industry* (New York: American Management Association, Inc., 1965). "The primary purpose of this book is to contribute toward an understanding of corporate long-range planning—an important area of managerial responsibility which so far has not received very much detailed analysis in business literature," especially in that dealing with retailing.

Weiss, E. B. "Classification Merchandising Topples Departmental Barriers," *Advertising Age,* August 9, 1965, pp. 75–76; and August 16, 1965, pp. 76 ff. The impact of current trends in merchandise grouping on the older department arrangement is examined by a close student of the retail field.

Wingate, J. W., and Friedlander, J. S. *The Management of Retail Buying* (Englewood Cliffs, N.J.: Prentice-Hall, Inc., 1963). Part I of this excellent book contains a helpful chapter on "Organization for Buying: Single and Multi-Unit Stores."

Woll, Milton. "Store Organization: How to Build in the Capacity for Change," *Stores,* October, 1961, pp. 18–21; "Modern Organization Structure for Large Stores," *ibid.,* November, 1961, pp. 36–38; and "Modern Retail Organization Structure," *ibid.,* December, 1961, pp. 15–17. These three authoritative discussions provide a thorough appraisal of the conditions responsible for recent changes in organization and reveal the nature of these changes. Also cf. the summary of a seminar on "The Management of Branch Stores," *ibid.,* May, 1965, pp. 10–14 ff.

8
CHAPTER

Retail Personnel Management

In the previous chapter the significance of personnel—the human factor —in the successful conduct of a retail enterprise was emphasized. Today, in stores of all types, personnel problems of various kinds confront management in both existing and new units; and these problems are intensified as old stores are expanded and new ones are opened.

SCOPE AND AIMS OF PERSONNEL MANAGEMENT

Personnel management in a retail organization involves the handling of the various problems connected directly with the organization's employees.[1] The more important activities include those of selecting, training, and compensating employees; maintaining adequate personnel performance; carrying out employee service activities; and hearing and seeking satisfactory adjustments to employees' complaints. To deal successfully with these activities, the retailer must both understand and apply the principles which have gradually been developed in the area of human relations.

Of course, the immediate aim of personnel activities is the development of a staff that will perform the other retail functions satisfactorily from both the retailer's and the customer's points of view. In other words, personnel work is a facilitating or service function, engaged in to make more effective the performance of other selling and sales-supporting activities. To accomplish this objective, there must be close cooperation between management personnel throughout the company and the members of the personnel division. As is true of other retail activities, the ultimate aim of personnel

---

[1] The student who lacks an overall understanding of the personnel field will benefit from the reading of one of the general texts in this area, such as D. S. Beach, *Personnel: The Management of People at Work* (New York: Macmillan Co., 1965).

management is to aid in maximizing the store's profit. In the final analysis, personnel management is a dollar-and-cents matter.

INCREASING EMPHASIS ON PERSONNEL MANAGEMENT

The primary significance of personnel management lies in the fact that retailing is a "humanized" business involving frequent contact between the firm's customers and its employees. In fact, it is often said that the impression the customer receives from employees does "as much as, if not more than, anything else to build and maintain the store's image."[2] Despite the importance of the employee, only in recent decades has personnel management been widely recognized as an important activity of the retailer. In 1882 the owner-operator of a general store handled many of his personnel problems simply by posting the following:

RULES FOR CLERKS

1. This store must be opened at Sunrise. No mistake. Open 6 o'clock A.M. Summer and Winter. Close about 8:30 or 9 P.M. the year round.

2. Store must be swept—dusted—doors and windows opened—lamps filled, trimmed and chimneys cleaned—counters, base shelves and show cases dusted—pens made—a pail of water also the coal must be brought in before breakfast, if there is time to do it and attend to all the customers who call.

3. The store is not to be opened on the Sabbath day unless absolutely necessary and then only for a few minutes.

4. Should the store be opened on Sunday the clerks must go in alone and get tobacco for customers in need.

5. The clerk who is in the habit of smoking Spanish Cigars—being shaved at the barbers—going to dancing parties and other places of amusement and being out late at night—will assuredly give his employer reason to be ever suspicious of his integrity and honesty.

6. Clerks are allowed to smoke in the store provided they do not wait on women with a "stogie" in the mouth.

7. Each clerk must pay not less than $5.00 per year to the Church and must attend Sunday School regularly.

8. Men clerks are given one evening a week off for courting and two if they go to prayer meeting.

9. After the 14 hours in the store the leisure hours should be spent mostly in reading.[3]

Today, however, good personnel management is considered so essential by the larger retailers that the personnel director sometimes occupies a position

---

[2] J. E. Stafford and T. V. Greer, "Consumer Preference for Types of Salesmen: A Study of Independence-Dependence Characteristics," *Journal of Retailing*, Vol. XLI, No. 2 (Summer, 1965), p. 27.

[3] Carson, Pirie, Scott & Co., *"We" and Our Business* (Chicago, 1927), p. 20.

in the retail organization comparable with that of the merchandise manager and operating manager. Increased attention is being devoted to problems of personnel in both small and large stores.

Some Overall Causal Factors

Among the factors which, over the past four decades, have made businessmen more personnel-conscious are these: a federal administration generally sympathetic to labor; legislation requiring collective bargaining with unions when desired by employees; the role now played by labor unions; federal and state wage and hour laws; social security legislation; state unemployment insurance laws; employee demands for a broad list of "fringe" benefits; and legislation banning job discrimination based on "race, color, religion, sex, or national origin."[4] Among retail stores the above developments alone would have led to the greatest emphasis on personnel in history; but this emphasis has been even more pronounced because of the gradual recognition of a number of other factors pertaining more specifically to retailing. The more important of these factors require analysis.

Causal Factors within Retailing

Good People Bring Good Results. Progressive retailers realize that the skillful handling of personnel activities—what W. H. Bingham, President, R. H. Macy & Company, once referred to as "the successful management of people"—is as important to the success of the store, for example, as the merchandise carried and the fixtures and equipment employed. As a matter of fact, competing stores are frequently quite similar in regard to merchandise, equipment, and sales promotion, so that personnel becomes the distinguishing feature. In big league baseball there is an old saying: "If you want to be a good manager, get good ball players." This saying is just as applicable to the general manager of a retail store: "If you want to run a successful store, get (and keep) good people."

Customer Good Will and Repeat Business. In the very small store, customer good will is the result of personal contact with the proprietor. But in other stores, as has already been emphasized, customer impression is built upon relationships with employees of all types—salespeople, telephone

---

[4] Title VII of the Civil Rights Act of 1964. An analysis of this Title will be found in Eileen Ahern, "Equal Employment Opportunity," *Personnel,* July–August, 1965, pp. 40–44; and "What the Civil Rights Act Means to Your Company," *Management Review,* January, 1966, pp. 38–41. For some of the Title's implications for retailers, cf. two columns by Samuel Feinberg in *Women's Wear Daily,* July 16, 1965, p. 7, and July 20, 1965, p. 10.

operators, elevator operators, credit department employees, deliverymen, and adjustment department employees. If the employees are courteous, alert, friendly, and helpful to the customer, customer good will is created; if they are not, the result is the development of ill will which even extensive advertising cannot overcome. Probably far more customers quit any store because of dissatisfaction with employees and their attitudes than leave because of discontent with the merchandise.

Human Relations in Retailing. In retailing, as in other fields, personnel management today seems to be entering a new era.[5] Thoughtful retailers have been impressed by such developments as the gradual deterioration in the quality of selling service offered by their salespeople, by lowered employee morale, and by the limited number of young people of ability who are entering retailing because of (what they consider to be) unsatisfactory working relationships. Consequently, these retailers have resolved to minimize such problems by improving human relations in their firms. Specifically, this means that they approach all aspects of personnel work from the point of view of the people involved. What is it about Mr. Jones in the interviewing office that seems to drive away applicants for positions, while the majority of those interviewed by Mr. White accept the jobs offered to them? What human factors are involved in the fact that employee morale is lower in Department A than in Department B (or Store A than in Store B) when the hours of work and compensation are the same? Is it because of differences in employees' attitudes that, in identical departments of two stores, many more customer complaints develop in one than in the other?

Out of this emphasis retailers have gradually come to recognize a number of human relations principles which can be applied not only in their personnel work, but in all their relationships with people. These may be stated as follows:

1. We do not like to be dominated by others.
2. We are more likely to agree with those we like personally.
3. All of us like to feel important, to be recognized as individuals, and to do work that is significant.
4. We want to be in the "know."
5. Emotions, as well as objective analysis, are important in our reactions to situations.
6. We accept change slowly.
7. In our job, we want good working conditions, a fair wage, a chance to get ahead, and to feel secure.

---

[5] The development and application of the "new era" concepts in personnel management are set forth in Elizabeth Marting and Dorothy Macdonald (Editors), *Management and Its People* (New York: American Management Association, Inc., 1965).

In applying the foregoing principles the retailer must exercise common sense if he is to achieve the proper balance. He must not be so "soft" in his relations with employees that they begin to feel sorry for themselves and fail to fulfill their assigned tasks. At the same time, he must not be so "tough" that employees lose all initiative because of their fear of him.

Many Inexperienced Employees.   Retail personnel work is particularly important because many of the employees of the usual retail store are young and lack previous business training. Large numbers of young people leaving high school, business school, or college find their first jobs in retail stores. Moreover, since many of these persons soon leave to seek work elsewhere, to get married, or for some other reason, it becomes necessary for the store to employ a constant stream of inexperienced people. In many stores two thirds of the women employees are less than twenty-five years of age. With a rising proportion of married women seeking employment, an increasing number of inexperienced older workers have also sought jobs in retailing.[6]

Rapid Rate of Employee Turnover.   The high rate of turnover among retail employees is the result of many factors including belief that better wages, hours, and working conditions are available elsewhere; poor supervision; poor training which leads to resignations or discharges; many young and inexperienced personnel; high percentage of women employed; dissatisfaction with immediate superiors or with the general management; dislike of a particular community; injuries; poor health; restlessness on employee's part; and low morale. Although the rate of turnover varies widely in stores of different sizes and types, it often rises to 50 percent or more[7] thereby adding substantially to the operating costs involved in hiring and training personnel and in unemployment compensation payments.

As a general rule, close management attention to the turnover problem is essential whenever the rate is higher than 25 to 35 percent. As we shall see in more detail in later paragraphs, the retailer may attempt to solve the turnover problem by the following methods:

1. More careful selection
2. Better training
3. Using a compensation plan which the employees consider fair and which results in an annual income at least equal to that which can be secured in similar work elsewhere
4. A well-conceived promotion policy

---

[6] Three out of ten married women now work outside the home. Half of the working women are over 40. Henry Levinson, "Managing Women at Work," *Management Review,* January, 1965, p. 50.

[7] A 50 percent turnover means that a number equal to 50 percent of the store's average number of employees left the store's employment in the course of a year.

5. Adequate employee service activities
6. Hearing and seeking satisfactory adjustments to employees' complaints and grievances
7. Introducing a pension system
8. Recognizing the importance of morale in effective performance, even to the point of employing outside agencies to conduct "morale surveys" as a step toward better human relations within the store

Substantial Cost of Executive Training and Replacement. By no means is the labor turnover problem confined to those below the management level. A variety chain executive has informed one of the authors that over a ten-year period 47 percent of those in his firm's manager training program withdrew or were let out within the first year of their employment. An additional 13 percent did not complete the second year of the program and 10 percent more failed to finish the third year. This executive estimates the cost of training a manager at $8,000. The situation in department and specialty stores, in supermarkets and discount houses, is much the same. When it is realized that department stores, for example, require one "executive" for every ten employees because of their decentralized structure, the magnitude of the executive turnover problem is apparent.

Large Number of Part-Time Employees. Wide fluctuations in retail sales, both from hour to hour and seasonally, have long encouraged retailers to employ part-time personnel. Among a broad sample of supermarkets, over 48 percent of all employers were on a part-time basis.[8] One authority claims that in retailing as a whole the use of part-time personnel is expanding far more rapidly than total retail employment.[9] Increasingly retailers are finding it difficult to locate a sufficient number of able people to "man" their part-time openings.[10] Consequently, they are taking on individuals less well educated and more difficult to train with the result that the personnel management task is made more difficult.

Expansion of Many Retail Firms. The personnel problems of some retailers are increasing simply because their companies are growing so rapidly. With over 250,000 employees already, each year the expansion program of Sears, Roebuck and Co. requires the hiring, training, and motivating of thousands of additional employees.[11] Over 24,000 new employees are called for during the 1964–72 period by the growth projected for

[8] *The Super Market Industry Speaks, 1966* (Chicago, Ill.: Super Market Institute, 1966), p. 29.
[9] Aaron Scheinfeld, board chairman of Manpower, Inc., quoted by Edward Gold, "Retail Part-Time Hiring Climbs 400% in Four Years," *Women's Wear Daily,* May 12, 1964, p. 18.
[10] "Jingle Bells Ring Out Call for Part-time Help," *Business Week,* November 27, 1965, pp. 38 and 40.
[11] "Inside Sears, Roebuck," *Printers' Ink,* October 22, 1965, p. 20.

Federated Department Stores, Inc.[12] And by no means is all the expansion confined to the large-scale retailers. As we have already noted, many of today's smaller retailers are modernizing and enlarging their establishments.[13] Among the food chains, many of the smaller ones are growing more rapidly than the large firms.[14]

High Wage-to-Sales Ratio. The fact that wages commonly represent more than one half of the retailer's total expense is another reason for the emphasis on personnel work. In a competitive market and with a low ratio of profit to sales, no retailer can ignore a factor responsible for such a large part of his total operating expense.

Various Kinds of Ability Needed. The significance of personnel work is further evidenced by the fact that, especially in the large retail store, employees perform many different kinds of jobs. Not only are people needed for selling positions which require different qualifications; the same also holds true for those engaged in sales-supporting activities. The retailer requires people of various degrees of skill and intelligence—checkout girls, stock room boys, store managers, basement salespeople, fur department saleswomen, heating engineers, watch repairmen, garage mechanics, testing laboratory technicians, registered nurses, dieticians, accountants, pharmacists, economists, and top management people.

Employees' Requirements. The retailer should realize that his employees have many legitimate wants which he must satisfy in varying degree; if he does not, he will pay the penalty of bad personnel relationships. His employees want good working conditions; satisfactory wages and hours; security of employment; recognition for good work and for suggestions; vacations with pay; the privilege of purchasing merchandise at a discount; treatment as individuals rather than as cogs in a machine; a feeling of importance; a chance to work to their full capacities and to use their maximum abilities and aptitudes; and, in many cases, an opportunity for advancement. Although it is expensive for the employer to meet the demands of his employees, it is sometimes even more expensive for him not to, especially if the result should be a strike with its costly consequences. It is the job of personnel management to reconcile the wishes of employees with the ability of the employer to meet them.

Retailers face a difficult task in meeting employees' demands because the conditions surrounding retail employment work against high wages, short

---

[12] *Women's Wear Daily,* February 21, 1963, p. 40.

[13] Cf. pp. 141–43, above.

[14] "A Profile of the Corporate Food Chains, 1960–1965," *Chain Store Age* (Supermarket Executives Ed.), May, 1965, p. 64b; and "Who The Expansionists Are," *ibid.,* April, 1966, p. 63.

hours, and security of employment. Faced with keen competition from other retailers, the individual retailer is in no position to raise prices as a means of paying higher wages; while a justification for relatively high wages is lacking in view of the low physical requirements and the fact that, in large measure, retail work does not require much education, experience, or formalized training. Customer buying habits frequently require him to operate his store for long hours—and currently the hours involved are even greater than those of a decade ago. As for security of employment, the seasonal fluctuation in retail sales is so large that it is difficult to provide security for all employees. Even in drugstores, with sales less subject to seasonal influences than for some other types of establishments, December business is twice that of January;[15] and many retailers experience additional sales peaks preceding Easter and during back-to-school days. Sales variations also take place among the different days of the week and hours of the day. Although in recent years retailers have greatly improved the stability of employment of "regular" employees by employing part-time workers and "extras"—to illustrate, the percentage of part-time employees in supermarkets increased steadily from 30 percent in 1951 to 48 percent in 1966[16]—what this does is to transfer the insecurity to these latter employees.

IMPORTANCE OF DEFINITE PERSONNEL POLICIES

In view of their significance to the retailer, much thought should be given to the formulation of his personnel policies. Like other policies, they should be clear and definite—which, where practicable, means they should be in writing; formulated with great care; administered consistently; stable, yet flexible enough to meet changing conditions; sufficiently comprehensive to cover all major aspects of employee-management relationships; and widely publicized among employees. Especially is the statement of definite policies important to the large-scale retailer since, in such firms, many decisions affecting personnel are made by minor executives. Unless these officers know and follow the firm's policies, employee ill will is inevitable.

Among the areas in which definite personnel policies should be formulated are these:

1. Authority and responsibility of the personnel division and its relationships with other divisions and departments
2. Recruiting personnel and developing sources of supply

---

[15] For a chart of monthly sales for drug departments in discount houses, cf. *Discount Store News,* August 22, 1966, p. 34.

[16] *The Super Market Industry Speaks, 1966, op. cit.,* p. 29.

3. Selecting personnel—number and types of interviews, use of tests, and similar devices
4. Training methods and content of training—for new and existing personnel
5. Compensation and compensation methods
6. Working conditions—hours of work, number of days per week, and vacations
7. Induction of new employees
8. Promotions, transfers, and terminations
9. Personnel reviews and ratings
10. Employee discounts on purchases
11. Employee cafeterias and lunchrooms
12. Personnel complaints and methods of handling them
13. Unions and labor organizations

CARRYING OUT PERSONNEL ACTIVITIES

Personnel activities in the small store are usually handled directly by the proprietor or manager. Since the number of employees is very small and since the close personal relationship between proprietor and employee frequently leads to understanding of one another's position, the proprietor need spend little time on personnel work. In the medium-sized retail organization, in which 15 or 20 people may be employed, personnel work is more exacting. For example, more time must be spent in hiring and training employees; perhaps training will take so much time that the task must be turned over to a "sponsor."[17] In the chain-store system operating fairly small units, some of these duties may be turned over to district managers or supervisors. Yet the majority of all personnel activities still center in the proprietor or store manager.

It is in the larger retail organization that personnel work begins to assume significant proportions, and that management must recognize the need for a constructive personnel program. In the chain-store company, the department store, and the giant discount house, the mere number of employees creates a hiring and training problem. Lack of direct association between the executives who formulate general policies and employees may result in misunderstandings and ill will, which must be minimized. Consequently, there is a need for supervisors who are acquainted with the firm's personnel policies and who are both able and willing to put these policies into effect. To fulfill this need, personnel departments or divisions have been created.[18]

In a real sense, however, it must be emphasized that personnel work is

---

[17] Cf. p. 234, below.
[18] Cf. the discussion on pp. 193 and 209, above.

performed by every employee and executive of a store, regardless of whether he is or is not in the personnel department. In part, this statement is valid since many retailers rely upon present employees for the training and development of new people: thus in the May Department Stores "every executive is responsible for developing his successor well in advance of when he may be needed."[19] But, more importantly, the statement is true because a successful personnel program is based on good human relations throughout the entire organization, and what each individual in the organization does is significant to this end. The superintendent in a chain operation who undermines the firm's manager-training program by referring to it as "impractical," does much to weaken the entire personnel program. And the department manager who is so lacking in his understanding of human relations that he attempts to dominate everyone in this department is merely complicating the personnel department's employee-selection program by increasing turnover among his employees.

EMPLOYMENT PROCEDURE

Recruiting an adequate force of retail employees involves at least four important steps: (1) making careful job analyses and preparing adequate job specifications or descriptions; (2) developing satisfactory sources of supply; (3) selecting from among the applicants by means of application forms, interviews, tests, and physical examinations; and (4) introducing the new employee to the store and to his job. In addition, large-scale retailers frequently find it essential to maintain a contingent force and a file of prospective employees.

Job Analyses and Job Specifications

A job analysis is a complete study of the job. It consists of studying the exact work to be done, the quantity and quality of work expected, the best ways to do it, and the desired characteristics of the employee. In the course of the analysis, facts are developed with respect to such matters as the physical effort required; the working conditions—work environment and safety hazards—involved; the experience that is necessary because of job complexity; the responsibility required for material and equipment; the need for dependability and accuracy in the handling of funds, figures, and facts; the mental keenness called for to meet situations and solve problems presented by the job; and the leadership qualities necessary to organize and

---

[19] "How Top Retailers Build Executives," *Business Week*, June 5, 1965, p. 88.

direct the work of others. The analysis should also include hours worked and job evaluation.[20]

When a job analysis has been completed, the results should be used to draw up what is known as a "job specification" or "job description" for the particular type of work.[21] This specification is useful in finding persons to fill jobs, in setting up tests for placement purposes, and in transferring certain of the store's present employees to jobs for which they are better equipped. It is a guide to the training department and to the department head or supervisor in deciding what kind of training is desirable for employees performing various jobs. It helps in making interstore comparisons since it gives common titles to similar jobs in other stores. In securing the data the management obtains a better understanding of working conditions and what is required of each employee; and such information is the first step toward improvement. In addition, the job specification facilitates the delegation process since it shows employees exactly what is expected of them, especially if the information is used by the management to set up employee guides or work charts.[22]

Sources of Personnel

With detailed job specifications available or—where these do not exist—with a fairly clear-cut idea of the type of person desired, the retailer is now ready to look for people who have the desired qualifications. For many positions, this will not be difficult since some people take the initiative and apply in person or by correspondence for jobs. Many stores keep availability files and hire qualified employees in order of application. Still other prospects are recommended to the store by its employees and customers.[23]

However, most retailers find it necessary to seek out people if they want the best available. High schools, business schools, and colleges are sources that may be utilized to advantage, including those specialized institutions which exist to develop personnel for definite fields, such as the Academy of Food Marketing at St. Joseph's College in Philadelphia, the Institute of Retail Management at New York University, the Fashion Institute of Tech-

---

[20] For a discussion of job evaluation, cf. pp. 253–55, below.

[21] This distinction between job analysis and job specification will be clear if it is remembered that the specification is the report of the type of work and the qualifications necessary therefor as discovered by the analysis. For a more extended treatment of this whole subject cf. J. A. Patton, C. L. Littlefield, and S. A. Self, *Job Evaluation* (3d ed.; Homewood, Ill.: Richard D. Irwin, Inc., 1964), Part II, "Job Analysis and Description."

[22] J. D. Miller, "Written Job Description Helps Delegation Process," *Administrative Management*, January, 1966, p. 45.

[23] J. C. Ullman, "Employee Referrals: Prime Tool for Recruiting Workers," *Personnel*, May–June, 1966, pp. 30–35.

nology, and the Food Distribution Center at the University of Southern California. Stockholders may be asked to suggest possible candidates for positions.[24] Government and private employment agencies may be approached. When a store needs a number of people, it may use classified or regular space advertisements in newspapers. If an executive position is open, the store's personnel should be reviewed carefully, inquiries should be made among vendors familiar with the organization and among executives of other stores, and specialized employment agencies may be called upon.

As a means of making the college a greater source of employees, some retailers regularly send representatives to interview members of the graduating class.[25] A few retailers, especially chains and department stores, have gone beyond this and established summer or part-time employment programs for college and high school students, hoping that such experience will "sell" participants on the particular retailer for their after-college years and encourage the participants to "talk up" retailing as a career to their classmates.[26] A drug chain, in addition to offers of loans and part-time jobs to pharmacy school students, also attempts to attract high school students through weekend work. Some retail trade associations—the National Retail Merchants Association, for example—have also undertaken programs to encourage more college students to enter the retail field.

Selecting Personnel

Long ago, in his *Republic,* Plato stated a truth that explains in part the difficulty in selecting employees: ". . . no two persons are born exactly alike, but each differs from each in natural endowments, one being suited for one occupation and another for another. . . ." After having decided upon the general characteristics needed by employees in various positions and having become familiar with the sources from which they may be drawn, the next important step is to acquire knowledge regarding candidates who differ "in natural endowments," so that the store may hire those persons best meeting its requirements. The sources of this knowledge are as follows: (1)

[24] A "Dear Stockholder" letter from the personnel vice-president of W. T. Grant Company reads, in part, as follows: "Perhaps you are aware of such a young man, preferably between the ages of 22 and 30, who is seeking a new career. If so, and you believe he might have some interest in our Company, would you list his name and address on the enclosed post card and drop it in the mail. We will arrange for interviews."

[25] And some of these representatives make the serious mistake of promising too much! Cf. E. L. Zwerski, "Oversell: A Major Pitfall in College Recruitment," *Personnel Journal,* March, 1966, pp. 167–68.

[26] The summer-time plan used by Neiman-Marcus (Dallas, Fort Worth, and Houston) is outlined in "New Approach to College Boards," *Women's Wear Daily,* July 20, 1965, p. 20.

application forms, (2) applicant's references, (3) preliminary interviews, (4) tests, (5) physical examinations, and (6) final interviews. Although the order may vary from firm to firm, these six sources of information about the applicant are employed by most large retailers. In contrast, the proprietor of the small store usually limits himself to the interview and references.

Application Forms and References.   Some retailers—Safeway Stores, Inc., for example—use a very simple one-page preliminary application form. The form, which calls for a brief description of the applicant's experience, education, type of job sought, and expected salary, is designed merely to eliminate the obviously undesirable candidates without going to the expense of processing the company's regular four-page application.

Regardless of whether a preliminary application form is or is not used, the regular application forms used by retailers—while not so lengthy as they once were—contain many questions. These questions relate to the applicant's personal and family background, his present living conditions, health, and previous employment. Information is sought in regard to schools attended and progress made before the applicant ended his formal education. In some cases the applicant may be asked to submit a transcript of his high school or college record as well as his photograph. Questions will be asked to ascertain why the applicant left previous employers, why he desires the type of work for which he is applying, and why he wishes to secure work with this particular retail organization. Finally, the applicant is asked to give the names of several persons as references.

Preliminary Interviews.   With the information provided by the application blank at hand and some candidates possibly eliminated, the personnel manager—or the proprietor in the case of the small store—is ready to proceed with a preliminary interview of prospective employees. These interviews are usually quite brief, sometimes lasting no more than fifteen minutes. The interviewer seeks information as to basic interests and fields of proficiency such as sales work, typing, or personnel activities, as well as voice, appearance, use of English, poise, self-confidence, and attitude toward work. He tries to study the applicant by getting him to do the talking.[27]

Tests.   There are wide differences of opinion among retail personnel men as to the value of the four main kinds of tests for applicants—intelligence, aptitude, skill, and personality.[28] Some retailers, especially in the

[27] An excellent guide to interview techniques is provided by G. A. Bassett, *Practical Interviewing* (New York: American Management Association, Inc., 1965).

[28] These various types of tests are discussed more fully in R. M. Guion, *Personnel Testing* (New York: McGraw-Hill Book Co., Inc., 1965); and Daniel Peck, "Personnel Tests and Services," reprinted from *Administrative Management,* December, 1965.

department store field, believe that intelligence or mental ability tests are so important that they require each applicant to take a test. They may even refuse to hire persons for specific jobs unless their intelligence quotients fall within certain ranges: if an applicant's I.Q. is too low, he may not be able to do the job; if it is too high, he may be bored with it so that employee turnover is rapid. However, it is doubtful if more than 25 to 30 percent of the department stores use intelligence tests and, even though one authority has recommended that they be given to all applicants for positions with food chains,[29] probably fewer than 15 percent of all largescale retailers require them.

Aptitude tests, which are probably somewhat more widely used by retailers than are intelligence tests, attempt to measure potential as distinguished from developed capacity for learning a certain kind of work. To illustrate, the New York State Employment Service has developed a sales aptitude test battery which—it is claimed by the Service—"is an effective instrument when combined with other pertinent information about an individual in making predictions of probable job performance in the sales field."[30] Some retailers claim considerable success with these aptitude tests, and certainly they are being used by a growing number of firms.[31] Yet many retailers have been disappointed in the results. Apparently, extensive and careful research is still needed. Consequently, the great majority of stores, particularly small ones, place but limited faith in aptitude tests.

For certain types of jobs, more reliance is placed by retailers on what are variously known as skill, job, or trade tests. These tests have been developed to show present skill along certain lines. For example, a stenographer may be given a test to indicate her speed in taking dictation and in typing, as well as to show the number of errors she makes. A deliveryman may be given a test on local geography. However, it is so difficult to devise job tests for selling positions that they are used for sales applicants by only a few companies.

Personality tests are based on the assumption that certain personality traits (friendliness, flexibility, sociability, stability) are essential to success and that, by measuring these traits in an individual, his success or failure may be predicted. There is no doubt that retailers and other businessmen are showing increased interest in personality tests but no reliable estimate of the extent of their use is presently available. Recently one observer gave

---

[29] E. M. Harwell, "Employee Tests for Food Chains," *Chain Store Age* (Supermarket Executives Ed.), July, 1965, p. 19.

[30] For an analysis of tests for selling positions, cf. "Can Salesmen Be Tested?" *Dun's Review and Modern Industry,* March, 1966, pp. 40–41 ff.

[31] "Psychological Aptitude Tests for Potential Execs Are Being Used Increasingly by Discount Chains," *Discount Store News,* May 16, 1966, p. 14.

this harsh opinion of personality tests: they "have had a dismal record as predictors of job success. This [result] is not because personality is unimportant, but because the questionnaires and objective check lists so far devised bear little relationship to the behavior of the person who fills them out."[32] And another student states his conviction that "a skilled interviewer can learn more about an applicant's personality traits . . . than all the personality tests combined."[33] However, other observers concluded that, properly used, these tests can make a contribution to the selection process.[34]

In summary, the use of various types of tests has grown considerably in recent years as psychologists have made improvements in techniques and as retailers have recognized their value in avoiding mistakes in the selection process.[35] In addition to tests which they give, some retailers use outside testing facilities of various kinds designed not only to assist in selection but also to help in the upgrading of persons already employed.[36] Yet most retail personnel people still consider tests of the kinds described chiefly as additional "screens" through which applicants must pass. They recognize that "tests are nothing more than tools designed to help management improve the accuracy of its personnel decisions relating to employment and promotion to key positions. They should never be the sole criterion for any decision."[37] In other words, they supplement other information upon which judgments are made concerning decisions to hire employees.

Physical Examinations. Physical examinations are not used by many small or medium-sized stores, and even in the large retail organization they are often on a voluntary basis. This policy is probably unwise. Retail store work is so hard on those who are not physically fit that all stores would do well to employ only persons who meet certain minimum requirements. In recognition of this fact, it is becoming more and more common to make mandatory some kind of a physical examination. In addition, "physicals" tend to minimize accidents and injuries, and such savings may offset the cost of the examination.

Final Interviews. After the results are available from tests and physical examinations, the applicant is usually given a final interview. At

---

[32] An anonymous psychological consultant quoted by Samuel Feinberg, "Psychological Aptitude Testing," *Women's Wear Daily,* November 26, 1965, p. 7.

[33] Harwell, *op. cit.,* p. 50.

[34] R. M. Guion and R. F. Gottier, "Validity of Personality Measures in Personnel Selection," *Personnel Psychology,* Summer, 1965, pp. 135–64.

[35] That tests are also being more widely used by industry in general is indicated by Roger Ricklefs, "How Companies are using Psychological Tests," *Management Review,* April, 1965, pp. 45–48.

[36] One of the better-known organizations affording such service is the Klein Institute for Aptitude Testing, Inc., of New York City.

[37] Harwell, *op. cit.,* p. 50.

this time, an effort is made to give the applicant additional information about the job and to judge his knowledge and reactions concerning the conditions and circumstances connected with it. In large stores the final interview is often conducted by the department manager or the applicant's "boss", perhaps assisted by one of the key interviewers from the personnel department. Chain-store firms typically schedule the final interview at the central or branch headquarters and by an experienced interviewer.

Because of the reliance placed upon the interview in the selecting process, it may be well to inquire: How satisfactory is the interview as a means of selecting employees? To this question it is difficult to give a direct answer. We do know that various interviewers frequently assign widely different ratings to applicants for the same job. Such differences are the result of lack of care in interviewing, disagreement as to qualities desired, and divergence of opinion concerning the outward indications of those qualities. While not all of these difficulties can be completely overcome, some of them can be minimized by carefully drawn specifications and by using experienced, trained interviewers.[38] Under such circumstances, the interview is a useful tool for selecting employees. In the future, the interviewers' conclusions may become even more valid when they are checked out against those of electronic data processing equipment into which have been fed both the job requirements and the characteristics of the applicant.[39]

Introducing the Employee to the Store and to His Job

Broadly speaking, the selection process has not been completed until the new employee has been introduced to his job and to his associates. All too frequently this step is neglected. In many stores no effort is made to give the new employee some enthusiasm for his job by acquainting him with the history of the firm, its organization, and its policies. Even the introduction of the employee to his immediate associates is perfunctory, and little effort is made to make him "feel at home." Yet this indoctrination task is essential if the new employee is to enter upon his work with the feeling that he really "belongs."

What can the retailer do to introduce the employee to the store and to the job with more satisfactory results? In the small store, the proprietor should inform the employee about the store and the promotion opportunities which it offers. He should also take the time to introduce the new worker to the

---

[38] For specific suggestions to improve the interview cf. F. M. Lopez, *Personnel Interviewing* (New York: McGraw-Hill Book Co., Inc., 1965) and S. A. Richardson *et al, Interviewing* (New York: Basic Books, Inc., 1965).

[39] On the use of EDP in this connection cf. "Picking Top Men—by Electronics," *Business Week,* March 6, 1965, pp. 97–98.

other employees and to explain the nature and extent of his duties, the hours, and other working conditions.

In the large retail organization, employee induction is a joint responsibility of the employment department and the training department. The original contracts with the store come with the employment department in the selecting process. After the applicant is employed, induction is taken over by the training department. Through store tours, classes, conferences, and handbooks, the employee is instructed in store organization, policy, and specific duties. Later, he may be introduced to his immediate colleagues by a sponsor, by the department or store manager, or by a member of the personnel division.

Contingent Force and Prospect File

Because most medium-size and large retail organizations need persons upon short notice, they usually keep on the payroll a number of persons who are not permanently assigned to a particular department. These persons make up the so-called "contingent force." In some stores this force is composed of the store's most experienced salespeople, who can serve even in departments with which they are not very familiar. Other organizations build their contingent force from part-time workers or from inexperienced new employees who give promise of being satisfactory workers after some service in the store.

A store's contingent force can only take care of sudden emergencies, such as special sales and sickness among employees. Where turnover of help is imminent, it is desirable to maintain a list of people who have been passed upon by the employment office. This list is referred to usually as the "prospect file." By keeping it up-to-date and by steadily adding new names to it, the employment office seeks to fill all personnel requisitions soon after they are received.

TRAINING EMPLOYEES

A second major responsibility of personnel management is employee training. Nowhere else, probably, is the axiom that "personnel work is a dollar-and-cents matter" more clearly demonstrated. Adequate training results in more effective job performance and greater productivity; it insures conformance with established rules and regulations, thus reducing errors and increasing customer satisfaction; it lowers selling costs both in the short run and the long run, thus enhancing profits; through better job performance, it increases the earnings of individual employees; it reduces employee turn-

over, improves morale, and strengthens loyalty; and it simplifies management's job by lessening the task of supervision. Small wonder, in view of
these significant advantages and the evidence of a decline in the quality of
service offered by many stores,[40] that retailers of all sizes and types have
turned their attention increasingly in recent years toward improving their
training programs.[41]

Centralized and Decentralized Training

Organized training, of course, does not necessarily mean centralized training, that is, training conducted solely by a central department. In the small
and medium-size store, training may be carried out by the proprietor or
manager from day to day, right on the job. Even in the large store or chain
organization, although the training plans may be formed by a central
training staff in cooperation with buyers, merchandise executives, and store
managers, the actual instruction may be given by persons employed
throughout the whole organization or even by qualified outsiders.[42] In practice, it seems that decentralized instruction is gaining at the expense of centralized training: many retail executives believe that individuals actually performing various jobs have much more knowledge of their work and can
better command the respect of the trainee than persons on the staff of the
training department.

In chain-store organizations the training provided within each store is
usually supplemented by additional training carried out by the headquarters
training staff. Goldblatt Brothers, Inc., a department store chain, centrally
prepares sales training films, copies of which are sent to each store. Others
centralize all training in one or a limited number of stores so that some
control from headquarters can be exerted. Still other retailers bring together
their employees in small groups for periodic training sessions.

Some Factors Determining Extent of the Training Program

The extent of a store's training programs is determined in part by the
quality of service the store wishes to render, the attitude of executives

[40] For a series of articles which look at the quality of present day retail salesmanship
from the manufacturers' point of view by asking: "What really happens in the store when
someone thinks of buying your product?" cf. "Sales Management Goes Shopping," *Sales
Management*, February 19, 1965, pp. 85–92 and succeeding issues.

[41] W. E. Wood, "Search for Better Retail Training," *Merchandising World*, February 7,
1966, pp. 16–19.

[42] For a specific decentralized program (Montgomery Ward & Company) cf. "Personnel Strategy," *Chain Store Age* (Variety Store—General Merchandise Managers Ed.),
December, 1964, pp. 164 ff.

toward training, and personnel turnover. If the store does not aim at a high service standard, if its executives cannot see any "profit" in training, and if personnel turnover is low, the store will often engage in a minimum of formal training for its employees. When the reverse of these statements is true, a comprehensive training program is likely to be found.

In addition to the factors just mentioned, the training program followed in a particular store is also dependent upon the size of the firm and the types of employees to be trained. Among small-scale retailers, training is limited mainly to salespeople, some of whom may be inexperienced, whereas others have had varying amounts of previous training. Since the small store specializes in a limited line of merchandise, a comparable training program can be used for practically all new employees, with some adjustments because of previous experience.

As the size of the firm increases, however, the training program becomes more complicated. Not only must a greater number of employees be trained, but the training must be broadened to include both selling and nonselling employees who perform a wide variety of jobs and handle many different types of goods. In addition, the training of part-time employees is a more serious problem. If a policy of promotion-from-within is followed, training of persons seeking advancement must also be provided. Finally, it is frequently in the large and growing firm that key executives appreciate the significance of an extensive program to train employees. The net result is a total training program at a cost which may run into many thousands of dollars each year.

The Training Program[43]

Broadly speaking, those trained in retail stores may be classified as follows: (1) new, inexperienced employees; (2) new, experienced employees; (3) regularly employed persons; and (4) "extras", that is, individuals employed for short intervals such as the pre-Christmas period.

Traning New, Inexperienced Employees. Although the training for both may have some basic similarities, we will divide this discussion into selling and sales-supporting personnel.

1. *Salespeople.* Training for employees in this group is the only kind of training which large numbers of retailers agree is worthwhile. In many organizations this training is offered in a selling school which requires two or three full days, or which is broken down to provide a two- or three-hour class on the first day of employment plus an hour-a-day class for the next

---

[43] Training programs for college trainees have already been covered in Chapter 3, "Retailing and the College Graduate," so they are excluded from the present discussion.

week or two.[44] The instruction given at these classes is very specific in nature. The salesperson-to-be is given a picture of the store's organization—made more vivid, perhaps, by a trip through the store. Store policies are explained concerning returned goods, credit, adjustments, absences from work, dress regulations, employee discounts, and safety regulations. Instructions are given in the making-out of sales slips, in the use of cash registers, and in stockkeeping. Usually there is also some consideration of how to greet customers, show merchandise, and close sales.

In the small store, whether independent or chain operated, training similar to that just described is conducted by the proprietor or manager on the sales floor. In medium-size and larger stores such training is provided through the "sponsor" system because it is believed that this method of training is more effective than the use of the formal class. A sponsor is the representative of the training department on the selling floor. It is his duty properly to introduce the new employee to other workers in the selling department, to review the firm's rules and regulations, to explain stockkeeping methods, to describe the sales systems employed, to teach selling techniques, to correct individual difficulties, and periodically to rate each new worker. The sponsor's major task, however, is that of morale building through regular follow-up.

Some retailers use written material to supplement classroom lectures, workshop groups, role playing demonstrations, or the information imparted by the sponsor. Store manuals, for example, may be used to explain the firm's organization, policies, and merchandise, as well as the fundamentals of salesmanship. Increasingly this written material is being reorganized for programmed instruction, that is, systematically presented so that the student can absorb it by himself either from a book or from a teaching machine.[45] Several retail trade associations have also prepared helpful manuals on selling for use by their members and some manufacturers provide details concerning the merchandise they sell. Comic-type posters may be used to stress such matters as courtesy to customers and the need for care in filling out sales slips.

A few large retailers—for example, Marshall Field & Company; Sears, Roebuck and Co.; and W. T. Grant Company—have developed slides or movies to demonstrate the right and the wrong tactics to use with various types of customers, to illustrate suggestion selling, and to instill pride of

---

[44] For a specific example of a three day program (Abraham & Straus, Inc., of Brooklyn) cf. David Gray, "The Future of Retail Salesmanship," *New York Retailer,* December, 1964, p. 24.

[45] For details cf. the excellent article by L. G. Schiffman, "Programmed Instruction: A Training Mode," *New York Retailer,* December, 1964, pp. 2–11.

service in their salespeople.[46] Visual aids are receiving increased attention from all retailers, and it is probable that this form of training will assume more importance in the next few years. Many chain stores employ traveling supervisors, both for checking on the training given by managers and for instructing employees, and they frequently employ visual aids.

During recent years many stores have turned to outside agencies for assistance in developing their training programs for inexperienced salespeople. Through joint participation with other stores in support of a central agency, the individual store or firm can give its new salespeople training as adequate as that given in the large store and at as low a cost per employee. Even fairly large stores may discover that the outside agency is attractive. Of course, such outside training has to be supplemented with a certain amount of internal training on the system used by the store in which the salesperson is actually employed.

Federal funds made available to the states under the George-Barden Act are being used, in part, for training inexperienced people for retail positions. To receive a grant for distributive education, a state must at least match each federal dollar. The resulting courses in salesmanship—as well as in such areas as window trimming, accounting, and showcard writing—are of value to persons interested in retailing.[47]

Despite all the training efforts referred to in the preceding paragraphs, there are observers who still believe "it is questionable whether management is securing and developing salespeople with the characteristics which reinforce the aims of the firm."[48] Some even state flatly that "sales personnel today rarely get the training or have the incentive to do a professional job in selling."[49] While these opinions may be somewhat harsh, they do emphasize the need for constant attention to the sales training program for new (and experienced) retail employees. Such programs offer the best possible means of raising the current "low prestige" image of personal selling.[50]

2. *Sales-Supporting Employees.* For persons engaged in sales-supporting activities such as deliverymen, elevator operators, and cashiers, the same two general training techniques are employed as for salespeople, that is, class

---

[46] The films used by the Bullock's-Magnin division of Federated Department Stores, Inc., are indicated in *Women's Wear Daily,* December 2, 1965, p. 12.

[47] For details cf. "Uncle Sam Will Train Your Workers," *Super Market Merchandising,* October, 1964, p. 37. For what purports to be a complete list of the schools offering high school or post high school courses in distributive education cf. Education Division of Super Market Institute, Inc., *Food Retailing Courses in Educational Institutions* (Chicago, Ill.: The Institute, 1966,), pp. 37–68.

[48] J. E. Stafford and T. V. Greer, *op. cit.,* p. 27.

[49] G. C. Engel, retail consultant, quoted in *New York Times,* November 21, 1965, p. 5.

[50] For other aspects of this image cf. J. L. Mason, "The Low Prestige of Personal Selling," *Journal of Marketing,* Vol. XXIX, No. 4 (October, 1965), pp. 7–10.

training for a short period and the sponsor system. Movies, demonstrations, group discussions, individual conferences, and store manuals are also used; and some attention is being given to the possibilities of programmed training.[51] Usually much of this type of training is decentralized, and even in stores where the program is planned by the central training office, the actual instruction is normally delegated to employees who perform the various jobs.

Too often in the past, training of nonselling employees was limited to the brief initial training period. Few stores ever took the trouble to give the receiving clerk or the marker an understanding of his place in the retail organization. This attitude undoubtedly has contributed to some unsatisfactory performance as well as easing the task of union leaders in organizing nonselling employees. If these workers are to feel that they are an essential part of the organization, their training should go beyond the question: How is my job performed?

Training New, Experienced Employees. New employees with previous retail experience do not need as elaborate introductory training as inexperienced employees. In the small store such employees are usually put quite completely on their own after a minimum of instruction concerning the exact duties of the job and peculiarities of the store's system. In the large retail organization, however, some formal training is necessary in regard to store organization, policies, and methods. This training may be carried out by means of a few class meetings or by putting the new employee under a sponsor for a brief period.

Training Regular Employees. Although training programs of retail stores are still centered largely on the new employees, increasing attention is being given to those already on the payroll. In other words, progressive retailers recognize that training should be a continuous process for all employees. In the few class hours of initial training given a new employee, so much material is set forth that few employees absorb all of it. Moreover, after they have actually worked in the store for a while, many questions come up that did not occur to them during the introductory training. Follow-up instruction is also essential because, to quote a retail executive, even "veteran cashiers (salespeople, stockroom personnel, and so on) get over-confident, careless, and forget the basic rules of courtesy, or just were not properly trained in the first place."[52] Other employees must be up-dated periodically in fashion and merchandise developments. Furthermore, most

---

[51] For a specific example of these techniques in use cf. "How Ralphs (a Los Angeles chain) Trains People," *Super Market Merchandising,* April, 1966, pp. 25–27.

[52] "Elm Farm's Training, Retraining Keeps Checker Performance High," *Chain Store Age* (Supermarket Executives Ed.), November, 1963, p. 72.

people need some prodding if they are to advance; and formal training even for those who are not new in the firm is a sound step in providing this necessary push. Finally, the ambitious employee—the one who wants to get ahead—expects his company to offer promotion training opportunities; and, if it does not, he will seek employment elsewhere. Consequently, although some retailers offer advanced training on a voluntary basis because they believe that it is a waste of money if the employee is not really interested in it, others make it known that such training is required of all those who expect future advancement.

1. *Follow-Up or Job Training.* Follow-up training often takes the form of individual conferences to discuss methods of improving the individual's performance. However, if the number of employees is large, the instruction may be given through a class. In a department store or a discount house the buyer may hold a weekly meeting with the employees of his department to disseminate information on fashion trends and new merchandise; increasingly, representatives of the manufacturers participate in these sessions, thus providing the sales personnel with additional information about their products.[53] The controller may lead a discussion of how salespeople may aid in expense control. The general manager may discuss the use of sales quotas and either the buyer or someone from the training office may give lectures on salesmanship. In the chain store system the foregoing in-store techniques are supplemented by a constant flow of follow-up training materials from headquarters: in Montgomery Ward & Company, for example, "pamphlets, films, information bulletins, selling tips—they've been trickling out of Chicago for years, keeping people on the sales floor abreast of what's new, different or important about the merchandise they're trying to move."[54]

Some firms carry out job training by switching employees from one branch of the business to another, thus providing a complete view of the firm's operations. Still another technique is to divide the sales force into small groups, sending a group from time to time to visit competing stores for purposes of observation. This technique stimulates interest and encourages employees to notice things that will improve their performance. Such observation trips are followed by group conferences in which experiences are exchanged.

2. *Promotional Training.* The majority of successful retailers agree that a policy of promotion from the ranks is highly desirable. Most of them

---

[53] For illustrations of manufacturers participating in training sessions with retail personnel cf. R. C. Rowe, "Wanamaker's Training Seminar," *Merchandising Week,* September 13, 1965, p. 48; and "DuPont's Stretch Corps," *Sales Management,* October 16, 1964, pp. 49–51.

[54] "Personnel Strategy," *op. cit.,* p. 176.

would echo the statement of Mr. Irving Edison, President of Edison Brothers Stores, Inc., a national shoe chain:

"For over 40 years, we have followed an inviolate policy of elevating our shoe salesman to the higher posts in our company. Our 508 stores are managed by 508 of our former salespeople. Our 30 regional managers are our former salespeople. Every buyer in our home office and most of our officers are former salespeople of our company. We believe that, if we do not have qualified, trained personnel in our company for the bigger positions that become available, the fault is ours."[55]

Not only does promotion from within build employee good will for the firm and improve morale; it also attracts forward-looking employees to the firm, provides officers who are well trained in the store's policies and practices, and is a relatively inexpensive method of securing executives.

For maximum effectiveness, a policy of promotion from within the firm should be accompanied with an adequate training program for promotable personnel.[56] Such a program may involve many aspects, including company-planned conferences and courses covering various aspects of the business, work-study arrangements with universities, evening courses in colleges, correspondence courses, rotation of employees among various jobs, and the sponsor system. In addition, the use of a house organ as an aid in training should not be overlooked. By presenting information about employees who have been granted promotions, it may stimulate other persons to greater efforts. Data on new lines of merchandise, on the use of good salesmanship, on outstanding or unusual services rendered to customers, and on certain of the store's policies may be covered in the store paper.

A few examples will indicate the "flavor" of these training programs:

1. The Bullock's-Magnin division of Federated Department Stores, Inc., relies heavily on rotation among selling and sales-supporting departments to give breadth of training to promotable people. Even key buyers may be rotated "to provide new challenges . . . new thoughts."[57]

2. In addition to its college trainee program, Montgomery Ward & Company has developed a whole series of educational activities for promotable personnel:

a) Sponsor Store Program—Trainees for department managers in such specialties as automotive service or repair service are given special training by outstanding department managers of stores: 177 employees were trained under this program in 1964.

---

[55] Quoted by Samuel Feinberg in *Women's Wear Daily,* May 28, 1965, p. 7.

[56] L. L. Ferguson, "Better Management of Managers' Careers," *Harvard Business Review,* Vol. XLIV, No. 2 (March–April, 1966), pp. 139–52.

[57] C. P. Schwarberg, Bullock's vice president for personnel, quoted in "Bullock's Buyer Rotation Helps Counter Stagnation," *Women's Wear Daily,* December 2, 1965, p. 12.

b) Correspondence Courses—These have been developed to familiarize employees with each credit function. One-half of our credit employees now are enrolled in these courses which will better equip them to serve the needs of our millions of credit customers.

c) Retail Department Manager Training Program—This is a special curriculum being given to all present and future store-level department managers. [Over] . . . 13,500 managerial employees . . . have completed this program.

d) Middle Management Training Program—An 11 to 15 week orientation course for 27 to 35-year-old men employed for specific sales and management positions at the middle management level; 132 men were employed and trained in this category last year.

e) Senior Management Training Program—This is a limited program for those senior executives who are employed to fill specific management positions in the Company; 19 persons were trained under this program last year.

f) Management Orientation Conferences—These are semiannual, two-week conferences for the intensive training of potentially-promotable executives to broaden their knowledge of all facets of Ward's corporate operations; 109 men have graduated from this course.[58]

3. Kroger Company—a supermarket chain—(1) sends carefully selected individuals to the executive development programs of major universities, (2) provides for rotational training and a 13-week training tour which gives the individual an opportunity to learn phases of the business with which he is not familiar, and (3) periodically offers 10-day and 4-day merchandising clinics handled by both company people and outside consultants. Biweekly four-hour class sessions are used by Elm Farm Foods Company for field supervisors, store managers, and assistant managers. Ralphs has a ten-week program for assistant managers which also includes four-hour class sessions, but on a weekly basis.[59]

It is unfortunate that most of the advanced training (and much of the other training as well) given by stores to employees other than executives is largely technical in nature and designed to explain how certain jobs are performed. This type of training is important, of course, but if the store is really eager to stir the interest of its workers in jobs in the retail field, the training needs to be broader. It should give the employee a picture of the significance of retailing in our economy, of major trends in the retail field, and of the importance of the individual to the success of the store.[60] Moreover, it is quite likely that most retailers have been too slow to

---

[58] *Annual Report,* year ended February 3, 1965, pp. 8–9.

[59] For details of these and other programs cf. *Chain Store Age* (Supermarket Executives Ed.) March, 1965, pp. 72–73; April, 1964, pp. 72–73 and 115; November, 1963, pp. 72–73.

[60] The case for broader training is well stated in "Specialists Try a Wider Track," *Business Week,* July 31, 1965, pp. 56–57.

advance those who have taken advantage of promotional training opportunities.[61] A decrease in this time lag could be a significant factor in educating retail personnel as to the dollar and cents advantage of such training.

3. *Training Supervisors.* No training program in retail stores can be really effective without the full support and cooperation of the supervisory force. And such cooperation will not be forthcoming unless supervisors are thoroughly familiar with their obligations and responsibilities in relation to the training of both selling and sales-supporting employees. Consequently, some large retailers have adopted measures to make their supervisors aware of the significance of training and to employ them in the actual training process. To these ends, special self-study programs for supervisors have been developed which make use of textbooks, correspondence courses, phonograph records, and (in a few instances) teaching machines.[62] Still other retailers have rather formalized training courses in which leadership qualities are emphasized and in which company personnel policies and procedures and their just application are stressed. Supervisors are taught that their job is to maintain good human relationships within their departments by proper indoctrination of employees; by on-the-job training; by frequent personnel reviews; by recommendations for promotions, transfers, and releases; and by initiation of salary recommendations. Lectures, films, and business games may be employed in these more formalized training courses for supervisors. In chain organizations the supervisors may meet from time to time at a regional or main office headquarters for all or parts of this type of training. Such activities, of course, should be carried out under the guidance of the personnel division and in accordance with the general policies of the firm.

Training Extras. The training of extras is complicated by the fact that such employees are seldom on the payroll long enough to make intensive training worthwhile; yet very often they may account for as much as one third or more of a store's sales. In addition, and as we have already noted, the current shortage of "extras" is forcing the retailer to take on less satisfactory employees, so that the training task is more difficult than at an earlier period.

In the larger stores, the "extras" are usually given a one- (sometimes two-) day "cram" session covering, in abbreviated fashion, the material given to new inexperienced employees.[63] From that point on, the employee is turned over to a sponsor. Some retailers, both large and small, rely

---

[61] On the need for more rapid promotion cf. J. L. Goldstucker, "Competent Retail Trainees—Where are They?" *Journal of Marketing,* Vol. XXVII, No. 2 (April, 1963), p. 41.

[62] Cf. "Are Teaching Machines For You?" *Super Market Merchandising,* November, 1964, pp. 42–43.

[63] Cf. pp. 233–36, above.

practically entirely on the sponsor system, perhaps supplemented by printed material. One variety chain gives each extra employee a short manual which covers such matters as store policies and regulations, care of stock, and the manner of approaching customers. In a few cases, retailers in a city have cooperated in getting the service of a local business school or college to give initial general training to holiday employees.

Regardless of the training given extras before they begin work, the retailer must depend in large measure upon the aid and advice extended to them by his regular employees. Marshall Field & Company uses its house organ as a medium of appealing to its employees for this necessary cooperation, as follows:

Let's Welcome Them

Christmas hiring has started. Between now and the end of November we will nearly double our number of employees. These new people come in to aid us during the greatest rush of the year—it is only through their efforts added to our own that we will be able to give our large number of holiday customers the traditional courtesy and service that spell FIELD'S.

Let's welcome them—remembering our own first days in the store, let's help them. We know the store. We know its systems, its locations, its habits and its people. And all these are strange to our new members. We can do much to help them overcome their strangeness, and to make their work here the pleasant experience we all want it to be. Let's increase our constant effort to do this during the next few weeks—let's resolve that each new member will learn of Field's courtesy and service from personal experience—will learn that these qualities are genuine and are extended to customers because they are practiced "at home."

Appraising the Training Program

It is very difficult to measure definitely the value of employee training.[64] Some checking techniques, however, are available which afford management an indication of what the training is accomplishing. Despite the human factors and the expense involved, shopping-service reports—a report on specific sales personnel usually made by an individual whose business it is to shop stores and turn in an analysis—are used quite widely by the larger retailers.[65] The average sale, the number of errors, and the number of complaints recorded are still other indicators which, when used with caution, have some merit. Periodic examinations sometimes afford a fairly satisfac-

---

[64] Cf. the discussion on pp. 231–32, above.

[65] That conclusions based on these reports must be reached with great care is indicated by the fact that the reports are influenced by the income of the shopper, the training given the shopper, and other factors.

tory check.[66] Personnel reviews at regular intervals are also used for this purpose.

In the final analysis, however, the effectiveness of the training program is measured by the general morale of the store's employees, the opportunities for advancement and the extent of promotion from within, the quality of supervision, the number of customer complaints, the rate of employee turnover, and—most important of all—the quality of customer service and its reflection in profits.

REVIEW AND DISCUSSION QUESTIONS

1. Explain fully the text statement that personnel "problems are intensified as old stores are expanded and new ones are opened."
2. "It is old-fashioned to think of personnel management as a dollar-and-cents matter; instead it must be thought of as a means of keeping people happy on their jobs." Discuss.
3. Discuss the main factors responsible for the increased emphasis on personnel management in retail stores in recent years.
4. Talk with the general manager of a department store, the manager of a discount house, and the manager of a food chain store to determine (1) the organization-chart position of their personnel directors and (2) the scope of the duties of these directors.
5. During the conversations referred to in question 4, inquire (and report to the class on) as to the impact of Title VII the Civil Rights Act of 1964 on each firm's personnel policies.
6. Select three of the seven "human relations principles" listed on page 218 and comment on some of your personal experiences which seem to support or invalidate these "principles."
7. Why are written personnel policies desirable in many stores? What should they include?
8. "It must be recognized that, in a sense, personnel work is performed by every employee and executive of a store, regardless of whether he is or is not in the personnel department." Give three illustrations of this statement.
9. Discuss the important steps involved in recruiting an adequate force of retail employees.
10. What are the most common sources from which a store may draw employees? Which sources seem the most satisfactory for (a) the small drugstore, (b) the large chain drug company, (c) the discount house, and (d) the department store? Would your answer be affected by the type of jobs available? Give your reasons.
11. Discuss the value and the use of each of the following factors in the selec-

---

[66] These tests do not have to be written. For salespeople the "test sale" is becoming a popular means of checking on the effectiveness of the training program. The employee who has finished her initial training is required to demonstrate the sale of specific merchandise with another salesperson or an employee of the training department as the customer.

tion of employees: the application blank, the preliminary interview, tests, the physical examination, and the final interview.

12. What is meant by the term "induction of employees"? Indicate the significance of the induction program from both employer and employee points of view.

13. Based on interviews or reading comment upon the degree of centralization (or decentralization) in the training programs of three large-scale retailers.

14. Compare and contrast the training program of a small retailer in your home town with that of a competing large-scale retailer handling the same general types of merchandise.

15. What kind of follow-up training would you recommend (a) in a small specialty shop, (b) in a large clothing store for men, and (c) in a department store?

SUPPLEMENTARY READINGS

Consult references at the close of Chapter 9.

9
CHAPTER

Retail Personnel Management—Continued

COMPENSATING RETAIL PERSONNEL

A third very important personnel responsibility involves working out compensation plans for selling and sales-supporting personnel, including such managerial personnel as buyers or department managers, store managers, and key executives. Dissatisfaction with compensation plans is a common source of complaint; yet it is very difficult to devise any method of payment which is satisfactory to personnel performing a wide variety of tasks that require different skills and abilities. Some of the difficulties may be made clear if we establish the requisites of an ideal plan and then see how closely the plans in use conform to this goal.

Goals of a Compensation Plan

An ideal compensation plan, designed to meet the requirements of both the store and the employee as far as this is practicable, should:

1. Keep wage cost under control. All too frequently the determination of wage costs for purposes of control is based upon past experience, thus perpetuating past errors. Comparisons of figures with those of fairly comparable stores should be made at frequent intervals, and management should take prompt action when important deviations are vealed.

2. Minimize discontent among employees and help to reduce labor turnover. It should not only *be* fair but should be *considered* fair by employees.

3. Be easily understood by employees and easily administered by management.

4. Provide an incentive for better work, rewarding improved performance and penalizing inefficiency.

5. Guarantee a minimum income and regular periodic payments, so as to give the employee a sense of security.

Compensating Salespeople

There are four main compensation plans for salespeople which should be reviewed in connection with the desirable requisites:

1. Straight salary
2. Salary plus commission of *all* net sales
3. Quota bonus, also known as salary-quota bonus
4. Straight commission (usually with drawing account)

Some stores use combinations of the foregoing plans to meet their particular requirements and practically all retailers employ various salary supplements to stimulate their salespeople.

Straight Salary. Under this plan the employee is paid a definite amount each payday—for example, $70 each Friday. It is the most common method of compensating salespeople, being almost universally used in the small store and in chain stores selling convenience goods.

The straight salary plan has a number of advantages. It is especially well adapted to the small store where the employee performs so many different jobs that it is difficult and perhaps unfair to pay him on any other basis. By setting the salary high enough, employee discontent is minimized; and by varying salaries among the employees, the store can hold those individuals who might be attracted to other firms. This plan is easily understood and, by providing a fixed regular payment, it meets the objections of many who dislike the insecurity associated with a fluctuating income.

These advantages of the straight salary are so significant that, when accompanied by a well-conceived personnel-rating program[1] to provide an incentive, it is probably the best single method of compensating retail salespeople. But, when used without personnel rating, it fails to offer an immediate incentive to greater efforts. The straight salary also lacks any degree of automatic flexibility so that the wage-cost ratio may get out of control. Especially is this disadvantage important in periods of falling sales when, because of such factors as fear of causing employee discontent, hope of a reversal of the sales trend, and union contracts, the retailer finds it very difficult to effect wage reductions. As a result, the payroll ratio may increase sharply.

Salary Plus Commission on All Net Sales. This plan, which is even more common in the very large stores than straight salary, usually calls for a salary which is somewhat less than would be paid in the absence of the commission but adds a relatively low commission rate on *all* net sales.

---

[1] Cf. pp. 255–56, below.

Currently, the commission rate ranges from ½ to 1 percent. Thus, a person with a $70 weekly salary and weekly net sales of $500 would receive an income of $72.50 (on a ½ of 1 percent commission) or $75 (with a 1 percent commission rate).

By combining a small commission with a salary, the objections frequently raised concerning the straight salary method are, to a degree, minimized. Some immediate incentive to greater effort is provided; and since the income from commissions will fluctuate with sales, a limited degree of flexibility in wage ratio is attained. At the same time, by keeping the basic salary large relative to the weekly pay, the main advantages of the straight salary plan are retained.

Quota Bonus. Increasingly, some of the larger retailers selling shopping and specialty goods are paying their sales people a basic salary plus a commission on all net sales in excess of a certain quota. Three steps are involved in putting this plan into operation, as follows:

1. The weekly (or monthly) quota should be determined. Typically, the record of past sales is the basis of this decision, with adjustment for changed conditions and for seasonal fluctuations. If records suggest that $900 of weekly sales is about average, this figure may be used as the quota. To be of the greatest value, the quota should remain within the reach of practically all the salespeople. Yet it cannot be too low, or it will be reached by all without much effort.

2. A basic weekly (or monthly) salary should be established. This salary, which may be looked upon as a drawing account, is usually determined on the basis of the past wage-cost ratio adjusted in the light of competitive practices. If this ratio has averaged about 7 percent, the basic salary may be established at 7 percent of the quota. With a quota of $900, the basic salary becomes $63.

3. A decision should be made in regard to the commission to be paid on sales in excess of the quota. In practice, there seems to be a tendency to set this commission considerably below the store's average wage cost. If 7 percent is the average wage cost, the commission may be set at 3 or 4 percent. In some cases the bonus is a specific dollar amount, rather than a percentage of sales in excess of the quota.

Does this type of compensation plan meet the requirements we have set up for an ideal plan? In regard to control of wage cost, the basic salary makes up the bulk of the total wage payment, so that not much flexibility is secured. The plan may minimize discontent since it gives each salesperson the chance to earn as much as any other salesperson. Any change in quotas, however, may be interpreted as an attempt to reduce wage payments and, hence, may lead to dissatisfaction. The plan involves some clerical work in computing total payments. Assuming the quotas are not set too high, the commission on sales in excess of the quota provides an incentive for greater effort. Yet it is difficult to keep the quota adjusted to periods of falling and rising sales. From the point of view of the employee, it is rather complicated; and if the commission is held off for a considerable period, there is a loss of incentive. Finally, the plan has the advantage of providing a steady income through a basic salary.[2]

Straight Commission. Under the straight commission plan of wage payment, salespeople receive a specified commission on all goods they sell. This commission varies from 3 to 8 percent of sales, depending on the type of merchandise and its profitableness, the store, and the season of the year. This method of payment is most common in stores and departments selling items of high unit value, such as furniture and rugs, women's apparel, and shoes.

In actual practice the straight commission is often supplemented with a drawing account. That is, payments are made to salespeople at regular intervals, and these are charged against commissions earned each month when reconciliations are made.

Better than any other plan the straight commission provides for a flexible wage which keeps the wage cost under control. It is a plan that is easily understood by employees, and the payment due is computed without difficulty. Since income varies directly with sales and payment follows closely upon the expenditure of effort, an incentive is offered. When supplemented with a drawing account, a regular income is assured.

Paradoxical though it may seem, the incentive provided by the straight commission plan has proved to be one of its weaknesses, especially for stores that desire to build a reputation for service to all customers. This result follows from the fact that salespeople may try to avoid persons who seem merely to be "looking" or who are interested in low-priced merchandise. In some cases, a store is able to minimize this disadvantage by the use of a call system, which usually provides for a man to welcome each customer and assign a salesperson to take care of her wishes. In this way, salespeople get an equal chance to make sales and cannot "pick" their customers. However, there is still the objection that the salesperson, trying to increase his income, may exert pressure on the customer to buy. Some customers object to such tactics. Another difficulty is that new salespeople, without a "following" or experience, often find it difficult to make a sufficient number of sales to obtain what they feel is an adequate income.

Salary Supplements for Salespeople. In addition to regular payments under the plans that have been discussed, some retailers provide their salespeople with opportunities for earning extra compensation which may add from 10 to 15 percent to regular salary. Sometimes this is done through

---

[2] Various kinds of bonus plans for food stores are evaluated in "Bonus Plans Build Morale," *Progressive Grocer,* June, 1964, pp. 110 ff.

profit sharing. Among supermarket chains, several years ago 14 percent of the firms shared profits with *all* employees.[3] While it was not until 1963 that Montgomery Ward & Company adopted a general profit-sharing plan covering sales and sales-supporting personnel as well as store managers, superintendents, and major executives,[4] the J. C. Penney Company and Sears, Roebuck and Co. have long had such plans and both firms cite them as a significant factor in their success.[5] In contrast, other retailers—Woodward and Lothrop, Washington, D.C., department store company, for instance— have abandoned profit sharing, believing the relatively small payments going to sales personnel and the lack of clear-cut evidence of relationship between effort and reward minimize the impact of this form of salary supplement.

Prize money (P.M.'s) or extra commissions, another kind of salary supplement, may be paid for selling certain kinds of merchandise, such as private brands. Dollar awards are used to encourage courteous treatment of customers. Increasingly in recent years retailers have distributed valuable prizes (trips to Florida, major appliances, and wardrobes) as incentives to encourage salespeople to reach the goals established for sales contests.

Even more common for employees of department and specialty stores are discounts on all purchases made in the store—and of late retailers are liberalizing this arrangement. Whereas, formerly, some weeks or months of service were quite typically required, today the privilege of obtaining discounts is granted almost immediately. Moreover, the discounts granted have been increased by many retailers; the 10 to 15 percent figures formerly provided have been replaced by 15 to 20 percent with the higher figure currently the one used by the majority of these stores. With over 4 percent of department store sales and 2 percent of specialty store sales accounted for by employee discount purchases, it is clear why these retailers consider the discount as a way to promote the store's merchandise to employees as well as an important aid in retaining personnel.[6] In contrast, just 6 percent of the food chains grant employee discounts and even in these firms the discounts

---

[3] An additional 26 percent have profit sharing limited to certain managerial personnel. *The Super Market Industry Speaks* (Chicago: Super Market Institute, Inc., 1961), p. 23. It is probable that at least these proportions exist today.

[4] "Personnel Strategy," *Chain Store Age* (Variety Store-General Merchandise Managers Edition), December, 1964, p. 166.

[5] "Inside Sears, Roebuck," *Printers' Ink,* October 22, 1965, p. 20. Profit-sharing at Sears is directly tied-in with the firm's pension program. Cf. John Osbon, "Profit Sharing Pension Paradise," *Women's Wear Daily,* October 7, 1964, pp. 1, 56; and "What Do You Mean, 'Only Money'?" *ibid.,* July 25, 1966, p. 9.

[6] Richard Rosenthal, "Employee Discount Buying Rings up 4% of Store Sales," *Women's Wear Daily,* December 1, 1965, p. 8. For further details on this study by the National Retail Merchants Association, cf. *Retail Employee Discounts* (New York: The Association, 1965).

are held within the 5 to 10 percent range; while the 10 percent discount is also used by the E. J. Korvette discount house.[7] With their relatively low mark-ups and the possibility that the discount privilege might be abused (employees purchasing for friends and relatives), these chains tend to minimize this form of salary supplement.

Still other salary supplements are the cash award given for usable suggestions and the special bonus, based on length of service or other factors, often given at Christmas time. To cite a single example of the bonus, the W. T. Grant Company distributes a Christmas bonus of $5 for each year of employee service with the firm. Finally, various pension programs have been developed; these provide for compensation in the years after the salesperson's retirement.[8]

Compensating Sales-Supporting Employees

The straight salary is the most popular way of compensating these employees. In part, such widespread use of the salary plan is a result of the difficulties involved in setting quotas or in finding a satisfactory basis for a commission. Yet there are nonselling jobs for which a standard unit of output can be set and a commission paid, based upon the number of units produced; and this area is being extended in department stores and chain-store systems through the use of industrial engineering principles and the establishment of "work-study" bureaus which have developed new methods and devices to measure productivity. By way of illustration, for those engaged in marking goods, the number of units marked may serve as the basis of a commission. For packers the number of packages put up may establish the commission basis, whereas for stenographers the number of pages or of lines typed may serve. But even in these instances, it is hard to get a standard unit of output. For the typist the number of lines typed depends somewhat upon the material, and this is a variable factor. Not all goods are marked in the same way, and various-sized packages have different time requirements for packing.

As to incentive plans for nonselling employees, they are limited almost entirely to the large retail firms. However, in retail stores of all sizes, sales-supporting employees are usually eligible for most of the salary supplements given to selling employees, especially discounts on purchases, profit sharing, cash awards, and special bonuses.

---

[7] "What Should You Do About Employee Discounts?" *Super Market Merchandising,* December, 1965, p. 29; and "Korvette Personnel to get 10% Off; Practice Spreads," *Discount Store News,* October 31, 1966, p. 1.

[8] Cf. p. 265, below.

Compensating Managerial Personnel[9]

At the managerial level, while the straight salary may be used by itself, in most cases compensation plans are adopted that provide an immediate incentive to greater efforts.

Department Store and Specialty-Store Buyers.[10]   Practically all department and specialty stores use some form of bonus payment, in addition to salary, to compensate their buyers; and the specific arrangement is usually set forth in a definite written contract.

Six common methods are employed for determining the bonus, as follows:

1. Bonus based on sales—either stated as a percentage of the total sales of the department (such as 1 percent) or as a stated percentage of the increase in sales over a quota. Frequently there is also the requirement that a stated minimum gross margin must be maintained.

2. Bonus based on increased sales plus increased gross margin or net profit. For example, a store may agree to pay "1 percent of sales increase over previous year plus 5 percent of additional net profits after income taxes."

3. Bonus based on total store operations. Such an arrangement is designed to induce buyers to "merchandise" with a store-wide approach to problems. The amount the buyer receives is dependent on a management review of the department's operation during the year.

4. Bonus based on departmental net profit, either before or after federal taxes. The bonus may vary from 1 to 10 percent and it may not apply until after a stated dollar amount of net profit has been reached, e.g., $10,000.

5. Bonus based on a department's contribution. "Contribution" is usually defined as the dollar gross margin of the department minus specified controllable expenses. The bonus is calculated as a percentage of the department's contribution and commonly ranges from 1 to 3 percent.

6. Bonus based on departmental gross margin, such as 3 percent or more of the gross margin realized.

Chain-Store Managers.   In variety, discount, and junior department store chains a common arrangement is to pay a salary and then give the manager from 10 to 15 percent of the profits made by his store. Other firms use a drawing account and give the manager from 10 to 20 percent of the profits minus what he has already received from the drawing account. Such compensation plans give the manager a direct incentive to make his store produce profits. Even when a salary is paid, it is kept relatively low, so that a large part of the manager's income results from his store's profit.

---

[9] Also cf. the discussion of top management compensation in Chapter 3, pp. 61–62, above.

[10] For additional treatment of this topic cf. the Caroline Stores, Inc. case in C. H. McGregor, *Retail Management Problems* (3rd ed.; Homewood, Ill.: Richard D. Irwin, Inc., 1962), pp. 87–88.

In contrast to the foregoing chains, the food and drug chains usually base their incentive payments on sales, a common plan being a salary plus from 1 to 2 percent on sales. Although this arrangement encourages the manager to produce volume irrespective of profits, in a foodstore or drugstore the profits realized are not so completely under the manager's control as they are in a variety store. In some cases the store manager is paid a straight commission on sales and, from his commission, he is expected to pay his employees. Such a plan has the major advantage of keeping wage costs under definite control.

Chain organizations in several fields—auto supplies, for example—also make use of a bonus based on the store's contribution to company profits. Frequently the percentage of bonus is paid only on the contribution above an established goal for the store; and the bonus may be divided between manager and assistant manager on a 3 to 1 or some other fixed basis.

Whatever compensation plan is adopted for the chain-store manager, it should be suited to the needs of the company. Specifically, it should help top management attract and hold the type of personnel wanted by providing incentive for above-average efforts and satisfactory operating results, furnishing extra rewards for outstanding accomplishment, and comparing favorably with the compensation plans of leading competitors.

Major Executives. Previous mention has been made of the search for executive talent.[11] While an attractive compensation plan is one of the major factors in attracting and retaining properly qualified retail executives, it is but *one* element. In fact, studies indicate that the fundamental satisfactions desired by those who operate their own stores or who serve in executive positions for others are as follows:

1. Financial rewards commensurate with the responsibilities of the position.
2. Freedom of action within the individual's sphere of responsibility with commensurate authority.
3. Adequate title and prestige of position.
4. Stability of position, with adequate provision for retirement.
5. Satisfactory working quarters and conditions. Many executives report that they want comfortable offices with adequate light and ventilation and good furnishings. One company president who had recently moved into a new office was heard to say: "I'd gladly take $5,000 a year off my present salary if it were necessary to justify my present office facilities."
6. Association with an organization that is "moving ahead," so that one may take pride in being a part of it.
7. A position that offers an opportunity of public service.

Despite the fact that financial reward is by no means the only consideration important to retail executives, a fact which is currently not given

---

[11] Cf. pp. 71–72 and 77–78, above.

sufficient attention in the retail field, dollar compensation *is* significant. What policies and practices are currently being followed?[12]

The majority of proprietors of small stores pay themselves a regular weekly or bi-weekly salary. The size of this salary may be adjusted from year to year according to the proprietor's judgment as to the expected profits. Moreover, it may be supplemented from time to time or at the end of each year by extra withdrawals of funds if the profit position is satisfactory.

While the executives of some large retail organizations are paid by salary only, the incentive aspect is so important that most of them receive a salary plus some form of bonus or profit sharing arrangement, all or part of which may be deferred until after retirement when the recipient will be (presumably) in a lower tax bracket.[13] Also common are option plans which permit the executive to benefit (by paying a capital gains tax rather than an income tax) from advances in the price of the firm's stock.[14] Still other typical elements in the executive compensation package are insurance payments and pension plans.[15]

In some instances the firm's bonus or profit-sharing arrangement is not formalized, the amount paid being determined each year by the president or the board of directors. In contrast, most firms set aside a fixed percentage of net profits as a bonus or profit-sharing fund, which is divided among key executives in ratio to their salaries or according to some other predetermined formula. That such profit sharing is effective is suggested by one careful study of 14 major chains. The seven chains with profit-sharing plans were substantially more successful than the seven lacking such plans.[16]

A compensation plan for executives should provide a means whereby the company can relieve itself of inefficient officials. In other words, some mistakes are inevitable in employing executives; in such cases a company's commitments should be such that the "mistakes" are not retained on the staff

[12] Current and possible future trends in executive compensation are analyzed in two articles by Arch Patton, "Executive Compensation by 1970," *Harvard Business Review,* Vol. XLII, No. 5 (September–October, 1964), pp. 137–46, and "Top Executive Pay: New Facts and Figures," *ibid.,* Vol. XLIV, No. 5 (September–October, 1966), pp. 94–97; and N. P. Clement, Jr., "Current Practices in Retail Executive Compensation," *Retail Control,* February, 1965, pp. 13–35.

[13] John Cunnion, *Tax Protected Compensation for the Executive* (Larchmont, New York: Business Reports, Inc., 1966).

[14] Cf. "How Stock Options Fatten Executive Wallets," *Business Management,* February, 1966, pp. 62–63; and "Stock Options: Still Going Strong," *Management Review,* June, 1966, pp. 57–59. For a report on stock options outstanding at Montgomery Ward & Company cf. *Annual Report* for year ended February 2, 1966, p. 16.

[15] An excellent review of "Trends in Corporate Pension Plans," which emphasizes that "the liberalization of pension benefits is proceeding at a fast clip," will be found in *Management Review,* April, 1966, pp. 65–69.

[16] J. J. Jehring and B. L. Metzger, *The Stockholder and Employee Profit Sharing* (Evanston, Ill.: Profit Sharing Research Foundation, 1960).

to retard the firm's progress. Perhaps the age of the executive is such that he can be retired; in other cases the compensation plan should allow the officer to be separated from the firm under an arrangement that is fair to both parties.

Finally, the compensation plan for executives should be subjected to frequent review. In part, such a review is necessary because constantly changing taxation and inheritance laws have an impact on the tax status of the different ways of remunerating executives. But the plan also needs periodic review from the point of view of individual executives. An executive's needs change with the various stages of his career cycle.[17] In his thirties and early forties his main requirement may be for cash; from forty-five until his mid-fifties, he may be able to forego some immediate cash in favor of stock options or a long range incentive bonus plan; and as he approaches retirement, a deferral arrangement may be attractive.

Job Evaluation and The Compensation Plan

Job evaluation is simply a carefully worked out program for appraising the value of jobs and obtaining an equitable relationship among them—a program founded upon common sense and good judgment. Consequently, it lies at the core of a firm's compensation plan.[18] Although job evaluation has been carried on in a more or less formal way in industrial plants for many years, only recently has it received the close attention it deserves from retail personnel executives.

Goals of Job Evaluation. There are five major objectives of job evaluation, as follows:

1. To implement a company policy of equal pay for equal work, thereby building employee good will.
2. To pay all employees in proportion to their responsibilities and to the difficulty of their work.
3. To recognize monetary differentials for different quality and quantity of work, thus giving employees an incentive for improved performance.
4. To provide a basis for explaining to employees why a job is valued as it is.
5. To establish pay rates in keeping with those for similar work in the community.

Job Evaluation Methods. A great variety of methods are employed to evaluate jobs in retail stores and the plan adapted by any specific firm should, of course, be tailored to its own conditions, reflect the considered

---

[17] Cf. G. H. Foote, "Executive Compensation and the Career Cycle," *Management Review*, July, 1965, pp. 19–22.

[18] On this point cf. J. D. Batten and D. H. Stouder, "Compensation and Job Evaluation," *Personnel Journal*, December, 1965, pp. 12 ff.

judgment of the firm's executives, and be based on adequate study of the pertinent factors involved. The techniques used may be illustrated by describing the practices of one progressive store.[19] This firm, utilizing a job evaluation plan based upon four major groups of factors common to all jobs, assigns weights within each group as follows:

1. *Skill requirement factors,* including education, 10 percent; job knowledge, 15 percent; customer contact, 10 percent; personal contact (other than customer contact), 10 percent; special aptitudes, 7 percent.
2. *Responsibility requirement factors,* including supervision, 12 percent; and responsibility, 15 percent.
3. *Effort requirement factors,* including mental effort, 9 percent; and physical effort, 6 percent.
4. *Working conditions factor,* 6 percent.

Using these factors as a yardstick, jobs are evaluated by a committee composed of the store superintendent, the personnel director, the industrial engineer, the controller, the merchandise manager, and the president of the store. Summaries are prepared for each division and distributed to the divisional manager concerned. Inequities are corrected promptly, after which the personnel manager prepares a total store summary and forwards it to top management.

Before any job evaluation program is instituted, steps should be taken to gain acceptance of it by all employees. Unless they understand the reasons for its adoption and how it will affect their work, the program will not produce its maximum results. Management should avoid such errors as lack of simplicity, failure to apply common sense, and general impatience for results. Job evaluation is a painstaking process, and its value will depend upon the care with which it is planned and carried out.[20]

Significant By-Products of Job Evaluation. In addition to the many direct advantages which accrue through properly conducted job evaluations, such as more equitable wage rates, better wage progression, and improved employee morale, important by-products also result. These include increased emphasis upon job study and improved personnel performance, stimulation of employees by presenting a clearer picture of promotional opportunities, a reduction in labor turnover, fair and frequent reviews of individual performance, suggestions for presenting management's point of view in collec-

---

[19] For a discussion of various methods used in job evaluation cf. J. A. Patton, C. L. Littlefield, and S. A. Self, *Job Evaluation* (3d ed.; Homewood, Ill.: Richard D. Irwin, Inc., 1964), chapters 6, 7 and 8.

[20] Other important aspects of these programs are developed in K. O. Mann, "Characteristics of Job Evaluation Programs," *Personnel Administration,* September, 1965, pp. 45–47.

tive bargaining on wages, and the information required by management to explain satisfactorily to employees the wage rates paid.

In a survey of 98 department stores some years ago 47 percent reported the use of some kind of job evaluation.[21] While this figure is far too high for retailing as a whole, the gains from job evaluation are so significant that the practice will undoubtedly receive greater attention from retail store executives in the future than ever before. Experience has proven it a necessary and useful tool in determining and maintaining a satisfactory compensation program.

OBTAINING SATISFACTORY PERSONNEL PERFORMANCE

As already emphasized, the responsibility of personnel management does not end with the hiring and initial training of employees. Some of the most important personnel functions are involved in keeping those persons who have been hired and trained at a satisfactory performance level. To a degree, achieving this goal depends upon the spirit which management injects into the firm's personnel—the birthday corsage to saleswomen, the breakfast for the contest winner, and the picture of the "best manager of the week" in the weekly house organ.

More than enthusiasm, however, is needed to stimulate employees toward a higher-level performance of their responsibilities: there must be personnel activities leading to a suitable compensation plan preferably based on sound job evaluation; continuous evaluation of personnel; promotion, transfer, demotion, and termination of the employment of some workers; maintenance of adequate working conditions; the carrying-out of certain employee service activities; and the successful handling of employees' complaints. Except for compensation plans and job evaluation, which have already been covered, these activities will be discussed in the remaining sections of this chapter.

Evaluating Personnel

Personnel evaluation seeks to give the retailer a carefully formed opinion as to the value of each employee to the firm. Such evaluation is important to management as the basis for salary adjustments, promotions, transfers, and terminations and also as a method of encouraging employees to do better work. It aids in detecting employees who are "slipping" before they have fallen to such a low performance level that termination of employment is

---

[21] I. L. Sands, "Personnel Practices in Department Stores," *New York Retailer,* June, 1957, p. 20. Comparable data for more recent years are not available.

necessary. In the process of evaluation the management is brought into closer relationship with the employee, which leads to a better understanding of the position of each.

Careful evaluation of personnel is difficult because the value of an employee to a firm depends, in part, on so many factors which cannot be measured objectively. Not only is the employee's production important; his ability, loyalty, honesty, and attitude toward the store and his work are also significant elements. How a particular worker rates on many of these latter elements is a matter of opinion, and there may be a variation in the opinions of the individuals rating the same employee. In spite of such difficulties, if the retailer will maintain adequate and up-to-date records, set up objective standards wherever possible, get opinions from a number of sources, and carry out the process on a regular schedule, the results will prove well worth the effort.

In the Small Store. In small stores personnel evaluation is performed by the proprietor, and all too often without any definite, objective standards; hence his opinions are greatly influenced by his personal likes and dislikes. Greater objectivity may be obtained, however, through recognition of the importance of evaluation and the establishment of certain criteria to use as a yardstick. In the case of a salesperson, for example, he might use records of sales, both in dollars and in number of transactions, customer complaints, errors in filling orders and recording sales, the number of times late to or absent from work, and the ratio of dollar value of goods returned to sales. If the store is large enough to have several employees, the proprietor may periodically ask each employee to rate the other employees as to a number of personal qualities—loyalty, honesty, courtesy, and attitude toward work. Occasionally, it may even be possible for the proprietor to get customer reaction to certain employees by interviewing a number of patrons. If the store has any sales-supporting employees, they may be evaluated by techniques fairly comparable to those just mentioned.

In the Large Store. In most large retail firms, periodic and systematic evaluation of personnel is commonly known as the "personnel review." A committee, frequently consisting of the personnel director and two or three other executives, carries out the review activities. This committee originates forms for recording the performance of each employee (see Figure 9–1) and forms for periodic employee ratings. Although each individual's rating may be made as often as once a month or as infrequently as once a year, about every six months is the usual frequency. To minimize the element of personal prejudice, each employee is usually rated by two to four of his associates. The factors appraised usually include some or all of the following: personality, attendance, sales, industry, initiative, cooperation, knowl-

TO: _____   DATE: ___2 - 15-___

_____*Guppy, Joseph*_____   *asst. Mgr.*   ___971-6___   _____
Name of Person to be Rated   Position   Department   House Number

Please check the appropriate squares below to indicate the above-named person's present job
performance. Give detailed comments below, on all ratings checked Deficient or Poor. For
example, if you have checked Quantity of Work as deficient, you might comment that the cause
is lack of interest; or lack of stamina; a personality clash with a fellow worker; lack of
knowledge of his job; or lack of planning.

	POOR	DEFIC	AVER	GOOD	EXCEL
QUANTITY OF WORK				✓	
QUALITY OF WORK					✓
LEADERSHIP (Includes training and supervision of subordinates)			✓		
INITIATIVE (Can he see things to be done?)					✓
AMOUNT OF SUPERVISION REQUIRED					✓
ATTITUDE TOWARD OTHERS (Is he pleasant, courteous, tactful, cooperative, self-confident and aggressive?)					✓
ORGANIZING ABILITY (Can he analyze a problem or a bad situation and effect a solution smoothly and easily?)					✓
OVER-ALL RATING					✓

COMMENTS: *Mr. Guppy has become a valuable assistant in the department. Is learning shoe know-how rapidly. Sees his job and does it thoroughly.*

PROMOTIONAL POSSIBILITIES: Is this person promotable immediately? _*Yes*_ What more
responsible position do you think he could fill ably? *Asst - larger shoe dept.*
What more responsible position does he have as a goal, if any? *Mgr - Shoes*
If not immediately promotable, when do you think he will be? _*6 months*_

M. Manager   *Joe Guppy*
Signature of Department Manager   Signature of Person Rated

D. Smith
Signature of Divisional Manager

After discussing this rating with the Employe, please return as soon as possible to the
Personnel Office

Courtesy: The Emporium, San Francisco

FIG. 9-1. Job performance form.

edge of the job, loyalty to the firm, accuracy, appearance, treatment of
customers, health, and willingness and ability to assume responsibility.

Another type of personnel evaluation for salespeople is the "shopping
report" prepared by an outside organization. This report covers important
points regarding salesmanship, the appearance of the salesperson and the
department, and the extent of compliance with the store system.

The individual performance records and ratings made available by the
foregoing practices are reviewed by the committee and employees are di-

vided into several groups as follows: (1) those who deserve promotion; (2) those who should stay where they are; (3) those who should be shifted to some other department in the organization in the hope that they will do better there; (4) those who should be discharged if they do not improve before the next periodic review; and (5) those who have previously been warned that they must improve, have failed to improve, and so should be discharged.

Relocating Personnel

The relocation of employees is common in retail stores, just as it is in practically every career field. Some of these relocations will be *promotions;* others will *transfer* the person to a job in another store or department or to a position within the same department where responsibility and pay remain about the same; still others will involve *demotion* because performance has been unsatisfactory.

Promotions. Promotion from within an organization serves both management and employees. It gives management the qualified manpower to fill responsible executive positions. It offers the employee with ability an opportunity to use and exercise that ability and the satisfaction which comes from being part of an organization in which ability is recognized and rewarded. There are few better ways of building employee good will, of offering an incentive for improved performance, and of holding valuable employees than assuring them that they have a "job with a future."

Transfers. Frequently there is much to be gained, both for employer and employee, by transferring a worker to another job. Some transfers are made in an effort to find an assignment for which the employee is better suited by training, ability, and temperament. Others result from the employer's desire to stimulate the employee's interest in the business by "getting him out of a rut" or by reducing the monotony associated with the steady performance of a certain task. Sometimes the transfer is designed to give the employee a broader background and to prepare him for advancement: this use of the transfer is important especially in chain and department stores.

Demotions. As a general rule, no demotion should take place until the retailer is convinced that successful transfer is impossible. Demoting employees requires a great amount of skill and understanding. All too often, the demoted employee takes his new job with a feeling that he has been "railroaded" and not treated fairly by the firm. Unless he can be demoted and his good will retained (or soon regained), it is best to sever connections with him. This statement is not to deny that satisfactory demotions can sometimes be carried out—for instance, during periods when the firm finds it necessary to contract its operations, or when it is evident to the employee that because of age or physical defects he cannot carry on in his present assignment. But the retailer should recognize the difficulties faced when he contemplates demoting an employee.

Terminations

Employers today are looking upon terminations with increasing disfavor. This attitude is partly the result of the growth of unions, with the employer hesitating to discharge a worker for fear he may be accused by the union of discharging the employee because of union activities. But other factors have also played a part. The unemployment compensation provisions of the federal Social Security Act and state laws relating thereto have caused many retailers affected by this legislation to intensify their efforts to maintain continuous employment and thus to effect savings in their payments. In addition, merchants realize that a number of terminations may cause other employees to worry about their jobs and, as a result, lower morale. Moreover, a termination means that the firm has lost its investment in the training of an employee. Since this investment may be considerable, termination should ordinarily be considered only after serious attempts at relocation have been made and the employee has been given adequate warning.

In spite of a growing dislike for terminations, when this course of action has been decided upon, management should not hesitate to face the employee with its decision. Certainly the employee has a right to expect at least an interview with the proprietor of the small store or with someone from the personnel department in the large organization and, in most cases, to receive the reasons leading to the termination. The store itself will reap benefits if it can discharge an employee and still keep some good will, so that he will not go into the community and spread unfavorable publicity concerning the store. Although not even the most carefully conducted termination procedure can always avoid this unfortunate result, much success can be achieved by a well-handled final interview.

Retail Working Conditions[22]

The personnel department has the duty of reviewing and suggesting improvements in working conditions. To this end there must be detailed

---

[22] Also cf. the discussion of this subject on pp. 62–64, above.

studies from the employee's point of view of such matters as lighting, heating, ventilation, rest periods, hours of work, safety, and vacations. Perhaps certain employees can be placed on somewhat reduced hours and still accomplish as much or more than when working longer hours. Certain rest periods may increase efficiency. An employees' cafeteria may meet an important need by providing good food at reasonable prices, and still pay its own way or at least cover the direct cost involved.

Store Hours and Employee Hours. The days and hours of the week the retailer should be open to serve his customers is a problem of increasing importance. Although preferences of customers is probably the chief determinant, competitors' policies, employee attitudes, and government regulations are also basic considerations.[23] Because of the retailer's desire to serve his customers, retail stores have long been noted for the length of time they remain open for business as compared with other firms. However, as a result of the current trend toward night and Sunday openings, store hours today are substantially greater than two decades ago. This trend is evident from reports to the authors by shoe retailers who have increased their "open hours" about 40 percent in the past twenty years, the 48-hour store week of the Forties becoming the 58-hour store week of the Fifties and the 68-hour week today. The typical supermarket east of the Mississippi River is open 72 hours each week, while those in the west average 81 hours.[24]

Traditionally, retail employees have been expected to work long hours but, in line with the general workweek, there has been a progressive shortening of these hours in recent years. Hence, and despite the trend for stores to remain open for longer hours, at present the 40-hour workweek has become fairly common for retail employees in cities with but a slightly longer workweek in other areas. When stores are open six or seven days, either a system of staggered hours or a double shift of employees is used.[25]

1. *Night Openings.* Probably beginning with supermarket operators in southern California, the movement toward night openings has spread rapidly throughout the United States. Faced with the inroads of discount houses and other competitors, many stores have reluctantly added evening (and in numerous cases, Sunday) openings. Downtown retailers have adopted eve-

---

[23] The impact of government regulation through wage and hour laws is covered on p. 269, below.

[24] *Facts about New Super Markets Opened in 1965* (Chicago: Super Market Institute, Inc., 1966), p. 17.

[25] The personnel-scheduling plan for a 24-hour store is discussed in "How Mayfair Makes the 24-Hour Store Work," *Chain Store Age* (Supermarket Executives Ed.), March, 1964, pp. 76–82. Also cf. "Unadorned Warehouse-Type Store Opens Around-the-Clock Operation in Nashville," *Business Week,* November 27, 1965, p. 123.

ning hours as a competitive tool to weaken the pulling power of shopping centers. The net result is that today almost all kinds of stores in all sections of the country are open some evening or evenings each week. Fifty-six percent of the supermarkets east of the Mississippi River and 96 percent of those west of it are open at least six nights each week; downtown Los Angeles stores are open just Monday nights but many outlying units operate six evenings. While downtown Chicago retailers are trying to hold to two nights, some have already gone to three, and stores in suburban Chicago are open as many as five nights. Evening hours have come to be considered essential by shopping center retailers.[26] Already many retailers find that 25 to 35 percent of their sales take place during evening hours, while for some stores the figure rises to 60 percent.

From the point of view of the individual retailer, the decision on night openings raises some major questions, such as:

1. Do the potential customers prefer this time for shopping? Since the retailer exists to serve his customers, this question is the key one.

2. Are night openings profitable? That is, do they result in an increase in sales without a proportionate advance in expenses, or do they merely shift part of the volume to different times with no over-all sales gain? (One student concludes that, while night openings may not be profitable to department stores, they "are probably a necessity by virtue of the fact that competition maintains the same practice.")[27]

3. Are night openings in downtown shopping areas necessary to retard the decentralization of shopping and to meet competition of branch and chain stores?

4. Is customer service impaired or improved through night openings?

5. Are personnel standards lowered or raised as a result of night openings? Does the practice aid or retard the retailer's ability to obtain qualified employees?

6. What combination of staggered hours, part-time employees, and "shift" schedules will be necessary for the store to be open at night and still give employees the shorter hours which they demand?

7. Assuming that it is decided to adopt a policy of night openings, then two additional questions must be answered:

a) Shall the store remain open one or more nights each week?

b) What night or nights and what hours shall be chosen?

2. *Sunday Retailing.* Although many drug and food stores, newspaper shops, and filling stations, to mention just a few, have long operated on

---

[26] *The Super Market Industry Speaks, 1965* (Chicago, Ill.: Super Market Institute, 1965), p. 26; "They Buy by Night: Keep Retailers Up," *Women's Wear Daily,* September 3, 1965, p. 9.

[27] Sam Flanel, Manager of Controllers' Congress of the National Retail Merchants Association, quoted in "Night Openings Overrated?" *Women's Wear Daily,* September 14, 1965, p. 11.

Sunday, only recently have other stores adopted the practice. One of the factors responsible for this growth is the rapid expansion of shopping center and highway shopping. Retailers in these locations—such as discount houses—quickly discovered that night and Saturday hours were especially important to them because of the possibility of family shopping. When they tried Sunday hours, they experienced another substantial increase in sales.[28]

Numerous efforts—most of them unsuccessful—have been made to prevent stores from opening on Sundays through state and local ordinance.[29] Retail trade unions have opposed Sunday selling, even when overtime wages are paid and a forty hour week is maintained through "staggering" of employees. Some retailers, strongly opposed to Sunday retailing, have sponsored joint advertisements condemning the practice and urging customers to stay out of stores on Sundays. Opinions differ regarding the effectiveness of the plea. In practice, however, increasingly stores are yielding to competitive pressure and remaining open on Sundays.[30]

The widespread adoption of Sunday openings by retail stores of almost all types has raised questions for management similar to those already mentioned for night openings and need not be repeated here. Careful consideration of them is essential, however, before a decision is made.

Safety Provisions. Today, retailers are more "safety conscious" than ever before. Safety provisions and preventive measures receive constant attention and have resulted in fewer accidents. In addition, the growing number of governmental regulations affecting working conditions has necessitated familiarity and compliance with safety provisions.

Employee Service Activities

In addition to governmental regulations governing the number of working hours per week and requiring unemployment insurance, workmen's compensation, new pay "floors," and old-age pensions, retailers are increasingly taking on still other service activities.[31] Sears, for example, probably spends more than $150 million each year to give its employees paid

[28] E. B. Weiss, "Sunday Retailing Forges Ahead," *Advertising Age,* September 28, 1964, pp. 90 ff.

[29] Cf., for example, "Sunday Selling Canons Fail to Evoke Clear-Cut Gospel," *Women's Wear Daily,* February 4, 1965, p. 11.

[30] Note the following statement in an advertisement by a variety store chain: "It has not been our policy to open Sunday. However, due to local conditions in the Denver area we are forced to open. We support the 'Save Our Sunday' movment but, until such time as the situation changes, we will be open every Sunday from 12 noon 'til 5:00 P.M."

[31] That the variety and cost of such service activities will continue to rise in the years ahead is suggested by T. H. Paine, "Employee Benefit Costs—Nowhere to Go But Up?" *Personnel,* January–February, 1966, pp. 8–16.

vacations, group life insurance, discounts on purchases, illness allowances and medical care, profit sharing, and other benefits; in fact, during a recent year, the Company contributed over $63 million just to its savings and profit sharing pension fund.[32] In addition, it contributes several million dollars each year to social security and state workmen's compensation funds. The survey of 98 department stores previously referred to disclosed that 73 percent of them sponsor athletic and recreational activities, 62 percent aid employees to locate living quarters, 62 percent offer a fully equipped medical department, 77 percent provide group insurance, and 43 percent offer savings and loan programs.[33] Still other retailers engage in educational activities, and offer counseling services on a wide variety of subjects, including preparation for retirement.[34]

Sometimes the cost of the service work immediately pays for itself, as when a retailer offers certain health services which lead to a rise in productivity. In other instances, such as providing a pension system, it is quite impossible to say whether or not the cost of the system is offset by greater effort. But the fact remains that the service activities of a retailer are important in attracting and keeping employees, and competition is forcing more and more employers to undertake them.

Medical and Health Services. In large retail organizations medical and health services may be available on a formalized, continuous basis, with one or more full-time doctors and a staff of nurses. The smaller firm uses a doctor only part time, often having regular hours during which he is at the store to serve employees. A visiting nurse may be retained to give aid to employees confined to their homes. Dental clinics have been set up by some organizations. Vacations, which are steadily being liberalized, are still another way to improve the health of employees.[35]

Increasingly retail organizations have encouraged and aided their employees to take medical and hospitalization insurance, often provided through organizations like "Blue Shield" and "Blue Cross." Under the plans of such a group, both the store and the employee pay part of the cost, the latter's contribution being deducted from his pay and, together with the store's share, sent to the insurance company. The present emphasis on medical care is also demonstrated by the attention given this matter in union negotiations; frequently greater medical and dental benefits are sought. And,

---

[32] *Annual Report,* year ended January 31, 1966, p. 8.

[33] Sands, *op. cit.,* pp. 20–21. More recent comparable data are not available.

[34] E. F. Lundgren, "Needed: Retirement Counseling Programs in Business," *Personnel Journal,* September, 1965, pp. 432–36.

[35] Cf. pp. 62–63, above; and A. A. Sloane, "Trends Toward More Liberalized Vacations," *Personnel,* January–February, 1966, pp. 56–61.

of course, both employer and employee are required to finance, through a compulsory payroll tax, the hospital and related care offered under the medicare program.[36]

Recreational and Educational Activities. One effective method of building good will is through store-sponsored recreational activities such as orchestras, glee clubs, dramatics, athletic events, all-store picnics, costume parties, dances, and many other kinds of social events. Some stores provide rented or store-owned facilities for the groups they sponsor: An auditorium in which the glee club and dramatic group may give entertainments, an athletic field, a hall for social gatherings. Management should go slowly in "pushing" recreational activities, and all signs of paternalism must be avoided. Probably the best approach is for the retailer to sponsor only those activities in which the employees take some initiative. A common method of ascertaining employee interest is to establish one or more recreation clubs which are partly supported by dues contributed by employees.[37]

Educational activities of retailers, other than those directly connected with the training program, are not widespread but are steadily becoming more common. Some of the larger firms have long maintained libraries, and increasingly they are offering financial assistance, through scholarships and work-study arrangements, to encourage employees to continue their education in business schools, colleges, and universities.

Employee Financial Benefit Plans. Retailers extend other kinds of financial aid to their employees through group insurance, mutual-aid associations, old-age pensions, and savings and loan programs.

1. *Group Insurance.* Group life insurance plans, under which both employer and employee make a contribution, are restricted chiefly to large stores and chain organizations. Employee contributions are deducted from pay checks. There are no restrictions because of age, and no physical examination is required. However, the insurance lapses when the employee terminates his connection with the company (although under some plans the employee may convert some or all of his group insurance to another kind of policy); and, since it is term insurance, it has no cash value.

2. *Mutual-Aid Associations.* These associations, which are voluntary in nature, have as their main aim the provision of sickness, accident, and death benefits for employees not covered by workmen's compensation and insurance plans. They also render extensive assistance in times of financial

---

[36] Under the current schedule, the payroll tax is 1 percent on the first $6,600 of earnings divided equally between employer and employee. In 1973 the rate advances to 1.1 percent.

[37] For an example of such a club within Montgomery Ward & Company cf. "Personnel Strategy," *op. cit.*, p. 174.

stress. They are usually incorporated, so that they have a legal existence separate from that of the store. Contributions come from both employees and employer; and, although employees and management may cooperate in the operation of the association, frequently control is largely in the hands of the employees. In some cases the employer underwrites the establishment of the association and then leaves it up to employee contributions to carry on from that point.

3. *Old-Age Pensions.* As in other fields the passage of the federal Social Security Act established a pension plan for retail employees.[38] The employer is required to match the payments being made by his employees, the payment of each being 3.9 (4.4 after 1968) percent on wages up to $6,600 per year. Upon reaching the age of 65, the individual who retired before 1965 may receive a monthly retirement benefit which, depending upon his and his employer's contributions, may range as high as $135.90 per month; while for those retiring after December 31, 1964, somewhat higher benefits will be paid.[39] There is also provision for partial benefits to a widow. In addition, an increasing number of organizations are supplementing these payments by old-age pension plans of their own.[40]

4. *Savings and Loan Plans.* Some large retailers have established savings plans. These usually call for periodic cash deposits on the part of employees, to be accompanied by a deposit to each employee's account by the employer; or the employer's deposit may be withheld until the employee has made his payment for a number of months or has saved a certain amount. For example, employees of one large retailer may deposit three percent of their annual pay in the savings plan and the company—depending upon its annual earnings—will contribute an amount equal to 25 to 50 percent of each employee's deposit. In a recent year, this firm contributed over $1.7 million to this savings plan.[41] Many retailers, both large and small, encourage the purchase of government savings bonds and make

---

[38] The unemployment insurance feature of the Social Security Act is covered in Chapter 27, "Retail Insurance."

[39] For details, cf. *Medicare and Social Security Benefits* (Chicago, Ill.: Commerce Clearing House, Inc., 1965), pp. 2–8 and 23.

[40] For a general study of private pension plans cf. United States Bureau of Labor Statistics, *Digest of 100 Selected Pension Plans Under Collective Bargaining* (Washington: The Bureau, 1965). An analysis of the plan at Sears, Roebuck and Co. is given in Osbon, *op. cit.,* pp. 1 and 56. For an inquiry into the actuarial uncertainties of the present and future costs of the pension plans adopted by retailing (and other) firms, cf. T. A. Wise, "Those Uncertain Actuaries," *Fortune,* Vol. LXXIII, No. 1, (January, 1966), pp. 164–66 ff. Some suggestions for limiting the cost of these plans will be found in "How Management Can Control Rising Pension Costs," *Business Management,* March, 1966, pp. 47–50 ff.

[41] Montgomery Ward & Company, *Annual Report* for year ended February 2, 1966, p. 16. For the plan of another retailer, cf. *Annual Report* of Mercantile Stores Company, Inc., year ended January 31, 1966, pp. 20–21.

deductions of agreed amounts from regular pay checks of employees to pay for them. Others may offer an emergency loan service through which an employee may secure funds repayable through deductions from his wages. Or, such loans may be handled through credit unions, many of which have been encouraged by management.[42]

Handling Employee Complaints

Employee complaints cover a wide range of subjects—hours, wages, promotions, working conditions, "fringe" benefits, and tactics of other salespeople. Many retailers go to great lengths to minimize or eliminate such complaints. The employee-service activities discussed in the previous section are important in this connection, as is also the case with practically all the work of the personnel division. So that remedial action may be taken, the so-called "exit interview" is used by some retailers to determine the factors which caused the employee to be dissatisfied with his job.[43] A checklist used by the exit interviewers employed by one retailer is given in Figure 9–2. Still other firms encourage their employees to elect representatives to meet

---

                                                                    Date

NAME   DEPARTMENT

DATE EMPLOYED   LAST DAY WORKED   SALARY OR RATE   ——

WHY IS EMPLOYEE LEAVING?   ——

WHAT, IF ANYTHING, WAS ESPECIALLY DISLIKED ABOUT WORK?

WERE WORKING CONDITIONS SATISFACTORY? (LIGHT, HEAT, ATMOSPHERE, ETC.)   ——

WAS EQUIPMENT FOR YOUR JOB SATISFACTORY?   ——

WERE YOUR REST PERIODS—EATING PERIODS SATISFACTORY?
WAS SALARY SATISFACTORY? (INCREASE?)   ——

DO YOU HAVE ANY UNFINISHED FINANCIAL BUSINESS WITH THE COMPANY?
   (CREDIT UNION, ETC.)   ——

WAS TREATMENT RECEIVED FROM THIS OFFICE SATISFACTORY?   ——

HOW WAS THE TREATMENT FROM THE OTHER EMPLOYEES?   ——

DO YOU THINK A PERSON HAS OPPORTUNITY FOR ADVANCEMENT IN THIS FIRM?   ——

DOES EMPLOYEE HAVE ANY SUGGESTIONS FOR IMPROVEMENT ON ANYTHING
   WITHIN ORGANIZATION?   ——

DOES EMPLOYEE THINK MANAGEMENT IS INTERESTED IN EMPLOYEE?   ——

WAS AMPLE TRAINING GIVEN ON JOB?   ——

WOULD EMPLOYEE BE INTERESTED IN WORKING AGAIN FOR THE COMPANY?   ——

OTHER COMMENTS: _____

SIGNATURE OF INTERVIEWER   SIGNATURE OF EMPLOYEE

FIG. 9–2.   Exit interview checklist.

---

[42] "Starting a Credit Union for your Firm," *Administrative Management,* March, 1966, pp. 32 ff.

[43] "Getting Full Value from Exit Interviews," *Supervisory Management,* March, 1965, pp. 49–51.

with management and discuss problems of mutual interests. Employer-employee committees are established to consider especially difficult problems, such as improving working conditions and the more advantageous planning of vacations.

Despite such efforts complaints continue to develop and provision should be made to handle them promptly and effectively. In the small store they are handled directly by the proprietor and usually on an informal basis; but in the large operation a definite procedure needs to be set up for dealing with them.[44] Such a procedure has been made imperative by the growth of trade unions in the retail field, since the union demands that there be some responsible executive with whom it can negotiate and from whom it can expect action when agreements have been reached. The net result has been that the personnel director, or a special assistant well versed in personnel relations, has been given the duty of dealing with complaints.

Labor Organizations in the Retail Field

Growth of Retail Labor Unions. Unions in the retail field are not a new development. As early as 1882, there existed several unions composed solely of store employees.[45] Their main aim of seeking shorter hours earned them the name of "Early Closing Societies." Although these early unions had some successes and experienced some growth, the limited development of trade unions that has taken place in the retail field has occurred mainly since the early 1930's.

The National Labor Relations Act, passed in 1935, although it specifically exempts those employed in a local retailing capacity, provides that employers shall not interfere in any way with unions, shall not discriminate against union members, and shall not refuse to bargain with their employees' representatives. In other words, if a majority of the employees of an interstate retail organization form a union and send representatives to talk over certain grievances, the management must negotiate concerning the complaints.[46] Whereas at an earlier time the setting up of an agency to handle employees' complaints was a matter for the store to decide, today the machinery must exist in retail establishments where employees are organ-

---

[44] For specific procedural suggestions cf. "How to Handle Employee Complaints," *Super Market Merchandising,* February, 1964, pp. 59 ff.

[45] P. H. Nystrom, *Economics of Retailing* (New York: Ronald Press Co., 1930), Vol. II, p. 281.)

[46] Actually, the union may represent the firm's employees in a given geographic area, such as greater Los Angeles, and not necessarily throughout the country. Moreover, it may represent just certain types of employees, such as restaurant workers, sales personnel, or clerical employees. Cf. "Unions Will Sell Harder in Stores," *Business Week,* February 6, 1965, p. 46.

ized. A few states have passed laws that place intrastate employees in the same position as employees of interstate retailers.

Despite both this favorable legal situation and success in obtaining the closed shop and the checkoff in some department and chain stores, the spread of unions in the retail field has been slow.[47] Probably no more than 5 to 10 percent of all nonmanagerial retail employees are unionized. Among sales-supporting personnel—truck drivers, warehouse employees, elevator operators, and maintenance staffs—the percentage is somewhat higher. The trend, however, is for retail unions to gain more ground. In the Southern California area 45,000 retail employees already belong to the Retail Clerks International Association; and about 55 percent of the supermarket chains of that area are organized, although in varying degrees.[48] Nationwide, the Retail Clerks International Association, which has become the "fastest growing union in the United States," has 428,000 members; while 167,000 belong to the AFL-CIO's Retail, Wholesale and Department Store Union and 341,000 to the Amalgamated Meat Cutters and Butcher Workmen.[49] Currently, these unions are seeking to make inroads among employees of discount houses, supermarkets, department stores, and specialty stores in major cities.[50] In some instances, long and costly strikes have resulted from these efforts.[51]

Union Aims. In general, retail unions have sought such goals as union recognition, the closed shop, shorter hours, higher wages, extra pay for overtime, paid vacations, health and welfare programs, grievance procedures, seniority rights, and job security.[52] In some cases substantial gains have been made, especially in regard to hours, wages, paid vacations, and overtime pay, and these gains have been recognized in formal contracts drawn up and signed by representatives of both employees and management.[53] To forestall union activities, retailers in some cities have formed

---

[47] "Retail Unions Run Into Roadblocks," *Women's Wear Daily,* December 7, 1965, p. 31.

[48] "Organizing with an Adman's Touch," *Business Week,* October 16, 1965, p. 76.

[49] The quotation is from "The Clerks Are Minding the Store," *Fortune,* Vol. LXVI, No. 2 (August, 1962), pp. 191–92; the membership figures are given in "Unions Gain Members, But the Going's Slow," *Business Week,* November 6, 1965, p. 114.

[50] For example, cf. John Osbon, "Chicago Stores Facing Strong Drive by Unions," *Women's Wear Daily,* October 22, 1965, p. 18; and "Department Stores Drive on Portland Retail Clerks Set," *ibid.,* March 23, 1966, p. 10.

[51] For the story of a three-month labor struggle in one area cf. "New Pact Ends Labor Dispute in Baltimore," *Super Market News,* July 27, 1964, p. 1.

[52] As an illustration of union efforts to achieve job security, in some areas the Amalgamated Meat Cutters have contracts which forbid retailers from selling pre-packaged meats. *Business Week,* May 7, 1966, p. 128.

[53] A 1965 three-year contract, the first drawn up between the RCIA and the Texas supermarket and home-center chain of J. Weingarten, Inc., increased weekly wages by

their own voluntary agreements as to hours, wages, and other matters, such agreements usually representing gains for their employees.

1. *Wage and Hour Laws.* As one step toward higher wages, unions have supported both state and federal wage and hour laws. A few states have had such laws for some time but it was not until 1961 that the federal government passed a law including a substantial number of retail workers.

Known as the Wage and Hour Law, this legislation (H.R. 3935) provided for a reduction in working hours per week and established minimum wage rates for workers in the larger retailing establishments. So far as hours of work are concerned, the law sets a 40 hour week with overtime at one and one-half times the standard rate. Salesmen receiving more than half their pay from commissions or who earn at least one and one-half times the minimum rate are excluded from overtime. Originally establishing $1.00 per hour as the minimum wage rate, in 1964 the minimum advanced to $1.15 per hour, in 1965 to $1.25 per hour, in 1967 to $1.40 per hour and in 1968 it goes to $1.60. Although in 1965 the minimum wage provisions applied to retailers having at least $1 million in sales, by 1971 the $1.60 minimum must be paid by retailers with annual sales in excess of $250,000.

Certain implications of the minimum wage and hour laws for the retailers covered are quite clear.[54] One is that retailers are compelled to maintain the differential between those whose wages are advanced by the minimum and other workers already exceeding it. Another is that the rising minimum has accelerated the move toward self-service and automation and caused many retailers to place greater emphasis on productivity.[55]

Management Response to Unions. Although management's first reaction to the spread of unionism was to look for some method of "smashing the union," increasing numbers of enlightened retailers, like alert businessmen in all fields, soon decided to make an effort to improve conditions and minimize grievances. In some cases the leading retailers of a city have agreed to a "code of ethics" calling for better working conditions, shorter hours, and higher wages. A number of retailers have actively encouraged a

---

$4–$5; set a 40-hour week with overtime pay features, including time-and-a-half for Sundays and night-time premium pay; guaranteed six paid holidays each year with daily paid rest periods; and added such additional benefits as life insurance, sick pay, and medication. *Super Market Merchandising,* August, 1965, p. 13. In such detail is the July 16, 1965 agreement between the San Francisco Retailers' Council and the Department Store Employes' Union that it fills a 39 page booklet.

[54] However, as to many other implications of these laws, there is widespread disagreement. Cf. "If Minimum Wage Moves Up to $1.75 an Hour," *U.S. News and World Report,* August 16, 1965, pp. 75–76; and New York Department of Labor, *Economic Effects of Minimum Wages* (Albany, N.Y.: The Department, 1964).

[55] D. E. Kahn, "Minimum Wages: Factor Substitution and the Marginal Producer," *Quarterly Journal of Economics,* August, 1965, pp. 478–86; and "Wage Legislation: What Does It Mean to Retailers?" *Department Store Economist,* February, 1966, p. 34.

degree of employee participation in management. Other companies are making serious efforts to acquaint employees with their labor policies, what management is already doing for its employees, and what it hopes to do in the future. To this end, "jobholders' annual reports" and employee policy books are distributed to employees. In the past, all too often, major difficulties in personnel relations have been caused by management weaknesses. Fortunately, alert executives recognize this fact and are taking measures to correct the situation.

As to the future of unions and collective bargaining in the retail field, certainly the facts that retailing is a field of relatively small establishments with close relationships between proprietor and employees, that many retail employees hope to establish their own stores at a later time, and that many employees are on a part-time basis while many others look upon retailing as a temporary means of making a living, are deterrents to labor organizations. Yet it seems likely that labor developments in the retail field are still in their early stages. Unions may well demonstrate greater strength and continue to grow.

There are many retailers who see only "bad" results from union growth, especially loss of control over personnel. In contrast, a few retailers argue that the end result may be employees who are more appreciative of the problems of management, more willing to cooperate in making suggestions for improving operations, and—because of a greater feeling of security—more enthusiastic about their jobs. In large measure, securing these benefits depends upon a progressive personnel program, which is believed in and adhered to by the management and made absolutely clear to all employees.

Regardless of a specific retailer's attitude toward retail unions, he can not afford to overlook his legal and moral responsibilities to his employees. Familiarity and full compliance with city, state, and federal labor regulations are essential. In addition, his personnel policies must be forward-looking in the sense that he must anticipate and prepare for future developments. Above all, he must provide an environment in which employees can work pleasantly and effectively.

REVIEW AND DISCUSSION QUESTIONS

1. Talk with five employees, selecting each one from a different type of store (food, drug, department store, and so on) to determine the validity or inaccuracy of the statement: "Employee dissatisfaction with compensation plans is a common source of employee complaint."
2. Are there any characteristics of retailing which make it difficult to devise a satisfactory compensation plan for retail personnel? Explain.
3. As the proprietor of a retail store, under what conditions or circum-

stances would you adopt each of the main methods of compensating sales-people?

4. Analyze the pros and cons for paying salespeople a straight commission in (1) a drugstore, (2) a new car agency, (3) a men's clothing store.
5. What is your opinion concerning equal pay for equal work regardless of sex? Defend your answer.
6. Through library or field research, determine the details of the employee profit-sharing plans in use by two retail firms. Make comparisons between them and formulate your own set of requirements for a good profit-sharing plan.
7. Evaluate the employee discount policies of three specific retailers in your area.
8. Explain the major current compensation plans for sales-supporting employees.
9. What do you think are the most satisfactory ways for compensating (a) department store buyers, (b) chain discount house managers, (c) chain women's ready-to-wear shop managers, (d) general managers of the branches of a mail-order house, and (e) major executives in large retail firms? Explain.
10. Discuss the meaning, objectives, and methods of job evaluation.
11. Talk with two employees of retailers using a systematic plan of personnel review. Report and analyze these individuals' opinions as to the benefits and limitations of the review.
12. What are the main current trends in retail working conditions? Discuss the impact of these trends on the activities of the personnel department.
13. Based on present employee service activities carried on by retailers, what, in your judgment, will be the directions in which they will move in the future? Give reasons for your answer.
14. How do you account for the relatively slow growth of retail trade unions in this country and what do you think of their future growth possibilities?
15. If a $2.00 per hour minimum wage law were adopted, effective six months from now, suggest its immediate and long view implications for retailing.

SUPPLEMENTARY READINGS

AHERN, EILEEN. "Equal Employment Opportunity," *Personnel,* July–August, 1965, pp. 40–44; and "What the Civil Rights Act Means to Your Company," *Management Review,* January, 1966, pp. 38–41. These analyses of Title VII of the Civil Rights Act of 1964 should be supplemented by the discussion of the Title's application to retailing in FEINBERG, SAMUEL, *Women's Wear Daily,* July 16, 1965, p. 7 and July 20, 1965, p. 10.

BEACH, D. S. *Personnel: The Management of People at Work* (New York: Macmillan Co., 1965). Although not specifically directed at the retailer, this general text can be read with great profit to the student of retailing.

CLARK, H. F., AND SLOAN, H. S. *Classrooms in the Stores* (New York: Institute for Instructional Improvement, Inc., 1962). This volume provides a close look at retail training and emphasizes the limitations of present methods and devices. For criticism of this study cf. "Union Blasts Report, Cites Rise in Retail Productivity," *Women's Wear Daily*, March 30, 1962, p. 2.

CLEMENT, N. P., JR. "Current Practices in Retail Executive Compensation," *Retail Control*, February, 1965, pp. 13–35. A study of current compensation practices of stores in the western part of the United States and an analysis of the goals and elements of a good compensation plan are presented in this article.

GOLDSTUCKER, J. L. "Competent Retail Trainees—Where Are They?" *Journal of Marketing*, Vol. XXVII, No. 2 (April, 1963), pp. 38–41. If trainees are to be attracted to the retail field, the author believes that appreciably higher salaries must be offered to them, and the more talented ones must be advanced more rapidly than in the past.

GUION, R. M. *Personnel Testing* (New York: McGraw-Hill Book Co., Inc., 1965). The types of employment tests, their validity, and current testing practices are included in this basic volume. Also cf. GUION, R. M., AND GOTTIER, R. F. "Validity of Personality Measures in Personnel Selection," *Personnel Psychology*, Summer, 1965, pp. 135–64.

"If Minimum Wage Moves Up to $1.75 an Hour," *U.S. News and World Report*, August 16, 1965, pp. 75–76. In addition to this general discussion concerning the impact of minimum wage laws, also cf. "Wage Legislation: What Does It Mean to Retailers?" *Department Store Economist*, February, 1966, p. 34.

JEHRING, J. J., AND METZGER, B. L. *The Stockholder and Employee Profit Sharing* (Evanston, Ill.: Profit Sharing Research Foundation, 1960). Drawing on an analysis of 14 retail chains, the authors conclude that profit sharing contributes to a successful company.

LOPEZ, F. M. *Personnel Interviewing* (New York: McGraw-Hill Book Co., Inc., 1965). The limitations of the interview, as well as suggestions for getting better results from it, are set forth in this volume. Other good sources are afforded by BASSETT, G. A. *Practical Interviewing* (New York: American Management Association, Inc., 1965) and RICHARDSON, S. A., et al. *Interviewing* (New York: Basic Books, Inc., 1965).

MARK, B. R. "Hiring and Training Personnel for the Bookstore," *Publishers' Weekly*, March 1, 1965, pp. 68–71. Personnel selecting and training practices in a specific retail field are detailed in this article. For retailing in general, cf. WOOD, W. E. "Search for Better Retail Training," *Merchandising World*, February 7, 1966, pp. 16–19.

MARTING, ELIZABETH, AND MACDONALD, DOROTHY (ed.). *Management and Its People* (New York: American Management Association, 1965). The development of today's personnel management philosophy during the past 45 years is set forth in this volume.

NATIONAL RETAIL MERCHANTS ASSOCIATION. *Retail Employee Discounts* (New York, 1965). Employee discount policies and practices in 270 department and specialty stores are analyzed in this study.

OSBON, JOHN. "Profit Sharing Pension Paradise," *Women's Wear Daily*, October 7, 1964, pp. 1 and 56. This report on the savings and profit-sharing pension fund of Sears, Roebuck and Company is based on an address by the fund's executive director. Also cf. "Trends in Corporate Pension Plans," *Management Review,* April, 1966, pp. 65–69.

PATTON, ARCH. "Executive Compensation by 1970," *Harvard Business Review,* Vol. XLII, No. 5 (September–October, 1964), pp. 137–46. Among other developments, the author sees a trend toward cash payments instead of stock options (but cf. "Stock Options: Still Going Strong," *Management Review,* June, 1966, pp. 57–59.) He also believes that increasingly incentive payments will be based on a "performance appraisal" of the execuive.

PATTON, J. A., LITTLEFIELD, C. L., AND SELF, S. A. *Job Evaluation* (3d ed.; Homewood, Ill.: Richard D. Irwin, Inc., 1964). By text and cases this volume covers (1) compensation policies and programs, (2) job analysis and descriptions, (3) job evaluation, (4) pricing jobs, and (5) administration of the compensation program. Also suggested is MILLER, J. D. "Written Job Description Helps Delegation Process," *Administrative Management,* January, 1966, p. 45.

"Personnel Strategy," *Chain Store Age* (Variety Store—General Merchandise Managers Edition), December, 1964, pp. 164, 166–82. Some of the personnel policies and practices of Montgomery Ward & Company are outlined in this article.

RICKLEFS, ROGER. "How Companies are Using Psychological Tests," *Management Review,* April, 1965, pp. 45–48. The increasing use of testing by business firms is detailed in this article. For testing by retailers cf. HARWELL, E. M., "Employee Tests for Food Chains," *Chain Store Age* (Supermarket Executives Edition), July, 1965, pp. 19 and 50; and FEINBERG, SAMUEL, "Psychological Aptitude Testing," *Women's Wear Daily,* November 26, 1965, p. 7.

SCHIFFMAN, L. G. "Programmed Instruction: A Training Mode," *New York Retailer,* December, 1964, pp. 2–11. Among the subjects covered in this article are: What is programmed instruction? What is a teaching machine? Where can one get programs? A good bibliography is also included.

STAFFORD, J. E., AND GREER, T. V. "Consumer Preference for Types of Salesmen: A Study of Independence-Dependence Characteristics," *Journal of Retailing,* Vol. XLI, No. 2 (Summer, 1965), pp. 27–33 ff. Since the selection and training of salespeople should result in the kind of personnel favored by customers, this study of what consumers really want is important to retail personnel management.

SUPER MARKET INSTITUTE, INC. *Testing, Selecting, and Motivating Employees for Superior Performance* (Chicago, 1964). The policies and practices of food chains in testing, selecting, and motivating employees are reported in the proceedings of the Institute's mid-year (1964) conference.

———. *Food Retailing Courses in Educational Institutions* (Chicago, 1966). This listing covers extension courses as well as those offered in secondary schools and colleges.

"What Should You Do About Employee Discounts," *Super Market Merchandising,* December, 1965, p. 29; and ROSENTHAL, RICHARD. "Employee Discount Buying Rings Up 4% of Store Sales," *Women's Wear Daily,* December 1, 1965, p. 8. These two reports cover employee discount practices in super- markets, department stores, and specialty stores.

WISE, T. A.   "Those Uncertain Actuaries," *Fortune,* Vol. LXXIII, No. 1 (January, 1966), pp. 164–66 ff. Many retail firms have pension plans. Some of the problems of determining how many dollars a firm should place in its plan, and when, are discussed in this article.

PART V

Merchandise Management:

Buying, Control, Receiving, and Pricing

10
CHAPTER

Buying to Meet Customers' Wants

There is an old saying among retailers that "goods well bought are half sold." Certainly there is much validity in this saying, and the retailer who neglects the buying function operates under a severe handicap. One might go further and add that goods not well bought cannot be profitably sold. Our most sucessful retailers are those who have placed much emphasis on the buying function.[1] It is important, therefore, that we examine this subject in some detail.

THE BUYING FUNCTION

In general conversation the term "buying" is used simply to connote the act of purchase. We speak of going to the grocery store to buy a can of peas; when we hand the grocer 30 cents and get the can of peas, we have engaged in buying. As used by the retailer, however, the term "buying" includes far more than the act of purchase. Specifically, it involves the following steps: (1) formulating effective buying policies; (2) determining customer wants; (3) selecting sources of supply; (4) determining suitability of the merchandise offered for sale; (5) negotiating terms of sale; and (6) transferring title. In this and the next two chapters, each of these steps will be considered.

It should be made clear at the outset, however, that the work of persons known in various retail organizations as "buyers" may consist of less or more

---

[1] For some examples, note the emphasis placed on buying by the J. C. Penney Company; Sears, Roebuck and Co.; and the Great Atlantic & Pacific Tea Company. Cf. John McDonald, "Sears Makes It Look Easy," *Fortune,* Vol. LXIX, No. 5 (May, 1964), especially pp. 123 and 125; and "Pinching 500,000,000,000 Pennies," *ibid.,* Vol. LXVII, No. 3 (March, 1963), p. 172.

than the six activities mentioned. In a large shoe chain the buyer may have nothing to do with the formulation of buying policies and spend little time on the determination of wants, the general manager assuming these activities. In contrast, in the smaller retail store the proprietor generally does the buying in addition to serving in such other capacities as salesman, advertising director, and general manager. Even in the large department store the buyer may be in charge of the selling as well as the buying activities of his department.[2] Our interest lies in how the buying function is performed, irrespective of the title carried by the individual or individuals engaged in performing that function.[3]

FORMULATING EFFECTIVE BUYING POLICIES[4]

The first step in buying is the establishment of clear-cut policies covering all aspects of the purchasing function. To illustrate, let us consider the policy with respect to selecting sources of supply. Since vendors differ widely in the quality and style of merchandise they handle and in their ability to deliver the goods ordered when promised, much care must be exercised in choosing particular suppliers. Decisions must be made as to buying from jobbers or wholesalers, as contrasted to purchase directly from manufacturers; the degree to which buying will be concentrated with a few resources; and whether joint purchasing will be undertaken with other retailers.

Naturally, there are wide differences between small stores and large stores as to the importance of the foregoing considerations. Small stores customarily buy from wholesalers, whereas large stores generally buy directly from manufacturers. Whereas proprietors of small stores make infrequent trips to market, buyers for large stores may go several times a year. In view of price and other advantages obtained by buying directly, small retailers should consider the advisability of joining cooperative buying associations while large stores often have a choice among cooperative-, group-, or centralized-buying arrangements. As we shall see later, along with their advantages these arrangements have serious limitations which store executives often fail to recognize. Full consideration of all the factors involved should precede any decision on this question.

---

[2] The trend toward the separation of these two functions in department store organization is discusses on pp. 206–9, above.

[3] The "personal qualifications needed for success" in performing the buying function are set forth in J. W. Wingate and J. S. Friedlander, *The Management of Retail Buying* (Englewood Cliffs, N.J.: Prentice-Hall, Inc., 1963), pp. 13–19.

[4] The reader will find it helpful to review the discussion of policies in Chapter 2, pp. 44–49, above.

Buying Policies Must Harmonize With Other Policies

In establishing his buying policies the retailer should bear in mind two basic considerations. First, his buying policies should be "in tune" with the general objectives of his organization. In discussing the retailing mix offered by any retailer, two careful students have suggested that this mix "is composed of three sub-mixes: a goods and service mix, a communications mix, and a physical distribution mix"[5]—and there should be harmony among all three sub-mixes. Put another way, the retailer who aims to sell expensive and high-style women's dresses should establish buying policies which will bring these dresses to his store, surround his dresses with the services and physical facilities expected by potential customers of such merchandise, and promote his apparel through advertising which reflects the character of his store.[6] But the type of merchandise handled is not the only guide to appropriate buying policies for a specific retailer; his policies are also influenced by such other factors as the stock assortment or "breadth of line" carried; the clientele to be served; the funds available in the merchandise budget; the knowledge, experience, and preferences of the buyer, merchandise manager, and proprietor; the nature and extent of competition; general business conditions, including seasonal and cyclical variations; and the general needs of the community as a whole.

Buying Policies Must Serve the Customer

The second basic consideration in establishing buying policies is to recognize the importance of the customer.[7] Actually, all successful purchasing begins with a clear-cut idea on the buyer's part of *what* is wanted, or at least what the buyer thinks will be wanted when it is called to the attention of potential customers. As one merchant puts it, "the merchant should develop an attitude and strategy for interpreting what people want and how big that want is."[8] The buyer's personal likes and dislikes are unimportant; he is the

[5] William Lazer and E. J. Kelley, "The Retailing Mix: Planning and Management," *Journal of Retailing,* Vol. XXXVII, No. 1 (Spring, 1961), p. 37.

[6] The need for a store to create a distinctive "image" in the customer's mind is well set forth in S. R. Flaster, "Diversified Image in Women's Specialty Stores: With A Look At Madison Avenue Shops," *New York Retailer,* December, 1965, pp. 7–12; and J. W. Wingate, "Revising the Store Image," *ibid.,* May, 1966, pp. 7–10.

[7] An understanding of consumer decision making is essential for effective buying. On this topic cf. J. V. McNeal (Ed.), *Dimensions of Consumer Behavior* (New York: Appleton-Century-Crofts, 1965).

[8] H. L. Seegal, writing in *The Buyer's Manual* (4th. ed.; New York: National Retail Merchants Association, 1965), p. 47.

"purchasing agent" of the customers.[9] He should know customers preferences as to price class of goods, quality, materials, styles, colors, and the like —a task which is growing in importance as customers achieve higher standards of living and become more discriminating ("fussy" is the word often used by retailers) in their purchases.[10]

Despite the key role of the customer, one retailer freely admits that "some department store retailers have had little understanding of their shoppers." Believing that too many managements "place complete reliance on instinct," he urges his fellow retailers to research the customer in order "to reevaluate their policies . . . to see if customer needs can be better served without undue additional operating cost."[11] Especially in relation to buying policies, this advice is of great value. In such a reevaluation, the shifts in consumer spending and buying habits growing out of the factors already outlined in Chapter 1 should be given careful consideration.[12]

In addition to considerable knowledge of what consumers want, the buyer must also form a judgment as to the quantity of the desired merchandise which he should purchase. The balance of this chapter, shall be used to investigate the ways in which stores of various sizes and in different fields obtain information concerning *what* particular goods their customers want and in what *quantities* the wanted goods should be purchased by the store.

DETERMINING THE GOODS CUSTOMERS WANT

Information as to the types, kinds, and prices of goods wanted by a retailer's present and potential customers may be gathered both inside and outside the store. The major sources may be classified as follows:

A. Inside sources
   1. Past sales
   2. Returned goods and adjustment data
   3. Credit department data

---

[9] And many retailers find that the majority of their customers are women. One authority suggests it is "the ever increasing duties of the wife who serves as household purchasing agent." H. O. Whiteside in Reavis Cox, Wroe Alderson, and S. J. Shapiro, *Theory in Marketing* (Homewood, Ill.: Richard D. Irwin, Inc., 1964), p. 270. In fact, "it has been estimated that they (women) purchase 75 percent of all goods and services sold in America." *Executives' Guide to Marketing for 1965* (New York: Printers' Ink, 1964), p. 33.

[10] These changes are set forth in George Katona, *The Mass Consumption Society* (New York: McGraw-Hill Book Company, 1964) and, more briefly, in R. L. Brown, "Compelling New Age of Elegance," *Sales Management,* February 19, 1965, pp. 25–27 ff.

[11] M. J. Rothenberg, Allied Stores Corporation, in a review of S. U. Rich, *Shopping Behavior of Department Store Customers* published in *Journal of Marketing Research,* Vol. II, No. 4 (November, 1965), p. 424.

[12] Cf. the discussion of "The Changing Environment of Retailing," pp. 9–15, above.

4. Customer inquiries
5. Suggestions of salespeople
6. Judgment of buyers
B. Outside sources
1. Other successful stores
2. Vendors' offerings
3. Central market representatives
4. Trade papers, newspapers, and general publications
5. Customer surveys

Past Sales

The most important inside source of information on customers' wants is found in a store's past sales. Although this source yields more information on staple merchandise than on fashion goods, it is an important source even for the latter.

The Basic Stock List for Staple Goods. Practically every kind of retail store has a large number of items which are little affected by fashion. At one extreme, we find the food store, with staples making up the bulk of its stock. Near the other extreme is the millinery shop, where staples are practically nonexistent. Between these extremes are stores with all degrees of combinations of staple and fashion merchandise. A detailed analysis of past sales of the more staple items will enable a store to determine a basic stock list for such items, and this list is of significant aid to the store buyer.

A basic stock list usually consists of (1) a list of the items to be carried in stock, classified as to size and other important factors; (2) the minimum quantities to have on hand at any time—adjusted, of course to seasonal requirements; and (3) the quantity to order when reordering takes place. In the establishment of such a list, an analysis of past sales is essential. Consider how a food store would get figures to place the X brand of ground coffee on its basic stock list. A study of the store's records shows sales of pounds averaging 36 per week and of two-pounds 3 per week. In no single week of the past year has the store sold over 48 pounds and 5 two-pounds. As the packer of the coffee guarantees delivery within one week from the time an order is placed, the store does not need to carry more than enough to meet the demand of its peak weeks. Consequently, 48 pounds and 5 two-pounds becomes the minimum stock.[13] Every time the stock falls to this point, the buyer should reorder.

---

[13] In terms of a formula, the minimum stock is equal to the quantity normally sold (36 pounds and 3 two-pounds) during the delivery period (one week, in this case) plus a safety factor (additional units to meet maximum possible demand—12 pounds and 2 two-pounds, in this case). Put briefly:

Minimum stock = Delivery-period quantity + Safety factor.

But how large an order should be placed? The answer will depend upon a number of factors—such as the quantity discounts allowed by the vendor, the cost of delivery for orders of various sizes, speed of deterioration of the product, and the unit in which the product is packed (12's, 24's, etc.).[14] In regard to coffee, such factors suggest that a new supply should come in every week. For the store mentioned, the order should not exceed an average week's need of 36 pounds and 3 two-pounds. This type of analysis can be applied to any staple merchandise.

Under the foregoing system some means should be used to make it clear to the sales staff when the minimum stock point has been reached; otherwise this information will not be given to the buyer. While periodic visual inspection of inventory may be relied upon for this purpose, many retailers find it helpful to develop some kind of "automatic reminder." Perhaps a cardboard divider or a tape may be employed to separate the minimum stock from other merchandise. Still other retailers prefer the two-bin system, under which one bin holds the merchandise for regular sale and the other holds the minimum inventory. As is discussed below, a perpetual inventory system—perhaps employing electronic equipment—is usable under certain conditions.

Many manufacturers offer aid to retailers of their products in the development of a basic stock list. For example, the Telechron division of the General Electric Company has prepared a forty-page booklet on *Retail-Tested Selling Ideas and Profit Pointers* which offers basic stock lists for electric clocks as well as ideas on inventory control, displays, promotions, and other aspects of retailing. The U.S. Plywood Corporation furnishes its retail lumber dealers with similar publications, which are supplemented with a Headquarters Dealer training program.[15] Regardless of his field, the retailer will find similar aids available to him from manufacturers and trade associations.

1. *Perpetual Inventory for Staple Goods.* Sometimes the basic stock list is supplemented by a perpetual inventory system which indicates the quantity of stock on hand at any time. A card showing the minimum stock and the reorder quantity may be kept for each item carried. Every time a quantity of an item is received by the store, this is entered on the card. Sales are also entered. Thus, a glance at the card will tell the quantity on hand. It is part of the duty of the person keeping the perpetual inventory control to inform the buyer when the stock reaches the minimum or reorder point.

For the large retailer, recent developments in electronic tabulating equipment suggest that he may eventually have more complete inventory data

---

[14] For details, cf. "Determining Quantity to Purchase," pp. 297–301, below.

[15] "New Growth Rings for U.S. Plywood," *Business Week,* July 24, 1965, p. 74.

and have it available more promptly than ever before.[16] Safeway Stores, Inc., Food Fair Stores, F. W. Woolworth, S. S. Kresge, and many other chains are already using electronic data processing, in part, to control inventories and furnish sales information to buyers.[17] The plan used by the J. C. Penney Company will illustrate the possibilities. About one third of the firm's year-round staple merchandise has been placed under a semiautomatic merchandising system which is based on punched tickets attached to each item. These tickets or tags contain all the necessary data for reordering. As merchandise is sold the tags are removed, sent to a central point, "fed" into a computer for a summary report which, in turn, is the basis of replacing the store's inventory.[18]

Most stores find that a perpetual inventory control system, regardless of whether it is based on clerical work or on electronic computers, is too complicated and expensive for their needs. Drug and grocery stores consider it too time-consuming to record every package of toothpaste or every pound of coffee sold. They consider it better for the buyer to take his basic stock list and spend a few hours each week canvassing the shelves in his store or his department to find out what items are down to or near the minimum requirements. Many chain organizations—for example, those selling convenience goods where the unit price is relatively low—follow this practice in their stores; however, in their warehouses, where the unit of sale is larger and goods are packed in larger units, they use a perpetual inventory system. Even as electronic computers are more widely used by retailers of lower-priced stable goods, it seems likely that they will be of greater aid in controlling warehouse stocks rather than merchandise already in stores.[19]

2. *Revision of Basic Stock List.* The basic stock list even for staples should be revised constantly. Not only do some kinds of goods gain in popularity as others lose, but there is a steady shift among the competing products of various manufacturers. In addition, revisions of the list, together with the minimum and reorder quantities, should reflect the fact that some staples are affected by seasonal shifts in demand. Sales of men's plain wool hose increase in the fall and winter and decrease in the spring. Food stores

[16] Cf. the previous discussion of EDP on pp. 138–41, above.

[17] For some illustrations, cf. "Automatic Ordering at Food Fair," *Super Market Merchandising,* December, 1965, p. 10; and "General Supers Dials Its Stores, Hears the Registers Ring," *Chain Store Age* (Supermarket Executives Edition), May, 1965, pp. 78–79.

[18] Edward Coyle, "Punch Card Plan Puts Stock in Penney Stores Pronto," *Women's Wear Daily,* April 16, 1963, pp. 1 and 44; and "Computers Begin to Solve the Marketing Puzzle," *Business Week,* April 17, 1965, p. 115.

[19] Cf. S. O. Kaylin's discussion of "Distribution Centers: Special Report on Automation and Data Processing Systems," *Chain Store Age* (Executives Edition), October, 1965, pp. E15–E25.

sell huge quantities of nuts during the Christmas holidays. In the drug departments of discount houses the "Christmas rush" results in December accounting for nearly 14 percent of annual sales, while November produces less than 8 percent and January 7 percent.[20] The coming of Easter, June graduation, and September's "back-to-school" days spell huge fluctuations in the sales of many staples.

Many buyers have found that a seasonal buying calendar is an ideal supplement to a basic stock list. Such a calendar sets forth all special events. It shows the dates on which the buyer should begin to consider each special need, when increased orders should be placed, when goods should be delivered and ready for display, and when the buyer should cease reordering or return to the more normal reorder quantity.

In summary, by a careful analysis of past sales, a basic stock list can be devised for staple merchandise. Kept up to date and supplemented with a buying calendar and—under certain circumstances—with a perpetual inventory control system, the basic stock list provides a method that makes the actual determination of wants for many staples quite automatic.

3. *Merchandise Flow by Brands.* Significant knowledge of customer preference for individual brands and families of brands can also be secured from an analysis of past sales, and the growth of self-service and self-selection has increased the importance of the brand factor. Information as to how rapidly particular brands move is important, since it enables the retailer or buyer to concentrate more on the "best sellers" and results in better service and prices from suppliers of such merchandise.

A major problem of many retailers is the duplication of merchandise among a variety of brands.[21] Manufacturers of lines of cosmetics, for example, present a problem for the retail druggist when they induce him to purchase a complete line which practically duplicates those of other suppliers. If the druggist has information concerning the sale of each manufacturer's brand, he is in a position to purchase needed, salable goods much more intelligently.

The Model Stock for Fashion Goods. For goods with fashion characteristics a basic stock list based entirely on an analysis of past sales may be of little value to the buyer. What sold well last year may, because of fashion changes, have few sales this year. Consequently, instead of establishing a list of specific items together with minimum and reorder quantities for each item, the retailer—taking into consideration both past sales and sales ex-

---

[20] Cf. the monthly sales chart of drug sales in *Discount Store News,* August 22, 1966, p. 34.

[21] Cf. "The Battle of the Brands," *Dun's Review and Modern Industry,* May, 1964 pp. 53 ff.

pected for the forthcoming period—tries to build up a picture of (1) the total dollar value of the stock and (2) the general breakdown of the stock to be carried as to such factors as sizes, types, and price lines. The result is known as a model stock. From the point of view of planned sales, it contains the merchandise that will enable those sales to be achieved most effectively.

Although a model stock is forward looking—that is, it is always built to meet expected or forthcoming sales—an analysis of past sales is essential to its existence. Even for such high-fashion goods as womens' ready-to-wear a study of past sales may suggest which colors and styles are gaining or losing in popularity. Records of past sales may also be of assistance in determining the dollar value of the goods to be carried as well as their general characteristics, that is, the model stock.

1. *Dollar Value of the Stock.* The dollar value of the model stock can be determined by past sales and past stocks supplemented by an estimate of the outlook for business. Beginning with the figures for a department or a store, the past sales should be broken down on a daily, weekly, or monthly basis. Usually a monthly breakdown, with adjustments for fluctuating seasons such as Easter, is sufficient. Let us assume that last year's sales for the month under consideration were $16,000. If the sales outlook is good, sales for this year may be adjusted upward from the preceding year, perhaps by 10 percent, or $1,600. Thus, we obtain an estimate of $17,600 for the month's total sales. Now we turn to past records again and discover that in this particular department or store a turnover of only once a month can be expected; that is, to achieve sales of $17,600, the average stock at retail should also equal $17,600. We conclude, therefore, that the dollar value of our model stock should be $17,600.[22]

2. *General Characteristics of Goods Carried.* For fashion goods, past sales can also yield information as to the type of merchandise to be carried in stock, sizes, price lines, and trends in materials and sales. In regard to type, consider a men's shoe store. Past sales indicate that, irrespective of fashion changes, for comparable months the store sells fairly consistent percentages of dress, street, and sport shoes. Variations in this percentage from month to month can be indicated on a buying calendar. A similar situation exists in the women's dress shop or department, which finds fairly consistent ratios to total sales for afternoon, evening, and sport dresses.

For most fashion goods the assortment as to size is also fairly constant. Hence, here is another factor around which the model stock should be planned. For example, irrespective of the year's fashion, a women's dress shop finds its percentage sales of dresses of various sizes as follows:

---

[22] This figure would have to be adjusted upward or downward if the department wished to add to or reduce its previous end-of-the-month inventory.

Size	*Percentage of Sales*
12	12
14	22
16	30
18	26
20	10

It should be recognized, however, that the model stock assortment as to size and type should not be necessarily the same as the actual sales distribution. Although 10 percent of all sales are in size 20 dresses, to provide an adequate assortment, this size may account for 15 percent of the model stock.

Past sales also furnish information as to the prices at which a store should offer merchandise. Although stores located in the less populated areas have to carry goods that appeal to broad income groups, city stores find it best to appeal more or less to specific income classes. Consequently, a store gradually becomes known as a high-priced, a medium-priced, or a low-priced establishment. Past sales trends, by indicating whether the best or the cheapest goods are moving, can show a buyer the merchandise items which appeal most to his customers. But past sales show more than this. Even if a store is buying merchandise to appeal to the middle class, it will find that sales tend to take place around certain price lines.[23] Once the price lines are adopted, analysis of past sales will reveal the percentage of total sales in each price line. Thus another fairly stable factor is found which can be used in planning a model stock, even for fashion goods.

Finally, and as already suggested, past sales offer information on trends in customer acceptance of materials, colors, and particular styles. By keeping a running check on these factors, the buyer is better prepared in placing reorders. Some buyers have found that the maintenance of a fashion calendar is highly desirable. On this calendar is indicated the progress of customer demand for each style—when the style was introduced, how rapidly customers accepted it, and when sales reached their peak.

In the medium-size retail organization the analysis leading to summary data on size assortments and types of merchandise is prepared typically by the accounting department or the merchandise office. Such analyses are made from time to time instead of on a continuous basis. In the smaller organizations, where there is even less division of labor, the buyer may merely guess at what past sales show in regard to these factors. In contrast, large retail organizations—the large department stores and chains—maintain unit-control bureaus, under the merchandising division, which make

---

[23] Price lining is discussed in some detail in Chapter 16.

this kind of analysis their main job.[24] From the unit-control bureau the buyer finds a continuous stream of information on past sales flowing into his office.

3. *Perpetual Inventory for Fashion Goods.* Many retail organizations find it desirable to maintain perpetual inventories of fashion goods, just as for staple goods. They accomplish this through unit-control systems of various types. By way of illustration, the system used in the dress shops of Diana Stores Corporation is very similar to that already described for the J. C. Penney Company.[25] Model stocks are devised, such stocks varying from month to month as seasons, fashions, and sales change. Each garment sent to a store is listed at headquarters. When the garment is sold, this is reported to headquarters by returning part of the ticket formerly attached to it. Hence, by a counting process (which is carried out by electronic computers) buyers at headquarters know exactly by unit prices, styles, sizes, and colors what a store has on hand and how fast various items are moving.

In one shoe chain the model stock of each store is set up on a large rectangular block to which a number of pegs are attached. Each peg represents a particular style, color, and the size of shoe. By using rings to represent pairs of shoes in stock, the store manager is able to note his stock on hand for any item by counting the number of rings on the correct peg. A colored ring is placed on each peg above the rings representing the minimum number of each kind of shoe the owner wishes to maintain in stock. As shoes are sold, rings are removed from the corresponding peg. When the colored ring is reached, the retailer is automatically informed that he needs to reorder.

So important is inventory control for fashion goods that some retailers—such as Diana Stores Corporation, referred to above—have installed electronic computers, in part, for stock control and buying purposes.[26] The Federated Department Stores and Woodward & Lothrop have invested heavily in electronics programs designed to put up-to-date figures in the hands of buyers.[27] Through its electronic equipment Sears, Roebuck and Co. expects to achieve complete merchandise and inventory control by 1970.[28] Early in 1966 both the National Cash Register Company and International Business Machines introduced unit stock control and automatic reorder

---

[24] Some stores locate this bureau in the controller's office.

[25] Cf. p. 283, above.

[26] Cf. the previous discussion of EDP on pp. 138–41, above.

[27] C. R. McBrier, "Management Uses EDP in Retailing," *Office,* January, 1965, pp. 143–44 ff; Bert Berger, "Accelerating Retail Velocity with EDP," *Chain Store Age* (Executives Edition), May, 1966, pp. E28–E32; and "Data Processing," *Women's Wear Daily,* June 20, 1966, pp. 14–23.

[28] John Osbon, "Buyers Not Losing Status Under EDP," *Women's Wear Daily,* June 28, 1965, p. 16.

systems which use the sales register tape to "feed" data into the computer.[29] Stores too small to have their own computers can have their tapes processed at nearby computer centers. Despite this "sharing" of computer time, however, the cost of the necessary equipment is so great that, at least for the immediate future, sales register types and electronic computers will be used mainly by large retailers—and even the majority of these will continue to use clerical personnel to get much of the data they need for buying purposes.

4. *Summary.* Even for fashion goods, there are a number of factors around which a model stock can be built. Past sales yield some indication of the types of merchandise, sizes, price lines, and trends regarding materials and colors. In addition, when adjusted according to the best available information as to the future, past sales and stocks provide a basis for estimating future sales and stocks. Thus, the buyer is provided with information about the dollar value of the model stock as well as about many of its important characteristics.

It needs to be reemphasized that the model stock in fashion goods is far from a *fait accompli.* Although it is often planned six months or more in advance, month-to-month or even more frequent changes are sometimes necessary. And it should not be forgotten that many stores make special purchases of goods outside of their regular assortments. Such purchases may include merchandise (1) for special promotions, (2) to help the sale of outmoded merchandise, and (3) for prestige. All of these purchases must be fitted into the model-stock plan.

Finally, the model-stock plan is as applicable to small stores as to the largest retail organization. This point is important since both students of retailing and small retailers frequently think that modern aids to buying have little applicability to the small store.

Returned Goods and Adjustment Data

Considerable information as to what a store's customers want can be obtained from returned goods and customer complaints. Some merchandise is of such inferior material or of such poor workmanship that it gives unsatisfactory service. Women's dresses may fade, and the collars of men's shirts may fray. Knowledge of such facts is obviously of importance to buyers.

In the small store, complaints about merchandise and service are usually taken directly to the owner-buyer, so that no special machinery is necessary to bring this information to the buyer's attention. In the large store, how-

---

[29] The National Cash Register system is described in a two-page advertisement in *Wall Street Journal,* January 5, 1966, pp. 16–17.

ever, complaints are registered with the adjustment department; it is necessary, therefore, to provide a method by which the information may be passed on to the buyer. For this purpose the "adjustment-department notice," which contains a brief description of the complaint and of the merchandise against which the complaint was registered, has been developed. These notices may be turned over directly to the buyer; or they may go through the merchandising office, with a summary to the buyer.

Credit Department Data

Retailers who extend credit can make good use of two chief kinds of information available in the credit department in determining what customers want. One has to do with the customers' records regarding purchases and the kinds and prices of merchandise they return for various reasons as indicated in the previous section.

The other kind of information is supplied in connection with the credit application. For example, names of credit customers may be classified as to nationality, occupation, age, marriage status, sex, and income. If the store is serving a large number of persons of a particular nationality, it may be well to devote more attention to goods appealing especially to these people. Occupational data give evidence as to whether working clothes or dress shirts should be featured. Income data are important in determining whether the store should stock low-, medium-, or high-priced goods. Data on age, marriage status, and sex also indicate customer wants: witness the great differences in goods desired by teen-agers, the 20 to 29 year old "singles," and "senior citizens."[30]

Credit application analysis is relatively simple for stores that require a large amount of information on each credit card, since the needed data are collected as by-products. In using credit data, however, the buyer should recognize that the store's credit customers may not form a typical sample of all its customers, so that this kind of inside-the-store information must be supplemented with customer data gathered outside the store.

Customer Inquiries

Customer inquiries are another helpful source of information to the buyer in determining what to purchase. In the very small store the buyer can learn a great deal merely by making a "mental record" of the various things

---

[30] For details, cf. Paul Gilkison, "What Influences the Buying Decisions of Teen-Agers?" *Journal of Retailing,* Vol. XLI, No. 3 (Fall, 1965), pp. 33–41 and 48; "Young, Single Spenders Pour It On The Market," *Business Week,* January 1, 1966, pp. 62–63.

customers request. A men's haberdashery retailer will do a better job of buying if he recalls that his customers are asking for a particular brand of shirts, for "executive length" stretch socks, and for blazer-type sport jackets.

As an aid to memory, even the smallest stores will find it desirable to keep a pad on which customer inquiries can be written down. In the store large enough to employ several salespeople, so that the owner-buyer does not talk with all customers, such a record of goods asked for but not stocked becomes nearly indispensable to sound purchasing. Ordinarily, a pad placed near the sales register or where merchandise is wrapped will suffice.

Want Slips. For the large retail organization, where the buyer is removed even farther from the customer, more care should be exercised in recording customer inquiries. Here a formal want-slip system is desirable and forms should be provided for entering requests for merchandise not carried in stock. Such slips usually go to the merchandising office for analysis, with a summary turned over to the buyer.

By no means will all the items suggested by a want-slip system be purchased for stock. For some items the number of requests will be so few that the buyer will decide that it is not worthwhile to make a purchase. Even where there are a number of requests over a period of several days, the trend may be downward; and the buyer may feel that the demand will disappear before he can get the merchandise in stock. The want slip should provide the buyer with information as to whether or not the customer making the inquiry for merchandise not in stock is willing to accept a substitute. If substitution is possible in practically all cases, the buyer may feel that the customer's desire for the item is insufficient to justify stocking it. Or again, the merchandise inquired about may not be available at a price that would appeal to the store's usual customers. The buyer should also realize that the want slip is open to the disadvantage that the customer inquiry which it is supposed to represent may have originated with a manufacturer who sends in "customers" to request his product; or it may have originated in the mind of a salesperson eager to show the manager that he is "on the job." But, in spite of the need for discretion on the part of the buyer, a want-slip system is highly desirable.

When want slips are adopted as a part of a store's system, it should be made clear to all salespeople that a slip should be made out for each inquiry. In other words, it is the buyer's job to exercise judgment as to the significance of the inquiry, not the salesperson's. Cooperation in filling out want slips is improved if the buyer constantly reminds employees that he is aided by these slips in making purchases. In the large store, where prospective salespeople are given formal training, instructions should be given during such training as to the necessity for want slips and the way to fill them out. In the small store, constant use of the want pad by the proprietor will lead his employees to do likewise.[31]

Suggestions of Salespeople

In cooperating to make possible the operation of a system of want slips, salespeople aid the buyer in forming an opinion of the desires of customers. But salespeople are customers in their own right, with wants that are frequently similar to those of other patrons. Consequently, salespersons afford the buyer a valuable sample of customer opinion. Urging salespeople to bring in suggestions for purchases and seeking the opinions of salespersons on the merchandise offered in the market help the buyer in his purchasing.

Other Successful Stores

Turning to outside sources of information concerning customers' wants, as listed on page 281 (we shall return later to the judgment of buyers on page 296), no buyer can afford to overlook the goods offered by other successful stores, both those with which he is in direct competition and those in other places. This source of information is especially important for smaller retailers who cannot afford to develop other more costly ways of finding out what customers want. Of course, in using other stores as a source of information, the buyer must realize that just because a store has stocked a particular item does not indicate that customers want it. In other words, along with other information, the retailer must develop means of finding out how fast such goods are moving.

Methods Available to Smaller Stores. For the small-store buyer, information on other stores can be obtained by visits to such stores and by studying their advertisements. Usually, visits are limited to noncompeting stores, either in the same city or elsewhere, since the small storekeeper may resent "snooping" on the part of a competitor. Visits to successful stores are typically an integral part of a trip to a central market. Many small-store buyers find it highly desirable to scrutinize the advertisements of local papers as well as those of leading retailers in the larger cities. For this purpose, subscriptions to a few large city newspapers are sometimes maintained. Since the buyer also wishes to know how customers responded to the advertisements, several firms exist to supply this type of service for a fee—

---

[31] Cf. Wingate and Friedlander, *op. cit.,* pp. 129–33, for the essentials of a good want-slip system and the chief objections to want slips.

gathering the desired information through persons they employ as "shoppers."[32]

Methods of Large Stores: Comparison Departments. In addition to the foregoing techniques, many large stores have comparison departments whose responsibility, among others, is to "shop" competitive stores in the trading area to determine merchandise offerings, prices, and customer response. Frequently goods are purchased for later detailed comparison with the store's own goods. Reports are prepared and submitted to the buyer for his guidance in building proper assortments and establishing prices.[33]

The widespread nature of "comparison shopping" is suggested by one student's conclusion: "Today the majority of large stores employ one or more persons specifically for the task of comparing merchandise and prices, as well as various aspects of service."[34] That the phrase "or more" is appropriate may be indicated by a few figures, as follows: Sears, Roebuck and Co. employs 50 comparison shoppers who make between 40,000 and 50,000 individual item comparisons each year. Another large retailer with headquarters in New York City also has a regular staff of about 50 shoppers who purchase up to $500,000 each year of comparison merchandise. A Chicago retailer employs 7 people for this purpose, one in Detroit uses more than 20, and 4 make purchases for a large Los Angeles store.[35]

Being Different. Despite the advantages of knowing what is being stocked and promoted by other successful stores, the retailer should not be a slave to such information. Put another way, some retailers owe their success to the fact that they operate unique stores—stores which offer "unusual merchandise." To use the words of one highly successful, small-town retailer: "'Tain't the money that puts your business up. It's having something that no one else has as good as."[36] In carrying out this philosophy, a small shop selling women's apparel builds its clientele on having "different" dresses.[37] A men's clothing retailer always tries to be ahead of his large-scale competitors in having the latest fashions. An independent supermarket may stress high-quality merchandise and fast service in a store of unusual design. In fact, one of the advantages of the smaller store is its buying

---

[32] One of the leading fashion-reporting firms is Tobé. The Retail News Bureau of New York City covers promotions in leading stores and customer response to them.

[33] For additional details on the organization, methods, and results of comparison shopping cf. K. R. Gillespie, "The Role of Espionage in Retailing," *Journal of Retailing,* Vol. XXXIX, No. 1 (Spring, 1963), pp. 7–12, and 48.

[34] *Ibid.,* p. 8.

[35] Figures supplied to the authors by the various firms.

[36] L. L. Bean, quoted in *Time,* December 7, 1962, p. 89.

[37] For some specific examples of such shops cf. S. R. Flaster, *op. cit.*

flexibility which gives it an opportunity to "be different" from the large retailer.

Vendors' Offerings

Stores of all sizes rely to a considerable degree on the offerings of vendors as a means of finding out what goods are "in demand." Especially do the smaller stores use this technique, since it involves a very limited expenditure of time and money. As a matter of fact, it is probably true that buyers rely too much on vendors, too many of whom still try to sell what they are producing rather than first studying customer demand to find out just what is wanted. Yet there is a definite trend for vendors to engage in more customer research, as is illustrated by the various surveys of the clothing preferences of high school girls and college women financed by Bobbie Brooks, Inc., a manufacturer of apparel.[38] As they do, their offerings will reflect more and more customers' needs and thus become a more dependable guide to the buyer.

Some vendors go to the expense of providing their customers (retailers) with bulletins to inform them what is selling. This practice is followed especially by vendors of fashion merchandise. Other vendors depend upon salesmen to pass along this information to retailers in their stores and at trade shows or when the retailers call on vendors during buying trips. A growing number of resources are even developing inventory control systems—some based on electronic computers—for their retail outlets, which provide the retailers with stock control, semiautomatic reordering, and information on what is selling in other stores supplied by the resource.[39] Vendors using the franchise system or servicing retailers through a voluntary chain arrangement place special emphasis on supplying "what is selling" data to their outlets.[40]

Central Market Representatives

Many retail organizations retain central market representatives, often referred to as MR's, one of whose functions is to provide the store buyers with information as to what is new in the market and what is proving popular with other buyers. These representatives study vendors' offerings,

---

[38] *How They Sell*, by the editors of *The Wall Street Journal* (New York: Dow Jones & Co., 1965), p. 137.

[39] Isadore Barmash, "Apparel Men Help Merchants Sort Goods, Order, and Reorder," *New York Times*, August 23, 1965, pp. 36 and 40.

[40] Cf. the discussion of franchising on pp. 66–67, above.

watch fashion trends, and check promotions in large city stores; and transmit their conclusions to buyers by means of bulletins as well as directly when the buyers visit the central markets. To quote one retailer: The MR "is a shopper, an analyst, a merchandise counselor . . . (He) is in the market eight hours a day, analyzing fashion trends, colors, fabrics, and any other factors of importance. He draws conclusions and gives directions to buyers and merchandisers in all our member stores."[41] Used by medium-size as well as large retail organizations, this source of information is important for a considerable number of retailers.

Trade Papers, Newspapers, and General Publications

Retailers of all sizes depend on magazines and newspapers for much information as to what customers want. Retailers of women's wear find it worthwhile to study such publications as *Mademoiselle, Seventeen, Charm, Harper's Bazaar,* and *Vogue,* in which the latest fashions are pictured and discussed. *Women's Wear Daily* is another standard source of information in this field. For retailers of men's wearing apparel, *Esquire, Daily News Record,* and *Men's Wear* offer considerable data on fashion trends. Many other fields are also supplied with tradepapers, as illustrated by *Drug Topics, Chain Store Age* (with various editions for retailers of drugs, variety store-general merchandise, restaurant, and supermarkets; and a special edition for retail executives), *Discount Store News, Progressive Grocer, National Jeweler, Hardware Retailer, Footwear News,* and *National Furniture Review.*

Customer Surveys

In a broad sense, any activity which aims at gathering information concerning wants directly from customers may be classified as a customer survey.[42] Thus, even the clothing retailer who visits social functions attended by his potential customers so that he can judge better the quality and style of the clothing they are wearing is making a very informal customer survey.

Use of Questionnaires and the Style Count. In some retail organizations, customer surveys are made by means of questionnaires. Although it is less expensive to mail these questionnaires, a higher percentage of returns

---

[41] W. T. French of Associated Merchandising Corporation, quoted in "AMC's Power on 7th Avenue—Peanuts or High Pressure?" *Women's Wear Daily,* April 27, 1964, p. 18.

[42] That retailers should engage in far more customer research than is now the case is suggested by H. L. Isaacson, "Why Not Research the Consumer?" *New York Retailer,* December, 1965, pp. 2–6.

and a better selection of customers can be obtained if personal interviews are conducted. Such surveys may be used to provide the store not only with data as to the goods customers want but also with information as to the surroundings and services they want with the goods. It is of the utmost importance that surveys be conducted and interpreted with great care; otherwise, the results may suggest actions on the retailer's part which are not warranted by the facts.

Stores or departments handling fashion goods find the style count an important source of customer information. The count is made by placing observers at certain points with instructions to record what people are wearing. For instance, a store may wish information on the fashion trend in dresses. It places observers in various restaurants, movie lobbies, and store entrances, with instructions to record the type, material, color, and silhouette of the dress on each woman observed. The observation points must be selected with care, so that information will be obtained on the middle- and lower-income classes as well as on the groups that act as local fashion leaders. If care is used in segregating these classes and if the count is retaken at intervals, the buyer gets information not only on what the fashion leaders are wearing but also on how fast the fashion cycle is progressing.

Consumer Advisory Committees.   Still another way of making a customer survey is offered by the consumer advisory group or jury.[43] Instead of questioning a large number of customers, the store attempts to organize a single small group which is representative of its customers. At times the group is broken down into subgroups, each representing one segment of the store's customers. Thus, one subgroup may be made up of high school or college students, another of newlyweds, and another of middle-income buyers. Aldens, a division of Gamble-Skogmo, Inc., which operates a combination mail-order house and chain-store business, has used advisory groups as an aid in fashion forecasting and reports their forecasts are more accurate than those made by the firm's buyers. Such groups or panels may be used not only to pass on merchandise offered by vendors but also to appraise goods already in the store, together with the store's operating policies.[44]

Other Surveys.   A number of qualified agencies conduct customer surveys for retailers or on their own initiative for the purpose of obtaining

[43] Wingate and Friedlander distinguish among five varieties of consumer panels: (1) the customer advisory group—which makes suggestions concerning store policies, services, and merchandise assortments; (2) the consumer jury that expresses opinion on advertising and sketches of styles; (3) the consumer experience group that reports on performance of products in use; (4) the home inventory group that reports the goods they have on hand; and (5) the continuous-purchase-record group which records and make monthly reports on their family purchasing. *Op. cit.,* p. 102.

[44] For a description of how one advisory board operates cf. "Halle Bros. Wins Bouquets With Its Consumer Board," *Women's Wear Daily,* June 6, 1966, p. 17.

data of value in buying. Many newspapers, such as the *Milwaukee Journal,* the *Cleveland Press,* the *Chicago Tribune,* and the *New York Times,* finance research designed to provide information on consumer buying habits.[45] The A. C. Nielsen Company, through its consumer and dealer panels, supplies valuable data, and the studies of R. L. Polk and Company and the Curtis Publishing Company are helpful to the retailer. Some resident buying organizations, especially those located in New York City, also undertake studies of various types for their members.

Judgment of Buyers

Even after a buyer has made full use of all or a number of the foregoing sources of information as to what customers want, he still has to exercise judgment as to the merchandise to purchase. In other words, all of the data he gathers needs to be interpreted. The successful buyer is frequently distinguished from the unsuccessful buyer by his "sense" in correctly interpreting the facts, which are also known by the unsuccessful buyer but which he cannot analyze satisfactorily.

One leading firm, which employs nearly 500 buyers (organized under some 50 product-line merchandise supervisors) to purchase from more than 18,000 resources,[46] acknowledges the significance of the buyer in these words:

For many years Sears management has recognized the importance of developing buyers who are experts in their lines. To assure mastery of the merchandise, the number of items purchased by any buyer is limited so that he will have the opportunity to specialize. Thus, the buyer must be an authority on manufacturing processes, materials, designs, colors, and trends in styling. In addition, he must be thoroughly familiar with the end use and performance of his merchandise, be it clothing or a power-operated appliance, household staples, or plumbing ware—in short, the buyer is responsible for every facet of the merchandise itself and everything that is essential to its production and marketing.[47]

Buying Committees. For new items retailers increasingly are substituting the judgment of a buying committee for that of a single buyer. To illustrate this trend, three out of every four supermarket chains report that they have established three- to eight-man committees which often include some or all of these: the buyer assigned to the particular group of products under consideration, his superior—head buyer or merchandise manager, the

---

[45] For a report on one of these newspaper (*Chicago Tribune*) studies cf. P. D. Martineau, "Customers' Shopping Center Habits Change Retailing," *Editor & Publisher,* October 26, 1964, pp. 16 and 56.

[46] "Inside Sears, Roebuck," *Printers' Ink,* October 22, 1965, p. 23.

[47] *Annual Report,* Sears, Roebuck and Co., fiscal year ended January 31, 1962, p. 10.

publicity manager, and two or three store supervisors. No new product can be added to stock without the approval of the committee which meets on a regular schedule or at the call of any buyer who has a product which demands immediate consideration.[48] Similar committees now exist in retail organizations dealing in many kinds of merchandise.

DETERMINING QUANTITY TO PURCHASE

Having formed his opinion as to *what* merchandise he should buy, the buyer now faces the question of *how much* to purchase at any particular time. His decision here will rest on these important factors: (1) the period for which purchasing shall be done, (2) estimated sales for the period, (3) goods on hand plus goods already on order, and (4) the desired stock at the end of the period.

Period for Which Purchasing Is Done

The chief purpose in making purchases, of course, is to fulfill customers' needs as reflected in sales. And customer acceptance of merchandise offerings (sales) cannot be estimated without considering a particular period of time. For some goods—fresh vegetables, for example—the period may be only one day. A longer period is in the mind of the buyer of women's winter coats, most likely the few months during which he expects such coats to sell. In this case, however, the selling season may be broken down into months, with purchases planned for each month. A similar breakdown into shorter periods may also be used by the buyer of staples which sell throughout the year.

Hand-to-Mouth Buying. Since World War I several factors have led retailers to practice "hand-to-mouth" buying, that is, to decrease the period for which they buy. The increasing emphasis on fashion has contributed to this development since such merchandise is subject to large markdowns unless it is sold before the crest of the fashion cycle has passed. The drastic price declines of the early twenties and of the early thirties, plus the more moderate declines on various occasions since that time for limited types of merchandise, taught retailers the importance of small inventories. Many retailers have discovered that a small inventory with a rapid turnover decreases storage and interest charges, results in a steady flow of new merchandise into the store and increased sales, and reduces the risks in-

---

[48] For interesting and valuable insights into the practices of buying committees as used by supermarkets cf. "Manufacturers' Headquarters Salesmen," *Progressive Grocer*, May, 1964, pp. 42–48; and *The Super Market Industry Speaks, 1966* (Chicago, Ill.: Super Market Institute, Inc., 1966), p. 26.

volved in long-term commitments. Finally, better inventory control and ordering systems—some of them based on electronic data processing; improvements in communication—the telephone, telegraph, and teletype; and more rapid delivery, resulting from branch and public warehouses near the retailer, the truck, air express, and fast freight, have made it possible to operate successfully on smaller stocks. Through a combination of an easier ordering system, lower inventories, less need for backroom space, and better adjustment of inventory to customer demand, supermarket chains have reported annual savings of over $8,000 per unit.[49] In addition, sales benefited from the fact that out-of-stock situations were substantially reduced.

Of course, hand-to-mouth buying is not without its disadvantages. It results in the loss of higher-bracket noncumulative quantity discounts. If carried too far, inadequate assortments and being out of stock of some items may result in a loss of sales and customer good will. Larger displays are an important sales stimulant, and such displays cannot be built with small inventories. The cost of placing, transporting, and receiving a large number of small orders is considerable. There are also the dangers that (1) on a rising market, higher prices will have to be paid on later orders and (2) the emphasis on smaller orders and speed in delivery will undermine quality standards on merchandise. But in spite of these disadvantages, hand-to-mouth buying carried to a reasonable limit is a sound policy.

Speculative Buying.[50]   Many retailers follow a policy of varying the length of the period for which they purchase according to whether they expect a rising or a falling price level. When rising prices are expected, buyers place large orders, in the hope of reselling at the higher prices and thus obtaining a larger gross margin than usual. When falling prices are anticipated, a very close hand-to-mouth buying policy is pursued. In regard to this policy, it may be said that, if the retailer is quite consistently right in predicting price-level changes, retailing is not the best field for him. He could make a much larger income speculating on some commodity exchange and not have the problems connected with the operation of a store. In other words, a retailer is in business to make a merchandising profit, not a speculative profit. If he wants to speculate, he does not need to bother with operating a store at the same time. To put it very bluntly: Speculation is a profession in itself and does not under any circumstances come under the head of buying.

---

[49] "How to Reduce Store Labor and Inventory Costs," *Super Market Merchandising,* August, 1965, p. 35.

[50] On this subject, the student should read the discussion on "Forward Buying versus Speculation" in W. B. England, *Procurement: Principles and Cases* (4th ed.; Homewood, Ill.: Richard D. Irwin, Inc., 1962), pp. 600–613.

The foregoing paragraph should not be taken as a complete condemnation of placing larger orders than usual when rising prices are expected. Sometimes it is necessary to place larger orders merely to increase the assurance of getting goods, especially when other retailers are placing larger orders in the expectancy of higher prices. But the paragraph does condemn the retailer who tends to forget his merchandising function in his scramble to get an inventory profit and who fails to recognize the dangers inherent in speculative buying.

It is also dangerous to trim inventories too far when the retailer expects a falling price level. In the words of one experienced retailer:

> Though it is considered sound practice to minimize losses by keeping small inventories in times of shrinking values, from a practical angle this is unsound, for the reputation of carrying a fine stock is more important than the expected loss. Over against the few occasions when normal inventories have been decreased to forestall losses can be set the great majority of occasions when insufficient inventories have given rise to a myriad of intangible costs—ill will, small repeat orders, and the extra expenses entailed in work stoppages, delays and extra efforts. Within a wide margin, inventory depreciation is the lesser of the two evils.[51]

In brief, although some inventory variation in response to expected price-level changes is desirable, it must not be carried to excess regardless of whether a higher or a lower price level is expected.

Other Considerations. Three other factors which influence the period for which purchasing is done are (1) quantity discounts, (2) supply conditions, and (3) the retailer's financial resources and storage facilities. Obviously, large discounts will encourage purchasing for a longer period. Likewise, if supply conditions are such that delivery is uncertain, the retailer may well "order ahead." The retailer's most important sources of information on the conditions of supply are the following: vendors, trade papers, newspapers, and central market representatives. Small retailers rely largely on the first three sources, whereas medium and large retailers find all four sources available to them. In the great majority of stores the buyer has to gather this material; but increasingly, in the larger organizations, research departments are being established to gather and interpret these data. Finally, it is clear that retailers with limited financial resources—including both cash and credit—and without adequate storage facilities are restricted as to the length of the period for which they can buy.[52]

---

[51] Oswald Knauth, *Managerial Enterprise* (New York: W. W. Norton & Co., Inc., 1948), p. 103.

[52] The significance of storage facilities in forward buying is emphasized in R. E. Buck, "Buy and Warehouse for Profit," *Super Market Merchandising,* November, 1964, pp. 44 ff.

Estimated Sales for the Period

The second major consideration in deciding how much to buy is the estimated sales for the period. This estimate usually is based on past sales, with allowance for changes in the competitive situation and business conditions. Without entering into the details of making sales estimates, three points need to be mentioned. First, the competitive situation is often the determining factor in the sales outlook for a particular store or department. Even though a store had sales of $10,000 for a certain month last year and business conditions are better this year, the sales estimate may be less for the comparable period this year because of the existence of a new competitor.

Second, the buyer should not be misled by the statistics on the business outlook for the country as a whole.[53] He should be much more interested in the outlook as to the incomes of his potential customers and their buying intentions. In other words, the general economic situation in the area in which his store is located, particularly as it affects the income of his customers and potential customers and reflects their willingness to spend this income, is far more important to the retailer in planning his sales than is the business outlook for the country as a whole.

Third, the importance of a careful estimate of sales varies both by kinds of goods and from time to time. Thus, for perishable and fashion goods, careful estimates are needed; otherwise, excessive purchases will result in spoilage of goods or in large markdowns. For staple goods, excessive purchases may mean merely larger-than-necessary inventories for a while, with a temporary tie-up of some working capital. Of course, in periods of falling prices, overestimates of sales for staples may result in significant inventory losses.

For new merchandise the buyer may feel it quite impossible to estimate sales even for a relatively short period; as a result, he may buy only a few units to test customer reaction. Although this solution may result in his quickly being out of stock, it may be better than taking markdowns when the new goods fail to sell. Or if the item is an expensive one, samples may be purchased with special orders being placed as sales are made to customers.

Stock on Hand and on Order

It is evident that the stock on hand and that for which orders already have been placed will affect the quantity to be purchased in a given period.

---

[53] He should also be aware that even general business forecasts frequently fail to "call the turns." Cf. "How to Rate the Forecasters," *Business Week*, January 9, 1965, pp. 39–40.

Information as to goods on hand may be obtained from observation, current merchandise control records, or physical inventories. In small stores observation is the usual method. Before placing orders with a salesman, the storekeeper or the buyer will look over his stock of the particular items involved. Preceding a buying trip he may make a more careful appraisal of his stock, perhaps going to the expense of an inventory of the items in which he is interested. In some lines a perpetual inventory system may be used,[54] thus providing the buyer with an up-to-the-minute picture of stock on hand.

In the larger stores buyers maintain or have access to merchandise records which reveal currently the quantity of most items on hand, since proper ticketing of goods permits accurate tabulation of goods purchased and sold. It is an easy matter, therefore, to determine the stock on hand at any given time. It is equally convenient to obtain data concerning merchandise on order from the buyer's own records. These records generally include a duplicate of every unfilled order which the buyer has placed.

Desired Stock at End of Period

The planned or desired stock at the end of the particular period, our final major consideration in determining how much to buy, represents the best judgment of the buyer after pertinent information has been evaluated. Because of an increasing sales trend, a rising fashion cycle for the goods, prospective price advances,[55] supply conditions which make stock replacement difficult, and the existence of substantial quantity discounts, he may decide to build a relatively large end-of-period stock. The reverse of these factors may induce him to reduce his inventory.

Trip Buying Plan

When a buyer is going to market, he frequently finds it desirable to develop a carefully worked out trip buying plan covering the specific items he wishes to purchase and the amount he intends to spend in the light of his "open-to-buy,"[56] merchandise budget, and the other sources of information which have been described in this chapter. Figure 10–1 shows the form used by one retailer in developing his trip buying plan.[57]

---

[54] See the description of the perpetual inventory system used in a chain shoe store, p. 287, above.

[55] But cf. the discussion on "Speculative Buying," pp. 298–99, above.

[56] For details on the "open-to-buy" cf. pp. 413–16, below.

[57] For a discussion of buying trips, cf. following chapter, pp. 318–20, below.

Stk. & Inv. on Hand Today $_____
On Order This Month Del._____
Est. Sales Bal. of Month_____
Planned Stock E. O. M._____
Open to Buy This Month_____
Planned Sales This Month_____

Trip Buying Limit_____ (MONTH) Delivery $_____
Planned Initial Mark-up %_____

On Order Next Month Del._____
Plan Purchases Next Month_____
Est. Sales Next Month_____

Dep't._____
Store_____
Date_____

ALL ABOVE SPACES ON THIS PLAN MUST BE FILLED OUT BEFORE BEING SIGNED BY BUYER

1 On Hand	2 On Order	3 Total	4 Estimated Sales Till Delivery	5 Stock Remaining	6 Planned Stock Desired	7 Open to Buy	8 Plan to Buy Now	9 DESCRIPTION OF MERCHANDISE	10 Cost	11 Retail	12 Total Retail	13 QUANTITY PURCHASED

Delivery Date_____ Signed_____ Approved_____
Buyer   Mdse. Mgr.

FIG. 10-1. Trip buying plan form.

In this chapter, we have reviewed various methods by which the buyer obtains information as to the merchandise his customers want and as to the quantities he should purchase. With this information available—and not before—he is in a position to start choosing his sources of supply. In the next chapter, we shall turn to this latter topic.

REVIEW AND DISCUSSION QUESTIONS

1. "It does not necessarily follow that all aspects of the buying function are performed by individuals known as buyers." Explain and illustrate.

2. List and evaluate five factors which have a bearing on the buying policies of a specific retailer.

3. Prepare a five minute class report on the article by S. R. Flaster referred to in footnote 6 on page 279.

4. In view of the importance of customer knowledge in effective buying, how can you explain the relatively small amount of customer research on the part of retailers?

5. Distinguish between a "basic stock list" and a "model stock." Discuss the problems involved in establishing a basic stock list for staple goods and a model stock for fashion goods.

6. Evaluate the relative difficulties in establishing perpetual inventory systems for staple and fashion goods in the retail store.

7. Visit some of the larger retail stores in your community or a nearby city and ascertain the extent to which electronic computers are being used to improve buying. Determine, for any firms using computers, the degree of satisfaction that exists.

8. Explain how the buyer is aided in determining customer wants by the information he obtains by analyzing returned goods and adjustments.

9. Summarize the advantages and disadvantages of using "want slips" to determine customer wants.

10. Assume that you are the owner-buyer of a men's clothing store or women's apparel shop in a city of 25,000 population. List and evaluate the methods you would use to determine what merchandise is being successfully sold by competing stores and by successful comparable stores in other cities.

11. Assume that you are the buyer for the shoe department in a large discount house. What kinds or types of information would you require to do an effective buying job? Where would you obtain this information?

12. Based on your reading, evaluate the buying aid given by vendors to their retail customers.

13. Prepare a report of some 1,500 words on the topic: "The Buying Committee: A Critical Appraisal of Its Functions under Existing Conditions."

14. Explain in some detail the main factors which determine the quantity of merchandise to be purchased at a given time.
15. Evaluate speculative buying as a policy.

SUPPLEMENTARY READINGS

BROWN, R. L. "Compelling New Age of Elegance," *Sales Management,* February 19, 1965, pp. 25–27 ff. "With a new taste for higher quality merchandise and the money to pay for it," is the description of today's customer as presented in this article.

COX, REAVIS; ALDERSON, WROE; AND SHAPIRO, S. J. *Theory in Marketing* (Homewood, Ill.: Richard D. Irwin, Inc., 1964), Part III, "Consumer Behavior" pp. 233–309. These six chapters, prepared by six different authors, provide an excellent background on the retailer's customers.

FRIEDLANDER, J. S. "The "Maximum' System for Reorder Open-to-buy," *New York Retailer,* June, 1962, pp. 8–11. The author presents concisely how mathematical formulae may be used in computing the reorder open-to-buy.

GILLESPIE, K. R. "The Role of Espionage in Retailing," *Journal of Retailing,* Vol. XXXIX, No. 1 (Spring, 1963), pp. 7–12, and 48. The role of comparison shopping (historical, organization, and activities) is the subject of this article.

GREER, T. V., AND WALTERS, C. G. "Credit Records: Information Tool for Planning," *Journal of Retailing,* Vol. XLII, No. 3 (Fall, 1966), pp. 11–18, 51. How credit records may aid the buyer is well presented by the authors.

JARNOW, J. A. AND JUDELLE, BEATRICE (eds.). *Inside the Fashion Business* (New York: John Wiley & Sons, Inc., 1965). The authors' survey of literature on fashion has produced a comprehensive book on the subject.

JUDELLE, BEATRICE. "The Fashion Buyer Today," *Stores,* September, 1964, pp. 21–36. Based on a survey of several hundred retailers and their resources, the author critically appraises how fashion buyers are responding to the increasing merchandising pressures of today.

KATONA, GEORGE. *The Mass Consumption Society* (New York: McGraw-Hill Book Co., 1964). In buying from the customers' point of view, the buyer needs the background offered by this study of consumer psychology in an affluent society.

KAYLIN, S. O. "Distribution Centers: Special Report on Automation and Data Processing Systems," *Chain Store Age* (Executives Edition), October, 1965, pp. E15–E25. That automation of the chain store warehouse has had an impact on chain buying practices is made clear by this special report.

LAZER, WILLIAM, AND KELLEY, E. J. "The Retailing Mix: Planning and Management," *Journal of Retailing,* Vol. XXXVII, No. 1 (Spring, 1961), pp. 34–41. The significance of coordinating the goods purchased with "the total package of goods and services that a store offers for sale to the public" is the emphasis of this article.

MCNEAL, J. V. (ed.). *Dimensions of Consumer Behavior* (New York: Appleton-Century-Crofts, 1965). In this book of readings an attempt is made "to bring together significant aspects of consumer behavior that, principally, have resulted from efforts generally classified as motivation research."

MONTGOMERY, V. E. *Buying Practices of Retailers in South Dakota* (Vermillion, S.D.: University of South Dakota, Business Research Bureau, 1965). The student will gain much from this careful presentation, especially as regards the practices of smaller retailers.

NATIONAL CASH REGISTER CO. *Buying to Sell Profitably* (Dayton, Ohio, n.d.). In this brief booklet the company outlines many aspects of buying from the point of view of the small retailer.

NATIONAL RETAIL MERCHANTS ASSOCIATION. *The Buyer's Manual* (4th ed.; New York: The Association, 1965). This volume, consisting of a number of articles written by individuals of long experience in the retail field, covers many aspects of the buying function.

————. *Want Slip Policies and Systems in Department Stores* (New York: The Association, n.d.). This publication presents the best discussion of want slips from the point of view of department store operation. Much of what is said has general applicability to all stores.

"Retailers Boldly Enter EDP Wonderland," *Women's Wear Daily,* June 28, 1965, pp. 1, 15–22; and "Data Processing," ibid., June 20, 1966, pp. 14–23. Among other uses of EDP, these reports cover its current aid to the retail buyer.

WINGATE, J. W. "Revising the Store Image," *New York Retailer,* May, 1966, pp. 7–10. The significance of buying policies and practices to a store's image is suggested by Professor Wingate.

WINGATE, J. W., AND FRIEDLANDER, J. S. *The Management of Retail Buying* (Englewood Cliffs, N.J.: Prentice-Hall, Inc., 1963). Although emphasizing the department store, this book is the best single volume on the retail buying function.

11
CHAPTER

Buying: Selecting Merchandise Resources
and Suitable Merchandise

Once the retailer (or buyer) has decided what merchandise to buy and the quantities necessary to meet the anticipated needs of his customers, he must locate satisfactory sources of supply. Some indication of the scope of this problem is found in the fact that an independent supermarket operator has to assemble from 3,000 to 6,000 different items and a drugstore up to 12,000 items. For the large-scale retailer even these figures seem small; a general merchandise store or a large discount house may stock as many as 40,000 different types, styles, sizes, or qualities of merchandise, and the 200,000 items sold by Sears, Roebuck and Co. come from over 18,000 suppliers.[1] The purposes of this chapter are to describe and to evaluate the "merchandise resources"—as they are known in the trade—from which the retailer purchases these goods. Attention is also devoted to selecting merchandise which is suitable to customers' requirements.

MAIN TYPES OF MERCHANDISE RESOURCES

Fundamentally, there are three major sources of supply open to the retailer: Middlemen, manufacturers, and farmers or growers. While each of these sources calls for some discussion, our treatment can be relatively brief in view of the typical reader's familiarity with them from his basic marketing course. In addition, it should be mentioned that a few retailers make some purchases from other retailers. Thus the retailer of men's clothing who is "out" of a shirt of a certain size may go to another retailer and secure one,

---

[1] "Inside Sears, Roebuck," *Printers' Ink,* October 22, 1965, p. 23.

rather than let his regular customer go there. Or again, so-called "discount" retailers find, on occasion, that some manufacturers and wholesalers refuse to sell them merchandise; their response may be to find other retailers to make the purchases for them. In view of the relative unimportance of these practices, however, they will not be discussed further in this chapter.

Middlemen As Merchandise Resources

The Wholesaler. Wholesalers are merchant middlemen who typically buy from manufacturers in relatively large quantities and sell to retailers in substantially smaller quantities. Probably almost half of all manufactured consumers' goods go through the hands of wholesalers. They may handle as much as 90 percent of all goods in the hardware trade and nearly 70 percent of all drugstore merchandise. Hence, wholesalers are a most important source of supply for the retailer.

1. *Service and Limited-Function Wholesalers.* The great majority of present-day wholesalers are best described as service wholesalers, despite the growth of those performing only limited functions. The service wholesaler's most important function is to serve as the retailers' "buying agent." He anticipates what retailers will want, goes out in the market to obtain these goods, and has them available when the retailers want them. This assembling of merchandise is a gigantic task, involving, as already suggested, so many different items.

The service wholesaler not only assembles goods for the retailer, but he also renders other valuable services, including storage of goods until they are wanted, rapid delivery upon order, financing through the extension of credit, and risk reduction through enabling the retailer to operate on smaller stocks and guaranteeing the goods sold. Finally, the service wholesaler is an important source of market information for the retailer.

Limited-function wholesalers do not extend many of the foregoing services to the retailer. The cash-and-carry wholesalers in the grocery and tobacco fields are good examples. By limiting themselves to a small stock of fast-moving items, eliminating salesmen, and offering no credit or delivery service, these middlemen reduce the cost of wholesaling. But most retailers, because of the important services they perform, still prefer the service wholesalers.

The services rendered by "regular" wholesalers are especially valuable to small- and medium-sized retailers; consequently, these retailers utilize this source of supply more than any other. In contrast, large-scale retailers such as chain stores, who are able to perform many of the wholesaler's functions within their own organizations, find it more economical to take over the buying, storing, financing, and similar services which the wholesaler performs for smaller retailers. Even large retailers, however, make some use of wholesalers, relying on them to obtain items temporarily out of stock or for which the demand is limited.[2]

2. *The Rack Jobber.* Essentially the rack jobber is a wholesaler of nonfood items who arranges with the managements of independent and chain supermarkets to stock and maintain an assortment of goods in a fixture or rack in a particular space in each store. A specific percentage of markup —usually 25 to 33 percent, depending upon the type of merchandise and competitive conditions[3]—is guaranteed to the supermarket. The wholesaler (jobber) selects the items and arranges proper displays, making shifts whenever he considers such action advisable.

There is no doubt but that the rack jobber is responsible for much of the rapidity with which supermarkets have added nonfoods. Without his specialized service, the retailer would have been very hesitant to add toys, housewares, children's books, hardware, and many other items to his inventory. But with the rack jobber to deliver the merchandise, arrange for its display, price it, provide for point-of-purchase material and special promotions, remove slow-selling items—and at a guaranteed gross profit margin— the retailer's resistance crumbled.[4] Today the rack jobber is the main source of supply for health and beauty aids in 48 percent of the independent and small-chain supermarkets, in 71 percent for housewares, and 65 percent for soft goods.[5]

While the larger chain supermarket operators have used the rack jobber as a means of introducing nonfoods to their stores—and many still continue to use him—there is a tendency for the chain to take over his functions. This step has been taken by such chains as Acme Markets, Inc., Mayfair Markets, and Food Fair Stores; and the trend is continuing, despite the switch back to rack jobbers by the Great Atlantic & Pacific Tea Company.[6] Among the large supermarket chains direct buying is used by 81 percent for health and

---

[2] Some students conclude that certain of the large national and regional supermarket chains should rely more on wholesalers than is currently the case. Cf. L. W. Stern, "Self-Sufficiency: A Fixation in Corporate Supermarket Chains?" *Journal of Retailing,* Vol. XLII, No. 1 (Spring, 1966), pp. 18–25 ff.

[3] I. W. Lazar, "Non-Food Sales and the Rack Jobber," *New York Retailer,* May, 1966, p. 22.

[4] For the operating methods and financial results of specific rack jobbers cf. "U.S. Consumer Products Rack Up New Advance in Operating Results," *Barrons,* August 23, 1965, p. 15; and "Sophistication in Supermarkets: Rack Jobbers Polish Technique," *Merchandising Week,* November 8, 1965, p. 37.

[5] "33rd Annual Report of the Grocery Industry," *Progressive Grocer,* April, 1966, p. 63.

[6] "Rack Jobbers Back at A & P In Non-Food Items Switch," *Women's Wear Daily,* June 2, 1965, p. 44.

beauty aids, 80 percent for housewares, and 53 percent for glassware.[7] The managements of these chains have become convinced that they can perform this jobber's services for less than, in effect, he charges for them. Of course, this trend is in line with the chain's desire for as complete integration as proves to be economically feasible. However, so far as many supermarket operators are concerned, as long as the rack jobber provides needed non-foods, gives good service, and prices his merchandise on a competitive basis, he will be widely used as a source of merchandise.

3. *Integration of Wholesale and Retail Functions.* In the typical chain store system there is often a high degree of integration of retail and wholesale activities within a single firm. The voluntary chain form of organization affords still another illustration of integration.[8] While in this case the wholesale and retail activities are not under common ownership, there is usually a contractual arrangement under which both wholesaler and retailer agree to coordinate their operations. In actual practice the line between chain and voluntary chain operations is becoming somewhat blurred: in addition to serving retailers under contract, the voluntary chain wholesaler may operate a chain of his own—or have a substantial financial investment in many of the so-called "independent" stores.[9] Or again, a retailer may own a whole group of stores (i.e., a chain) and yet have them supplied by merchandise from a voluntary chain wholesaler.[10] Finally, the retailers may actually own the wholesale organization, an arrangement usually referred to as a cooperative chain.[11] In brief, like on a muddy football field, it's becoming difficult to tell the players even with a program.

While voluntary and cooperative wholesalers have developed outside

---

[7] "Non-food Merchandising Practices," *Super Market Merchandising,* January, 1966, p. 53.

[8] For details on this form of organization cf. Chapter VII, "Group Activities of Independent Retailers," in C. F. Phillips and D. J. Duncan, *Marketing Principles and Methods* (5th ed.; Homewood, Ill.: Richard D. Irwin, Inc., 1964) and K. A. Adams, "Achieving Market Organization Through Voluntary and Cooperative Groups," *Journal of Retailing,* Vol. XLII, No. 2 (Summer, 1966), pp. 19–28, 60.

[9] For a specific illustration of such arrangements cf. "W. T. Benson: Profile of the New Thrust in Food Distribution," *Chain Store Age* (Supermarket Executives Edition), January, 1965, p. 82 l.

[10] Of all the supermarket chains in the United States belonging to the Super Market Institute, 30 percent (with 7 percent of the stores) are supplied through voluntary chain wholesalers and 33 percent (with 10 percent of the stores) through cooperative wholesalers. While these chains typically operate but a few units each, there are notable exceptions. Cf. *The Super Market Industry Speaks,* 1965 (Chicago, Ill.: Super Market Institute, 1965), pp. 25–26. For a specific example, cf. "Shop-Rite Foodarama," *Super Market Merchandising,* December, 1965, pp. 18–23; and Glenn Snyder, "Shop-Rite," *Progressive Grocer,* April, 1966, pp. 312–23.

[11] An illustration: "Twin County Grocers," *Super Market Merchandising,* June, 1966, pp. 22–24.

the food field, it is in food that they play their greatest role. As recently as 1958 their annual sales in this area were $5.2 billion; five years later they reached $8.3 billion.[12] If we also take into account the integration of wholesale and retail activities through (1) chain store organizations, (2) voluntary and cooperative wholesalers in nonfood fields, and (3) group buying arrangements,[13] the magnitude of this development comes into focus.

Other Middlemen.   Other middlemen—brokers, commission men, manufacturers' agents, selling agents, and auctions—are used as sources of needed merchandise by some retailers. But, as already noted, the volume of goods bought through these resources is far less than that purchased from wholesalers. The reasons are clear if we examine each one briefly.

1. *Brokers.*   The broker's main service is to bring buyer and seller together. He is used chiefly in buying and selling grocery specialties, dry goods, and fruits and vegetables. Although he is more useful to large retailers than to small-scale operators, even small retailers of men's and women's wear, household appliances, furniture, jewelry, hardware, and drugs employ his services to some degree.[14] As an example of the way the broker operates, consider the large food chain which wishes to purchase several tons of sugar. Instead of having its own buyer go from refiner to refiner to see what is available and at what prices, the chain will secure the services of a broker. Perhaps he is told the highest price the chain will pay for its sugar. Since he is a specialist in sugar, he knows prices and the supplies available; hence, he can quickly locate a proper source of supply and carry out the buyer's orders. Title passes not through the broker but directly from the seller of the sugar to the food chain. For bringing buyer and seller together, the broker receives a fee or commission.

2. *Commission Men.*   Commission men likewise constitute a source of supply mainly for large retailers, especially for those interested in buying dry goods, grocery specialties, and fruits and vegetables. Although they are often confused with brokers, commission men differ in that they usually handle the merchandise. They operate typically in central markets, receive merchandise that they display and sell, deduct their commission and other charges from the proceeds of the sale, and remit the balance to their principals.

3. *Selling Agents and Manufacturers' Agents.*   Selling agents are independent businessmen who take over the entire sales function for their clients. They are employed mostly by small manufacturers of piece goods, clothing, and food specialties who are not large enough to have their own

---

[12] Census of Business data in *Super Market Merchandising,* January, 1966, p. 14.

[13] Cf. pp. 324–25, below.

[14] Cf. the discussion of the merchandise broker on p. 321, below.

sales organizations. In addition to selling for their clients, selling agents often give advice on styling, extend financial aid, and make collections. Manufacturers' agents sell goods similar to those sold by selling agents; but manufacturers' agents have less authority over prices and terms of sale, are restricted to a more limited area, and sell only part of their clients' output.

4. *Auctions.* Auctions are an important source of supply for the larger retailers of fruits and vegetables. At the auction, produce is placed on display and sold quickly to the highest bidder, the proceeds going to the shipper after commissions and other charges have been deducted. Because of the skill needed to be a good buyer as well as the time involved in attending the auction, most smaller retailers buy their fruits and vegetables from wholesalers, many of whom may have used the auction as their source of supply.

The Manufacturer As A Merchandise Resource

Why Retailers Like to Buy Direct.   Many retailers, of course, purchase their merchandise directly from the manufacturer. They believe that there is much to be gained in so doing, even though they lose some of the services offered by the regular wholesaler. The manufacturer's salesman may be better trained and better informed regarding the particular kind of merchandise in which he specializes. Consequently, he is able to give the retailer advice on such elements as advertising and display methods being used by other retailers and on the stock needed. Especially is the advice of the manufacturer's salesman of value in regard to high-fashion merchandise. Also, direct buying is frequently accompanied by the manufacturer's cooperation in training the retailer's salesmen in how to sell certain merchandise; providing demonstrators; training employees to repair and install merchandise (by way of illustration, oil burners); and providing advertising and display material.

In regard to fashion merchandise, not only does direct buying allow the retailer to secure advice from the manufacturer, but it frequently enables him to get merchandise into his store more quickly than if a middleman intervenes. For high-fashion items, time is an important consideration. Even for manufactured goods which are somewhat perishable—crackers and cookies, for example—speed in getting merchandise from manufacturer to retailer is also of significance, and increasingly so since customers are constantly demanding fresher merchandise. Consequently, on perishable products, it is sometimes to the retailer's advantage to buy direct from the manufacturer.

For the large retailer direct buying makes possible the purchase of goods made according to his own specifications. And purchasing by specification is on the increase: Montgomery Ward & Company reports many "new and improved product lines to its own specifications" while Sears, Roebuck and Co. "is responsible for the design details of 95 percent of the goods it sells."[15] Drug chains, furniture chains, department stores, and discount houses are among the other retailers buying on this basis. Being close to the customer, the retailer is in a good position to assess customer wants; and his testing laboratory[16] can often serve as an ideal place for drawing up the specifications for a product.

Even if direct buying did not offer the foregoing benefits, it would still be favored by many retailers, especially by large-scale operators, because they find that it allows them to obtain lower net prices. In other words—partly by eliminating some of the middleman's functions, partly by absorbing these functions, and partly by having them performed by the manufacturer—the cost of marketing is reduced, with the result that prices to the retailer are also reduced.

In view of the many advantages to the direct-buying retailer, it is not surprising that smaller retailers have joined together to achieve at least some of these gains. In Cleveland, direct buying by a group of hardware retailers has resulted in a reported 10 to 20 percent reduction in purchase prices; and savings are also being achieved by an association of appliance and TV retailers in the Chicago-Milwaukee area.[17] In another retail field, the ability to purchase directly from manufacturers was a major reason for the formation of Casual Corner Associates, an association of independently owned sportswear shops.[18]

Why Some Manufacturers Sell Direct. Although we are mainly interested in the retailer's point of view, by no means is all direct sale solely a result of his desire to buy direct. Many manufacturers prefer to sell directly to retailers because they consider it "good business."

The necessity of speed in getting fashion and perishable merchandise to the retailer is as important to the manufacturer as it is to the retailer. Moreover, the growth of retailers who are willing to buy in large amounts, who perform part of the storage function, and who are good credit risks encourages the manufacturer to sell direct. In some cases, even relatively small retailers concentrate their buying with a few manufacturers so that they can buy in sufficiently large quantities to make direct sale economical.

---

[15] Montgomery Ward *Annual Report,* fiscal year ended February 3, 1965, p. 6; and John McDonald, "Sears Makes It Look Easy," *Fortune,* Vol. LXIX, No. 5 (May, 1964), p. 123.

[16] Cf. pp. 331–32, below.

[17] *Wall Street Journal,* March 14, 1963, p. 1

[18] "Casual Corner Sets 40 Units in '66," *Women's Wear Daily,* September 14, 1965, p. 18. Also cf. the discussion of "Group Buying" on pp. 324–25, below.

In the men's clothing field, for instance, many small retailers buy a major part of their suits and overcoats from a small number of sources. Also, they tend to buy a large part of their goods for each season at one time, thus further increasing the size of their orders.

Some manufacturers sell directly to secure more aggressive selling, as in the grocery field where wholesalers have developed their own private brands. The availability of public warehouses and manufacturers' branches as distributing points and the tendency on the part of some manufacturers to store their products near the retailer are other elements which are partly the cause and partly the effect of direct selling.

Manufacturer-Retailer Integration. Just as integration has taken place between wholesaler and retailer, the manufacturer and the retailer have also been drawn together. Some retailers, having purchased for some time from certain manufacturers, have taken the initiative and "bought out" —in whole or in part—some of their resources. Currently, Sears, Roebuck and Co. has from 9 to 100 percent ownership of the manufacturers producing 30 percent of the merchandise it sells.[19] In other cases, the retailer has established his own manufacturing divisions or subsidiary companies. Thus the Great Atlantic & Pacific Tea Company owns—among many others— bakeries, candy factories, ice cream plants, cheese factories, and French-fried potato plants; Bond Stores, Inc., manufactures men's suits, coats, and shirts; and the Thom McAn Shoe Company produces its own shoes.

Importance of Manufacturer as a Resource. It should be clear from the foregoing discussion that the importance of direct sale varies according to the size of the retailer and the type of merchandise carried. The location of the retailer is still another consideration. Large department stores, mail-order companies, and chain stores negotiate directly with manufacturers for a great part of their purchases—perhaps 75 percent or more. Although the percentage of their total purchases from manufacturers is much less, even small grocery retailers buy from producers such merchandise as cookies, crackers, breads, many kinds of cheese, some breakfast cereals, mayonnaise, and some coffee. Proprietary medicines, millinery, men's and women's clothing, nationally advertised men's hats, higher-priced hosiery, and men's shirts are also sold direct.

The Farmer as a Merchandise Resource

Although he should be mentioned as a third merchandise resource, the grower is not an important source of supply for retailers, except in the food field. In this field, even small retailers may draw a considerable part of their

---

[19] McDonald, *op. cit.*, p. 127. Also cf. "Sears' Suppliers," *Financial World,* November 3, 1965, pp. 5 ff.

fresh fruits and vegetables directly from local growers; with the retailer taking his truck and going directly to the farmer, or the latter bringing his output to town where he peddles it from store to store.

Turning to the large chain retailers, they may even send buyers to distant farmers, as it well illustrated by the practices of the Great Atlantic & Pacific Tea Company. "Its produce-buying division is the largest single factor in the market. Three teams of buyers—on the West Coast, in the Mississippi Valley, and on the East Coast—follow the crops northward as they ripen and keep in constant communication with the central office, and with one another, over a national teletype system."[20] While smaller chains cover a less extensive geographic area, they, too, frequently by-pass central markets and go directly to growers or, more often, to cooperative marketing associations to which the growers belong. This trend toward direct buying, however, should not blind us to the fact that most agricultural consumers' goods are still brought to the retailer by means of one or more of the various middlemen already discussed.[21]

VENDOR INITIATIVE TO FIND A BUYER

The initiative in bringing the retailer and the source of supply together may be taken by the seller or by the retailer himself, acting individually or in cooperation with other retailers. We begin with those cases in which the seller takes the initiative.

Catalogs and Price Lists

To provide information concerning their offerings at the time it is wanted by the retailer rather than when the salesman calls, both manufacturers and wholesalers issue catalogs. Although they were at one time of considerable importance and are still widely used by vendors of some kinds of merchandise, today catalogs are used by retailers largely for the purchase of fill-in merchandise. Even for such merchandise, which consists chiefly of staples, catalogs are used mainly by retailers located in areas where the total business of vendors is not sufficient to justify frequent visits by salesmen. As catalog sales have fallen off, some vendors have substituted shorter price lists, with less complete descriptions of the items offered for sale than formerly appeared in their catalogs.

---

[20] "Pinching 500,000,000,000 Pennies," *Fortune,* Vol. LXVII, No. 3 (March, 1963), p. 172. Also cf. "Produce Buying Practices at Safeway," *Super Market Merchandising,* December, 1966, pp. 30–31, 47.

[21] Cf. pp. 307–11, above.

Some vendors prepare catalogs for use mainly by the small-town retailer as a means of selling merchandise which he does not carry in stock. This type of catalog seems to be gaining in popularity since a rising percentage of the customer's dollar is spent for the kinds of merchandise which can be sold through this medium. As recently as ten years ago the John Plain & Company catalog listed about 8,000 items of merchandise; the catalog now in the hands of 58,000 retailers contains over 19,000 items—and Company sales have advanced from an estimated $15–$20 million to $40–50 million.[22]

Catalogs are also used by some resident buying offices located in cities such as New York as a means of assisting their client stores in making purchases. One office, for example, issues a notion catalog describing all the items carried by the stores in its affiliated group. Another publishes a housewares catalog in mineographed form containing the chief offerings of over 1,200 suppliers.[23]

Salesmen

Probably the most important activity initiated by the vendor desiring to sell his products is the use of salesmen to call upon prospective purchasers. When goods sell quite rapidly, i.e., have a good turnover, salesmen may call upon each of their customers as frequently as once a week, thus making it easier for the retailer to practice hand-to-mouth buying. As a matter of fact, in the grocery, drug, and hardware fields, some wholesalers' salesmen telephone their retailer customers daily. In other fields—men's clothing, for instance—where the retailer finds it satisfactory to place a smaller number of larger orders, visits by the salesmen are less frequent. To some degree the frequency of salesmen visits also depends on business conditions. The more difficult it is to sell, the greater the likelihood that calls will be made more often and additional selling "pressure" exerted.

Purchasing through salesmen usually does not permit the buyer to compare directly the merchandise offerings of various manufacturers before placing his order, but it does offer some important advantages. It takes from the buyer the burden of looking for sources of supply. When samples are brought to the store the buyer can get the opinions of his salespeople before purchases are made. The salesman serves as a source of market information; consequently, many buyers make it a practice at least to talk with all the salesmen who call. When buying is done on the premises of the buyer, he can more deliberately check the stock on hand; and feeling less rushed and more at ease in his own store, he probably does a better job of purchasing.

---

[22] For further details on this firm cf. Arthur Weinberg, "Catalogs Keep Rural Touch, Cater to Urban Tastes," *Women's Wear Daily*, September 18, 1964, p. 13.

[23] Resident buying offices are discussed on pp. 320–24, below.

RETAILER INITIATIVE TO FIND A VENDOR

Increasingly, retailers are taking the initiative and seeking sources of supply, rather than depending on vendors coming to them. They prefer to compare more closely the offerings of several vendors, survey "the market," and exchange ideas with various sellers and retailers in the same line of business. Moreover, many manufacturers of such high-fashion goods as women's dresses are so small and concentrated in such a limited area that it is more economical for the large retailer to take the initiative than for the manufacturer to send out salesmen.

Visits to Local Markets

Most vendors located near retailers take the initiative and call on them, but occasionally retailers find it desirable to go to the vendors. As already indicated, even small food store retailers may find it advisable to seek out local growers of fruits and vegetables. At times, such direct buying may give the retailer his produce at lower prices. Large food retailers also send their buyers into local markets to assure themselves of an ample supply at the lowest possible price. Usually the buyers for the large organizations do not buy from individual farmers; rather, they deal with the local middlemen who have brought together the output of a number of farmers. Retailers may also take the initiative in dealing with cash-and-carry wholesalers in the local market and, on occasion, may find it advisable to call on certain local manufacturers.

Visits to Central Markets

Central Market Facilities. Central market buying, which takes the retailer to certain major cities in his search for merchandise resources, is practiced especially by medium-size and large-scale retailers and, to some degree, by all retailers of fashion goods. Most retailers look upon New York City as the dominant central market for many types of merchandise and, especially, as the important market for women's wear, since it produces about two thirds of all the dresses manufactured in this country. But, other cities are gaining as central markets, and for certain goods they overshadow New York. On the West Coast, San Francisco and Los Angeles have become so important, especially for department stores, that even buyers from eastern stores are visiting these cities. For furniture, Chicago; Grand

Rapids, Michigan; High Point, North Carolina; and Jamestown, New York, are important markets, in addition to New York City. For many retailers, St. Louis, Dallas, and New Orleans are important central markets.

Central market buyers typically visit the display quarters of individual vendors as well as joint display centers. In most cities the vendors of competing goods are located close together so that suppliers' offerings can be easily compared, that is, fairly distinct markets or locations exist within the confines of these cities. Permanent displays in one large building are also frequently maintained by competing vendors. Chicago's American Furniture Mart houses the permanent displays of many sellers of furniture and related products; the gigantic Merchandise Mart in the same city is used for display and selling purposes by vendors in practically all fields, with home furnishings increasing in importance; Atlanta's Merchandise Mart likewise has displays covering many lines of merchandise; while the Apparel Mart in Dallas concentrates on all kinds of apparel.[24]

Where central permanent displays are not used, competing vendors often sponsor a temporary joint showing of their goods. Thus, New York City has its house-furnishings show and its toy fair; Chicago, its home-furnishings show, its millinery-fashion display, its semiannual furniture markets, and its national shoe fair; Grand Rapids, its furniture show; and San Francisco, its home-furnishings show.

Benefits and Methods of Central Market Buying. Although the excitement of the large "showings" is not conducive to careful buying, there is much to be said from the buyer's point of view in favor of the joint showing. In many instances—as concerns furniture, for example—catalog illustrations may be misleading, so that it is wise for the buyer to see samples of the actual goods before they are purchased. The show meets this need. Moreover, it allows the buyer to view all offerings in a minimum of time, to make direct comparisons, to exchange ideas with other buyers, and to see what they are purchasing.

Buying in central markets is carried on mainly (1) through store buyers who make periodic trips to market, (2) through store buyers assisted by resident buying offices, and (3) through central market representatives. When the store buyer goes to market and buys without assistance from a resident buying office, he has full authority. Although he still retains full authority when he makes use of the resident buying office, actually the office is important in determining what shall be purchased. Where central market representatives are used, the local buyer loses to them much of his authority.

---

[24] For details on some of these marts cf. "Atlanta Merchandise Mart Set to Double Size by Fall, 1968," and "Dallas Mart: Deep in Heart of Stores," *Women's Wear Daily,* November 9, 1966, pp. 30, 60.

Central Market Buying Trips. Buying visits to central markets may occur as often as every few days or may be made only once in several years if ever. The frequency of these trips is determined by such factors as: (1) whether or not the buyer's store has a resident buying office; (2) the type of merchandise involved, i.e., staple or fashion goods; (3) the size of the store; (4) business and supply conditions; and (5) the location of the retailer in relation to the central market.

Since "the average market trip lasts three to five days, except at the beginning of a season, . . . [and since] so much work is crowded into these few days . . . , intensive preparation is essential."[25] As part of this pre-trip activity, a buying plan is usually prepared. Once in the market, the buyer must "make every minute count," as is suggested by the discussion which follows.

1. *"Scouting" the Market.* Visits to central markets, especially for fashion merchandise, afford the buyer the opportunity to obtain merchandise knowledge before he actually starts to make purchases. A buyer who does not have the assistance of a resident buying office usually utilizes his first visit to each vendor as a "sight-seeing" trip, merely to note what is available. But much depends, of course, upon supply and demand conditions. When goods are in short supply, delays in making purchases may result in failure to obtain the goods desired. Even though the buyer is not interested in expensive goods, he will find it advantageous to call on the vendors of such goods, because he may learn much from them as to the styles that are in fashion. Then, by visiting the low- and medium-priced vendors, the buyer can form some idea of how far the fashion cycle has developed for each style. In addition, by visiting the various price-class vendors, he obtains valuable price information.

On this first excursion the buyer should keep rather complete notes as to prices, materials, styles, and the best offerings of each vendor. Before he makes his second trip, during which he will probably place orders, careful study should be made of these notes. This practice saves him the trouble of again calling upon *all* vendors and reviewing *all* their offerings.

Many buyers find it helpful to visit stores located in the central market city either before or after exploring the offerings of vendors, thus observing merchandise being displayed. On occasion, the entire reason for a trip to a certain city may be to observe other stores. To illustrate, the fashion reputation of Neiman-Marcus of Dallas, Texas, is so great that its various fashion expositions attract store buyers from all parts of the country.

At times the buyer will want to make another round of visits in the

---

[25] F. A. Coy, writing in *The Buyer's Manual* (4th ed.; New York: National Retail Merchants Association, 1965), p. 56.

central market city before placing orders, this time to observe some of the factories that make merchandise in which he is interested. From such a trip he may get ideas as to goods being produced but not yet placed on sale. He may discover special goods being manufactured or held for others. And, in some cases, he may pick up special lots of items at low prices.

2. *Selecting Vendors: Many or a Few?* With full information concerning the merchandise which is available, the buyer is ready to practice the sound rule of selecting the items he believes best adapted to the needs of his customers. Through a careful study of his notes, the buyer is able to determine quickly the sources of supply which have the goods he requires at the most favorable terms. These resources he visits for the second time to check more carefully on specific goods, to negotiate prices and terms, and to place his orders.

Because of the information that such a practice provides, it is desirable for the buyer to shop all vendors in the central market who handle the type of merchandise in which he is interested. Widespread shopping, however, does not necessarily imply he will spread his purchases among many vendors.[26] In fact, by concentrating his purchases, the buyer saves time, earns the good will of vendors, obtains better credit terms and improved deliveries, assures that his orders are filled more accurately, and that his claims are more cheerfully adjusted. The good will generated may prove of considerable help in obtaining favorable treatment during periods when deliveries are uncertain, in having the buyer's attention called to especially good "buys," and in securing lower prices. Moreover, concentrating orders allows the buyer to secure larger quantity discounts.

At the same time, the buyer must recognize there are advantages in spreading his orders among several resources. This practice gives him a greater assurance of supply, in that not all suppliers might be shut down at the same time by floods, fires, or strikes. The resulting competition among the several suppliers may lead to the granting of better prices or terms of sale as each tries to enlarge his share of the buyer's order. For the large retailer, whose purchases might account for a significant part of the vendor's sales, concentration of purchasing involves certain responsibilities which the vendor may not wish to assume.

In brief, the retailer must weigh the advantages of both concentrating and spreading his orders. While each specific situation must be weighed carefully, as a general rule many experienced retailers have concluded they

---

[26] The discussion which follows is applicable to the selection of vendors in all markets and not in central markets alone. For a detailed analysis of this subject cf. E. W. Crooks, "The Case for Concentration of Purchases," *Journal of Retailing*, Vol. XLII, No. 1 (Spring, 1966), pp. 14–18.

should not spread their purchases among more vendors than is necessary to get the best goods available. Hence, when they find sources of supply which (1) have merchandise meeting their needs, (2) can be counted on as steady sources of supply, (3) are in sound financial condition, (4) have fair prices and terms of sale, (5) give good delivery service, (6) make adjustments promptly on all reasonable complaints, (7) are fair and honest in their dealings, (8) have progressive managements, and (9) deliver goods identical with their samples, they tend to concentrate their purchases with them. To cite a specific illustration, since 1963 Montgomery Ward & Company has been steadily reducing the number of its resources in an effort to simplify product lines, build up the best resources, improve product quality, and achieve greater control over the specifications of products.[27] For a wide variety of reasons, it appears that many other retailers will pursue a similar policy.[28]

3. *The Resource File.* Maintained by many buyers as an aid in deciding which vendors shall get the bulk of their orders, this file consists of a card record for each vendor with whom business has been done, with notations on the card to indicate results of past dealings. For example, the card will show discounts allowed by the vendor and whether or not the goods delivered were identical with samples. Such information is valuable especially when an organization finds it necessary to change buyers. When a resident buying office is used, the resource file may be maintained in that office.[29]

Resident Buying Offices To Assist Local Buyers. Resident buying offices have assumed increased importance in recent years, gradually expanding their services until today they are literally merchandising consultants for their client stores. They now serve probably as many as 90 percent of the country's department and specialty stores and also play an important role for discount houses.[30]

1. *Classification of Resident Buying Offices.* Although resident buying offices may be classified in various ways, probably the clearest grouping is as follows:

[27] Cf. *Annual Report,* fiscal year ended February 3, 1965, p. 6; and *Women's Wear Daily,* February 7, 1966, p. 8.

[28] Some of these reasons are developed in E. B. Weiss, "Collaboration vs. Confrontation Between Major Suppliers and Major Retailers," *Advertising Age,* January 31, 1966, pp. 92 and 95; and "Programmed Merchandising, The New Way to Work with Key Resources," *Department Store Economist,* October, 1964, pp. 22–27.

[29] The rating of resources and the forms used by retailers to record resource information are discussed by C. G. Taylor in *The Buyer's Manual, op. cit.,* pp. 67–74.

[30] For a detailed listing of resident buying offices cf. *Phelon's Resident Buyers and Merchandise Brokers of Department Store Merchandise, Ready-to-Wear, Millinery* (New York: Phelon-Sheldon Publications, Inc., 1967).

1. Independent offices
   a) Salaried or paid offices
   b) Merchandise brokers
2. Store-owned offices
   a) Private offices
   b) Associated offices
   c) Syndicate and chain offices[31]

2. Independent Offices. The independent resident buying office is a private company with an ownership different from that of the several stores which it serves. In the salaried or paid type of office, contracts are usually drawn up which provide for the buyers to have the use of the services offered for a certain period of time, typically one year. Some contracts set a minimum fee of as low as $100 a month, with larger payments according to annual sales or services rendered. Other contracts call for the fee to equal a certain percentage of the sales of the store or of the departments involved, ¼ of 1 percent being the common figure for large stores.

The merchandise broker, another type of independent office formerly known as a commission resident buying office, exists to serve smaller retailers who cannot afford the minimum cost of the salaried type of resident buying office. Whereas it is estimated that a department or specialty store needs annual sales of at least $75,000 before it is economical to sign a contract with a salaried buying office, the merchandise broker can be used by much smaller stores. This result follows from the fact that these offices are paid by the vendors with whom orders are placed, a fee of 3 percent on all orders being a common figure. No contract exists between the store and the merchandise broker, and in practice a store may use one merchandise broker for a while and then abruptly shift to another.

3. Store-Owned Offices. The store-owned buying office is owned outright by a single large store or group of stores. When operated as a definite division of one organization such as Meier & Frank Co. of Portland, Oregon, or the Belk Stores Service Corporation of the group of Belk stores, it is known as a "private" buying office.[32] When the office is owned and directed by several independent or ownership-group stores for their own benefit, it is known as an "associated" buying office. Probably the best-known offices of this type are the Associated Merchandising Corporation which serves some 30 to 40 major department stores, including all divisions

---

[31] This classification is based on J. W. Wingate, "Some Data on Resident Buying," *New York Retailer,* October, 1962, pp. 2–6. Also cf. J. W. Wingate and J. S. Friedlander, *The Management of Retail Buying* (Englewood Cliffs, N. J.: Prentice-Hall, Inc., 1963), p. 65. For another classification cf. A. C. Elgart, writing in *The Buyer's Manual, op. cit.,* pp. 401–2.

[32] The operations of the Belk Stores Service Corporation are outlined in "Holdout In a World of Chains," *Business Week,* October 23, 1965, especially p. 116.

of the Federated Department Stores, Inc.; and Frederick Atkins, Inc., with some 50 department stores as members.[33]

The syndicate office, the third type of store-owned resident buying office, is best exemplified by the chain-store or ownership-group buying office, which purchases centrally or otherwise for the stores involved. It resembles the associated buying office in many respects but is able to force adoption of its recommendations to a much greater degree because of common owner- ship of the stores. Examples of the syndicate type of the resident buying office are Associated Dry Goods Corporation and the Allied Purchasing Corporation. The latter organization, for example, serves the more than 100 stores of the Allied Stores Corporation through buying offices in New York, Chicago, Los Angeles, Miami, and Dallas and a foreign-buying subsidiary which operates buying offices in several cities abroad. While the buyers within each store have considerable authority to make direct purchases to meet local market demand, even on these purchases the buyers are aided by the advice and recommendations of the resident buying office staff. In fact, after deciding what he wants, a local buyer will frequently ask a resident buyer to go into the market and make the actual purchase. For staple merchandise, full buying authority resides with the resident buying staff. Finally, buyer committees for various lines of merchandise composed of both store buyers and those from the Allied Purchasing Corporation, select many items which must be carried by all stores.[34]

4. *Location and Merchandise Lines.* All of these present-day types of resident buying offices have seen their greatest development in the New York market because this area is the major central market for many kinds of goods. Some resident buying offices exist elsewhere, as in Chicago, Los Angeles and St. Louis. Although the majority of resident buyers operate in the women's and children's apparel trades, many offer service in the pur- chase of furs, men's wear, millinery, home furnishings, jewelry, and other merchandise lines. Some are fairly small, serving a limited number of stores in the purchase of a few lines; others are set up to serve buyers of goods in a large number of fields.

5. *Services Rendered Buyers.* Resident buying offices furnish several important services to store buyers which enable them to do a much better job than they could do without such assistance. This help is provided the store buyer both while he is in his home city and while he is visiting the

---

[33] A list of the stores served by the Associated Merchandising Corporation and a description of its activities are included in "AMC's Power on 7th Avenue: Peanuts or High Pressure?" *Women's Wear Daily,* April 27, 1964, pp. 1 and 18.

[34] Cf. the comments on "individual store" and "central" buying in the Allied organiza- tion in Wingate and Friedlander, *op. cit.,* pp. 40–41.

central market on a buying trip. Let us review some of these forms of assistance.

Employees of the resident buying office are in the market center all the time; consequently, they can place orders upon request, check on deliveries, handle adjustments, and provide the store buyer with a vast amount of information as to goods available, fashion trends, prices, and the best sources of supply. The store buyer gets his information from experts, and he gets it quickly. When in the market, someone from the resident buying office accompanies the buyer from vendor to vendor so that both can pass judgment on merchandise offers. This arrangement enables the resident buyer to point out the "best buys" while the local buyer concentrates on which of the "best buys" can be sold to *his* customers. The office may arrange for a "showing" at which the offerings of many vendors are put on display, thus conserving the buyer's time. In some instances, vendors, knowing that resident buyers will influence the purchasing of several store buyers, are more willing to grant price concessions to the resident buyers. Hence, merchandise may be purchased at lower prices.[35] The resident buying office also provides facilities for the buyer when he is in the central market, such as office space, stenographic aid, and sample rooms where vendors may display their goods. Finally, the resident buying office often plays an important role in making arrangements for carrying out group buying.[36]

When the store buyer is not in the central market, the resident buying office may aid him through a constant stream of market information in the form of letters, special reports, or regular weekly or monthly bulletins. Thus the buyer is kept informed concerning fashion and price trends and special buys. During recent years there has been a tendency for resident buying offices to purchase more items for the stores they serve. In some cases, samples of new goods or of execptional values are forwarded to the buyer. If the store buyer decides to purchase some of these goods, he may so inform the resident buying office and ask it to place the order. A considerable number of fill-in purchases are placed through the resident buying office. The office may even consolidate shipment on a number of small orders placed with several vendors, thus reducing the cost of transportation. For staple or "never-out" merchandise, the buying office—aided by a unit-control system worked out between the store and the office—may make all the purchases, thus giving the local store buyers more time for the buying of other merchandise. Some offices actually merchandise fashion departments

---

[35] The merchandise broker type of resident buying offices does not attempt to get price reductions from vendors. Of course, any price reductions which are obtained should be considered in relationship to the Robinson-Patman Act. Cf. pp. 340–50, below.

[36] Cf. the next section.

in the stores they serve. After agreeing on a model stock, a unit-control system is installed. Based on sales tabs flowing to the resident buying office, the office assumes all purchasing responsibility. Since leading offices have foreign branches or are closely associated with similar groups abroad, they also do some purchasing of foreign merchandise.

The resident buying office sometimes offers the store two other services which, although not directly related to buying, are very valuable. It may suggest goods for promotional events, prepare advertising copy, and outline the whole campaign. This kind of service is especially valuable to the medium-size store which cannot afford to maintain a highly-paid advertising executive. The other service is operating as a clearinghouse for information from all the stores served. For example, the resident office may gather data on expenses, markdowns, training systems, and sales promotions and distribute these data to all the stores of the group. Such information may be very important to a retailer in improving his own operations.

Group Buying. Group buying involves joint purchasing by a group of buyers representing noncompeting stores.[37] As already suggested, resident buying offices frequently play an important role in group buying, especially as it is practiced by department and specialty stores. Typically, they gather the samples from various vendors and place them on display at their offices or, in some cases, in hotel sample rooms. Sometimes all vendors' labels are removed so that buying may be as objective as possible. After the samples have been considered, the committee of buyers decides, by a majority or two-thirds vote, on the items to be bought, each buyer usually taking at least a minimum quantity of the merchandise so selected.

By no means is group buying restricted to department and department-ized specialty stores; it is also practiced by retailers of hardware, appliances, foods, drugs, and other merchandise lines.[38] For reasons mentioned in the following paragraphs, more retailers will likely turn to group buying to improve their competitive position.

1. *Benefits of Group Buying.* A number of expected advantages explain why department and specialty stores practice group buying and, with quite obvious modification, these same factors are applicable to group buying as practiced by other retailers. First, there is the desire to place large orders on certain goods and thus secure large discounts. Second, the pooling of knowledge as to what customers want, goods available, and fashion trends enables buyers to select items that will sell to better advantage. Third, group buying saves the buyer's time while he is in the market. Fourth, the direct compari-

---

[37] When the selecting of items is done by a committee of buyers chosen to act for the buyers of all the stores, it is referred to as "committee buying."

[38] Cf. the earlier discussion of joint-buying on page 312, above.

son of merchandise—which is possible because samples of several vendors are available in one place—makes for better buying. Fifth, in some cases, buying groups do enough purchasing to enable them to develop standards for certain items which they can have produced according to their own specifications. Sixth, group buying may result also in other than just buying advantages such as the promotional activities which some groups have sponsored. After buying certain goods, a group may develop brand names which are placed on the goods and then widely advertised. The resident buying office is important in planning these group promotions.

2. *Limitations of Group Buying.* In addition to the objections raised by vendors,[39] there are difficulties with group buying even from the point of view of the retail store. Too often, the store buyer feels that group buying is just a step toward his elimination, with his buying function taken over by central buyers. As a result, he may not give his full cooperation in "pushing" goods selected by the group and in placing orders for his minimum quantity of the selected goods. In the latter case, his action makes it difficult for the group to present a united front in asking lower prices of the vendor. Moreover, at least in part, it must be recognized that the buyer's objection that the goods are not purchased with *his* particular customers in mind is true. Consequently, a buyer may find that he is getting some goods on which he has to take large markdowns. Group buying, in practice, has also proven to be time consuming; and not all of the groups have really shown the better selection of goods which many hold to be the main advantage of such buying.

It should also be pointed out that group buying is best suited to stores handling medium-priced lines. The low-priced store finds that most of the goods it buys are made by manufacturers for stock, so that the manufacturer has no production savings to share with a group placing a single large order. Also, the selection problem for customers of low-priced goods is easier than for more discriminating customers who buy somewhat more expensive goods. The retailer of high-priced goods finds that the customer-demanded individuality of his stock precludes his entering into extensive group-buying arrangements.

Central Buying. Central buying implies that a large part of the authority over buying lies outside the retail store. It is well illustrated by the buying practices of many leading chain-store organizations, especially those handling convenience goods. Instead of allowing the store manager to

---

[39] Vendors raise these objections, among others, against group buying: It results in too many price concessions, causes manufacturers to reduce quality, and encourages style piracy while samples are in the sample room of the buying committee. On the matter of price concessions, cf. the discussion in "AMC's Power on 7th Ave.," *op. cit.*

choose sources of supply, this activity is performed by headquarters executives. The central buyer is made responsible for purchasing, and the store manager specializes in selling.

1. *Trend Toward Central Buying.* Two careful students of retail buying write that "perhaps the major trend in modern merchandising has been for two or more stores to unite to centralize their buying activities. Central buyers replace buyers for individual stores."[40] Even department stores have adopted some central-buying practices.[41] For example, certain of the ownership-group department stores—Allied Stores Corporation and Associated Dry Goods Corporation—have long used central buyers for some staples and lower-priced fashion merchandise. A few independent stores also have made arrangements for a very limited amount of central buying. However, the loss of authority over buying on the part of the department store buyer up to the present time must not be overemphasized. In the main the practice has not made much headway outside of staples, and some firms have even returned to individual store buying after experimenting with central buying.[42]

Actually, organizations with central buyers depend to a degree on store buyers, especially in regard to shopping goods. Even such large chains as W. T. Grant Company, F. W. Woolworth Company, Sears, Roebuck and Co., and J. C. Penney Company let their store managers select much of their merchandise from lists supplied by headquarters. In other instances the managers meet and make their selections from the samples gathered by the central buyers, with blanket orders being placed on the items selected. In the department store ownership groups, the accepted practice is to let the store buyers refuse goods selected by central buyers. Yet it cannot be denied that the trend toward central buying has taken away from many store buyers an appreciable part of their authority over buying.[43]

Central buyers must have at their disposal a constant stream of information as to what customers are demanding. In obtaining this information, use is made of all the methods that we have discussed in a preceding section. Through perpetual inventory systems and unit inventory control plans— which increasingly are being made more complete, more accurate, and more up to date by the use of electronic computers—as well as through general

[40] Wingate and Friedlander, *op. cit.,* p. 39.

[41] The type of department stores engaging in more central buying is illustrated by those listed in E. B. Weiss, "Meet Our Newest Mass Retailers," *Advertising Age,* June 7, 1965, pp. 124 ff.

[42] For an example cf. "Fedway Completes Buying Switch to Individual Stores," *Women's Wear Daily,* July 7, 1964, p. 2.

[43] For supporting evidence cf. "Manufacturers Accuse Retailers of Downgrading the Buyer's Role," *Merchandising Week,* March 7, 1966, p. 25.

reports from the store to the central buyer as to how goods are moving, what goods are in stock, and what goods are being asked for by customers, many central buyers know as much or more about the wants of customers they never see as the store buyers who come in daily contact with their customers.

2. *Advantages and Disadvantages of Central Buying.*[44] In part, the advantages claimed for central buying are similar to those claimed for group buying. At least this statement is true in regard to the lower prices secured by quantity buying and the possibility of central planning of sales promotions. But the claims for central buying go beyond these two considerations. The central buyer spends his full time in just buying; consequently, he becomes an expert in buying and should do a better job than the store buyer, for whom buying is a part-time activity. Being located in the central market, or at least keeping closely in touch with it, the central buyer secures new merchandise as soon as it appears. The traveling expenses incident to many trips to central markets are reduced; and being in the central market, he is often in a position to inspect goods, especially fashion goods, before they are shipped. It is also argued that to relieve the store buyer of purchasing leaves him free to devote his attention to selling, which results in a better selling job.

Although there is general agreement that central buying of staples has much in its favor, this agreement is lacking when fashion goods are under consideration. It is contended that, for such goods, the buyer must be in touch with the store's customers. Moreover, customers' wants differ from store to store, so that the central buyer may find himself unable to buy in sufficient quantities to get any important quantity discounts. Certainly there is some truth in these contentions—so much, perhaps, that fashion goods in many large organizations, especially those appealing to the buyers for upper-income groups, will never be purchased by central buyers. Yet the development of methods of keeping central buyers informed as to what customers want is proceeding so rapidly that in years to come this limitation may look less serious than it has in the past.

3. *Ordering for Specific Stores in Chain Systems.* One of the problems growing out of central buying by chain organizations is that of devising an adequate system (1) to inform the store managers of the goods already purchased by the central buyers and (2) to enable the managers to requisition stock for their stores from these centrally purchased goods. The food chains can be used to illustrate the factors involved. For many years it has

---

[44] Also cf. the discussion of the merits and limitations of separating the buying and selling functions in departmentized stores on pp. 206–8, above.

been the practice of these chains to provide store managers with a list of all the items carried in company warehouses. Usually these merchandise lists are printed on a form which can also be used for placing orders. For dry groceries, the store manager takes his list and, on a given day each week or perhaps more often, walks around his store, noting the quantity on hand for each item and entering the amount he wishes to order. This form then goes to the nearest company warehouse where the order is filled.

Today the food chains are speeding up this ordering process by the use of electronic equipment.[45] Many units of Safeway Stores, Inc., are equipped with an ordering machine which produces a tape listing the wanted merchandise. In turn, the symbols on this tape are transmitted electronically to a warehouse from which the order is filled. Acme Markets, Inc. is experimenting with a somewhat similar system, except that the warehouse can—at its convenience, perhaps at night hours—dial the store and receive the order over a regular telephone wire.[46] The National Tea Company system has store employees place the order on cards. These cards are sent to headquarters where they are "read" by an electronic machine which automatically transmits shipping orders to the warehouse. However, this Company has experimented with a telephone wire transmission system which reduces the time between placing an order and receiving the merchandise in the store from three days (when cards are mailed) to one day.[47] Many chains in other fields—variety, drug, shoe, general merchandise, to mention a few—are also using electronic equipment to speed up the flow of orders to their retail units.[48]

Of course, not all chain systems depend on the store manager to make the decision as to merchandise that should be handled by a specific store. In other words, some firms "merchandise" individual stores from headquarters or a branch headquarters. Previously, Diana Stores Corporation and, for some lines, the J. C. Penney Company, have been cited as examples of this type of electronic operation.[49] Through a combination of model stocks, the flow of sales tags or tickets to headquarters, and the rapid analysis of these tags, headquarters can quickly decide what merchandise is needed in the store.

---

[45] Cf. the previous discussion of this subject on pp. 138–41, 282–83, and 287–88, above.

[46] *Annual Report,* fiscal year ended April 3, 1965, p. 8.

[47] "Test Two Computer Ordering Systems," *Super Market Merchandising,* November, 1965, p. 12.

[48] For the practices of two specific companies cf. "From Warehouse to Stores: Simplified Merchandise Control," (S. S. Kresge Company) *Chain Store Age* (Executives Ed.), December, 1965, pp. E22–27; and "EDP Network Links 365 Stores with 8 Warehouses," (Walgreen Company) *ibid.,* March, 1966, pp. E38–E41.

[49] Cf. p. 287, above.

Buying in Foreign Markets

The past three decades have seen significant fluctuations in the use of foreign markets as sources of supply. During the period of World War II the inflow of goods from many foreign markets dropped abruptly. Recently, however, an increased interest in foreign-made goods has been manifested with some large stores featuring extensively imports from Mexico, France, Italy, Japan, and other countries.[50] Although reliable data concerning the ratio of sales of foreign merchandise to total sales in such stores are not available, it is probable that it seldom exceeds 5 percent. For Sears, Roebuck and Co. and for Montgomery Ward & Company imports account for from one half of 1 percent to 2 percent of sales, while approximately 5 percent of the sales of W. T. Grant Company consists of merchandise from abroad.[51]

Many retailers believe, however, that the goods obtained from abroad— laces from Belgium, furniture from Denmark, sporting goods and wood carvings from Switzerland, linen from Ireland, men's wear and sportswear from England—are important both in giving prestige to the store and, because of the high markup which is sometimes possible, in contributing to net profits. Moreover, in some lines the percentage of business done in foreign merchandise is high: An Atlanta retailer expects that one third of his sales of handbags and jewelry will involve foreign-made products and Sears sells more imported sewing machines than domestic machines. In view of the attractiveness of many imported items, together with the price appeal which some of them offer, it seems likely that retailers will desire to increase still further their purchases in foreign markets.

The bulk of foreign goods bought by retailers come through importers located in New York City, although a considerable quantity enters through Pacific Coast importers.[52] Many of these importers send out catalogs and/or salesmen to retailers, but retailers often take the initiative and call on importers.

Other retailers make purchases from foreign sellers by correspondence or through their resident buying offices, if those offices maintain foreign con-

---

[50] As an example of the emphasis on foreign goods, cf. the report of Dayton's (Minneapolis department store) *fiesta* of Mexican goods in "Trend-Setting Store Imports," *Business Week*, July 31, 1965, p. 62; Isadore Barmash "Retailers Offer Foreign Motifs," *New York Times*, September 25, 1966, pp. F1, 12; and "The Import Syndrome," *Women's Wear Daily*, November 28, 1966, pp. 1, 23.

[51] Statement of L. C. Lustenberger, President of W. T. Grant Company, at stockholders annual meeting, April 26, 1966, p. 4 (mimeographed).

[52] Various guides are available to help a buyer locate importers of specific goods, such as the annual *Buyers Guide to Imported German Products* (New York: Nordeman Publishing Co., Inc., annually).

nections. Among the larger retailers, it is not uncommon to send buyers abroad or to have foreign store-owned buying offices. Thus the Associated Dry Goods Corporation maintains a buying office in London and the Great Atlantic & Pacific Tea Company has coffee-buying offices in Colombia and Brazil.[53] Those who send buyers abroad often employ a foreign resident buying office; such an office assists buyers in the same way they are aided in domestic central markets by similar offices.

SELECTING SUITABLE MERCHANDISE

A knowledge of available sources of supply and of buying methods and arrangements does not furnish the buyer with all the information he requires to do a good job. He should possess facts that will enable him to determine correctly the suitability of the merchandise for the purposes for which it is bought.

Some General Rules

Determination of merchandise suitability may be carried out by inspection of the merchandise, by means of a sample, or by a description. It needs to be stressed that, regardless of the actual procedure, determination of suitability is impossible (1) unless the buyer knows what his customers want and (2) unless the buyer can recognize what he wants when he examines the merchandise offered by various resources. We have discussed in detail how the buyer can find out what his customers want. To make certain that he obtains goods that meet these requirements, the buyer must possess a broad, as well as a detailed, knowledge of raw materials, of manufacturing techniques, of workmanship, and of possible finishes.

Despite the attention the buyer gives to customers' requirements when making purchases, he is constantly being surprised by the rapidity of sale of some items he has bought with considerable trepidation. In other words, he often finds that many of his customers will buy things that he does not consider to be in "good taste." This situation emphasizes two points: (1) some items should be bought in limited quantities on a "tryout" basis to test their acceptability by the store's customers, and (2) the buyer should be open-minded at all times in judging the advisability of purchasing available goods.

In part, the suitability of goods may be determined by the buying plan. If laid out with care, so that the plan really shows what customers want, few

---

[53] Associated Dry Goods Corporation *Annual Report,* fiscal year ended January 30, 1965, frontispiece; and "Pinching 500,000,000,000 Pennies," *op. cit.,* p. 172.

purchases should be made which do not fit into it. The buyer also needs to be sure that the goods being purchased will not compete too directly with other purchases or with goods in stock.

Suitability depends on the probable appeal of the merchandise to the store's customers, its physical features, and its price. The significance of price, of course, varies from store to store. Whereas a chain store with a low-price reputation must rely largely on goods that can be resold at such low prices that they "sell themselves," an old-line department store can resell at a much higher markup. Yet, as concerns each item, the buyer will do well to ask himself: What price will *my* customers pay for this item? With this price in mind, the markup can be deducted, thus arriving at the price the buyer can afford to pay.

The Role of Testing Bureaus

In recent years testing bureaus have become of material aid to the buyer in determining the suitability of goods. The steady gain in the number of these bureaus makes it clear that retailers are increasingly recognizing the importance of providing the highest quality of merchandise commensurate with the price, the value of presenting accurate information about the goods offered for sale, and the necessity of guarding customers against unserviceable merchandise. In fact, one retailer goes so far as to say: "Final authority in purchasing rests with the laboratory. Buyers must secure the laboratory's approval before making the merchandise available" to customers.[54] However, the foregoing policy is exceptional, that of the J. C. Penney Company being more typical in that the buying decision remains with the buyer—the laboratory limiting its role to advice "on the quality of the product and whether it stands up to the claims made for it by the manufacturer."[55]

Testing bureaus may be used by buyers for such purposes as: (1) to test merchandise for fading, shrinking, and wearing ability before ordering; (2) to determine the uniformity of sizes in wearing apparel before commitments are made; (3) to devise specifications to be used in making purchases; (4) to check on the quality of goods delivered and their adherence to specifications; (5) to compare merchandise offered for sale in competing stores with that in the buyer's store; and (6) to suggest product innovation or improvements. But others than buyers may also gain from such testing: Adjustment departments are provided with facts for dealing with customer merchandise

---

[54] *Annual Report,* Sears, Roebuck and Co., fiscal year ended January 31, 1962, p. 11.

[55] Statement by P. J. Flynn, Penney's testing center director, in "Test, Test, Test Is Credo, and Penney's Practices It," *Women's Wear Daily,* March 24, 1965, p. 26

complaints and top management is assured that the claims presented in the store's advertising are valid.

Testing bureaus are of two main types: store owned and commercial, the latter being bureaus that offer their services to retailers and others on a fee basis.[56] Because of the expense involved in store-owned testing bureaus, they are usually operated only by large-scale retailers—such as Sears, Roebuck and Co., J. C. Penney Company, Montgomery Ward & Company, R. H. Macy & Company, Marshall Field & Company—whereas the commercial bureaus are used by both large and small retailers.[57] In some instances groups of stores operate jointly owned bureaus. Hence, testing by retailers is not necessarily confined to the large retail organizations. In practice, however, the large retailers have made the most use of testing as a means of determining the capacity of certain goods to meet customer wants.

Many retailers review the periodic bulletins published by such consumer-supported testing and reporting organizations as Consumers' Research, Inc., and Consumers Union and, especially in the case of reports on their own brands of merchandise, use the ratings (where favorable) in promoting sales. Aware of the increasing acceptance by consumers of the recommendations of these agencies, retailers also use the information to determine the suitability of goods. These bulletins are of special assistance to the small retailer who finds the use of testing bureaus too expensive.

REVIEW AND DISCUSSION QUESTIONS

1. Give examples of the integration of wholesale and retail activities and suggest the buying implications of these developments.
2. Evaluate the future of the rack jobber.
3. Explain briefly the reasons why many retailers prefer to buy directly from the manufacturer. In view of this preference, how do you account for the fact that wholesalers are used so widely as sources of supply?
4. Explain the meaning and give some specific examples of specification buying by a large retailer with whom you are familiar.
5. What is your opinion as to the integration of manufacturing and retailing during the next decade?

---

[56] Two of the better known "outside" laboratories are the United States Testing Company of Hoboken, New Jersey, and the Better Fabrics Testing Bureau of New York City. Product testing by manufacturers is also carried on through "independent" agencies; witness the testing by the Underwriters' Laboratories of the American Insurance Association. Cf. "The Public Gives UL Its Seal of Approval," *Business Week,* September 18, 1965, pp. 92 and 96.

[57] It costs Sears about $2 million annually to operate its testing laboratory, which employs 180 scientists and technicians. "Inside Sears, Roebuck," *op. cit.,* p. 23. Consequently, even large-scale retailers find the store-owned bureau expensive. A few years ago, after three years of its own testing, The Kroger Co. shifted to commercial testing.

6. Choose any five central markets for particular types of merchandise and discuss the factors responsible for their development in the specific areas of the country in which they are located.

7. Describe the physical facilities which exist in each of the five central markets you selected in question 6.

8. How do you explain the fact that certain retailers send buyers frequently into central markets, whereas others send buyers quite infrequently?

9. Talk with a store buyer who recently visited a central market. Report to the class the exact steps taken by the buyer in making his purchases. Evaluate his program in terms of its buying effectiveness.

10. Discuss the pros and cons of spreading purchases among a large number of resources.

11. Prepare a paper of some 1,500 words on the subject: "Resident Buying Offices: Their Development, Services and Probable Future."

12. Differentiate clearly between group buying and central buying. In your judgment which form will enjoy the greatest growth under present conditions? Why?

13. "Organizations with central buyers still depend to a considerable degree on the judgment of personnel in the local store." Illustrate and justify this statement.

14. As the key buying executive of a large department store chain, you wish to expand your purchases of foreign goods. What ways of buying are open to you? Evaluate each.

15. Explain the types of testing bureaus available to the buyer and the services they perform.

SUPPLEMENTARY READINGS

Some of the suggestions for reading included at the end of Chapter 10 are also applicable to this chapter. In addition, the following will be helpful:

"AMC's Power on 7th Ave.: Peanuts or High Pressure," *Women's Wear Daily,* April 27, 1964, pp. 1 and 18. The development, methods, and influence of a major resident buying organization (Associated Merchandising Corporation) are presented by the staff of *Women's Wear Daily.*

Buyers Guide to Imported German Products (New York: Nordeman Publishing Co., Inc., annually). This volume is a good illustration of the material available to help the buyer in locating foreign merchandise.

"Holdout in a World of Chains," *Business Week,* October 23, 1965, pp. 113–16. Among other developments in the Belk department store group, this article makes it clear that buying policies and methods are also gradually being adjusted to meet today's requirements.

McDONALD, JOHN. "Sears Makes It Look Easy," *Fortune,* Vol. LXIX, No. 5 (May, 1964), pp. 120–27 ff. Various aspects of buying (degree of centralization, use of specifications, buying organization, integration with manufacturers) by this gigantic retailer are treated in this typical *Fortune*-type article.

For supplementary material cf. "Inside Sears, Roebuck," *Printers' Ink,* October 22, 1965, pp. 15–30; and "Sears' Suppliers," *Financial World,* November 3, 1965, pp. 5 ff.

MOONEY, ED. "The New Thrust in Food Distribution: Today's Voluntary and Cooperative Chains," *Chain Store Age* (Supermarket Executives Edition), January, 1965, pp. 82a–82l. In a special report, this leading trade journal treats many aspects of group activities, including buying. Also cf. "The Three Faces of Food Retailing: Corporate Chains, Cooperative Groups, Voluntary Groups," *Progressive Grocer,* April, 1966, pp. 299–340.

NATIONAL RETAIL MERCHANTS ASSOCIATION. *The Buyer's Manual* (4th ed.; New York: The Association, 1965). Chaps. 6, 7, and 40 of this volume are of particular interest in connection with merchandise resources.

STERN, L. W. "Self-Sufficiency: A Fixation in Corporate Supermarket Chains?" *Journal of Retailing,* Vol. XLII, No. 1 (Spring, 1966), pp. 18–25 ff. Despite the advantages of vertical integration, the author concludes "that many large national and regional corporate supermarket chains could find that engaging the services of specialty wholesalers would be more beneficial, at least in the short run, than increasing the size of their organizations."

"Test, Test, Test Is Credo, and Penney's Practices It," *Women's Wear Daily,* March 24, 1965, p. 26. Some policies and practices of a company-owned testing bureau (J. C. Penney Company) are described in this brief article.

"Trend-Setting Store Imports," *Business Week,* July 31, 1965, p. 62. The current emphasis on foreign goods in retail establishments is illustrated by this report of the *fiesta* from Mexico held at Dayton's, Minneapolis department store.

SHAFFER, VESTA. "The Evolution of the Modern Resident Buying Office," *New York Retailer,* April, 1962, pp. 11–13. The types of offices, expansion of services, and recent developments are covered by this article. Also cf. FUCHSBERG, SEYMOUR. "New Vistas for Central Merchandising," *ibid.,* February, 1962, pp. 11–12.

LAZAR, I. W. "Non-Food Sales and the Rack Jobber," *New York Retailer,* May, 1966, pp. 19–24. The author presents a clear picture of the operations of the rack jobber in this article. In addition, the operations of a specific rack jobber are set forth in "U. S. Consumer Products Racks Up New Advance in Operating Results," *Barrons,* August 23, 1965, p. 15; and the role of this middleman in the wholesaling of housewares is described in "Sophistication in Supermarkets: Rack Jobbers Polish Techniques," *Merchandising Week,* November 8, 1965, p. 37.

WARSHAW, M. R. *Effective Selling Through Wholesalers* (Ann Arbor: Bureau of Business Research, University of Michigan, 1961). Although approached from the manufacturer's rather than the retailer's point of view, the author develops marketing strategies which are of interest to the retailer and the student.

WEISS, E. B. *Management and The Marketing Revolution* (New York: McGraw-Hill Book Co., Inc., 1964). In his usual pungent manner, Mr. Weiss forecasts the future for various aspects of buying, such as the need for the small independent to associate himself with a voluntary chain.

————. "Meet Our Newest Mass Retailers," *Advertising Age,* June 7, 1965, pp. 124 ff. The existence of the one hundred department store chains listed in this article explains much about today's trend toward central buying.

WINGATE, I. B. *Textile Fashion and their Selection* (5th ed.; Englewood Cliffs, N.J.: Prentice-Hall, Inc., 1964); and WINGATE, I. B.; GILLESPIE, K. R.; AND ADDISON, B. G. *Know Your Merchandise* (3d ed.; McGraw-Hill Book Co., 1964). One essential prerequisite of good buying is to "know your merchandise." These two volumes are stepping stones to that goal.

WINGATE, J. W., AND FRIEDLANDER, J. S. *The Management of Retail Buying* (Englewood Cliffs, N.J.: Prentice-Hall, Inc., 1963). In connection with this chapter cf. Chapter III, "Resident Buying and other Associated Buying Activities"; Chapter IX, "Merchandise Resources"; and Chapter X, "Techniques of Merchandise Selection."

12
CHAPTER

.

Buying: Negotiating with Merchandise Resources

When the buyer has decided that certain merchandise best fulfills his customers' needs, he must negotiate on a number of factors before a purchase agreement is made. A major element is the price of the merchandise. What the retailer actually pays for his merchandise, however, depends not only on the vendor's list price but also upon the various discounts which may be secured. The retailer is also interested in the period of time allowed for the taking of discounts and the date when the bill finally becomes payable, that is, the dating that may be obtained. These two elements—discounts and dating—are known as the "terms of sale." Sometimes the retailer would also like the vendor to guarantee prices against decline for a certain period; and the vendor may seek an "escalator clause," providing for upward price adjustments under certain circumstances. Finally, negotiations may also take place over transportation charges and the exclusiveness of the merchandise. In this chapter we turn our attention to these various aspects of negotiations, also giving some consideration to the transfer of title and vendor relations.

SOME GUIDELINES FOR NEGOTIATIONS

In negotiating purchases with vendors, the buyer should keep certain matters in mind. He should recognize that he has more chance of selling the merchandise he purchases if it is what his customers want, even though he has to sell it at a relatively high price, than he has of selling unwanted merchandise at a relatively low price. In other words, getting the right merchandise is more important than getting a price concession on the wrong merchandise. And the buyer must not expect unreasonable price concessions from the vendor. Some buyers make such "stiff" demands that they lose the good will of the vendors; as a result, vendors retaliate by devoting less attention and granting fewer favors to such buyers. Prompt delivery and information as to special buying opportunities are more likely to go to those with whom the vendors are on friendly terms. Consequently, an important asset of a buyer is the ability to secure the friendship and respect of vendors.[1]

The preceding paragraph should not be interpreted as an argument for the buyer to be "soft" in his negotiations. When he knows the vendor is giving concessions to other comparable buyers, he should be firm in refusing to purchase except at comparable prices. Neither is the foregoing an argument for buyers to purchase just from their friends. But it does mean that it is to the buyer's own long-run interest not to take unreasonable advantage of a seller. Negotiations should be based on a considered understanding of the vendor's position. Similarly, the vendor must recognize the buyer's position and treat him accordingly.

The buyer will do well in his negotiations not to give the vendor the idea that he "knows all the answers." The buyer who blusters around trying to impress everyone with his knowledge as to prices, quality of goods, and market trends usually ends up by incurring the vendors' ill will. Most vendors have sufficient knowledge of their own goods and of other offerings in the market to pick out quickly the well-informed buyer from the uninformed buyer, and vendors sometimes take great pleasure in selling to buyers who pretend to "know it all" the goods they should *not* buy.

Before the buyer begins his price negotiations he should accumulate a vast amount of price information. The sources of these data are too numerous to mention completely but include conversations with salesmen, newspaper items, trade journals, luncheon and telephone conversations with vendors and other retailers, past purchases, commodity market quotations, catalogs and price lists of vendors, and prices in other stores. Some retailers attempt to carry most of this knowledge in their heads, whereas others maintain notebooks in which each bit of pertinent information is entered.

The buyer should also realize that the degree of concession from the asking price varies from vendor to vendor and from field to field. In those fields where the vendors are small and some of the buyers are large, asking prices are subject to a considerable amount of higgling. By way of illustration, the buyer for a large department store may represent such an important

---

[1] On this topic cf. Harold Hoffman, "The Myths and Folklore of Vendor Relations," *New York Retailer*, April, 1962, pp. 2–5.

outlet for a small dress manufacturer that the latter may be willing to grant a significant price concession rather than lose the account.[2] The case for a price concession might be even stronger if the buyer represented a large chain-store organization which was the sole outlet for the manufacturer. To a large food manufacturer, in contrast, the account of a single small grocer is so unimportant that the manufacturer's price is not subject to bargaining.

TERMS OF SALE: DISCOUNTS

A discount is any reduction in the list or quoted price of merchandise which is allowed the purchaser by the seller. In practice, discounts may be placed in a sixfold classification: quantity, trade, seasonal, advertising or promotional, brokerage, and cash. Although the significance of these kinds of discounts differs for various retailers, the retailer needs an understanding of each kind.

Quantity Discounts

Nature and Types. A quantity discount is a reduction allowed from the invoice price because of the quantity purchased. Such discounts are based typically on the quantity ordered[3] at a given time—the noncumulative quantity discount. Thus, a vendor might quote a price of $9.75 per dozen with a discount of 25 cents per dozen for purchases of from 3 to 5 dozen at a time, 50 cents off for purchases of from 6 to 15 dozen, and 75 cents off for orders of over 15 dozen.[4] Some use is also made of the cumulative quantity discount, sometimes referred to as a "deferred discount" or a "patronage discount." In this case the discount applies to the total purchases made within a period. For example, a manufacturer of tooth paste may allow a discount of 5 percent if total purchases for the year amount to $10,000, 7 percent if purchases amount to $15,000, and 10 percent if they reach or exceed $20,000. A similar arrangement may be based on the number of units purchased rather than the dollar amount.

Closely related to the quantity discount, or in fact a variation of it, is the "free deal" or "free goods." This practice involves including in the shipment

[2] Cf. Kay Dalton, "Big Stores Cited as Price Hagglers," *Women's Wear Daily*, February 8, 1962, p. 10.

[3] Sometimes the "quantity ordered" refers to the quantity of a *single* item; at other times, it refers to the quantity of *all* items included in the order.

[4] For a mathematical approach to the construction of a quantity discount schedule, cf. J. F. Crowther, "Rationale for Quantity Discounts," *Harvard Business Review*, Vol. XLII, No. 2 (March–April, 1964), pp. 121–27.

certain goods in excess of those ordered; such as, if six dozen of an item are ordered, an extra half dozen may be shipped without charge.

Why Quantity Discounts Are Granted: 1. *Economies of Large Orders.* Among the major reasons for granting quantity discounts is the economies made possible for the vendor. Salesmen's cost may be reduced when a retailer, who has formerly given a small order each week, adopts a policy of placing one large order every two months. The cost of billing and collecting may be little more on a large order than on a small one. The packaging and transportation cost per unit is less on large orders. If the vendor is a manufacturer, the large order may also aid him in cutting his cost of production through buying his raw materials and other supplies in larger quantities and operating his plant more steadily. If the large orders are placed during what would otherwise be a dull season, production economies may be especially large.

The cumulative quantity discount, of course, does not encourage the kind of buying which results in reducing the vendor's cost so much as does the noncumulative quantity discount. Under the former the goods may be shipped in small lots at various times, thus involving higher billing, packing, transporting, and collecting costs. Although the buyer's concentration of purchases with a single vendor may give the latter a more certain market which enables him (1) to reduce the frequency of calls by his salesmen, (2) to cut down his advertising somewhat, and (3) to plan his production schedule to better advantage, such savings are small at best and, in the majority of cases, probably do not exist. Even when buying is concentrated, discounts may be so high that the same result could have been obtained at a lower cost by some form of sales promotion.[5] From the retailer's point of view, however, cumulative quantity discounts have the merit of not encouraging him to overbuy at any one particular time, except perhaps near the end of the discount period when he may be eager to qualify for a higher discount.

Why Quantity Discounts Are Granted: 2. *Buyer Pressures.* In addition to the economies of large orders which may accrue to the vendor, the pressure from the buyer for quantity discounts was also responsible for bringing them into existence. Such pressure has even been exerted in cases where higher unit costs actually resulted from the large order. For instance, many fashion goods, such as women's dresses, are produced by relatively small-scale manufacturers whose costs are largely direct costs. In such cases, production economies are limited. When the larger order has to be fulfilled

---

[5] Cf. the excellent analysis in C. E. Griffin, "When Is a Price Reduction Profitable?" *Harvard Business Review,* Vol. XXXVIII, No. 3 (September, 1960), pp. 125–32.

by overtime work and the hiring of inexperienced help, unit production cost may even be increased.

Robinson-Patman Act. Quantity discounts are subject to limits other than those resulting from the bargaining ability of buyer and seller. Under the Robinson-Patman Act, passed by Congress in 1936, a vendor selling in interstate trade may not give a lower price to one buyer than to another under the following circumstances:

1. If the buyers take commodities of the same grade and quality
2. If the price difference
   a) Substantially lessens competition
   b) Tends to create a monopoly
   c) Injures, destroys, or prevents competition with vendor or buyer, or customers of either; and
3. If the price difference is not one merely making "due allowance for differences in the cost of manufacture, sale, or delivery resulting from the differing methods or quantities in which such commodities are to such purchasers sold or delivered."

1. *Overall Appraisal of the Act.* An excellent case, with which the present authors concur, can be made that the Robinson-Patman Act is inconsistent with the principles of a competitive economy. Through its emphasis (1) on cost as the basis of price differentials and (2) on "proportionately equal terms" for advertising allowances,[6] it inhibits a seller from achieving the best possible competitive "mix" of price and nonprice strategy and has "the effect of limiting the decision-making freedom of businessmen."[7] Another authority concludes that the Act, as interpreted by the Federal Trade Commission and the courts, has "rigidified price structures, deprived the economy of the advantages of free bargaining, prevented innovation in marketing techniques, and moved us in the direction of a cartelized distribution system."[8] And, as Professor Grether points out, action taken under the Act has "often [been] contrary to the purposes of antitrust enforcement."[9]

It should also be emphasized that the Robinson-Patman Act has not achieved its real goal which was "to protect the small independent retailer . . . (by curbing) the growth of multiunit retail operations."[10] In fact,

[6] Cf. pp. 346–47, below.

[7] L. X. Tarpey, Sr., "The Woman's Day Case and Cooperative Advertising," *Journal of Marketing,* Vol. XXIX, No. 3 (July, 1965), p. 39.

[8] Milton Handler, "Recent Antitrust Developments," *Yale Law Journal,* November, 1961, p. 98.

[9] E. T. Grether, *Marketing and Public Policy* (Englewood Cliffs, N. J.: Prentice-Hall, Inc., 1966), p. 59.

[10] L. G. Schiffman, " 'Like Grade and Quality': The Borden Case," *New York Retailer,* December, 1965, p. 13.

the same authority suggested that effective support can be found for the conclusion that the Act has resulted in "a strengthening of the market position of the large retailer."

In view of the foregoing implications it is not surprising that many voices have long urged a careful revision of the Robinson-Patman Act.[11] However, Congress has not heeded these suggestions, with the result that the original Act is still the law: it must be taken into account in establishing discounts. Under it, once the Federal Trade Commission has established the facts that (1) the commodities are of "like grade and quality", (2) there is a price difference between buyers, and (3) the buyers are in competition, the burden of proof is upon the alleged violator; he is held guilty unless he can prove himself innocent.[12] In all cases in which price discrimination is found to exist, the buyer is equally guilty with the vendor if he "knowingly" receives the discount.

2. *"Like Grade and Quality."*   For many years the Commission attempted to define "like grade and quality" by applying the test of physical likeness. It decided that if the Borden Company sold chemically identical cans of evaporated milk, they were of "like grade and quality"—even though some of the cans were marketed under a national brand while others were distributed as private brands. But prior to March, 1966, the court, by accepting the market as its testing ground of likeness, had ruled otherwise, saying

[We cannot] ignore the fact that a brand name product may be able to command a higher price than an unknown brand because of its public acceptance . . . [We] do not believe it was the intention of Congress that such clearly demonstrable consumer preferences should simply be ignored in determining when products may be priced differently . . . [When] labels are proven to have demonstrable commercial significance . . . they can change the grade of a product."[13]

In brief, for two commodities to be of "like grade and quality," the court held that they must be alike physically and have somewhat similar consumer acceptance in the market.[14]

---

[11] In 1966, revision of the Act was recommended by the Report of the National Commission on Food Marketing, *Food from Farmer to Consumer* (Washington, D.C.: U.S. Government Printing Office, 1966), p. 107.

[12] The rule that the burden of proof is upon the alleged violator has been accepted by the courts in many cases under the Act. For an example, cf. *Bergjans Farm Dairy Co. v. Sanitary Milk Producers*, D.C. E. Mo. (March, 1965).

[13] *The Borden Company v. Federal Trade Commission* 339 F. 2d 133 (CA-5, December, 1964).

[14] The decision by the U.S. Court of Appeals in the Borden case is carefully discussed in Schiffman, *op. cit.*, pp. 13–19; and by L. X. Tarpey, Sr., in *Journal of Marketing*, Vol. XXIX, No. 3 (July, 1965), pp. 67–8. Also cf. S. A. Diamond, "Private Brands and The Federal Trade Commission," *Advertising Age*, January 18, 1965, p. 85.

In March of 1966, however, the United States Supreme Court reversed the lower court by accepting the Commission's "identical composition" test and rejecting the market test.[15] This decision is so in conflict with the marketing policies and practices of so many firms that it is doubtful if it will stand unchallenged.[16]

Legality of Quantity Discounts. Under the Robinson-Patman Act, most of the firms that have been called upon to defend their quantity discounts have done so under item 3. That is, they have claimed a cost differential as the basis of their discount schedule. In many of these instances the Federal Trade Commission, which has instituted most of the cases under the Act, has decided that the evidence of a sufficient cost differential has been lacking and has held the discount schedule illegal. Moreover, based upon the cases which have been appealed to the courts, "the record shows that few firms have been able, in litigation, to justify price differences on the basis of cost."[17]

In view of the foregoing actions, it is now clear that, unless it can distinctly be established that the resulting lower price was made in good faith "to meet a competitor's equally low price," the Commission and the courts will throw out any quantity discount schedule not based on a careful allocation of costs (including overhead costs) in relationship to the quantity.[18] For example, a seller cannot assume that all his manufacturing overhead is allocated against his first 100,000 units of production, so that a price just covering direct costs plus a small profit can be granted to a large-quantity buyer. In addition, all sales costs involved in selling to a quantity buyer must be assigned to him, plus his share of all general selling costs. However, the Commission's attempt to set an upper limit on a quantity discount schedule, despite the fact that higher discounts might be justified on a cost basis for larger orders, has been overruled by the courts.[19]

Since the buyer who "knowingly" benefits from price discrimination is equally guilty with the vendor, the retailer must resist the temptation to bargain for a larger quantity discount than can be justified by the cost differential. To many authorities this section of the law, literally interpreted

---

[15] *Federal Trade Commission* v. *Borden Co.,* 383 U.S. 637, March 23, 1966.

[16] S. A. Diamond, "Private Brands: The Borden Case is Not Over Yet," *Advertising Age,* April 18, 1966, pp. 80 ff.

[17] M. C. Howard, *Legal Aspects of Marketing* (New York: McGraw-Hill Book Co., Inc., 1964), p. 62.

[18] For an excellent study of the Commission's position and a summary of the court cases dealing with the cost defense, cf. R. A. Lynn, "Is the Cost Defense Workable?" *Journal of Marketing,* Vol. XXIX, No. 1 (January, 1965), pp. 37–42. For the cost defense in a specific case cf. H. F. Taggert, *Cost Justification: Thomasville Chair Company* (Ann Arbor, Michigan: University of Michigan, Bureau of Business Research, 1964).

[19] *Federal Trade Commission* v. *B. F. Goodrich Co.,* 242 F. 2d 31 (CCA D.C., February, 1957).

—which it probably would not be—makes the unrealistic assumption that the buyer knows the vendor's cost, and so does not make sense. In this connection, and partly to aid the buyer, one student of the subject suggests that (1) the seller's price schedule should contain a statement that it is based on cost differences and (2) the cost defense should be denied any seller who has not determined his cost savings *before* being called upon to justify his discounts.[20] But such is *not* the present situation, so the buyer must exercise restraint. He should be especially wary in urging vendors to give him cumulative quantity discounts, since such discounts are especially difficult to justify on a cost basis.[21]

Trade Discounts

Defined and Illustrated. The trade discount, sometimes called a functional discount, "is a reduction in price given to a certain category of customer to cover the cost of performing a particular trading function."[22] A manufacturer selling to service wholesalers, drop-shipment wholesalers, chain stores, and independent retailers may offer a 50 percent trade discount to all service wholesalers and chains, 45 percent to drop-shipment wholesalers, and 35 percent to the smaller retailers. This discount bears no relationship to the quantity purchased at any given time. It may be given in addition to a quantity discount.

In some instances the retailer will find that vendors who deal with several trade groups use a string or chain of discounts. Thus, a particular vendor might offer the chain-store and wholesaler buyers a trade discount of 30, 20, 10 or, as it would usually be stated, "less 30, less 20, and less 10." When such a chain of discounts is used, the discounts are deducted from the list price shown on the invoice in the order stated; that is, 30 percent off the list price, 20 percent off the balance, and 10 per cent off the second balance. As a result the chain store and wholesaler would receive a cost price amounting to 50.4 percent of the list price. Such a percentage, which may be applied to the list price to determine actual cost, is known as the "on" percentage.[23] For sales to drop-shipment wholesalers the 10 percent discount

[20] Cf. D. J. Fennelly, "On the Judging of Mince Pies," *Harvard Business Review,* Vol. XLII, No. 6 (November–December, 1964), pp. 77–86.

[21] J. E. Martin, "Justifying Price Differentials," *Management Accounting,* November, 1965, pp. 56–62.

[22] M. P. Brown, W. B. England, and J. B. Matthews, Jr., *Problems in Marketing* (3d ed.; New York: McGraw-Hill Book Co., Inc., 1961), p. 857.

[23] The "on" percentage, based on the figures given, is calculated as follows: Let 100 percent represent the list price shown on the invoice. Thirty percent of 100 is 30, and this amount deducted from 100 is 70. Twenty percent of 70 is 14, leaving 56 as the balance. Ten percent of 56 is 5.6, leaving 50.4 percent as the "on" percentage.

may disappear, making the "on" percentage 56 percent. For sales to independent retailers the "on" percentage would be 70 percent.

Frequently, the manufacturer's list price is the suggested resale price at the consumer level and, when trade discounts are considered, also provides the resale price at the wholesale level. To illustrate: A drug manufacturer, selling through wholesalers for distribution to retailers, lists his product at $12 per dozen. His trade discounts are "less 33⅓ and less 15." Under these circumstances, the wholesaler would pay $6.80 per dozen.[24] He would resell to the retailer at $8.00 a dozen, realizing a 15 percent markup on his selling price and allowing the retailer a 33⅓ percent markup on his selling price of $1.00 each, or $12 per dozen.

Some Reasons for Trade Discounts. There is ample justification from the retailer's point of view for the practice of offering trade discounts. As illustrated in the preceding paragraph, often the manufacturer's list price is approximately the resale price. Therefore, if the retailer is to resell at this suggested price, he must buy at a discount in order to get a margin to cover his operating costs and profit.

But what is the retailer's point of view when a manufacturer offers trade discounts which vary according to the status of the buyer, as, for instance, 50 percent to wholesalers and 35 percent to independent retailers? Such discounts are usually justified by one or both of two quite different reasons. First, there may be a significant variation in the vendor's cost of selling to the different trade groups. To illustrate: It is less costly for a manufacturer to sell 5,000 dozen units of his product to a single wholesaler than it is to sell the same quantity to 200 independent retailers. Particularly would sales to the latter trade group be expensive in terms of salesmen's time, number of shipments and invoices, and collection problems.

Second, different trade discounts are sometimes justified by variations in the buyers' costs of operation. This point may be made clear by a hypothetical case. Let us assume that it costs a vendor exactly the same to sell to wholesalers and cooperative chain retailers but that the latter have a lower operating cost as compared to the wholesaler-independent retailer channel. Under these conditions, if both buy at the same price, the wholesaler-independent channel can be undersold and may withdraw from the sale of the vendor's product. This possible step could be prevented by a larger trade discount to the wholesaler as compared with the cooperative chain retailer. In such a case the trade discount would be used to keep the product on sale in more retail outlets, that is, to broaden its retail distribution.

Legality of Trade Discounts. Discounts based on trade status are

---

[24] Calculated as follows: $12.00 − $4.00 (33⅓ percent) = $8.00; $8.00 − $1.20 (15 percent) = $6.80.

not mentioned in the Robinson-Patman Act. However, to the layman it would seem that, under item 3, page 340, vendors would have to justify the prices that result from their trade discounts on the basis of "cost of manufacture, sale, or delivery." But the Federal Trade Commission and the courts have not taken this position; instead, they have ruled that, as long as the various trade discounts are offered equally to all buyers in a specific grouping, they are legal. In other words, the present interpretation is that different trade discounts to various trade groups result in no injury to competition and therefore constitute no violation of the Act. As long as the Commission and the courts take this position, the retailer should bargain for the best trade-discount classification he can get.

It should be emphasized, however, that the trading groupings recognized by a seller must have a factual base.[25] Put another way, a manufacturer could not arbitrarily classify one variety store as a "retailer" and give a "wholesale" rating to two other variety stores which have joined together for group buying.[26]

Seasonal Discounts

Seasonal discounts are percentage reductions in the billed price given to encourage ordering, and sometimes accepting delivery, in the so-called "off" seasons of the year. Vendors of toys may grant seasonal discounts to encourage buyers to place orders and to accept delivery in June, rather than to wait until August; and paint manufacturers may give such discounts to secure orders for spring stock in October, November, and December.

From the retailer's point of view, the seasonal discount should be large enough to compensate him for storing the goods purchased for several weeks or months and for the interest on the investment involved when he pays for the merchandise soon after it is delivered. The main justification for the seasonal discount, however, is the economies which may accrue to the manufacturer. These include (1) obtaining business during normal "slack" periods, thus keeping his factory in operation and enabling him to distribute his overhead costs more evenly; (2) reducing his storage costs; and (3) minimizing his risks due to price changes.

---

[25] For a case involving this principle cf. *General Auto Supplies, Inc., et al. v. Federal Trade Commission,* CA-7 (April, 1965). Also cf. the discussion of "Qualify for the Functional Discount of the Wholesaler," in J. W. Wingate and J. S. Friedlander, *The Management of Retail Buying* (Englewood Cliffs, N.J.: Prentice-Hall, Inc., 1963), pp. 287–88.

[26] "Selling to Buying Group at Prices Lower than Individual Members are Entitled to Violates Clayton Act, F.T.C. Rules," *Air Conditioning, Heating & Refrigeration News,* October 5, 1964, p. 39.

The Robinson-Patman Act still allows a vendor to make use of the seasonal discount, as long as the same discount is given to all competing comparable buyers who purchase at approximately the same time. Moreover, the discount can be altered from time to time as the seasons change. Hence, the seasonal discount is still subject to negotiation.

Advertising Discounts or Allowances

Sometimes it is possible for retailers to obtain allowances for various forms of sales promotional effort. A manufacturer may prefer to have his product advertised in each city over the name of a local department store. Not only does this action result in some carry-over of the prestige of each store to the manufacturer's product, but it also lowers his advertising cost, since local advertising rates are substantially lower than national rates.[27] Other manufacturers wish to be sure that their goods are given adequate window and interior displays, as well as being called to the customer's attention by the salespeople. A promotional allowance may be used for securing these services.[28]

Accounting for Advertising Allowances. A problem arises as to how advertising discounts should be handled by the retailer. Should he treat them as reductions in his cost of merchandise or in his advertising cost? On the one hand, it would seem logical to treat these discounts as reductions in advertising cost. For is not the manufacturer paying the retailer to advertise for him, and does this not increase the retailer's advertising cost over what it would be if such promotional work were not undertaken? But, on the other hand, when the payment is really for promotional work, it is a payment for a trading function or service, like the trade discount. Consequently, both kinds of discounts should be and are usually treated the same way, that is, as reductions in the cost of the merchandise.

Impact of the Robinson-Patman Act. For *competing* buyers the Robinson-Patman Act limits discounts for promotional purposes to those made available on "proportionately equal terms," but "proportional *to what* is not stated . . ."[29] Various cases coming under this section of the Act,

---

[27] Cf. C. H. Sandage and Vernon Fryburger, *Advertising Theory and Practice* (6th ed.; Homewood, Ill.: Richard D. Irwin, Inc., 1963), p. 435.

[28] For a specific example of a manufacturer using a promotional allowance to buy a point-of-sale display service, cf. Whitehall Pharmacal Company case in H. L. Hansen, *Marketing: Text, Cases, and Readings* (rev. ed.; Homewood, Ill.: Richard D. Irwin, Inc., 1961), pp. 498–501. For a long, but what the author refers to as a "very incomplete," list of various kinds of promotional allowances cf. E. B. Weiss, *Non-Merchandising Income: The Next Great Revolution in Mass Retailing* (New York: Doyle Dane Bernbach, Inc., 1960), pp. 45–47.

[29] Howard, *op. cit.,* p. 52.

however, make it clear that a vendor should not offer, nor should a buyer accept, a promotional allowance unless (1) it is a reasonable payment for the service; (2) it is made for a service which competing dealers in this product similarly and proportionally furnish to the vendor; and (3) it is proportionalized between the dealers furnishing a similar service.[30] Likewise, a retailer should not accept a merchandising service, such as store demonstrators, from a vendor unless the service is similarly and proportionally furnished to competing dealers.[31] In some cases, however, the Federal Trade Commission has suggested that a "substitute service" rather than the "same service" might justify a promotional payment. For example, although the store demonstrators offered by some cosmetic manufacturers might be economical in large retail stores with a heavy traffic of customers, they would be impractical in small stores. In such a situation, therefore, the manufacturer could continue to use demonstrators in the large store but offer the smaller retailers a substitute service.

As a practical matter, the "proportionally equal terms" rule may not allow the seller buying a promotional service to pay what the services of competing buyers are really worth to him. "For example, a high-class store buying no more than a discount store performs a more valuable service in advertising the manufacturer's product, in that the high-class store's sponsorship carries more weight with the public and with the buyers of other stores who are considering the purchase of the manufacturer's line. But the lack of objectivity in such a concept of proportionality will in all probability make it unacceptable to the Federal Trade Commission."[32] The Commission and the courts have also placed restrictions on the advertising purchased in a publication owned by a buyer.[33] And in a recent case, the Commission has held that the buyer who "induced" the allowance is guilty and subject to punishment, along with the manufacturer who granted it.[34]

Brokerage Discounts or Allowances

Their Nature. The brokerage allowance or discount is a reduction granted by the vendor because the retailer makes it unnecessary for the

---

[30] For discussions of two recent rulings of the Federal Trade Commission on advertising allowances cf. "F.T.C. Hits Best [& Co.] with Unfair Ad Allowance Charge," *Advertising Age,* November 15, 1965, p. 135; and "Ace Book and Distributors Told to Stop Discriminating," *Publishers' Weekly,* July 26, 1965, pp. 31–32.

[31] Cf. the discussion in Howard, *op. cit.,* pp. 69–73.

[32] Wingate and Friedlander, *op. cit.,* p. 326.

[33] L. X. Tarpey, Sr., "The Woman's Day Case and Cooperative Advertising," *op. cit.,* pp. 35–9.

[34] *Fred Meyer, Inc., et al* v. *Federal Trade Commission* (CA-9, March, 1966).

vendor to use a broker. Thus, the payment goes to the retailer rather than to an independent broker.

A look at the buying organization of the Great Atlantic & Pacific Tea Company will make it clear how a retailer can render a brokerage service to the vendor.[35] This company maintains buying offices scattered throughout the United States, each office more or less specializing in buying products raised or packed in its district. Thus the firm's San Francisco office buys (among other things) California canned fruits and vegetables, dried fruits, nuts, and fresh fruits. Buyers from these offices deal directly with the sellers, so that the packer of canned goods or dried fruits need not pay a broker for selling his product. If this packer is pricing his goods on the assumption that he will pay a fee to an independent broker, it would seem logical that the A & P, which in this case performs the brokerage function, should receive either a lower price or the brokerage charge.

Legal Situation. No matter how logical it may seem, however, a long line of Federal Trade Commission and court cases makes it clear that, *if a vendor uses brokers for part of his sales,* he may not grant lower prices to reflect the nonpayment of brokerage to any sellers on direct sales.[36] And this statement is true even when the vendor can show that the performance of a brokerage service by the buyer resulted in a saving to the vendor. In other words, only those vendors who sell *all* their output directly to retailers may grant lower prices than they might ask if using brokers.

The conclusions of the preceding paragraph give rise to one of the paradoxical elements in the Robinson-Patman Act. The brokerage provision keeps "manufacturers and processors from turning over to voluntary and cooperative chain headquarters the selling commissions that they save on the large-scale direct orders they receive from these organizations. Thus an act that was intended to aid small merchants, particularly independent grocers, has served to eliminate a major potential support for the type of organization that seems necessary to the survival of many of these small merchants."[37]

Cash Discounts

Definition and Types. A cash discount is a reduction in price given by a vendor in return for prompt payment of his invoices. It is typically

---

[35] Some aspects of the Company's buying operations are treated in "Pinching 500,000,000,000 Pennies," *Fortune,* Vol. LXVII, No. 3 (March, 1963), especially p. 172.

[36] Cf. *Southgate Brokerage Company Inc.* v. *Federal Trade Commission,* 150 F. (2d) 607 (4th Cir., 1945).

[37] S. C. Hollander, *Restraints Upon Retail Competition,* (East Lansing, Michigan: Graduate School of Business Administration, Michigan State University, 1965), p. 37.

computed as a percentage of the amount that remains after other discounts have been deducted from the billed amount. A very common cash discount is 2 percent for payment within 10 days of the date of the invoice, which may be stated on the invoice as 2/10. If such terms appear on an invoice dated April 1, the buyer may take 2 percent from the total invoice if it is paid not later than April 11.

What if payment is not made by April 11? In this case it is customary for the buyer to wait 20 days longer and pay the total invoice price at that time. In other words, the terms are usually stated on the invoice as 2/10, net 30. When the net-payment day is not stated, it is assumed to be 30 days from the date of the invoice or whatever period is customary in the particular trade. If payment is not made within 30 days, the vendor has the legal right to add an interest charge, usually 6 percent.

Other terms for cash discounts are also quite common. Under a bill with terms of 2/10–30 extra, the 2 percent cash discount is extended for a 30-day period in addition to the 10-day period, a total of 40 days from the date of the invoice. Terms of 2/10 E.O.M. mean that the cash discount period runs for 10 days following the end of the month in which the purchase was made. For example, for a purchase made on April 1 with terms of 2/10 E.O.M., the 2 percent discount could be taken at any time through May 10.

Significance and Legality of Cash Discounts.   The retailer should take advantage of cash discounts, even if he has to borrow the money to do so. Not only is taking the discount a means of gaining the good will of vendors, but it is immediately profitable from the retailer's point of view— so much so that one successful retailer refers to the cash discount as "a profit cushion."[38] Terms of 2/10, n/30 mean that, if the retailer does not pay within 10 days, he is paying 2 percent for the use of the money for the remaining 20 days until full payment is due. Since there are approximately eighteen 20-day periods in a year, this is equivalent to about 36 percent interest. For terms of 3/10, n/60, the equivalent interest rate would be 21.6 percent;[39] and it would be even higher in those fields, like women's coats and suits, where the cash discount is as much as 8 percent.[40]

As long as uniform cash discounts are granted to all competing comparable buyers, there is no danger that they will result in price discrimination and thus run afoul of the Robinson-Patman Act. In general, cash discounts

---

[38] J. M. Ney, writing in *The Buyer's Manual* (4th ed.; New York: National Retail Merchants Association, 1965), p. 88.

[39] In figuring interest, the year is assumed to contain 360 days.

[40] "Reduce 8% Cash Discount? Makers Cool to Hot Potato," *Women's Wear Daily*, September 4, 1964, p. 20.

have been used in a nondiscriminatory manner. But this has not always been true. One buyer may be given terms of 2/10, n/30, whereas a comparable buyer, after exerting sufficient pressure, may obtain 4/20, n/90. If both buyers take the cash discount, the second buyer gets his merchandise at a lower net cost than the first buyer. If the second buyer does not take the discount, he still gets the advantage of a longer credit period. In either case, we have an example of a price differential which is illegal. As a practical matter, however, "the difficulties in the way of apprehension and prosecution are so great that the Act tends to penalize the 'gentlemen' or 'ethical' buyer in his competition with the 'tough' buyer."[41]

Price Negotiation Still Legal and Important

Despite the limitations placed on price bargaining by the Robinson-Patman Act, the buyer still has ample opportunity to negotiate for lower prices.[42] There is nothing in the Act to prevent a buyer from buying at the lowest lawful prices that sellers are willing to offer or accept. To this end, he should take advantage of all savings (other than brokerage) which sellers realize by reason of the buyer's methods of purchasing and the quantities he buys. Likewise he should attempt to benefit from all lawful fluctuations in market prices and from the best trade-discount classification and seasonal discount he can get.

It should be emphasized that the act neither *requires* nor *prevents* the use of discounts of any kind; it simply places limits on discounts when they are used.[43] Hence, a vendor may decide not to grant discounts. In such a case the buyer may need to bargain with the vendor to get even the discount that the law makes legal. As a matter of fact, some large buyers often do not receive discounts as large as the actual difference in cost, that is, as large as are legal. Moreover, in all cases in which competition does not exist, the buyer can negotiate for larger discounts. To illustrate: If the buyer takes the entire output of a vendor, there is no competition, so that any price or any discount

---

[41] Wingate and Friedlander, *op. cit.,* p. 293.

[42] Perhaps the best analysis of what *can* be done under the Act is found in F. D. Buggie, "Lawful Discrimination in Marketing," *Journal of Marketing,* Vol. XXVI, No. 2 (April, 1962), pp. 1–8. Also cf. "The Borden Decision," *New York Retailer,* May, 1966, p. 6.

[43] In 1962 Senator Hubert Humphrey of Minnesota introduced a bill (S 3255) which would *require* trade discounts. His goal (which was not achieved since the bill failed to pass) : to aid the small retailer by forcing the manufacturer to give the same trade discount to all retailers, regardless of whether the retailer buys direct (large retailer) or through a wholesaler (small retailer). For an analysis which concludes that mandatory trade discounts, "however well intended, are bad law . . . [and] cannot be justified on grounds of economic efficiency. . . ." cf. J. F. Barron "Mandatory Functional Discounts: An Appraisal," *Journal of Business,* Vol. XXXV, No. 3 (July, 1962), p. 316.

he may obtain is legal. With the seller legally able to cut prices "in good faith" to meet competitors' prices, the buyer must frequently bargain to achieve the prices made possible by this provision.[44]

The buyer should also be aware that many states have not adopted provisions similar to those of the Robinson-Patman Act; consequently, for buyers and vendors within these states, price differentials are not bound by cost differentials. Also, by making up his own specifications and thus receiving a product that is not of "like grade and quality" with the vendor's other goods—the buyer opens the way for price concessions.

In brief, negotiating over price is still an important part of the buyer's activities. As already suggested, he "has the right and obligation to seek the lowest prices given to competitors of his class . . . [For him] to assume routinely that quoted prices are standard and fixed merely because the vendor claims a one-price policy, is to be naive."[45]

TERMS OF SALE: DATINGS

The dating of an invoice "refers both to the time before which the specified amount of discount may be taken and to the time at which payment for the merchandise will become due."[46] In our earlier discussion, we mentioned that terms of 2/10, n/30 mean that a 2 percent discount may be taken within a 10-day period and that payment of the billed amount is due in 30 days from the date of the invoice. These periods of 10 days and 30 days make up the dating of the bill. Of course, when no discounts are granted, the dating refers simply to the length of the period before which full payment is expected. Usually the retailer considers an invoice dating more favorable the longer the period during which discounts may be taken and/or during which payment may be made. In contrast, sellers usually want payment as soon as possible. Thus datings become a subject of negotiation.

Datings fall into two general groups: those indicating no lapse of time before the discount may be taken and payment becomes due, and those allowing some lapse of time. The only type of dating falling in the first group is the C.O.D. dating. The second group, which may be referred to as delayed or future datings, contains a number of types.

---

[44] For cases upholding the principle of freedom to meet competitors' prices cf. *Federal Trade Commission* v. *Standard Oil Co.*, 78 S. Ct. 369 (January, 1958); and *Continental Baking Co., Carnation Co., and Pet Milk Co.* v. *Utah Pie Corporation*, CA-10 (May, 1965).

[45] Wingate and Friedlander, *op. cit.*, p. 298.

[46] Brown, England, and Matthews, *op. cit.*, p. 856.

Immediate Dating: C.O.D.

When merchandise is sold with a C.O.D. (cash on delivery) dating, discounts must be taken and payment made at once. In practice, when goods are shipped C.O.D., the common carrier makes the collection from the buyer, the collection usually taking place before the buyer inspects the goods. But C.O.D. datings are relatively rare. They are so disliked by buyers that they are used by sellers only when the latter are quite uncertain of a buyer's ability and willingness to pay. For instance, a buyer may be in the central market and decide to place an order with a vendor from whom no previous purchases have been made. The buyer may want the goods shipped at once, but the vendor may refuse to extend credit until an investigation has been made. In such circumstances the buyer may agree to C.O.D. terms on the shipment. Some buyers are in such poor financial position that they can get goods only on C.O.D. terms. In practically all other cases, however, future datings can be arranged.

Future Datings

Kinds of Future Datings. Some illustrations of future datings already have been given. The *ordinary dating* of "net 30 days" is a good example. As noted, when no specific dating is placed on the invoice, "n/30" may usually be assumed to be the period covered, that is, the bill falls due 30 days from the date of the invoice.

In *extra datings* the vendor allows an added number of days before the ordinary dating period begins. Thus, when the terms are "2/10, 60 days extra," the buyer has 60 days before the ordinary dating of 2/10, n/30 begins. In other words, the discount may be taken up to 70 days from the invoice date, and the full payment falls due 90 days from the invoice date. Actually, however, the 90-day due date of the invoice means little, since in practically every case the cash discount will be taken near or at the end of the 70-day period. As we have seen, *E.O.M. dating* means that the ordinary dating period begins at the end of the month in which the purchase is made. Consequently, on an invoice dated March 4, with terms 3/10 E.O.M., the 3 percent cash discount can be taken through April 10.[47]

Three kinds of future datings are in fairly common usage when the invoice date is not the point from which either the discount or the due date

[47] In practice, under E.O.M. terms, purchases made on and after the 25th of the month usually go into the following month. Thus, on a purchase made on April 26 with terms of 2/10 E.O.M., the cash discount could be taken through June 10.

of the invoice is calculated. *Advance dating* simply sets some date following the invoice date from which the ordinary dating period begins. Thus, an invoice made out on May 15 may be dated "as of September 1," so that the buyer does not have to make payment in full until 30 days following the advance date, that is, October 1. *Seasonal dating* is similar to advanced dating except that the date from which the ordinary dating begins is related to the seasons. To illustrate: Many retailers may want to place orders for their Christmas merchandise during the summer months but do not wish to make payment until the goods have been sold. To accommodate these retailers, vendors may use a seasonal dating of December 1. Full payment is due 30 days after December 1, although there is considerable variation in the practices of various fields in this regard.

An *R.O.G.* (receipt of goods) *dating* means that the ordinary dating period begins on the date the goods are received by the retailer. Goods with a 2/10, n/30, R.O.G. dating which are received on April 11 must be paid for on or before April 21 to obtain the cash discount; and the invoice becomes due and payable on May 11.

Reason for Future Datings. In general, future datings are used because most retailers are in need of an extension of credit, especially the smaller ones whose finances are decidedly limited. Although there are many exceptions, most vendors extend credit for a period long enough to allow the retailers to turn at least a part of their purchases into cash. Since the turnover of groceries is fairly rapid, terms of 2/10, n/30 are quite satisfactory to the buyer. Many hardware items turn over very slowly; here 60- or 90-day periods seem desirable. R.O.G. datings are preferred by retailers located at considerable distances from vendors, since a large part or all of the credit period under an ordinary dating would be gone before the goods arrived. The R.O.G. dating merely puts these operators in a position comparable to that of retailers who get ordinary datings but who are located nearer their sources of supply. E.O.M. datings, which are often urged by retailers who desire to make a single monthly payment for all purchases from a vendor, are granted by sellers chiefly as a convenience to their customers. Competition among vendors results in terms desired by the majority of retailers.

Anticipation. Although most retailers require that credit be extended by vendors, some, particularly the large operators, are financially able to pay their bills before the due dates. Such prepayments, made primarily to keep their funds "at work" by earning an extra discount, are referred to as anticipation. Typically computed at a 6 percent rate of interest, during various "tight" money periods retailers have demanded—without much success—an increase in the anticipation rate to 7 and even 8 percent.

The general rule for anticipation taken before the end of the cash discount period is as follows:[48] The retailer may take the cash discount plus 6 percent interest on the balance for the number of days remaining until the end of the cash discount period. For example, an invoice for $1,000 with terms of 2/10, n/30 is paid 5 days before the end of the discount period. The 2 percent cash discount is equal to $20, leaving $980 to be paid. But this $980 balance is subject to a reduction equal to 6 percent interest for 5 days, that is $0.82.[49] Hence, the actual payment made by the retailer is $979.18. Or again, an invoice with terms of 2/10–30 extra, paid in 10 days, is anticipated 30 days prior to the expiration of the cash discount period. In this case, both the 2 percent cash discount and the 6 percent interest for 30 days are deductible.

Many retailers consider anticipation good practice, in that it gains for them the good will of vendors; and they consider the 6 percent interest a good return on their money. As a result, anticipating is more prevalent than is realized by most students of retailing, especially among department stores and departmentized specialty stores. However, from time to time—especially during periods of rising prices and strong demand for merchandise—some vendors attempt to eliminate the practice. Such efforts are usually vigorously opposed by retailers.[50] Whether or not a specific retailer can anticipate depends upon this rule: He has no legal right to take anticipation "unless it is part of the contract express[ed] or implied, that is, unless the right to take anticipation is noted on the invoice, or unless anticipation is an established custom of the trade, an established practice of the parties concerned, or otherwise a part of the agreement between purchaser and seller."[51]

Discount Loading. A number of retailers follow the practice of "loading," that is, of charging to selling departments any excess in the amount of the cash discount arbitrarily set by the management above the cash discount actually received from the vendor. To illustrate: A retail store may establish 6 percent as the cash discount which all buyers must receive from resources. On a particular purchase the buyer receives only 4 percent. As a result, the department is charged, or "loaded," with the extra 2 percent. Or, more specifically, assume that the amount of an invoice before cash discounts was $100. After the 4 percent is deducted the actual cost is $96.

---

[48] In rare instances anticipation may be allowed after the expiration of the discount period for the number of days by which the date of payment precedes the time the invoice falls due.

[49] Six percent interest on $980 for a year is $58.80. Five days is 1/72 of a year of 360 days, the number of days used for computing interest on anticipation. One seventy-second of $58.80 is $0.817.

[50] For a specific example, cf. "Protest Logan Move to Bar Anticipation," *Women's Wear Daily,* February 11, 1966, p. 3.

[51] M. P. McNair, E. A. Burnham, and A. C. Hersum, *Cases in Retail Management* (New York: McGraw-Hill Book Co., Inc., 1957), p. 63.

But the buyer should have received 6 percent and the actual cost should have been $94. Consequently, the department is charged $102.13, arrived at as follows: $96 = 100 percent − 6 percent = 94 percent of the loaded cost. The loaded cost equals 100 percent, or $102.13.

Retailers who practice loading do so mainly for three reasons: (1) the large cash discount set arbitrarily induces the buyer to drive harder bargains or have the net profit of his department—and his bonus—reduced; (2) all inventory and purchase figures are placed on a comparable basis; and (3) higher markups are obtained when based on inflated invoice costs, particularly in stores applying fixed percentages of markups.

OTHER NEGOTIATIONS FOR MERCHANDISE

Price Guaranties

Sometimes a buyer seeks guaranties against possible future price declines. In return for placing orders early, he may ask for both a seasonal discount and a price guaranty; and, to obtain the advantages of the early order, the vendor may be willing to make these concessions. For instance, on an early winter order for goods to be delivered in the spring, the vendor may agree that, if he lowers his price after the order is placed, he will refund to the buyer the difference between the price at which the order was placed and the price asked when the goods are shipped in the spring. If the price has advanced by spring, there is no refund; but the buyer pays only the price at which he placed the order. Thus, he is protected against both price rises and price declines.[52] In some instances the guaranty applies against the prices of the major competitors of the vendor, as well as against his own prices.

The price guaranty is fairly common for seasonal items for which the vendor is especially eager to encourage early orders. Some manufacturers also use the price guaranty along with the quantity discount to encourage buyers to place extra-large orders on staples. The guaranty is of particular value to retailers who must carry a full line of a vendor's goods, so that there is a substantial investment in inventory. And, finally, the price guaranty is especially desirable during a period when the price structure is uncertain.

Transportation Terms

The transportation terms offered by the vendor may take any one of several forms. When prices are quoted f.o.b. (free on board) factory, the

---

[52] Sometimes, sellers insist on "escalator clauses," which permit them to advance prices under certain conditions.

buyer pays all transportation charges from the vendor's delivery platform. In such cases, however, the vendor usually arranges for transportation with the transportation agency or agencies decided upon by the buyer. For merchandise sold at prices quoted f.o.b. shipping point, the vendor assumes the cost of transportation to his local shipping point, such as the local railroad station; but the buyer pays all further transportation charges. Sometimes, vendors quote prices f.o.b. certain cities, for example, f.o.b. Chicago or f.o.b. Detroit. Under these terms a buyer located in Saginaw, Michigan, would pay only the transportation charges from Detroit to Saginaw. When goods are sold f.o.b. store, the buyer has no transportation charges to pay.

A retailer may cut transportation cost in other ways than by having the vendor absorb it. Carloads travel at lower unit rates than small shipments, so that the large buyer who concentrates his purchases has an advantage. Even when purchases are not concentrated, it may be possible for the buyer to have his representative or a private packing company consolidate purchases from several vendors in the city where the merchandise was bought, thus achieving a lower cost of transportation.[53] More careful planning of routes may reduce this cost. Perhaps a cheaper method of transportation can be used. For goods not needed at once, a slower and less expensive way of delivery is quite satisfactory. Moreover, by inducing the vendor to exercise some ingenuity in his packing, perhaps the weight and size of the package may be reduced. When the retailer pays the freight, it is to his advantage to have all packages shipped in the cheapest possible freight classification. To insure this saving, he carefully checks all the freight bills prior to paying them; such auditing sometimes results in substantial savings on transportation bills.[54]

Exclusiveness of Goods

It is often as important to a store to be the only retailer in a city to handle certain goods as it is to buy them at low prices. In fact, many retailers of specialty goods are willing to pay higher prices for goods for which they act as exclusive distributors than for other merchandise of comparable quality. A shoe retailer knows that a certain shoe manufacturer has built up over a number of years a wide acceptance for his shoes. The retailer reasons that if he can get the exclusive agency for these shoes he will reap the benefits of

---

[53] For example, freight-pooling cooperatives have been established to allow smaller stores to take advantage of volume rates on hanger shipments of apparel. Savings of 20–25 percent have been achieved with faster deliveries and no unpacking and ironing problems.

[54] For a checklist useful to retailers in analyzing their transportation costs and the impact of various operations on them cf. *Reducing Transportation Costs* (Washington, D.C.: Small Business Administration, Management Aids No. 139, April, 1962).

the good will the manufacturer has acquired, and also eliminate all direct price competition, since no other retailers in his immediate area can undersell him on the same brand of shoes. Even if the retailer is located in a city large enough to justify the manufacturer having several so-called "exclusive" agents, price competition will still be held within a narrow range.

Certain risks are present when a retailer becomes the exclusive agent for a single manufacturer. The retailer may lose the agency through no fault of his own. Perhaps the manufacturer will change his policy, or he may decide that he would prefer to use some other nearby retailer. If this happens, the first agent will immediately lose some part of his clientele. In addition, to get the exclusive agency, the retailer may have to agree not to carry competing products placed on the market by other manufacturers.[55] This step will limit his sales to those customers who are willing to buy the particular line he carries.

The retailer may also negotiate over the temporary exclusive distribution of certain goods, especially for new fashion items. Here the retailer is interested in being the exclusive distributor because it enables him to acquire the reputation of being ahead of his competitors with "the last word" in merchandise. Also, the temporary limitation on competition gives him a chance to sell his new goods at a higher markup than would be possible otherwise.

THE PURCHASE ORDER

When negotiations have been completed and the buyer is ready to place his order, he prepares a purchase order form. In the small store the vendor's order form is usually used. As a matter of fact, many small storekeepers depend upon the vendor's representative to make out the order, after which they examine it and sign it.

The large retail organization usually provides its buyers with its own order forms, an example of which is given in Figure 12–1. This practice is definitely to the advantage of the store for the following reasons: (1) it allows the store to plan an order form suited to its own requirements, thus permitting the printing of desired information on the form and the preparation of sufficient copies to allow distribution to all interested departments; (2) it provides protection against some vendors who enter on their own forms (usually in small type) certain conditions often unacceptable to the

[55] When exclusive contracts of this type (that is, which forbid the retailer from selling competitors' products) cover so many of the retail outlets in a given market that they tend "substantially to lessen competition," they become illegal. Cf. discussion in C. F. Phillips and D. J. Duncan, *Marketing: Principles and Methods* (5th ed.; Homewood, Ill.: Richard D. Irwin, Inc., 1964), p. 616.

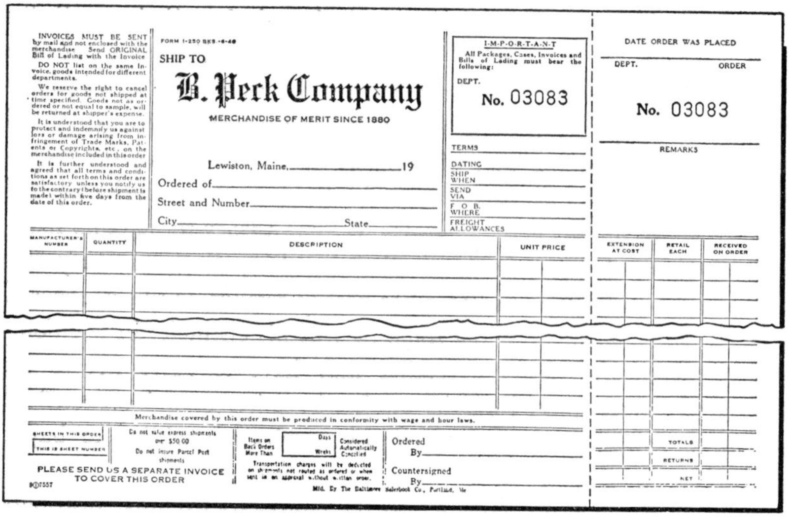
INVOICES MUST BE SENT by mail and not enclosed with the merchandise. Send ORIGINAL Bill of Lading with the Invoice.

DO NOT list on the same Invoice, goods intended for different departments.

We reserve the right to cancel orders for goods not shipped at time specified. Goods not as ordered or not equal to sample, will be returned at shipper's expense.

It is understood that you are to protect and indemnify us against loss or damage arising from infringement of Trade Marks, Patents or Copyrights, etc., on the merchandise included in this order.

It is further understood and agreed that all terms and conditions as set forth on this order are satisfactory unless you notify us to the contrary (before shipment is made) within five days from the date of this order.

FORM 1-250 BKS.-6-48

SHIP TO

B. Peck Company

MERCHANDISE OF MERIT SINCE 1880

Lewiston, Maine, ______ 19

Ordered of ______

Street and Number ______

City ______ State ______

I-M-P-O-R-T-A-N-T

All Packages, Cases, Invoices and Bills of Lading must bear the following:

DEPT.

No. 03083

TERMS

DATING

SHIP WHEN

SEND VIA

F. O. B. WHERE

FREIGHT ALLOWANCES

DATE ORDER WAS PLACED

DEPT. ORDER

No. 03083

REMARKS

MANUFACTURER'S NUMBER	QUANTITY	DESCRIPTION	UNIT PRICE	EXTENSION AT COST	RETAIL EACH	RECEIVED ON ORDER

Merchandise covered by this order must be produced in conformity with wage and hour laws.

SHEETS IN THIS ORDER

THIS IS SHEET NUMBER

Do not value express shipments over $50.00

Do not insure Parcel Post shipments

Items on Back Orders More Than ____ Days ____ Weeks Considered Automatically Cancelled

Transportation charges will be deducted on shipments not routed as ordered or when sent in on approval without written order.

Ordered By ______

Countersigned By ______

TOTALS

RETURNS

NET

PLEASE SEND US A SEPARATE INVOICE TO COVER THIS ORDER

9D7557

Mfd. By The Baltimore Salesbook Co., Portland, Me

Courtesy: B. Peck Company, Lewiston, Maine

FIG. 12–1. Purchase order form.

buyer; and (3) it furnishes an ideal medium through which vendors may be given shipping instructions and a statement of the conditions under which the store will accept the merchandise ordered.

Preretailing

Preretailing, practiced mainly by large retailers, refers to the practice of placing the retail price of the items being bought on the store's copies of the purchase order (1) at the time the order is placed or (2) at least before the actual receipt of the merchandise. When the shipment is received, the marking department may proceed without delay to attach price tickets.

TRANSFER OF TITLE

Transfer of title, the final major step in the buying process, usually takes place when the vendor releases the merchandise to a common carrier for delivery. From this moment on, responsibility for the merchandise lies with the buyer; if goods are damaged in shipment, the buyer's recourse is against the common carrier, not the vendor. In dealing with certain vendors, however, buyers sometimes find it possible to get physical possession of goods without taking title.

Consignment Buying

When goods are bought on consignment, title to the merchandise remains with the vendor. Consequently, the retailer is relieved from assuming such risks as those of price decline and absolescence. These risks remain with the vendor, since he agrees to accept the return of any merchandise not sold. The retailer, however, is not relieved of all risks since he is responsible for anything resulting from his neglect, such as the loss of merchandise through theft and fire as well as from physical damage from other causes. Yet most of the noninsurable risks remain with the titleholder.

To understand the retailer's attitude toward consigned merchandise one must examine the reasons why vendors engage in this practice. First, and most important, manufacturers accept the added risks of consignment selling only when they find it necessary to get retailers to stock their goods. In other words, consignment selling is adopted usually when no other sales strategy will work. Second, when goods are sold on consignment, the vendor has the legal right to fix the resale price.[56] As a practical matter, however, this right is being increasingly restricted by court decisions.[57]

Some Limitations from the Retailer's Point of View. As previously indicated, on consignment merchandise the retailer is free from certain risks which go with outright ownership; and he does not tie up additional funds in inventory. Yet most retailers are hesitant to accept consignment merchandise. They are afraid that such goods may be inferior and that vendors are offering them on consignment because they cannot be sold by other methods. Since the vendor accepts the risks of the titleholder, his prices are advanced. Some retailers object to having their resale prices set by vendors. On returned goods the vendor may claim that the goods have been damaged or that they could have been sold if the retailer had merchandised them aggressively. This attitude, which may be justified in many cases, may lead to ill will between vendor and retailer. Some retailers may also take on too many consigned items and use display space which might have been employed to better advantage for other merchandise.

In view of these disadvantages, alert retailers scrutinize with care the merchandise offered them on consignment. Even in cases where it seems wise to place the first order for a new item on this basis, it is probably best for the retailer to purchase outright as soon as he is in a position to judge sales potentialities.

Memorandum Buying. While the exact meaning of memorandum buying varies with the wording of the document drawn up between seller and buyer,[58] in general it is a method of obtaining merchandise which involves features of both outright purchase and consignment buying. As

---

[56] Cf. the discussion of resale price maintenance in Chapter 17, below.

[57] For example, the courts have held that consignment selling cannot involve (1) coercion on the seller's part and (2) an agreement among buyers to fix prices. Cf. *Sun Oil Co.* v. *Federal Trade Commission,* (CA-7, August, 1965); and *Atlantic Refining Co.* v. *Federal Trade Commission,* (CA-6, April, 1965).

[58] Wingate and Friedlander, *op. cit.,* p. 319.

contrasted with consignment buying, title usually passes legally to the buyer; but, since the buyer retains the same privilege of returning goods which he enjoys under consignment buying, most of the risks that usually go with the transfer of title remain with the vendor. As a result, the retailer—as the owner of the merchandise—is free to price it as he wishes; otherwise the situation in regard to memorandum buying from the retailer's point of view is quite comparable to that of buying on consignment.

Returns of Merchandise to Vendors

In some instances merchandise returns are attempted that are quite unjustified. Prices may have declined since the goods in question were ordered or placed in stock, and the retailer may wish to pass the loss from inventory depreciation back onto the vendor. Or a fashion change not foreseen by a number of buyers may result in an increase in refusals. Unless there are other factors involved, a vendor should not be expected to take back goods merely because the retailer did a poor job of buying. Price and fashion changes are part of the risks going with the title to merchandise; and once the retailer has accepted title, these risks are his.

There are many cases, however, in which the retailer is fully justified in refusing shipments or returning merchandise already in stock. The goods shipped may not be as described in the vendor's catalog, or they may fail to conform to specifications or samples. Goods may be defective, a fact that may not become apparent until revealed by consumer use. Merchandise may have arrived before or after the date specified by the buyer: early arrival causing excess inventories requiring payment before the date planned upon by the buyer; late arrival resulting in markdowns if the peak of demand has already passed. When the vendor ships less or more than the quantity ordered, the retailer is also justified in refusing the goods, since the smaller or larger quantity may upset his planned stock. Likewise, merchandise should not be accepted when the vendor insists on terms of sale different from those originally agreed upon.

It is considered good practice for the retailer to send immediately to the vendor a full explanation for each refusal. Moreover, the goods should be returned at once; otherwise, especially if fashion goods are involved, the vendor may suffer unnecessary loss. If the vendor is one with whom the retailer has maintained connections for some time, it is not uncommon for the retailer to accept the goods and then to seek an adjustment. When the goods are not suited to the retailer's requirements, however, immediate return is the next best step.[59]

---

[59] For a more extensive discussion of cancellations and returns cf. D. E. Moeser, "Sound Buying Practices," in *The Buyer's Manual, op. cit.,* pp. 81–4.

Joint Retailer-Manufacturer Agreements. To minimize disagreements between retailers and vendors on cancellations and merchandise returns, these subjects are sometimes dealt with in "basic trade provisions" prepared jointly by retailer and manufacturer trade groups. Such a statement exists in the apparel trade and the pertinent sections read, in part, as follows:

Purchaser may not cancel this Order for any reason before date for completion of delivery; cancellation after date for completion of delivery shall be effective only upon Purchaser's written notice to Seller, but shall not be effective with respect to any shipments made by the Seller within three (3) working days after receipt of such notice.

No returns of merchandise shall be made except for defects therein, or for non-conformity with some material provision of this Order. Where defects are discoverable upon reasonable inspection, or where non-conformity is claimed, such returns shall be made within five (5) working days after the receipt of the goods affected. The Purchaser shall send the Seller a separate written notice, setting forth the nature of the defects or non-conformity claimed, prior to or simultaneously with the return. Seller may replace such return merchandise, provided such replacement is made within five (5) days after the last permissible delivery date.

In the event of the material interruption of the business of either the Seller or Purchaser by reason of fire, war, Act of God, governmental action, or strikes which materially affect the performance of this contract, the party so affected may cancel the order for such merchandise as has not been delivered, upon notice to the other party, notwithstanding any other provisions herein.[60]

The agreement also provides that "any controversy or claim rising out of or relating to any of the provisions of this Order shall be settled by arbitration in accordance with the rules of the American Arbitration Association." Finally, both buyer and seller are automatically bound by the agreement unless they both accept, in writing, some other terms.

REVIEW AND DISCUSSION QUESTIONS

1. Carefully evaluate three of the several guidelines for negotiations suggested on pages 336–38.
2. As a buyer of household furniture, list the price-information sources available to you.
3. What elements are included in the phrase "terms of sale"? Define each element.
4. Discuss the quantity discount from the point of view of (a) the retailer, (b) the vendor, and (c) society at large. Does this type of discount seem justified from all three points of view?
5. Appraise the legality of quantity discounts under the Robinson-Patman Act.

---

[60] Statement of the Apparel Industries Inter-Association Committee, *Women's Wear Daily,* December 16, 1965, p. 35.

6. What is a "trade discount?" What purposes does the trade discount serve that are not already afforded by the quantity discount?

7. Under the Robinson-Patman Act, the Federal Trade Commission and some courts have used different standards in applying the phrase "like grade and quality." State and evaluate the standards used by each.

8. Explain the meaning, uses, and legality of seasonal discounts, advertising allowances, and brokerage discounts.

9. Assume that merchandise shipped on May 15 was billed at $1,950 with terms of 2/10–30 extra, f.o.b. destination, and that the bill was paid on the day the cash discount expired. On what date was the bill paid and what was the amount of the check?

10. Assuming the same terms and figures given in (9) above, plus the fact that anticipation was allowed, what amount should be remitted to the vendor if the bill was paid on June 1?

11. An invoice for $1,000, dated August 10, carries a dating of 2/10 E.O.M. and trade discounts of "25, less 10, less 5." To take all discounts, when must the bill be paid? What would be the amount of the check?

12. Define "loading" in your own words and explain the reasons why some retailers follow this practice.

13. Under the conditions of today, how important to the buyer are negotiations with the vendor concerning exclusiveness of merchandise? Explain your answer.

14. Appraise consignment buying from the retailer's point of view.

15. List five situations under which you feel the return of merchandise to vendors would be justified. Defend your answer. Suggest three instances of unjustified returns.

SUPPLEMENTARY READINGS

BAUM, D. J. *The Robinson-Patman Act* (Syracuse, N.Y.: Syracuse University Press, 1964). Stressing the need for great care in interpreting the various court decisions which have resulted from the Robinson-Patman Act, the author provides a useful comprehensive study of this controversial law.

BLISS, J. J., AND MILLSTEIN, I. M. (eds.). *Manual of Federal Trade Regulations Affecting Retailers* (New York: National Retail Merchants Association, 1963). Prepared as a practical guide for retailers, the manual—among other subjects—covers the impact on retailing of the Federal Trade Commission Act and the Robinson-Patman Act. An appendix includes much of the text of these laws.

BUGGIE, F. D. "Lawful Discrimination in Marketing," *Journal of Marketing,* Vol. XXVI, No. 2 (April, 1962), pp. 1–8. "The purpose of this article is to . . . [point] up some types of techniques and situations whereby the businessman may *lawfully* discriminate" under the Robinson-Patman Act.

CROWTHER, J. F. "Rationale for Quantity Discounts," *Harvard Business Review,* Vol. XLII, No. 2 (March–April, 1964), pp. 121–27. Among other aspects of quantity discounts, the author suggests a mathematical approach to their construction.

ENGLAND, W. B. *Procurement: Principles and Cases* (4th ed.; Homewood, Ill.: Richard D. Irwin, Inc., 1962). The discussion of price negotiations in Chapter XI, and especially pp. 567–69 concerning escalator clauses, is of particular interest.

FENNELLY, D. J. "On the Judging of Mince Pies," *Harvard Business Review,* Vol. XLII, No. 6 (November–December, 1964), pp. 77–86. A number of valuable suggestions on accounting for a cost defense under the Robinson-Patman Act are suggested by the author.

GRETHER, E. T. *Marketing and Public Policy* (Englewood Cliffs, N.J.: Prentice-Hall, Inc., 1966). In a 120 page volume, a long-time student of marketing examines "the interrelationships between marketing and the marketing system and the public policies and governmental regulations that pertain to them in the United States." He has many pertinent comments on the Robinson-Patman Act, especially on pp. 58–68.

HOWARD, M. C. *Legal Aspects of Marketing* (New York: McGraw-Hill Book Co., Inc., 1964). Chapter 3, "Price Discounts," offers a good discussion of the Robinson-Patman Act and its relation to various kinds of discounts and allowances.

KINTER, E. W. *An Antitrust Primer* (New York: Macmillan Company, 1964). The former chairman of the Federal Trade Commission draws on his experience to provide, in the words of the book's subtitle, "a guide to antitrust and trade regulation laws for businessmen." Special attention is given to the Robinson-Patman Act.

LYNN, R. A. "Is the Cost Defense Workable?" *Journal of Marketing,* Vol. XXIX, No. 1 (January, 1965), pp. 37–42. The author answers "Yes," but adds qualifications which limit the positive character of his affirmation.

MARTIN, J. E. "Justifying Price Differentials," *Management Accounting,* November, 1965, pp. 56–62. The cost data needed to support the cost defense for price discrimination are suggested in this article.

NATIONAL RETAIL MERCHANTS ASSOCIATION. *The Buyer's Manual* (4th ed., New York, 1965). Written by leading retailers, chapters 7, 8, 9, 10, 11, and 43 have special applicability to the present chapter.

SCHIFFMAN, L. G. " 'Like Grade and Quality': The Borden Case," *New York Retailer,* December, 1965, pp. 13–19. To his careful analysis of the Federal Trade Commission's action against the Borden Company, the author adds a valuable bibliography on the subject. Also cf. "The Borden Decision," *ibid.,* May, 1966, p. 6; and DIAMOND, S. A. "Private Brands: The Borden Case Not Over Yet," *Advertising Age,* April 18, 1966, pp. 80 ff.

TAGGERT, H. F. *Cost Justification: Thomasville Chair Company* (Ann Arbor, Mich.: University of Michigan, Bureau of Business Reasearch, 1964). A specific instance of the cost defense to justify price differentials is analyzed by Professor Taggert.

TARPEY, L. X., SR. "The Woman's Day Case and Cooperative Advertising," *Journal of Marketing,* Vol. XXIX, No. 3 (July, 1965), pp. 35–9. After analyzing this particular use of Section 2(d) of the Robinson-Patman Act to regulate cooperative advertising, the author concludes that the "Court of Appeals turned its back on the bulk of the marketing facts which, if considered, might have changed the decision."

WINGATE, J. W., AND FRIEDLANDER, J. S. *The Management of Retail Buying* (Englewood Cliffs, N.J.: Prentice-Hall, Inc., 1963). Chapter XI, "Negotiating the Wholesale Price;" Chapter XII, "Vendor Services Available to the Buyer"; and Chapter XIII, "The Buyer's Order and Vendor Relations," offer excellent supplementary material for the present chapter.

13

CHAPTER

Merchandise Management

INTRODUCTION

It is evident from our discussion of retail buying in previous chapters that effective purchasing is based on adequate controls to insure prompt reordering of goods that are selling and to prevent additional purchases of merchandise unacceptable to customers. But proper merchandise management should also minimize the investment in inventory consistent with the satisfactory fulfillment of customers' wants. The rapid growth of multistore operations has intensified the need for prompt, accurate, and complete data upon which to base merchandising decisions.

Finding satisfactory solutions to merchandising problems is no easy matter. Not only should carefully thought-out policies governing all aspects of merchandise management be formulated, but these policies should be implemented with effective procedures adapted to the needs of the particular store, regardless of its size.[1]

Although some form of inventory management or control is needed in all stores, the methods employed to attain this goal differ widely. In small stores the desired relationship between stocks and sales is secured through close supervision by the proprietor, who studies his records and inspects his stock at various periods. As stores grow in size, however, and as the assortments of merchandise they handle become greater, the maintenance of a balanced relationship between stocks and sales becomes increasingly difficult. Consequently, personal inspection becomes less practicable; and more

---

[1] Cf. Ralph Guppy, "An Approach to Sound Inventory Management," *Retail Control*, January, 1964, pp. 44–51. Also cf. E. L. Harling, "The Theory of Merchandise Control," in *The Buyer's Manual* (4th ed.; New York: National Retail Merchants Association, 1965), pp. 150–63.

written merchandise records of various types are required as aids to the judgment of the buyer. These records constitute an important phase of merchandise control.[2]

With an appreciation of the value of basic policies as the foundation upon which effective merchandise management may be built, we may proceed (1) to examine the nature and purposes of merchandise control; (2) to explain the two common methods used to assist in controlling merchandise inventories—dollar control and unit control; (3) to explore the use of EDP in this area; (4) to indicate the value of the physical inventory as a tool of merchandise management; (5) to describe the relationship and use of the rate of stockturn and the stock-sales ratio in connection with merchandise management activities; and (6) to indicate the nature and importance of stock shortages. In the next chapter, we shall discuss what is probably the most complete and, for many stores, the most satisfactory form of dollar merchandise control—the merchandise budget.

THE NATURE AND PURPOSES OF MERCHANDISE MANAGEMENT

Broadly speaking, merchandise management or stock control refers to the maintenance, in a store or a department, of a stock of merchandise that is adjusted to the demands of customers and prospective customers. Stated in more detail, and in terms of the large-scale retailer, it involves a "procedurally organized system, supported with continuous research, which permits and causes the prompt factual economic evaluation of profit planning and profit results of inventory units and dollars invested for satisfaction of customers' service and merchandise needs, in compliance with top management's directive and desire for store image."[3]

The balanced relationship which merchandise management seeks between stocks and sales is obtained (1) through an appreciation on the part of proprietors, buyers, and others of its benefits; (2) through the development and use of various procedures and forms which will provide promptly, accurately, and in usable form the information needed by buyers to know when, what, and how much to buy; (3) through the revision of procedures and forms to meet changing requirements and conditions; and (4) through the analysis and interpretation of the data collected and the actions taken as

---

[2] Merchandise management or control in most stores is a joint responsibility of the merchandise manager and the controller. Therefore, it may be considered as a major function of either or both executives and is often discussed from the point of control as in the case of expense control or financial control. The present authors believe it advisable to examine the various aspects of merchandise management at this particular point because of its close relationship to buying.

[3] John Gotlinger, "Merchandise Management," *Retail Control*, May, 1966, p. 21

a result thereof. It is in connection with the last-mentioned point that real control takes place. That is, it is the *use* of the information gathered that makes control possible.

Purposes of Merchandise Control

As already indicated, the over-all objective of merchandise management is to bring about and to maintain a complete, well-assorted stock of goods based upon current and anticipated customer demand. When such a balanced stock is achieved, it enables the retailer to realize the following purposes or goals.

To Meet Customer Demands Satisfactorily. As the "purchasing agent" for his customers, the retailer has the responsibility of having on hand the merchandise his customers want, at prices they are willing and able to pay. This responsibility is a difficult one to meet, since customer demand will vary from day to day and from season to season. However, if merchandise control procedures are successful, they will help the retailer to attain this goal.

To Improve Profits. A balanced stock frequently leads directly to greater sales and fewer markdowns, thereby bringing about an improvement in the dollar gross margin. Consequently, if expenses remain the same or if they do not increase proportionately, profits will be increased. In like manner, but less directly, methods and devices employed to control merchandise contribute to increased profit by indicating trends and conditions that require attention by executives, by focusing attention on fast- and slow-moving items, by helping to keep stocks "clean" and "fresh," by assisting in the planning of more effective advertising and sales-promotion events, and by enabling the buyer to reorder more frequently.

To Provide Buying Information. Buyers need a continuous stream of information if they are to know what, when, and how much to buy. Merchandise control really begins before goods are purchased rather than after. Certainly the buyer should study the sales of his department or store by types and prices of merchandise, the returns by customers, the markdowns taken to sell goods, and other information of a similar nature as a guide in making purchasing commitments, but plans should be made sufficiently in advance of buying commitments to insure a properly balanced stock. Review of past experience is essential, of course, if buying mistakes are to be minimized and fast-selling merchandise is to be reordered as promptly as needed.

To Minimize Investment in Inventory. The desirability of keeping the investment in merchandise inventory at the lowest possible point consistent with the fulfillment of customer demand is evident. Such action, of course, results in a better rate of stockturn. But increasing the rate of stockturn should not be thought of as a major purpose of merchandise control; the chief objective is to maintain well-assorted, balanced stocks in relationship to sales. If this is done the rate of stockturn will take care of itself; and the advantages of a satisfactory rate of stockturn will accrue to the management of the business.

In addition to the major purposes of merchandise control we have discussed, others may be mentioned in summary form: (1) to reduce the amount of slow-selling merchandise carried; (2) to make selling easier through improved assortments and cleaner stocks, thus reducing selling expense; and (3) to develop an appreciation of the continuous fundamental relationship between stocks and sales and the importance of this relationship in the final determination of profits.

Limitations of Merchandise Control

No retailer should undertake a program designed to provide a better balance between his stocks and his sales, i.e., merchandise control, without a full understanding of the limitations involved.

Control Methods an Aid to Judgment. Control methods are never an adequate substitute for knowledge, experience, and wisdom on the part of the buyer: they should be looked upon as aids to judgment and not as substitutes for it. This statement is equally true for staple items and fashion goods, although the systematic reorder of staples requires less of the buyer's attention. Regardless of the "automatic" nature of the procedures that may be established, there still remains the necessity of analyzing and interpreting the information supplied.

Frequent Appraisal of Systems Necessary. All too often systems devised for providing necessary information to buyers are continued in use long past the time they contribute data of value. Since routines or procedures are set up to provide specific types of information under a given set of circumstances, they need to be reviewed frequently to determine their suitability in the light of new situations.

Costly to Operate. Merchandise control systems are costly to install and their maintenance is a continuing expense. Moreover, since they need to be revised quite frequently, additional expenses are involved in retraining personnel to use the new methods. This cost problem is particularly acute because of the increasing computerization of merchandise control data.[4]

---

[4] Cf. "EDP and Merchandise Management," pp. 380–82, below.

Many retailers, fearing the high costs of a suitable system, hesitate to install one and later find that their competitors are far ahead of them. Others fail to recognize the technical knowledge of design, programming, and operation required for conversion to computers as well as the necessary retraining of members of their own staff.

In any case, the type of system to use is a matter of judgment based upon experience. It is clear that the advantages of the system must be measured against the cost involved. But any system to be most useful should provide information that is accurate, timely, and complete enough to meet the purposes for which it is gathered.

"Control" a Misnomer? Some retailers, aware of the benefits that have accrued to their competitors through carefully established systems of merchandise control, have adopted similar methods under the false impression that "control" would result automatically and without further attention. But the control forms provide only helpful information; continuous follow-up is essential. Or, as it is often stated: "Control exists only when information is interpreted and translated into action." It should also be emphasized that, despite improvements in recent years, effective control of merchandise inventories still constitutes one of the major problems of retail executives.[5] Although every suitable method and device should be employed to develop the information essential for sound decision-making in balancing stocks and sales, buyers should not expect the impossible or abrogate their responsibility for deciding what, when, and how much to buy.

Responsibility for Merchandise Management[6]

In small stores responsibility for all merchandising activities rests upon the proprietor or upon someone designated by him. In larger stores, merchandise management becomes more complicated; and responsibility for it is divided among a number of people. In department stores this task usually falls upon the merchandise manager, who shares it with his buyers (department heads) because these individuals handle all buying, and the information collected is most useful for this purpose. In fact, the job may be so great that a merchandise controller, under the direction of the merchandise manager or even the president may supervise these activities and work closely with the various buyers. Sometimes the controller exercises supervision over

---

[5] Cf. Ed Gold, "Stock Woes Lead Store Headaches," *Women's Wear Daily,* September 2, 1965, pp. 1, 25.

[6] For excellent discussions of the buying function and of organization for buying and control of merchandise in single and multiunit stores, cf. J. W. Wingate and J. S. Friedlander, *The Management of Retail Buying* (Englewood Cliffs, N.J.: Prentice-Hall, Inc., 1963), chaps. i and ii.

stock control activities as part of his responsibility for all systems and records. In such instances close cooperation between the controller and the merchandise manager is necessary.

In chain stores responsibility for merchandise control is usually centered in the headquarters office under either the controller or a special control executive who reports to the head buyer or merchandise manager. Considerable reliance is placed upon information supplied by warehouse and store managers, who make frequent and detailed reports to merchandise managers in the headquarters city. These reports include information on sales of important individual items and on the condition of stock as revealed by daily checks by department heads for "shorts" and by checks at less frequent intervals when regular orders for goods are placed. Automation has been of considerable assistance here.[7]

Merchandise Control in Stores of Different Size and Type

Fundamentally, merchandise is controlled in one or both of two ways—in dollars and in physical units. *Dollar control* is exercised in terms of the amount of money at retail prices invested in merchandise. Control by physical units, commonly known as *unit control*, is usually accomplished in terms of individual items or pieces of merchandise. Whereas dollar control answers the question, "How much?" unit control goes further and attempts to tell "what."

Either dollar or unit control may be very simple, as illustrated by the case of unit control exercised through personal inspection of the items in stock at either regular or irregular intervals. This inspection should include the stock on the shelves and in the stock room. In most small stores the proprietor depends upon this method to determine which goods are selling, which are not, and the proper time to reorder. In some instances, he may rely upon the vendor's salesman to suggest what is needed to complete his stock, a common practice in the grocery, drug, and variety goods fields when the salesman and the retailer have had long and satisfactory dealings.

In somewhat larger stores, where the proprietor finds personal inspection impracticable, salespeople are assigned definite sections of the stock to watch. They are asked to report to the proprietor or buyer when the supply of any item is low or when sales are unusually heavy for specific merchandise. In some stores handling staple items—such as drug, grocery, and hardware stores—this reporting responsibility is assigned to stockmen.

---

[7] Cf. the discussion on pp. 381–82, below.

Such relatively simple methods of controlling stocks frequently fail to provide adequate control. Therefore, more formal methods have to be adopted. In medium-size stores and particularly the larger ones, carefully designed procedures are essential because of the size and value of the merchandise inventory, the need for more detailed information for buying purposes, and the element of fashion. The specific methods used by any particular retailer will depend upon the size of his establishment, methods employed by similar stores, the kind and amount of data he desires, the use he expects to make of this information, and his own preferences. We now turn to a discussion of the two more formal procedures of stock control—dollar control and unit control.

DOLLAR CONTROL[8]

General Forms

Dollar control usually involves the maintenance of records designed to provide the desired information in terms of retail prices and the use of such data as a guide in buying. In small stores this method of control is commonly used for the entire stores as a unit. In departmentized stores, however, it may be applied to departments, merchandise sections, or be extended to classifications and even to specific price lines.

Departmental Control. This form of control refers to the use of dollar control on a departmental basis. Through records of sales, returns by customers, purchases, returns to vendors, markup, gross margin, markdowns, rate of stockturn, and physical inventories, it is possible to judge the profitableness of each department and the performance of each buyer. Strong and weak departments may thus be determined and measures adopted that will improve operation. It is not possible under this method, however, to detect points of strength and weakness within each department. Since effective control must often go further than the overall figures for each department, controls by classification and price-line have been developed.

Classification Control. Classification control, increasingly referred to as "classification merchandising," is that form of dollar control based upon classifications of related types of merchandise within departments. All the essential information recorded departmentally under departmental control is recorded by merchandise classification under classification control. Thus, in a

---

[8] For a detailed explanation of dollar control cf. C.S. Thompson, "The Dollar Merchandise Plan" in *The Buyer's Manual, op. cit.,* pp. 134–49. Also cf. J. S. Meyer, "Mathematics of Merchandise Control," *ibid.,* pp. 164–180.

men's furnishings department, information may be recorded separately for such classifications as shirts, neckties, hosiery, pajamas, underwear, robes, and sweaters.

No aspect of retailing, with the possible exception of EDP and its various applications, has received greater attention in recent years than classification merchandising.[9] Many retailers, dissatisfied with the negative connotation of "control," have adopted the new term and instituted programs placing emphasis on "the discovery of opportunities for increased sales" and a better "balancing of stocks in relation to sales."[10] As a part of these programs, there has been a tendency not only to subdivide broad classifications into smaller groups but also to reclassify them into categories of items "considered by the customer as essentially interchangeable from the standpoint of end use."[11] As individual firms have established classifications and categories suited to their particular requirements, an urgent need has developed for a common no-menclature for retailers as well as for their suppliers.[12]

Price-Line Control. This form of dollar control is based on price lines. A price line is a single retail price at which an assortment of merchandise is offered to the public. Just as a department may be divided into classifications for the purpose of effecting better control, so departments or classifications may be broken down into price lines to obtain more detailed information about the movement of smaller groups of closely related merchandise. Price-line control, however, does not naturally follow classification control. In fact, many departments use price-line control as a substitute for, or in place of, classification control. Moreover, price lines may be broken down into classifications, according to material, size, style, or some other desired basis.

Dollar-Control Systems

Department, classification, and price-line control may be operated either through a perpetual or a periodic inventory system. Subject to many exceptions, it may be said that, in general, the smaller independent stores tend to

[9] Cf. C. E. Ebert, "Merchandise Classification . . . How Far, How Fast, What Cost?", *Retail Control,* February, 1966, pp. 22–31.

[10] Hugo Frank, "Problems in Introducing Classification Programs Successfully," *Retail Control,* February, 1966, p. 12, and C. E. Ebert, *op. cit.,* pp. 22–31.

[11] Matt Wigginton, "Concerted Action Now," *Retail Control,* April, 1965, p. 50. Also cf. E. B. Weiss, "Classification Merchandising Topples Departmental Barriers," *Advertising Age,* August 9, 1965, pp. 75–76, and August 16, 1965, pp. 76 ff.

[12] As this is written, the National Retail Merchants Association is engaged in developing standardized merchandise classifications based on consumer needs and preferences, rather than on traditional buying categories. These classifications are expected to be useful in both manually and electronically controlled systems.

use the periodic inventory system, whereas larger units and chain organizations employ in some measure the perpetual inventory system.

Perpetual Inventory System. Under the perpetual inventory method, it is necessary either (1) to operate the complete retail inventory method of accounting[13] for the store as a whole or for each department, classification, or price line; or (2) at least to analyze data on sales and inventories without attempting to determine the initial markup or the gross margin. Because of the detailed records required, the major problem under the perpetual inventory method is to obtain complete and accurate information. Several retailers have recently installed EDP equipment to provide needed data more quickly.[14] Others still use clerical help. But whether handled by electronic equipment or by people, for merchandise to which it is applicable the perpetual inventory method provides a cumulative record of stocks on hand and sales and makes possible prompt adjustments through providing current, useful information.

Periodic Inventory System. The periodic inventory method of dollar control involves the keeping of three important records for the store as a whole or by departments, classifications, or price lines. The records needed—all at retail prices—cover inventories, purchases, and markdowns. From these records, sales data and other valuable information may be obtained semiannually or at other intervals, as desired. For example, sales for the whole store or by departments, classifications, or price lines may be derived from the three figures as follows:

Retail stock on hand, August 1	$ 50,000
Retail purchases, August 1–January 31	100,000
Total retail stock handled	$150,000
Inventory at retail, January 31	60,000
Sales and markdowns, August 1–January 31	$ 90,000
Markdowns, August 1–January 31	10,000
Derived sales (including stock shortages)	$ 80,000

When an estimated amount for stock shortages is deducted, based on previous experience, actual sales may be determined.

The periodic inventory method may be extended beyond this simple illustration. By recording the opening inventory and the purchases both at cost price and at retail price, a markup percentage may be obtained; and by using the cost complement of this markup percentage (100 percent — markup percent = cost percent), the retail value of the stock on hand may be reduced to a cost basis. This procedure permits the calculation of the

[13] The retail inventory method is explained in Chapter 24.
[14] Cf. pp. 138–41, 282–83, 287–88, 328, above, and pp. 380–82, below.

gross cost of merchandise sold, and the gross margin figures may be obtained by department, classification, or price line, provided, of course, that stock shortages are closely estimated. The chief advantages of this form of dollar control are its simplicity and its economy in use, but since information is provided only semiannually or whenever inventories are taken its usefulness is considerably reduced.

UNIT CONTROL

Unit control, the second basic form of merchandise control, involves the maintenance of records in terms of physical units, rather than in terms of dollars. Although closely related to dollar control, unit control should not be thought of as a substitute for dollar control but rather as a supplement to it. In other words, both types are essential in keeping stocks adjusted to customer demand. Unit control is operated most frequently in ready-to-wear and other departments where merchandise of high-unit value is carried. It may be used, however, in any department where the need for this type of system is evident and where its cost is warranted.

Unit-Control Systems

Unit-control systems vary widely from store to store and even from department to department within a store, but they have a common characteristic: they provide information quickly by day, week, month, or any other period. This physical unit information may include, for instance, data on sales and stocks by style number, color, size, material, or any other characteristics of the merchandise. It may also include data on markups, markdowns, gross margin, and rate of stockturn, by price, merchandise classification, vendor, or any other desired breakdown. The information that is obtained will depend upon the particular needs of the buyer and upon the information required by the merchandising office. A major reason for the rapid growth of EDP is that it provides the required data quickly and accurately.

Like dollar control, unit control may also be effectuated through either a perpetual inventory or a periodic physical inventory system.

Perpetual Inventory Systems. These systems of unit control operate in a similar manner to the perpetual inventory method explained in connection with dollar control. Through a continuous record of the movement of merchandise into and out of the department, adjustments in stock may be made promptly to meet sales requirements. Moreover, the perpetual inventory form of control affords a check on stock shortages[15] by making possible the determination of these shortages at the time physical inventories are taken. This system of control is used frequently for merchandise such as men's clothing, women's apparel, and shoes, where sales are easily recorded by units and reorders are common. It is not practicable where the unit of sale is small and record-keeping costs are high in relationship to their value, as would be true, for example, in drugs, cosmetics, and notions.

Physical Inventory Systems. These systems are based upon periodic physical inventories which may be taken as frequently as desired—weekly, monthly, or semiannually. No attempt is made to record sales by units as they occur. A figure for sales is obtained, however, by adding the beginning inventory of each unit to the purchases and then subtracting the ending inventory. This figure, of course, includes both sales and stock shortages. Information for control purposes is obtained at the time of the physical inventory by analyzing the rate at which items are being sold and by comparing the goods in the previous inventory with those in the current inventory. Purchases, of course, must be analyzed in a similar manner.

Other Systems of Unit Control. Used with either or both of the unit-control systems described—that is, the perpetual or periodic inventory systems—other forms have been developed to meet special requirements and conditions. They are designed chiefly to minimize lost sales caused by merchandise being out of stock and to maintain adequate assortments of goods in the light of customer demand.

1. *Requisition or Reserve Stock Control.* This system operates through the reserve stock, and provides needed control over goods such as drugs and cosmetics, where unit control in the selling department is not feasible. Requisitions are drawn on the stock room by the selling department for groups of items known as "units," and such withdrawals are considered as sales. It is evident, of course, that over a period of time the withdrawals will be equal to the sales if the forward stocks are properly maintained. The system, therefore, amounts to a perpetual inventory control within the reserve stock room.

2. *Tickler Control.* Under tickler control the periodic inventories usually cover only certain sections of the stock, but they are taken at frequent intervals. The word "tickler" is used to describe this form of control because the lists of items to be inventoried each day are placed in a tickler file, and the list for any particular day automatically comes to the attention of the

---

[15] Broadly speaking, a stock shortage is the amount of merchandise in terms of retail prices which has "disappeared" during a particular period. In other words, a shortage exists when the amount of merchandise on hand is less than the store records indicate should be on hand. Cf. the discussion in the following chapter.

buyer. The tickler system may be used for forward stocks, reserve stocks, or for a combination of the two, depending on whether goods pass through a reserve stock room before reaching the selling floor. It is most useful for articles having a steady rate of sales.[16]

3. *Checklist System.* Under the checklist system goods on hand are checked against a basic or model stock list[17] at regular, short intervals. The quantity of each item on hand at the time may or may not be counted, but the personal inspection of the stock is supposed to reveal the need for reorder.[18] This system reveals overstocked or understocked conditions and aids in the correction of such situations. Its effectiveness depends on three main factors: (1) the care with which the list is checked against the actual stock; (2) the maintenance of a uniform arrangement of the stock; and (3) the alertness shown by salespeople and other responsible persons in not permitting any item to be completely "sold out." Otherwise, the inspector has to guess what belongs in a vacant space.

4. *Warehouse Control System.* Control over such "warehouse items" as furniture, stoves, refrigerators, and television sets—commonly sold from samples in the store, with delivery made from warehouse stock—may be exercised either in the store or in the warehouse, or in both places. When sales are made, the sales checks are usually sent to a control operator who stamps the warehouse copy of the sales check to indicate that he has entered it. This step permits prompt entries in the control books, which are always accessible to department managers and assistants for review. Thus overselling, with subsequent inability to deliver, is eliminated. These records still necessitate, however, the maintainance of some records at the warehouse such as bin or shelf stock cards, or a visual index system to facilitate inventory taking and to assist stockmen.

Some stores follow a practice of attaching books of gummed labels to

---

[16] The term "tickler control" is also used to refer to the practice of placing cards, slips, or gummed labels at certain places in the stock as reminders to the buyers. As goods are sold and the "reminders" are reached, the cards are removed and placed in containers provided for the purpose. At frequent intervals, the cards are collected and reviewed as to the advisability of reorder. It is apparent that these reminder cards should contain sufficient information to permit the prompt placing of orders. This form of control is also termed "reorder control" and "reminder control."

[17] A basic stock list represents the *minimum* assortment and quantities of items that should be on hand at a given time to meet reasonable demands of customers. A model stock list includes a complete, *well-balanced* assortment of merchandise designed to meet a specific sales volume. Automatic reorder quantities are frequently used with a basic stock list. Cf. discussion on pp. 281–84, above.

[18] Closely related to the checklist system is the "never-out" list used by some stores. The "never-out" list contains only the names of items, usually staples, for which there is a large and steady demand and which the store must have on hand at all times or risk losing sales and customers. Items on the list are checked against the stock on hand at frequent intervals.

store samples of warehouse articles. These labels are numbered consecutively, and the books contain the same number of labels as the quantity of items in the warehouse and on the floor. When a sale is made, the highest-numbered label is torn out of the book and pasted on the warehouse copy of the sales check. The highest number remaining in the book at any time, therefore, represents the number of items still on hand. To insure that all sales are properly recorded, it is essential that stockmen in the warehouse fill no order unless the sales check bears a gummed label or the control operator's stamp, depending on the system used.[19]

Benefits of Unit Control

Unit control was developed to meet a need that remained unfulfilled by the use of various forms of dollar control. Specifically it sought to provide information relative to physical characteristics of merchandise which would prove useful in buying and selling. Consequently, it is logical to summarize its benefits from the buying and selling points of view.

As a *buying* tool, unit control yields these benefits:

1. It reveals what merchandise is selling best, to the end that similar merchandise can be bought, with proper allowance being given to current sales and fashion trends.

2. It indicates the merchandise that is selling slowly and that should not be reordered. It furnishes a valuable guide, therefore, in reducing the number of price lines, styles, and colors which are carried.

3. It shows the proper time to buy merchandise, thus insuring a stock of goods to meet customers' requirements. In like manner, by showing goods on order, it tends to prevent unnecessary duplicate reorders.

4. It aids in establishing model stock plans, thus insuring complete, well-balanced stocks.

5. It reveals, where the perpetual inventory system is used, the quantity of stock on hand at any time without taking a physical inventory. Moreover, by comparing this book figure with that obtained when the physical inventory is taken, the stock shortage may be found. This comparison focuses attention on stock shortages and assists in controlling them.

As a *selling* tool, unit control provides assistance as follows:

1. It shows the age condition of the stock, thereby drawing attention to the items upon which markdowns should be taken or indicating those that require special promotion. Losses are reduced when markdowns and other required actions are taken promptly.

---

[19] On stock handling in warehouses of retailers of various kinds, cf. "Distribution Centers," comprising the entire issue of *Chain Store Age* (Executives Edition), October, 1965.

2. It reveals the most popular merchandise or best-selling items which may be further promoted.

3. It minimizes the number of "out-of-stock" situations.

4. It serves as a guide in planning special sales events by providing information on the nature and amount of goods available for promotion.

5. It often saves time for the customer by giving precise information on particular items in stock without the necessity of locating these items in the stock itself. This advantage is especially significant when unusual items are called for and when a large stock is maintained.

Reasons for Limited Use of Unit Control

In view of the important buying and selling benefits which accrue from a well-planned and operated system of unit control, it would seem that all stores able to afford it would adopt this method. But many have failed to do so and it is advisable to inquire as to the reasons.

1. Many retail store executives believe that the cost of maintaining the necessary records exceeds the benefits derived from the information supplied. Frequently this is not a disadvantage of unit control but a fault of the system as planned and a reflection upon the judgment of those who make use of the data.

2. The publicity given to the elaborate systems used in large stores with their expensive forms, numerous recapitulations, and involved handling of records has instilled skepticism in the minds of proprietors of smaller stores as to the usefulness of similar, though less elaborate, systems in their stores.

3. The failure of some proprietors and buyers to define the specific purposes and uses to which the information will be put prior to the time it is collected often results in the gathering of considerable data which are not useful and are consequently disregarded.

4. The opposition of some inexperienced buyers is based on their belief that unit-control systems are established to furnish information to merchandise managers and the controller regarding the buyers' incompetence, rather than as a means of helping them to become better buyers through the possession of additional facts.

5. The fear of many buyers that the unit-control system, by supplying detailed merchandise information, would decrease their importance and value in the store has furthered their opposition. Most buyers dislike the term "automatic buying."

6. The strong conviction of many buying executives that effective control over merchandise can be maintained successfully only through study of the merchandise itself and not by placing dependence upon records concerning that merchandise.

7. The unsatisfactory experience of some buyers with unit-control systems has caused them to look with disfavor upon such systems. This experience may have been caused by poorly planned systems, by expecting too much of the system installed, by attempting to make the records tie in completely with dollar control, or by failure to build an adequate organization to do the unit-control job. Frequently, the "unsatisfactory experience" is exaggerated in the buyer's

mind because he is temperamentally opposed to the systematic records required for unit control. His major interests lie in buying and selling, not in accounting.

Establishing a Unit-Control System

If a careful review of the advantages and disadvantages of unit control, supplemented by an investigation of the conditions under which such a system of control would operate, results in a decision to set up this type of control for a store or for a particular department, the proprietor or department head should proceed as follows:

1. Make a complete list of all the information that it would be advisable to obtain from the system. In doing so, secure the opinion of other merchants and of employees in the store or particular department who understand the purposes of such control.

2. Examine the methods by which the desired information may be obtained to determine their suitability for the purposes in mind. This study should involve such factors as the type of merchandise, including size, color, and variety handled; the unit price; the manner in which goods are purchased and stored, that is, the frequency of orders, their size, and whether regular use is made of the reserve stock room; and the rate of stockturn.

3. When the particular method has been chosen, forms or records should be devised to provide information of the kind and in the form wanted. The guides in this connection should be brevity, simplicity, and clarity. Detailed explanation of the use of the forms should accompany their distribution.

4. A physical inventory should be taken to determine what items are in stock and the quantities of each. This step furnishes a basis upon which records may be built and also permits the desired segregation to be accomplished without difficulty. When the goods are properly segregated, they are ready to be re-marked according to the plans made.

5. Goods should be marked to permit the recording of necessary information. Marking involves (*a*) preparing suitable price tickets with symbols, letters, or numbers used to designate style, color, size, vendor, and the like; and (*b*) attaching the tickets to the merchandise. Without markings that will enable the necessary information to be recorded, unit control is impossible for most types of goods.

6. Provision should be made for the accurate recording of sales. Although there are numerous ways of doing this, the most common methods consist of price ticket stubs, copies of sales checks, sales register receipt stubs, salespeople's tallies, and reserve stock requisitions. Very recent years, however, have witnessed many changes in methods of recording sales, particularly by the more progressive firms, as technological improvements have enabled them to speed up transactions, obtain more complete information, and reduce the number of errors. New-type sales registers, for example, are now available that permit sales transactions to be recorded quickly as one of the first steps in a complete system of merchandise management.[20]

---

[20] Cf. *General Information: The Values of Total System Reports for Retailers* (Dayton, Ohio: National Cash Register Company, 1966). Also cf. footnote 23, p. 380, below.

7. Complete and accurate control records should be maintained in such a manner that the unit-control information can be summarized, tabulated, and recorded promptly and fully, and checked frequently.

When a unit-control system has been set up in the manner outlined, control has been only partially accomplished. The data recorded must be analyzed, interpreted, and used. It is in this connection that the value of the system is tested. Unless the data provided are translated into improved buying practices and better-balanced stocks in relationship to sales, the system is a failure.

EDP AND MERCHANDISE MANAGEMENT

Preceding chapters have indicated that many progressive stores have adopted EDP equipment to supply information to decision-making executives on many aspects of retail operation.[21] At this point we need add but a few paragraphs to illustrate the use of such equipment in the control of merchandise inventories, an area for which EDP is particularly suited. As one executive has stated, so far as inventories are concerned, "Everything you do is with individuals. You deal with thousands of strangers and with each sex at every age level. You have the seasonal factor and various income levels. And, beyond that, the vagaries of fashion."[22] The need is great, therefore, for detailed data, available promptly and accurately, to insure correct decisions on merchandise matters. The computer has helped fulfill this need.[23]

EDP in Department Stores: A Specific Illustration

The use and benefits of EDP for merchandise control in department stores is well illustrated by the equipment installed by Woodward & Lothrop of Washington, D.C. Besides its main store, this organization operates eight suburban branches and its total annual sales exceed $100 million. Its EDP setup, "perhaps the country's most sophisticated . . . system," includes "more than $2.5 million worth of electronic computers and supporting ware [permitting] executives and buyers [to make a] close check on the

[21] Cf. the discussion on pp. 138–41, 282–83, 287–88, and 328.

[22] L. J. Amtmann, Woodward & Lothrop, Washington, D.C., in "Where the Computers Care, Too," *Business Week,* March 12, 1966, p. 141. Also cf. "Now Retailers Put It All on Tape," *ibid.,* January 16, 1965, p. 31.

[23] Unit control as well as financial data are captured at the point of sale in form suitable for computer input by a new register and system developed by the National Cash Register Company and called REACT (Register Enforced Automated Control Technique).

performance of specific product lines and on customer tastes."[24] This installation was preceded by the design of a model department store computer system developed over a period of two years. All sales registers were replaced with new machines which record on tape for each transaction the department number, the classification of item, the amount of sale, and the salesperson. Executives expect to add the individual item number and a code number for the customer in the near future, thus enabling the store to build a profile of each customer's purchasing habits.

Presently the system, operating 24 hours a day, shows only how some staple items are moving but executives hope that similar data will soon cover the "volatile trends" in women's fashions. Each night tapes are fed into a computer and each morning executives are furnished a "flash report" of the previous day's sales. By afternoon detailed data are available by dpartment, sub-department, and buyer, and a careful evaluation of results is made.

Woodward & Lothrop has plans to extend its data processing activities still further in the future. The use of computers to prepare purchase orders based on buyers' forecasts already is being tested as is the prediction of future sales based on past experience. And, its executives hope, company computers will be linked with the EDP equipment of suppliers permitting purchase orders to be issued and filled electronically. This step has already been taken on an experimental basis by Bobbie Brooks, Inc., a well-known ready-to-wear manufacturer, and one of its major retail accounts.[25] Each evening the retailer's computer transmits information on sales by style, color, and size to the Brooks firm and merchandise needed to maintain a balanced inventory is shipped the next morning.

EDP in Chain Stores

Chain stores also have been active in updating their methods and equipment to improve their control over merchandise inventories. In a previous chapter we referred to a telephone-ordering system, such as the one developed by Digitronics Corporation.[26]

Called Data-Verter, it is supposed to allow orders to be relayed much faster. A store manager punches his requirements on a special adding machine-tape recorder. Then a transmitter beeps the order via a telephone to a central

[24] "Where the Computers Care, Too," *op. cit.,* pp. 140–41. The remainder of this discussion is based on the same source.
[25] Cf. "B. Brooks Computer Tie-in with Big Store Set Up in Test," *Women's Wear Daily,* August 26, 1965, p. 37.
[26] Cf. p. 328, above.

computer. Transmission takes about three minutes, and the branch can have its merchandise overnight. Several large food and general merchandise chains are now trying the system.[27]

Another example of merchandising data resulting from EDP is afforded by the Kroger Company, a large food chain. This firm recently developed a Product Movement Index, a by-product of its computerized system. The Index furnishes grocery manufacturers with weekly data on shipments of branded goods from Kroger warehouses to its 1,300 stores in twenty states. Charges are $150 per week for each product group, with lower prices if five or more groups are purchased. Through the data supplied, manufacturers learn their weekly sales in Kroger stores, the sales of competing brands, their share of total market, and the prices paid by consumers.[28]

EDP in Smaller Stores

It should also be emphasized again that various arrangements are now available under which smaller stores can realize the advantages of EDP. In February, 1966, 21 stores were using a group EDP Service developed by the National Retail Merchants Association, 30 more had completed arrangements for installing the system, and 78 additional ones were in the preparatory stage.[29] Under this system stores send taped sales and inventory data to the NRMA computer service bureau, which sorts the transactions into merchandise classifications and sends back printed sales and inventory reports by classifications and by departments, as well as for the total store.

THE PHYSICAL INVENTORY

The physical inventory—an actual counting and listing of the goods in stock at a given time, together with the cost or retail price of each item—is normally thought of as a "necessary evil" occurring once or twice a year in order to determine whether the retail store has made a profit during the past fiscal period.[30] But in addition to this financial purpose, the physical inventory is an important aspect of merchandise control.

As of a specific date, the physical inventory shows the kinds, quantities, and values of the items in stock for the store as a whole and by departments.

---

[27] "Marketing Briefs," *Business Week,* November 13, 1965, p. 196.

[28] "Kroger Co. Adds Data to Its Wares," *Business Week,* September 4, 1965, p. 38.

[29] "How Smaller Stores Use EDP," *Stores,* February, 1966, pp. 64–66. Also cf. E. J. Watson, "Computer Services for Small Business," *Management Accounting,* October, 1965, pp. 11–13; and David Coleman and Theodore Cohn, "How Companies are Using Data Processing Centers," *Management Review,* November, 1965, pp. 30–33.

[30] For its significance in determining operating results of the business, cf. Chapter 23.

Moreover—depending on the store, the types of merchandise handled, and the information placed on the price ticket—the physical inventory makes possible the classification of items by sections or divisions of departments, by age groups, by price lines, by physical units, or by other desired groupings. With this information, the retailer may improve the effectiveness of his buying and also adopt proper selling methods to move the merchandise on hand.

The physical inventory also provides a basis for checking and correcting unit control and other stock records. In this connection the physical inventory furnishes the figures with which book inventories are compared in order to determine the amount of stock shortage or overage. When this amount is known, corrective measures may be adopted.

The reliability of the physical inventory figures is dependent, of course, upon their accuracy and completeness. Consequently, considerable care must be exercised in entering quantities on hand and controlling inventory cards or sheets. To minimize errors the physical inventory should be planned carefully, the required information listed by qualified personnel, the calculations and summaries carefully checked, and the inventory reports issued promptly. The importance of these factors varies with the size and kind of store, but none of them should be neglected by any retailer.

Taking the Physical Inventory

In Chain Stores Selling Standardized Goods. There is no standard procedure for taking the physical inventory in all types of stores and practices vary widely. At one extreme, for example, is the monthly inventory of the grocery chain for which there is little advance preparation. The inventory crew, usually consisting of at least two men, comes into a store quite unexpectedly. As one man goes through the stock, calling off the number of units at each price, the other records; or perhaps a tape or wire recorder is used, so that both men can count. Although headquarters may want to know the quantities on hand for a few specific items, in general all it desires is the total value of the goods in the store; consequently, only the price-quantity relationships are required. When the count has been completed, the sheet is sent to headquarters, where the value of the stock is computed.

In Department Stores. At the other extreme in taking the physical inventory is the department store where advance preparation for the inventory is essential.[31] Commonly, the process is divided into four stages:

---

[31] Cf. National Retail Merchants Association, *Inventory Taking Manual* (New York: The Association, 1965).

(1) the planning stage; (2) the counting and recording of the goods on hand; (3) the calculation of the value of the stock; and (4) the issuance of inventory reports.

Before the actual count is made, the buyer of each department, acting under the direction of the controller or an inventory supervisor, usually takes the following steps:

1. Classifies and groups merchandise by type, price, and style to increase the speed of the count, to be sure all merchandise is included, and to increase the buyer's own information as to what he has in stock.
2. Adjusts prices so that they are market prices. (If the buyer has done this from day to day, no special adjustments will be called for at inventory time.) The buyer will also check to see that all necessary information is on the price tickets.
3. If time is available before the inventory, sometimes plans a sale to reduce stock to a minimum and to clear out undesirable merchandise disclosed by step 1.
4. Prepares a layout chart of the department, showing the location of each fixture with merchandise. This chart enables the controller to issue inventory sheets or tags marked for specific sections in each department, thus assuring that all merchandise is included when the count is taken.
5. Obtains the necessary inventory sheets or tags from the controller.
6. Checks up on the salespeople's knowledge of inventory instructions if

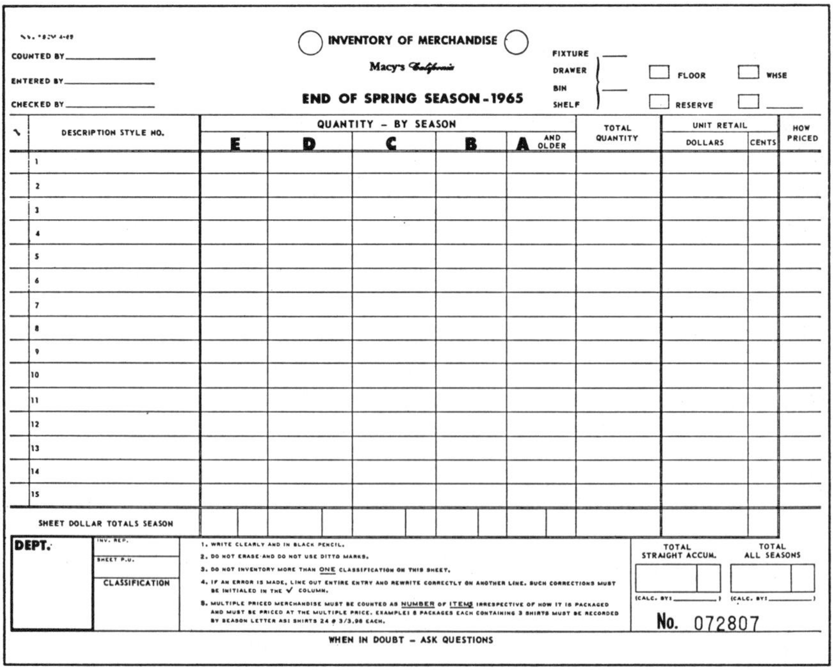

INVENTORY OF MERCHANDISE

Macy's California

END OF SPRING SEASON - 1965

COUNTED BY ______

ENTERED BY ______

CHECKED BY ______

FIXTURE ___ DRAWER BIN ___ SHELF

☐ FLOOR ☐ WHSE

☐ RESERVE ☐ ______

✓	DESCRIPTION STYLE NO.	QUANTITY – BY SEASON E	D	C	B	A AND OLDER	TOTAL QUANTITY	UNIT RETAIL DOLLARS	CENTS	HOW PRICED
	1									
	2									
	3									
	4									
	5									
	6									
	7									
	8									
	9									
	10									
	11									
	12									
	13									
	14									
	15									
SHEET DOLLAR TOTALS SEASON										

DEPT. | INV. REP. | SHEET P.U. | CLASSIFICATION

1. WRITE CLEARLY AND IN BLACK PENCIL.
2. DO NOT ERASE AND DO NOT USE DITTO MARKS.
3. DO NOT INVENTORY MORE THAN ONE CLASSIFICATION ON THIS SHEET.
4. IF AN ERROR IS MADE, LINE OUT ENTIRE ENTRY AND REWRITE CORRECTLY ON ANOTHER LINE. SUCH CORRECTIONS MUST BE INITIALED IN THE ✓ COLUMN.
5. MULTIPLE PRICED MERCHANDISE MUST BE COUNTED AS NUMBER OF ITEMS IRRESPECTIVE OF HOW IT IS PACKAGED AND MUST BE PRICED AT THE MULTIPLE PRICE. EXAMPLE: 8 PACKAGES EACH CONTAINING 3 SHIRTS MUST BE RECORDED BY SEASON LETTER AS: SHIRTS 24 @ 3/3.98 EACH.

TOTAL STRAIGHT ACCUM. (CALC. BY: ______) TOTAL ALL SEASONS (CALC. BY: ______)

No. 072807

WHEN IN DOUBT – ASK QUESTIONS

Courtesy: Macy's, California

FIG. 13–1. Example of a form for taking inventory.

these have been provided by the controller; or instructs salespeople in the technique of inventory taking, and shows them the need for accuracy and speed.

After plans have been completed and the designated inventory date arrives, the actual counting and recording begin. Usually employees work in pairs, one calling and one recording. In some stores, however, items are listed by individual salespeople a day or so in advance of the actual "taking." The recording may take place on inventory sheets or inventory tags but the former are used by the vast majority of firms. When sheets are used, a number of items (including description, quantity, price, and other desired characteristics) are recorded on each sheet (see Figure 13–1); with tags or tickets only one item of a particular size or type appears on each ticket (see Figure 13–2). Since selling may be going on while the inventory taking is in progress, all sales are recorded either on the tags or on special deduction sheets, thus allowing the computation of the stock on hand when the inventory taking has been completed. To increase accuracy, some retailers have the recorder change places with the counter and a recount is made. But a complete retake slows down the taking of the inventory, so spot checks or partial retakes are frequently used; and unless such checks indicate the existence of numerous errors, the inventory is assumed to be correct. Since most large department stores use the retail inventory method, they maintain perpetual or book inventories and are thus able further to check the accuracy of their book figures against the physical inventory. In fact, an important purpose of the physical inventory is to check the accuracy of the book figures.

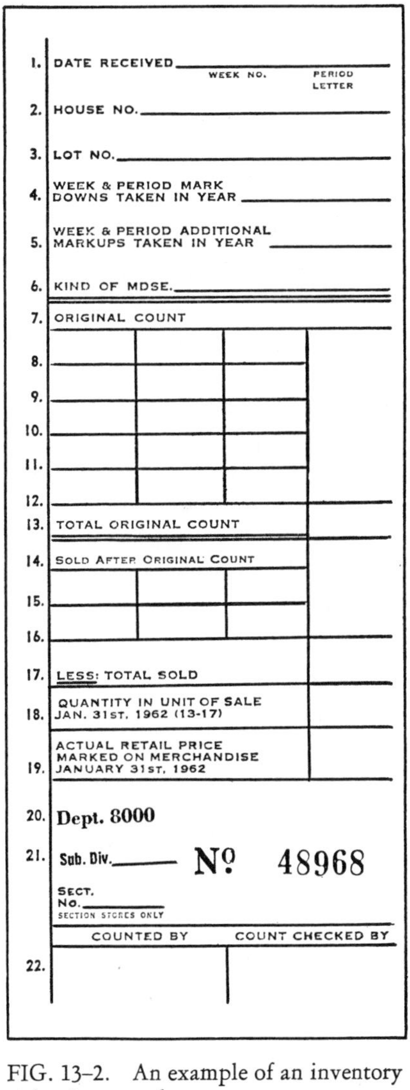
1. DATE RECEIVED ____ WEEK NO. PERIOD LETTER
2. HOUSE NO. ____
3. LOT NO. ____
4. WEEK & PERIOD MARK DOWNS TAKEN IN YEAR ____
5. WEEK & PERIOD ADDITIONAL MARKUPS TAKEN IN YEAR ____
6. KIND OF MDSE. ____
7. ORIGINAL COUNT
8.
9.
10.
11.
12.
13. TOTAL ORIGINAL COUNT
14. SOLD AFTER ORIGINAL COUNT
15.
16.
17. LESS: TOTAL SOLD
18. QUANTITY IN UNIT OF SALE JAN. 31ST, 1962 (13-17)
19. ACTUAL RETAIL PRICE MARKED ON MERCHANDISE JANUARY 31ST, 1962
20. Dept. 8000
21. Sub. Div. ____ № 48968
SECT. NO. ____
SECTION STORES ONLY
COUNTED BY COUNT CHECKED BY
22.

FIG. 13–2. An example of an inventory ticket in general use.

Once the counting, recording, and checking are completed, all sheets and tags are sent to the controller's office for calculating and summarizing. The final step is to prepare and issue the necessary reports, including those which relate to the age of goods as compared with the previous inventory, stock shortages and overages by departments, imported merchandise on hand, and warehouse stocks.

In Small Stores. In between the simplicity of the physical inventory of the standardized chain-store unit and the rather complex procedure necessary in the department store stands the system suitable for small independent stores. Since a physical inventory is taken only once or twice a year, the retailer should inspect his stock rather carefully prior to making the actual count. Such an examination will acquaint him with the items on hand and enable him to sort out the slow-moving ones, or "sleepers," which should be cleared out through a preinventory sale. Moreover, it will permit him to adjust costs and retail prices to market levels. The employees used to assist him should be instructed in inventory taking and the need for care and accuracy stressed. Standardized forms suitable for recording the desired information are available from a number of salesbook companies and trade associations, and it is advisable to make use of these forms.

Stock Turnover[32]

Stock turnover, or rate of stockturn, is the number of times during a given period—usually a year—that the average amount of stock on hand is sold. Although stockturn rates are universally computed on a yearly basis, they may be derived for any period desired.

The rate of stockturn is most commonly determined by dividing the average inventory at cost into the cost of the merchandise sold. Quite frequently, however, it is computed by dividing the average inventory at retail into the net sales figure. A much less common, but equally satisfactory, method is to divide the average inventory in physical units into sales in physical units. To illustrate: Assume that a clothing merchant begins the year with 100 suits which cost $50 each and which are marked to retail at $75 each. During the year, other suits are purchased for resale; at the end of the year the retailer has in stock 60 suits which cost him $40 each and which carry a retail price of $60 each. For the year, his net sales of 360 suits

---

[32] For a clear statement of the stockturn problem cf. Max Robb, "Turnover," in *The Buyer's Manual* (4th. ed.; New York: National Retail Merchants Association, 1965), pp. 265–74; "Turnover: Insight into Your Most Basic Problem," *Department Store Economist,* November, 1964, pp. 26–27, 32; and D. J. Dalrymple, "How Important Is Stock Turnover?" *Journal of Retailing,* Vol. XL, No. 4 (Winter 1964–65), pp. 1–5.

amount to $24,975; the cost of goods sold is $16,650. Upon the basis of these figures the annual rate of stockturn may be computed in three ways, as follows:[33]

1. Opening inventory at cost... $ 5,000
    Closing inventory at cost.. 2,400
                                                                                2/$ 7,400
    Average inventory at cost... 3,700
    Cost of goods sold.. 16,650

$$\frac{\$16,650}{\$3,700} = 4.5 = \text{Stockturn rate}$$

2. Opening inventory at retail.. $ 7,500
    Closing inventory at retail...................................... 3,600
                                                                                2/$11,100
    Average inventory at retail...................................... 5,550
    Net sales.. 24,975

$$\frac{\$24,975}{\$5,550} = 4.5 = \text{Stockturn rate}$$

3. Opening inventory in units... 100
    Closing inventory in units.. 60
                                                                                2/160
    Average inventory in units....................................... 80
    Net sales in units... 360

$$\frac{360}{80} = 4.5 = \text{Stockturn rate}$$

Caution Signals in Computing Stock Turnover

Sales and Average Stock Figures Must Be Comparable. It is apparent from the foregoing illustration that both the sales and the average stock figures must cover the same operating period and that *both* of them be either on a cost or on a retail basis. Actually, it does not make much difference whether the retailer decides to use cost or retail figures, since they produce nearly the same result.[34] Retailers using the retail method of inventory will find the use of retail figures quite convenient, whereas retailers using the cost method of inventory will have the necessary figures to make the computation based on cost. The main consideration is that the retailer should be consistent from year to year; otherwise, his annual stock turnover figures will not be comparable and will be of little practical value as a guide to better operations.

---

[33] Sometimes businessmen and students alike confuse stock turnover and capital turnover. The latter, however, is calculated by dividing the average inventory at cost into the net sales for the period.

[34] Cost figures, however, will usually give a slightly higher rate of stockturn than retail figures, because of the influence of markdowns.

Average Stock Must Be Representative. To obtain a reliable stock turnover figure, a truly representative average, rather than just any statistical average, is needed. Lack of records on the part of many retailers, however, forces them to use an average that is not representative. Many small retailers using the cost method of inventory and taking a physical inventory but once a year are forced to find the average stock by using the opening and closing inventories, as follows:

Average stock = ½(Opening cost inventory + Closing cost inventory)

As a typical or representative figure, the foregoing average is unsatisfactory, since it does not accurately reflect stock conditions throughout the entire year. For example, if the retailer takes his physical inventories in January when stock is relatively low, the average reflects only low stock periods, and the resultant turnover figure is exaggerated. But the lack of a better stock figure should not keep the retailer from computing his stock turnover. Even a figure computed in this manner is of value to the retailer in comparing his stock turnover with that of other retailers using the same method of computation; it also gives him a picture of the year-to-year trend within his own store, both by departments and for the store as a whole.

Some retailers go one step further and also inventory their stocks in the middle of their fiscal year. Such retailers are in a position to compute their average stock by averaging their opening, midyear, and closing inventories as follows:

Average stock = ⅓(Opening cost inventory + Midyear cost inventory
+ Closing cost inventory)

Although this method may give a somewhat more representative average than when just two inventories are used, it should be noted that, for many retailers, July (when the midyear physical inventory is usually made) is a dull month, with the result that stocks are also low at this time. The final figure for turnover, therefore, again appears higher than is actually the case.

For practical purposes, those retailers who take monthly physical inventories or who maintain perpetual inventories so that monthly figures are available, are in the best position to get a truly representative average stock. Such retailers, by including their opening inventory with their twelve monthly closing inventories, are able to obtain an average stock figure which reflects stock conditions throughout the year.[35] For retailers with the

---

[35] This statement may not be exactly true for all retailers, since some of them make a conscious effort to bring their end-of-month stocks to a relatively low level. To take

data available, this method is far superior to the two methods discussed above. Yet, unless they have the information available for other reasons, it is too costly to develop figures just for this purpose. What is important is consistency in methods of computation to insure comparability within the firm as well as with other retailers using the same method. When this goal is achieved, any of the foregoing three methods of obtaining an average stock will be satisfactory.

Advantages of Rapid Stockturn

The advantages to the retailer of a rapid rate of stockturn are so evident that no extended discussion is necessary. By limiting his investment in inventory he reduces such expenses as those for interest, taxes, insurance on merchandise, and store and storage space. By having "fresher" merchandise on hand he may actually achieve greater sales with a smaller stock than with a larger one made up of soiled and shopworn goods. Markdowns also may be reduced. Finally, the retailer with a relatively high stockturn finds that his return on invested capital may rise.[36]

Despite the advantages of a rapid rate of stockturn, the statistical evidence of Table 13–1 and 13–2 makes it clear that successful retailers operate with wide variations in their rates of stock turnover. To understand this situation, we need to examine the reasons for such variations, the relationship of turnover to profits, and the possible disadvantages of a relatively high turnover rate.

Causes of Variations in the Rate of Stockturn

Variations in the rate of stockturn that exist among retail stores are caused by many factors, only four of which can be examined here: type of goods sold, store policy, store location, and the aid provided by manufacturers.

Type of Goods Sold. Table 13–1 shows the rates of stockturn for retail stores in a number of fields. At one extreme are service stations (25.3) and food stores (18.1); whereas at the other extreme, jewelry stores turned their stock only 1.5 times a year. Reasons for this wide variation are

---

account of this element, a few stores go so far as to compute an average stock figure based on weekly data, as follows:

$$\text{Average stock} = 1/53 \ (\text{Opening inventory} + \text{Closing inventories at the end of the 52 weeks})$$

Such a refinement is not necessary for ordinary purposes.

[36] "Schnucks, St. Louis: Averages 35 Turns per Store," *Super Market Merchandising* August, 1965, pp. 26–31 ff.

not difficult to find; they lie both in the characteristics of the goods and in consumers' buying habits for each type of merchandise. Gasoline and oil are sold in only a few grades; and since many items sold in food stores are perishable, customers prefer to purchase at frequent intervals, thus enabling this type of retailer to operate with a relatively limited stock in relation to his sales. In contrast, jewelry is bought less frequently than most other items, and a large and costly stock is usually necessary to meet customers' demands for an adequate assortment.

TABLE 13–1

RATES OF STOCKTURN IN SELECTED RETAIL STORES

Kind of Business	Rate of Stockturn
Book stores	3.3
Department stores (sales $1–$2 million)	2.8
Drygoods and general merchandise (sales $200,000 and over)	3.1
Drug stores (retail pharmacies) (sales $100,000 to $120,000)	3.2
Food stores (chains with sales below $20 million)	18.1
Furniture stores (sales less than $250,000)	2.2
Hardware stores (profit makers)	2.2
Jewelry stores (Installment credit—sales over $100,000)	1.5
Office supply and equipment dealers	3.3
Service stations (proprietorships)	25.3
Specialty stores (sales $1–$5 million)	3.2
Toy stores (sales $60,000 and less)	3.0

Source: National Cash Register Company, *Expenses in Retail Businesses* (Dayton, Ohio: The Company, 1965). The food store figure is from *Progressive Grocer*, April, 1966, p. 69.

Store Policy and Location. Differences in policies naturally influence variations in rates of stockturn among retail stores. For instance, those which may lead to relatively high rates of stockturn include the following, among others: hand-to-mouth buying; elimination of slow-selling items; fewer price lines; minimizing number of styles, sizes, and colors; promotional activity and low-margin pricing; and concentration on fast-moving national brands. In the drug field, for example, independent cut-rate stores and many chain-store organizations follow policies of limiting their stocks to fast-moving items, engaging in much promotional activity, and pricing their goods with a relatively small markup. In contrast, other drug retailers prefer to follow policies of full stocks and "regular" prices. These two groups of retailers will obviously have different rates of stockturn.

The location of a store or of a branch is another very important factor in contributing to a low (or high) stock turnover. Some stores are so located —perhaps in small towns or in city neighborhood sections—that it is impossible to secure very large sales. Since a certain minimum stock is necessary, these stores will show relatively low rates of stockturn. In contrast, stores which are located where customer traffic is heavy and large sales are possible will experience higher rates of stockturn; that is, their stocks will not increase proportionately with their sales.

Aid Provided by Manufacturers. As some retailers have limited their stocks to achieve a better stockturn, they have been criticized by manufacturers for giving up one of their major functions, that is, providing an adequate assortment of merchandise from which the customer may make a selection. Especially are manufacturers critical of the retailer's hesitancy to stock a new item until the manufacturer, through advertising, has created customer demand for it.

Some manufacturers, well aware of the retailer's need for strict inventory control, have faced this situation in a positive manner. In cooperation with the retailer, they have developed stock-control plans giving the manufacturer a reasonable display of his product and, at the same time, providing the retailer with a good turnover figure. One skirt manufacturer helps the retailer set up a model stock, sends in salesmen to take a weekly inventory, and offers to replace slow-selling items with fast-selling merchandise. Such aid from the manufacturer is of particular value to the smaller retailer who often lacks the stock-control programs of the larger firms.

Stock Turnover and Profits

It is often stated that there is a direct relationship between stock turnover and profits and that the retailer may increase his profits by increasing his stock turnover. In support of this position, data such as those summarized in Table 13–2 are presented which indicate in every case that the firms of the same kind with the highest rate of turnover realized the greatest profit ratio to sales.

It should be made perfectly clear, however, that there is no such causation between stock turnover and profits as these statistics might lead one to believe. In other words, mere improvement in stock turnovers does not necessarily mean an increase in profits. *Whether or not profits increase with stock turnover depends entirely upon the methods by which the higher stock turnover is obtained.* To illustrate: One way in which a retailer may increase his stock turnover is to reduce his average stock without reducing his sales. To this end, slow-moving items may be eliminated. Perhaps some price lines or competing brands can be dropped. A hand-to-mouth buying policy may be adopted. The net result *may* be increased profits, since the smaller stock may decrease both markdowns and operating expenses.

Increased profits are not sure to result from reducing stock, however, even if sales are maintained. Purchasing in small quantities may result in additional correspondence and clerical cost; a greater expense in receiving, checking, and marking merchandise; and in the loss of quantity discounts which may more than balance the gains from a faster stock turnover. The

TABLE 13–2

RATE OF STOCKTURN AND PROFITS IN SELECTED TYPES
OF RETAIL TRADE, 1965

Retail Trade	Rate of Stockturn*	Net Profit as Percentage of Net Sales
Clothing Stores—Men's and Boys'	5.0	4.42
	3.7	2.63
	2.8	1.49
Department Stores	7.3	3.21
	5.4	2.18
	3.9	1.22
Discount Stores	7.5	3.01
	5.8	1.75
	4.4	1.07
Furniture Stores	6.2	5.04
	4.8	2.39
	3.6	0.92
Grocery and meat stores (independent)	23.0	1.80
	16.6	1.30
	12.7	0.81
Hardware Stores	4.9	3.88
	3.4	2.16
	2.9	0.74
Shoe Stores—Men's, Women's, Children's	4.5	4.49
	3.5	2.69
	2.5	1.05
Women's specialty shops	9.4	4.02
	6.7	1.91
	4.8	0.81

Source: "The Ratios of Retailing," *Dun's Review and Modern Industry*, September, 1966, p. 53.
* This column does not show true stockturn figures, since it is calculated by dividing net sales by inventory at cost.

proprietor or buyer may have to spend so much of his time in small-lot buying that he is unable to continue other activities which formerly added considerably to profits. Moreover, transportation costs on small orders are relatively greater than on larger orders. Finally, over a period of time, it may be impossible to maintain sales on the reduced stock. In other words, assortments may become so inadequate that customer ill will is engendered, and sales and profits will eventually decline.[37]

Conclusions on Stock Turnover. The preceding discussion makes it clear that a mere increase in stock turnover is not what the retailer wants. Rather, he wants increased profit. Sometimes this goal is achieved by steps that also lead to a higher stock turnover, but at other times the path lies in some other direction. If the retailer will concentrate on such matters as careful buying, judicious pricing, a well-balanced stock, effective sales promotion, and properly trained personnel, he will not have to worry about stock turnover. Adequate stock turnover is a result of good merchandising and, therefore, a measure of the alertness and ability of the management.

STOCK-SALES RATIOS

The stock-sales ratio is a useful device in controlling merchandise. It indicates the relationship that exists between the stock on hand at the beginning of a period (usually a month) in terms of retail prices and the sales for that month.[38] If, for example, the retail value of goods on hand in a department on October 1 was $40,000 and the sales for October were $20,000, the stock-sales ratio for the month would be 2 to 1.

Through a knowledge of his own past stock-sales ratios and those of other retailers, a retailer has a good basis for planning the stock he needs to meet anticipated sales.[39] Especially will the retailer find the stock-sales ratio of value if he remembers that, like other merchandise statistics, it is an *aid to,* and not a *substitute for* judgment. The stock-sales ratio should not be considered a mere formula which answers all questions relating to stock and sales relationships.

STOCK SHORTAGES

An important and continuous problem of merchandise management is the control of stock shortages—the unaccounted-for disappearance of merchandise at retail prices. Such shortages may develop at many points in the

---

[37] Cf. George Baylis, "Are the Brakes Too Tight to Let the Train Roll?", *Retail Control,* October, 1965, pp. 15–26.

[38] It is possible, of course, to express this relationship in terms of the end-of-the-month stock rather than that at the beginning of the month, or even to use physical units.

[39] Departmental stock-sales ratios for selected departments by store size are given in Sam Flanel, *Departmental Merchandising and Operating Results of Department and Specialty Stores in 1965* (New York: National Retail Merchants Association, 1966).

operation of a retail store.[40] To illustrate: Merchandise may be mistakenly sold for less than the price tag indicates, some breakage is inevitable, and shrinkage and mismeasuring play a role. But the two chief causes of stock shortages are dishonesty and errors in records.

Dishonesty as a Cause of Shortages

Stock shortages caused by thefts of merchandise by employees,[41] customers, amateur and professional shoplifters, and even armed robbers have plagued retail stores for many years. And the problem has been magnified in recent years with the growth of self-service and the increase in the number of supermarkets and discount houses. A recent report of the Federal Bureau of Investigation reveals that shoplifting is now the nation's fastest growing form of larceny, increasing 93 percent in a five year period.[42] Annual losses for all retailers are now estimated in excess of $2 billion; the Kroger Company alone has annual shoplifting losses of more than $8 million.[43] Among department stores with sales of from $10 to $20 million in 1965 the stock-shortage figure was 1.4 percent of sales and among departmentized specialty stores with annual sales of from $1 million to $5 million during the same year the figure was 1.0 percent.[44] It is not possible to determine what proportions of these shortages are caused by thefts.

To minimize stock shortages resulting from dishonesty, retailers take many steps. Burglar alarm systems and regular police protection are important against the professional burglar. The careful selection, training, and constant supervision of employees is another essential aspect of an antishortage program. Shoplifting is fought by the use of human "spotters" and

---

[40] Cf. S. D. Astor, "The Positive Approach to Shortage Control," *Stores,* September, 1965, pp. 58–59. Also cf. his "The Inventory Shortage Enigma of the Discount Industry," *Journal of Retailing,* Vol. XL, No. 2 (Summer, 1964), pp. 31–42. On the buyer's responsibility for controlling shortages cf. W. E. Miller, "The Buyer and Inventory Shortages," *The Buyer's Manual, op. cit.,* pp. 248–55.

[41] Cf. "Eye-Popping Shortages Grow as Insiders Rob Stores Blind," *Women's Wear Daily,* March 16, 1966, pp. 1, 23. The situation in ten major cities is reviewed. Also cf. "Pilferage, a View from the Top," *Progressive Grocer,* January, 1966, pp. 117–19. This article summarizes the techniques employed to curb losses in 12,000 supermarkets in 34 states.

[42] "FBI Notes Increase of 93% in Shoplifting," *New York Times,* December 2, 1965, p. 37. Also cf. "Store Security," *Chain Store Age* (Executives Ed.), February, 1966, pp. 60–62; and the discussion of fraud detection in P. M. Comerford, "Fraud," *Retail Control,* October, 1965, pp. 26–40.

[43] "Larceny in Everyday Life," *Time,* September 9, 1966, p. 26; and "Policing the Grocery Store," *ibid.,* September 16, 1966, p. 111.

[44] Sam Flanel, *Financial and Operating Results of Department and Specialty Stores in 1965* (New York: National Retail Merchants Association, Controllers' Congress, 1966), pp. 31, 59.

television "eyes" throughout the store, and the training of employees to recognize the characteristics of the typical shoplifter—the customer who (1) hangs around without buying, (2) carries a shopping bag, (3) has a large purse, and (4) wears a topcoat in mild weather. In many cities, retailers exchange information on shoplifters, thus aiding each other to detect them.

Municipal and state laws designed to afford better protection to the retailer who brings about the arrest of the shoplifter are also encouraged by retailer groups. Such laws are necessary since, without them, the retailer who apprehends a shoplifter runs the risk of being sued for false arrest or false imprisonment. The Florida law, for example, minimizes this danger for the retailer by allowing him to take a suspect into custody for a "reasonable length of time" in an attempt to recover the goods. Even though the merchant has made a mistake, he cannot be sued successfully if he can satisfy a court that he had a "probable cause" for acting as he did. At least seven states now have such laws—Arizona, Pennsylvania, West Virginia, Ohio, Illinois, Florida, and Kentucky. Moreover, the courts are gradually taking a more serious view of shoplifting. In California a district court of appeals has held, in effect, that a retailer no longer needs delay detention until after the shoplifter leaves the store: if he carries the merchandise through a check-out stand without paying, the retailer may take action to recover the goods without risking a suit for false arrest.

Errors as Cause of Shortages

The honest mistakes which cause stock shortages are almost legion: errors in marking, in inventory taking, in handling returns, in delivering the wrong merchandise, in billing credit customers, in making change for cash customers, and in recording markdowns. While the selection, training, and supervision of employees will minimize these errors, they will not eliminate them—any more than stock shortages caused by dishonesty can be eliminated. As a result, even after taking all reasonable steps, stock shortages will exist; so the retailer needs to give continuous attention to this problem.[45]

REVIEW AND DISCUSSION QUESTIONS

1. Without reference to the textbook, formulate what you consider to be a satisfactory definition of "merchandise management." Account for its growing importance.

---

[45] Cf. Marvin Adler, "Inventory Shortage . . . New Ways to Control It," *Retail Control,* December, 1965, pp. 45–65.

2. Despite the growth of mechanization in control operations, merchandise management methods and devices are an aid to judgment and not a substitute for it. Discuss.

3. Define "dollar control" and explain briefly the major forms which such control may take.

4. How do you account for the growth of "classification merchandising?"

5. Summarize the essential differences between dollar control and unit control of merchandise.

6. Prepare an outline of the steps you would follow if you were charged with the responsibility of instituting departmental dollar control in a supermarket.

7. As manager of a large store selling women's clothing, you are interested in instituting a unit-control system. Explain in detail the specific kind of system you would want and the procedure you would follow in adopting it.

8. Assume you were asked to speak for 10 minutes before your Retailing Class on the topic "Electronic Data Processing and Merchandise Management." What points would you cover and why?

9. Discuss the value of the physical inventory as an aid in merchandise management.

10. Calculate the rate of stockturn based on the following figures: beginning inventory at cost $20,400, ending inventory at cost $16,200, and cost of merchandise sold $64,050.

11. Upon the basis of the evidence presented in the textbook, what useful generalizations can you formulate concerning the relationship between stock turnover and net profit?

12. Distinguish between the terms "stock turnover" and "stock-sales ratio." In your judgment, why are not stock-sales ratios used more widely as a merchandise-control device as compared to rates of stockturn?

13. Explain the term "stock shortage," outline the chief causes of such shortages, and suggest ways by which these shortages may be reduced.

14. Visit your local library and examine operating and merchandising results of department and specialty stores during the past five years to determine the changes in stock shortages during this period. Summarize your findings and comment on their significance.

15. Visit a few leading retailers in your community and ascertain the extent to which they have adopted EDP. Also report on their opinions regarding the advantages and disadvantages of EDP.

SUPPLEMENTARY READINGS

BARBER, HAROLD, AND HELFANT, SEYMOUR. *Retail Merchandising and Management With Electronic Data Processing* (New York: National Retail Merchants Association, 1965). This manual, covering the steps in a storewide system, describes and illustrates coding systems, merchandise classification breakdowns, and required reports. It is "must reading" for retailers interested in EDP.

CAMERON, M. G. *The Booster and the Snitch: Department Store Shoplifting.* (New York: The Macmillan Company, 1964). Based on the 10-year experience of a large department store, this volume covers the activities of the two major groups of shoplifters (1) the professionals (boosters), and (2) the pilferers (snitches).

"Data Processing in U.S. Retailing," *Retail Business,* November, 1965, pp. 37–43. The rapid increase in the use of EDP systems to provide merchandise data and the benefits that have resulted are detailed in this material.

Department Store Economist. "The Surge in Data Processing." November, 1965, pp. 27–34. A special report on the 7th annual EDP Conference of the Retail Research Institute, this article summarizes the latest developments in the use of equipment and methods.

HARLING, E. L. *Merchandise Control and Budgeting* (New York: National Retail Merchants Association, 1965). An updated revision of *Dollar and Unit Merchandising Planning and Budgeting,* the author discusses when and how to buy and shows how to figure open-to-buy.

JUDELLE, BEATRICE. "Classification Merchandising in the Fashion Departments," *Stores,* September 25, 1965, pp. 13–26. In this depth study of department stores, the use and benefits of classification merchandising are reviewed.

KAYLIN, S. O. "Distribution Centers," *Chain Store Age* (Executives Edition), October, 1965, pp. E15–E25. In a "Special Report on Automation and Data Processing Systems the Chains Use to Cut Costs, Shrink Inventory, and Control Outs," the author has assembled data on all aspects of the problem. Also cf. "From Warehouse to Stores: Simplified Merchandise Control [at S. S. Kresge's]," *ibid.,* December, 1965, pp. 22 ff.

MCGUIRE, J. E. *The Computer—Its Present and Future Impact on Retail Executives.* (Rochester, N.Y.: School of Retailing, Rochester Institute of Technology, 1965). A brief report on a student research study designed to assess the impact of computer technology on managerial personnel, this publication is well worth reading.

NATIONAL RETAIL MERCHANTS ASSOCIATION. *The Buyer's Manual* (4th ed., New York, 1965). Written by 43 experienced retailers, this fourth edition of a widely used book includes 5 new chapters on current problems and careful updating of the other 38. Chapters XIV through XVII are particularly pertinent to the discussion in this chapter: THOMPSON, C. S., "The Dollar Merchandise Plan," pp. 134–49; HARLING, E. L., "The Theory of Merchandise Control," pp. 150–63; MEYER, J. S., "The Mathematics of Merchandise Control," pp. 164–80; and BURNSIDE, FRANK, "Merchandising by Classification," pp. 181–92.

———. *Profitable Fashion Merchandise Coordination* (New York, 1965). Discussing the successful coordination of merchandising and promoting fashion goods, this revised treatment has added a chapter on home furnishings.

———; CONTROLLERS' CONGRESS. *Inventory Taking Manual* and *Stock Control Manual* (New York, 1965). These two publications are of particular interest in connection with this chapter.

———. *Retail Control.* Published monthly September through June by the

Controllers' Congress of the Association, this journal contains numerous pertinent articles in connection with the discussion in this chapter as follows: TOLLE, EMERSON, "Inventory Management," pp. 92–134, and WEINER, I. J., "Introduction to EDP," pp. 36–64, October, 1965; POND, DEWEY, "EDP— How to Get Started," pp. 3–28 and GARBER, H. S., and LENNOX, J. E., "Small Store EDP Course—Applications," pp. 161–88, November, 1965; WATERBURY, E. S., "Gathering Classification Data by Mechanical and Manual Systems," pp. 15–21, February, 1966; and GOTLINGER, JOHN, "Merchandise Management," pp. 20–27, May, 1966.

"Programmed Merchandising—The New Way to Work with Key Resources," *Chain Store Age* (Executives Edition), October, 1965, pp. 16–17; and "How Stores Benefit from Programmed Merchandising," January, 1966, pp. 30–33. In these two articles a new technique in merchandise management is discussed.

SALKIN, E. L. "Linear Programming for Merchandise Decisions," *Journal of Retailing,* Vol. XL, No. 4 (Winter, 1964–65), pp. 37–41 ff. In this short treatment the author uses a hypothetical case to illustrate a scientific approach to decision making.

SHERMAN, K. N. *Inventory Control* (Washington, D.C.: Small Business Administration, 1964). In this 12 page booklet sources related to inventory control systems are listed.

WEISS, E. B. "The Future of Electronics in Coordinated Inventory Management," *Advertising Age,* May 2, 1966, p. 92. Emphasizing the high cost of distribution, Mr. Weiss foresees electronic mutual assistance between the distributing trades and manufacturers.

WINGATE, J. W.; SCHALLER, E. O.; AND GOLDENTHAL, IRVING. *Problems in Retail Merchandising,* (5th ed.; Englewood Cliffs, N.J.: Prentice-Hall, Inc., 1961). Aid in connection with the current chapter will be found in the discussion of "How to Take Inventory," pp. 99–103; "How to Measure Stock-Turn," pp. 142–53; and "How to Increase Stock-Turn," pp. 154–62.

14

CHAPTER

Merchandise Management through the Budget

In the previous chapter the general purposes of merchandise management and control were emphasized and the methods employed to accomplish these objectives were discussed. In this chapter we consider the merchandise budget, the most comprehensive device available to the retailer for effectuating dollar control over his merchandise.

MERCHANDISE BUDGETING: MEANING AND OBJECTIVES

Broadly speaking, a merchandise budget or plan is a forecast of specified merchandise activities for a definite period of time. It usually involves setting down on paper the desired results (plan) for a specific period and the appropriate methods by which these results will be accomplished. Although variations exist among stores with respect to the factors included in the merchandise budget, the essential elements are sales; stocks; reductions, including markdowns, employee and other discounts, and stock shortages; purchases; and gross margin. Other elements often included, however, are stock turnover, total and direct expense, net profit or controllable net profit, merchandise returns by customers, number of transactions, and average sales.

Purposes of Merchandise Budgeting

The fundamental purpose of a merchandise budget is to provide a clear-cut plan of merchandising operations for a specific period of time based upon careful study of existing needs and foreseeable conditions. Individuals

399

or firms contemplating the expenditure of several thousand dollars for the construction or renovation of a building would never think of going ahead without drafting definite plans, reviewing these plans carefully, and then abiding by them. Today, however, in many small stores and in a few large ones, investments of substantial amounts are made in merchandise without any definite plans and with little judgment being exercised. Proprietors of such stores are proceeding in the dark, not knowing what to expect or what lies ahead of them. Often the result is the accumulation of heavy merchandise inventories which bear no relationship to sales and which must eventually be cleared through large markdowns.

The merchandise budget provides both a definite course of future action and a yardstick for evaluating current performance. It enables the retailer to obtain sales by timely buying of merchandise, to adjust his inventories to meet sales requirements, and to plan promotional efforts more effectively. It also provides information through which management may check the effectiveness of merchandise executives and buyers in performing their duties. Without such a standard of measurement, for example, a buyer might be congratulated for showing a small increase in sales over last year when, in view of the facts of the situation, he should have turned in a larger increase. The merchandise budget also makes it easier to place authority and to fix responsibility for performance; and it helps to coordinate all of the departments of the store into a profit-making entity. Moreover, it assists the chief financial officer in planning the funds needed for the purchase of merchandise.

Still another purpose served by the budget is the provision of a cumulative record of past results, both planned and actual. Such a record is essential to the retailer in judging the accuracy of past estimates and in improving his future estimates. The budget also develops a "planning consciousness" and a realization on the part of buyers of the need for facts rather than guesswork and hunches in buying and selling activities. As a matter of fact, even the drawing-up of a budget has significance: many retail executives believe that the planning involved is more valuable to them than the formal budget itself.

Essentials of a Good Merchandise Budget

To accomplish its purposes, a merchandise budget (1) should be planned some weeks in advance of its effective date; (2) should be as simple as possible and still include the elements that are considered necessary to successful merchandising operations; (3) should represent the combined judgment of those whose activities influence the success of the budget; (4)

should cover a period not longer than that for which reliable estimates may be made; and (5) should be flexible enough to permit necessary adjustments.

Most of the foregoing requisites of a good merchandise budget are self-evident and require little further explanation. It is clear, for example, that in the large organization—since the budget will be much more complex than in the small store—advanced, careful planning is essential. Such planning involves a review of past years' experience, a reconsideration of the elements to be included, and the inclusion of new factors influencing future results. All these steps are designed to improve the accuracy of forecasts; and the more closely the plans approximate actual results, the more valuable are the budgeted figures.

In the small store where the owner is closely associated with all operations, relatively few elements need to be included in the budget.[1] It is perhaps enough to plan his sales, stocks, reductions, purchases, and gross margin; and this much can be done by reviewing past records, examining stock periodically, and by estimating future needs. As the store grows in size, however, and the owner becomes further removed from the details of his business, it will be increasingly difficult for him to make future plans on such a simple basis as that used in the small store.[2] A system must be established to provide him with a flow of information and additional aspects of his business must be included in his budget. Although details of the budget may vary, no store is too large or too small to plan its future operations.

A workable merchandise budget requires that, in the preparation of estimates, proper weight be given to the opinions of various individuals whose activities influence the success of the plan. This step makes it easier to obtain each executive's cooperation in securing the results set forth therein. Consequently, after the buyers, store managers, and other have submitted their estimates, but before the plan becomes effective, the budget should be reviewed by such executives as the merchandise manager and the controller. These individuals will usually suggest revisions to improve the reliability of the estimates. Thus, the final figures represent the composite judgment of a number of persons.

It is clear that the longer the period covered by the budget the more difficult it is to make dependable estimates. Although the usual period covered by the budget is one season of six months, in practice this period

---

[1] Cf. Figs. 14–1, 14–2, and 14–3, below.

[2] For a specific illustration of this point cf. the Wayman Department Store cases (A and B) in C. H. McGregor, *Retail Management Problems* (3rd ed.; Homewood, Ill.: Richard D. Irwin, Inc., 1962), pp. 138–44.

often is broken down into monthly, semimonthly, or even ten-day or weekly periods. Some stores make preliminary estimates one year in advance and revise them from month to month. Final budget figures should represent reasonable expectations in the light of prevailing conditions and other facts known at the time.

A merchandise budget should be sufficiently flexible to permit adjustments, but it should not merely represent a rough estimate of what might be expected. Whenever prepared, it should represent the closest possible calculations based on available data. But despite extreme care, all possible contingencies cannot be foreseen; and it is inevitable that actual results will show deviations from those planned. When these occur, revisions should be made promptly; to neglect such action will serve to decrease the value of the budgeted figures.

Form of the Merchandise Budget

The form of the merchandise budget in a retail store depends upon such factors as the purposes for which the information is to be used, the kinds and amounts of data included, the period or periods covered, and the preferences of those collecting and using the information. Although there are numerous forms of the merchandise budget, for retailers of fairly comparable operations the forms differ largely in the manner in which the data are presented rather than in the information itself.

Some trade associations in the retail field have encouraged the use of standardized forms by their memberships. Figures 14–1, 14–2, and 14–3 show the profit-planning sheet and the business control form recommended by the National Retail Hardware Association and used by its members for several years. It will be noted that the profit-planning sheet explains the various steps involved in the budget, and the business control form emphasizes planned and actual figures, monthly and cumulatively, for the period covered but does not show the past year's figures. This information, however, may be obtained easily from the comparable form for the previous year.[3] More elaborate forms used in a department store are shown later in this chapter. As emphasized previously, the best form for any store to use is that which provides the desired information in a manner suitable for use, in as simple a form as possible, and for the period or periods required.

---

[3] In most budgets, it is customary to include the previous year's figures in addition to planned figures for the budgeted period.

Profit Planning Sheet
For Business Control
Devised by
THE NATIONAL RETAIL HARDWARE ASSOCIATION

Firm_____

Address_____

FIRST STEP: Plan expense for this year.

Enter actual expense for last year in each classification. If classifications do not agree with yours, change to agree with your records. In no case include shop labor and freight with expense. Then enter planned expense for this year.

	(Use nearest dollar figures)			(Use nearest dollar figures)	
Expense Item	Actual Last Year	Planned This Year	Expense Item	Actual Last Year	Planned This Year
A Salaries, Owner			M Depreciation, Delivery Equipm't		
B Salaries, Clerks			N Depreciation, Furniture and Fixtures		
C Salaries, Office			O Depreciation, Building		
D Office Supplies and Postage			P Rent		
E Advertising			Q Repairs		
F Donations			R Heat, Light and Water		
G Store Supplies			S Insurance		
H Telephone and Telegraph			T Taxes		
I Losses, Notes & Accounts			U Interest on Borrowed Money		
K Salaries, Delivery			V Association and Other Dues		
L Other Delivery Expense			X Unclassified		
			Y Total Actual Expense Last Year and Planned This Year		

SECOND STEP: Plan margin for this year.

Determine percentage of margin for the past five years by filling in columns below.

(Use nearest dollar figures)

	19 —	19 —	19 —	19 —	19 —
1. Enter year for which figures are given.					
2. Enter under each year the amount of merchandise inventory at beginning of that year.					
3. Enter total amount of merchandise purchased each year. Include shop labor and freight.					
4. Add amounts on lines 2 and 3.					
5. Enter amount of merchandise inventory at end of each year.					
6. Subtract amounts on line 5 from those on line 4 giving cost of goods sold during year.					
7. Enter total net sales for each year Merchandise returned by customers should be deducted first.					
8. Enter cost of goods sold from line 6, same column.					
9. Subtract amounts on line 8 from those on line 7. The result is the margin.					
10. Divide amounts on line 9 by those on line 7. The result is percentage of margin on sales.	%	%	%	%	%

11. Planned margin that can reasonably be expected, based on experience as shown on line 10.................................%

THIRD STEP: Find sales required to pay expenses and leave 5% for profit.

12. Deduct 5% for profit from planned margin (line 11)_____% which leaves percentage available for expense of _____%

13. Expense_____% (line 12) equals planned expense of $_____ (Line Y, planned column)

14. 1% equals $_____ 100% will then be the amount of sales necessary ....$_____

Example: If expense is 20% of the planned sales and amounts to $10,000, 1% will be 1/20 of $10,000 or $500. 100% will equal 100 times $500 or $50,000, amount of sales.

Courtesy: National Retail Hardware Association

FIG. 14–1. Profit-planning sheet for business control.

FOURTH STEP: Plan monthly sales.

In the first three columns below enter net sales by months for the past three years.

In Column A, add the sales for each month for the three years. Thus line 15, Column A will be the total of January sales for three years Line 27, Column A, will be the sum of the total sales for three years.

In Column B, enter the percentage of total sales usually obtained in each month. To find, divide total sales for each month, Column A, by the sum of the total sales for three years, line 27, Column A.

Column A. Thus, if total sales for three years are $150,000 and total sales for three Januaries, $7,500, the probable sales for January will be 7,500 ÷ 150,000 or 5%.

In Column C, enter the planned sales for each month. First, enter in Column C, line 27, the planned sales for the year from line 14 in Third Step Then multiply the planned sales for the year by the percentages in Column B. Enter result in Column C. Thus, if planned sales are $50,000 and it is found in Column B that 5% of the yearly sales result in January the planned sales for January will be $50,000 multiplied by .05 or $2,500.

(Use nearest dollar figures.)

	19 __	19 __	19 __	Column A Total of Months	Column B Mthly. Pctgs.	Column C Planned Sales	
15. January					%		January
16. February					%		February
17. March					%		March
18. April					%		April
19. May					%		May
20. June					%		June
21. July					%		July
22. August					%		August
23. September					%		September
24. October					%		October
25. November					%		November
26. December					%		December
27. Total					100 0 %		Total

FIFTH STEP: Determine the amount of purchases required to leave a desired investment in merchandise inventory at end of the year. Follow instructions below.

(Use nearest dollar)

28. Enter planned sales for this year (line 14, Third Step)	
29. Enter planned margin (planned sales as above, multiplied by per cent. of margin, line 11, Second Step)	
30. Deduct amount on line 29 from that on line 28. The result is the approximate cost of goods sold	
31 Enter amount of merchandise inventory desired at end of this year	
32. Add amounts on line 30 and 31	
33. Enter actual inventory at beginning of this year	
34. Deduct amount on line 33 from that on line 32. The result is planned purchases for this year	

SIXTH STEP: Plan monthly purchases. (Follow similar procedure as in Fourth Step.)

In the first three columns below enter net purchases by months for the past three years The amounts should include freight paid, also shop labor Merchandise returned to wholesalers or manufacturers and credited by them during a given month should be deducted from purchases for the month.

In Column D, add the purchases for each month for the three years.

In Column E, enter the percentage of total purchases usually

obtained in each month To find, divide total purchases for each month Column D, by the sum of the total purchases for three years, line 47, Column D.

In Column F, enter the planned purchases for each month. First, enter in Column F, line 47, the planned purchases for the year from line 34, Fifth Step. Then multiply the planned purchases for the year by the percentages in Column E. Enter result in Column F.

(Use nearest dollar figures)

	19 __	19 __	19 __	Column D Total of Months	Column E Mthly. Pctgs.	Column F Pl. Purchases	
35. January					%		January
36. February					%		February
37. March					%		March
38. April					%		April
39. May					%		May
40. June					%		June
41. July					%		July
42. August					%		August
43. September					%		September
44. October					%		October
45. November					%		November
46. December					%		December
47. Total					100 0 %		Total

FIG. 14–2. Profit-planning sheet, reverse side.

BUSINESS CONTROL FORM

Beginning Inventory $_____   Estimated Margin _____%

19	SALES Planned A Monthly	B Cumulative	SALES Actual C Monthly	D Cumulative	EXPENSE Planned E Monthly	F Cumulative	EXPENSE Actual G Monthly	H Cumulative	Percent of Sales (Cumulative Figures) I Estimated	J Actual	PURCHASES Planned K Monthly	L Cumulative	PURCHASES Actual M Monthly	N Cumulative	Percent of Sales (Cumulative Figures) O Estimated	P Actual	ESTIMATED Book Inventory Q	Profit or Loss R	LINE NO.
January																			1
February																			2
March																			3
April																			4
May																			5
June																			6
July																			7
August																			8
September																			9
October																			10
November																			11
December																			12

FIG. 14-3. Business control form.

BASIC STEPS IN MERCHANDISE BUDGETING[4]

Planned Sales

In most large stores the first step in setting up a merchandise budget is to plan sales rather than expenses as recommended by the National Retail Hardware Association (Fig. 14–1). This planning is done either in units by price lines or in dollars for the period of time involved. Either approach, of course, is dependent on the availability of relevant information. Forecasting sales by units and translating these into total sales figures for the department or store, for instance, is impossible wthout records upon which to base estimates and to obtain the final results. Similarly, sales in dollars cannot be estimated without reliable data of the following kinds: (1) long-term trend of sales reflecting the normal rate of growth of the business; (2) conditions outside the particular business which affects its sales volume; and (3) conditions within the particular business which influence future sales. Planning sales in dollars rather than units is almost universally practiced.

Long-Term Trend of Sales. The past experience of the store or department is of special importance in planning sales. Sales by months for several years should be listed and trends noted. Has there been a steady and regular growth in sales volume, or is the sales record characterized by variations upward and downward? If variations have taken place, the reasons for them should be considered carefully. After past results have been examined, conditions affecting future sales possibilities should be investigated.

Outside Conditions. Among the major conditions outside the business which influence the planned sales volume are the following:

1. The general business conditions expected during the coming period in the country as a whole and in the particular area where the store is located. Although such conditions usually cannot be forecast accurately, considerable information from a variety of sources is now available to the retailer which makes his estimates more reliable than formerly. Not only does the retailer have access to the opinions of qualified forecasting experts through various economic services to which he may subscribe, but an increasing number of large stores are employing their own economic advisers.[5] To supplement his own judgment, the retailer will find invaluable the data provided by his trade association, the Census Bureau, and many others.

2. The trend of population in the trading area in which the store is located.

---

[4] As a general background to a detailed examination of merchandise budgeting cf. Morey Sostrin, "Merchandising to a Profit," *The Buyer's Manual* (4th ed.; New York: National Retail Merchants Association, 1965), pp. 281–89.

[5] For an illustration of factors considered by economists in their forecasts, cf. "Take Aim at Lower Sales Target in 1966, Stores Told," *Women's Wear Daily,* January 3, 1966, p. 2. Also cf "5% Rise in Retail Sales, GNP Looms in '66 Crystal Ball," *ibid.,* October 18, 1965, p. 2.

Important shifts in trading areas are constantly taking place; the retailer should recognize these changes and make whatever adjustments in his figures seem necessary.

3. Changes in the purchasing power of the store's customers and prospective customers caused by shifts in business activity in the particular trading area.

4. Differences in the competitive situation. Changes of this nature may result from the addition of new stores, through the modernization of existing ones, or through changes in sales promotional activity.

5. Evidence of broad fashion movements which affect merchandise of the type handled by the store. Recent emphasis on teen-age fashions, for example, should be evaluated in the light of the store's policies and practices.

Inside Conditions. Analysis of present conditions within the store, and those likely to prevail in the foreseeable future as compared with previous years are vital considerations in any sales forecast. Examples of such conditions are the following:

1. Possible revisions of promotional and credit policies. To illustrate: it might be decided to increase or decrease advertising expenditures; trading stamps might be adopted to attract customers; or credit policies liberalized.

2. Shifts made in the location or amount of space occupied by a particular department.

3. Changes or contemplated changes in the arrangement or physical facilities of a department, such as the consolidation or further division of existing departments.

4. Addition of new merchandise lines. One of the reasons for the continued increase in food store sales during the past several years is attributable to this factor.

5. Possible expansion of parking facilities for customers.

6. Change in store hours, particularly night and Sunday openings.

7. Opening of new stores and branches, or the modernization of existing ones, together with the estimated effect of these developments on the "parent" store or other company stores operated in the area.[6]

Beating Last Year's Figures. It should now be clear that estimating future sales requires considerable judgment. Yet many retailers take the easy way out and set their goal as that of "beating last year's figures." Unfortunately, the solution as to "what lies ahead" for the sales of any retailer is not this simple. For some lines of merchandise and perhaps for some entire departments, consumer demand may be on an uptrend; but for others, demand may be leveling off or actually in the declining stage.[7] As an illustration of such divergent trends, there is ample evidence that a "new

---

[6] Modernization of its 17-year-old Flatbush unit by R. H. Macy & Company at a cost of $1 million was expected to increase the store's sales by 35 to 40 percent. "Macy's Flatbush Uplift Elevates Sales Sights 40%," *Women's Wear Daily*, November 24, 1965, p. 39.

[7] Cf. 1963 *Census of Business, Retail Trade, Merchandise Line Sales, United States Summary*, Advance Report BC 63 (A)–RS7A (Washington, D.C.: U.S. Department of Commerce, July, 1965).

customer" is developing—one with wants quite different from the customer of twenty years ago—who is interested in better quality merchandise and whose desire for a higher standard of living even exceeds the rapid growth in his personal income during recent years.[8] And the "old-age" and "teen-age" markets mentioned in Chapter 1 are creating opportunities for retailers not anticipated a decade or more ago.

Every retailer, regardless of size, should analyze his sales outlook by his major lines of merchandise. As the late Kenneth Collins wrote, he must "roll with the punch . . . give up volume one place while making it up in another . . . [If he always tried] to beat last year's figures every place, . . . [he might] wind up beating them no place."[9]

Monthly Sales Estimates. When sales for the budget period have been estimated, the next step is to break down this figure by months or some other short period. This step requires an analysis of past experience, weather conditions, seasonal variation, the number of selling days in each month, the special sales events planned for each month, and the dates of such important holidays as Easter.[10] Even so, certain developments may occur that are impossible to forecast and necessitate revisions in estimates. Newspaper strikes in such cities as Detroit, Pittsburgh, and New York City are illustrative of such happenings.[11]

Sales Forecasts for New Stores. Most of the factors enumerated do not apply to new stores but rather to established ones. When new stores are contemplated, no past-sales records are available to serve as a guide. It is advisable, therefore, to review the sales volume of other comparable stores or departments in similar locations. It is desirable, also, for the prospective store proprietor to visit other stores, to observe the amount of customer traffic, to talk with as many of his potential competitors and his retailer friends as possible, and attempt to judge by all suitable means what his sales volume will be. Despite the care exercised, the retailer may find that his sales estimates for new stores are subject to a substantial margin of error.[12]

---

[8] Cf. William Royce and John Baumeister, *Home Furnishings Trends to 1975* (Chicago: National Retail Furniture Association, 1965).

[9] "Today and Yesterday in Retailing," *Women's Wear Daily,* April 19, 1957, p. 8.

[10] Some stores also forecast sales in terms of number of transactions, particularly during periods of price stabilization following periods of price increases. Through studying the trend in the number of transactions, an estimate may be made of the forthcoming period. The same is true of the average sale. By multiplying the two figures, the total sales figure for the budget period may be determined.

[11] The sales effects of the 134-day Detroit newspaper strike on the various cities within the Detroit Metropolitan Area are discussed in Rikuma Ito, "Effects of a Newspaper Strike on Retail Sales," *Journal of Marketing,* Vol. XXX, No. 3 (July, 1966), pp. 54–58.

[12] Among supermarkets opened in 1965, approximately 42 percent experienced sales above those estimated and 50 percent below. Only 8 percent obtained approximately the sales anticipated. Cf. *Facts About New Super Markets Opened in 1965* (Chicago: Super

Planned Stock

The second important step in merchandise budgeting is planning stock to meet expected sales. In this planning, the objective is the same as we have emphasized previously—to maintain a balanced inventory in relation to anticipated sales. To accomplish this objective successfully, the retailer should (1) maintain an assortment of sufficient length and breadth to satisfy the needs of his customers,[13] (2) adjust his inventory to conform to the forward movement of the selling season,[14] and (3) keep his inventory investment under such control that his stock turnover is satisfactory from a profit standpoint. Usually, as in the planning of sales, it is advisable to make estimates of the season's requirements and then to break down these estimates into months.

Methods of Planning Stocks. Retailers commonly employ one or more of the four following methods to plan needed stocks:

1. *The Basic Stock Method.* Under this plan the beginning-of-the-month (B.O.M.) stock is determined for any particular month by adding planned sales for the period to the basic stock figure. This computation may be expressed as a formula in terms of retail prices, as follows:

B.O.M. stock = Planned sales for the month + (Average stock at retail − Average monthly sales)

2. *The Percentage Variation (or Deviation) Method.* Here the beginning-of-the-month stock is increased or decreased from the planned average stock by 50 percent of the sales variations from the average monthly sales. Or, in terms of retail prices,

$$\text{B.O.M. stock} = \text{Average stock} \times \tfrac{1}{2}\left(1 + \frac{\text{Sales for the month}}{\text{Average monthly sales}}\right)$$

3. *The Weeks' Supply Method.* When this method is used the planned stock is based upon a predetermined number of weeks' supply as judged by

Market Institute, Inc., 1966), p. 4. How the computer may be used to estimate sales for a new retail development is suggested by D. L. Huff and Larry Blue, in *A Programmed Solution for Estimating Retail Sales Potentials* (Lawrence, Kansas: University of Kansas, 1966).

[13] For the difficulties involved in this task cf. A. R. Dodd, Jr., "Why Do Consumers Want More than Retailers Stock?" *Printer's Ink,* November 26, 1965, pp. 11–12. Also cf. H. B. Wess, "Merchandising Assortment and Items," *The Buyer's Manual, op. cit.,* pp. 240–47.

[14] Cf. "Stores Load Shelves, Brace for Record Yule," *Business Week,* November 6, 1965, pp. 30–31; and William Burston, "Christmas Merchandising," *The Buyer's Manual, op. cit.,* pp. 217–28.

the planned sales for this period. In practice, the planned stock is related specifically to a desired stock turnover.

4. *The Stock-Sales Ratio Method.* In this case the planned sales volume for the month is multiplied by the planned beginning-of-the-month stock-sales ratio to ascertain the planned B.O.M. stock.

Regardless of the method or methods used, it is evident that planning stock involves a decision as to the merchandise that should be on hand at the beginning of the period; that which is to be bought during the period; and that expected to be on hand at the end of the period.

It is important for the retailer to bear in mind that stocks and sales do not necessarily increase or decrease proportionately. As sales increase, for example, stocks may actually decrease, and stock turnover may increase. He should recognize also that some merchandise in which size is important, such as shoes and dresses, have minimum levels below which stock cannot go, regardless of volume. It is also evident that stocks should be adjusted to the forward movement of the selling season; and that the general business outlook, including availability of merchandise and the price trend, needs to be considered.

Planned Reductions

Planning of reductions is a third essential step in merchandise budgeting. Reductions include markdowns, discounts given to employees and certain types of customers such as clergymen, and stock shortages. Since discounts to special customers and to employees usually are included in markdowns, only planned figures for markdowns and stock shortages are shown on most budget forms. These figures, like others on the budget form, are stated in retail prices.

Markdowns.[15] A retailer marks down his merchandise so that at all times his prices will reflect the level at which sales can be made at a satisfactory rate to his customers. In other words, the retailer does not *take* markdowns; rather, the markdown is merely his recognition and recording of something that has happened or in his judgment will take place. Consequently, in practice, markdowns are inevitable and failure to recognize them in the budget is a short-sighted policy. Actually, planning markdowns results in reducing their size and frequency because the buyer is made more conscious of them and is encouraged to take the steps necessary to minimize them.

The effective planning of markdowns required that their causes be deter-

---

[15] Cf. S. L. Solomon, "Markdowns," *The Buyer's Manual, op. cit.,* pp. 256–64, but especially pp. 260–62. As a pricing problem, markdowns are discussed in Chapter 17.

mined and summarized clearly for the benefit of buyers and others concerned with such price reductions in the period ahead. Although the causes of markdowns are numerous, they may be grouped under four main headings: (1) markdowns growing out of preventable causes, or errors in buying caused by failure of the buyer to analyze customer demand adequately and to buy accordingly, such as wrong styles, sizes, or workmanship; (2) markdowns caused by price adjustments outside the buyer's control, such as declining price levels, changes in price lines, and competitors' prices; (3) markdowns attributable to store promotional policies, such as special sales events and multiple pricing, which are also outside the buyer's control; and (4) normal operational markdowns, such as price reductions on soiled and damaged goods, sample cuts and remnants, and breakage, which are practically inevitable in buying and selling merchandise.[16]

In addition to understanding the causes of markdowns in the past, consideration should be given to other factors, both within and without the department, which will probably influence the amount of markdowns in the budget period ahead. Among the more important of these are the sales promotional events planned for the period; the trend in business conditions, with particular attention being given to price trends; the types of merchandise handled and the condition of the stock at the beginning of the period; the markdowns taken by comparable stores, as revealed by published figures; and contemplated changes in policies and in the personnel of the department.

Stock Shortages. Like markdowns, stock shortages—the unaccounted-for disappearance of merchandise at retail prices—are inevitable in retail stores despite all the efforts made to prevent them. Consequently, they should be included in the merchandise budget.

In planning the stock-shortage figure, which is commonly done on a percentage-of-sales basis, particular attention should be given to the past experience of the store or department and that of similar stores or departments of such stores.[17] Wide variations exist among stores of different types and departments selling different merchandise. To illustrate: discount houses will have larger shortages than jewelry stores and costume jewelry sections of department stores will have smaller ones than those in self-service variety stores. Contemplated changes in price-change procedure, in checking incoming and outgoing merchandise, in the personnel of the department, and

---

[16] On the causes of markdowns cf. Chapter 17.

[17] The stock shortages experienced by department and specialty stores are shown in the annual reports on merchandising and operating results published by the Controllers' Congress, National Retail Merchants Association. Also cf. the discussion in Chapter 13, p. 394, above; and that of Marvin Adler in "Inventory Shortages . . . New Tools to Combat It," *Retail Control,* December, 1965, pp. 45–65.

in the frequency of price reductions should also receive study. Moreover, planned "drives" by the management to make employees more "stock-shortage conscious" should be considered. Based on such information, the retailer arrives at a budget figure for his stock shortages. Usually, however, he will place chief reliance on his previous experience.

Planned Purchases

When figures for sales, opening and closing stocks, and reductions have been planned, the planning of purchases in dollars—the fourth major step in merchandise budgeting—becomes merely a mechanical or mathematical operation through the use of certain formulas. Although the calculations are in terms of retail prices, they may readily be converted into cost figures by applying the cost complement of the markup percentage. The formulas in common usage are as follows:

1. Planned purchases = Planned sales + Planned reductions
   + Planned increase in stock, or −
   Planned decrease in stock
2. Planned purchases = Planned stock at end of period +
   Planned sales + Planned reductions
   − Stock at beginning of period

These formulas may be clarified by illustrations:

Formula 1, as applied to the month of September:

Planned sales		$10,000	
Planned reductions		1,000	
Markdowns	$900		
Shortages	100		
Total			$11,000
Stock on hand, September 1		$20,000	
Planned stock, September 30		22,000	
Planned increase in stock			2,000
Planned purchases in dollars			$13,000

Formula 2, also applied to September:

Planned stock, September 30	$22,000	
Planned sales	10,000	
Planned reductions	1,000	
Total		$33,000
Stock on hand, September 1		20,000
Planned purchases in dollars		$13,000

These formulas may be applied to an entire store, a department, a classification, or a price line for the budget period or for any part of the period. Moreover, they are applicable to control in physical units as well as in dollars. But they should not be thought of as automatic in operation; they are useful only when the figures upon which they are based are accurate, timely, and tempered with the buyer's judgment. Improved equipment and

EDP have speeded up the availability of the information required for sound decisions and for prompt revisions in estimates. When such adjustments are made, then the computed purchase figure adequately fulfills its function—as a guide to the buyer's judgment, not a substitute for it.[18]

The Open-to-Buy. "Open-to-buy" may be defined as that amount, either in terms of retail prices or at cost, which a buyer is open to receive into stock during a certain period on the basis of the plans formulated. To illustrate, and using retail prices, let us assume that planned purchases for the month of October are $1,000. Obviously, on October 1, the buyer is open-to-buy $1,000 in merchandise during the month. By October 20, he has spent $700 for merchandise that has arrived or will arrive before the end of the month, leaving $300 for him to spend for goods to be received during the remaining ten days of the month. In other words, he is open-to-buy $300 on October 20. In practice, however, open-to-buy calculations are not so simple.[19] Adjustments in inventories during the budget period, fluctuations in sales volume, markdowns, and goods ordered but not yet received—all serve to complicate the determination of the amount that still may be spent.

As indicated above, open-to-buy figures may also be stated in terms of cost, although it is customary to state them at retail. Cost figures may be obtained by applying the cost complement of the initial markup percentage[20] to the retail figure. For example, if the initial markup is 40 percent on retail, then the open-to-buy figure at cost may be found by multiplying the retail figure by 60 percent (100 percent-40 percent).

In many stores it is customary for buyers to make trips to market to examine offerings of manufacturers and to make purchases of needed merchandise. In preparing for such trips, one of the first things buyers do is to determine how much they are open-to-buy for the remainder of the budget period. It is essential, therefore, that this information be available currently, a need increasingly being fulfilled by automated equipment of various types. The data are incorporated in departmental reports, prepared at weekly or ten-day intervals, which show the amount that still may be purchased as well as other information of interest to the buyer.

[18] The amount and percentage of markup to be placed on goods purchased is an important phase of purchase planning, since the planned stock figures are at retail, whereas the store buyer is faced with cost prices in the wholesale market. Because the initial markup is discussed at some length in the following chapter, further attention is not given to it here.

[19] For an example of the problems in determining the open-to-buy figure for a specific retailer, cf. the Dills & Harms case in C. H. McGregor, *op. cit.,* pp. 150–53.

[20] The initial markup is the difference between the cost of merchandise and the first retail price placed on the goods. The initial markup percentage is obtained by dividing the initial markup by the initial or first retail price and multiplying the result by 100.

As an example, let us review how the open-to-buy figure may be determined for a store or a department of a large store in the middle of a budget period. Assume the following figures for the month of April.

Actual stock, April 1	$37,000
Planned sales for the month	75,000
Planned markdowns and shortages for the month	2,500
Planned stock, April 30	35,000
Planned initial markup	40 percent

Assume further that, during the first half of April, net sales were $28,000; markdowns and shortages, $900; and receipts of goods, $30,000. On April 15, goods on order for April delivery amounted to $20,000 at retail prices. The amount the department is open to buy may be calculated as follows:

Needed Stock		*Available Stock*	
Planned stock, April 30 ....$35,000		Stock on hand at present	
Planned sales for remainder of month		($67,000–$28,900)	$38,100
($75,000–$28,000) 47,000		Actual stock, April 1 .....$37,000	
Planned markdowns and shortages for		Receipts of goods......... 30,000	
remainder of month ($2,500–		Total stock handled......$67,000	
$900) 1,600		Markdowns and shortages	
		to date............. 900	
		Sales to date............ 28,000	
		Total deductions........$28,900	
		Goods on order for April de-	
		livery................	20,000
Total......................$83,600		Total...............	$58,100

Needed stock ($83,600) – Available stock ($58,100) = $25,500 Open-to-buy at retail
Open-to-buy at cost = $25,500 × 0.60 = $15,300

If the available stock exceeded the needed stock, the department would be overbought.[21]

The open-to-buy form used by the retailer does not need to be complicated or elaborate. In fact, simplicity is highly desirable. The best form is one that furnishes the needed information in the most concise manner possible. One store uses the form shown in Figure 14–4.

It is important to remember that the open-to-buy figure is a guide rather than a set amount which cannot be exceeded. In other words, even though a store or department has used the amount set up in the budget for purchases during a given period, this fact does not mean that further purchases are impossible if stock is needed to meet customers' requirements. A department may be overbought, for instance, but still be in urgent need of staple, fast-selling merchandise. To refuse its buyer further funds to make purchases

---

[21] For other explanations of calculating the open-to-buy cf. J. S. Meyer, "Mathematics of Merchandise Control," *The Buyer's Manual, op. cit.,* pp. 167–70.

DEPT.	YOUR SALES LAST YEAR	ESTIMATED SALES SAME PERIOD THIS YEAR	INVENTORY	UNFILLED ORDERS	YOUR INVENTORY AND UNFILLED ORDERS TOTAL ON	IF YOU PURCHASED NOTHING MORE YOUR INVENTORY WOULD BE ON	HOWEVER YOUR INVENTORY SHOULD BE ON	THEREFORE YOU ARE OPEN TO BUY ABOUT	
	FROM___ TO___							RETAIL	COST

FIG. 14-4 A simple open-to-buy form which provides essential information.

Courtesy: Gano-Downs Company, Denver, Colorado

would be increasing the difficulties of the department and of the store.[22] Causes of the overbought condition should be ascertained, however, and measures taken to prevent their recurrence. To condone such a situation without penalizing those responsible for it would be to encourage the repetition of mistakes.

Although small retailers do not collect information of the type described in as great detail or as frequently as large stores, they nevertheless formulate definite buying plans and adhere to them rather closely. Since small operators make fewer trips to market, they must make the best possible use of their time and their finances while there. Therefore, although they may not set up formal purchasing limits, they should have rather definite ideas about such limits before they go to market.

Planned Gross Margin and Operating Profit

Determining gross margin is the fifth essential step in merchandise budgeting. Because net profit is ascertained by deducting expenses from the gross margin, the significance of the latter figure is obvious. The selling price, of course, may or may not be the price at which the goods are originally offered for sale to the public. In other words, the gross margin is the initial markup adjusted for price changes, stock shortages, and discounts to employees.[23]

It is evident from the preceding statements that, once the initial markup and retail reductions have been planned, the planned gross margin may be computed by the following formula:

$$\text{Gross margin} = [\text{Initial markup} \times (100 \text{ percent} + \text{Retail reductions})] - \text{Retail reductions}$$

In practice, however, the gross margin is often determined from a table, which indicates gross margin percentage figures for initial markup, cash discounts, and retail reductions of various sizes.[24]

During recent years, many retailers have found themselves faced with a rising expense ratio so that it has been necessary to plan for a higher gross margin to protect their net profit. But it has been difficult to accomplish this

---

[22] States one retailer: "To give buyers the greatest chance to do their best job . . . put the Open-to-Buy where the demand lies by recognizing that the traditional retail dollar Open-to-Buy by department often works to squelch action on the known factors of current interest. Free money for new adventures in merchandise by giving the buyers up-to-date tools for the efficient management of inventory." George Baylis, "Are the Brakes Too Tight to Let the Train Roll?" *Retail Control,* October, 1965, p. 25.

[23] Cf. the discussion of the relationship between initial markup and gross margin in Chapter 16.

[24] In the formula given, gross margin and maintained markup are considered to be the same. When cash discounts received by the retailer and alteration costs are considered, the former is added and the latter subtracted from the result to obtain a true gross margin.

objective. As a result, some types of retailers have experienced a "profit squeeze"; that is, while their sales have increased, they have found it impossible to improve gross margin sufficiently to offset the advance in expenses. Among supermarkets, for example, between 1960 and 1965 gross margin increased from 21.62 percent to 22.48 percent but the rise in operating expenses reduced net operating profit from 1.38 percent to 1.20 percent during this period.[25] In contrast, some retailers have achieved either higher gross margins or kept their expenses sufficiently under control to increase their profit ratios.[26]

Whether competitive factors in retailing will allow still higher markups is for the future to determine. In the meantime, the basic problem as related to budgeting remains—how best to forecast an attainable gross margin figure that will yield, after the deduction of expenses, a satisfactory and reasonable net profit. As in the case of stock shortages and other budgeted figures, the retailer has as guides his previous experience and that of comparable stores and departments. He should make certain that he uses all the pertinent information that is available so that his planning efforts may be worthwhile.

MERCHANDISE BUDGETING PROCEDURE

The elements that are involved and the care that should be exercised in setting up a merchandise budget have been emphasized. Only casual mention has been made, however, of the actual steps required in the formation of the budget. Moreover, little attention has been given to the constant follow-up which is necessary to determine if the plans are adequate and if revisions are advisable in the light of developments that have taken place. A brief description of the budgetary procedure in a department store will illustrate the steps leading to the formation of the budget and show how the budget is used as an operating tool. But again it should be emphasized that the procedure followed, the information assembled, and the timing and use of the data should be adopted to the particular needs of the firm.

Initial Planning of Merchandise Budget

About three months in advance of the date on which the merchandise budget is to become effective, a preliminary six-month merchandise budget

---

[25] "33rd Annual Report of the Grocery Industry," *Progressive Grocer,* April, 1966, p. 70.

[26] R. J. Robichaud, "Retail Profit Rise—What Does It Mean?" *Journal of Retailing,* Vol. XLII, No. 3 (Fall, 1966), pp. 52–67. Also cf. Sam Flanel, *Financial and Operating Results of Department and Specialty Stores in 1965* (New York: National Retail Merchants Association, Controllers' Congress, 1966).

DEPT. NO.																					
NAME																					
SPRING 19____																					
FALL 19____																					

CLASSIFICATION	TOTAL SALES FOR THE SEASON			FEBRUARY–AUGUST			MARCH–SEPTEMBER			APRIL–OCTOBER			MAY–NOVEMBER			JUNE–DECEMBER			JULY–JANUARY		
				PLAN	ACTUAL		PLAN	ACTUAL		PLAN	ACTUAL		PLAN	ACTUAL		PLAN	ACTUAL		PLAN	ACTUAL	
	PLAN	LAST YEAR			THIS YEAR	LAST YEAR		THIS YEAR	LAST YEAR		THIS YEAR	LAST YEAR		THIS YEAR	LAST YEAR		THIS YEAR	LAST YEAR		THIS YEAR	LAST YEAR
			SALES																		
			SALES																		
			TOTAL																		
			STOCK																		
			SALES																		
			SALES																		
			TOTAL																		
			STOCK																		
			SALES																		
			SALES																		
			TOTAL																		
			STOCK																		
			SALES																		
			SALES																		
			TOTAL																		
			STOCK																		
			SALES																		
			SALES																		
			TOTAL																		
			STOCK																		
			SALES																		
			SALES																		
			TOTAL																		
			STOCK																		
			SALES																		
			SALES																		
			TOTAL																		
			STOCK																		
			SALES																		
			SALES																		
			TOTAL																		
			STOCK																		
			SALES																		
			SALES																		
			TOTAL																		
			STOCK																		
			SALES																		
			SALES																		
			TOTAL																		
			STOCK																		

FORM 257

FIG. 14–5. Preliminary six-months merchandise plan by department and classification. The form may be used for either the spring season beginning in February or the fall season beginning in August.

form for each department by the appropriate classifications[27] and showing the results of the previous year, is prepared in the merchandise manager's office.[28] This form, shown in Figure 14–5, is sent to each buyer for insertion of similar figures for the season being planned. The buyer reviews past experience and, with the assistance of the divisional merchandise manager, makes his estimates on the basis of all available information. These estimates are then discussed with the general merchandise manager, and the buyer and/or the divisional manager is asked to justify them.

In this discussion the estimates are reviewed carefully and comparisons are made with the previous year's operations and, in some cases, with the operations of several past years. Comparisons may also be made against standards previously set up and also against "outside" statistics, such as those issued by the Controllers' Congress of the National Retail Merchants Association, and Fairchild Publications. Considerable care is spent on this review to insure that plans are realistic and all relevant information is considered. Sometimes it is decided that the anticipated sales should be higher or lower than those estimated; that the ending monthly stocks should be "peaked" earlier or later; or that the timing of purchases should be changed. On such occasions, adjustments are made in the figures so that they represent the best judgment of the group.

Monthly Departmental Merchandise Plan

The preparation of a merchandise plan for each sales department is the second step in the store's merchandise budgeting procedure. This plan is mainly a recapitulation of the figures shown on the seasonal plan (Figure 14–5), but it is for the department as a whole rather than by classifications within the department. The specific form used (Figure 14–6) also provides for additional information on deliveries, average stock, rate of stockturn, cash discounts, cumulative markup, and markdowns.

Merchandise Statistics Report

The next stage in merchandise planning involves the development of a merchandise statistics report for each selling department by classifications. This report (Figure 14–7) shows both planned and actual sales for the

---

[27] New developments in systems and equipment are causing changes in classification merchandising. Increasing attention is being given to stock-keeping units (SKU) "for in the not too distant future . . . classification will be inadequate to maintain the competitive requirements of merchandise management." John Gotlinger, "Merchandise Management," *Retail Control,* May, 1966, p. 27.

[28] Retailers using a thirteen-month year often replace the two six-month budgets with three budgets, two covering sixteen weeks each and one covering twenty weeks—the so-called 4-5-4 calendar.

FROM							DEPARTMENT		
TO		**MERCHANDISE PLAN** (ALL FIGURES AT RETAIL)							

		ACTUAL LAST YEAR	PLANNED THIS YEAR	% INC. - DEC.			ACTUAL LAST YEAR	PLANNED THIS YEAR	% INC. - DEC.
SALES						DELIVERIES			
						AVERAGE STOCK			X X X
	TOTAL					STOCK TURN			X X X
% CASH DISCOUNT				X X X		% MARKDOWN		X X X	X X X

CUMULATIVE MARKUP %	JANUARY JULY	FEBRUARY AUGUST	MARCH SEPTEMBER	APRIL OCTOBER	MAY NOVEMBER	JUNE DECEMBER	JULY JANUARY
PLANNED THIS YEAR: LAST YEAR							
ACTUAL THIS YEAR							

SPRING FALL		JANUARY JULY	FEBRUARY AUGUST	MARCH SEPTEMBER	APRIL OCTOBER	MAY NOVEMBER	JUNE DECEMBER	JULY JANUARY
STOCK END OF MONTH	TOTAL · LAST YEAR							
	PLANNED THIS YEAR							
	ACTUAL THIS YEAR							
DELIV- ERIES	TOTAL · LAST YEAR							
	PLANNED THIS YEAR							
	ACTUAL THIS YEAR							
	LAST YEAR							
	PLANNED THIS YEAR							
	ACTUAL THIS YEAR							
SALES	LAST YEAR							
	PLANNED THIS YEAR							
	ACTUAL THIS YEAR							
	TOTAL · LAST YEAR							
	PLANNED THIS YEAR							
	ACTUAL THIS YEAR							
MARK DOWNS (DOLLARS)	TOTAL · ACTUAL LAST YEAR							
	ACTUAL THIS YEAR							

F385   BUYER   DIV. MGR.   GEN. MDSE. MGR.   CONTROLLER

FIG. 14-6. Monthly departmental merchandise plan.

particular month and for the season (year) to date. It should be noted also that data are provided on the end-of-month stock situation as well as outstanding commitments *on a cost basis*. To permit better control of markdowns, dollar amounts for each classification are shown monthly.

Three-Month Summary and Buyers' Guide

Each month, following a study of the data on the merchandise statistics report, projections of anticipated results and a record of current perform-

MERCHANDISE STATISTICS REPORT

Period _____ to _____

CLASS	SAN FRANCISCO SALES				OAKLAND SALES				TOTAL SALES				TOTAL PLANNED SALES		E.O.M. STOCK			OUTSTANDINGS AT COST		MARK DOWNS
	Period		Year to Date		Period		Year to Date		Period		Year to Date		Period	Year to Date	TY	LY	Plan			
	TY	LY	TY	LY	TY	LY	TY	LY	TY	LY	TY	LY								
1A Panels																				
2A Novelty Curtains																				
3A Drapes																				
4A Rugs and Bath Sets																				
5A Decorator Pillows and Chair Covers																				
6A Slip Covers																				
TOTAL																				

DEPARTMENT __Draperies, Curtains, and Rugs__

ALL FIGURES TO NEAREST HUNDRED $ RETAIL EXCEPT OUTSTANDINGS AT COST

FIG. 14-7. Monthly departmental statistics report by classifications.

DEPT. OR CLASSIFICATION									

PERIOD									
ADJ. DATES									
1. SALES									
2. MODEL E. O. M.									
3. TOTAL REQ.									
4. STOCK O.H.									
5. RETAIL O.T.B.									
6. COST O.T.B.									
7. ON ORDER									
8. BALANCE O.T.B.									

REMARKS	DATE	ORDERS	BALANCE	DATE	ORDERS	BALANCE	DATE	ORDERS	BALANCE

FIG. 14–8.   Three-months summary and buyers' guide.

ances are made for each department—and sometimes each classification—for a three-month period. These forecasts, based on the most recent available information, are related to current activity so closely that this overall report (Figure 14–8) is often referred to as "The Buyers' Bible."

Let us refer to Figure 14–8 and note the eight figures used for improving the buyers' performance. (1) "Sales" refers to those planned for the current month; (2) "Model E.O.M." is the planned end-of-month stock taken from the preliminary six-months plan shown in Figure 14–5; (3) "Total Requirements" represents the total merchandise needed and is obtained by adding the planned sales to the planned E.O.M. stock; (4) "Stock on Hand" is available from the merchandise statistics report (Figure 14–7); (5) "Retail Open-to-Buy" is determined by subtracting the stock on hand from the total requirements; (6) "Cost Open-to-Buy" is obtained by multiplying the retail open-to-buy by the cost complement of the cumulative markup; (7) the "Goods-on-Order" figure is easily found by referring to the "outstandings at cost" shown on the merchandise statistics report (Figure 14–7); and (8) the "Balance O.T.B." is simply the cost open-to-buy minus the cost of the goods on order.

To keep the buyer's position clear with respect to his open-to-buy at any time, each purchase order is entered on the lower part of the form. Thus, by subtracting the amount of the order from the "Balance O.T.B." shown in number 8, the buyer knows exactly how much he may spend during the remainder of the month.

Monthly Operating Statement

The final step in the merchandise budgeting process is the preparation of a monthly operating statement. This statement, shown in Figure 14–9, is

MONTHLY OPERATING STATEMENT

FORM [illegible]

MONTH: L.Y.	%	MONTH: T.Y.	%		YEAR TO DATE: L.Y.	%	YEAR TO DATE: T.Y.	%
				1 NET SALES - Increase or Decrease %				
				2 RETURNS - % to Gross Sales				
				3 NUMBER OF TRANSACTIONS				
				4 AVERAGE GROSS SALE				
				5 MARKDOWNS AND ALLOWANCES - % to Sales				
				6 EMPLOYEES' DISCOUNT - % to Sales				
				7 INVENTORY SHORTAGE AND SHRINKAGE				
				8 RETAIL PURCHASES - MARKUP %				
				9 CASH DISCOUNT - % to Cost Purchases				
				10 RETAIL STOCK E.O.M. - CUMULATED MARKUP %				
				11 NET WORKROOM COST				
				12 GROSS MARGIN - % to Sales				
				EXPENSES				
				13 SPACE CHARGE - STORE				
				14 SPACE CHARGE - WAREHOUSE				
				15 TAXES AND INSURANCE				
				16 INTEREST ON MERCHANDISE				
				17 MAINTENANCE				
				18 NEWSPAPER ADVERTISING				
				19 ADVERTISING PREPARATION				
				20 WINDOWS				
				21 SIGN SHOP				
				22 OTHER PUBLICITY - DIRECT				
				23 RECEIVING AND MARKING				
				24 DELIVERY				
				25 DIRECT SELLING				
				26 STOCK AND CLERICAL				
				27 MAIL AND TELEPHONE ORDERS				
				28 CASHIER WRAPPING				
				29 CRATING AND PACKING				
				30 BUYING EXPENSES				
				31 RETURN TO VENDOR				
				32				
				33 TOTAL CONTROLLABLE EXPENSE				
				34 INDIRECT EXPENSE				
				35 TOTAL EXPENSES				
				36 NET PROFIT				

DEPARTMENT____________________

FIG. 14–9. Monthly operating statement. L.Y. refers to last year, T.Y. to this year.

issued at the end of each month for each department showing the actual results of the merchandising operations for the month. It is cumulative or progressive in nature and furnishes the desired information for each month and for the season to date.

Data on the twelve items listed at the top of the form, beginning with net sales and ending with gross margin, are available for the buyers'—and their superiors'—review and guidance. Comparable figures for the previous year and percentage changes in results between the two years are also entered on the form. As the form indicates, some of the figures are in dollars and some in percentages. When the expenses are entered it is possible to determine the net profit for the department for the latest month as well as for the season to date. By means of this form a detailed picture of each department is thus provided and corrective action is made possible.

LIMITATIONS OF THE MERCHANDISE BUDGET

Despite its widespread use as a tool of management, the merchandise budget has limitations which should be recognized. First, and as indicated previously, it is an aid to the judgment of those who use it and is not designed to control their thinking. If the budget is expected to provide an automatic control over merchandise inventories, if it is not reviewed at frequent intervals, and if the information it contains is incomplete and not current, then the budget will be a failure.

Second, the planning and the operation of a suitable merchandise budget involve considerable time, effort, and expense. If the benefits that accrue from its use are not greater than the cost involved in preparing and maintaining it—and they may not be if the system cost is as much as one-half of one percent of the sales of the controlled merchandise—then it should be discontinued.

Third, some buyers claim that a merchandise budget often so restricts their actions that they are unable to take advantage of exceptional buying opportunities which may arise. Since the budget is designed to aid the buyer in his operations rather than to curtail his activities, this complaint deserves further examination. In practice, the buyer ordinarily has a voice in preparing the merchandising budget, so that the planned figures reflect his judgment as well as that of his associates. If he believes that some of the figures are unattainable or unreasonable in view of the facts as he knows them and in the light of anticipated conditions, then he should object strenuously to these particular items and attempt to convince his associates of the merit of his stand. At the same time, store officials should provide their buyers with merchandising data quickly and assist them to interpret and use this information. After all, the responsibility of buyers and other employees is conditioned upon the knowledge and authority given them.

Fourth, since the planned figures in the merchandise budget are based upon analysis and interpretation of known facts and probable future conditions, it is evident that these figures are of value only as long as conditions closely approximate those anticipated. When changes occur, revisions in estimates should be made in the light of these conditions. In other words, flexibility of the budget is essential.

RESPONSIBILITY FOR THE MERCHANDISE BUDGET

Responsibility for the merchandise budget may be divided into two distinct parts: responsibility for its formation and responsibility for its supervision in operation.

Budget Formation

In small stores the sole responsibility for developing a merchandise budget rests with the proprietor. The form the budget takes, the type of information collected, and the use made of these data will depend upon the needs of the store and the proprietor's attitude toward merchandise planning. Before anything of a formal nature is undertaken, the retailer should appreciate the value of budgeting and be willing to expend the necessary time and effort to establish the system and afford it a chance to work. Too often, in small stores the fault with a budget system that fails to work lies not in the system itself but rather in the attitude of those affected by it.

In most large stores responsibility for budget formation is usually shared by the merchandise manager and the controller or treasurer. The actual formation of the budget, however, is based to a large degree upon estimates prepared by buyers or divisional managers in department stores and discount houses and by merchandise assistants, supervisors, and store managers in chain stores. These latter individuals, of course, submit their estimates to their superiors for final approval. When approved, departmental or store budgets are commonly consolidated into divisions, and the divisions into a complete store or company plan. In some organizations sales plans or quotas are made by the major executives for the company as a whole, after which the sales are divided among stores or departments upon the basis of experience and reasonable future expectations.

Budget Supervision

If the merchandise budget is to function effectively in either the large or the small store, it must be supervised properly. Supervision includes more than mere checking of actual results against planned figures. It involves, in addition, follow-up to determine if information in the form desired is being supplied promptly and accurately; if purchases and markdowns are properly authorized; if the open-to-buy figure is being exceeded frequently and, if so, who has approved such action; and if the budgeted figures are being revised when necessary. Furthermore, supervision involves the review of the budget at frequent and regular intervals by merchandise and control executives.

Responsibility for the activities described rests with the proprietor in small stores. In large stores, it is divided between the merchandise manager and the controller, aided by the same individuals who assist in formulating the merchandise budget, that is, divisional merchandise managers, buyers, merchandise assistants, supervisors, and store managers. Wherever responsibility lies, supervision should be thorough, consistent, and continuous.

REVIEW AND DISCUSSION QUESTIONS

1. Explain briefly the purposes and requisites of a good merchandise budget.
2. Discuss the relationships between EDP and merchandise budgeting. Include the benefits that EDP make possible in the budgetary process.
3. Suppose you were told by a small retailer, following your explanation of the advantages of merchandise budgeting to the small store, that budgeting was useful only to large stores and that he had been successful for years without doing any budgeting. How would you reply?
4. Summarize the six steps recommended by the National Retail Hardware Association in its Profit Planning Sheet for Business Control. How do you explain "expense planning" as the first step when department stores and specialty stores start with "planned sales"?
5. Explain briefly the major factors that should be taken into account in planning sales for a budget period. To what extent do these factors vary in importance among stores of different kinds and sizes?
6. As the prospective proprietor of a new grocery (or hardware, or drug, or discount) store, how would you proceed to estimate your sales for the first year of operation? Be specific.
7. Discuss the main purposes of stock planning and the four main methods employed to attain these objectives.
8. What is meant by the term "retail reductions"? Suggest methods of making realistic estimates of each type of reduction for budgeting purposes.
9. What is involved in the process of planning purchases as an element in merchandise budgeting? Be sure to indicate the relationships of the various factors.
10. How much is the department manager open-to-buy at retail for the month of May in the following situation?

> Stock on hand April 1 at retail $13,450
> Outstanding orders for delivery in April at retail. 1,825
> Planned sales for April 4,800
> Planned stock at retail May 1 9,650

11. How do you account for the differences (size) in the figures for gross margin and for net profit (stated as a percentage of net sales) among supermarkets as a group and department stores as a group? Is any trend evident in either type of store?

12. Visit a progressive retail store in your community and determine the merchandise budgeting procedure employed. Describe this procedure in detail, using whatever forms and illustrations are necessay to make your description clear.

13. In your opinion, what are the chief limitations of the merchandise budget? How may these limitations be minimized?

14. Assume that you have recommended the use of the merchandise budget to a small retailer who has not employed it previously. What words of caution would you give him regarding its adoption and the results he might expect from its use?

15. Compare and contrast the responsibility for the formation and the supervision of the merchandise budget in small stores and in large stores.

SUPPLEMENTARY READINGS

The references included at the end of Chapter 13 are also applicable to this chapter and should be consulted for further information. In addition, the following will prove helpful:

GOTLINGER, JOHN. "Merchandise Management," *Retail Control,* May, 1966, pp. 20–27. An executive of Peck & Peck, New York City, suggests that "the retail controller . . . should take the lead in developing merchandise management programs in his organization."

MEYERS, J. S., *et al. Merchandise Control and Budgeting* (New York: National Retail Merchants Association, 1965). A completely revised edition of *Dollar and Unit Merchandise Planning and Budgeting,* this volume discusses techniques and controls governing what, when, and how much to buy.

NATIONAL RETAIL MERCHANTS ASSOCIATION. *The Buyer's Manual* (4th ed.; New York, 1965). The following discussions have particular relevance to the topics in this chapter: THOMPSON, C. S., "The Dollar Merchandise Plan," pp. 134–49; BURNSIDE, FRANK, "Merchandising By Classification," pp. 181–92; DANIELS, A. F., "Fashion Merchandising," pp. 193–201; and SOLOMON, S. L., "Markdowns," pp. 256–64.

RADOLF, HERMAN. "Retail Operating Ratios," *Journal of Retailing,* Vol. XLI, No. 4 (Winter 1965–1966), pp. 50–51, 61; and ROBICHAUD, R. J. "Retail Profit Rise—What Does It Mean?" *ibid.,* Vol. XLII, No. 3 (Fall, 1966), pp. 52–67. Pointing out the improved sales and profit results for 1964 and 1965, the authors review, among others, results for department and specialty stores, apparel shops, discount houses, and variety stores.

The Value of Total System Reports for Retailers (Dayton, Ohio: National Cash Register Co., Marketing Services Department, 1965). The section on "Merchandise Management Reports," the heart of the NCR Total System, is of special interest in connection with this chapter.

WINGATE, J. W.; SCHALLER, E. O.; AND GOLDENTHAL, IRVING. *Problems in Retail Merchandising* (5th ed.; Englewood Cliffs, N.J.: Prentice-Hall, Inc., 1961). In this rather old but excellent volume, the discussions of "How to Control Markdowns," pp. 92–97; "How to Determine and Control Stock Shortages," pp. 104–12; "How to Plan Sales and Markdowns," pp. 179–94; "How to Plan Stock in Dollars," pp. 195–207; and "How to Plan Purchases and Open-to-Buy," pp. 208–15, are helpful in connection with this chapter.

15
CHAPTER

Managing Incoming Merchandise

A moment's reflection will readily reveal that after merchandise is purchased it must be delivered to the store and made available for inspection by customers. This process is necessary in stores of all kinds and sizes and involves the performance of several closely related activities including receiving, checking, marking, distributing, and traffic.

ACTIVITIES RELATED TO INCOMING MERCHANDISE

Receiving refers to the activities necessary in taking physical possession of merchandise (and also supplies and equipment) at the store and its movement to the area where it is opened and checked. Checking includes a matching of the purchase order against the invoice, the opening of containers, the removal and sorting of merchandise, and a comparison of the quantity and quality of the goods with the specifications of the order. Marking consists of placing certain types of information on the merchandise or on price tickets attached to or placed near the merchandise, to aid the customer and the salesperson in making selections and to provide information for certain aspects of control. Distributing refers to the activities involved in moving merchandise from the marking room to the stock room, if one is used, or otherwise to the sales floor. Traffic has to do with the choice of routes for shipments, the filing and collection of damage claims, the auditing of transportation bills, and similar matters.

An adequate performance level for these related activities is significant both to the customer, who gains from the resulting better service, and to the retailer, who benefits from greater profits. Exclusive of incoming transportation, these activities may cost as much as 1 percent of sales and they afford many opportunities through mechanization and automation to help relieve the "profit squeeze" prevalent in many retail stores today. Despite the foregoing, many students of retailing agree that "merchandise handling has not yet received sufficient attention" from top management.[1]

Requirements of Effective Performance

Although the methods used to carry out the activities discussed in this chapter will vary according to both type and size of store, certain basic requirements for their effective performance are common to all retailers. These requirements are as follows: (1) use of specialized employees when the amount of work is sufficient to justify the cost, (2) development (through work simplification programs[2]) of standardized routines, with specialized procedures for the handling of exceptional cases, to increase the speed and accuracy with which the activities are performed; (3) centralization of all receiving operations and provision of adequate space for this purpose; (4) maximum use of mechanical equipment to reduce cost wherever feasible; and (5) maintenance of adequate control records.[3]

Today retailers, faced with the handling of merchandise in unprecedented volume, are turning more than ever before to the mechanization of receiving, marking, and related functions. Space shortages, higher labor and material costs, and keener competition are forcing top management attention upon these all-too-often neglected activities.

Centralization of Activities Common

Many small stores perform the activities of receiving, checking, and marking on the sales floor or in a back storage room. In the medium-size and large stores, however, "experience has shown" the wisdom of centralizing these operations in a separate receiving room or in a checking and marking room.[4] This centralization yields the following advantages: (1) It affords

---

[1] A. S. Boykoff, quoted in "Says Top Brass Fumbles Dollars in Handling Merchandise," *Women's Wear Daily,* January 13, 1966, p. 52.

[2] Work simplification is defined "as the organized application of common sense or logic to the problem of finding better and easier ways of doing a job." L. J. Konopa, "Are Work Simplifications Systems Adaptable to Retailing?" *Journal of Retailing,* Vol. XXXVIII, No. 4 (Winter, 1962–63), p. 45.

[3] To this list, some retailers would add a sixth, that is, the use of special bonuses or incentive payments to encourage speed and accuracy on the part of personnel performing these activities. For the incentive program used by one retailer, cf. John Osbon, "Saks-5th Receiving Room Checks, Saves—Earns Cash," *Women's Wear Daily,* April 20, 1966, p. 12.

[4] E. H. Wabler, "Traffic, Receiving, and Marking," in *The Buyer's Manual* (4th ed.; New York: National Retail Merchants Association, 1965), pp. 382.

better control over incoming merchandise by lessening the danger of lost invoices and of expiration of discount periods before payments are made. (2) It permits use of specialized employees rather than salespeople; this insures a more uniform and better quality of work and reduces the cost. (3) It overcomes the objections of salespeople, who consider (and properly so) that waiting on customers is their main job, and who dislike doing work not related to actual selling. (4) It avoids the confusion and congestion associated with opening and marking goods on the sales floor, which detracts from the appearance of the store and irritates customers.

Frequently, ready-to-wear merchandise is opened and checked in a separate room (1) to facilitate its removal from containers, thus avoiding wrinkling, and (2) to speed up its movement to the selling floors. Both of these factors have become less important in recent years, however, because of the widespread practice of shipping apparel by truck and on hangers. As a precaution against theft, jewelry and other merchandise of high value is usually received in a separate receiving room or in a special section of the main receiving area. Furniture and other heavy household items are customarily received and stored in warehouses or at subsidiary receiving points located near the elevator leading to the furniture department. If a basement store is operated and the size of the store warrants it, a separate receiving room is sometimes used for merchandise going to this store, especially when checking and marking are carried on several stories above the main floor. With these main exceptions, however, a centralized receiving room is superior to decentralized or sales floor receiving.

As branch stores first developed, most large organizations had the goods received, checked, and marked in a central facility—and, to a considerable degree this practice is still common. Increasingly, however, to hasten the movement of merchandise to selling floors, many firms have provided space, equipment, and personnel at the branches to perform these operations.

Factors Determining Location of Centralized Department

Value of the Space. As a general rule, receiving and related activities should be centralized in space that has a relatively low value for selling purposes. In the small store operating on a single floor, the rear of the store is least valuable for selling; consequently, receiving activities may well be centralized in the back room. This arrangement is typical in small grocery, drug, hardware, and ready-to-wear stores. In the large store occupying several floors, the upper floors have least value for selling purposes; and receiving, checking, and marking activities are usually concentrated on one of these floors, although a receiving point will be located on the ground floor. In such cases the receiving point and the checking and marking room are connected by elevators.

Adequacy of the Space. The space must be adequate to meet the everyday needs of the store and also to provide room for handling merchandise at peak periods, such as Christmas and Easter. In most cases, however, checking and marking rooms will be congested at such times, necessitating the employment of additional help to speed up the flow of merchandise to the sales floor.

Location in Relationship to Stock Rooms. Is it customary to have merchandise opened, checked, and marked on the same floor as the stock room and adjacent to it. Such a location minimizes the handling of merchandise and therefore reduces costs. As a practical matter, however, general stock rooms are not so important as they were years ago; in part because of changes in retailers' buying habits,[5] but also in part because a growing number of retailers tend to carry much of their extra stock with their selling stock. Thus when the S. S. Kresge Company converted some of its traditional variety stores to Jupiter stores (limited selection of variety-store merchandise with a bargain atmosphere), the storage areas were incorporated into the selling space; and when Giant Foods, a supermarket chain, wished to add nonfood items to some of its conventional-size stores, it did so by using former backroom areas.[6] Moreover, some of the more recently designed stores have many storage areas with each kind of merchandise stored next to or near its appropriate selling department. Thus, in the circular store that Macy's has built in Queens (Figure 5–4, page 127), stockrooms are on the periphery of each floor.[7]

Location in Relationship to the Selling Floor. Since most merchants still place incoming merchandise on the selling floor as needed, it is desirable that the receiving room and the stock room be readily accessible to the selling floor or floors. This requirement does not mean that the receiving room should necessarily be located on the main floor of the small store; however, there is a trend toward this arrangement and even large stores have found that the proximity of stock space and selling departments has brought savings in personnel, better customer service, and greater sales. Despite this trend, the previous discussion has made it clear that, as long as convenient mechanisms for transferring merchandise are available, the receiving room and the sales floor may be separated by several stories.

---

[5] Cf. the discussion of hand-to-mouth buying on pp. 297–98, above.

[6] "Kresge's Triple-Threat Retailing," *Business Week,* January 29, 1966, p. 134; and "First the Warehouse Store . . . Now the Warehouse Department," *Chain Store Age* (Supermarket Executives Edition), May, 1966, pp. 68–69.

[7] "Shopping Go-Round at Macy's," *Business Week,* February 15, 1964, p. 34.

It should also be emphasized that, for merchandise sold by sample, such as furniture, radios, stoves, and refrigerators, warehouses are operated by large stores in relatively low-rent districts, often at some distance from the stores. For this merchandise, receiving, checking, marking (if any), and storage are performed in the warehouse, with delivery made direct to the customer's home. To cite a specific instance, 85 percent of the warehouse space that Montgomery Ward & Company has in the Detroit area is used for direct delivery to customers who have bought through Ward stores scattered throughout the greater Detroit area.[8]

LAYOUT AND EQUIPMENT FOR RECEIVING

Efficiency in receiving merchandise and the activities associated therewith is dependent in part upon adequate space and its proper utilization. To quote one study of supermarkets: "The best equipment and work methods in the world [will not] do any good unless you have the proper backroom layout."[9] At the same time, the equipment provided and the work methods employed are also significant. And there are important differences among stores of various size and kind in dealing with these activities.

In Small Stores

Receiving, checking, and marking are frequently carried on without the aid of any special facilities and without any particular layout in the receiving areas of small stores. This statement is true even in the small units operated by chain-store firms. Merchandise is commonly unloaded from trucks onto the sidewalk or is carried into the back room (occasionally even the sales area is used) and piled on the floor. It is unpacked and marked at the convenience of the manager or a salesperson. Some stores have stationary or double-deck, portable tables in the receiving area. As merchandise is unpacked, it is sorted, placed on these tables, checked, and marked.

In Medium-Size and Larger Stores

Among somewhat larger stores the layout of the receiving room—also known as the checking and marking room—depends upon the system used

---

[8] "Inventory Reduction: Target of Distribution Program," *Chain Store Age* (Executives Edition), December, 1963, p. E39.

[9] Cf. "The Backroom: 'A Hornet's Nest,'" *Super Market Merchandising*, April, 1962, p. 44. The importance of receiving room layout is also emphasized by the receiving department head of G. Fox & Co., Hartford, Connecticut, in Sam Linderman, "Stores Try to Trace Route to Uniform Traffic Pattern," *Women's Wear Daily*, January 12, 1966, p. 28.

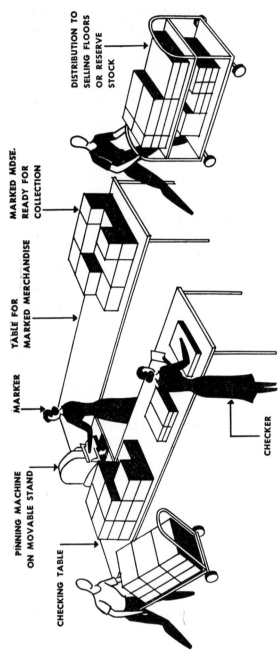

PINNING MACHINE
ON MOVABLE STAND

CHECKING TABLE

MARKER

TABLE FOR
MARKED MERCHANDISE

MARKED MDSE.
READY FOR
COLLECTION

DISTRIBUTION TO
SELLING FLOORS
OR RESERVE
STOCK

CHECKER

This method of operation is based on parallel stationary tables, with attaching machine on movable stand between them. Tables and machine stand are exactly the same height (about 36") and space between tables is just wide enough for marker and machine. Overhead electric connection permits machine to move the length of the table. The operating method is as follows:

1. Receiver or stockman brings packages containing merchandise to be machine-marked to checking table.
2. Checker matches invoice to package, opens, piles merchandise on table, invoice checks, leaving retailed invoice with merchandise.
3. Marker moves pinning machine opposite merchandise, and ma-

chine-marks, piling marked merchandise on the table at her right. As piles of boxes are marked, she moves machine so that merchandise to be marked, and space to pile it after marking, always are right at hand.

4. Stockman collects marked merchandise from table, takes to forward or reserve stock.

This operating plan shows a single unit for one attaching machine. It is capable of indefinite expansion by increasing the length of the tables and adding more pinning machines. It is adaptable to portable table operation by using lines of portable tables in place of the stationary tables; or to a combination of the two systems by having the checking table stationary and the tables for marked merchandise portable.

Courtesy: Dennison Manufacturing Co.

FIG. 15-1. Flow chart showing checking and marking operation with stationary tables.

in handling, checking, and marking merchandise. Three methods are widely employed, while a fourth—which involves the use of mechanized conveyors—is used by the large retailers. Perhaps the most common is the use of *stationary tables* or *check-marking tables,* as illustrated in Figure 15–1. These tables are frequently placed in a room large enough to allow cases to be brought in and unpacked. The merchandise is then sorted as it is placed on each table. After being checked and marked, the merchandise is moved to the stock room or to the sales floor.

The use of the *portable table*—the second method employed in handling and checking merchandise—involves placing the goods on tables with wheels. After the merchandise has been sorted and checked for quantity, the

Courtesy: Rapids-Standard Co., Inc.

FIG. 15–2. Use of conveyor in receiving and checking. From the receiving point, packages are moved to the checking area by the roller gravity conveyor in the immediate foreground. Then they are pushed off and slide down the incline to the appropriate unpacking and checking station before going on to the marking areas.

tables are moved to another section of the receiving room, where marking takes place. This method minimizes one major disadvantage of systems employing check-marking tables, just described. When both checking and marking are performed in one location, it sometimes happens that buyers, entering the receiving room to check the quality of goods that they are eager to place on sale, remove merchandise before the quantity check has been completed. By not allowing buyers in the section where quantity checking is done, there is less danger of their removing merchandise before the quantity check is completed.

A third method used to facilitate the checking and marking of merchandise is known as the *bin method*. The receiving room is divided into two sections, one for checking and one for marking, with a series of bins or openings dividing the sections. As merchandise is checked on tables in one section, it is shoved through the bins onto tables in the other section, where marking takes place. As with the portable-table system, this method tends to keep buyers from removing merchandise that has not been checked, since they are not allowed in the checking sections of the receiving room. How-

FIG. 15–3. Use of conveyor in marking. The picture shows the central conveyor and several spurs.

ever, the system has the disadvantages of an extra handling of all goods and of creating some confusion in marking because of an occasional mixing of unlike goods in a bin.

Larger retailers with a sufficient volume to justify the investment have moved to a fourth method, which involves *mechanical* conveyor belts or roller conveyors to move merchandise from the receiving point through the checking and marking operations. At the appropriate checking point, for example, the merchandise may be moved off the central conveyor (Figure 15–2), it is then returned to the central conveyor, moved on to the marking area where a conveyor spur detours it while marking is performed (Figure 15–3). Even the movement to the selling area or to the stock room may be by mechanical equipment. With today's high wage scales, even moderate-sized retailers can well give careful consideration to the employment of mechanized facilities for these activities.

RECEIVING PROCEDURE

To clarify our discussion of layout and the facilities required for effective performance of receiving and related functions, some of the methods employed in handling and checking merchandise have been mentioned in previous paragraphs. But let us now return to the actual receiving of merchandise and note the various steps which are necessary before goods are placed on sale.

Activities at the Receiving Point

The place a store takes physical possession of the merchandise is usually referred to as the receiving point, station, or dock. In the small store the receiving point and the receiving room may be the same; or goods may be accepted on the front sidewalk or at the rear of the store and then sent to a basement receiving room by chute. When out-of-doors receiving is practiced, incoming merchandise may be damaged by the elements unless it is promptly moved into the store. Other disadvantages of this practice are found in the additional lifting of cartons and in the blocking of pedestrian traffic.

In the larger store, specific physical facilities may exist at the receiving point. Frequently, the store erects an unloading or receiving platform at the rear of the store, constructed to the tailboard height of the majority of trucks and covered by a roof to protect merchandise from the elements. If a platform is not possible because of space limitation, a rear sidewalk may be used, but merchandise should be moved into the receiving room by means of trucks, elevators, chutes, and roller conveyors (see Figure 15–4) as soon as possible.[10]

At the receiving point all boxes and cartons should be inspected to determine possible damage to merchandise. If there is no such indication, the receiving clerk merely signs the carrier's receipt; but if there is evidence of damage, the receipt will be signed only after the word "Damaged" has been written upon it. Such action facilitates the filing of damage claims later. It should be noted that this receiving point inspection of the containers does not involve any examination of the merchandise itself. Consequently, damage or loss concealed by the containers will not be revealed until the

---

[10] On merchandise handling in a department store (Jordan Marsh Company, Boston) cf. "No-Driver Tractor Cuts Handling 50 Percent," *Chain Store Age* (Executives Edition), November, 1965, p. 26.

Courtesy: Rapids-Standard Company, Inc.

FIG. 15–4. Moving merchandise from delivery truck into receiving room of super-market by conveyor.

containers are opened and the goods removed for checking. If damaged merchandise is then found, or if shortages exist, claims should be filed promptly against the transportation agency or the person responsible for the damage or shortage.

Receiving Records

In the very small store where the proprietor himself or a member of his family handles the receiving of merchandise it is probably unnecessary to record its receipt. In the store large enough to have any degree of specialization of activities, however, recording of incoming shipments is essential. The information required varies among stores but commonly includes such data as: date and hour of arrival; apparent condition of the shipment (e.g., any damage); weight; delivery charges, if paid by the retailer; shipper's name and location; form of transportation, such as railroad, express, or parcel post; person making the delivery (e.g., name of truck driver); number of pieces;

amount and number of invoice,[11] and the department for which the merchandise is intended. Figure 15–5 shows a typical receiving record. Currently, some large retailers are replacing or supplementing this type of receiving record with punched cards which can be "fed" directly into a computer.[12]

Importance of the Receiving Record. Several benefits result from the use of the receiving record: It provides a record to which the store can turn in case disagreement arises between vendor and the store relative to the receipt of a particular shipment. By placing the invoice number on the receiving record, the store is assured that each invoice is associated with the proper merchandise. The need for this action is especially important when

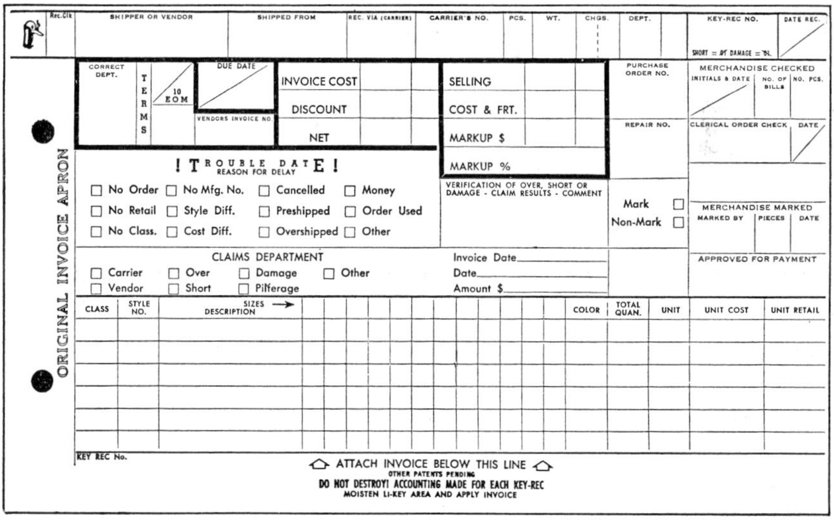
ORIGINAL INVOICE APRON
Rec. Clk | SHIPPER OR VENDOR | SHIPPED FROM | REC. VIA (CARRIER) | CARRIER'S NO. | PCS. | WT. | CHGS. | DEPT. | KEY-REC NO. | DATE REC.
SHORT = DAMAGE =
CORRECT DEPT. | TERMS | 10 EOM | DUE DATE | VENDORS INVOICE NO.
INVOICE COST | DISCOUNT | NET
SELLING | COST & FRT. | MARKUP $ | MARKUP %
PURCHASE ORDER NO. | REPAIR NO.
MERCHANDISE CHECKED: INITIALS & DATE | NO. OF BILLS | NO. PCS.
CLERICAL ORDER CHECK | DATE
! TROUBLE DATE ! REASON FOR DELAY
☐ No Order ☐ No Mfg. No. ☐ Cancelled ☐ Money
☐ No Retail ☐ Style Diff. ☐ Preshipped ☐ Order Used
☐ No Class. ☐ Cost Diff. ☐ Overshipped ☐ Other
VERIFICATION OF OVER, SHORT OR DAMAGE - CLAIM RESULTS - COMMENT
Mark ☐ Non-Mark ☐
MERCHANDISE MARKED: MARKED BY | PIECES | DATE
CLAIMS DEPARTMENT
☐ Carrier ☐ Over ☐ Damage ☐ Other
☐ Vendor ☐ Short ☐ Pilferage
Invoice Date____ Date____ Amount $____
APPROVED FOR PAYMENT
CLASS | STYLE NO. | DESCRIPTION | SIZES → | COLOR | TOTAL QUAN. | UNIT | UNIT COST | UNIT RETAIL
KEY REC No.
ATTACH INVOICE BELOW THIS LINE
OTHER PATENTS PENDING
DO NOT DESTROY! ACCOUNTING MADE FOR EACH KEY-REC
MOISTEN LI-KEY AREA AND APPLY INVOICE

FIG. 15–5. A receiving record which permits attachment of the invoice.

partial shipments are involved and when many shipments are received from one vendor. Moreover, the receiving record allows management to check on the length of time invoices and merchandise are held in the receiving room. Finally, by requiring that all invoices be checked against the receiving record

[11] Invoices from local vendors and, to an increasing extent, from those located at a distance when shipments are made by truck, usually arrive with the merchandise, so that they are available to the receiving clerk when he makes out the receiving record. On other out-of-town shipments, invoices come by mail and usually arrive before the merchandise. If so, they sometimes go to the receiving point, where they are held until the arrival of the merchandise. The receiving record number is placed on the invoice and on the receiving sheet or slip, if the latter is used.

[12] The system used by Wieboldt's of Chicago is described by Samuel Feinberg, "EDP and Retail Traffic Operations," *Women's Wear Daily,* April 27, 1966, p. 10.

before payment, invoices covering merchandise not yet received by the store will not be paid.[13]

When the receiving records are completed and the proper notations placed upon containers, the merchandise is moved to the checking and marking room. Again depending upon the size of the store and the location of the two areas, this movement may be by hand, by movable tables, by chutes, or by some mechanical means such as trucks, elevators, or roller conveyors.

CHECKING PROCEDURE

Checking consists of four quite distinct steps: First, the invoice is checked against the purchase order; second, the merchandise is removed from the shipping containers and sorted; third, the merchandise is checked for quantity; and, finally, the goods are checked for quality. In smaller stores and in many large stores, two or more of the steps may be performed by the same employee.

Checking Invoice against Purchase Order

The main purposes of comparing the invoice with the purchase order are to ascertain (1) if the description and quantity of the goods billed are the same as those ordered and (2) if the terms of sale (dating and discounts) on the invoice are as stipulated on the purchase order. This matching process is important and should be conducted with care.

Opening and Sorting Merchandise

Despite the trend to ship wearing apparel by truck in garment bags,[14] most merchandise still arrives at retail stores in boxes, cartons, crates, and similar containers. Many retailers consider it good practice not to open these containers and remove merchandise until invoices are available, although much depends upon the type of goods. They reason that if merchandise is removed from the containers and cannot be checked immediately against the invoice, either of two possibilities may result: If the merchandise is sorted and placed on tables ready for checking, some of it may be removed before

---

[13] This requirement is not always fulfilled, especially in cases in which buyers are located at some distance from vendors. If past relationships have been satisfactory, goods are sometimes paid for before their receipt in order to take advantage of the cash discount. If discrepancies arise, adjustments are made without difficulty.

[14] Dresses, blouses, coats, and similar items are frequently placed in garment bags and hung in trucks for shipment. Upon arrival at destination, the garments are easily removed, marked, and transferred to the selling floor. Problems of unpacking, eliminating wrinkles, and marking are simplified.

the invoice arrives without any record being made; consequently, a shortage will be shown when the goods are checked. Or if the store makes a record of the merchandise removed from the container, places the goods in stock, and later finds a discrepancy when the invoice arrives, there is no way of rechecking the shipment. Although, as a general rule, it seems wise to avoid opening containers until invoices are available, it is probably best—if the goods are needed on the sales floor—to take the chances involved and open the merchandise at once.

Checking for Quantity

The most frequently used methods of checking incoming merchandise for quantity are the direct check and the blind check. Variations of these methods—the semiblind check and the combination check—are also used by some retailers. A few retailers use a spot check, that is, just checking at random on a few items or packages, but this method can overlook so many errors that it is not recommended. Basically, the problem involved in selecting the method for a particular store depends upon the attitude of management regarding the tightness of control and upon whom it wishes to place responsibility for careful checking. The direct check, for example, places responsibility entirely upon the checker; in most of the other methods, however, responsibility is shared by at least two employees.

The Direct Check. Under this system of checking for quantity, incoming shipments are usually checked directly against the invoice. If the invoice is not available on receipt of the merchandise, the shipment is usually held unopened in the receiving room until the invoice arrives. However, if the checking room becomes crowded or if certain merchandise is needed on the selling floor, "dummy" invoices are made out; checking then proceeds as if these dummy invoices were the originals. In some firms the direct check is against the purchase order rather than the invoice.

The main advantages of the direct checking method lie in its speed and simplicity, in its economy, and in the possibility of a recheck in case of a discrepancy between the checker's count and the invoice quantity. Probably the main disadvantage of this method is the possibility of careless checking. When the checker is given the invoice with the quantities entered, he may more or less assume that the quantities are correct. In addition, there is some possibility of goods piling up in the receiving room waiting for invoices, with the result that merchandise does not flow rapidly to the selling floor. This danger has been minimized in recent years, however, by the increased number of vendors enclosing duplicate invoices with their shipments. Despite limitations, the direct check continues to be the most common method of checking for quantity in small stores, and probably in large ones.

The Blind Check.   This method of checking merchandise consists of providing the checker with a blank prepared form or merely a sheet of paper on which he enters for each shipment the kinds and description of the merchandise, the quantities, the shipper, and other pertinent information. The completed form or list is then checked against the original invoice by another employee, possibly one from the invoice office if the store is large. This procedure usually results in more careful checking, since the checker has no idea what each shipment is supposed to contain; consequently, he has to count each item to obtain a quantity figure to enter on the blank form. Other advantages of this method of checking are that (1) it allows immediate checking and placing of merchandise on sale, even if the original invoice is delayed; (2) cost figures are kept from the checkers; and (3) invoices are not left lying around the receiving room, where they may be soiled, lost, or delayed in reaching the accounts payable office.

As for disadvantages, the blind check is more expensive than the direct check. It involves extra time in placing the necessary data on the blank form and in having another employee check this information against the original invoice. In addition, if merchandise is removed from the receiving room before a check has been made against the original invoice, a recheck is impossible. And, here again, the practice of many vendors to include packing slips in their shipments has removed the uncertainty regarding the contents and has led some checkers to use the packing ships to make up their list to be checked against the invoice.

Other Checking Methods.   The *semiblind method* of checking attempts to save both time and cost as compared with the blind check. Instead of providing the checker with a completely blank form, he is given one upon which are listed the items in the shipment but with the quantities omitted. Consequently, the checker merely has to count the merchandise and enter the quantities, with the result that greater speed is attained and checking costs are reduced. This economy in the checker's time is partially offset, however, by the fact that an employee in the invoice office must enter the additional data for the checkers, such as a description of the merchandise, upon the forms used for checking purposes.

The *combination check* is a combination of the direct and blind checks. Its object is to obtain an accurate count of the merchandise and to speed up the removal of the goods from the receiving room. When invoices are available at the time the merchandise is received, the direct check is used, thus securing the greater economy which that method makes possible; when merchandise is received and invoices are not available, however, the blind check is used.

Regardless of the method or methods employed to check merchandise, it is a common practice in medium-size and large stores to check quantities merely on the basis of the quantities listed on the outside of the packages included in the shipment. To illustrate: A shipment of nylon hosiery, packed three pairs to the box, would be checked for quantity simply by counting the boxes and multiplying by three. Checking each box to make sure that three pairs of hosiery were inside would be left to the marker when he places a price ticket on each pair. This checking of individual items is facilitated by marking machines which make it possible to print any specific number of price tickets. The use of such equipment is explained on pages 450–51.

It is apparent that the checking of *bulk merchandise* presents a different problem from that of other goods. When such merchandise is received, it is necessary to check both the number of bulk containers and the weight of the contents of each container. Particular care is needed in examining containers for substandard weights. Fruits and vegetables are often repacked by shippers and, in the process, loss of weight sometimes occurs; or the time element alone may be responsible for shrinkage. A similar situation exists with respect to meat received for cutting and resale.

Handling Quantity Discrepancies. When the quantity check reveals a discrepancy with the invoice, and when the merchandise still remains in the receiving room—as it will if the direct check is used—the checker should call the supervisor or manager to make a recheck. In the small store, of course, where checking is done by the proprietor or by a salesperson, the procedure is for the proprietor to make the recheck. When the merchandise has already been placed in stock and a recheck is not possible, the original check will have to serve as a basis of a claim against the shipper—or against the carrier, if there is evidence that the discrepancy was occasioned by the latter. If the shipment contains less than indicated on the original invoice, it is customary for the retailer to make a compensating deduction from the total of the invoice when payment is made to the vendor. If the shipment contains more merchandise than shown on the invoice, the opinion of the buyer is sought as to how to handle the situation. If he feels that the extra merchandise can be sold, an addition to the invoice total will be made; otherwise, just the payment called for by the invoice will be made, and the extra merchandise will be returned to the vendor.

Checking for Quality

All too frequently, in an effort to get goods on the selling floor promptly, emphasis is placed on the quantity check and insufficient attention is given to the quality of the merchandise received. This emphasis is unfortunate because the quality factor is important in building customer satisfaction and sales volume.

In the small firm, where the proprietor or a salesperson opens containers, removes merchandise, and checks for quantity, checking for quality is usually performed by the same individual. In large firms, quality checking is not the responsibility of the quantity checker, who is not an expert in merchandise, but usually rests with the buyers or special quality inspectors. For example, some large chains and department stores use special inspectors to check the quality of women's ready-to-wear arriving in the receiving room in the chain's central warehouse or in the receiving room of the department store. As already suggested, to avoid removal of merchandise before it has been checked for quantity, buyers in such stores are not usually allowed to check for quality until the quantity check has been completed.

The usual basis of quality checking is the buyer's experience, his knowledge of quality and values, and his memory of the merchandise purchased. In stores of all sizes, this basis of checking dominates. Increasingly, however, there is a tendency in the large firm to see that the buyer has a more objective standard by which quality may be judged. Some buyers purchase samples in showrooms and check merchandise received against these samples. Other buyers are aided by standards and specifications established by the government, the trade, the vendor, or the retailer himself. By way of illustration, the National Bureau of Standards has established standards for some items; and it allows manufacturers to certify that their products conform to these standards. In such cases, quality may be checked by examining the merchandise to see if a label is attached giving such certification. A few of the large department stores, mail-order firms, and chain stores have testing laboratories in which samples of incoming merchandise are tested for quality.[15] In addition, the facilities of outside testing organizations are available at a reasonable cost to stores of all sizes. These more objective ways of determining quality are of great aid to the buyer in the discharge of his duty of checking quality.

MARKING MERCHANDISE

The marking of merchandise by means of price tickets, gummed stickers, an automatic imprinting system, or even by hand before placing it on sale is an almost universal practice among retailers. Among the exceptions are those stores in which merchandise is highly standardized or well marked by the manufacturer. Similarly, some retailers selling merchandise at a single price also dispense with price marking. Even in these cases, however, some marking may be necessary to provide better control over stocks and to facilitate the taking of inventory. As one retailer has written: "In the light of

---

[15] Cf. the discussion of testing bureaus on pp. 331–32, above.

present day recording and stock control, price marking has become an important field in its own right. Simply attaching a price ticket to an article no longer constitutes good marking."[16] We can better understand his emphasis on marking by glancing at some of the guidelines and reasons for this activity.

Some Guidelines for Marking

Certain basic principles guide the retailer in marking the merchandise he offers for sale, regardless of the methods or devices he uses in the process.

1. The merchandise should be marked legibly, neatly, and in as permanent a manner as possible without damage to the goods. The use of rubber stamps and marking machines has practically solved this problem, particularly when the marker uses good judgment in placing the price or choosing the type of price ticket to be attached to the merchandise and in properly locating the ticket on the item.

2. All necessary information should be placed on the price ticket, if one is used, at the time the merchandise is marked. These data should be limited to facts that supply needed information to those handling the goods, including customers, and to facts that are used by buyers for merchandise control purposes and for guidance in future purchasing.[17] In small stores the cost of the item, in code, and the retail price will usually be given. The code may consist of some word or phrase which does not contain a duplication of letters. Thus, the phrase "trade quick" might be used, with each letter representing a figure, as follows:

$$1\ 2\ 3\ 4\ 5\ 6\ 7\ 8\ 9\ 0^{18}$$
$$t\ r\ a\ d\ e\ q\ u\ i\ c\ k$$

Under this code an item that cost \$1.75 would be marked with the letters "tue."

In department and specialty stores the information will ordinarily include the season letter and week in the season, the department number, the size and color of the goods, and the retail price. It is also a fairly common practice in such stores to place a number upon the price ticket indicating

---

[16] Wabler, *op. cit.,* p. 384.

[17] As an aid to customers, increasingly more information is being placed on price tickets, on shelf tickets, or on special inserts or attachments. As an illustration of this trend cf. "Chicago Co-op Grocer Tests Use of Shelf Tickets with Price/Ounce Information," *Advertising Age,* April 4, 1966, p. 32.

[18] Other cost codes in common use are "blacksmith," "rusty nail x," and "young blade."

the source of the merchandise and, when practicable, the manufacturer's or supplier's style number.

3. Merchandise should be so marked as to minimize manipulation of prices either by employees of the store or by customers. This end is usually accomplished (1) by the use of marking machines and specially prepared ink and (2) by attaching tickets to merchandise so securely that customers and employees will have difficulty in changing them from one article of merchandise to another. Unused price tickets should not be allowed in selling departments.

4. When a record of articles sold daily is desired for control purposes, price tickets with perforated stubs should be used. After sorting, these stubs may be forwarded to the department head or the buyer. They furnish information as to the particular articles selling best and as to the colors, styles, and sizes that are proving most popular. In addition, they enable the department head to maintain a perpetual inventory of the merchandise in his department.

5. Certain items should be marked in some manner, usually in addition to the price ticket, which will prevent their wear or use by the customer before they are returned. A common practice in this connection is to seal a tag upon the article so that the customer cannot or will not wear the item without removing the tag. To millinery, for instance, some retail stores attach a tag reading: "If this tag is removed, this merchandise may not be returned for credit." It may be advisable to mark particular merchandise so as to convey to the customer the information that it is not returnable or that precautions should be taken by the user in the care of the article. Some stores use specially printed price tickets indicating that certain goods cannot be returned for sanitary reasons.

6. Merchandise should be marked as quickly as possible and at as low a cost as possible consistent with accuracy and the type of merchandise handled. The actual application of this principle is, of course, a matter of good management. In practice, there is a wide difference in the efficiency of marking departments in retail stores; this difference is caused, among other things, by the various methods employed in the individual stores, the types of personnel and equipment used, and the effectiveness of supervision.

Additional Reasons for Marking

Although some of the reasons for marking merchandise have been indicated in the preceding section, others are clearly apparent: (1) Marking merchandise with the price, size, color, and other data is an aid to the salesperson in serving the customer. (2) Customer good will is created by marking; customers prefer to deal with retailers who treat all patrons the same, and marking is an indication (but not a guaranty) that the store follows such a practice. (3) The markings, especially the price, encourage the customer to serve herself, thus reducing sales effort.[19] (4) A physical inventory is greatly simplified if all merchandise is plainly marked, perhaps with both retail price and cost price. (5) Marking the date the merchandise was received aids the buyer or proprietor in selecting goods to be moved by price reductions, thus keeping fresh merchandise in stock.

Marking Procedures

At least three procedures are followed in marking merchandise. *Immediate marking,* the first and most common practice, involves the marking of each item of merchandise in the desired manner as promptly as possible after its receipt.

The second method, known as *delayed marking,* refers to the practice of writing the retail price and other necessary information on the outside of the containers only. Then the merchandise is moved to a reserve stock room. When part or all of these goods are ready to be moved to the sales floor, the containers are opened and the individual items marked. This procedure is practicable for some items such as canned goods and fast-selling staples. It is also highly effective in the case of merchandise on which prices change frequently; in such a case, bulk marking,[20] saves the expense of re-marking. Perhaps its chief disadvantage is that insufficient information may be given by the markings to provide adequate control of merchandise.

The third procedure may be termed *group marking.* Under this plan, as goods are received the containers are marked on the outside as in delayed marking, and the goods are then sent to the reserve stock room. Later, they are moved to the selling floor *without* the individual items being marked; instead, the merchandise is grouped in bins or trays or on tables or shelves with the price indicated by a nearby price tag. This procedure has developed primarily as a means of reducing the cost of marking and re-marking goods and to speed up the delivery of goods to the selling floor. It is widely used by stores selling meats, groceries, low-priced variety goods, drug accessories, and the less expensive automobile supplies. Supermarkets and other stores which have turned to self-service operation, however, have found it necessary to

[19] The significance of markings as a means of encouraging self selection by the customer is emphasized in P. Daignault, "Those Punched Tickets," *Sales Management,* July 16, 1965, pp. 51–2 ff.

[20] The term "bulk marking" is used by some retailers, however, to denote other practices. When a grocer, for example, places a large box of soap chips on his sales floor and writes "60¢ per pound" on the box, he considers such action to be bulk marking.

place at least the retail price on individual items; otherwise, the check-out step is very slow and many errors are made.

How Merchandise Is Marked

Placing the desired information on merchandise may be accomplished by writing the price and other information on the merchandise or on its container; by using a rubber stamp; or by attaching gummed labels, pin

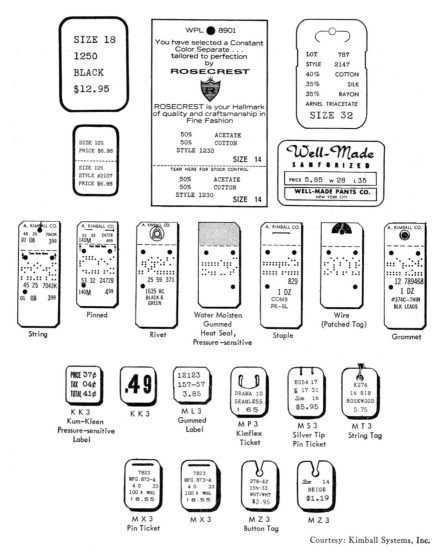

Courtesy: Kimball Systems, Inc.

FIG. 15–6.　Some forms of price tags and tickets in common use.

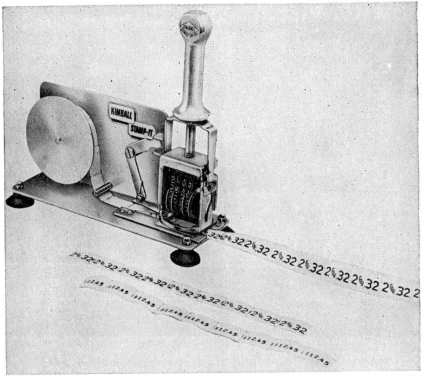

Courtesy: Kimball Systems, Inc.

FIG. 15-7. A low-cost, hand-operated labeling machine, the Kimball Stamp-It.

tickets, button tickets, clip tickets, or string tickets to the merchandise either by hand or by using a machine designed for this purpose.

Hand and Rubber-Stamp Marking. Hand marking, of course, is most common in small retail stores. In the hardware and paint store, for example, the salesperson may write "$1.98" on each quart can of paint as he places it on the shelf; or he may write the price on a gummed label which he attaches to the merchandise. The writing may be done with a lead pencil, grease pencil or crayon.

Rubber stamps have largely superseded the use of gummed labels, pin tickets, and string tickets in many stores for marking a wide variety of merchandise. In stores selling packaged foods, drugs, and cosmetics, for instance, the retail price is often stamped on the top of each package prior to removal from the bulk container.

Price Tickets. To overcome the limitations of marking by hand and by rubber stamps, including the time required, frequent errors, and the fact that the markings may be rubbed off before the merchandise is sold, many small retailers and practically all large ones find it worthwhile to attach

FIG. 15–8. The Monarch Model 116 for printing and applying labels.

price tickets to merchandise. The kinds of tickets used vary widely, even within a single store, since it is desirable to adapt the price ticket to the merchandise. Some of the common types of tickets are shown in Figure 15–6.

When price tickets are used, it is customary to employ electric or hand-operated equipment for the purpose of printing the designated information on the tickets and, in many cases, to attach the price tickets to the merchandise. Recent improvements in such equipment permit the use of all kinds of paper stocks—gummed, ungummed, heat-seal, pressure-sensitive as well as heavy tag or board stocks. The hand-operated Kimball Stamp-It (Figure 15–7) prints on a fast-peeling label which is easily attached to the product by being hand-pressed against it. Still another hand-operated machine, the Monarch Model 116 (Figure 15–8), both prints and applies the label as the operator squeezes the handle. Figure 15–9 shows the Dennison Spin-print Portable Label Printer, which weighs 18 ounces yet prints 300 pressure-sensitive labels a minute. For the retailer wishing a somewhat more automatic operation, the Kimball Series 2000 (Figure 15–10) imprints and applies pressure-sensitive labels to conveyorized or hand-fed merchandise at the rate of 150 per minute; while the Monarch Sensomatic (Figure 15–11) applies the label with a jet of compressed air. Many of these machines turn

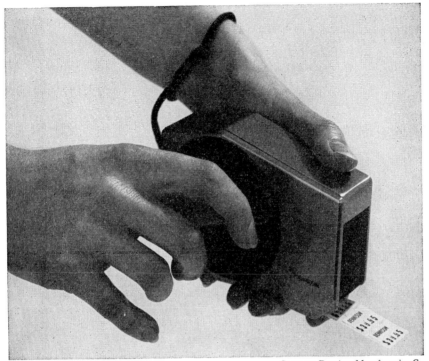

Courtesy: Dennison Manufacturing Co.

FIG. 15-9.   The hand-operated Dennison Spin-print Portable Label Printer.

out such complete price and inventory tickets that the stubs are picked up by mechanical or electronic means and the resulting tabulations are used for stock control purposes.

Where Merchandise Is Marked

Some retailers, particularly small ones, have their marking activities performed by salespeople on the selling floor. This practice should be followed only as a last resort because any cost saving resulting from having salespeople do marking in their spare time is usually more than offset by other factors. These include the following: (1) the ticket is not so neat as that obtained in the marking room, where the marker is not interrupted by customers; (2) more frequent mistakes occur, both because there are interruptions and because the invoice often is not available throughout the marking process; (3) marking is slower; and (4) an added burden is placed on the buyer or manager when he has to oversee marking activities. It is desirable, therefore, to have marking concentrated in the receiving room or in a checking and marking room. Such a location also facilitates the use

FIG. 15–10. The Kimball Series 2000 for imprinting and applying labels.

of marking machines. In the large store, marking will be performed by full-time markers; in smaller stores, by a person who also engages in other activities.

Authorizing Marking. Regardless of who does the actual marking of merchandise, proper authorization is necessary to insure that the desired information is provided for the marker and that he knows when to proceed with the task. In the small store, the proprietor may enter on the invoice the proposed price, perhaps even before the goods arrive in the store. If an employee does the marking, he may be given the invoice to insure more accurate work.

In the large store the most common means of instructing the markers is also through the invoice or a copy thereof. As soon as the invoice arrives, and after it is time-stamped and properly entered in the accounts payable department to insure payment within the discount period, it is usually sent to an invoice office, where it is attached to and checked against a copy of the purchase order. It then flows to the room where the buyer checks the quality of the merchandise; and during the quality check, the buyer inserts the retail prices.

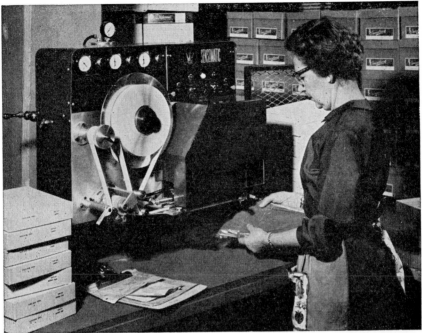

Courtesy: Monarch Marking System Co.

FIG. 15–11. A highly automatic printing and labeling machine, the Monarch Sensomatic.

Some stores use the priced sample to instruct the markers. Under this plan the buyer takes a sample of the merchandise when he makes his quality check and places on it a ticket that contains the information desired on all the items. The sample is then turned over to the markers.

More and more stores are now authorizing marking through a process known as *preretailing*. This practice, which requires that the buyer place the retail prices of the items being bought upon the store's copy of the purchase order at the time the order is placed, affords two main advantages. First, it forces the buyer to consider the retail price at the time of purchase, thereby discouraging him from making purchases which do not seem likely to give him the desired markon. Second, marking is expedited in that it can begin as soon as the goods arrive. In addition, some retailers have discovered that preretailing, by allowing practically all records to be maintained at retail (rather than both at retail and at cost) prices, simplifies and speeds up their accounting systems.

Premarking Merchandise. Some large retailers, to reduce marking expenses and to hasten the movement of goods to the selling floor, have induced vendors to mark merchandise prior to shipment, a practice known as premarking.[21] In some cases the stores make out the price tickets and send them to vendors for attaching to the goods; in other cases, vendors furnish the price tickets, enter the necessary information (which the retailer must provide for them), and affix them to the merchandise. Although staples and fair-traded goods, since they have a greater degree of price stability, are the best candidates for premarking, men's clothing, women's hosiery, and greeting cards are also frequently premarked and some retailers even report success with the premarking of fashion goods.

It should be noted, however, that manufacturers marking merchandise for their retailer customers must let all competing customers know that the service is available; otherwise they will run afoul of the Robinson-Patman Act.[22] Practically all retailers are in agreement that a further extension of premarking is to be encouraged as a method of reducing retail costs.

Outside Marking of Fashion Merchandise. A trend in marking practice continuing to gain momentum is the hiring of outside carrier firms to mark fashion goods. Stimulated by the opening of new stores or branches and the inability of the central location to expand its processing space fast enough to permit prompt movement of merchandise to the other stores, many retailers now engage in this practice, including Montgomery Ward, Gimbels, Marshall Field, The Fair (Chicago), Alexander's, Goldblatt's, and Davidson Bros. (Atlanta).

In addition to space pressure, the relatively short life of fashion items has also contributed to the use of carriers to mark fashion goods. Some retailers believe that, since under this practice incoming merchandise can be checked and moved immediately to the selling floor, three or four days are added to the "life" of an item, with a resulting reduction in markdowns.

Re-Marking. Frequently, after merchandise has been marked and placed on the sales floor, markdowns are necessary; some additional markups may be advisable; some merchandise returned by customers must be re-marked; price tickets become soiled, torn, or lost; and departmental transfers of merchandise may call for re-marking. As a general rule, it is desirable that *all* marking remain under the control of receiving-room markers, although it is not necessary in every case for the merchandise to be returned to the receiving room for re-marking. When a department desires to take markdowns on certain items, a marker may be called to the department to do the re-marking there. As previously suggested, by centralizing responsibility for

---

[21] Where manufacturers have placed fictitious prices (that is, relatively high prices to mislead customers) on the tickets, the Federal Trade Commission has opposed the practice. Cf. "FTC Consent," *Women's Wear Daily,* September 24, 1965, p. 2.

[22] Cf. the discussion on pp. 340–43, above. Section 2(e) of the Robinson-Patman Act outlaws discriminatory furnishing of "services or facilities connected with the processing, handling, sale or offering for sale" of commodities.

marking, this activity is performed by specialists who are faster and more accurate; control over price tickets is maintained; and there is more assurance that all price changes will be properly recorded.

In re-marking merchandise, retailers follow two quite different policies so far as the original price is concerned. Some retailers believe that the original price should remain on the merchandise, perhaps just crossed out, with the new price added. This procedure makes it clear to the customer that a "bargain" is available. Other retailers prefer to replace the entire price tag and show just the new price. They reason that the re-marking cost is not increased by this procedure, the resulting price tag is clearer and more attractive to the customer, and the pricing psychology is better—they want to avoid the implication of: "We tried to get you to pay $19.95 for it; you didn't fall for that high price, so we'll now try a lower one."

DISTRIBUTION OF MERCHANDISE

After incoming merchandise has been marked, it is ready for distribution to the reserve stock room or to the selling floor. Information as to where the merchandise shall go is supplied by the proprietor in the small store, by the store manager in the chain store, and by the buyer or department head in the large store. Usually, the receiving-room manager knows from past experience and from the particular type of merchandise where to move the goods. In the case of the large store, however, the buyer may give distributing instructions at the time he "retails" the merchandise. If the merchandise is placed in the stock room, it is released only on requisition from the buyer. The manager or proprietor of the smaller store typically informs the employee who will mark the merchandise some time before the marking step is completed just what is to be done with the goods. Ordinarily, all employees of the small store are allowed in the stock room to get merchandise any time it is needed on the sales floor.

TRAFFIC DEPARTMENT

Up to this point, the discussion of this chapter has been concerned largely with the movement of merchandise *after* it reaches the store. But the retailer is also vitally concerned with the transportation of merchandise from vendor to his receiving point, not only to obtain more rapid deliveries but also to reduce costs and thereby increase his profits. Since "no buyer can, in addition to his other duties, be familiar with the ever-changing transportation field, nor can the average vendor know or employ a traffic expert who knows the best routes and schedules to the hundreds of points to which the company's

product is shipped,"[23] large scale retailers have established traffic departments to fill this gap.

When a retail store has a traffic department, its functions include the
selection of the more desirable routes for shipments of incoming merchandise; the tracing of shipments, when necessary; the checking of freight
classifications and rates, including the auditing of transportation bills of all
kinds; the payment of transportation charges; the placement and collection
of loss and/or damage claims; and other activities associated with the
physical movement of merchandise from vendors.

Savings and benefits realized usually far exceed the cost of performing
these functions.[24] Since the routing of merchandise will affect the transportation cost, the speed of delivery, and the care with which the merchandise is
handled en route to the store, the traffic manager should work with buyers
and assist them in instructing vendors as to how merchandise should be
shipped.[25] Some traffic departments actually hold classes for buyers to make
them "transportation conscious" so that they buy with the transport problem
in mind.[26] When overcharges result from failure to follow instructions,
vendors should be billed for the amounts involved. It is also good practice to
audit all freight bills at regular intervals, that is, to ascertain that merchandise has been shipped in the correct classification, that the proper classification rate has been charged, and that all computations on the bills are correct.

The tracing of delayed shipments is also important. Usually, this means
getting in touch with—and keeping in touch with—the carrier until the
shipment is located. When it is necessary to file claims for loss or damage,
either against the vendor or the carrier, this action should be taken promptly
and full information supplied in support of such claims.

As already noted, a formal department to perform traffic functions is
found only in large retail organizations, such as chain store systems, department stores, and mail order houses. Yet the activities enumerated should be
carried out in stores of all kinds. To this end, in the medium-size store, an
employee performs these tasks under the direction of the store superintendent; and in the small store, responsibility may be assumed by the proprietor
or delegated to an assistant.

---

[23] Wabler, *op. cit.,* p. 378.

[24] The traffic manager at Foley's of Houston, a division of Federated Department Stores,
reports that over a three year period the careful performance of these functions resulted in
a savings of 0.3 percent of sales. *Women's Wear Daily,* April 20, 1966, p. 12.

[25] A helpful "Glossary of Shipping Terms" will be found in J. W. Wingate and J. S.
Friedlander, *The Management of Retail Buying* (Englewood Cliffs, N. J.: Prentice-Hall,
Inc., 1963), pp. 301–3.

[26] For examples, cf. "Ward Attack on Traffic Costs: A Broad Educational Program,"
Chain Store Age (Executives Edition), December, 1963, pp. E33–E36; and the program
of Stewart Dry Goods Co.. Louisville, in *Women's Wear Daily,* May 7, 1963, p. 6.

CHAIN STORE MANAGEMENT OF INCOMING MERCHANDISE

Among chain-store firms operating their own warehouses, there is a considerable variation from the procedures so far discussed. In these firms, receiving and checking are performed at two points—in the warehouse and again in the store. In the former, special facilities are employed to handle the large volume of goods, such as pallets moved by highlift trucks, overhead track towveyor systems, towline arrangements, roller conveyors, and electronic controls.[27] The sizable distributing centers or warehouses operated by food chains are illustrated by Safeway's Distributing Center in Denver, Colorado, which is shown in Figure 15–12.

At the individual stores receiving typically consists of little more than having the truck back up to a rear door (or a front one), with the merchandise moved by conveyor or by hand inside the store. Sometimes goods are stored in a rear room until they can be moved to the shelves for choice by customers. Often, the manager and other employees help the truck driver unload and carry merchandise. Before the unloading starts, the truck driver hands the manager an invoice. As the merchandise is carried in, the manager checks for quantity, returning the invoice to the driver or sending it back to headquarters by mail. The driver is usually required to sign for all shortages. Checking for quality is performed at the warehouse.

In some of the large retail units operated by chain organizations, the handling of merchandise within the store is substantially mechanized. The J. C. Penney Company is experimenting in one store with 1,200 feet of overhead conveyor track which electrically moves aluminum carriers from loading dock to eight different stock areas. Since the merchandise has already been received, checked, and marked at a warehouse, it is ready for sale within 30 minutes after reaching the store.[28]

In chain firms operating relatively small units, the determination of prices is a function of headquarters; and notification of retail prices to be used in a particular store is sent to the manager. Actual marking is usually performed in the store, although there are many exceptions to this general rule. Even in supermarkets operated by chains "there are nearly as many methods of price-marking merchandise as grandmother's remedies for hiccups. In actual practice . . . cases may be price-marked at the warehouse or when they are received at the store. Individual cans or packages may be price-marked as

---

[27] On the problems of receiving, marking and allied activities in the warehouses of chain stores cf. a special report on "Distribution Centers," *Chain Store Age* (Executives Edition), October, 1965, pp. E15–E25. That the fully automatic warehouse is still far in the future is indicated by "Automation," *ibid.,* November, 1965, pp. E22–E26.

[28] Max Shapiro, "Penney's In-Store Distribution Saves Time, Cost, and Bother," *Women's Wear Daily,* November 11, 1966, p. 27.

Courtesy: Safeway Stores, Inc.

FIG. 15–12. Safeway's distributing center in Denver, Colorado. This large center consists of eight buildings designed to meet the company's warehousing needs in the area. Reading from left to right in the center of the picture the various buildings provide storage for (1) groceries, (2) frozen foods, (3) bakery goods, (4) milk products, (5) produce, and (6) meat. The building on the left at the bottom of the picture contains boxes, containers, and salvaged materials and the one on the right houses truck repair activities.

they are received at the store, in the backroom as needed, or at the shelf during the stocking operation."[29] Women's apparel chains quite typically place price tickets on garments before shipment from their warehouses. Even many of the drug, variety, and hard-lines chains have installed the latest type of pricing devices at their warehouses, where they premark some merchandise, with a resulting decrease in cost and an increase in accuracy. Grocery, drug, hardware, and variety chains depend to a large degree on group marking—writing prices on large containers and bins for floor displays and using shelf tickets—with self-service stores commonly writing or stamping the price on the individual item. Store employees usually perform whatever re-marking is necessary as a result of markdowns.

Merchandise shipped directly from vendors to the individual chain store is received, checked, and marked by methods somewhat comparable to those used in the independent store. Even in such situations, however, quality checking is frequently under the control of headquarters employees, who will make spot checks. Price determination may also be performed at headquarters, but the actual marking will be carried out in the store. Invoices are usually sent by vendors directly to headquarters for payment.

ORGANIZATION FOR INCOMING MERCHANDISE

As already suggested, in small stores it is the proprietor—perhaps assisted by a sales person—who handles incoming merchandise. The store large enough to have two or three buyers may make each of them responsible for receiving the lines he purchases.

The advantages of centralizing are so significant, however, that as soon as a retail organization is large enough, receiving, checking, marking, distributing, and traffic are usually placed under the operations manager or superintendent, with a receiving manager or a traffic manager exercising day-by-day responsibility.[30] In contrast, some large and medium-size organizations place these activities under the controller or under the merchandise manager. As a matter of fact, both of these latter arrangements may be entirely logical. In making the decision as to where to place responsibility, probably the most important factor is that of executive personalities and previous experience. If the controller or the merchandise manager is particularly qualified to handle receiving, it is quite likely that the responsibility will be delegated to him rather than to the operating manager or superintendent.

Regardless of the specific assignment of responsibility for these activities in the present organizational structure, it is evident that management must give increased attention to them in the years ahead. To this end, some firms are creating distribution managers (sometimes with the rank of a vice president) with broad responsibility over traffic, warehousing, and inventory control.[31] It seems likely that still other retailers will seek the benefits which flow from this step.

REVIEW AND DISCUSSION QUESTIONS

1. Discuss: "An adequate performance level for the activities related to incoming merchandise is significant both to the customer and to the retailer."
2. Based on your personal observations in five stores, do you agree or disagree (and why) with Mr. Boykoff's opinion that "merchandise handling has not yet received sufficient attention" from top management?

---

[30] Cf. R. C. Bond, "Department Store Organization," in *The Buyer's Manual, op. cit.,* pp. 14–15.

[31] For details cf. H. J. Bullen, "The Growing Importance of Physical Distribution Management," *Management Review,* July, 1965, pp. 31–34; and "The Next Place for Paring Costs," *Business Week,* May 1, 1965, pp. 132–36.

3. Summarize the merits and limitations of centralizing receiving, checking, and marking activities. What do you consider to be the best solution for handling these activities when branch or suburban stores are operated by the "parent"?

4. What factors are decisive in choosing a physical location for the receiving department? How do these differ among large stores and small stores?

5. How do you account for the fact that general reserve stock rooms are not so important as they were three decades ago?

6. Visit the receiving departments of (*a*) a small neighborhood grocery store, (*b*) a supermarket, (*c*) a men's shop, and (*d*) a discount house. Prepare a report evaluating the layout of this department in each store.

7. Prepare a five minute report on this subject: Mechanization of Receiving, Checking, and Marking Activities.

8. "Checking consists of four quite distinct steps." Explain each.

9. Based on conversations with (1) the proprietor of a women's ready-to-wear shop, (2) the dress buyer for a department store, and (3) a women's apparel chain buyer, discuss the shipment of dresses on hangers, covering extent of the practice, advantages, disadvantages, and future possibilities.

10. Differentiate clearly among the chief methods of checking merchandise for *quantity*. Which method seems most practical for the small store? for the larger store?

11. Visit a department store and a supermarket in your area and determine the methods each employs to mark the merchandise it sells. Ascertain the reasoning behind their marking policies.

12. Discuss the major functions of the traffic department.

13. What means are used by retailers to create a "transportation consciousness" on the part of buyers?

14. In what ways do the receiving, checking, and marking activities of chain stores differ from those of single-unit retail establishments?

15. Describe the organization structure for handling incoming merchandise in department stores, chain store systems, and small stores. Are there any significant organizational trends?

SUPPLEMENTARY READINGS

Helpful booklets and descriptions of equipment used in receiving and related activities are available from many equipment manufacturers, such as Dennison Manufacturing Co., Framingham, Massachusetts; Kimball Systems, Inc. (a division of Litton Industries), 15 Daniel Street, Farmingdale, New York; Lamson Corporation, 625 Lamson Street, Syracuse, New York; Monarch Marking System Co., Dayton, Ohio; and Rapids-Standard Co., Inc., 825 Rapistan Building, Grand Rapids, Michigan.

BRINKMANN, T. H. "There's a Device for Repetitively Marking Just About Anything," *Office,* December, 1965, pp. 72–73 ff. The author reviews modern devices for marking.

Chain Store Age (Executives Edition) "Distribution Centers" (October, 1965), pp. E15–25; and "Automation" (November, 1965), pp. E22–E25. In these two articles the reader will find comprehensive explanations of merchandise handling in a variety of chain-store warehouses. The methods used by Montgomery Ward & Company to reduce the cost of merchandise movement are detailed in "Ward Attack on Traffic Costs: A Broad Educational Program" (December, 1964), pp. E33–E36.

Handling Groceries from Warehouse to Retail Store Shelves (Washington, D.C.: U.S. Department of Agriculture, Agriculture Marketing Service, 1961). Based on a study of leading chain organizations, this booklet reviews all the activities involved in the handling of groceries in the warehouse and moving them to the retail store.

LOCKLIN, D. P. *Economics of Transportation* (6th ed.; Homewood, Ill.: Richard D. Irwin, Inc., 1966). With transportation playing an ever-increasing role in the problems associated with incoming merchandise, the retailer needs the overall understanding of this field which is provided by this volume.

MONGEON, L. F. (ed.). *Receiving Department Operations Manual* (New York: National Retail Merchants Association, 1961). Written by a number of successful retailers, this volume covers all aspects of the receiving function and related activites.

MOSSMAN, F. H., AND MORTON, NEWTON. *Logistics of Distribution Systems* (Boston, Mass.: Allyn and Bacon, Inc., 1965). Warehousing and inventory controls are emphasized in this text on physical distribution.

NATIONAL RETAIL MERCHANTS ASSOCIATION. *The Buyer's Manual* (4th ed.; New York: The Association, 1965). Chap. 38 of this valuable reference guide, written by E. H. Wabler, summarizes information on traffic, receiving, and marking. Also cf. *Marking Methods Manual,* which describes the best methods of price-ticketing some 2,600 lines of merchandise, and *Manual for Reducing Transportation Costs,* which contains numerous suggestions for minimizing transportation costs as well as a list of 805 shipping points for different kinds of goods. Also of interest is *Traffic Topics.* Issued ten times a year by the Association, this publication summarizes recent developments (1) in systems and procedures related to merchandise handling and (2) in transportation rates and shipping regulations.

OI, W. Y., AND HURTER, A. P., JR. *Economics of Private Truck Transportation* (Dubuque, Iowa: Wm. C. Brown Company, 1965). The second volume in a three-volume study, the authors analyze the growth of private trucking, who uses it, and why.

PRICHARD, J. W., AND EAGLE, R. H. *Modern Inventory Management* (New York: John Wiley & Sons, Inc., 1965). In this primer on inventory management—and, it should be emphasized, merchandise being received, checked, marked, and distributed is part of the inventory—the authors treat both "practical" and theoretical aspects of the subject.

TAFF, C. A. *Management of Traffic and Physical Distribution* (3d ed.; Homewood, Ill.: Richard D. Irwin, Inc., 1964). Although dealing mainly with traffic management from the manufacturer's point of view, the retailer can also benefit from this complete coverage of the subject.

16
CHAPTER

Pricing Merchandise

SUCCESSFUL PRICING CONTRIBUTES TO MAXIMUM PROFITS

It is the aim of each retailer to get the largest total profit which his store will yield, considering both his ability and the effort he is willing to put forth.[1] To this end, his store location must be chosen with care; and the store's layout must be well planned. Buying must be peformed with full knowledge of what the customer wants and of where the needed merchandise may be secured at the lowest cost. Merchandise and budgetary control contribute to the same end—larger net profits. So it is with pricing. Although successful pricing is often put forth as *the* means of maximizing profits, actually it is only one of several steps the store must take to secure such profits. Yet pricing is an important step and needs to be given careful consideration. The retailer who fails to establish adequate pricing policies may eventually discover that he is on the road to failure.

Pricing from the Long-Run Point of View

Several things need to be made clear concerning pricing for maximum profits. The first of these is that a long-run point of view must be maintained by the retailer. When a retailer begins business, he may plan to sell at such low prices that he will no more than "break even" during the first months while he is building up a clientele. In the short run, such a low-price policy

---

[1] Of course, the retailer (like every other businessman) also has secondary goals in mind, such as growth of his company and the firm's prestige in the community. Cf. the discussions by W. J. Baumol, "Company Goals, Growth, and the Multiproduct Firm," in Reavis Cox, Wroe Alderson, and S. J. Shapiro, *Theory in Marketing* (Homewood, Ill.: Richard D. Irwin, Inc., 1964), pp. 324–26 and 332; and by E. T. Grether, *Marketing and Public Policy* (Englewood Cliffs, N.J.: Prentice-Hall, Inc., 1966), chap. 4, "Environment and Goals of the Enterprise."

may not maximize profits; but if it enables him to build a sufficient volume of business, this policy may be maximizing his profits when a long-run period is considered.

Individual Item Profit and Total Profit

For the retailer to price his goods so as to maximize profits does not mean that each item sold must carry a profit. As a matter of fact, some of the most successful retailers have found that one of the best ways to attract customers is to price certain items very low.[2] When customers are in the store to purchase the low-priced items, sufficient amounts of other goods may be purchased to make the retailer's total profit larger than if he had made no use of "leaders." In other words, it is the *total* profit which the retailer wants to maximize, not the profit on any particular good.

Maximum Profits and Height of Prices

A third point concerning maximum profits is that they do not result necessarily from selling at relatively high prices. Every retailer should keep firmly in mind the fact that profits are the result of the relationships among sales, prices, costs of merchandise, and expenses of operation. Sometimes these factors will indicate maximum profits with prices higher than those now being charged, but they may also suggest that profits will be increased if prices are reduced.

The foregoing may be made clear by an illustration: Retailer A is following a high-price policy which limits his sales to those customers who are located especially close to his store plus those who feel that he has somewhat superior merchandise as compared with his competitors. His total annual volume is $50,000, merchandise cost $35,000, operating expenses $13,000, leaving $2,000 as net profit. Not satisfied with this profit, Mr. A decides to experiment with lower prices. His lower prices prove so attractive that his sales gradually expand to $75,000 a year. In view of larger purchases which give rise to greater discounts, his cost of merchandise expands in a somewhat smaller ratio than sales, thus becoming $52,000 and leaving him a gross margin of $23,000. Although the added sales result in higher operating expenses, many of his expense items do not increase very much. For example, his rent remains the same; and heat, light, and power costs advance but little. Even his total payroll expands only slightly, since those employed previously are able to handle most of the added business. As a net

---

[2] Cf. the discussion of "Leader Merchandising," pp. 498–503, below.

result, operating expenses rise just to $17,000. Thus, in spite of selling at lower prices, Mr. A's profit gains from $2,000 to $6,000.

The recognition that relatively low prices may lead to a sufficient sales growth to increase total profits lies at the root of the pricing policies followed by many retailers.[3] As a general statement it may be said that, among others, chain stores, mail-order companies, supermarkets, and discount houses have priced according to this concept. The net result, of course, has been a rise in the standard of living of their customers—as well as an advance in their profits. Unfortunately, the majority of retailers in many other countries continue to practice a high markup, low-volume concept, although there are an encouraging number of exceptions to this statement.[4]

Pricing as an Art

Finally, it needs to be emphasized that pricing for maximum profits is an art as well as a science. As one authority has written: ". . . to view pricing *solely* as a problem in the economics of price determination is to miss the flavor of the real pricing problem."[5] Customer response to prices established by a retailer cannot be forecast with any high degree of accuracy. Nor can the retailer say with assurance that prices at a certain level will result in the creation of good will which, in turn, will build a long-run repeat business. Put another way, although the retailer should make use of all the scientific evidence he can find, he should recognize that a vast amount of intuition, as well as trial and error, is an essential ingredient to successful pricing at the retail level. In fact, it is probably not too much to say that intuition "enters to some degree in most pricing decisions" throughout the entire channel of distribution.[6]

ONE-PRICE POLICY

At least apparent adherence to a one-price policy is customary among retailers in this country. Following this policy, a retailer offers each item for

---

[3] For a specific example of a food chain pricing on this principle cf. "Competitive Pricing," *Food Merchandising,* March–April, 1964, p. 40. However, some authorities caution that the expected sales gain from lower prices may easily be overstated. Cf. C. E. Griffin, "When Is Price Reduction Profitable?" *Harvard Business Review,* Vol. XXXVIII, No. 5 (September–October, 1960), pp. 125–32.

[4] For evidence on the high markup, low-volume concept in Spain, cf. E. H. Lewis, "Marketing in Spain," *Journal of Marketing,* Vol. XXVIII, No. 4 (October, 1964), p. 20.

[5] J. A. Howard, *Marketing Management* (rev. ed.; Homewood, Ill.: Richard D. Irwin, Inc., 1963), p. 350.

[6] Wroe Alderson and P. E. Green, *Planning and Problem Solving in Marketing* (Homewood, Ill.: Richard D. Irwin, Inc., 1964), p. 242.

sale at one price to all patrons who purchase in comparable quantities and under similar conditions. By way of illustration, a particular brand of women's hose is priced at $1.35 a pair, or two pairs for $2.65; and no matter who happens to be the buyer, the price will not vary. Ordinarily, the price is attached to the hose by means of a price ticket or in some other manner is made evident to all potential customers.

Development and Advantages of One-Price Policy

We are so accustomed to a one-price policy that we usually overlook the possibility of a retailer's following a variable-price policy, under which retail prices are determined by direct bargaining between customers and store-keeper. However, such bargaining is still common throughout much of the world and was the practice in this country until a fairly recent period.[7] In fact, it seems that the practice of placing definite prices on goods, which customers were free to accept or reject, did not spread among retailers until after the Civil War. A study of contemporary newspaper advertisements indicates that Mid-western retailers were shifting from a varying price policy to a one-price system in the latter half of the 1860's and the early 1870's.[8] Apparently, A. T. Stewart and Tiffany & Company of New York and John Wanamaker of Philadelphia were among the leaders in the movement. In 1881 when J. L. Hudson founded the store which still bears his name in Detroit, he advertised: "We have adopted the 'strictly one-price' policy and mark all our goods in plain figures."[9] These retailers found that the one-price policy increased the confidence people had in their stores, since under the old system no customer knew whether or not he was getting the best possible treatment. In addition, individual bargaining was found to be time-consuming for both salesman and customer. The advantages of the plan caused others to follow the lead of these merchants, so that today the store professing to follow a varying-price policy is the exception to the rule.

Varying-Price Policy Still Common. In actual practice, however, there is more use of a varying-price policy than is apparent. Retailers of

---

[7] Concerning Nigeria, R. W. Baker reports: "Bargaining is the general rule, sometimes animated and vociferous, sometimes quite subtle. A price once offered can be changed if accepted too quickly, thereby reinitiating the bargaining process." Cf. his "Marketing in Nigeria," *Journal of Marketing,* Vol. XXXIX, No. 3 (July, 1965), p. 46. Also cf. H. L. Munn, "Retailing in Nigeria," *Journal of Retailing,* Vol. XLII, No. 3 (Fall, 1966), pp. 26–32, 40, esp. p. 27.

[8] W. A. Tonning, "The Beginnings of the Money-Back Guarantee and the One-Price Policy in Champaign-Urbana, Illinois, 1833–1880," *Business History Review,* June, 1956, pp. 196–210.

[9] Oscar Webber, *J. L. Hudson: The Man and the Store* (New York: Newcomen Society in North America, 1954), p. 11.

automobiles, electric refrigerators, radios, television sets, and other consumer durable goods find that many of their customers offer "trade-ins" and that, in the bargaining necessary to establish a value for trade-ins, the one-price policy disappears. Frequently, it vanishes even when no trade-in is involved: one student, who in an earlier study of automobile dealers found them giving discounts of 14 to 18 percent off list on new cars when no used car was turned in, summarized his various studies of high-unit value goods by reporting that "the price had to be determined through negotiations."[10] And many a discount house customer knows from experience that if he does not like the quoted price on (say) a washing machine, he can dicker at the store—and frequently wind up with a better one. Moreover, in many of the smaller and medium-size stores, expecially those dealing in other than convenience goods, "price-shading" is fairly common. In fact, it seems likely that a major portion of discount buying for high-unit value consumer durable goods is not being carried on by discount houses as such, but by retail dealers who will cut prices before they lose a sale.

Some retailers maintain that a reduction in the quoted price is all right if it can be covered up. Perhaps the customer can be talked into taking two items for a sum less than the two usual prices, thus making the reduction appear as a quantity discount. Or the retailer may explain that he is planning to take a markdown on the item in the near future so that he is merely taking it a few days sooner than he planned. In such a case, it might be made clear to the customer that this is an exceptional case, not to be repeated. Or perhaps the retailer may agree to make a certain amount of alterations at no charge. However, it seems to the authors that the risks of becoming known as a retailer who is willing to bargain are too great. A one-price policy builds confidence, and successful retailing is built on confidence.[11]

Single-Price Policy: A Type of One-Price Policy

Sometimes a one-price policy is confused with a single-price policy, although the latter is really only one of the forms that a one-price policy may take. Under a single-price policy, all merchandise of the same general type is offered for sale at the same price. Thus a store selling inexpensive millinery may price all its hats at $5.88, offering customers a wide assortment at this single price.

---

[10] A. F. Jung, "Retail Pricing Policies on Small Appliances," *Journal of Retailing*, Vol. XLI, No. 1 (Spring, 1965), p. 17.

[11] As a matter of fact, throughout the whole field of marketing students of the subject usually agree that a one-price system is "sound marketing policy." For example, cf. W. B. England, *Procurement: Principles and Cases* (4th ed.; Homewood, Ill.: Richard D. Irwin, Inc., 1962), p. 579.

MARKUP

Meaning of Markup

A helpful approach to the factors influencing the prices asked by a retailer is through a discussion of markup. "Retail markup" means the amount that is added to the cost price to arrive at the retail price, a relationship which is frequently stated in the phrase "cost plus markup equals retail." This amount may be expressed in dollars or as a percentage of the retail price.[12] For instance, an item costing $0.80 and sold for $1.20 carried a markup of $0.40, or 33⅓ percent. Markup may refer to a single item, as in the preceding sentence; or it may be used concerning a department, a store, or a chain of stores. Thus, if a toy department operating merely during the Christmas season places prices totaling $10,000 on goods costing $6,000, the markup is $4,000, or 40 percent.

Initial Markup versus Gross Margin. It is essential to distinguish between the initial markup and the maintained markup or gross margin. The initial markup, also known as the "original markup" or the "markon," is the difference between the cost and the first retail price placed on the goods. Using the same figures as those of the preceding paragraph, an item costing $0.80 and originally priced at $1.20 carried an initial markup of $0.40, or 33⅓ percent. However, perhaps customers refused to buy this item at $1.20, and it was finally cut to $0.98 before it was sold. The difference between the cost and the actual selling price, $0.18, or 18.4 percent in this case, is referred to as the "maintained markup" or "gross margin." In other words, whereas the initial markup represents the amount by which the original retail price of goods exceeds their cost, the maintained markup or gross margin is the amount above cost realized when the goods are sold. It should be evident that, from the point of view of profitable operation, the maintained markup is more important than the initial markup. If, in the preceding case, it cost the store more than $0.18 to sell the item, the store lost money on that particular item.

Cost of Merchandise. In speaking of the markup as the difference between the cost of merchandise and its selling price, exactly what is meant by cost? To clarify: A shipment of goods carries an invoice total of $100. However, this $100 is subject to a quantity discount of 10 percent,[13] a cash discount of 2 percent, and a freight charge of $5.00. Is the cost of merchandise $100 (face of invoice), $105 (invoice plus transportation), $88.20

---

[12] Some retailers still follow the older practice of expressing this difference as a percentage of the cost.

[13] The quantity discount would be this high only in a few fields. Cf. discussion of quantity discounts, pp. 338–43, above.

(all discounts deducted),[14] or some other figure? Since we want to know exactly what the goods cost the retailer delivered to his store, we would find the figure as follows: $100 minus $10 (quantity discount), minus $1.80 (cash discount), plus $5.00 (freight), or $93.20. In other words, "cost of merchandise" means the invoice cost of merchandise minus discounts plus inward transportation charges paid by the retailer. If on a net cost of merchandise of $93.20 the retailer wants an initial markup of 40 percent, he would price these goods at $155.33.[15]

It should be noted, however, that many retailers prefer to overstate their cost of merchandise so that they have a "cushion," or an extra margin, as protection. These retailers do not deduct their cash discounts from the face of the invoice in determining their merchandise cost.[16] Using this method in the preceding case, the cost of merchandise would be stated as $95 and, since a 40 percent retail markup is equal to 66⅔ percent markup on cost, the goods would be priced to return $158.33. The $3.00 increase in the total retail figure is the "cushion" provided by using the higher cost figure.

Role of Markup in Pricing

It might be thought that the markup can be used as a simple mechanistic method of setting prices, as follows: The proprietor of a store determines from his past records that his operating costs equal 29 percent of sales and his profit is 3 percent on sales. Thus, by pricing his goods so that a gross margin of 32 percent on sales is secured, he will be able to meet his costs and make a profit. However, this procedure demands more than a 32 percent initial markup; after being put into stock, some goods may be subject to markdowns or lost through pilferage. In addition, stores commonly have a policy of selling to employees at a discount. Perhaps the total reductions (markdowns, shortages, and discounts to employees) are estimated as 6 percent of sales. Using the formula

$$\text{Initial markup percentage} = \frac{\text{Gross margin} + \text{Retail reductions}}{100 \text{ percent} + \text{Retail reductions}},$$

the proprietor arrives at the following initial markup percentage:

$$\frac{32 \text{ percent} + 6 \text{ percent}}{100 \text{ percent} + 6 \text{ percent}} = \frac{38 \text{ percent}}{106 \text{ percent}} = 35.85 \text{ percent.}$$

---

[14] Ten percent from $100 leaves $90. Two percent from $90 leaves $88.20.

[15] In other words, 66⅔ percent of $93.20 is $155.33. In practice, of course, the unit price multiplied by the number of units would just approximate this figure.

[16] That is, some store executives prefer to treat the cash discount as a financial earning and enter it as part of "other income" on the operating statement. Most businessmen, however, consider the cash discount to be a merchandise earning, as it is treated in the preceding paragraph.

Thus, to get a gross margin of 32 percent, an initial markup of approximately 36 percent is needed.

A question typical of those that frequently confront the retailer is the following: What price should be placed on each of 24 items having a total cost of $7.80 to provide an initial markup of 36 percent? To answer this question, the retailer might use the formula given below:

$$\text{Retail price} = \frac{\text{Cost}}{100 \text{ percent} - \text{Markup}} \times 100 = \frac{\$7.80}{64} \times 100 = \$12.19$$

Consequently, he would sell each of the 24 items for approximately $0.50.

Rather than use the preceding formula, many retailers prefer to convert the markup on retail into a markup on cost, so that the markup can be

TABLE 16–1

MARKUP TABLE

Find the desired retail markup percentage in the left-hand column. Multiply the cost of the article by the corresponding percentage in the right-hand or cost-markup column. The result added to the cost gives the correct selling price.

Markup Percent of Selling Price	Markup Percent of Cost	Markup Percent of Selling Price	Markup Percent of Cost	Markup Percent of Selling Price	Markup Percent of Cost
5.0	5.3	18.5	22.7	33.3	50.0
6.0	6.4	19.0	23.5	34.0	51.5
7.0	7.5	20.0	25.0	35.0	53.9
8.0	8.7	21.0	26.6	35.5	55.0
9.0	10.0	22.0	28.2	36.0	56.3
10.0	11.1	22.5	29.0	37.0	58.8
10.7	12.0	23.0	29.9	37.5	60.0
11.0	12.4	23.1	30.0	38.0	61.3
11.1	12.5	24.0	31.6	39.0	64.0
12.0	13.6	25.0	33.3	39.5	65.5
12.5	14.3	26.0	35.0	40.0	66.7
13.0	15.0	27.0	37.0	41.0	70.0
14.0	16.3	27.3	37.5	42.0	72.4
15.0	17.7	28.0	39.0	42.8	75.0
16.0	19.1	28.5	40.0	44.4	80.0
16.7	20.0	29.0	40.9	46.1	85.0
17.0	20.5	30.0	42.9	47.5	90.0
17.5	21.2	31.0	45.0	48.7	95.0
18.0	22.0	32.0	47.1	50.0	100.0

SOURCE: National Cash Register Company, *Expenses in Retail Businesses* (Dayton, Ohio: The Company, n.d.), p. 44.

multiplied by the cost and the result then added to the cost to give the selling price. In this case, the retailer will want to know what percentage on cost is equal to 36 percent on retail. Although he will usually consult a markup table, such as is illustrated in Table 16–1, he may make the conversion by means of the following formula:

$$\text{Markup on cost} = \frac{\text{Markup on retail}}{100 \text{ percent} - \text{Markup on retail}} \times 100 \text{ percent}$$

$$\text{Markup on cost} = \frac{36 \text{ percent}}{100 \text{ percent} - 36 \text{ percent}} \times 100 \text{ percent} = 56.25 \text{ percent.}$$

Since 56.25 percent of the cost of $7.80 is $4.39, the 24 items should be sold to yield $12.19.

Using a Single Markup. Once a retailer has decided upon the *average* markup needed, by no means has he solved all his pricing problems. In practice he finds it unwise to add the same markup to all his goods.[17] It may be that, for some goods, a markup of 5 percent on retail is most advantageous; at the other extreme, some goods may carry a markup as high as 75 percent. Table 16–2 presents indirect evidence on this point by showing the margins secured by a supermarket chain.

TABLE 16–2

RETAIL MARGINS FOR A SUPERMARKET CHAIN
(Expressed as Percentage of Sales)

Item	Margin
Sugar	9.2
Coffee	11.1
Soaps	13.0
Baby foods	13.2
Soups	17.1
Cereals	20.7
Canned meat	22.5
Paper products	22.7
Condiments	25.0
Spices	30.7
Household accessories	35.0
Bulbs	48.0

SOURCE: P. J. Cifrino, "Cifrino's Space Yield Formula," *Chain Store Age* (Supermarket Executives Edition), November, 1963, p. 85.

Let us consider just a few of the reasons why the use of a single markup for all the goods in a store is usually considered an unwise policy. Goods having the same cost may vary markedly in appeal to customers. Competition may be too strong on some items to allow the store to get its desired average markup. Some goods may be so subject to markdowns that they are unprofitable unless their initial markup is very high. Also, it costs more to sell some goods than others; they require more display, more time from the salesperson, and more advertising. A higher-than-average markup is needed to offset this greater cost. Furthermore, the retailer will find customary

---

[17] For a short-time exception cf. the story of a supermarket operator who priced all the merchandise in his grocery department at his wholesale cost plus 10 percent added during the checkout operation, However, within two years the firm discontinued business. Cf. "Discount Test Not Right for Justrite," *Super Market Merchandising,* September, 1964, p. 12.

markups—some high and some low—in wide use; and he usually finds it desirable to adhere rather closely to these markups. Hence, even though a retailer makes use of a single markup percentage as a point of departure in his pricing, the actual price established may vary considerably from that indicated by the application of the average markup percentage.

Using Several Markups. One step away from the use of a single markup is the practice followed by many retailers of dividing their stocks into several groups and applying different markups to each group.[18] A food retailer realizes that he may have to take large markdowns on his fresh fruits and vegetables to clear his shelves, or he may even have to throw some away. In contrast, he expects a steady turnover with no significant markdown on his canned fruits and vegetables. Consequently, he reasons that a 30 percent initial markup is necessary on fresh fruits and vegetables, whereas 20 percent is satisfactory for canned goods. The shopkeeper dealing in women's dresses as well as more staple women's apparel items also finds it necessary to use different markups. On goods most subject to markdowns, perhaps an initial markup of 50 percent is needed; more staple goods can be carried profitably on a 30–40 percent markup.

Individual Item Pricing.[19] Increasingly, retailers are recognizing that even the use of several markups for different commodity groups does not result in maximum profits. As a result, they are looking more at the profitability of each item and setting a price which maximizes the item's contribution to dollar profit, regardless of whether this price gives a percentage margin in line with that historically expected.

Specifically, under this concept it may be more profitable for a retailer to sell an item at a 24 percent markup than at his customary 40 percent. In other words, the resulting increase in total dollar margin from the more rapid turnover at the lower percentage margin may more than offset the added operating cost of handling more units. To use some figures: assume that a retailer is selling daily an average of two units of an electric appliance at $100 each. His merchandise cost is $60 each so that his gross dollar margin is $40 each (40 percent of retail) or $80 per day on this item ($40 each × 2 units sold). Assume further that by reducing his price to $79 his daily sales increase to six units. While his percentage margin now drops approximately to 24 percent ($19 on a selling price of $79), his *total* dollar margin on this item becomes $114 ($19 each × 6 units sold). Unless his direct cost

---

[18] Some pricing students refer to the use of a single markup as "cost-plus pricing" and employ the phrase "flexible markup pricing" when markup varies by groups of products. Cf. A. R. Oxenfeldt, *Pricing for Executives* (Belmont, Calif.: Wadsworth Publishing Co., Inc., 1961), p. 70.

[19] This subject is treated more fully in the discussion of merchandise management accounting in Chapter 24, below.

resulting from the sale of six units instead of two units increases by more than $34 (the additional dollar gross margin), his total dollar profits will show a gain.

To implement individual item pricing, some large scale retailers have undertaken careful (and costly) studies of the turnover of various items when sold at different markups. Voluntary chain wholesalers prepare price guides which suggest to their retailers the "most profitable" markups for each item they carry.[20] Some retail trade associations offer a similar service to their members.[21] Careful academic investigations and analyses have also been made.[22] These studies should add to the retailer's ability to maximize his profits through better pricing practices.

SOME FACTORS INFLUENCING MARKUP

Even retailers who have tried to break down their stocks into groups to which they apply various markups or who attempt individual item pricing often find it necessary to deviate from their usual markups. Moreover, markup policies vary from retailer to retailer. We now turn to some of the many factors causing such deviations in markup. No significance is to be attached to the order in which these factors are presented, since their importance varies from case to case.

Customer Appeal of the Goods

If one is realistic, he will recognize that the cost of an item sometimes has little relationship to how much the item appeals to customers. Of two dresses purchased at $8.75, one may move readily at $16.75; the other may hang on the rack even after being marked down to $9.75. Women's hats are another case in point. The important thing is the appeal of the hat, not its cost. One of the most difficult things in pricing is to recognize the goods that will or will not appeal to customers and to price the merchandise accordingly. Consequently, one successful retailer offers this advice: "Buyers should spend enough time in the receiving room properly appraising goods in terms

---

[20] An illustration of such a guide for food retailers is given in C. E. Shaffer "How We Balance Pricing," *Super Market Merchandising,* September, 1965, pp. 48–50 and 72.

[21] Cf. The National Retail Hardware Association's Stock Selection Guide as described in R. R. Mueller, "Shortest Route to Increased Profits," *Hardware Retailer,* December, 1965, p. 15.

[22] For example, cf. R. D. Buzzell *et al, Product Profitability Measurement and Merchandising Decisions* (Boston, Mass.: Harvard Graduate School of Business Administration, 1965).

of *what prices they will bring.* They should also examine the merchandise in their departments rather than rely on stock figures or unit control records exclusively. They must develop a 'feel for merchandise' that tells them almost instinctively what items and styles will sell at a profit."[23]

Pricing at Competitors' Level

A retailer may decide to deviate from the price necessary to give him his usual markup to meet a competitor's price. That this policy is not new is indicated by its inclusion in the Wanamaker Guarantee, announced in the early days of this well-known concern: "We hereby guarantee . . . that the prices of our goods shall be as low as the same quality of material and manufacture as sold anywhere in the United States."[24]

Today, many retailers meet competitors' prices—some of them going so far as to meet *all* prices of *all* competitors, but with the majority being more selective both as to the items and the competitors. This price policy is followed by the majority of the supermarket chains, with each chain typically matching the advertised "leader" prices of its main competitor rather than trying to meet all competitors.[25] In the department store field, the units of the Federated Department Stores and J. L. Hudson Company of Detroit, are advocates of the "meet competitors' prices" policy. Even on merchandise sold by discount houses, they follow this policy—Hudson's refunding to its customers any differential between its prices and those of any competitor and ". . . Federated's stores meet(ing) competitive prices even if it means operating a whole department at a loss."[26] To provide the facts necessary for the implementation of this price policy, "today the majority of large stores employ one or more persons [comparison shoppers] specifically for the task of comparing merchandise and prices, as well as various aspects of service" in competing stores.[27]

---

[23] Morey Sostrin, "Merchandising To a Profit," *The Buyer's Manual* (4th ed.; New York: National Retail Merchants Association, 1965), p. 282.

[24] J. H. Appel, *The Business Biography of John Wanamaker* (New York: Macmillan Co., 1930), p. 70.

[25] George Fisk, S. J. Shapiro, and Lawrence Nein, "Price Rivalry among Philadelphia Food Chains," *Journal of Advertising Research,* June, 1964, p. 12: and Wroe Alderson, *et al., The Structure of Retail Competition in the Philadelphia Market* (Philadelphia: Wharton School of Finance and Commerce, 1960), p. 23.

[26] C. E. Silberman, "The Department Stores Are Waking Up," *Fortune,* Vol. LXVI, No. 1 (July, 1962), p. 246.

[27] K. R. Gillespie, "The Role of Espionage in Retailing," *Journal of Retailing,* Vol. XXXIX, No. 1 (Spring, 1963), p. 8. For the comparison shopping practices of food, variety, and drug chains, cf. "How Competition Is Checking You," *Chain Store Age* (Grocery Executives Edition), July, 1961, pp. 30–32.

Pricing below Competitors' Level

Markups in some stores are influenced by the policy of going one step beyond meeting competition, that is, actually underselling competition. Many discount houses and some supermarket operators are avid pursuers of this pricing policy.[28] R. H. Macy & Company of New York advertises widely that—"with reasonable exceptions which include goods price-controlled by the manufacturer"—it attempts to price its merchandise 6 percent below its credit-granting competitors. Sears, Roebuck and Co. stated its underselling policy in these words which appeared in one of its nation-wide advertisements: "If Sears cannot offer an equal product for less money or a superior product for the same amount, Sears does not offer you this product at all." Comparison shopping is employed by the firm to be sure this policy is put into practice.

Price Wars.[29]   While an underselling policy is often effective with customers, it does not make those practicing it popular with competing retailers. In fact, like the use of loss leaders which is discussed in the next chapter, the policy may lead to a price war, that is, a "head-on conflict between (or among) vendors . . . [which] is characterized by successive moves and countermoves with resulting downward spiraling of prices."[30]

Usually confined to a single product or to a limited number of fast-moving items, price wars can bring prices to a relatively low point. When one supermarket operator in the Minneapolis–St. Paul area reduced bread by 8 cents a loaf, his competitors made even deeper cuts and soon the normal 23-cent loaf was selling two for 29 cents. In Indianapolis, a price war reduced the price of a half gallon of milk from 36 cents to 10 cents, far below even the wholesale cost of the milk which was about 26 cents. Gasoline normally selling at 31.9 cents per gallon in a California city dropped to 19.9 cents, although 5 to 10 cent discounts are more common in gasoline price conflicts.[31] Why the original price-cutter may be unpopular with his competitors is suggested by the report that during a San Antonio gasoline price war, more than 150 out of 250 private-brand service stations went out of business.[32]

---

[28] For some evidence as to "considerable price variations and differences among prices charged by retail institutions," cf. another of the several studies by A. F. Jung, "A Different Retail Price Pattern: The Case of Carpeting," *Journal of Business,* Vol. XXXVIII, No. 2 (April, 1965), pp. 180–5.

[29] Also cf. the discussion of price wars on pp. 502–3, below.

[30] Ralph Cassady, Jr., "Price Warfare—A Form of Business Rivalry," in Cox, Alderson, and Shapiro, *op. cit.,* p. 356.

[31] For other examples of price reductions resulting from price warfare cf. *ibid.,* pp. 362, 369, and 371.

[32] "Gasoline War," *Wall Street Journal,* May 2, 1962, p. 1.

Characteristics of Low-Price Retailers. Underselling retailers usually have certain definite characteristics. One of these is that they are "hard" buyers; to get a markup high enough to let them show a profit, they must have a low cost of merchandise. Frequently they operate with low-cost physical facilities, one such store being described as follows: "Floors are bare cement; walls are exposed cinderblock; the ceiling is unfinished—fluorescent lights are hung on exposed steel girders and dry groceries are sold out of cut cases displayed in warehouse bags."[33] Such stores also try to keep expenses at a minimum by dispensing with many of the services offered by other stores. They may limit their stocks to the fast-moving items; customers may be expected to assist themselves to some degree; and credit and delivery services may not be offered or may be extended on a very restricted basis. Their advertising consists largely of comparative prices on the merchandise offered for sale. In other words, retailers who adopt this particular price policy must adopt consistent policies in other areas: those who do not will soon find themselves characterized by the sign in a window of a vacant store—"We undersold everybody." In addition, such stores frequently are strong advocates of private brands, the use of which limits direct price comparisons between the "low-price" stores and their competitors.

1. *Discount House Pricing.* Many of the characteristics of low-price retailers mentioned in the preceding paragraph are well illustrated by the discount houses.[34] Consequently, they have been able to achieve relatively low operating cost ratios: One study of 28 such firms reports an interquartile average cost-to-sales ratio of 27.0 percent which may be contrasted with 30.5 percent for department stores with about the same annual sales per store.[35] In turn, they can cover their total operating expenses and earn a satisfactory profit with prices below those of many competitors.[36] Not infrequently, merchants operating leased departments in discount houses are required to sell at a fixed low markup or to price their merchandise at a certain percentage below competitors' prices.[37] While few careful price studies are available,

[33] "24-Hour Merchandising Laboratory," *Chain Store Age* (Supermarket Executives Edition), February, 1966, p. 56.

[34] Cf. our earlier discussion of this important retail institution, pp. 15–18, above.

[35] "University of Massachusetts Issues Pilot Study of Discount Stores," *Discount Store News,* May 17, 1965, p. 3; and *Operating Results of Self-Service Discount Department Stores* (Amherst, Mass.: University of Massachusetts, School of Business Administration, 1966).

[36] For the reaction of department stores to discount house competition cf. Walter Gross, "Strategies Used by Major Department Stores to Compete with Low-Margin Retailers," *Journal of Retailing,* Vol. XL, No. 2 (Summer, 1964), pp. 11–14.

[37] In the Gibson operation, for illustration, the drug prescription lessees must have prices "at least 25% lower than the prices prevailing in the state." Cf. "Gibson: Rx Price Must Be 25% Off," *Discount Store News,* March 7, 1966, p. 25.

the consensus is that discount nonfood prices range from 5 to 15 percent lower than those of competing stores, with the advantage in food at the lower end of this range.[38]

2. *Pricing in Farmers' Markets.* Another retailing institution which, like the discount house, engages in below-competitor pricing based on low operating costs, is the farmers' market. An outgrowth of foreign bazaars and early American markets in which farmers really were the dominant sellers, today's farmers' markets—while used by some farmers as a means of selling fresh fruits and vegetables—are dominated by middlemen. Like the shopping center, the grounds and buildings are usually centrally owned but leased to many retailers, a wide variety of merchandise is offered for sale, and most of the markets are located in suburban or rural areas; but, unlike the shopping center, the facilities are frequently very simple (open sheds, quonset huts, and unpaved parking lots are not uncommon), they may be used largely on weekends, and the auction method of sale is used for some merchandise. Large-scale promotions supported by all the retailers in the market create a carnival or circus atmosphere and attract large crowds. A few years ago it was estimated that there were about 1,000 farmers' markets with annual sales in excess of $1 billion; but it seems likely that their current number is considerably less as some have "traded up" to become regular shopping centers, others have been converted to discount houses, and some have gone out of business.[39]

Pricing above Competitors' Level

In contrast to those retailers who adjust their markups so as to meet or to undersell competition are those who follow a policy of selling some or all of their merchandise at higher-than-competitor prices.[40] These retailers recognize that customers are attracted to a store by many considerations other than price;[41] and, as a result, that it is perfectly possible for two stores with

[38] A study of prices in four conventional supermarkets and three discount supermarkets in Rhode Island disclosed the latter stores undersold the former by an average of 5.8 percent. "How Much Lower Are Discount Prices?" *Super Market Merchandising,* April, 1966, pp. 32–33. Also cf. Ruth and Edward Brecher, "How Big are Bargains in Discount Stores?" *Reader's Digest,* July, 1965, p. 81; E. W. Cundiff and R. C. Andersen, "Competitive Food Pricing of Discounters," *Journal of Retailing,* Vol. XXXIX, No. 1 (Spring, 1963), p. 16; and A. F. Jung, "Retail Pricing Policies on Small Appliances," *op. cit.,* p. 18.

[39] "Farmers' Market Fading, Stung by Soaring Cost," *Women's Wear Daily,* February 12, 1962, p. 21.

[40] This policy is also followed by manufacturers. For an example (Green Giant Co.) cf. "What's New, Besides Ho-Ho-Ho," *Business Week,* October 23, 1965, p. 138.

[41] Of those who base their buying on price alone, John Ruskin had this to say: "There is hardly anything in the world that some man can't make a little worse and sell a little cheaper, and the people who consider price only are this man's lawful prey."

different prices to exist side by side and both to be successful. What are some of these nonprice considerations that attract customers?

Nonprice Competition. Among the major factors which tend to keep retailers from coming into direct price competition with others in their field are the following:

1. *Services.* One very important factor is the service offered. One store may be more generous in its delivery policy, in its extension of credit, or in its acceptance of returned goods. By way of illustration, most of the older department stores are more liberal in rendering these services than are the stores that have been opened by Sears, Roebuck and Co. and Montgomery Ward & Company. Many people want added services and are willing to pay for them. Consequently, the operators of the older department stores find that they can get somewhat higher prices for their goods and yet not lose many of their customers to the lower-priced stores. In the marketing of gasoline, the services rendered through the service station (windshield wash, roadmaps, restrooms) are so important in attracting customers that one oil company executive is quoted as saying: "It's what comes with the gas that makes the difference."[42]

2. *Prestige.* The prestige that a store has acquired is another factor taking it out of direct price competition with its competitors. A store that has existed for some time in a community where it has set the standard for quality may have acquired considerable prestige in the eyes of its customers. Buyers are willing to pay something more for the goods sold by that store merely because of the store's "name." Thus, a woman's coat carrying a label from Saks Fifth Avenue, Neiman-Marcus, I. Magnin, or Marshall Field becomes a different coat in the eyes of the buyer than the same coat sold by a mail-order firm. Because the coat is looked upon by the customer as a "different" coat, the store with prestige may obtain a higher price than other stores.

3. *Location.* For some customers the location of a store is a factor taking it out of direct price competition with other stores. Price surveys show that the downtown stores tend to have prices below those of neighborhood stores, thus reflecting the fact that competition is keener when stores are located close together. However, surrounding the neighborhood store are a number of families who desire to buy some goods where they can be purchased conveniently. Rather than walk or drive four blocks to a lower-priced establishment, they will pay a few cents more for the convenience of the nearer store.

4. *Store Hours.* Retailers also limit the price competition facing them by

---

[42] *Time,* July 9, 1965, p. 90.

varying the hours they remain open. There are small neighborhood stores successfully following a high-price policy because they are open at hours when other stores are closed; many of them do the bulk of their business during the evenings and on Sundays.

5. *Private Brands.* Other retailers find that the necessity of meeting the prices of competitors can be avoided to some degree by stocking goods that are not comparable in brand to those handled by others. This practice makes it difficult for customers to compare prices among stores and, if comparisons are made, enables the retailer to explain that noncomparable goods are being compared.[43] To illustrate: If a drugstore handles a well-known brand of tooth paste at $0.45 and a nearby store reduces its price on the same brand to $0.39, the first store must admit that it is being undersold—and may be forced to cut its price to meet competition. However, if the first store has its own brand of tooth paste, it might claim that its tooth paste is better by at least the difference in price.

The foregoing paragraph should not be interpreted as indicating that private brands are usually sold at prices which exceed those of national brands; typically, the opposite is the case.[44] In fact, policies widely followed by many chains in all merchandise fields requires that private brands (*a*) must be at least equal in quality to competing national brands; (*b*) must sell at lower prices for the same size packages or at similar prices for larger packages; and (*c*) must provide larger gross margins. To quote an executive of the Great Atlantic & Pacific Tea Company: "There are two reasons we will put a product under our own label. One, we are able to price it under advertised [national] brands; two, we are able to make more money on it."[45]

Based on the foregoing policies, private brands have been widely developed by voluntary and cooperative chain organizations, department stores, and such leading chains as Sears, Roebuck; Montgomery Ward; Safeway Stores; A & P; Woolworth; Grant; and Penney. Sears and Ward report that over 90 percent of their sales in branded merchandise are private brands.[46]

---

[43] Many private brands, of course, are manufactured by firms selling nationally advertised brands. For example, cf. the packaging of physically identical evaporated milk under private labels and its own label by the Borden Company. *Journal of Marketing,* Vol. XXIX, No. 3 (July, 1965), pp. 67–68. While sometimes the merchandise sold under the two kinds of brands is quite comparable, in other instances there are significant quality differences.

[44] For evidence in the food field cf. L. J. Konopa, "Fluctuating Food Prices—A Survey," *Journal of Retailing,* Vol. XL, No. 4 (Winter, 1964–65), Table I, p. 18; and Report of the National Commission on Food Marketing, *Food from Farmer to Consumer* (Washington, D.C.: U.S. Government Printing Office, 1966), p. 75.

[45] "New Crowd Minds Store for the Tea Company," *Business Week,* June 13, 1964, p. 94.

[46] Victor Wortman, "Inside Sears, Roebuck," *Printers' Ink,* October 22, 1965, p. 95; and Montgomery Ward & Company *Annual Report,* year ended February 3, 1965, p. 6.

For the A & P, which probably carries "more of its own-brand merchandise than any other food chain," private brands account for 20 percent of total sales.[47] R. H. Macy & Company expects its company-owned brands, which now account for 10 percent of sales, to double in relative importance over the next few years.[48] Private brands already account for over 50 percent of the sales of W. T. Grant Company; and one of the firm's objectives is "to develop and steadily increase outstanding items, in all lines, to our own specifications, to be identified as Grant's Own Brands."[49] Despite the fact that sales of advertised brands of dry groceries gained 21.4 percent in the 1961–65 period while private brand sales advanced by 10.8 percent,[50] some authorities predict that by 1975 the private brand will be even more deeply entrenched throughout the retail field than it is today.[51]

6. *Arrangements with Manufacturers.* In addition to avoiding direct price comparisons by using private brands, a store may try to achieve this same end by getting goods on an exclusive basis. Sometimes the store becomes the exclusive agent for the products of a certain manufacturer, thus making sure that none of its immediate competitors can get the same goods. As an illustration of this possibility, a letter from the president of a cosmetic manufacturer to his exclusive retailer in Passaic, New Jersey, states: ". . . yours is the only outlet for Charles of the Ritz products in the entire city. In the entire State of New Jersey, we have no city in which more than three stores handle the distribution of Charles of the Ritz, and in our entire nationwide distribution we sell to no store known as a price cutter or with a past history of price cutting. We therefore believe that the store will have no problem as to maintaining its full retail markup on Charles of the Ritz products." In fashion goods, a store will try to get vendors to agree that no other retailer located within a certain radius from it will be allowed to purchase the same styles.

Extent of Escape from Price Competition. Professor Backman points out that many "businessmen prefer nonprice competition to price competition . . . because

1. They generally believe that the goodwill derived from nonprice factors will be more lasting than that based on price appeal.

---

[47] "New Crowd Minds Store for the Tea Company," *op. cit.,* p. 94.

[48] "Private Brands at Macy's," *New York Retailer,* February, 1963, p. 15; and *Business Week,* October 2, 1965, p. 70.

[49] *This We Believe: A Statement of the Policies that Guide Decisions in the W. T. Grant Co.* (New York: The Company, 1966), p. 13.

[50] *Chain Store Age* (Supermarket Executives Edition), December, 1965, p. 3.

[51] E. B. Weiss, "Controlled Labels to Expand More," *Advertising Age,* July 12, 1965, p. 1.

2. Competitors may find it more difficult to match nonprice factors than to meet price changes."[52]

In view of this preference, three points need to be emphasized concerning a store's ability to escape direct price competition. First, no store can completely escape price competition. Although its prestige, the services rendered, its location, and its hours may enable it to sell at somewhat higher prices, too broad a price difference will cause it to lose customers. In fact, any price difference causes a store to lose some customers, since there are some who have little regard for a store's services or prestige. The wider the price differences become, the more customers leave and go over to the lower-priced store.

A specific instance demonstrating the point of the preceding paragraph is afforded by the efforts of a number of "prestige" retailers to place higher-than-normal markups on some lines. Urged on by their relatively low net profit margins, Saks Fifth Avenue and similar retailers placed, for example, $55.00 and $65.00 prices on garments they previously would have sold for $49.95 and $59.95, thus increasing their dollar markup by $5.05 for each item. However, within two years these stores had abandoned their new markon policy since it had resulted in lower sales.

Second, it should be noted that this tendency for a price above that of a competitor to drive customers elsewhere is true especially in regard to staple and well-known branded merchandise. For such merchandise the more thrifty buyers can go from store to store and get information as to the prices being asked by the various retailers on fairly comparable merchandise. Since it is more difficult to make price comparisons on style goods, prices asked by the retailer selling such goods are less influenced by prices being asked in competing stores.

Third, most stores find that they have some competitors who have about as much prestige and offer as many services as they do. Hence, it may not take a very wide price differential between such stores to cause a fairly rapid shift of trade. It is the prices of such comparable competition that each retailer must keep especially in mind when he is pricing his goods. If the application of his usual markup gives him a price in excess of what these competitors are asking, it may be best for him to be satisfied with a lower markup.

Price Lines

Price lining consists of selecting certain prices and carrying assortments of merchandise only at these prices, except when markdowns are taken. For

[52] Jules Backman, "Pricing," in George Schwartz (Ed.), *Science in Marketing* (New York: John Wiley & Sons, Inc., 1965), p. 251.

example, men's ties may be carried at $1.50, $2.50, and $3.50; and women's dresses at $17.98, $22.98, and $29.98.

Reasons for Price Lines. It is easy to see why price lining developed. In shopping goods, to which price lining is especially applicable, the customer desires a wide assortment from which to choose; but she is confused if there are small price differences among the various goods shown. By carrying full assortments only at certain price levels, this confusion, which hinders purchasing, is reduced. The customer merely indicates to the salesperson the price she is willing to pay, and the salesperson can show her a wide assortment from which to choose. Many customers are attracted to the store that makes their buying problems easier by carrying price lines meeting the demands of their incomes. By selling at a few price lines, salespeople become well acquainted with the prices, so that they make fewer mistakes. Thus selling is facilitated, and the store gains the good will of customers. At the same time the size of the store's stock may be reduced, turnover increased, markdowns decreased, and stock control simplified. Interest and storage charges are reduced. As we have seen in another connection, price lining is also of aid to the buyer.[53]

Establishing Price Lines.[54] Price lines are usually established through a careful analysis of past sales, picking out those prices at which the bulk of the sales were made. In some cases, however, past sales are disregarded: The retailer simply selects a number of price classes and then it is up to the salespeople to "push" the selected price lines to get them established. Although it is unwise to be too definite as to the number of price lines needed, seldom will a store want fewer than three which provide it with a low-, medium-, and high-price group.[55] One popular-priced women's sportwear chain has selected four price lines;[56] and for such merchandise as hosiery, a large store may find that half a dozen or more price lines are necessary to meet the needs of its customers. Once the price lines are chosen, all new purchases are planned to fit within these price classes.

Some of the advantages of price lining are lost when the price lines are not far enough apart so that it is evident to the customer that they represent definite differences in quality. Otherwise, the customer will still be confused with several goods selling at fairly comparable prices. To serve customers of the income group to which each of his price lines will appeal, the retailer

[53] P. 286, ff., above.

[54] On this subject also cf. the discussion of "Principles of Price-Line Determination," in J. W. Wingate and J. S. Friedlander, *The Management of Retail Buying* (Englewood Cliffs, N.J.: Prentice-Hall, Inc., 1963), pp. 382–3.

[55] Three price lines are also common among manufacturers who "fair trade" their products. Cf. "Samsonite: On Land, in the Air, on the Sea," *Business Week*, February 27, 1965, p. 100.

[56] *Women's Wear Daily*, October 13, 1965, p. 52.

should make plans to have full assortments at each price line. He should also check his price lines against those established by his competitors to be sure that they have not found price lines with more customer appeal than those he has established. The significance of constant attention to and reappraisal of price lines is suggested by one retailer in these words: "The price line picture can seldom be considered static; testing and checking are always helpful—above and below and in between the established price lines."[57]

Price Lines in Periods of General Price Changes. As the incomes of the retailer's customers and wholesale prices change, the retailer may want to shift his price lines somewhat. Some retailers follow a policy of maintaining the same price lines and lowering the quality sold at each price as prices rise, whereas others think that the quality should be maintained with the price rising to absorb significant increases in wholesale prices. Still other retailers believe that periods of rising prices should be met by raising both the quality and the prices. Those taking this third point of view feel that, during periods of rising prices and rising incomes, people have a desire—and the income—for better things. These retailers point out that, because of a large number of relatively fixed expenditures, a 5 percent rise in income allows customers to spend more than 5 percent for many shopping goods. Although there is some truth in this argument, it would seem better policy for the store to maintain the quality of its price lines and try to "step up" some of its customers to its next higher price line.

During periods of falling prices, there is a tendency for a store to "trade down" its price lines, that is, to lower its price lines and also to reduce quality. This policy is tempting, for the store finds the incomes of its customers so reduced that they want to "trade down." Yet the policy is dangerous, especially since it breaks down whatever quality standards a store has tried to build up for each price line. It seems wise to lower the price line as long as this can be done without sacrificing quality; but beyond this, a store should not go. Customers who demand lower-quality merchandise than that purchased in "good" times should be encouraged to drop to the next lowest-price line.

In brief, during periods of price and income changes—whether rising or falling—a retailer will do well to change his price lines only when he can or must do so to maintain quality. Customers demanding higher or lower qualities should be traded up or down to other price lines.

Limitations of Price Lining. Price lines exert a significant influence on a store's prices. At least temporarily, prices are fixed so that the pricing problem is solved before the goods are even bought. As a result, it is up to

---

[57] F. S. Hirschler, "Price Lines and Price Lining," *The Buyer's Manual, op. cit.*, p. 125.

the buyer to get merchandise that will carry a sufficient markup when placed in a certain price line to allow the store to show a profit. This forcing of the buyer to get adequate assortments sometimes proves difficult and, in part, offsets the advantage to the buyer of having to consider only goods that can be sold at the price lines his store has established. Price lining also limits the ability of a store to meet competitors' prices. Still other disadvantages include (1) the danger that the price lines selected will not be suited to the preferences of customers and prospective customers, (2) the difficulty of maintaining price lines and uniform quality during periods of changes in price levels, (3) the likelihood that price lines will multiply over a period of time, and (4) the tendency to focus attention on price rather than on the merchandise. In spite of these drawbacks, the advantages of price lining have resulted in a widespread use of the practice.

Price Level Adjustments

The retailer will find it necessary to vary his markup on goods according to whether the general price level is declining or advancing. Consider, first, the situation when the general price level is falling. Men's hose purchased at $8.00 a dozen pairs and sold at $1.00 a pair for a markup of 33⅓ percent yield a gross margin of $4.00. If the store's operating expenses absorb $3.00 of this gross margin, the store has $9.00 in place of the $8.00 it had before the hose were bought and sold. Now, as a result of a fall in the general price level, the retailer is able to replace the dozen pairs of hose in stock at a cost of $7.00 a dozen. In addition to the $1.00 profit realized, the store has an extra $1.00 with which to buy goods. In such circumstances the retailer might well consider using a markup of less than 33⅓ percent. Or he might accomplish the same result by converting his retail markup of 33⅓ percent to a cost markup of 50 percent[58] and applying this to the expected replacement cost rather than to his actual cost. If competition is keen, he may have little choice in the matter, since he will be forced to sell his hose for less than $1.00 a pair.

In a period of rising prices, the retailer will have to take a higher-than-usual markup, or else his working capital will decrease. This situation may be illustrated by assuming that after the hose costing $8.00 a dozen pairs have been sold for $12.00, they cannot be replaced for less than $9.50. After deducting operating expenses, the store has left only $9.00 of its receipts of $12.00; to replenish its stock, the store must draw cash from some other sources. In view of the higher replacement cost, the store has lost

---

[58] Cf. pp. 468–70, above.

money on the transaction. Sound pricing would lead the retailer to take a larger markup during periods of rising prices or to consider his cost as the replacement cost. Unfortunately, from the retailer's point of view, competition usually keeps him from advancing his prices as rapidly as wholesale prices rise, so that his working capital may decrease during such periods.

Seasonal and Fashion Goods

For seasonal goods the initial markup is influenced by the time and weather of the season. Early in the season, there is a tendency to place higher markups on goods than when the season is advanced, the assumption being that early buyers are less price-conscious than those holding off, since the early shoppers are buying to take advantage of a better selection. Also, especially on fashion goods, the retailer realizes that he may later have to close out part of his stock by heavy markdowns; consequently, he needs a larger markup on early sales.

Customary Prices

Prices on certain goods have been more or less fixed as a result of their having prevailed for a considerable period of time. Examples are afforded by such items as chewing gum, candy bars, and soft drinks. For these goods the retailer's markup is determined for him almost as effectively as when the manufacturer requires him to resell his goods at fixed prices; for if the retailer tries to increase the customary price, sales may fall off so rapidly that a return to the customary price seems necessary.

Odd Prices

Several studies of newspaper advertisements of retailers reveal the widespread use of odd prices, that is, prices ending in such uneven amounts as 29 cents rather than the round number of 30 cents. In the food store advertisements included in one study, for example, by far the most popular prices were 29 cents, 39 cents, and 49 cents: in fact, 57 percent of the entire 2,597 prices ended in "9" while in second place was "5" with 15 percent.[59]

From the predominance of odd prices it is evident that retailers believe they have advantages over even prices. For one thing, while waiting for her change, the customer may look around and make additional purchases. The fact that the salesperson is forced to make change encourages the use of the sales register, so that the sale is recorded and its proceeds remain less easily in

[59] D. W. Twedt, "Does The '9 Fixation' in Retail Pricing Really Promote Sales?" *Journal of Marketing,* Vol. XXIX, No. 4 (October, 1964), p. 55.

the employee's hands. But most important is the supposed psychological effect of odd prices. It is claimed that a price of 19 cents may move many more units of an article than a 20-cent price, simply because people believe that they are getting a bargain, the odd price being a sign that the price has been cut as far as possible.

It is not at all certain, however, that odd prices have the psychological effect attributed to them. Several years ago one of the leading mail-order companies experimented with odd and even prices by pricing a specific item all the way from $1.88 to $1.99 in catalogs going to different customers. The results were inconclusive. Moreover, a higher standard of living and the increased use of sales taxes in many states have lessened the force of the odd-price argument.

In view of the foregoing, with the exception of the food line, retailers are increasingly accepting the conclusion that there is no particular "magic" about odd prices: that odd prices may attract customers who are penny-conscious, but repel other customers. Consequently there is a marked shift toward even prices by department stores and by manufacturers who preticket their products.[60] The retailer will do well to experiment in his community to discover whether odd prices are liked or disliked by his patrons.

Cost of Merchandise

It might be thought that the cost of merchandise would have no influence on the markup that a product might carry; however, it does. As a result of a special "buy," the retailer may be able to place a high markup on certain goods and still meet or "beat" the prices of competitors. In contrast, a high cost of merchandise may force a store to operate on a smaller markup than it deems advisable. One drug manufacturer has even urged retailers of his products to place substantially smaller markups on high-cost items than on those having a lower wholesale cost—his theory being that customers for expensive drugs now pay a disproportionate share of the retailer's total operating expenses.

Rate of Turnover

The markup placed on an item is affected decidedly by the retailer's opinion of the stock turnover he can expect when various prices are asked. It may well be that with a low markup the retailer can sell the good in such large quantities as to give him a larger total profit than if he sells fewer

---

[60] "More Stores are Getting Even as Odd Price Endings Fade," *Women's Wear Daily*, August 24, 1964, p. 9; "Even Prices Gaining in Intimate Apparel," *ibid.*, October 22, 1964, p. 1.

items at a higher markup. We have discussed this point in some detail in preceding sections of this chapter.[61]

Advertising Value of an Item or of a Department

The markup on some items is influenced by the retailer's opinion of their advertising value. At times, certain items may be selected to carry a very low markup to attract people into the store. As we shall see in the following chapter,[62] well-known branded items—typically "big volume items are the ones most often selected for advertising"[63]—are ideal for this purpose; the quality of the items is usually recognized quickly by the customer, and her familiarity with the regular price enables her to appreciate the significance of the price reduction.

At times a retailer may decide to keep a whole department in operation even though it is not realizing a markup sufficient to show a profit. Department stores, for instance, often operate their restaurants or tearooms on this basis. Realizing that quality food well served in attractive surroundings may be an important way to get people into the store, the retailer may deliberately lose money in this department. Usually, an attempt is made to realize a markup at least large enough to cover direct costs—food, wages, and other costs varying with the number of people served—and overhead is absorbed by the other departments. Some discount houses follow a policy of operating their dry grocery departments on low margins, placing them in the rear of their stores to act as a "traffic magnet". One discount retailer, who operates his grocery area on a 7 percent markup, maintains he could reduce this figure "to zero percent and still do well in this store;"[64] while another goes so far as to say: "If the food operator in a discount house is to serve his purpose (attract customers for the non-food departments), he *cannot* make a profit."[65]

Operating Cost

As has been suggested at several points in this chapter, the freedom of a retailer to vary his markup is determined, in part, by his operating cost.

---

[61] See "Maximum Profits and Height of Prices," pp. 463–64, above, and "Individual Item Pricing," pp. 471–72, above.

[62] See pp. 498–503.

[63] "National Survey: Non-Food Merchandising Practices," *Super Market Merchandising*, January, 1966, p. 52.

[64] "Discount vs. Conventional: Perskey's Figures," *Super Market Merchandising*, October, 1965, p. 50.

[65] Quoted in C. E. Silberman, "The Discounters Choose Their Weapons," *Fortune*, Vol. LXV, No. 5 (May, 1962), p. 186.

That chain food stores, in general, have long undersold independent food retailers is a well-established fact.[66] While several factors are responsible for the chain's price advantage, it is quite clear that relatively low operating cost plays a major role.

Price Legislation

Markups on some goods are influenced by federal and state laws, the most important being those that legalize resale price maintenance and minimize price cutting. Since these laws are discussed in some detail in the next chapter, at this point we need only recognize their existence and emphasize their bearing on the retailer's pricing freedom.

Conclusions on Markup

On the basis of our discussion, it seems reasonable to formulate the following conclusions concerning the markup policies of retailers:

First, in establishing the general level of the average markup used by a specific retailer, one of three policies may be followed: he may aim at prices which are (1) at, (2) below, or (3) above those of his competitors.

Second, some retailers find it possible to solve most of their pricing problems by using an average markup which they apply to practically everything they sell. This situation is most likely to exist in the small specialty shop.

Third, a larger number of retailers handle their pricing problem by dividing the goods they sell into a number of classes and applying a set markup to all goods falling into a particular class. These classes may be based on differences in the cost of handling the goods, variations in markdowns, differences in cost of merchandise, or some other factor. As the number of classes increases, the retailer approaches a policy of individual-item pricing.

Fourth, the great majority of retailers find it necessary to deviate widely from any rule of a set markup, even for a limited class of goods. Factors of customer appeal, competition, price lining, time of season, customary prices, odd prices, cost of merchandise, considerations of turnover, the advertising value of an item, operating cost, price maintenance by manufacturers, and government price laws, play a part in the determination of actual markups. The retailer should always remember that he is interested in *total profits,*

---

[66] C. F. Phillips and D. J. Duncan, *Marketing: Principles and Methods* (5th ed.; Homewood, Ill.: Richard D. Irwin, Inc., 1964), p. 211.

not in profits on any particular item. Markups on specific items should be in a process of constant adjustment in an effort to reach this goal.

It should be noted that this constant process of adjusting markups involves the retailer in trying to forecast results and that such forecasts may not be very accurate. As Professor Oxenfeldt says, "pricing decisions necessarily involve considerable guessing."[67] Among other things he must try to forecast the effect on turnover of a certain price reduction, the effect on cost if sales increase, and how markdowns will be affected by a higher or lower initial markup. All of these forecasts are subject to correction when the change is actually put into effect. In other words, adjustments on a trial-and-error basis are a "must." If a certain reduction in markup does not bring the expected increase in turnover, the retailer should try some other markup. Correct retail pricing involves a willingness to experiment. The retailer who tries to simplify his pricing by the mechanistic use of a single markup will usually find that he is losing out to more aggressive retailers.

REVIEW AND DISCUSSION QUESTIONS

1. Discuss: "While the retailer wants a profit, he does not seek the maximum profit. He simply will not work hard enough to achieve the latter goal."
2. Pricing is sometimes put forward as *the* means by which the retailer attempts to maximize his profits. What do you think of this point of view?
3. Distinguish between the short-run and the long-run points of view in pricing at retail, giving several illustrations to make clear your analysis.
4. "Pricing is an art as well as a science." Do you agree or disagree? Justify your answer.
5. List and evaluate the advantages and the disadvantages of a one-price policy.
6. From your own experience, give an illustration of a retailer following a "varying-price policy." How common is such a policy in this country?
7. Talk with three local retailers with different lines of merchandise and ascertain their use (if any) of markup in pricing.
8. Eighteen coats are purchased at $57.00 each. If a 40 percent markup is desired, what is the retail price per coat? What is the total retail of the purchase?
9. How much can a buyer afford to pay for a dress to retail at $65.00 if his markup is 45 percent?
10. Ten bookcases have an invoice cost of $20 each. Cartage charges are $24. At what price must the bookcases be retailed if the markup is 38 percent?
11. What is "individual-item pricing?" As a retailer of furniture, how would you implement such a policy?

---

[67] Oxenfeldt, *op. cit.*, p. 20.

12. Through conversations with local retailers or the reading of trade papers report on which competitors the retailer has in mind when he says, "We meet competitors' prices."
13. "Underselling retailers usually have certain definite characteristics." What are they?
14. Explain carefully how a specific retailer is able to hold customers despite prices somewhat above those of nearby competitors.
15. Evaluate the practice of price lining in a ready-to-wear shop? hardware store?

SUPPLEMENTARY READINGS

ALDERSON, WROE, et al. The Structure of Retail Competition in the Philadelphia Market (Philadelphia: Wharton School of Finance and Commerce, 1960). The pricing reactions of four food chains are revealed in this groundbreaking study.

ALDERSON, WROE, AND GREEN, P. E. Planning and Problem Solving in Marketing (Homewood, Ill.: Richard D. Irwin, Inc., 1964), Chapter 9, "Pricing Decisions." While not an easy chapter to read, the authors present some valuable insights, especially in their discussion of "How Businessmen Set Prices," pp. 241–43; and "Contributions of Economic Theory to Price Determination," pp. 243–44.

BACKMAN, JULES. "Pricing," in SCHWARTZ, GEORGE (Ed.). Science in Marketing (New York: John Wiley & Sons, Inc., 1965), Chapter 10. In addition to sections on prices in theory and in practice, pricing objectives, and industrial prices, pages 275–78 deal directly with retail pricing.

BUZZELL, R. D., et al. Product Profitability Measurement and Merchandising Decisions (Boston, Mass.: Harvard Graduate School of Business Administration, 1965). A "direct product profit" concept for individual food products is outlined in this ground-breaking study. Although the author deals with food, his techniques and conclusions are helpful to successful individual pricing in other commodity areas.

Chain Store Age. "24-Hour Merchandising Laboratory," (Supermarket Executives Edition), February, 1966, pp. 56–58. The physical facilities and operating methods of a so-called "farmers' market" are described in this article.

COX, REAVIS; ALDERSON, WROE; AND SHAPIRO, S. J. Theory in Marketing (Homewood, Ill.: Richard D. Irwin, Inc., 1964). An excellent discussion of price wars is included in this volume. Cf. CASSADY, RALPH, JR. "Price Warfare—A Form of Business Rivalry," pp. 355–79. On the subject of profit maximization as the retailer's goal, cf. BAUMOL, W. J., "Company Goals, Growth, and the Multi-product Firm," especially pp. 324–46.

GROSS, WALTER. "Strategies Used by Major Department Stores to Compete with Low-Margin Retailers," Journal of Retailing, Vol. XL, No. 2 (Summer, 1964), pp. 11–14. The author reports a survey of this subject which is based on opinions expressed by department store executives.

HOLLANDER, S. C. *Retail Price Policies* (East Lansing: Michigan State University, Bureau of Business Research, 1958). An outstanding student of retailing is responsible for this volume.

HOWARD, J. A. *Marketing Management* (rev. ed.; Homewood, Ill.: Richard D. Irwin, Inc., 1963), Chapter 12, "Price Decisions." While not directed specifically at retail pricing, the retailer can benefit from this analysis which recognizes that "pricing is probably more laden with folklore than any other area of marketing decisions."

JUNG, A. F. "A Different Retail Price Pattern: The Case of Carpeting," *Journal of Business,* Vol. XXXVIII, No. 2 (April, 1965), pp. 180–85. One in a long and valuable series of retail price studies, this particular article discloses that retailers price carpeting far closer to the list price than is true for consumer durables of high unit value. Also cf. "How Much Lower are Discount Prices?" *Super Market Merchandising,* April, 1966, pp. 32–33.

NATIONAL RETAIL MERCHANTS ASSOCIATION. *The Buyer's Manual* (4th ed.; New York, 1965). Chapter 13, by HIRSCHLER, F. S., "Price Lines and Price Lining," and Chapter 28, by SOSTRIN, MOREY, "Merchandising to a Profit," are helpful in connection with the present chapter.

RACHMAN, D. J. "How Manufacturer Pricing Methods are Adapted to Retailer Use," *Journal of Retailing,* Vol. XXXVI, No. 1 (Spring, 1960), pp. 7–10 ff. The student who fails to see similarities between pricing by manufacturers and by retailers will benefit from this presentation.

TWEDT, D. W. "Does the '9-Fixation' in Retail Pricing Really Promote Sales?" *Journal of Marketing,* Vol. XXIX, No. 4 (October, 1965), pp. 54–55. After reporting two new studies illustrating the '9 fixation,' the author proceeds to raise questions as to its validity.

WINGATE, J. W. AND FRIEDLANDER, J. S. *The Management of Retail Buying* (Englewood Cliffs, N.J.: Prentice-Hall, Inc., 1963), Chapter XIV, "Pricing and Selling Merchandise Purchased." Pricing objectives, profit margin controls, pricing individual items, price lines, and repricing are among the subjects included in this valuable chapter.

17
CHAPTER

Pricing Merchandise—Continued

In this chapter we continue our discussion of retail pricing, placing particular emphasis on price adjustments, leadership pricing, and legislation affecting pricing policies and practices.

ADJUSTMENTS IN SELLING PRICES

Since prices are constantly on trial, quite often it becomes desirable to change those originally placed on various items. The changes usually represent decreases in prices and are referred to as markdowns; but sometimes advances, or additional markups, are made.

Markdowns

It is customary in retail accounting to express markdowns as percentages of net sales; consequently, a price reduction on an individual item is usually stated as a percentage of the new and lower (actual selling) price. To illustrate: When a dress priced at $25 is marked down to $20 to find a customer, it is said that the dress has been given a 25 percent markdown.[1] The formula that will give the correct percentage markdown is as follows:

$$\text{Percentage markdown} = \frac{\text{Dollar markdown}}{\text{New (or actual) selling price}} \times 100 \text{ percent.}$$

Some Reasons for Markdowns. Some markdowns arise directly from buying and pricing mistakes on the retailer's part. Buying mistakes are illustrated by the men's clothing merchant who added a line of men's cos-

---

[1] Of course, from the customer's point of view, this markdown is thought of as a 20 percent reduction.

metics and then discovered that his particular customers were not interested in purchasing them, and by the women's apparel operator who reordered many items too close to Easter—a practice referred to as "going to the well once too often." As for pricing mistakes, every retailer must recognize that it is impossible to set exactly the right price on all the merchandise flowing through the store: To quote two authorities, "the original pricing of merchandise represents only a temporary decision, subject to revision in the light of customer reaction to the initial price."[2] When experience proves certain items are overpriced, markdowns are necessary.

However, it does not necessarily follow that, because a markdown is taken, the original asking price was too high from the store's point of view, or that the store buyer was at fault. Perhaps there was a decline in the wholesale price level, so that competitors who bought later had a lower cost of merchandise and set lower prices on their goods. Or new products— perhaps made of other materials; in more acceptable designs, styles, or colors; and of better quality—may have been placed on the market. Other markdowns are a result of goods having become shopworn. Even more important—in fact, they constitute one of the major reasons for markdowns—items may be reduced in price to provide the store with attractive merchandise for promotional purposes.

In many instances markdowns result from the store buyer's policy of deliberately purchasing more items than he expected to sell at the original price, so as to provide a good assortment throughout the heavy selling season. Frequently, on a shipment of fashion goods, the retailer is not sure which particular items will sell well. Consequently, he concludes that the safe course is to place a fairly high initial markup on all the dresses, for example, and later clear out those that remain by means of a markdown. Likewise, retailers of seasonable goods often find it necessary to use markdowns to dispose of remaining stocks of such goods at or near the end of the season. Perhaps a large number of Italian silk suits have been purchased but, because of a relatively cold and rainy summer, late July finds most of them still in stock. A drastic markdown may be the only way to move them.

Salespeople sometimes cause markdowns when they take the line of least resistance and merely show the customer what she asks to see. As a result, other goods lie in stock until it is too late to sell them at regular prices. Other salespeople may be too aggressive and get customers to take several items home to let the family help to decide whether or not to buy. When some of these goods are returned to the store, markdowns may be necessary, especially because of improper handling of the merchandise while it is in the

[2] J. W. Wingate and J. S. Friedlander, *The Management of Retail Buying* (Englewood Cliffs, N.J.: Prentice-Hall, Inc., 1963), p. 384.

customer's hands or because of the loss of possible sales while the goods are out of stock.

Every retailer finds that he gradually accumulates "odds and ends." If he handles men's shirts, he may find that he sold most of his blues but that his grays are still in stock; that customers have purchased his 14½ and 15 collar sizes and left the 15½ and 16's. Or perhaps he has not found customers for his sport shirts or his shirts with button-down collars. If he handles piece goods, he may accumulate a large number of small pieces of cloth which remain on each bolt. Such odds and ends usually require substantial markdowns to find buyers.

Finally, poor stock control is also a cause of markdowns. Because of inadequate records or failure to use those available, the retailer does not learn early enough which items are "slow sellers," that he is approaching the end of a selling season with too much seasonal merchandise on hand, or that his salespeople are concentrating their efforts on a few special items and neglecting others. Some of the larger retailers are now using electronic equipment to provide such information quickly and at a reasonable cost, so that markdowns growing out of inadequate records can be reduced.[3]

Markdowns as a Merchandising Tool. The foregoing paragraphs make it clear that markdowns are both inevitable and not necessarily an unmitigated evil. Indeed, the successful retailer looks upon them as "an effective tool of retail merchandising to dispose of merchandise which is unsalable at its present selling price and thereby to keep stocks constantly liquid; to assist in the promotion of sales; and to meet competition."[4] And, since they are unavoidable, markdowns are planned for in the store's budget.[5]

Timing of Markdowns. There is wide disagreement among merchants as to the best time to take markdowns. Some retailers delay taking markdowns in the hope of additional sales at the higher prices, a policy which can be more easily followed by a downtown store which relies more on transient (and, hence, less frequent) trade than by a suburban retailer whose store is visited more often by the same customers. Other retailers follow a policy of no markdowns except during two or three large sales each year: these yearly clearance sales become established in the minds of economy-conscious customers and serve to unload the shelves of the least desirable merchandise. Exclusive shops delay markdowns to discourage bargain

---

[3] Cf. the discussion of electronic data processing on pp. 138–41, 282–83, and 287–88, above, and pp. 630–32 and 729–30, below.

[4] S. L. Solomon, "Markdowns," in *The Buyer's Manual* (4th ed.; New York: National Retail Merchants Association, 1965), p. 256.

[5] Cf. "Planned Reductions," pp. 410–11, above.

hunters who detract from the store's class appeal; although some of them take markdowns early and still avoid large numbers of bargain hunters by placing garments in the next lower-price line without indicating that reductions have been made.

In contrast, other retailers believe that markdowns should be taken early. By making room for a steady flow of new goods to the store, this policy keeps their stock fresh. It reduces the size of the markdowns needed to move goods, since the merchandise is more in fashion than it would be four months later when the next clearance sale might take place. Because some marked-down goods are always available, it encourages thrifty buyers to shop there. It also avoids the cost of special sales.

1. *Some General Rules on Timing.* These advantages of early markdowns have encouraged retailers offering goods at comparatively low prices to adopt certain general rules to speed up the taking of markdowns. On fashion goods, retailers maintain that as soon as sales on an item begin to fall off, that is, as soon as the peak of the fashion cycle has been reached, a markdown should be taken *if* the store has any appreciable quantity on hand. Staples are given markdowns before they have been in the store long enough to get shopworn. Seasonal goods which are also fashion goods are sold before the end of the season. This rule requires that as soon as the first rush of buying for the season is over, the retailer should take inventory and judge whether his stock can be cleared out at the original prices; if not, markdowns are in order. For instance, although many men's winter suits are purchased in the months after Christmas, the majority of clothing stores take markdowns on such goods immediately after the first of the year.

Even the more aggressive retailers are in disagreement as to the best policy to follow regarding markdowns on seasonal goods of a staple nature. Toys not sold this Christmas might be sold the next. Marbles not moving this spring may find buyers next spring. Is it best to take markdowns on such goods so that one can begin each season with a new stock, or is it best to carry this merchandise into the next selling season? To such a question there is no "correct" answer. If the retailer has space available, he may find it most profitable to store the goods. However, he must realize that this practice ties up some of his money, that it involves storage cost, that some breakage or other damage (depending on the goods) is to be expected, and that it takes the time of his salespeople to put such goods away. In view of these disadvantages, if a moderate markdown will move the merchandise, it may be most profitable to sell it.

2. *Automatic Markdowns.* In general, it may be said that there is today a tendency toward taking markdowns earlier than ever before. Fashion merchandise retailers, who find it especially necessary to keep goods moving

out of the store, may follow a policy of taking a markdown on any garment in stock for four weeks. A few of them have even adopted an automatic markdown plan which controls both the time when the markdowns shall take place and their amount. By way of illustration, in the basement store of William Filene's Sons Company of Boston, after twelve selling days unsold merchandise is repriced at 75 percent of its original prices; after six more days, at 50 percent; after another six days, at 25 percent; and after a final six days, is given to charity. A somewhat similar policy is followed by the Ohrbach store in New York City, which begins a series of 10 percent automatic reductions after any garment has been in stock for two weeks.

While the Filene and Ohrbach plans have apparently proven successful for these particular retailers, they have not been adopted by many merchants. Typically the retailer prefers to adjust both the amount and timing of the markdown to the specific situation, rather than have these two elements set by an inflexible rule.[6]

Size of the Markdowns. The data of Table 17–1 make it evident that markdowns vary widely from one line of merchandise to another. For individual items, of course, the range would be much more than that indicated by the table.

To be effective, a markdown must be large enough to induce customers to buy the merchandise. Marking down a dress from $16.75 to $15.75 is

TABLE 17–1

Typical Figures For Markdowns in Selected Departments of
Department Stores, 1965
Based on Annual Sales Volume of Main and Branch Stores
(Net Sales = 100 Percent)

DEPARTMENT	STORES WITH ANNUAL SALES OF			
	$1–2 Million	$2–5 Million	$5–10 Million	$10–20 Million
Piece goods....................	8.1	7.7	10.1	9.2
Cosmetics and drug sundries....	1.5	1.8	2.1	2.4
Women's shoes...............	10.3	10.9	9.8	12.2
Women's and misses' coats......	13.4	11.2	11.8	11.8
Women's and misses' dresses....	15.4	14.3	14.3	15.3
Men's furnishings.............	5.6	4.8	4.6	4.4
Men's clothing................	8.8	10.4	10.0	8.5
Furniture.....................	16.5	9.6	8.5	8.2
Major household appliances.....	5.4	4.4	3.9	5.9
Millinery.....................	17.5	15.1	11.8	11.7

Source: Sam Flanel, *Departmental Merchandising and Operating Results of Department and Specialty Stores in 1965* (New York: National Retail Merchants Association, 1966).

[6] Solomon, *op. cit.,* p. 264.

probably not adequate, since most people who are willing to pay $15.75 will probably pay $16.75. Perhaps a reduction to $12.75 is necessary to reach the desired number of people. In this connection, the retailer can well keep in mind the old retail adage that "the first markdown is the least expensive." Put another way, when the merchant wants to clear stock he should not nibble away at the price by small successive reductions; the major correction should generally be made in one step.

Of course, the ideal markdown is the one that is just enough to sell the goods under consideration. But defining the "ideal" markdown is quite different from deciding what it is in a specific case. The retailer's decision must take into account not only tangible factors such as quantity of merchandise on hand and rate of movement but also those intangibles such as how competitors will respond to a price cut and how customers who bought at the higher price will react.

The size of the markdown necessary to sell the merchandise involved is also related directly to the promotional effort put forth by the retailer and the selling effort made by sales personnel. A "P.M." with a moderate markdown may move more merchandise than a larger markdown without an incentive to the sales staff.

Markdowns under Price Lining. Two general policies are used for handling markdowns on price-lined merchandise. Perhaps the usual policy is to require that a markdown be sufficient to place the item in at least the next lower-price line.[7] This policy has the advantage of keeping the price structure simple, so that the customer is not confused; and it also automatically determines the extent of the markdown.

The second policy consists of having special price lines which fall in between the regular price lines and which are used only for marked-down merchandise. It is argued that such a policy enables a store to reduce the size of the markdowns it has to take and helps the customer to distinguish clearly between regular-priced and marked-down merchandise. As a result of quicker recognition of the price-reduced merchandise, it may move more rapidly. In addition, segregation of price-reduced merchandise is a further factor enabling the store to build up the idea of a price line standing for a certain quality. When a given assortment is increased by merchandise marked down from a higher-price line, it loses its homogeneity.

Recording Markdowns. There are several reasons for maintaining a record of all markdowns. Perhaps most important, knowledge of past markdowns is essential to an intelligent decision upon an initial markup. The

---

[7] Some retailers state this general rule as "the next lower *active* price range." What they mean is that the merchandise must go into a price line where goods are selling in considerable volume.

validity of this statement may be made clear by inquiring what a retailer must know to establish an initial markup which will prove profitable. It will be recalled that the formula for initial markup is as follows:

$$\text{Initial markup percent} = \frac{\text{Percent gross margin} + \text{Percent retail reductions}}{100 \text{ percent} + \text{Percent retail reductions}}$$

Consequently, even if a retailer can estimate his operating expenses at 26 percent and places his desired net profit at 4 percent (thus necessitating a gross margin of 30 percent), he cannot determine his desired markup until he is able to calculate a figure for retail reductions, the size of which will be influenced significantly by markdowns.

Information on markdowns is also important as a check on pilferage. Retail reductions may be considered as consisting of markdowns, stock shortages, and discounts to employees and others. Assume that, in the case mentioned in the preceding paragraph, 7 percent is allowed to cover these retail reductions, making 34.58 percent the initial markup. Of this 7 percent figure, 2 percent is to cover stock shortages. However, at the end of the period in which the 34.58 percent markup has been used, net profit is discovered to be 2 percent rather than the desired 4 percent. With records of markdowns and discounts available, the cause of the lower profit ratio can be determined. If expenses have been held to 26 percent, markdowns to 3 percent, and discounts to 2 percent, then the lower profit ratio must be a result of a larger-than-expected stock shortage. Without records of markdowns and discounts, the retailer could locate his problem only in a very general way; that is, he would know that his retail reductions were too large, but he would not know whether he had a markdown, a discount, or a stock-shortage problem.

Finally, a knowledge of markdowns on various types of goods and on goods of specific manufacturers is an important managerial and buying aid. It may be discovered that certain types of goods are subject to such large markdowns that the retailer may be better off not to handle them. Or he may find that goods purchased from certain sources of supply are sold only with the aid of larger markdowns than merchandise bought from other sources.

Additional Markups

Additional markups—the amount by which the existing retail prices are advanced to new prices—are usually limited to periods of rapidly advancing prices. Whenever a retailer discovers that he cannot replace his present stock except at higher prices, he should not hesitate—if competition makes it possible—to advance his prices. Otherwise, he will find that he does not achieve the inventory gain needed to offset the inventory loss which will come if prices fall.

Once in a while a retailer may find that an item will sell better if its price is advanced. It may happen that the original price was so low that customers hesitated to buy, believing that the low price indicated low quality. In such cases, additional markups are advisable.

LEADER MERCHANDISING

In a general way, we may define a "leader" or "special" as any article sold with a markup that is less than the retailer's average cost (total expenses) of doing business. Evidence of the existence of leaders was illustrated in the previous chapter in Table 16–2 which showed a number of food store items sold on margins of less than 20 percent, whereas the average expense for a group of food chains in the same year was 20.2 percent.[8] Some retailers use just a few leaders at a time, as is true of the supermarket advertising eight or ten "weekend specials." In contrast, a discount house may price practically all of its food items as leaders.[9] Why do many retailers follow a policy of leader merchandising?

Why Retailers Use Leaders

Some leaders develop when a retailer stocks a new item which he tries to get "established" by price cutting. Still others result from the desirability of speeding up the turnover of merchandise in stock—for example, perishables in a grocery store on a Saturday evening. Passing by these situations, retailers advance five main arguments in favor of leaders, as follows:

Meeting Competition. Many retailers make use of leaders simply because they feel that they must meet competitors' prices, and their competitors use leaders.[10] Those following such a policy may meet (1) all the price cuts of all competitors, (2) all price cuts of some competitors, or (3) just price reductions on certain items made by a limited number of retailers. At one time Safeway Stores set forth its policy as meeting "the lowest price of every competitor item by item, day by day, and town by town." More recently this policy has been revised, with a resulting improvement in Safeway's profits, to define "competitors" as "major or effective competitors."

---

[8] Progressive Grocer, *Grocery Business Annual Report* (New York: Progressive Grocer, 1965), p. F19.

[9] Cf. discussion on pp. 475–76, above.

[10] Cf. discussion of this point in "Pricing at Competitors' Level," p. 473, above.

Variation in Expenses of Handling Merchandise. A second argument in favor of leaders arises from the fact that there are many items of merchandise which can be handled profitably for less than the average expenses of retailing. Such items are usually highly standardized, have a high turnover with minimum markdowns, occupy relatively little space in the store, and are readily accepted by customers so that they involve little selling time on the part of salespeople. Cigarettes afford a good illustration of these characteristics, and they are sold on a low markup. Despite their relatively low gross margin, however, one investigation of grocery store products concluded that "cigarettes produce by far the greatest space yield of any department we have studied."[11]

There is validity to the foregoing argument, but it is doubtful if it carries much weight in the minds of retailers when they price their merchandise. Until recent years, few retailers have tried to analyze their operating expenses by specific items or even by narrow groups of items. Indeed, in view of the overhead costs of retailing which would be allocated against various items in an arbitrary manner, it is doubtful that any analysis of operating expenses by specific items would be valid. Moreover, at least in the food field, it is frequently the heavy, bulky items like potatoes and sugar that are used as leaders. Consequently, it must be concluded that there are significant factors influencing the choice of leaders other than handling costs.

Increased Sales with Small Profit Margin. An argument for leaders is sometimes based on the greater net profit which can be made by selling a large quantity of an item at a very low profit margin. Of course, the validity of this argument rests upon the shape of the demand and operating expense curves for the item under consideration. If the demand curve facing the individual retailer is very elastic, a price reduction will produce a large increase in sales; and even though the unit profit is less, total profits may increase.

The serious shortcoming in this argument is that price reductions made by one seller are soon matched or bettered by his competitors.[12] In this situation the retailer initiating the price cut may find that his sales do not expand as much as he had expected. To minimize the influence of this factor, there is a constant shifting of leaders in an effort to keep ahead of competition; and by

---

[11] J. P. DeLuca, "Space Yield Findings on Cigarettes," *Chain Store Age* (Supermarket Executives Edition), January, 1965, p. 85.

[12] And careful studies support the validity of this matching move by competitors. Concludes one investigation of gasoline pricing: "The results of this study clearly indicate that operators of the sample stations should counter lower competitive prices immediately if they wish to maximize revenue." H. C. Claycamp, "Dynamic Effects of Short Duration Price Differentials on Retail Gasoline Sales," *Journal of Marketing Research,* Vol. III, No. 2 (May, 1966), p. 178.

means of this shifting, it seems likely that some retailers do increase their total profits by price reductions on certain items. When a number of competing retailers continue week after week to use the same items as leaders, this argument has little validity; and all too many retailers are guilty of this practice.

Retailers who base their case for leader merchandising on increased sales at the reduced price frequently overlook the great addition to sales which is necessary if profits are to be maintained. To illustrate: Consider an item which normally carries a 25 percent markup. If the price is cut by 10 percent, sales must increase by 66⅔ percent even to maintain the same dollar gross margin. Since the retailer may find some of his operating expenses increased as a result of greater sales, it may well be that, even for a 10 percent price cut, sales must double to maintain the profit he had before the cut took place.

Low Markup on New Items. The leader is sometimes justified on the grounds that any markup on new items in excess of the direct cost involved results in increased profits. Recognition of this fact has led some retailers to search for new customer-attracting items. The addition of such nonfoods as drug sundries and health and beauty aids to chain food store stocks is a case in point. Years ago, these items were not stocked by food chains. However, chain operators discovered that their sale at relatively low prices (as compared with prices in drugstores) resulted in a substantial volume of business. Since many stores already had enough space for these new products, practically no addition to retail overhead was necessary; and even in such variable expenses as wages and wrapping materials, little increase was shown. As a result, much of the gross margin on these items was carried through to net profit. Even today, some merchants believe that "with (nonfood) sales of 10 percent of the food volume, you will generate a profit equal to 50 percent of your food profit. You will also make a 30 to 40 percent return on your (additional) investment."[13]

Leaders as Means of Advertising. The most important argument for the leader lies in its advertising value; that is, it "brings people into the store." As one successful supermarket operator puts it: A leader program ". . . has a place in building volume. The fact remains that the more merchandise you give away, the more people you attract and the more volume and profits you get."[14]

At first glance, it may be thought that this argument for leaders is

---

[13] L. D. Jalkut, "City Products Bares Non-food Figures," *Super Market Merchandising,* December, 1965, p. 13.

[14] Statement of Fred Montesi in "The Montesi Magic—Sales: $10 Million Per Store," *Super Market Merchandising,* August, 1962, pp. 42–43.

practically the same as the two we have just considered. However, there is an important degree of difference among these three arguments. Whereas both of the preceding arguments imply markups high enough to allow the merchant to add to his profit *by increased sales of the leader itself,* this fifth argument does not necessarily require that the retailer show a profit on the leader. Rather, this argument recognizes the validity of the theory of joint pricing as applied to retailing—that the retailer wants the mix or combination of prices on the items he sells which will maximize his total profit, irrespective of the markup shown on any specific item. To quote one trade paper writer:

> Merchandise should be priced in line with what it will sell for rather than what it cost. Every item should bring a profit and/or a customer. Competition demands some promotional goods priced solely to produce traffic. Promotion programs offered by manufacturers and wholesalers, backed by consumer circulars, are helping greatly to meet this need. Reduced margins at all levels of distribution are necessary to answer some promotional problems.
>
> Longer margins must be obtained from other than promotional goods if average margins are going to be satisfactory. The profitmaker today can't be without long-margin merchandise any more than he can do without his short-margin traffic builders. *Through variable pricing he can have both . . . and increased profits!*[15]

It will be noted that the heart of the argument for this kind of leader pricing is this: the leader will attract a large number of customers who will also buy items carrying sufficiently large markups, so that the retailer's total profits will be increased. While the success of many retailers following this pricing policy testifies to its validity, it should be emphasized that the implementation of this policy requires a great deal of skill. Even such an outstanding firm as R. H. Macy & Company, which has long used cigarettes in its New York store to attract customers, has only recently discovered that most of its cigarette customers leave the store without making other purchases.[16] To discourage such shoppers, retailers frequently restrict the number of units of the leader which can be purchased by each customer; but, of course, this limitation decreases the pulling power of the leader for customers who might also purchase additional items in the store.

In pricing leaders as a means of advertising, the retailer should be aware that his pricing of other merchandise should be consistent with such a policy. In other words, since he is attracting customers by a price appeal, the use of leaders does not allow him to so overprice other merchandise that his price-conscious customers are disenchanted with his nonleader merchandise.

---

[15] R. R. Mueller, "Hard-Ware Comments," *Hardware Retailer,* December, 1965, p. 15.
[16] "Take Me to Your Loss Leader," *Wall Street Journal,* February 7, 1966, p. 14.

He should also recognize that a very large price reduction for some kinds of merchandise may repel, rather than attract, customers. What this means is that at some point a growing number of customers refuse to believe the retailer's claim as to savings. In a study of 2,051 buyers in 11 cities, public acceptance dropped off when the savings claimed was increased from 30 percent to 40 percent. In other words, when a "$10 value" was offered at $6 rather than $7, those who believed the saving was "real" decreased substantially.[17] However, on nationally advertised brands and standardized merchandise such a decrease in public acceptance would be much less likely.[18]

1. *Leaders and Price Wars.* A serious disadvantage which may result from using leaders to advertise a store is that it may set off a price war.[19] Naturally, competitors of the price-cutter do not like to lose their position in the market. Although they may refrain from matching the price reductions for a period, if the cuts are continued and if they prove effective in attracting customers, some competitors will eventually make similar or perhaps even greater reductions. The net result may be a price war which reduces the profits of all the competing retailers over a period of many weeks or months.

Price wars are terminated in various ways. Many of them end after a short preliminary skirmish—a period in which the competitors make downward price adjustments and, finding that their reductions are matched by others, quickly retire from the battle.[20] On other occasions, a specific retailer will attempt to check the downward spiraling of prices. When a Spokane, Washington, grocer found some of his competitors advertising prices below his wholesale cost, he rented a bus and transported his regular customers so they could buy the specials only—his goal being to increase his competitors' losses and force them to end their price war. During a Los Angeles milk war, which reduced the price of a quart of milk to one cent, one retailer gave pennies to his customers and urged them to "go across the street and buy the one-cent milk from his competitor."[21]

---

[17] Cf. review of a study by Professor T. J. Hogan of Duquesne University in *Advertising Age,* April 16, 1962, p. 104.

[18] Even the argument sometimes used by manufacturers, that price-cutting on a well-known branded product reduces its prestige, seems invalid. Cf. L. A. Skeock, "The Abolition of Resale Price Maintenance: Some Notes on Canadian Experience," *Economica,* August, 1964, pp. 260–69.

[19] Also cf. the discussion of price wars on p. 474, above.

[20] For details, cf. Ralph Cassady, Jr., "The Price Skirmish—A Distinctive Pattern of Competitive Behavior," *California Management Review,* Winter, 1964, pp. 11–16.

[21] Ralph Cassady, Jr., "Price Warfare—A Form of Business Rivalry," in Reavis Cox, Wroe Alderson, and S. J. Shapiro, *Theory in Marketing* (Homewood, Ill.: Richard D. Irwin, Inc., 1964), p. 363.

In the majority of cases, however, some kind of joint action by retailers or manufacturers is required before the upward price move takes place. Perhaps a group of retailers other than the warring principles will send in "employees . . . to buy stocks of goods at prices lower than their own wholesalers could provide."[22] Persuasive committees of retailers may call upon the price cutters, or the latter may be invited to a meeting for a discussion of the evils of price wars.[23] Gasoline price wars in several cities were terminated, at least temporarily, when the major oil suppliers refused to follow their usual practice of sharing the price cuts with their outlets. In effect, they said to their dealers: "Go ahead with your price war if you want to, but the wholesale price will not change. Any loss is out of your pocket."[24] Some major oil suppliers have attempted to end wars by consigning gasoline to retail outlets, thus enabling the supplier to fix the retail price.[25] While legislative action to eliminate price wars has been suggested, one careful student of the subject—with whom the present writers concur—concludes that such a program would reduce still further "competitive activity in an era in which competition is, if anything, too soft."[26]

RETAIL PRICE LEGISLATION

Retail Price Maintenance

For some products the retailer finds that he has only limited control of the markup he adopts, since the manufacturer plays a major role in determining the resale price. Concerning the manufacturer's right to set retail prices, there is a long legal history, most of which we do not need to review. The essential facts can be stated briefly as follows.

Legal Developments. Until less than four decades ago contracts between manufacturers and retailers by which the latter were required to resell at manufacturer established prices were illegal. However, beginning with

---

[22] K. R. Gillespie, "The Role of Espionage in Retailing," *Journal of Retailing,* Vol. XXXIX, No. 1 (Spring, 1963), p. 9.

[23] For specific instances of these tactics, cf. S. C. Hollander, *Restraints Upon Retail Competition* (East Lansing, Michigan: Michigan State University, Graduate School of Business Administration, 1965), pp. 54–55.

[24] This technique is illustrated in "Are Gas Price Wars at an End?" *Business Week,* May 29, 1965, especially p. 138.

[25] Some courts have cast doubt on the legality of this technique, especially when there is any evidence (1) that dealers were coerced into accepting the new program or (2) that dealers were brought together in groups, thus implying horizontal price-fixing. *Sun Oil Co.* v. *Federal Trade Commission,* CA-7 (August, 1965).

[26] Cassady, "Price Warfare—A Form of Business Rivalry," *op. cit.,* p. 379.

California in 1931, forty-six states—the exceptions being Alaska, Missouri, Texas, and Vermont plus the District of Columbia—passed so-called "fair-trade" laws, which made it legal for the manufacturer of a branded good in open competition to sign a contract with the retailer to assure maintenance of the retail price. These laws contained a "nonsigner's" clause which made them binding upon other retailers as soon as they were notified.

Under the state laws resale price maintenance was limited to intrastate commerce. However, by passing the Miller-Tydings Act of 1937, Congress legalized this practice in interstate commerce. Then the Supreme Court delivered what looked like a deathblow to fair trade: in the Schwegmann decision of May, 1951, the nonsigner's clause was ruled illegal under federal law.[27] Consequently, the manufacturer who wanted to fair trade his product was required to sign contracts with all his outlets, an act which was quite impossible for practically all producers.

The Schwegmann-decision restriction on fair trade did not last long. In 1952 Congress passed, and President Truman signed—despite his earlier statement that fair trade is "not in accord with our program"—the McGuire amendment to the Federal Trade Commission Act, and once again the nonsigner's clause was legal in interstate commerce. However, court decisions against the constitutionality of the nonsigner's clause and legislative action (the fair trade laws have been repealed in Kansas, Nebraska, and Nevada) have gradually reduced to 20 the number of states in which resale price maintenance is legally effective. Although most of these laws include the nonsigner's clause, three of them—Ohio, North Dakota, and Virginia—are illustrative of the current trend which substitutes the doctrine of implied contract.[28] That is, in these three states the law says that a retailer has automatically "contracted" to resell at the stated price if he accepts goods from a manufacturer who has notified him of his price maintenance program.[29]

Legal Situation Today. As a result of the foregoing legal developments, it is now possible for a manufacturer of a branded good which is in competition with other goods to fix the retail price of his product within any one of the twenty states in which retail price maintenance is legal by (in seventeen states) signing a contract with a single retailer in that state and notifying other retailers or (in three states) merely by notifying retailers of the resale price. Even the required notification may be carried out in a simple

---

[27] *Schwegmann Bros.* v. *Calvert Distillers,* 341 U.S. 384.

[28] Cf. M. C. Howard, "Legal Developments in Marketing," *Journal of Marketing,* Vol. XXIX, No. 4 (October, 1965), p. 64.

[29] The Virginia law will be found in Va. Code Ann. §§ 59–8.1 to 59–8.9 (Supp. 1960). The North Dakota law is reported in Commerce Clearing House, section 33,720.02a and 33,720.04 (March, 1965).

fashion, perhaps by stating resale prices in the manufacturer's price list, sales contracts, invoices, or by means of a bulletin to resellers.

It should be noted, however, that not all manufacturers who sell within the 20 states can fair trade their products. This privilege is given only to manufacturers and distributors of products (1) that carry "the trademark, brand, or name of the producer or distributor," and (2) that are in "free and open competition with commodities of the same general class produced or distributed by others."[30] Moreover, the manufacturer's influence over price must be in a vertical line only, that is, from manufacturer to wholesaler to retailer. Any attempt to effect horizontal price agreements among manufacturers, among wholesalers, or among retailers is still illegal. In California and Hawaii, for example, court action has been taken against drug retailers who, through the activities of their trade association, exerted "pressure" on other drug retailers to maintain prices on prescription drugs.[31] Moreover, the court has held that a drug manufacturer who is also a drug wholesaler cannot fix resale prices for other drug wholesalers who are in competition with his own wholesale outlets.[32]

Of course, under some circumstances a retailer may still sell below the fair-trade price. Court decisions grant pricing freedom on mail-order sales from a nonfair-trade state to a buyer in a fair-trade state, the argument being that the customer takes title where the seller releases the merchandise to a common carrier for delivery.[33] Even within fair-trade states, the retailer may undersell the established price if the trade-mark, brand, or manufacturer's name is removed from the product. Closing-out sales are exempted from the established price, although in some states the manufacturer must be given an opportunity to buy back his merchandise at cost. Likewise, damaged or deteriorated merchandise may be sold without pricing restrictions, usually after public notice has been given as to the condition of the merchandise. But, for the great majority of his sales of products for which fair-trade prices have been established, these prices are binding on the retailer.

The enforcement provisions under the state fair-trade laws are quite clear—and unsatisfactory, so far as fair-trade advocates are concerned. In general, those who "knowingly and wilfully" sell under the fair-trade price

---

[30] These limitations, stated in the Miller-Tydings Act of 1937, were not changed by the Schwegmann decision or the McGuire amendment.

[31] For a long list of states in which legal action has been taken against retail groups for pressure activities, cf. S. C. Hollander, *Restraints Upon Retail Competition, op. cit.*, pp. 51–2.

[32] *United States* v. *McKesson-Robbins*, 76 S.Ct. 937 (June, 1956).

[33] Cf. discussion of "Transfer of Title," pp. 358–61, above; *General Electric Co.* v. *Masters Mail Order Co.*, 335 U.S. 824 (1957); and M. C. Howard, *Legal Aspects of Marketing* (New York: McGraw-Hill Book Company, 1964), p. 41.

may be sued for damages. In addition, court injunctions may be obtained to enjoin such price cutting. But note that selling below the fair-trade price is not a statutory offense against which the state will take action. In other words, it is up to the manufacturer, wholesaler, or retailer to police those selling fair-traded goods and to institute action; and, increasingly, court decisions have limited the action which may be taken to enforce fair-trade agreements.[34] In view of court decisions as well as the expense and executive time required, the majority of manufacturers do a poor policing job, with the result that many retailers complain bitterly of the present enforcement situation.[35]

Economic Attack on Fair Trade. Not only has fair trade been losing ground in its legal battles of the past fifteen years, it has suffered even greater defeats on the economic front. Many manufacturers have gradually come to realize that their resale price maintenance programs contain the seeds of their own destruction. That is, by creating such a wide margin between wholesale and retail prices, manufacturers have encouraged the growth of discount houses and the spread of discounting among "legitimate" retailers; in turn, these developments have made it impossible for the manufacturer to enforce resale price-control contracts against other retailers. The net result is that fair trade has been abandoned for all or part of their products by many of its strongest and oldest supporters—W. A. Sheaffer Pen Company (after spending $2 million dollars over a two-year period in a futile attempt to enforce its resale price-maintenance contracts), General Electric Company (which also spent about $1 million a year on its enforcement programs), Sunbeam Corporation, Eastman Kodak Company (which had been fair-trading its products for nineteen years), Bell & Howell, Parker, Davis & Co., Schick, Inc., Royal McBee Corporation (Royal typewriters), Ronson Corporation, International Silver Company, E. Ingraham Company (clocks and watches), and Revere Copper & Brass. However, it should be noted that some of these firms have sought to minimize resale price cutting on certain products by other means, such as by consignment selling (Sunbeam Corporation for its Vista line) and by franchise agreements with each retailer (General Electric Company for its Premier products).

---

[34] As examples, cf. the limitations which the courts have placed on consignment selling (footnote 57, p. 359, above) and their conflicting decisions in the liquor price war conducted by R. H. Macy & Company in New York City, 1964–65. ("Two New York Courts Rule Opposite Ways in Battle Over State Retail Liquor Prices," *Wall Street Journal,* December 28, 1965, p. 4).

[35] A systematic analysis of the ability of manufacturers to enforce fair trade for their products is available in L. W. Stern, "Economic Factors Influencing Manufacturers' Decisions Concerning Price Maintenance," *Journal of Retailing,* Vol. XLI, No. 1 (Spring, 1965), pp. 30–37, 55.

Present Extent of Fair Trade. Even before its recent legal and economic defeats, manufacturers attempting to follow a resale price maintenance policy were mainly in such fields as drugs, toilet goods and cosmetics, household appliances, photographic supplies and equipment, books, sporting goods, and liquor. As a practical matter it seems doubtful if more than 5 to 10 percent of all retail volume has ever been in fair-traded merchandise,[36] and certainly even these figures are too high for the current situation. Yet some retailers still find the goods they sell under manufacturer price control. Consequently, the retailer needs some understanding of whether or not resale price maintenance is in his interest.

The Retailer's Point of View—1. *In the Short Run.* Retailers are divided into two groups, one strongly in favor of resale price maintenance and the other just as strongly opposed to it. Typically, those retailers who desire to sell at "regular" prices are the small operators who lack buying advantages and who offer services that necessitate a relatively high operating cost and hence a high markup. To these retailers, price maintenance by the manufacturer looks like a haven of refuge from the price competition of the low-price store. Just how severe this price competition can be is made clear by these comparisons: Sea & Ski listing at $1.49 advertised at 97 cents; $15.00 General Electric automatic toothbrushes for $11.27; Gillette's $1.60 Right Guard deodorant at $1.18; 99-cent Woodbury Shampoo for 79 cents; and the $3.50 Worthmore garden hose from the Plymouth Rubber Company at $2.39.[37] Retailers favoring fair trade reason that if such price differentials on well-known brands are abolished, a large part of the "pull" of the low-price store will be lost. As a result, "regular-price" retailers, especially those in the drug field, have prompted legislatures to pass fair-trade laws. Then, through their trade associations, they have brought pressure on manufacturers to put their products under resale price-maintenance contracts. These retailers are the active proponents of fair trade; they have literally forced many manufacturers to become at least apparent advocates of retail price maintenance.[38]

Retailers who oppose fair-trade laws claim that a large part of the price cutting denounced by many manufacturers and retailers is justified on the basis of low operating cost, low cost of merchandise, and the acceptance of a low profit margin. By way of illustration, studies have consistently demon-

---

[36] S. C. Hollander, "Retail Price Policies," in *The Relationship of Prices to Economic Stability and Growth,* Joint Economic Committee, 85th Cong. 2nd Sess. (Washington, D.C.: U.S. Government Printing Office, 1958), p. 428.

[37] *Discount Store News,* May 30, 1966, p. 8.

[38] The case for resale price maintenance as stated by its strongest advocates will be found in *The Case for Quality Stabilization* (Washington, D.C.: Quality Brands Associates of America, Inc., n.d.).

strated that chain-store organizations undersell many independent merchants on broad lists of well-known goods, and yet the chains have shown good earnings. Likewise, some discount houses have made substantial profits. Studies by various disinterested groups have shown wide variations in operating costs and in merchandise costs. As long as such differences are present, it seems economically sound that retail price differences should exist. Yet it is very common to hear a regular-price retailer denounce all price-cutters as "chiselers." In fact, this denunciation is so typical that one wit has defined a "chiseler" as anyone who is able to sell at a lower price than his competitors.

The Retailer's Point of View—2. In the Long Run. It may not be amiss to ask: Will resale price fixing by manufacturers serve to increase the profits of retailers who sell at "regular" prices? Certainly this is the assumption on which these retailers sponsored the fair-trade laws; and there is evidence that gross margins and prices to customers have increased under these laws. To illustrate: A United States Justice Department study of 132 rapid turnover items compared fair trade prices with actual prices in eight nonfair-trade cities. On the average there were no savings on 55 of the items, but for the remaining 77 items prices in the eight cities were 24 percent below fair-trade prices.[39] Further, it has been estimated that if fair trade pricing were extended throughout the country, the Consumer Price Index might advance from 4 to 5 percent.[40]

However, the higher profits which some retailers believe will result from resale price maintenance may well prove much less than expected. In spite of the illegality of price cutting on price-fixed goods, experience proves that some price cutting may continue. There is also a movement for price-cutting retailers to use private-brands, nonprice-controlled manufacturers' brands, or unbranded lines as sources of "leader" merchandise. Hence, they will still try to pull people into their stores by aggressive merchandising, thus holding back the sales increase expected by regular-price retailers as a result of resale price maintenance. If the profits of retailing do advance, more people will be encouraged to enter the field, competition will be increased, and profits will probably be reduced to their former level. As an example of this relationship, we have already noted that the rapid growth of the discount house is in part a result of the wide margins set under fair-trade contracts.[41] It must also be recognized that since fair-trade laws will serve to encourage nonprice competition as a substitute for price competition—i.e., more free services and broader stocks—profits may not advance, even though there is some decrease

---

[39] J. C. Darnell, "The Impact of Quality Stabilization," *Journal of Marketing Research,* Vol. II, No. 3 (August, 1965), p. 276.

[40] *Ibid.,* pp. 280–81.

[41] Cf. 475–76, above.

in price cutting.[42] It is probably some combination of these various factors which is responsible for the conclusion of a careful study of retail failures in fair trade and nonfair-trade states:

The best data available do not support the contention that the enactment of fair-trade laws lessens the number of retail failures or bankruptcies or increases the number of retail stores. Whatever effect they have apparently had has been slight and in an opposite direction to the one claimed by proponents of fair trade.[43]

All in all, the fair-trade laws may not have the long-run effect on retail profits which their sponsors expect.

Outlook for Fair-Trade Laws. The past decade and more have seen resale maintenance increasingly under attack both abroad and in this country. In Canada, Sweden, and Denmark the practice is now specifically prohibited and it is severely restricted in Finland.[44] In Britain, where as recently as 1964 "one quarter of all personal consumer expenditure [was] price maintained,"[45] resale price maintenance has been banned by Parliament, except for those manufacturers who can convince a Restrictive Practices Court that free pricing would be detrimental, that is, because of such possible results as lower quality goods, unnecessary services, or higher prices in the long run.[46]

In the United States, the attack on fair trade has been spearheaded by the Federal Trade Commission, which has consistently recommended the repeal of the Miller-Tydings Act as "economically unsound and undesirable in a competitive economy." For similar reasons the Justice Department has consistently stated its opposition to resale price maintenance; perhaps more significantly, the Department has instituted suits to limit the fair-trade enforcement actions of manufacturers.[47] The Attorney General's National Committee to Study the Anti-Trust Laws urged repeal of both the Miller-Tydings

---

[42] On the tendency of resale price maintenance to attract more firms and add to the services performed by retailers, cf. E. T. Grether, *Marketing and Public Policy* (Englewood Cliffs, N.J.: Prentice-Hall, Inc., 1966), p. 78.

[43] S. M. Lee, "The Impact of Fair-Trade Laws on Retailing," *Journal of Retailing,* Vol. XLI, No. 1 (Spring, 1965), p. 6.

[44] Skeoch, *op. cit., Journal of Marketing,* Vol. XXIX, No. 2 (April, 1965), p. 85; and B. S. Yamey (ed.), *Resale Price Maintenance* (Chicago, Ill.: Aldine Publishing Co., 1966).

[45] Christina Fulop, *Competition for Consumers* (London: The Institute of Economic Affairs, 1964), p. 55.

[46] That the shift to free pricing has stimulated price competition to the consumers' benefit is reported in "British Consumer Gets First Taste of Unfixed Prices; More to Follow," *Business Week,* March 13, 1965, p. 118; and "British Shoppers Get Spate of Price Cuts as 'Fair Trade' Fades," *Wall Street Journal,* March 4, 1965, p. 14.

[47] James Lee, "Fair Trade Faces Blistering Attack," *Women's Wear Daily,* April 27, 1964, p. 1, 36; and "Antitrust Lunges Again at Fair Trade," *Business Week,* July 4, 1964, pp. 20, 22.

and McGuire Acts. The Twentieth Century Fund's Committee on Cartels and Monopoly went even further and recommended repeal of both the Miller-Tydings Act and the fair-trade laws. On the economic front, as we have already seen, the growth of discount houses and the widespread disregard of their stated resale prices have led many manufacturers either to abandon fair trade or to question the wisdom of all-out efforts to enforce their resale price contracts.

Despite the strength of the antifair-trade forces and their considerable success to date, it seems doubtful that the attack will lead to the complete elimination of resale price maintenance. Abandoned by many manufacturers, it is still strongly supported by others. Never adopted by four states and made legally ineffective in 26 others, it is still lawful in 20 states, including such heavily populated areas as California, Illinois, Ohio, and New York. Moreover, Congress continues to consider bills to establish resale price maintenance on a nationwide basis. Under the so-called Quality Stabilization Bill it would be lawful for the manufacturer of a branded good to establish resale prices anywhere in the United States merely by notifying wholesalers and retailers through advertising or by a notice attached to the product.[48] Opposed by the Agriculture, Commerce, and Justice Departments, as well as by the Federal Trade Commission, the bill appeals to those congressmen who seek votes on the basis of having "done something for the little fellow."

Regardless of whether or not the Quality Stabilization Bill is passed, the fight for a national bill will continue.[49] The United States has gone far down the road toward extending protection to many groups who wish to escape from the impact of a competitive economy. As long as we have tariffs to protect producers and subsidy programs to aid farmers, we may expect fair-trade laws in some form to remain on our statute books.

Unfair-Sales and Unfair-Trade Practices Acts

About 31 states have passed (and in 26 they are still constitutional) unfair-sales acts, unfair-trade practices acts, or sales-below-cost laws known by some other name which aim at giving the retailer relief from price cutting. Whereas fair-trade laws are permissive[50] and apply to branded

[48] The bill is summarized in *The Case for Quality Stabilization, op. cit.,* pp. 4–5.

[49] In June, 1966, the bill was (temporarily?) renamed the "Truth-in-Pricing" bill and an effort was made to attach it as a rider to the "Truth-in-Packaging" bill. However, the move was defeated in the Senate, 51–29. *Discount Store News,* June 27, 1966, p. 1.

[50] In eleven states the liquor laws provide that resale price maintenance shall be compulsory. To illustrate: For many years (but not now) the New York State Liquor Authority applied this principle "to promote temperance and provide for more orderly distribution of alcoholic beverages."

merchandise, these laws are mandatory and apply to all goods. For example, Minnesota's Unfair Sales Act requires retailers to add at least 8 percent to their invoice cost of goods, and wholesalers to add at least 2 percent; the only exception being that lower prices may be charged if necessary to meet the legal prices of competitors. Since the minimum costs of retailing for practically all merchandise necessarily involves a margin in excess of 8 percent of sales, this type of law does not force any retailer to raise his prices above those justified by low costs of operation, low merchandise costs, and low net profit margins; but it does forbid the practice of deep price cutting. In other words, such a law seems to put a floor to price cutting without trying to get uniform prices in stores operating under various conditions. In a few states the "floor" has been defined as the cost of merchandise without the addition of a small markup.

Some states have adopted acts that may have less favorable results than those growing out of the Minnesota act. In Arizona the retailer must take a markup of at least 12 percent. Since this is in excess of the markup required for the retailing of some goods (cf. Table 16–2, p. 470), it may result in higher prices to the consumer. In California, the law forbids sales below cost except to meet competition, but then defines cost as "the invoice or replacement cost, whichever is lower, of the article or product to the distributor and vendor, *plus the cost of doing business by said distributor and vendor.*"[51]

The California type of statute has at least two serious faults: an administrative difficulty and an economic fallacy. The administrative difficulty is that it involves the determination of the cost of operation of every retailer accused of violating the law. The economic fallacy is that it seems to require each product sold to carry a markup equal to the merchant's average cost of doing business. Since many items can be sold on a margin considerably under the average cost of doing business, there seems no sound reason for raising the prices of such merchandise. Yet, in the states where these laws exist, the retailer must take them into account in establishing the markup on his goods.

"No administrative agency has been established with the special responsibility of administering or enforcing" the majority of these laws.[52] Although violations are statutory offenses against which the attorneys general of the various states may take action, in practice aggressive enforcement programs have not been followed. As a consequence, in certain states wholesalers and

[51] Statutes of 1935, chap. 477.

[52] Howard, *Legal Aspects of Marketing, op. cit.,* p. 47. But there are exceptions. For example, Connecticut has a Commissioner of Consumer Protection who may raise complaints "whenever he has reason to believe" a retailer has violated the State's sales below cost law. *Journal of Marketing,* Vol. XXX, No. 1 (January, 1966), p. 71.

retailers have formed associations, partly for the purpose of bringing alleged violations to the attention of the attorneys general and of encouraging the enforcement of the laws. In some instances these associations have themselves been prosecuted on the grounds that they were being used to encourage horizontal price fixing contrary to both state and federal laws.[53]

Restrictions on Pricing Freedom

Fair-trade laws and unfair-sales acts are examples of laws which restrict the pricing freedom of retailers. Yet competitive pricing, which requires pricing freedom, is the very heart of the free-enterprise system. How far we can limit that freedom and still retain our type of economy is one of today's major questions. At some point—if we want the advantages of freedom and the high standard of living which our system offers—we must be willing to accept the rigors of price competition and not try to protect everyone from its impact. And there is a very encouraging aspect of these restrictive laws: After a careful evaluation of their history, Professor Hollander concludes that "if we take a long enough view . . . these restraints seem to lose much of their force."[54] Apparently (and fortunately) it is difficult to remove the impact of competitive factors in the retail field.

REVIEW AND DISCUSSION QUESTIONS

1. Define "markdowns". Using a hypothetical example, compute the dollar and percentage markdown.
2. Explain fully why markdowns are referred to as "an effective merchandising tool".
3. "It does not necessarily follow that, because a markdown is taken, the original asking price was too high." Do you agree? Explain your answer.
4. Inquire of several local retailers as to their policies on taking markdowns, both as to timing and amount. Analyze each policy. Is there any disagreement among them as to when to take markdowns? Explain.
5. Explain the statement: "The first markdown is the least expensive." Do you agree or disagree? Why?
6. "There are two general policies in use for the handling of markdowns on price-lined merchandise." What are these policies, and how are they applied?
7. Analyze the advantages and disadvantages of an automatic markdown policy for (*a*) the used-car dealer, (*b*) the exclusive women's apparel shop, and (*c*) the basement operation of a department store.

---

[53] Hollander, *Restraints Upon Retail Competition, op. cit.,* p. 39.
[54] *Ibid.,* p. 84.

8. Investigate the markdown-recording practices of a (*a*) discount house, (*b*) supermarket, and (*c*) woman's apparel shop. Do you agree or disagree with the practices being followed in each store? Why?

9. Define "markup." Compute the dollar and percentage markup in a hypothetical example.

10. Identify "leader merchandising." How widespread is this pricing policy?

11. State the various arguments for the use of leaders; appraise each from the point of view of (*a*) the exclusive women's apparel shop, (*b*) the service food store, (*c*) the neighborhood drugstore, and (*d*) the discount house.

12. What is the current legal situation regarding fair trade?

13. Analyze the advantages and disadvantages of fair trade from the point of view of a (*a*) neighborhood drugstore, (*b*) supermarket chain, and (*c*) department store.

14. How do you account for the fact that retail failures are about the same in both fair trade and non-fair trade areas?

15. "Fair trade is not dead, but sleeping. Twenty years from today it will be more widespread than it was in the early 1950's." Do you agree? Why or why not?

SUPPLEMENTARY READINGS

In addition to the list suggested for the previous chapter cf. the following:

ALDERSON, WROE. *Dynamic Marketing Behavior* (Homewood, Ill.: Richard D. Irwin, Inc., 1965), chap. 4, "Negotiated Price, Price Leadership, and Market Price," and pp. 218–32 of chap. 9, "Toward a Theory of Retailing." Important aspects of price theory and actual prices in retail markets are considered in these sections.

CASSADY, RALPH, JR. "The Price Skirmish—A Distinctive Pattern of Competitive Behavior," *California Management Review,* Winter, 1964, pp. 11–16. In this article, a leading student of price wars develops this thesis: Many potential price wars end after a preliminary skirmish—a period in which the competitors "try out each other" and then retire from the scene.

CLAYCAMP, H. J. "Dynamic Effects of Short Duration Price Differentials on Retail Gasoline Sales," *Journal of Marketing Research,* Vol. III, No. 2 (May, 1966), pp. 175–78. This study supports the thesis that price cuts of a competitor should be met immediately "to maximize revenue."

DARNELL, J. C. "The Impact of Quality Stabilization," *Journal of Marketing Research,* Vol. II, No. 3 (August, 1965), pp. 274–82. "The objective of this article is to make estimates, based on a variety of assumptions, of the effect that (a national fair-trade) law might have on the Consumer Price Index."

GRETHER, E. T. *Marketing and Public Policy* (Englewood Cliffs, N.J.: Prentice-Hall, Inc., 1966). Resale price maintenance is analyzed on pp. 74–79 of this volume.

HOLLANDER, S. C. *Restraints Upon Retail Competition* (East Lansing, Michigan: Michigan State University, Graduate School of Business Administration,

1965). In this study "of the forces that tend to limit competition in retailing," Professor Hollander discusses (among many other subjects) resale price maintenance, unfair practices acts, and price wars.

HOWARD, M. C. *Legal Aspects of Marketing* (New York: McGraw-Hill Book Company, 1964). Fair trade legislation and sales-below-cost laws are covered in chapter II of this helpful volume.

Journal of Marketing. "Legal Developments in Marketing." Each issue of the *Journal* includes this valuable section on legal developments. A subsection on "Regulation of Price Competition" lists and comments upon legal actions concerning fair trade and sales-below-cost laws.

LEE, S. M. "The Impact of Fair-Trade Laws on Retailing," *Journal of Retailing,* Vol. XLI, No. 1 (Spring, 1965), pp. 1–6. The author examines the plea that fair trade is "necessary to save small retailers from extinction," and—based upon failure rates in fair trade and nonfair trade areas—finds it wanting. Also cf. DIRLAM, J. B. "Fair Trade in Rhode Island: A Continuing Controversy," *Rhode Island Business Quarterly,* Vol. II, No. 1 (March, 1966), pp. 3–5.

NATIONAL RETAIL MERCHANTS ASSOCIATION. *Markdowns: Their Causes, Their Prevention, Their Correction* (New York: The Association, 1957). Adequately described by its title, this booklet continues to be one of the best available on markdowns.

QUALITY BRANDS ASSOCIATES OF AMERICA, INC. *The Case for Quality Stabilization* (Washington, D.C., n.d.) In this pamphlet the advocates of a national fair trade law state their case.

SILBERMAN, C. E. "The Revolutionists of Retailing," *Fortune,* Vol. LXV, No. 4 (April, 1962), pp. 99–102 ff. The author emphasizes the part played by a low-price policy in the growth of the discount house.

SOLOMON, S. L. "Markdowns," in *The Buyer's Manual* (4th ed., New York: National Retail Merchants Association, 1965), Chapter 25. In this chapter the Chairman of the Board, Abraham & Straus, Brooklyn, comments on the causes, control, timing, and recording of markdowns.

STERN, L. W. "Economic Factors Influencing Manufacturers' Decisions Concerning Price Maintenance," *Journal of Retailing,* Vol. XLI, No. 1 (Spring, 1965), pp. 30–37, 55. Using "theoretical examples of several competitive situations," the author concludes that "the extent of concentration of sales may have a profound influence" on the success of a manufacturer's fair trade program.

STRASSER, WILLIAM. "Markdowns Not a Curse—But a Cure," *New York Retailer,* December, 1957, pp. 13–15. The author discusses markdowns from the point of view that they (1) correct errors that have been made and (2) promote sales.

WINGATE, J. W. AND FRIEDLANDER, J. S. *The Management of Retail Buying* (Englewood Cliffs, N.J.: Prentice-Hall, Inc., 1963). Chapter XIV of this college text discusses various aspects of leader merchandising and markdown policies.

WINGATE, J. W.; SCHALLER, E. O.; AND GOLDENTHAL, I. *Problems in Retail Merchandising* (5th ed.; Englewood Cliffs, N.J.: Prentice-Hall, Inc., 1961),

Sec. X, "How to Control Markdowns," pp. 92–97. The problems on these pages will increase the student's ability to compute markdowns.

YAMEY, B. S. (ed.). *Resale Price Maintenance* (Chicago, Ill.: Aldine Publishing Co., 1966). The seven studies of resale price maintenance included in this volume cover Canada, the United States, Sweden, Denmark, Ireland, the United Kingdom, and the European Economic Community.

PART VI

Sales Promotion and Customer Services

18
CHAPTER

Retail Advertising and Display

Once a store has been properly equipped and well-balanced assortments of merchandise have been assembled to meet the needs of prospective customers, measures must be adopted to attract these customers into the store and to induce them to make purchases. Moreover, such measures—to be really effective—should build good will for the store so that continuous patronage from satisfied customers will result. When this is done, sales volume will be maintained on a profitable level. The function of sales promotion is to accomplish these purposes.

Sales promotion efforts are of two major types: (1) those of a nonpersonal nature, involving the presentation of goods, ideas, or services to individuals, singly or in groups; and (2) those of a personal nature, involving such a presentation on a personal or face-to-face basis. The first type is illustrated by advertising, display, and mail-order catalogs; the second type involves "personal salesmanship." Sales promotion, then, is concerned with efforts both nonpersonal and personal in nature and with the effective coordination of these efforts to maximize profits.[1] In the present and next chapters attention will be devoted to the nonpersonal forms of sales promotion. Personal salesmanship will be discussed in Chapter 20.

THE ROLE OF RETAIL ADVERTISING

Advertising is "any paid form of nonpersonal presentation and promotion of ideas, goods, or services by an identified sponsor."[2] It is used by the re-

---

[1] For other explanations of these terms cf. C. H. Sandage and Vernon Fryburger, *Advertising Theory and Practice* (7th ed.; Homewood, Ill.: Richard D. Irwin, Inc., 1967), pp. 4–5; Otto Kleppner, *Advertising Procedure* (5th ed.; Englewood Cliffs, N.J.: Prentice-Hall, Inc., 1966), chapter I; and J. S. Wright and D. S. Warner, *Advertising* (2d ed.; New York: McGraw-Hill Book Co., 1966), pp. 4–5.

[2] This definition was formulated by the Definitions Committee of the American Marketing Association. Cf. the report of this Committee in the *Journal of Marketing,* Vol. XIII, No. 2 (October, 1948), p. 205. It continues to be widely accepted.

tailer to stimulate desire for the different kinds of merchandise and services he has for sale, to tell people what goods and services he has available, to keep people interested in his store between visits, to encourage customers to fulfill all their needs in his lines at his store, and to develop good will for his business. In other words, its main job from the retailer's standpoint is to create in the minds of his customers the image he desires;[3] and this image is the composite of many factors.

Even retailers who a decade ago did not use advertising for some or all of these purposes are now tending to do so. To cite one example: After relying mainly on window displays for many years, in 1958 the F. W. Woolworth Company embarked on an ambitious newspaper advertising program with highly successful results. Today it uses radio, television, and magazines to supplement its more than 45 million lines of newspaper advertising and special promotions at the local level, all designed to "make the public aware of the upgraded lines, the wider assortments, and the new merchandise that form the foundation of Woolworth's new image."[4]

To achieve its goals, advertising must conform to the policies formulated by the management and must be carefully planned, prepared, tested, and inserted in appropriate media at the right times. In addition, if maximum benefits are to be realized, it must be coordinated with other activities of the store.

Limitations of Retail Advertising

Advertising must not be thought of as a panacea for all the management deficiencies of the retailer. As a matter of fact, retailers who recognize the limitations of advertising programs and, consequently, do not expect the impossible from these programs are the ones who derive the greatest benefit from them. Certainly, retailers should understand the warning voiced by two students of advertising some years ago that:

1. Advertising cannot sell merchandise that people do not want to buy;
2. Advertising cannot sell merchandise in profitable quantities without the backing of every other division of the store; and
3. Advertising cannot succeed to the fullest extent unless it is used continuously.[5]

---

[3] A study by Foote, Cone and Belding revealed that "Women's Opinion of Stores [is] Formed from Advertising." Cf. *Advertising Age,* March 1, 1965, p. 10.

[4] *Annual Report* [of the F. W. Woolworth Company] *for 1965,* p. 12; and R. C. Kirkwood, *Report of Annual Meeting of Stockholders, F. W. Woolworth Co.* (New York, 1965), p. 9.

[5] C. M. Edwards, Jr., and R. A. Brown, *Retail Advertising and Sales Promotion* (3d ed.; Englewood Cliffs, N.J.: Prentice-Hall, Inc., 1959), p. 14.

This clear statement of the limitations of advertising by retailers emphasizes the fact that advertising, to be most effective, must serve the customer as well as the store.[6] Rather than attempting to sell unwanted goods, as its critics sometimes claim, advertising recognizes "that certain desires exist, that these are part of the human condition and a reflection of the progress that any society has made. Advertising can determine that the means are available for fulfilling those desires. And advertising can accelerate the fulfillment by bridging a communications gap, by telling the public that the goods can be had, what they are like, what satisfaction they may bring, and their price. This assignment is one that is basic to our economy, just as any communications job is basic to modern society."[7]

Two Main Types of Retail Advertising

For purposes of analysis, there are two types of retail advertising: (1) promotional or direct action, and (2) institutional or indirect action. As a practical matter, however, the majority of advertisements represent various degrees in the blending of these two main types.

Promotional or Direct-Action Advertising. The main purpose of this type of advertising is to bring customers into the store to purchase specific items of merchandise. Advertising with this emphasis constitutes the greater proportion of total retail advertising. It may take any one of three different forms: (1) regular-price advertising, in which merchandise is offered at its regular price and the appeal is based on the desirability of the goods (Figure 18–1); (2) "bargain" advertising, in which the price appeal is dominant, as in the case of store-wide sales or "specials" (Figure 18–2); and (3) clearance-sale advertising, in which the price factor is also important, but the main purpose is to close out slow-moving items, broken assortments, and remnants (Figure 18–3).

Institutional or Indirect-Action Advertising. Designed to develop good will for the store—to build confidence in its merchandise and services (Figure 18–4) and thus to establish permanent patronage, institutional advertising takes two chief forms—prestige advertising and service advertising. Prestige advertising aims to lend "atmosphere" to a store by acquainting present and prospective customers with the retailer's alertness and progressiveness in assembling adequate varieties of merchandise embodying the

---

[6] What customers expect from advertising is discussed by L. P. Bucklin, "The Informative Role of Advertising," *Journal of Advertising Research*, Vol. V, No. 3 (September, 1965), pp. 11–15.

[7] Roy Larsen, "Advertising and the Affluent Society," in C. H. Sandage (ed.), *The Promise of Advertising* (Urbana, Ill.: University of Illinois, 1961), pp. 167–68.

COME TO THRIFTY MACY*S
FOR THE BEST OF
EVERYTHING IN STEREO

COMPLETE STEREO SYSTEM
WITH FABULOUS NEW SCOTT 342
ALL-TRANSISTOR FM STEREO RECEIVER

299.95*

with Garrard, Shure, Radio Craftsmen components

• Scott 342 FM stereo receiver has 65-watt amplifier (at 4 ohms). Stereo tuner has 'excellent sensitivity, automatic stereo switching, Scott Comparatron circuitry
• Garrard 50 4-speed automatic turntable has counterweighted arm, 4-pole motor, intermix, oiled walnut base
• Shure M3D dynetic stereo cartridge with diamond needle
• Two RC 50 "Royale" wide range speaker systems in handsome oiled walnut finish enclosures

Walnut case for Scott optional 18.94

FIG. 18–1.   A regular-price promotional advertisement for a stereo system.

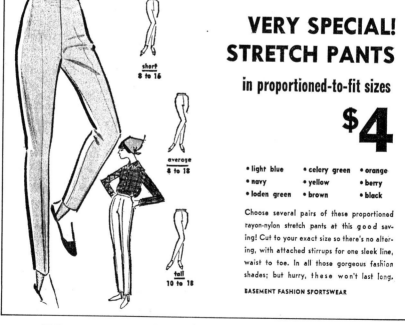

VERY SPECIAL!
STRETCH PANTS

in proportioned-to-fit sizes

$4

short
8 to 16

average
8 to 18

tall
10 to 18

• light blue	• celery green	• orange
• navy	• yellow	• berry
• loden green	• brown	• black

Choose several pairs of these proportioned rayon-nylon stretch pants at this good saving! Cut to your exact size so there's no altering, with attached stirrups for one sleek line, waist to toe. In all those gorgeous fashion shades; but hurry, these won't last long.

BASEMENT FASHION SPORTSWEAR

FIG. 18–2.   A promotional advertisement featuring price and value.

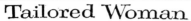

Tailored Woman

WE DO NOT PUBLICIZE COMPARATIVE PRICES

AFTER-EASTER

CLEARANCE

*If "Good Taste" is your watchword—
don't miss the substantial savings
on these wearable Spring Fashions
in Junior, Misses', Women's
and Demi-sizes!*

DESIGNER COATS..... now $98 to $118

DESIGNER SUITS .... now $118

fourth floor

SALON DRESSES & GOWNS: $18 to $98

FRENCH IMPORTS..GREATLY REDUCED

second floor

ALL-WEATHER COATS.. now $18 to $58

JUNIOR DRESSES & GOWNS: $12 to $48

2 & 3 PIECE KNITS ... now $28 to $38

SWEATERS & SKIRTS... now $10 to $13

Young Utopia • third floor

---

no c.o.d's • all sales final

EUGENE K. DENTON, Pres.   FIFTH AVE. at 57th ST.

STORE HOURS: 9:30 A.M. to 5:30 P.M.
Monday thru Saturday
Telephone: EXbrook 7-4500

OUR "346" DEPARTMENT
Brooks Brothers quality and taste
...and made on our own models

Our popular "346" Department offers an excellent opportunity to become acquainted with Brooks Brothers distinctive styling and quality at moderate prices. All our "346" suits, sport jackets and fine evening wear are made to our exacting specifications...on our own exclusive models...mostly of materials woven especially for us. The suits—made on our traditional 3-button, single-breasted model, feature our comfortable and correct natural shoulders, trousers without pleats, and matching vests...in a range of sizes from 36 to 46, including shorts, regulars, medium longs, longs...and extra longs for the tall, slender man.

Our "346" Tropical Suits, from $100 · Regular Weight, from $110
Our "346" Blazers and Sport Jackets, from $70

ESTABLISHED 1818

Brooks Brothers
CLOTHING
Men's & Boys' Furnishings, Hats & Shoes
201 POST ST., COR. GRANT AVE., SAN FRANCISCO, CAL. 94108
NEW YORK • BOSTON • PITTSBURGH • CHICAGO • LOS ANGELES

FIG. 18–3. A clearance-sale promotional advertisement. Note that comparative prices are not used.

FIG. 18–4. An institutional advertisement stressing quality and styling of merchandise.

newest ideas in style, design, and material.[8] Service advertising seeks to attract patronage by pointing out the various services and facilities offered by the store which make it a desirable place in which to buy. This basic appeal has been found effective by many retailers.

Blending of Promotional and Institutional Advertising. Although advertising which is predominately promotional in character continues to dominate the retail scene, a growing number of advertisements combine

---

[8] One leading store uses national magazines to maintain its image. Cf. James Feehery, Marshall Field & Company Uses Ads in *New Yorker* to Maintain Image," *Advertising Age,* October 5, 1964, p. 134. About 50 percent of the advertising of the Joseph Horne Company, Pittsburgh, Pa., is institutional in nature. "Horne's Sell Merchandise, Horne's in Ads," *Women's Wear Daily,* November 17, 1965, pp. 1, 51.

both the promotional and the institutional type of copy. Merchandise in competing stores is often so similar that advertising which attempts to sell merchandise simply as merchandise usually cannot be made effective enough to draw customers to one particular store. By weaving a considerable amount of store character into his promotional advertising, one prominent retailer seeks to achieve three purposes: "(1) build traffic, (2) reflect the personality of the whole store, and (3) sell the item advertised—in that order."[9]

Food-store advertising, which is often cited (incorrectly) as being strictly promotional in character, well illustrates the trend toward combining the two main types of retail advertising. A study of the advertisements prepared by four competing food chains in Philadelphia concluded that they used advertising to create a favorable image so that customers would visit their stores—not necessarily for the items mentioned but for the general classification of products in stock. To this end, the typical advertisement contained three general classes of items, with the first two classes predominating: (1) those to differentiate the advertiser from competitors, such as items not stocked by the other chains; (2) those serving as a reminder list—to keep customers informed of the breadth of stock; and (3) those so priced as to neutralize the previous advertisements of competitors, that is, items on which competitors' prices were met.[10]

Cooperative Advertising

Typically, the retailer assumes complete responsibility for the preparation and cost of the advertising which appears over his name. But on occasion he may engage in what is known as cooperative advertising, in which he shares responsibility and cost with a manufacturer or wholesaler. In such cases, the product is advertised over the retailer's name with the resource paying part—typically, 50 percent—of the cost up to a maximum amount—commonly 5 percent of the retailer's purchases. Perhaps as much as $2 billion is spent each year by manufacturers on cooperative advertising.[11] In

[9] Samuel Feinberg, "From Where I Sit," *Women's Wear Daily,* November 12, 1965, p. 8. Also cf. his "Vital Store Identity Within a Community," *ibid.,* September 25, 1965, p. 10.

[10] Wroe Alderson *et al, The Structure of Retail Competition in the Philadelphia Market* (Philadelphia: Wharton School of Finance and Commerce, 1960), p. 32. An A. C. Nielsen survey of readership of newspaper food advertisements revealed that "Food Stores Ads [are] Essential to Shoppers." Cf. *Editor and Publisher,* December 25, 1965, p. 16. Also cf. "72.4% of Supermart Shoppers Read Food Ads," *Advertising Age,* December 13, 1965, p. 61.

[11] The Federal Trade Commission pursues an active program designed to eliminate any discriminatory use of cooperative advertising. Cf. "FTC Confirms Korvette Probe, New Coop Rules," *Women's Wear Daily,* November 23, 1965, p. 2; and L. X. Tarpey, "Women's Day Case and Cooperative Advertising," *Journal of Marketing,* Vol. XXIX, No. 3 (July, 1965), pp. 35–39.

return for this expenditure, the resource gains from the added interest which the retailer may take in his product and from the retailer's prestige, as well as from local advertising rates which are below those for national advertisers.

Despite these advantages, however, many manufacturers dislike cooperative advertising. They are dissatisfied with the return they obtain from the advertising allowance, and prefer to advertise directly rather than through retailers. Consequently, the trade press often publishes stories of manufacturer dissatisfaction with cooperative advertising.[12]

To the retailer, cooperative advertising yields benefits such as assistance from the resource in the preparation of advertisements, tie-in posters and displays for use inside the store, and an increase in the total space he can afford. But the retailer should be sure that the product is one with which he wants his reputation associated, and be fully aware of the obligations he assumes in such arrangements. On balance, although the retailer will probably want to engage in some cooperative advertising, he should carefully select the best deals from all those offered to him by various manufacturers.

Expenditures for Retail Advertising

The amount of money spent for advertising in the United States is large and continues to grow even larger. The 1965 annual total exceeded $15 billion—and in 1966 probably reached the $16.3 billion level—with local advertisers (mainly retailers) increasing their expenditures at a faster rate than national advertisers.[13] Probably retail advertising approximated one third of the total.[14] This latter sum includes the limited amounts spent by small retailers who prepare their own advertisements—often with the advice and assistance of a local printer or newspaper publisher—as well as the large expenditures of discount houses, department, and chain stores, which operate extensive advertising departments often working in cooperation with advertising agencies. Thus, in the course of a year, the small neighborhood food store may spend less than a hundred dollars for the printing and distribution of a few hand bills, while the advertising expenditures of Sears, Roebuck and Co. reached $93 million in 1965 and exceeded $100 million in 1966.[15]

---

[12] Cf., for example, "Cooperative Advertising: The Millions of Ad Dollars that Never Get Spent," *Sales Management*, October 16, 1964, pp. 61–62 ff; and "R & K Originals Discontinues Store Cooperative Plan," *Women's Wear Daily*, June 6, 1966, p. 15.

[13] "1966 Ad Volume Shows 7% Gain," *Printers' Ink*, October 28, 1966, p. 23.

[14] National Conference Board, Inc., *A Graphic Guide to Consumer Markets* (New York: The Board, 1965), p. 81.

[15] "Sears Plans $100 Million Ad Spending," *San Francisco Chronicle*, July 14, 1966, p. 59.

Reliable figures showing the percentage of net sales spent for advertising by retailers as a group are not available. We do know, however, that the proportion spent varies widely among both large and small stores because of such factors as the type of store, its size and location, and the competitive situation. Among department stores, for example, which are large and consistent advertisers, advertising expenditures in 1965 varied from 2.62 percent of net sales for the smaller stores to 2.19 percent for the larger firms.[16] For specialty stores the range for the same year was 2.49 percent to 3.10 percent.[17] For a group of 19 discount houses the median expenditure for advertising was 3.2 percent of sales.[18] Among supermarket chains the ratio is 2.43 percent of sales, but this figure includes the cost of trading stamps and other similar promotions.[19]

STEPS IN PROGRAMMING RETAIL ADVERTISING[20]

In practice, retail advertising involves the determination of the advertising appropriation, planning the advertising, preparing the actual advertisements, testing the advertising, and selecting appropriate media. The retailer must coordinate these steps into a complete advertising program, perhaps—in the case of large-scale retailers—with the aid of an advertising agency.[21] To assist the smaller retailer, retail trade associations prepare helpful materials at frequent intervals for distribution to their members. Among those performing this service is the National Retail Furniture Association and the National Retail Hardware Association. The former association, for instance, often prepares brochures such as "25 Ideas That Will Make Your Advertising Easier to Produce and More effective in Results."

The Advertising Appropriation[22]

The amount a store *needs* to spend for advertising will depend upon the objectives it is seeking to accomplish, together with such factors as the store's

---

[16] Sam Flanel, *Financial and Operating Results of Department and Specialty Stores in 1965* (New York: National Retail Merchants Association, Controllers' Congress, 1966), p. ix.

[17] *Ibid.*, p. x.

[18] *Discount Store News,* May 17, 1965, p. 3.

[19] "Margins: Why Are They Rising?" *Progressive Grocer,* April, 1966, pp. 219–20.

[20] Since most students of retailing will have had or will be taking a course in advertising concurrently with their study of retailing, this section is restricted to a concise restatement of some fundamentals of advertising. The student without this background should read further in one or more of the basic texts listed in the supplementary readings at the end of this chapter.

[21] The assistance which may be given by an advertising agency is discussed by Wright and Warner, *op. cit.,* pp. 152–57.

[22] Cf. Chapter 25 for a discussion of budgeting for advertising.

age, policies, size, location, trading area, competition, and its past success in attracting customers. It will also be influenced by the rates and circulation of media and by business conditions, as well as by what is done by other stores of similar type.

The amount of money a retailer *needs* to spend for advertising, however, and what he can *afford* to spend are not always the same. The soundest approach for the retailer to follow in deciding how much money to spend for advertising during a given period is (1) to analyze his own situation carefully, (2) to define the objectives that he wishes to accomplish, (3) to decide upon the methods he proposes to follow in attaining these objectives, and (4) to set aside the amount of money needed to utilize these methods effectively, provided he can afford to do so. Often, it is financially impossible to carry out desirable and logical activities. In such a case the retailer must either postpone his course of action, carry it out on a more limited basis, or adopt other desirable alternatives.

The retailer's success in advertising also is influenced by factors independent of the actual money involved. Choice of the right merchandise and selling appeals, proper timing, judicious pricing, effective presentation, and coordination of the program among different media—all of these factors strongly influence the productiveness of his expenditure.

Effective Planning

After the appropriation has been decided upon, the retailer is ready to make detailed plans to use it most advantageously. As in other phases of store operation, the care with which plans are made will determine their usefulness and the value of the results they produce. Careful planning offers such advantages as the following: (1) it provides a definite concrete plan based on facts rather than indefinite, last-minute decisions based on opinions and guesswork; (2) it forces a review of past experience, thus focusing attention on past mistakes as well as on past successes; (3) it requires looking ahead to future advertising efforts, thus contributing to their effectiveness; (4) it takes into account all phases of the advertising program, thus insuring that each receives attention individually and in its relationship to others; (5) in departmentized and chain stores, it insures proper attention to the needs of each department and each store; (6) it anticipates new developments through projecting plans into the future for a specific period of time; (7) it considers probable changes in the status of competitors and their policies; and (8) it facilitates coordination of the advertising activities with those of merchandising, store management, and control.

Advertising should be planned in stores of all sizes, even in the small shop where the proprietor exercises direct supervision over all promotion.

Like the merchandise plan or budget, the advertising plan for the store or department may cover a period of several months, which may be further subdivided into months, weeks, or special promotions of one or more days. It will set forth programs for various types of promotions, including selection of merchandise to be advertised and choice of advertising media; and it will provide for the coordination of advertising and special forms of sales promotion, as well as for adjustments to meet unforeseen conditions.

Proper Timing.   Proper timing is an essential in the planning of advertising efforts. Food retailers in some cities, since they believe that Thursday, Friday, and Saturday of each week are the days when customers usually make large purchases, concentrate their advertising in Wednesday afternoon and Thursday morning papers. Department and specialty stores often advertise heavily on Sunday on the assumption that Sunday newspapers are read more thoroughly than those published on weekdays.

For retailers of high-fashion goods, timing in terms of weather is a factor of special importance. A large amount spent on advertising fall fashions during a warm spell may produce few sales. Likewise, the promotion of lightweight summer dresses during a summer cold spell may result in a large outlay with little customer response. In an effort to improve their timing, some retailers study the monthly weather forecasts of the United States Weather Bureau and adjust their promotions accordingly. Others go far beyond this and subscribe to weather forecasting services.[23]

Recognizing that their members require assistance in developing advertising plans and timing these plans most effectively, many of the leading trade associations, such as the National Association of Retail Druggists and the National Retail Merchants Association, prepare promotional calendars and guides for various months and events throughout the year.[24] Trade publications offer a similar service.[25]

Suitable Merchandise.   Special attention to the selection of merchandise to be advertised should be given by the retailer. Perhaps the greatest waste of retail advertising dollars occurs when the wrong merchandise is promoted. Even the best of advertisements cannot sell goods the customer does not want. In contrast relatively poor advertising is often effective in

---

[23] The *American Investor,* the magazine of the American Stock Exchange, reports a study that revealed a loss of retail sales of 1 percent for every degree of temperature below normal any day in the spring or above normal any day in the fall. It was found, also, that "every one-tenth inch of rain that falls between 7:00 and 11:00 A.M. on any day inevitably depresses sales by 1 percent." *Time,* "Economic Theory," March 19, 1965, p. 98.

[24] For illustrations of these aids cf. *Attracting and Holding Customers* (Dayton, Ohio: National Cash Register Company, Merchants Service, 1963), pp. 13–16.

[25] As an illustration cf. "66 Sales Promotion Ideas for 1966," *Super Market Merchandising,* July, 1966, pp. 28–29.

moving wanted merchandise. Since a major purpose of retail advertising therefore is to broaden the sale of *wanted* merchandise, every effort should be directed toward this objective.

In making his selection of goods to advertise, the retailer should be guided by past experience regarding proven best sellers; merchandise that is selling well in other stores; pretesting of goods to determine probable rate of sale; his desire to promote private brands; the advice of his salespeople (and department heads in larger stores); and considerations of timeliness, buying habits of the community, variety, and frequency of purchase.

Finally in selecting merchandise to advertise, a word of caution is in order. Too often retailers—especially small ones—advertise certain items without first making certain that adequate quantities are on hand to meet reasonable sales expectations. When quantities are exhausted customers unable to buy the goods advertised are annoyed and encouraged to make their purchases elsewhere. Many alert retailers, aware that their stocks may be inadequate to meet customer demands, specify limited quantities or broken sizes and colors in their advertising copy.

Preparing the Written Advertisement

When the overall advertising plan has been completed, the retailer can turn to the three factors involved in the preparation of the actual advertisements: developing and writing the copy; choosing the illustration; and making the layout.

The Copy. The term "copy" refers to the reading matter of an advertisement, including both the text and the headline. Copy may be said to be the heart of a retail advertisement, although color, illustrations, and typography must be coordinated with it to obtain the desired results.

Since human wants and needs are the basic influences motivating behavior, it is important that the retailer's advertising copy reflects a close familiarity with them. In other words, advertising copy should "interpret the want-satisfying qualities of [the retailer's offerings] . . . in terms of the consumer's [needs and desires]."[26] The retailer should also bear in mind that "efficiency in advertising seems to depend on the use of simple language—simple direct presentation of sales arguments—and the avoidance of tricky attention-getting devices unrelated to the product itself."[27] Unless these

---

[26] Sandage and Fryburger, *op. cit.,* p. 249. Also cf. Denis Higgins, *The Art of Writing Advertising* (Chicago: Advertising Publications, Inc., 1965).

[27] Alfred Politz, "The Dilemma of Creative Advertising," *Journal of Marketing,* Vol. XXV, No. 2 (October, 1960), pp. 1–2. Also cf. "How to Write Better Ads," *Progressive Grocer,* July, 1964, pp. 85–86; and C. W. Birchard, "Distinctive Advertising for Small Stores," *Journal of Retailing,* Vol. XLII, No. 1 (Spring, 1964), pp. 23–29.

guiding principles are followed the store operator is certain to be disappointed in the results of his advertising.

When the copy has been written, it should be subjected to certain tests to determine its value. Kleppner enumerates the qualities that should be examined, as follows: Does it present the benefits that the product offers to the reader? Is it clear? Is anything in it liable to be misunderstood? Is the most important benefit given the most prominence? Does it give adequate information? Is it accurate? Is it plausible? Can it be made more specific? Can the story be told in fewer words, in shorter words, or in fewer sentences? Does it make the reader want the product advertised?[28] As to the headline, does it attract attention and create interest in the rest of the copy?

The Illustration. There is an old saying that one picture is worth a thousand words. Although it is not essential that the retail advertisement contain an illustration—effective food advertising, for example, often contains no picture—retailers find it advisable to use illustrations frequently (1) to attract attention, (2) to show the merchandise itself and/or its use, (3) to lend "atmosphere," and (4) to concentrate the reader's observation within the confines of the advertisement and to direct attention to other parts of it. Small retailers find the advice and assistance of the local printer and the advertising aids of manufacturers whose products they handle of much value in choosing illustrations. Large retailers have their own specialists who, singly or in cooperation with advertising agencies or newspaper artists, devise appropriate illustrations to suggest the effect desired.

When an illustration is used in the advertisement, it should be simple, clear, and appropriate; it should not focus attention mainly on itself, but rather on the store or the merchandise or service being sold; it should contribute to the value of the advertisement more than would an alternative use of the space; and it should face into the advertisement and toward the copy if possible—otherwise there is danger that the reader's "gaze motion" will be directed toward the advertisement of a competitor in an adjoining column.

The Layout. The layout of an advertisement is usually in the form of a sketch showing the location of the text, headline, and illustration in relationship to each other. Its chief purposes are to enable the advertiser to visualize the complete advertisement and to provide instructions to the printer as to how the advertisement should be set up. How detailed the layout will be depends upon the preferences of the person in charge of the advertising and the instructions required by the printer.

Just as there are certain principles to guide the retailer in other phases of

---

[28] Otto Kleppner, *Advertising Procedure* (5th ed.; Englewood Cliffs, N.J.: Prentice-Hall, Inc., 1966), pp. 108–9.

his advertising plans, so, in making his layout, he has certain factors to direct him. Specifically, the layout (1) should have attention value, presenting a complete and balanced picture pleasing to the reader; (2) should provide the desired emphasis through focusing attention on the more important part or parts of the advertisement; (3) should reflect the character of the store and the things for which it stands; and (4) should make effective use of type faces and sizes, white space, slogans, and photoengravings in conformity with the best standards of advertising practice.[29]

Testing Retail Advertising

Today it is becoming increasingly necessary for retailers to check or test the effectiveness of their advertising.[30] These tests commonly take one or both of two forms: (1) checking of the advertisements prior to their insertion in chosen media—the precheck; and (2) checking of the results produced by the insertion of the advertisements in particular media—the aftercheck.

To insure proper coverage of all essential points in the precheck, check lists have been developed. The advertising department of the *Chicago Tribune* has long used the following:

1. Has the advertisement maximum attention value?
2. Is it "in character" for the store it represents?
3. Does it dramatize the offer? This point includes the appeal to the reader's emotions.
4. Does it satisfy the sense of value of the prospective purchaser? This point could be elaborated to ask: Does it give conviction that price is right, that quality is good, that the merchandise will be beneficial and useful?
5. Does it inspire confidence in the advertiser?
6. Have necessary details been included as to size, color, style, price, address, phone, store hours, time of sale, free parking?
7. Has it a selling "hook" or unusual inducement for direct action?

The aftercheck of advertising is equally as important to the retailer as is the precheck. Sales results should be ascertained and compared with those expected, not only for the particular item but for the department and the entire store. Such action permits analysis of the reasons for the results and thus helps the retailer to avoid past mistakes and to repeat past successes.

The retailer must recognize, however, the numerous difficulties involved

---

[29] For other factors cf. J. W. Crawford, *Advertising* (2d. ed.; Boston: Allyn and Bacon, Inc., 1965), pp. 212–23.

[30] "An ounce of copy pretesting is worth a pound of presumptions," says the copy research director of Grey Advertising. Cf. "Pretesting of Ads Essential, Kominek Tells Montreal Club," *Advertising Age,* October 18, 1965, p. 92.

in measuring accurately the effectiveness of his advertising.[31] Writes one economist: "It is almost impossible to measure the effects of past sales promotion efforts. And it is even more difficult to predict the effects of any combination of sales promotion devices in the future."[32] Although "keyed" advertisements are employed and offerings of certain merchandise are restricted to particular media, for example, other relevant factors cannot be held constant. Thus, a customer entering a store to purchase one item may see another advertised item on display and purchase it.

Selecting Appropriate Advertising Media

The retailer has numerous advertising media from which to choose in carrying out his advertising plans. The more important ones, each of which may be divided into several forms, are as follows:

1. Newspapers	6. Public vehicles
2. Direct mail	7. Motion-picture theaters
3. Radio	8. Personal distribution
4. Television	9. Classified
5. Outdoor	10. In-store

Newspapers. Newspapers constitute the most widely used advertising medium for large retail organizations and for many small stores with a fairly large trading area in relationship to the total area covered by the local papers.[33] Among food chains newspapers are the predominant medium, accounting for almost 60 percent of the advertising dollars.[34] The S.S. Kresge Company, which operates both variety stores and discount houses, spends 98 percent of its advertising budget in newspapers,[35] and Sears, Roebuck and Co. 71 percent.[36] Perhaps 65 percent or more of the depart-

---

[31] Also important in the measurement of advertising effectiveness is the development of the proper conceptual framework and the application of the proper methodology. Cf. J. W. Taylor, "Two Requirements for Measuring the Effectiveness of Promotion," *Journal of Marketing,* Vol. XXIV, No. 2 (April, 1965), pp. 43–45. Also cf. R. H. Campbell, "A Managerial Approach to Advertising Management," *ibid.,* October, 1965, pp. 1–6.

[32] A. R. Oxenfeldt, *Pricing for Marketing Executives* (Belmont, Calif.: Wadsworth Publishing Company, 1961), pp. 11–12. But cf. "What We Know about Measuring Ad Effectiveness," *Printers' Ink,* July 9, 1965, pp. 47–53.

[33] For factors determining the readership of newspaper advertisements cf. V. C. Troldahl and R. L. Jones, "Predictors of Newspaper Advertising Readership," *Journal of Advertising Research,* March, 1965, pp. 23–27.

[34] "18,000 Grocery Ads Show How Newspaper Space is Used," *Progressive Grocer,* April, 1966, p. 173.

[35] "Kresge Will Spend 98% of Ad Budget in Papers," *Women's Wear Daily,* July 15, 1966, p. 2.

[36] *New York Times,* July 13, 1966, p. 66.

ment and specialty stores' advertising budgets are spent for newspaper advertising. In contrast, newspaper advertising is too costly for the small retailer—the grocer, for example—who has a very limited marketing area.

Many retailers who stress fashion merchandise try to get publicity on the women's pages of the newspapers. Since the editors of such pages are eager to provide their readers with newsworthy developments in fashions, buyers who provide such information have little difficulty in obtaining recognition for themselves and for their stores.

Newspapers are popular among retailers because of their low cost per reader, market coverage, readership, quick response, quick check on results, availability for regular and frequent advertising, flexibility and speed, fewer size restrictions, and acceptance.[37] Despite these advantages, however, they possess obvious limitations which should be recognized by the retailer. They have considerable waste circulation in certain areas and among people who are not potential customers; with numerous editions, their "home coverage" is not proportionately large; their life is short, often being restricted to an hour or less; because of the numerous advertisements they contain, the competition for the reader's attention is keen; and despite recent advances in production methods, the quality of paper used still limits effective reproduction.

Direct Mail. In some small stores, direct mail affords the major form of advertising. A small Pennsylvania shop specializing in women's sportswear, for instance, found that five direct-mail pieces each year were sufficient for its purposes, so that no newspaper advertising of any kind was used. And a small fur store on Long Island, while inserting some advertisements in a local paper, relies heavily on three or four direct mailings each year to a list of 5,000 names, plus more frequent mailings to 500 to 1,000 names. Even among department stores and specialty stores, direct mail ranks second in importance.

Properly used, direct-mail advertising enables the retailer to select the audience he wishes to read his advertising, thus permitting him to make his message personal in nature; it obtains concentrated attention without distraction from competing advertisements, particularly when it is sent to the home; it makes possible a more accurate check of results; and it provides a number of methods of conveying a message, any one or more of which may be used. But it also has definite limitations. Its effectiveness is dependent on a mailing list which may involve considerable expense if it is kept up-to-date, specialized skill is required in the preparation of material, and the cost per

[37] Cf. C. J. Dirksen and Arthur Kroeger, *Advertising Principles and Problems* (Rev. ed.; Homewood, Ill.: Richard D. Irwin, Inc., 1964), pp. 366–76.

unit is quite high for materials, printing or typing, postage, and preparation for mailing.[38]

Radio and Television. The universal use of radio in homes, places of business, passenger cars and elsewhere makes it an advertising vehicle of significance to many retailers. Likewise, television has become an important media for a more limited number of retail organizations.[39] To be more specific, among food chains almost 10 percent of their advertising dollar is spent for radio and about 6 percent for television.[40]

The retailer using the radio or television may choose from a wide variety of programs and vary his appeals so as to reach all members of the family. He may reach them at times when they are receptive to suggestions of merchandise suited to their needs, and he may make last-minute changes which appear advisable.[41] Finally, radio and television advertising lend prestige to some types of retailers and create confidence and enthusiasm among employees.[42]

Perhaps the major disadvantage of radio and television is the fact that, because of their cost, their use is restricted mainly to large- or medium-size stores, or to combinations of small stores, although spot announcements are often within the cost possibilities of the small retailer. Also, many retailers do not appreciate the fact that these media demand special talents; some programs are ineffective because they are developed without professional aid.

Personal Distribution. The shopping-news type of publication, one form of personal distribution, is typically owned cooperatively by the retailers who advertise in it, but some are nonretailer controlled. Usually published once or twice a week, each issue consists of retail advertisements and brief articles on matters such as fashions and recent developments of interest to prospective customers. These papers are distributed free to homes and apartments in the city or within designated boundaries.

---

[38] For guides on using direct mail effectively, cf. Henry Hoke, Sr., *What You Should Know About Direct Mail* (Dobbs Ferry, N.Y.: Oceana Publications, Inc., 1966).

[39] Cf. Milton Gross, "Department Stores Hiked TV Use 35 Per Cent," *Advertising Age,* April 5, 1965, p. 141; H. P. Abrahams, "Why Retailers are Moving Into TV; Slow but Accelerating Trend," *Broadcasting,* January 17, 1966, pp. 36–37; and "Chain Soars from 36 to Over 100 Stores on Wings of Color TV," *ibid.,* January 3, 1966, p. 100.

[40] Cf. "18,000 Grocery Ads Show How Newspaper Space is Used," *op. cit.,* p. 173.

[41] One supermarket chain uses TV to acquaint viewers with quick price changes. Cf. "Three Second Color TV Spots . . . for Buddies," *Advertising Age,* December 13, 1965, p. 62.

[42] Some firms have used network television programs under joint sponsorship to their mutual advantage. One such instance is the promotion undertaken by three middlewestern stores affiliated with the Associated Merchandising Corporation—Shillito's of Cincinnati, Rike's of Dayton, and L. S. Ayers of Indianapolis. Cf. "Coop TV Ad Venture of Three AMC Stores Perking Sales," *Women's Wear Daily,* December 27, 1965, p. 21.

Some stores, especially those in small cities, often use hand bills or dodgers. Even some large stores make extensive use of dodgers in the form of circulars. Properly prepared, these are quite effective in stimulating the sale of food products, household items, and other goods. They are used especially in connection with special sales.

Which Advertising Media? Before "running" his advertising, the retailer should study carefully the merits and limitations of the various media available to him. Each medium should be evaluated in terms of (1) the store's present and prospective customers—their location, buying habits, reading habits, and income; (2) its cost in relationship to the money the retailer can afford to spend; (3) the advertising media used by competitors; (4) the trading area of the store; (5) the size of the store; and (6) the kind of message to be sent—whether it shall be of limited or general interest, or whether it shall be institutional or promotional. There is no medium that is "correct" for all retailers under all conditions. The retailer's skill is well tested in selecting that combination of media which best meets his needs.

TRUTH IN ADVERTISING

The effectiveness of retail advertising is dependent upon the confidence of readers in the honesty of the advertiser. As two students have written: "If advertising does not have the confidence of most consumers, it will lose its influence and surely die. If people grow to disbelieve a substantial percentage of the advertising messages that come to them, they will soon tend to reject most or all advertising."[43] Yet some retailers continue to be guilty of misleading and exaggerated claims in their advertising, thus bringing discredit to themselves and, in addition, making readers skeptical of advertising in general.[44] Consequently, leading retailers, manufacturers, advertising men, the government, and others have long been active in curbing the unfair advertising practices of this minority group. Among other ways, this program has been furthered through the work of Better Business Bureaus,[45] the *Printers' Ink* model statute against unfair advertising, which has been adopted in whole or in part by forty-four states and the District of Columbia; the work of the Federal Trade Commission; and such federal acts as the Wheeler-Lea Act of 1938 and the Food, Drug and Cosmetic Act of

---

[43] Sandage and Fryburger, *op. cit.,* p. 88.

[44] Cf. "FTC Warns: Clean up Phony Ads," *Women's Wear Daily,* June 29, 1966, pp. 1, 31. What constitutes misleading advertising is discussed in E. J. Kottman, "A Semantic Evaluation of Misleading Advertising," *Journal of Communications,* September, 1964, pp. 151–56.

[45] Cf. "Comparative Price Use in Ads Gets BBB Back-of-the-Hand," *Women's Wear Daily,* October, 26, 1965, p. 2.

1938.[46] Each merchant owes to his fellow retailers his full support of activities looking toward the elimination of untruthful advertising.

SPECIAL SALES EVENTS

An important part of the retailer's advertising program is the planning and execution of special promotions or special sales events—that is, the heavy promotion of merchandise at reduced prices for a limited period of time. While avoided by some stores, most retailers believe these events contribute significantly to sales and profits, and that they maintain the customers' interest in the store. A few firms place so much emphasis on these promotional events that a Special Events Office has been established to direct and coordinate them.[47] As one successful retailer has said: "Store business is show business."

One authoritative source distinguishes among three kinds of special sales events: (1) distress sales—"those held primarily to raise money quickly" and "often necessary regardless of their effect on" future business; (2) turnover sales—those "conducted principally for the purpose of selling slow-moving merchandise or closing out a line, brand, or department"; and (3) promotion sales—those designed usually to attract new customers, introduce new goods, or secure favorably publicity.[48] Among the many forms which these events may take are the following: clearance sale, stock-taking sale, department managers' sale, anniversary sale, white-goods sale, back-to-school sale, Mother's Day sale, store-wide sale, off-season sale, one-cent sale, birthday sale, two-for-the-price-of-one sale, home furnishings sale, food sale, and fire sale. Many trade associations and trade papers provide their members and readers with information on special sales events being held by retailers throughout the country. To illustrate, each year *Super Market Merchandising* presents such "a compilation of promotional ideas" for super-market operators.

The particular types of sales events used by a given retailer, and the frequency with which they are held, will depend upon the store's past experience, the competitive situation, ability to obtain aid from manufacturers, the seasonableness of the weather, the accumulation of slow-moving merchandise, and similar factors. Although many large stores probably rely more upon special sales to obtain a satisfactory sales volume than upon any other

---

[46] For details cf. C. F. Phillips and D. J. Duncan, *Marketing: Principles and Methods* (5th ed.; Homewood, Ill.: Richard D. Irwin, Inc., 1964), pp. 110–20.

[47] This step has been taken, for example, by Titche's, Dallas, Texas. Cf. Dorothy Gaines, "Youth Market Writes Titche's Success Story," *Women's Wear Daily*, February 1, 1966, p. 26.

[48] *Attracting and Holding Customers, op. cit.,* p. 19.

single factor, it is easy for the retailer to fall into the fatal error of holding too many special sales. Used too frequently, they undermine customer confidence in "regular" prices. In addition, customers become indifferent to such events, employees lose their enthusiasm, accounting and control problems are complicated, and merchandise returns are increased.

Joint Promotions

To an increasing extent special sales events are being organized by groups of retailers. This practice is not new as evidenced by the long-established annual or semiannual "dollar days" held in many cities.[49] But the development of the shopping center has brought group promotional activities to a new peak. From their very beginning, the retailers of those centers engaged in joint promotions, often organized around the visit of a celebrity, a circus, an outdoor party on the parking lot, an art exhibit, a concert, or a beauty contest. As more shopping centers were built and became competitive with one another, special sales events became even more important as a means of drawing customers to a particular center; and this trend was furthered as free standing discount houses grew in number and gave the center formidable competition for customers. In turn, the special events of shopping centers and outlying discount houses have forced downtown merchants to organize and carry out a growing number of joint events.

Planning Special Sales Events

Regardless of whether the special sales event is used by an individual retailer or by a group of retailers, it must be planned with care so that all activities are effectively coordinated. Store-wide sales, for instance, are often planned three to six months in advance. To obtain the best prices, buyers should approach resources in ample time to arrange for price concessions, which are frequently made possible through production in dull periods or because of vendors' overstocks. When these arrangements are completed, time is required for production, delivery to the store, receiving, and marking. Time is necessary, also, for the preparation and release of advertising—a task superimposed on the regular daily activities of the advertising staff— and for the securing of additional selling and nonselling employees to meet anticipated requirements. Otherwise, the value of the advertising in bringing

---

[49] On the joint promotional events of retailers cf. R. C. Judd, "Patterns in Smaller City Promotion of Retail Trade," *Journal of Retailing,* Vol. XL, No. 3 (Fall, 1964), pp. 10–16.

customers into the store is diminished, since sales are lost and customers become disgruntled because of poor service.

STORE DISPLAY

The growth of self-service in retail stores has brought increased emphasis on store display in establishments of all kinds and sizes.[50] Both window and interior displays have undergone a renaissance and retailers are devoting more attention to their coordination with advertising efforts and personal salesmanship to build a balanced and effective sales promotion program.[51] Yet the display head of Saks Fifth Avenue believes that many retailers still continue to misdirect the talents of their display people, fail to criticize displays constructively, neglect fashion, and encourage banality.[52]

Window Displays

Importance in Promoting Sales. The primary purpose of window displays is to prevent passers-by from passing by. One authority states: "Store windows act as magnets to attract people into a store. Windows proclaim the character of the store and the merchandise for sale. Good displays make people stop and look. Looking arouses desire to possess and this brings people into the store."[53] In addition, window displays encourage the sale of specific merchandise and create prestige for the store. The end result is that sales are increased and profit possibilities are enhanced.

The value of the space they occupy should make management continuously aware of the importance of window displays and the need for care in planning and evaluating them. Notes one observer: "With Manhattan real estate worth about $6 per cubic foot—and with just one child mannequin in each of Ohrbach's 34th Street displays—the space the tots take up is worth millions."[54] Evidence that many retailers manifest such an awareness is furnished by the considerable expense they assume to prepare their window displays. Some of the chains even have headquarter experts set up the

[50] Cf. "Greater Importance for Displays," a special report of *Printers' Ink,* February 25, 1966, pp. 53–58. Also cf. Richard Rosenthal, "Display Firms Regain Choice Place in Sun," *Women's Wear Daily,* December 7, 1965, pp. 1, 51.

[51] The close relationship between store layout and display has already been discussed. Cf. pp. 162–65, above.

[52] Cf. Richard Rosenthal, "Callahan Raps Display Industry for Banality," *Women's Wear Daily,* February 8, 1966, p. 46; and "Scolding Sets Display Men on Ear & Edge," *ibid.,* February 15, 1966, pp. 1, 66. For another point of view, that of the National Display Manager of J. C. Penney Company, cf. "Parker Says Display Needs 'Creative Responsibility'," *ibid.,* December 14, 1965, p. 43.

[53] *Attracting and Holding Customers, op. cit.,* p. 21.

[54] "Lester Gaba Looks at Display," *Women's Wear Daily,* March 2, 1966, p. 33.

forthcoming displays, and then send photographs and complete instructions for their reproduction to their store managers. In the department store field, window display experts are part of the regular staff, but even these are supplemented with outside professionals who provide ideas and materials for such special occasions as the Christmas season.

Most display money is still allocated to windows, 55 percent of display budgets being used in this manner as compared with 40 percent for interior display and 5 percent for other purposes.[55] Yet some retailers believe that window displays are rapidly losing their former significance. A Sears, Roebuck and Co. executive has stated: "Show windows to display merchandise were justified when people rode buses and streetcars. Now most of our customers come by automobile. They enter the stores through the rear parking lot. Advertising, not display windows, brings them in."[56] As a result, except in downtown areas where foot traffic is heavy, his company is replacing display windows with visual fronts, thereby achieving an increase in valuable selling space.

Effectiveness of Window Displays.   For most retailers, however, display windows are still vital to successful operation and it is unfortunate that they neglect to plan them properly, to "dress" them effectively, and to change them frequently. Too many merchants still consider window dressing as a necessary evil, delegate the responsibility to employees who are often uninterested in such work, and refuse to spend money on window fixtures and supplies necessary to do the job properly. The inevitable result is that sales are lost because the store is looked upon as unprogressive. Such a situation is more common among small retailers than among large ones. Large stores, as a rule, plan their window displays several weeks in advance, carefully select merchandise to be displayed, arrange definite time schedules for each window, and assign display space to various departments upon the basis of need, prevailing conditions, and other similar factors. The benefits that accrue from such action are well known and can be secured by the small retailer who is willing and able to plan ahead.

The retailer should not forget that a good window display can usually convey effectively only one message. This message, of course, may relate to any one of a number of ideas—the variety of values offered; the fashion leadership of the store; or the tie-in with holidays such as Easter, Independence Day, Thanksgiving, and Christmas, or with special occasions such as Mother's Day.

---

[55] Cf. a survey by the National Association of Display Industries as reported in "Most Display $'s Go to Windows," *ibid.,* January 25, 1966, p. 53.

[56] "Sears Stores Gain Selling Space by Junking the Display Windows," *Business Week,* May 21, 1960, p. 185.

An important factor determining the effectiveness of window displays is the frequency with which the displays are changed. Although much depends on the location of the store, both in regard to the size of the city and the particular site occupied, it is probably true that stores in small cities *should* change their displays more frequently than stores in the central shopping areas of the large cities. In actual practice, however, the reverse is more likely to be the case, although small city retailers are showing much improvement in this connection.

Interior Displays

Interior displays, the second form of store display, constitute practically the only method of sales promotion other than window displays in some stores—particularly supermarkets, variety stores, and many small grocery, drug, and hardware stores. Other retailers coordinate such displays with newspaper advertising featuring the same kinds of merchandise. Or they use them to induce customers to purchase additional items: their importance in this connection is indicated by various surveys which show that one half or more of the purchases made in some types of stores are the result of decisions made by the customer *after* entering the store.[57] With impulse buying so important, the correct use of interior displays should be of concern to the retailer.[58]

Types of Interior Displays. Interior displays may be conveniently classified into three groups: (1) merchandise displays, (2) dealer displays, and (3) store signs and decorations. These classifications are rather arbitrary and overlappings among them are inevitable.

1. *Merchandise Displays.* Merchandise displays constitute the most important type of interior display. Three main forms may be distinguished: open, closed, and architectural displays.

Open displays are those that make merchandise accessible to customers for handling or examination without the aid of a salesperson. Their variety is legion—shelf displays, as in self-service food stores; counter-top displays, as in drugstores; island displays and mass displays, as in supermarkets; and table-top displays and rack displays, as in department stores. Open displays permit customers to handle merchandise, are readily adjustable to meet variations in customers' demands, are simple and inexpensive to set

---

[57] Cf. du Pont's 7th Consumer Buying Habits Study as reported in *Super Market Merchandising,* June, 1966, p. 10; and Hawkins Stern, "The Significance of Impulse Buying Today," *Journal of Marketing,* Vol. XXVI, No. 2 (April, 1962), p. 60.

[58] Cf. G. M. Valenti, "Interior Display: A Way to Increase Sales," *Alabama Retail Trade,* November 30, 1965, p. 2. The author emphasizes the importance of showmanship in stopping traffic and turning shoppers into buyers.

up, and employ advantageously space that otherwise might not be used. Interestingly enough, some experiments have concluded that "jumble" (rather than neatly stacked) displays encourage the customer to handle, and to buy, more merchandise.

Closed displays consist of merchandise shown inside a wall case or showcase and inaccessible to customers without the aid of a salesperson. Their chief advantages are protection against theft and maintenance of merchandise in salable condition. For example, merchandise such as jewelry, fur coats, silverware, and expensive cosmetics is so valuable that close control must be exercised. Men's and women's clothing needs protection from excessive handling to prevent soiling and wrinkling.

Architectural displays provide an appropriate setting showing various articles of merchandise in use, such as model homes or complete kitchens or complete bathrooms. Their main advantage is that they dramatize the merchandise by showing it in a realistic setting.

2. *Dealer Displays.* Dealer displays, also known as point-of-sale (or point-of-purchase) advertising, consist of signs, banners, display racks, and other selling aids provided by the manufacturer, including those used in windows. When these displays are well planned by the manufacturer and judiciously used by the retailer, they encourage sales in two ways. First, they remind the sales personnel of the product and its merits, thus encouraging them to engage in suggestion selling. Second, and far more significant, dealer displays inform the shopper of a product at the very moment she is in a buying mood. From the manufacturer's point of view, dealer displays can present the advantages of his product pictorially, dramatically, and effectively; and to the very people who may be most interested in it, as evidenced by the fact that they are in a store where such a product is sold.[59]

Although many valuable displays are furnished retailers by manufacturers either as a gift or at a moderate charge, the increasing volume of point-of-sale display material, coupled with the much slower expansion of available space in the store where this material may be placed, has created problems both for the retailer and the supplier.[60] From the manufacturer's point of view, greater difficulty is encountered in getting his display material used. The retailer's problems are revealed by the results of a recent survey by a West Virginia company. About 50 percent of the four to eight display

---

[59] An analysis of the effective use of dealer displays will be found in Kleppner, *op. cit.,* p. 410 ff.

[60] For an expanded discussion of these problems cf. *Four Keys to Managing Grocery Advertising and Display Programs More Effectively* (New York: McKinsey & Co., Inc., 1965).

stands received by retailers each week were considered inferior for display purposes. Major complaints were that the displays were too large, poorly designed, not very original, and ineffective as "salesmen."[61]

In view of the situation outlined in the preceding paragraph it is evident that the retailer needs to consider each display piece on its own merits. He should ask himself such questions as: Is the display suitable to my type of operation? Does the merchandise displayed justify the area occupied by the display? If the item being displayed is an assortment item, does the display show an assortment? Does the attached sign, taken in conjunction with the merchandise, tell the customer the full sales story, or is the salesperson still needed? How much do I have to pay for the display rack or case?

3. *Store Signs and Decorations.* The term "store signs" includes counter signs, price cards, window signs, hanging signs, posters, elevator cards, flags, banners, and similar devices. Such signs are used by all retailers, but especially by stores making frequent use of special promotions and sales events. They are helpful in directing customers to merchandise being featured and in calling attention to special merchandise values.

Decorations refer to distinctive displays and other related preparations for such special occasions as Christmas, Halloween, and for anniversary and birthday sales. Seeking to generate a spirit that will be conducive to buying, retailers probably devote more attention to their Christmas decorations than to those of any other time.

RESPONSIBILITY FOR ADVERTISING AND DISPLAY

Regardless of store size, responsibility for advertising and display activities carries with it the obligation to originate and to appraise such activities and to combine them effectively to attain the objectives toward which they are directed. In small stores the responsibility rests with the proprietor. As stores grow in size, however, this responsibility must be delegated to qualified individuals, so that the proprietory may devote his attention to coordinating all activities of the business.

In department stores, responsibility for these activities is centered in the publicity director or the sales promotion manager, who may have the assistance of an advertising agency in planning and carrying out his assignment. Under him may be a display manager who is responsible for window and interior displays; an advertising manager who directs the work of the advertising department—including copy, art work, and production for var-

---

[61] "P-O-P: What It Needs Most," *Printers' Ink,* November 26, 1965, p. 3. Also cf. R. A. Carter, "Uses and Abuses of Point-of-Sale Material," *Publishers' Weekly,* January 4, 1966, p. 53–56.

ious media; and an individual in charge of miscellaneous methods of promoting sales of the types mentioned in the previous section. Sometimes this person may be called the "fashion coordinator."

Among chain stores problems are encountered unlike those in single-store operation. For example, traveling window-display crews may be employed, and advertisements in the form of matrices may be sent to individual stores for insertion in local newspapers. Lines of responsibility are similar to those in department stores, however, and, depending upon the size of the firm and its policies, an advertising agency may or may not be used in carrying out the advertising function.[62]

REVIEW AND DISCUSSION QUESTIONS

1. Explain the term "sales promotion" in your own words. What factors determine the part played by advertising in a retail store's sales promotional program?
2. Argue the "pro" and "con" sides of the statement: "Retail Advertising Today is a Sad Reflection on the Intelligence of Its Readers."
3. Distinguish among the main types of retail advertising and indicate the considerations that influence the use of each type. Under what conditions is a combination of the types advisable?
4. Define "co-operative advertising" and point out some of the recent developments in connection with its use.
5. Account for the wide variations among different types of stores in the amounts spent for advertising.
6. Explain briefly the nature and importance of each of the steps involved in programming retail advertising.
7. Assume that you have been asked to prepare an advertisement for a small retail store of your own choosing in your particular community. How would you proceed and what information would you want to fulfill this assignment?
8. Prepare the advertisement referred to in the previous question.
9. What factors should be taken into account in selecting merchandise to be advertised by (a) a food retailer, (b) a discount house operator, and (c) a department store?
10. How do you explain the increasing recognition retailers are giving to the pre-checking and after-checking of their advertising?
11. How should a retailer proceed in evaluating the various advertising media available to him? What major factors should govern his final choice?

---

[62] Some 38 percent of the Super Market Institute members have a full time advertising manager and 28 percent, mostly the larger firms, use advertising agencies. Over 50 percent of the companies employing an advertising agency also have full-time advertising managers. "The Super Market Industry Speaks," *Progressive Grocer*, July, 1966, p. 90.

12. Visit your local Better Business Bureau or one in a nearby city and investigate and report on its activities in connection with retail advertising.
13. List the chief characteristics of "special sales events" and explain the steps involved in planning and executing them.
14. Discuss the importance of store display and the need for coordinating it with the store's overall sales promotional program.
15. Suggest desirable guidelines for the retailer in planning (a) his window displays and (b) his interior displays.

SUPPLEMENTARY READINGS

ASSOCIATION OF BETTER BUSINESS BUREAUS. *A Guide for Retail Advertising and Selling* (New York, 1964). Designed to provide assistance to retailers in their sales promotional efforts, this volume can be of value in the preparation of truthful copy.

ASSOCIATION OF NATIONAL ADVERTISERS. *Prevailing Cooperative Advertising Practices and Trends* (New York, 1965). Recent changes in cooperative advertising based on the analysis of 170 agreements are examined in this ANA study. Also cf. MALLOY, FRANK. "A Hard Look at Cooperative Advertising," *Western Advertising,* October, 1965, pp. 13–17.

———. *Educational Preparation for Positions in Advertising Management* (New York, 1966). The student of retailing interested in sales promotional activities will find this booklet of value. It reveals the personal attributes sought by employers in the people they select for such positions.

BOYD, H. W., JR., AND NEWMAN, J. W. (eds.). *Advertising Management: Selected Readings* (Homewood, Ill.: Richard D. Irwin, Inc., 1965). Sections IV, "Developing the Advertising Message," and VI, "Evaluating Advertising Effectiveness," contain valuable readings of particular interest to the retailing student seeking additional information on advertising.

CRANE, EDGAR. *Marketing Communications* (New York: John Wiley & Sons, Inc., 1965). This "behavioral approach to men, managers, and media" provides new insights in communications for everyone interested in advertising.

CRAWFORD, J. W. *Advertising* (2d. ed.; Boston: Allyn and Bacon, Inc., 1965). Covering all aspects of advertising, this publication provides current information of value to the student of retailing.

EDWARDS, C. M., JR., AND BROWN, R. A. *Retail Advertising and Sales Promotion* (3d ed.; Englewood Cliffs, N.J.: Prentice-Hall, Inc., 1959). Although rather old, this volume continues as one of the best single sources on advertising and display from the retailer's point of view.

GODFREY, M. L. *Applying Today's Computer Technology to Advertising and Marketing* (New York: Association of National Advertisers, 1966). The types of computer applications directly related to advertising problems are emphasized in this ANA analysis.

JANEZECK, G. *Store Arrangement and Display* (Small Business Bibliography No. 52). (Washington, D.C.: Small Business Administration, 1965). This 8-

page pamphlet provides a selection of annotated references on display principles and techniques.

KLEPPNER, OTTO. *Advertising Procedure* (5th ed.; Englewood Cliffs, N.J.: Prentice-Hall, Inc., 1966). Updating one of the earlier "standard" textbooks in advertising, this latest edition provides the interested reader with knowledge of recent developments in the advertising field.

KIRKPATRICK, C. A. *Advertising: Mass Communication in Marketing* (2d. ed.; Boston: Houghton, Mifflin Company, 1964). The author treats the numerous goals and role of advertising in marketing communications.

LEHMANN, J. N. *Promotion of Home Goods* (Los Angeles: Maylay Publishing Company, 1965). This book constitutes a ready reference to the advertising, display, and miscellaneous promotion of house furnishings.

MAUGER, E. M. *Modern Display Techniques* (New York: Fairchild Publications, Inc., 1965). As the title indicates, this book reviews display techniques helpful to the retailer in promoting sales.

NATIONAL CASH REGISTER COMPANY. *Attracting and Holding Customers* (Dayton, Ohio, 1963). In sections 3 and 4 of this booklet are found excellent suggestions for promoting sales and conducting special sales events.

NATIONAL RETAIL MERCHANTS ASSOCIATION. *Sales Promotion Calendar* (New York, published annually). This comprehensive planning tool is designed to provide assistance to large and small retailers in their budgeting and sales promotion.

PAYNE, G. K. *Creative Display* (New York: National Retail Merchants Association, 1965). Full of ideas for the display man, the author offers a practical guide in the preparation of displays.

ROSENBLUM, M. L. *How to Design Effective Store Advertising* (New York: National Retail Merchants Association, 1962). Dealing basically with illustrations and layout, both large and small retailers will find a wealth of helpful material in this volume.

SANDAGE, C. H., AND FRYBURGER, VERNON. *Advertising: Theory and Practice* (7th ed.; Homewood, Ill.: Richard D. Irwin, Inc., 1967). Although covering the broad field of advertising, the authors' discussions of the preparation and reproduction of the advertising message, the testing of advertising effectiveness, and the advertising organization are of particular interest to retailers and students. Chap. xxxi relates solely to retail advertising.

WRIGHT, J. S., AND WARNER, D. S. *Advertising* (2d ed.; New York: McGraw-Hill Book Co., Inc., 1966). This interesting volume, although general in nature, gives attention to retail advertising in the pertinent areas of application.

19
CHAPTER

Retail Sales Promotion by Other
Nonpersonal Methods

In addition to advertising and display as discussed in the previous chapter, a variety of other nonpersonal methods of retail sales promotion are used by retailers. Among those of importance today are telephone and mail-order selling, packaging, labeling, and consumer premiums, including trading stamps.

TELEPHONE AND MAIL-ORDER SELLING

Soliciting purchases or accepting orders by telephone or mail on the part of retail stores is not a new development.[1] As long ago as 1905, the Strawbridge and Clothier store of Philadelphia was using a full-page advertisement to tell potential customers that it was "The Telephone Store."[2] Progress was slow, however, and it was not until the depression of the 1930's that a substantial growth in telephone selling took place. In contrast, mail-order selling by retail stores has long been accepted as an easy and convenient method by which customers could make known their wants and have goods delivered.

Today the large majority of newspaper readers and telephone users are familiar with attempts to obtain their business through these media. Many large stores actively encourage readers of their advertisements to telephone or mail their orders. To facilitate such action some stores provide telephone

---

[1] As used throughout this section, "mail orders" refer to such sales made by retailers who predominantly sell over the counter.

[2] *Philadelphia Bulletin,* June 3, 1905.

service to their customers on Sunday and during morning and evening hours when the stores are not open. In fact, the practice of ordering by telephone and by mail has become so prevalent that on occasions customers must be reminded that no mail or telephone orders will be accepted for special merchandise offerings. In addition to the solicitation of telephone and mail orders through newspapers, a growing number of retailers periodically issue small catalogs or booklets, especially just prior to the Christmas season, to emphasize fashion, seasonal, and other merchandise.[3]

Extent and Importance of Telephone and Mail-Order Selling

The extent to which retail stores offer telephone and mail-order service is suggested by their advertisements in a Sunday issue of the *New York Times* (April 17, 1966) and a Thursday issue of the *San Francisco Chronicle* (April 21, 1966). Practically all of the larger stores and several of the smaller ones invited telephone and mail orders with such statements as "Mail and Phone Orders Filled" (some mentioning "within five days of receipt of order," and some noting the minimum-size order that would be accepted). Readers were reminded to add a sales tax and specified amounts, such as 75 cents for deliveries beyond motor delivery areas and 40 cents for C.O.D. orders. In many instances reply coupons were used to facilitate ordering by mail (see Figure 19–1). On special-sale offerings, however, some stores reminded their potential customers: "No Mail or Phone Orders Please!"

Outside the New York and San Francisco areas many illustrations of telephone and mail-order selling by other retailers are readily available. The

The Emporium Market Street, S.F. • YU 2-1111
Please send the following:

Quan.	Style	Size	Color	Price

Name__________

Address__________

City__________ State__________

☐ Cash ☐ Charge ☐ Send Charge Application

Please add 4% tax in Calif., if beyond UP zone, add 35c handling charge.

FIG. 19–1. Coupon used by department store to facilitate ordering by mail.

[3] Marshall Field & Co.'s *Fashions of the Hour* is a good example of this practice.

J. C. Penney Company has purchased one of the smaller mail-order firms and is placing order desks in many of its stores; by the early 1970's the firm expects to offer a nationwide mail-order service.[4] Sears, Roebuck and Co. attributes a substantial part of its post-World War II increase in sales to the growing popularity of its telephone selling. Sales of this type have grown so rapidly in recent years, now accounting for an estimated 5–10 percent of total sales,[5] that the company's retail promotion manager terms the development to be the result of "a telephone class of customers." To serve this customer the company has installed telephone sales service in each of its 786 stores, 11 mail-order plants, 1,294 catalog sales offices, and 58 telephone sales offices.[6] Telephone service is available, also, in 76 service and parts centers supporting retail and catalog order service operations. Favorable results from telephone selling are also being shown by such other firms as Montgomery Ward & Company, Spiegel, Inc., and Aldens, Inc., each providing telephone service through telephone offices, catalog offices, and retail stores.

In the department store field, many firms now sell 5 to 13 percent of their volume by telephone.[7] Carson, Pirie, Scott & Co. of Chicago; T. Eaton Company, Ltd. of Toronto, Canada; J. L. Hudson Company of Detroit; and numerous others have long promoted sales by this medium.[8] The same is true for many small and large retailers of various types in all parts of the country. In fact, many neighborhood and downtown drug and food stores have long depended on the telephone to bring in many of their orders. Among specialty stores, telephone selling is also an effective sales tool: witness the experimental telephone selling campaign by Best & Company, New York, termed the "Client Calling Program" and conducted in October, 1965:

Some 580 full-time employees in Best's Fifth Avenue store and eight New York area branches made an estimated 20,000 calls during that first trial month. Out of these, about 1,000 resulted in sales, representing a surprising 5 percent effectiveness, with an average $47 per transaction in the adult ready-to-wear section and $20 in the children's departments. Telephone orders in the latter represented about 60 percent of the total.

---

[4] Statement by Penney's chief executive officer, *Women's Wear Daily*, June 17, 1966, p. 35.

[5] The company does not publish sales figures revealing telephone business as distinct from order desk and catalog sales office business. Our 5–10 percent estimate is based on various statements made by Sears' executives. Cf. John Osbon, "Catalog Chains Find Mail is No Longer King," *Women's Wear Daily*, July 29, 1965, p. 23.

[6] *Annual Report*, fiscal year ended January 31, 1966, p. 10.

[7] National Cash Register Company, *Attracting and Holding Customers* (Dayton, Ohio, 1963), p. 27.

[8] Cf. "Your Telephones: Are You Using Them Enough?," *Department Store Economist*, September, 1965, pp. 31–33.

This amounted to an extra sales total of some $30,000 for the initial month of the project. Subsequent checks on the project revealed the continuity of the results.[9]

The success of the Best & Company program has encouraged telephone company officials to propose similar ones to stores in other parts of the country.

Factors Encouraging Telephone and Mail-Order Selling

Customer's Point of View. The present emphasis upon telephone and mail-order selling is quite understandable. The telephone has come into widespread use in homes[10] and business, so that buying by telephone is convenient and is demanded by many buyers as a customer service. It enables them to avoid the inconveniences of shopping; they have no tiresome walking to do and no driving and parking problems to solve.

Some significant conclusions about telephone customers resulted from a survey conducted by students at the Harvard Graduate School of Business Administration, as follows:

1. Telephone sales are plus sales. They do not replace floor sales.[11] Half of the women interviewed shop by phone in one store and in person in another.

2. Half of the women interviewed stated they shop by phone for many items not advertised in the newspapers.

3. The average sales check on phone orders is 40 percent higher than on floor sales.

4. Other factors, like distance from the store, inclement weather, lack of babysitter, illness, and sundry other problems favor telephone shopping in many instances.[12]

Retailer's Point of View. To the retailer the telephone offers an easy method to contact present and prospective customers to point out especially advantageous purchases of seasonal and other merchandise. A contributing factor is the development of improved telephone-selling equipment closely adapted to the retailer's needs. As for mail-order selling, since retailers advertise widely in newspapers, it is easy for them to insert a few words indicating that the same merchandise can be purchased by mail. As customers have moved into suburban areas and as traffic and parking conditions

[9] Fred Eichelbaum, "Bells are Ringing Up Extra Sales in Best's Campaign," *Women's Wear Daily,* March 29, 1966, p. 48.

[10] In March, 1960, the Bureau of the Census reports that about 39.3 million households (75 percent of the total) had telephones. The number and proportion have probably grown since that time.

[11] On the validity of this point also cf. the discussion in section one of S. U. Rich, *Shopping Behavior of Department Store Customers* (Boston, Mass.: Harvard University, Graduate School of Business Administration, 1963).

[12] Eichelbaum, *op. cit.* The survey covered 52 major department stores in seven cities.

have worked against downtown shopping, progressive retailers have seized upon mail-order selling as well as the telephone to maintain contact with their customers. Sales by these means have increased, this fact has been widely publicized, and other stores have followed the practice.

Many large stores also feature a "Shopping Service" designed to assist telephone or mail-order customers in finding suitable merchandise for all types of occasions. Some of them use special names to identify this service. In San Francisco, for example, the Emporium has its "Barbara Lee" and I. Magnin and Company its "Kitty Steele."

Telephone Selling as a Business Builder

Among the most important ways in which the retailer can use the telephone to build business are the following:

1. Customers can be notified of the receipt of merchandise which was not in stock at the time of their visit to the store or which has been ordered especially for them. Such service prevents lost sales and builds customer goodwill.

2. As the business grows and each of the employees builds up a personal following, there is an increasing opportunity to make use of the telephone to get business by personal calls to customers who are pleased to be notified when some new merchandise arrives.

3. New residents can be tactfully solicited on the telephone, although this practice should be followed carefully. Some shop owners do not approve of it, as they claim that a blind solicitation by telephone often annoys a customer; if she is a busy housewife any interruption of her duties may be considered a nuisance. Therefore, it is often better to build customers' confidence by securing their permission to telephone them.

4. The telephone can be used in an effort to revive inactive credit accounts. With friendliness and a desire to obtain facts, one can:

   (a) express regret over the decreasing volume of business from such credit customers;

   (b) ascertain any cause for dissatisfaction;

   (c) make what commitments you feel are deserved by the circumstance; and

   (d) solicit an increase of future business.[13]

Disadvantages of Telephone and Mail-Order Selling

Despite the growth of telephone and mail-order selling, and despite considerable evidence to the contrary, many retailers are still reluctant to employ these forms of sales promotion because they fear customers will be

---

[13] *Attracting and Holding Customers, op. cit.,* p. 27.

kept from visiting their stores. Consequently, some of them still run the line "no mail, no phone, no C.O.D." on special promotions, hoping that this will cause store visits and result in other purchases being made.

Another common objection to telephone and mail-order selling is that the merchandise sold is more likely to be returned than merchandise bought when the customer visits the store, with the result that costs are increased and profits reduced. Of course, if a retailer trains his telephone staff to say, "Let us send you several dresses from which you can select one or two," high returns on telephone sales are to be expected. A similar result follows the sending out of merchandise—for instance, fruits and vegetables—which over-the-counter customers refuse to purchase. If the store makes an honest effort to treat telephone and mail-order customers as well as it treats those who come to the store, there is no reason for excessive returns on such sales.

Some practical operating disadvantages must also be overcome in telephone and mail-order selling. The retailer must maintain sufficient stock to permit fulfillment of all orders, thus avoiding customer disappointment when goods are unavailable and the cost of sending refunds and letters of explanation. Delivery service must be provided. Arrangements must be made to collect on C.O.D. transactions and/or to extend credit to telephone customers who desire to purchase on this basis. The telephone salesperson also is at a disadvantage in that she cannot see the customer and thus note facial reactions to suggestions and fit her approach to the income scale suggested by the customer's appearance. Moreover, some expense and trouble are involved in training and maintaining a telephone and mail-order staff.

The Future of Telephone and Mail-Order Selling

Disagreement exists among retailers concerning the future importance of this business. Those who have obtained satisfactory results from these sales promotion methods are convinced they have a bright future, but those who have not obtained the benefits expected frequently reach an opposite conclusion. On balance, it seems to the authors that the current sales increases from these methods of selling are in line with fundamental trends, and that further gains may be expected. But each retailer must determine the extent to which he will utilize these sales promotional devices based on his judgment of their effect on his sales volume, the costs involved, and the relationship of these devices to the other forms of selling effort he is employing.

In conclusion, it should be emphasized that sales by telephone and mail order do not just happen; they are the result of proper planning and the continuous, effective execution of these plans. Successful telephone selling, for example, depends in no small degree upon (1) proper selection and training of personnel; (2) a satisfactory wage scale, which will attract the desired type of employee; (3) proper working conditions, including the provision of adequate facilities; and (4) competent supervision.

IMPROVED PACKAGING TO PROMOTE RETAIL SALES

The past two decades have witnessed a sharp increase in the attention given to packaging by manufacturers and by retailers. Today, well-conceived packages are essential both in stores where displays must carry a major part of the sales task and in retail outlets which rely mainly on salespeople.[14] In turn, packaging has influence both on store layout and display, since the maximum effectiveness of packages cannot be obtained without good display techniques and appropriate fixtures.[15] Assuming that manufacturers and retailers combine these elements into well conceived programs, packaging should become even more important over the years just ahead.

Present Emphasis on Packaging

From the point of view of the manufacturer and retailer, four main factors have led to the growing interest in packaging: their desire to meet their customers' wishes, the realization that the package is an effective tool of sales promotion, the growth of the self-service and self-selection store, and various technological changes. All of these factors are interrelated; each factor is partly cause and partly effect of the others.

So far as customers are concerned, they have favored the "packaging revolution" since it aids them in buying convenient amounts, assures a higher degree of sanitation, protects fragile items, provides convenient containers for the storing of items while being used in the home, and offers a way to communicate "a product difference and product information."[16]

In addition to pleasing his customers, the manufacturer or the private-branding retailer who packages his product discovers he has achieved a valuable sales promotion tool.[17] In fact, some marketing experts rate pack-

---

[14] Cf. Julia Morse, "A Package is More than a Container," *Advertising & Sales Promotion,* March, 1966, pp. 29–32.

[15] Cf. David Breedon, "The Effect of Packaging on Store Fixtures and Vice Versa," *Stores,* October, 1965, pp. 37–46.

[16] Cf. the Arthur D. Little study reported in "Packaging Lags Behind Economy but Its Benefits to Consumer Grow: Little," *Advertising Age,* April 11, 1966, p. 112.

[17] For many illustrations of this point cf. "The Power of Proper Packaging," a special report by the staff of *Business Week,* in the issue of February 20, 1965, pp. 90–114.

age appeal as the main reason why a consumer buys one product rather than another. Although the authors are not in agreement with this statement, because in the long run it is the customer's satisfaction with the contents of the package which results in repeat purchases, there is little doubt but that the appeal of the package—including its style, color, utility, and attractiveness—plays a role in determining the product's salability. Consequently, the manufacturer who devises an attractive package often finds he has increased his competitive advantage over his competitors. This competitive factor has been especially significant in self-service stores, where there are no salesmen to extol the merits of the less distinguished package or the unpackaged merchandise.

Technological changes have made possible the greater emphasis on packaging. To illustrate, when the packaging of fresh meat was first attempted the available materials led to discoloration. Gradually the research laboratory turned out today's plastics, including transparent trays, which allow the meat to "breathe" and retain its natural color, thus increasing its salability.[18] Similar technological changes in the wood, paper, metal, and glass industries have produced an almost unbelievable variety of containers.[19]

Retailer Preferences in Packaging

Retailers want packages that attract customer attention, protect the product, make the product available in proper amounts or sizes, reflect the nature and use of the product, offer convenience in handling and placing on the shelves and in customer use, make effective displays, are moisture-proof, and are easily identified so that the customer is aided both in the selection process and in the rejection of substitutes. The great majority of retailers also want packages which are not deceptive to the customer, such as results from slack filling. Many customers believe deception through packaging still exists, a condition substantiated by their buying experiences. Manufacturers and private-branding retailers who engage in deceptive packaging have only themselves to blame when the late President Kennedy found it necessary to urge a government program looking toward "improving packaging standards

---

[18] Cf. "Transparent Trays Make New Bid for Meat Packaging," *Modern Packaging,* February, 1966, pp. 102–3 ff.

[19] Important trends in packaging, including the measurement of the package's impact on consumers, are discussed in the American Management Association's *Profitability and Penetration Through Packaging* (New York: The Association, 1965); "New Directions for Packaging," *Printers' Ink,* June 10, 1966, pp. 15–33; and "The Sophisticated Materials," *Dun's Review and Modern Industry,* November, 1966, pp. 144–47.

and achieving more specific disclosure of the quantity and ingredients of the product inside the package. . . ."[20]

LABELING TO PROMOTE RETAIL SALES

Labeling is the placing of text or pictorial material upon a product or attaching such information to its container. It is illustrated by the gummed paper sheet on the package, the printed material placed inside the container, and the tag attached to the product itself.

Labeling has long been used for such purposes as identifying the manufacturer or distributor of a product, disclosing the quantity of product in the package and the materials from which it is made, and informing the customer as to how the product should be used.[21] In recent years—with the expansion of self-service stores and federal legislation requiring certain product information on various consumer goods—labeling has become an important tool of sales promotion. On a tag attached to a television set appears a brief listing of the set's special features. Directions on a tag attached to a woman's orlon sweater emphasizes the ease with which the sweater can be washed. The gummed label on a package of cake mix employs both text and picture to convey the message that in a few minutes the customer can produce a cake superior to that "which mother made."

Retailer's Interest in Labeling

The retailer has much to gain from the awakened interest in labeling. Insofar as labels promote additional sales, he benefits from the extra volume. When the customer purchases with less aid from the salesman, the retailer's selling cost ratio is reduced. Since the added information should help his customers to purchase merchandise better suited to their needs, the retailer gains customer good will and returns of merchandise are reduced. As with packaging, however, the retailer suffers if the labeling is misleading. Consequently, regardless of whether the manufacturer or the retailer does the labeling, the retailer should insist upon accuracy on all labels.

Truth in Packaging and Labeling

Governmental efforts are also being directed toward better labeling practices: witness the 1966 enactment of the "Fair Packaging and Labeling

---

[20] Message to Congress of March 15, 1961, as reported in full in the *New York Times,* March 16, 1962.

[21] On the importance of correct labeling, particularly in the drug business where errors may be fatal, cf. "Error-proof Labeling," *Modern Packaging,* August, 1965, pp. 99–102 ff.

Bill," commonly referred to as the "Truth-in-Packaging Bill."[22] Although the highly controversial provision requiring standardization of packages was deleted from the measure, the remaining sections improve labeling by, among other things, prohibiting the use of misleading pictorial matter, requiring a list of the ingredients on the package or label, forcing a definition of size of serving when a package or label specifies it will serve any stated number of people, and eliminating such words as "jumbo" quart.[23] In addition, a net-quantity statement must appear on the label.[24]

Despite the need to eliminate deception in packages and labels, there is real concern among some retailers and manufacturers that government regulations in this area may result in unnecessary restraints on private business.[25] Specifically, they "fear that negative rules against misrepresentation and deception may lead into detailed, positive regulative requirements and standards" which will weaken the competitive positions of honest companies. Consequently, it is important that Congress "strike a proper balance so that only packaging and labeling that in fact do confuse and deceive consumer are proscribed."[26]

CONSUMER PREMIUMS TO PROMOTE RETAIL SALES[27]

The use of consumer premiums as traffic builders and as sales stimulators for retailers, particularly those in the food field, has assumed boom proportions in recent years. Used to some degree since the early years of this century, currently the premium business approximates $3 billion annually.[28] The retailer may use them to induce his customers to pay their bills on time, to watch demonstrations, to sell specific merchandise identified by his own brand, and to promote continuous customer patronage.[29]

---

[22] Some of the conditions which the bill seeks to correct are suggested in E. T. Grether, "Sharp Practice in Merchandising and Advertising," *Annals of the American Academy of Political and Social Science,* Vol. CCCLXIII (January, 1966), pp. 108–16.

[23] For details cf. *Modern Packaging,* June, 1965, p. 110; and *Business Week,* November 5, 1966, p. 88.

[24] In fact, this requirement had already been effected by a National Conference on Weights and Measures.

[25] Cf. C. S. Mayer, "Requiem for the Truth in Packaging Bill?," *Journal of Marketing,* Vol. XXX, No. 2 (April, 1966), pp. 1–5.

[26] E. T. Grether, *Marketing and Public Policy* (Englewood Cliffs, N.J.: Prentice-Hall, Inc., 1966), p. 47.

[27] Although many manufacturers use premiums to promote the sale of their merchandise, the present discussion is restricted primarily to activities of retailers. Cf., however, "Redemption of Manufacturers' Coupons" in a later section of this chapter.

[28] Cf. "The Premium Urge," *Sales Management,* October 1, 1965, pp. 51–56.

[29] Some of these various goals of premiums are illustrated in "How Retailers Can Stop Hating and Learn to Love the Premium," *Merchandising Week,* May 3, 1965, p. 46.

Types of Consumer Premiums

Considered from the continuous customer-patronage point of view, a premium may be defined as a tie-in arrangement in which a product (the premium) not part of a seller's regular sales assortment is sold at a discount or given away in return for purchases made in the regular sales assortment. From the point of view of the retailer, two major types of such arrangements may be distinguished: (1) the single transaction offer in which the customer may obtain the premium with a single purchase either as a gift or for the payment of a small additional amount; and (2) the continuity offer involving a series of purchases to accumulate coupons, cash register tapes, trading stamps, or the like to obtain a premium. Illustrations of the first type are: (*a*) a pair of nylon stretch stockings (retail value $1.00) for fifty cents plus one coupon from a Kraft Cheese package, and (*b*) the gift of the *Encyclopedia of Sports* with a Gillette Razor. As already suggested, an example of the continuity offer is provided by the trading-stamp plans which are discussed in the next section of this chapter.

Regardless of the type of consumer premium used by the retailer, the careful planning and proper execution of a premium program is essential. These steps include: (1) establishing guides or standards for selecting the right products to use as premiums; (2) providing adequate publicity to insure customer familiarity with the program, (3) arranging operating details, and (4) maintaining close cooperation with the manufacturer.

Promoting Sales with Trading Stamps

For many years trading stamps have been used by retailers to promote sales.[30] Currently, they are offered to customers by retailers accounting for an estimated 12 to 18 percent of all retail sales.[31] In the supermarket field, where stamps are especially effective in attracting customers, they are given by 22 percent of the independent stores and by 77 percent of those operated by chains.[32] While these figures represent a decline from those for the

[30] Although relatively less important than in the United States, trading stamps are also used abroad. To illustrate the point: Since their introduction in the late 1950's, "trading stamps have rapidly increased in importance" in Japan. A. J. Alton and G. O. Totten, "Trading Stamps in Japan—Boom in the Making?," *Journal of Marketing*, Vol. XXIX, No. 2 (April, 1965), pp. 12–17.

[31] "What's Going on in Trading Stamps?," *Progressive Grocer*, February, 1965, p. 54; and Richard Rosenthal, "Stamp Industry Talking Maturity Not Growth," *Women's Wear Daily*, July 2, 1965, p. 2.

[32] "33rd Annual Report of the Grocery Industry," *Progressive Grocer*, April, 1966, p. 56; and *The Super Market Industry Speaks: 1966* (Chicago: Super Market Institute, Inc., 1966), p. 22.

preceding year, the percentage of supermarket customers saving trading stamps continues to advance—reaching 92.5 percent in 1965.[33]

How and Why Trading Stamps Are Used.   When the customer in the stamp-giving store pays for her purchases, a number of the stamps (typically, at the rate of one stamp for each 10 cents in purchases) are handed to her. These stamps are accumulated and eventually turned in for merchandise at a stamp-redemption store or mail-order center: Over 850 such stores and centers are operated throughout the country just by the leading stamp company, the Sperry & Hutchinson Company.[34] The retailer buys his stamps from one of the many companies set up to sell and redeem them, or, if he is large enough, he may form his own stamp company.

To the retailer the added cost of the trading stamps (.002¢ to .003¢ per stamp) plus the time involved in handling them may be offset by certain advantages. Customers are attracted by the opportunity to obtain desirable merchandise, so that the retailer's volume may be increased. In turn, higher sales may result in greater total profits. A stamp promotion may make "regular" customers out of periodic shoppers. Also the retailer's competitors may react less quickly to his promotional use of a trading-stamp plan than they would to other promotional methods. Some studies even show that a small number of extra stamps offered with a particular commodity will increase sales more, and cost less to the retailer, than a price reduction.

Why Customers Like Trading Stamps.   While there are customers who react negatively to sales promotion through the trading stamp, the evidence is clear that stamps do appeal to many buyers. To cite a study in four midwestern cities, "trading stamps were saved by 90 percent of all the respondents" and, in general, "respondents in all four cities had favorable attitudes toward trading stamps."[35] Why do stamps have such a strong customer acceptance?

Without doubt there are many factors involved in answering this question. To some customers, stamps are a relatively painless way of saving. To others, they offer certain psychological satisfactions: A reputation for being thrifty, a response to the collecting instinct, and a sense of accomplishment in filling one's stamp books and redeeming them for merchandise. But the basic answer is economic in nature: The belief that the store offering trading stamps gives them more per dollar spent (when both the merchandise

---

[33] B. L. Schapker, "Behavior Patterns of Supermarket Shoppers," *Journal of Marketing,* Vol. XXX, No. 4 (October, 1966), p. 48.

[34] S. H. Brown, "Sperry & Hutchinson's Very Successful Stagnation," *Fortune,* Vol. LXX, No. 5 (November, 1964), p. 157.

[35] J. G. Udell, "Can Attitude Measurement Predict Consumer Behavior?," *Journal of Marketing,* Vol. XXIX, No. 4 (October, 1965), p. 50.

purchased and that obtained through the stamps are considered) than does the nonstamp store. Is the customer correct in this belief?

That filled stamp books have real value for the customer is both obvious and attested to by many studies, although the investigations differ somewhat as to the exact dollar value they report. Typical of these studies is one by Professors Vredenburg and Frisinger of Colorado State University. They report that a filled book can be redeemed for merchandise which has a value of $3.21 in traditional stores, or $2.82 in discount stores, the "all store" average being $3.11.[36]

Does the customer make any payment, in the form of higher prices, for trading stamps? In answer, several things can be said. First, since stamps are merely a form of sales promotion, this question is really another way of stating the old question: Does advertising raise prices? Second, while some customers believe prices in stamp-giving stores exceed those in nonstamp stores, the majority of customers agree with those in one four-city study, "that they had not noticed any difference between the prices in stores that did and those that did not offer stamps."[37] Third, despite some conflicting evidence, the various price studies which have been made were fairly summarized by an English writer in these words: "There is no conclusive evidence from the USA . . . that trading [stamps] have raised prices."[38] Fourth, even the studies which indicate somewhat higher prices in stamp-giving stores make it clear that the higher prices are more than offset by the value of the merchandise for which the stamps are redeemed.[39]

Requirements for Successful Use of the Trading Stamp. Despite the customer appeal of trading stamps, they are not a panacea for all retailers. Since competitive conditions will not usually allow a retailer to raise his prices to compensate for the cost of stamps, and since the discontinuance of stamps involves many serious problems,[40] before adopting stamps the retailer needs to be reasonably sure that he can increase his sales or

---

[36] H. L. Vredenburg and H. H. Frisinger, "The Value of Trading Stamps as Measured by Retail Prices," *Journal of Retailing,* Vol. XLI, No. 3 (Fall, 1965), p. 31.

[37] Udell, *op. cit.,* p. 50.

[38] Christina Fulop, *The Role of Trading Stamps in Retail Competition* (London: Institute of Economic Affairs Limited, 1964), p. 65. For a similar conclusion cf. V. A. Bunn, *Trading Stamps and Retail Food Prices, 1960–65* (Kansas City, Mo.: Midwest Research Institute, 1966).

[39] One government study concludes that "adjustments for stamps produce a minimal effect on the movement of the total CPI [Consumer Price Index] when cumulated over a fifteen-year period." Cf. E. D. Hoover and M. L. Drake, "Trading Stamps and the CPI," *Monthly Labor Review,* April, 1965, pp. 429–33.

[40] Some of these problems are suggested by Nathaniel Schwartz, "Trading Stamps— Should We Drop Them?," *Super Market Merchandising,* April, 1965, p. 40.

reduce his other operating costs. A retailer can usually achieve these goals only if he has some or all of these characteristics:

First, he needs a sufficient excess capacity in his retail operation so that he can absorb a 10 to 20 percent increase in his sales without any appreciable change in his total overhead costs.

Second, the retailer should have a location which places him reasonably close to a group of stores in various fields of retail business, with these stores using the same brand of stamp. In this group there should be a supermarket or a department store, or both, i.e., some retailer from whom the consumer will purchase in large volume, thereby rapidly accumulating stamps so that she has an incentive to save them.

Third, he must be willing to promote the stamps. In other words, if the retailer is to gain from his stamp operation, he must encourage customers to take them, save them, and redeem them.

Fourth, and perhaps most important of all, the retailer must meet his competitors in terms of convenience of location, prices, selection and quality of merchandise, courteous and friendly service, cleanliness of housekeeping, and type and quality of services rendered. Put another way, and using the words of an executive of a successful chain of supermarkets: "Whether stamp or discount, the *best operated* store is the one which succeeds."[41]

Since not all retailers have these four characteristics, or do not have them in the same degree, the success they have achieved with stamps varies widely. Some have so increased their sales that their profits have advanced, despite the cost of the stamps; others have suffered lower profits. Each retailer needs to analyze his particular operations with great care, including "the practices and attitudes of [his] competitors and customers,"[42] before he decides for or against trading stamps as part of his sales promotion program.

Factors in Growth of Premium Merchandising

Some attempts have been made to interpret the current widespread use of premiums by retailers "merely as a phase of a cycle entirely comparable with the past." A few years ago one authority in this field emphasized several causal factors in the present situation that indicate such an interpretation was not justified. These factors, which are still pertinent and bear repeating, are as follows:

---

[41] Avram Goldberg of Stop & Shop, Inc., in *Chain Store Age* (Supermarket Executives Edition), March, 1966, p. 15.

[42] R. W. Mueller, "The Present and Future of Trading Stamps," *Progressive Grocer,* October, 1965, p. 6.

1. The dominance and increasing trend toward limited service distribution of food and allied products at retail. . . . Consequently, (*a*) manufacturers of grocery products can expect little help from dealers through personal selling efforts and (*b*) shelf positions, display, and price are much more important relatively in influencing purchases by consumer-buyers.

2. Paralleling this trend is that toward one-stop shopping by consumer-buyers at single enterprises or in integrated shopping centers. Consequently, (*a*) competition among manufacturers for consumer attention is focused more sharply and (*b*) endeavors to find relief by seeking distribution through unorthodox outlets run into increasing resistance.

3. The high degree of concentration of volume in the hands of chains, supermarkets, voluntary chains, cooperatives, and large-scale or organized groups, together with the preceding two influences has made it increasingly essential for manufacturers to focus their promotional efforts more sharply and more effectively, especially in the food field. It is much simpler relatively to hold the whip-hand over an army of unorganized small dealers. . . . The bargaining position of large-scale and organized dealers has been greatly improved by their demonstrated capacity to sell products under their own private labels.

4. Sales promotional difficulties and necessities have been accentuated in recent years by three developments in brand promotion: (*a*) the rather complete knowledge and acceptance of the commodity as such by consumers in many product fields involving heavy consumer expenditures (that is, the pioneering, learning phase of market promotion is past); (*b*) the general acceptance of several brands of such products as almost entirely interchangeable (for example, the lack of recognition by many consumers of basic product differentiation, as among the major brands of gasoline); and (*c*) the growing importance of chain and other controlled brands. This latter expansion in itself, of course, reflects to a considerable extent the previous two factors.

5. An exceptional opportunity for premium selling directed at children has been created by (*a*) the increasing proportion of the population in the lower age levels arising out of the increase in the birth rate during and since World War II, and (*b*) the enormous increase in the number of TV sets in American households.

6. Finally, the widespread presence of fair trade, unfair practices, unfair sales, and anti-discrimination laws on the statute books of the states and the evolving code of fair competition in federal law and regulation have raised legal issues quite different from those prior to World War I. Among these issues, perhaps the most interesting and as yet unresolved one is just what a nonusing seller may do lawfully in good faith in meeting the competition of competitors offering premiums, trading stamps, and similar inducements. Under about half of the fair trade laws such practices are supposed to be prohibited. Under the other fair trade laws and the unfair practices acts, and under special forms of legislation, the legal issues are greatly beclouded.[43]

---

[43] E. T. Grether, "External Product and Enterprise Differentiation and Consumer Behavior," in R. H. Cole (ed.), *Consumer Behavior and Motivation* (Urbana: Bureau of Economic and Business Research, University of Illinois, 1956), pp. 91–93.

Redemption of Manufacturers' Coupons

Of growing concern to many retailers is their role in handling the coupons used by manufacturers to induce consumers to try their products.[44] These coupons are made available to the consumer in a variety of ways, most commonly through newspapers and magazines, by direct mailings, and on packages.[45] The face value of the coupons range from 3 cents to $5, with a 10-cent coupon being used most frequently, so that they are attractive to value-conscious shoppers.[46] A survey conducted by the A. C. Nielsen Company revealed that more than one billion coupons—10 percent of those distributed—and representing savings of $100 million off the regular price of new soaps, foods, cereals, and other products, were redeemed at retail outlets in 1965.[47] With at least 800 manufacturers presently using coupons, the retailer faces a heavy task in redeeming them and returning them to the issuing manufacturers for credit. The benefits he derives from this service are a matter of considerable conjecture on his part.

OTHER METHODS USED TO PROMOTE SALES

In addition to the methods and devices described, retailers use numerous other ways and means to attract customers to their stores and to retain their permanent patronage. Merchandise stunts, such as inviting a star baseball or football player to a sporting-goods store or department to meet customers and assist them in their purchases or to autograph goods purchased, afford a type of showmanship which often stimulates sales. Fashion shows, in which the newest designs in women's ready-to-wear are featured on live models, are widely used by department stores and by some specialty and limited-line stores. Flower shows, such as those held by Macy's of San Francisco and the May Company in its Denver store, attract numerous "observers" and undoubtedly many buyers. Contests of various sorts—related to cooking, photography, and craftsmanship—are sometimes used by retailers.

In many communities, retailers cooperate in the planning and execution of an annual "Dollar Day" to attract customers to the shopping district and

---

[44] Cf. A. C. Nielsen, Jr., "The Impact of Retail Coupons," *Journal of Marketing,* Vol. XXIX, No. 4 (October, 1965), pp. 11–15.

[45] Cf. Alvin Schwartz, "The Influence of Media Characteristics on Coupon Redemption," *ibid.,* Vol. XXX, No. 1 (January, 1966), pp. 41–46.

[46] "Companies Offering Coupons Increase; Dailies Used Most," *Advertising Age,* April 4, 1966, p. 10.

[47] "Moms Redeemed Billion Coupons in '65: Nielsen," *ibid.,* February 28, 1966, p. 24. Also cf. "The Era of the Giveaway," *Printers' Ink,* November 25, 1966, pp. 35–36 ff.

thus to increase sales. Some stores sponsor parades to advertise the store and promote business. R. H. Macy & Company's parade inaugurating the Christmas season and using mammoth balloon animals and comic-strip characters is probably one of the best known.

Stix, Baer & Fuller, a St. Louis department store, used a "Salute to St. Louis" as a sales promotion device. This two-week tribute to local industry featured the exhibits of 45 of the city's largest manufacturing and commercial enterprises who spent $100,000 to tell their stories on the store's selling floors. Attendance at the shows approximated 500,000, and included many individuals who had not previously visited the store. Not to be outdone, Famous-Barr (Stix, Baer & Fuller's leading competitor) featured a German-Irish-Italian "Special" for two weeks preceding the "Salute to St. Louis." It also promoted heavily its regular anniversary event which it ran simultaneously with its competitor's salute to local industry.[48]

Still other illustrations of techniques used to encourage sales include games of various kinds by supermarket chains—Bonus Bingo, Three of a Kind, Let's Go to the Races, and Win-A-Check, for examples.[49] In addition, many stores provide a sampling of foods and candy; and still others conduct demonstrations, either in the store or in the home, to promote the sale of appliances.

Although there is no question that all of these methods attract crowds and stimulate sales, recent consumer opposition and boycotting of stores have forced users to re-evaluate their programs. Numerous people are attracted merely to observe rather than to buy, and the resulting congestion may interfere with regular business and increase the stolen-goods problem. Yet, used with discretion, these sales promotion methods can prove very effective. Above all, they should be carefully planned in the light of the store's standing in the community and should denote originality and distinctiveness in the minds of customers.

GOVERNMENTAL CONCERN OVER SALES PROMOTION PRACTICES

In addition to seeking the improvements in packaging and labeling referred to previously,[50] the federal government has evidenced its concern for

---

[48] "Soft-Sell 'Salute' Boosts St. Louis—and a Store," *Business Week,* October 16, 1965, pp. 96–97.

[49] In 1966 Safeway Stores, Inc. was emphasizing its Bonus Programs, Program No. 80 offering 83,062 cash prizes totaling over $212,000 and Program No. 180 offering "over $250,000." No purchase was required to participate. These programs were discontinued in January, 1967. Also cf. "Selling Goods Through Games," *Dun's Review and Modern Industry,* July, 1964, pp. 49 ff; and "Game Playing Hits Peak!" *Chain Store Age* (Supermarket Executives Edition), September, 1966, pp. 45–49.

[50] Cf. pp. 554–55, above.

the consumer in other ways. To cite one prominent example: In 1964 President Johnson, motivated by the increasing disparity in the prices received by farmers and the prices paid by consumers in retail stores, appointed a National Commission on Food Marketing to examine the causes of this development. The report of the Commission[51] contains certain suggestions or proposals related to sales promotion methods and devices which are of particular interest to the student of retailing. Considerable controversy was provoked by the report and a strong dissent to various findings of the Commission was issued by six of its fifteen members. They deplored the summary presented in the "overview and appraisal" as well as the "conclusions" of the majority because they considered them "unsupported and unsupportable."[52] The advertising industry also was highly critical of the Commission's analysis.[53]

It is not possible here to analyze in detail either the Commission's proposals or the arguments against them. Let it suffice at this point, therefore, to quote both majority and minority excerpts from the report related specifically to grade labeling and standards, packaging, trading stamps, and to the difficulties encountered by the consumer in buying foods, all pertinent to the previous discussion in this chapter. But arguments for and against the Commission's proposals are certain to continue!

CONSUMER GRADES

A. Majority Statement:

Consumer grades should be developed and required to appear on all foods for which such grades are feasible, that are sold in substantial volume to consumers, and that belong to a recognized product category.

The grades should prominently appear on consumer packages if the product is ordinarily sold in such packages by manufacturers. Except for foods for which other nomenclature is well established, the grades should be in the form A, B, C . . . as established by the responsible Government agency.

It is not intended that genuinely new products should carry consumer grades when first put on the market. If a new product becomes widely used and takes on an identity of its own, it should then be considered for consumer grading. Nor is it intended that products sold in highly heterogeneous or perishable form should be consumer graded. In our view, rigid rules should not be laid down in this field but, rather, a flexible program of consumer grading should be adopted.

Although the principal purpose of this suggestion is to inform consumers, it

---

[51] National Commission on Food Marketing, *Food from Farmer to Consumer* (Washington, D.C.: U.S. Government Printing Office, 1966).

[52] *Ibid.*, p. 126. For statements by the minority members cf. pp. 125–89.

[53] Cf., for example, W. H. Chase, "How Can the Food Industry Answer that Damning Report?," *Printers' Ink*, July, 22, 1966, pp. 21–24, 29; and "First Toll of a Death Knell," *ibid.*, p. 26.

may also serve to reduce the excessive use of promotion, thus contributing to a better performance of the food industry.

To carry out the program, the Department of Agriculture could be authorized to promulgate consumer grades, determine the products for which they are feasible and required to be used, and check on compliance. The unit charged with this work would have ready access to the technical skills available in the Department. Provision should be made for hearing the views of the food industry before new grades are put into effect.[54]

B. Minority Statement:

There is no evidence before the Commission that this scheme [mandatory consumer-grade labeling] was sensible, or workable, or rewarding to the consumer even when first advocated in the 1920's and 1930's. It is unthinkable today, as we explain more thoroughly in our section III. One reason—administrative rigidity—was shared with the Commission by Max E. Brunk, Professor of Marketing at Cornell University. He cited a study he made for the Government of consumer reactions to Government-graded applesauce. The vast majority of consumers participating in the test preferred applesauce graded "C" or "substandard" over applesauce graded "A" or "B." Despite this finding, the consumer views were spurned, the standards were retained, and governmental preference prevailed. Quality judgments, we believe, are highly personal. They are not a special gift of people in the public employ. The simple truth is that individual, sectional, and regional preferences of 200 million Americans can never be captured, cataloged, and compressed into meaningful and workable Federal standards. We believe these personal value judgments are best left with the consumer. This should also be noted—the majority's chapter 12 indicates that consumer grades would involve "little or no extra cost." But here—once again—we have supposition, not fact. No study was made of what grade labeling and its attendant bureaucracy would cost the food industry, consumers through increased prices, and the taxpaying public.[55]

STANDARDS OF IDENTITY

A. Majority Statement:

The Food and Drug Administration should establish standards of identity for all foods recognized by the public as belonging to a definite product category and for which standards are practicable.

Standards of identity define what a given food product is, so that consumers will not be misled and reputable processors will not be exposed to unfair competition.

In numerous instances where either standards of identity or consumer grades are not in use, it would be practicable to give consumers needed information by requiring labels on processed foods to state certain facts determined to be especially indicative of quality. For example, butterfat content and overrun (indicating the air in the product) are important measures of quality in ice cream and should be shown on labels as long as grades are not used.[56]

---

[54] *Food from Farmer to Consumer, op. cit.,* p. 109.

[55] *Ibid.,* p. 130.

[56] *Ibid.,* p. 109.

B. Minority Statement:

The Food and Drug Administration has complete and comprehensive power to establish standards of identity. Rather than utilizing this authority wherever "practicable," as the majority proposes, we believe that such standards should be established only where necessary to advance the public interest. But since the matter was not analyzed by the Commission, no "conclusion" should be reached by the Commission in this area.[57]

PACKAGING AND LABELING

A. Majority Statement:

Packages and their labels should assist consumers in gaining an accurate impression of the contents and in making price comparisons.

There are positive values for consumers, to be sought wherever they do not necessitate unreasonable cost. They are distinct from but merge into another matter, that of preventing deception through packaging and labeling. We urge the Federal Trade Commission and the Food and Drug Administration to give more attention to this area, and we favor further legislation if needed to give them authority they lack.[58]

B. Minority Statement:

Of course packaging and labeling should be informative and honest. The FDA and FTC have ample authority to assure that they are. Current legislative proposals in this area, however, are directed not against fraud and deceit but toward the subjection of packaging to Federal control. The results of such proposals would be higher consumer costs, blighted innovation, impairment of competition, and a transfer of consumer decisions to the Federal apparatus. The majority recommendation, let it be noted, endorses this legislation only "if needed." It isn't.[59]

TRADING STAMPS

A. Majority Statement:

Trading stamps have come to be the outstanding form of nonprice competition. Starting in the mid-1950's, more and more food retailers distributed trading stamps to customers. Now perhaps 50 percent of retail food sales are made in stores using trading stamps. Some retailers have dropped trading stamps, but they are still an extremely significant factor in the promotion of retail food sales.

When stamps were first introduced, retailers giving them frequently attained additional volume to more than pay for the stamps. Consumers, therefore, did not have to pay higher prices for stamps. As more and more of the industry adopted stamps and competing forms of promotion, however, it was no longer possible for retailers as a whole to obtain additional volume by using trading stamp promotion. As a result, the cost of the stamps represented an additional cost of retailing, and prices rose. All too often consumers buying food also were

---

[57] *Ibid.,* p. 131.

[58] *Ibid.,* p. 109.

[59] *Ibid.,* p. 131.

required, in effect, to make tie-in purchases of premiums being offered for trading stamps.[60]

B. Since there is no minority statement on trading stamps, consult the analysis presented earlier in this chapter on pp. 556–59.

DIFFICULTIES ENCOUNTERED BY CONSUMERS

A. Majority Statement:

Some advertising is misleading or downright deceptive; some package sizes and designs exaggerate the contents; essential information that should be contained in labels is often hard to find, illegible, and even missing; package contents may be in odd or nonstandard amounts for no technical reason, making price comparisons difficult; per-pound prices of the "large economy size" occasionally are higher than per-pound prices of smaller sizes; "cents-off" labels proclaim price reductions that may not be genuine; special prices create confusion as to what the going price is; not all products advertised as weekend features are sold at special prices; consumer grades are confined to a few products and are by no means uniformly used even for those; and standards of identity are lacking for many products. At little or no extra cost, consumers could be given more information; and the more skillful shopping this would make possible would more than offset any costs of providing additional information.[61]

B. Minority Statement:

The majority subscribe to a view (ch. 12 of the majority report) that the consumer as a buyer has great difficulty in getting her money's worth in her food purchases. This is allegedly due to such things as fractional-ounce packages, or slack fill, or supposedly misleading pictures on labels, or confusion of unit cost between economy-size and regular size packages. We are reminded of a recent statement by Professor George J. Stigler of the University of Chicago, who said that if consumers were as stupid as they are alleged to be, boxes of cereals would soon be empty, as competitors put less and less in the box—but then, he added, the boxes would sell for the price of cardboard.[62]

Again we quote from Professor Max Brunk of Cornell. He states, "Mrs. Housewife isn't dumb and she isn't being 'taken' in the marketplace. She knows that food today is far more than 'just something to eat.' In it she has found pleasure, romance, adventure, convenience, amusement, and neither can the greatest merchandiser keep up with her demands nor the wisest of men predict the true values she will want and buy."[63]

The majority lament that consumers are not "highly skilled buyers," and hold that the consumer would be less influenced by advertising appeals, a less frequent impulse buyer, a more avid student of cheaper substitutes—and that

---

[60] *Ibid.*, p. 77.

[61] *Ibid.*, p. 101.

[62] George J. Stigler, "The Unjoined Debate," *Chicago Today,* University of Chicago, Winter, 1966, p. 8.

[63] Paper presented at Purdue University, Apr. 5, 1966.

she would turn a deaf ear to her children—if only she would become more skilled as a shopper. They complain, even, that food retailers' weekly price specials create confusion in consumers' minds "as to what the going price is." If this is true, how do they explain the very large purchase response—often several times the normal rate of sales—for the items that are put on special? We regard the whole list of criticisms of the consumer as considerably strained. We do not contend that she makes no mistakes. We do contend that the mistakes are few, of neither large nor lasting consequence, and quickly corrected.

1. Most consumers have learned what brands satisfy them and their families, and also which stores can be relied upon. Both the brand processor and the store operator face quick and certain retribution if the consumer is displeased. No other consumers in the world have a food marketing industry as responsive to their reactions.

2. Food is at least a weekly purchase in almost all homes. It is purchased, used up, and more is purchased. The repeat business goes to the items that please. Unsatisfactory experiences are not repeated. Moreover, the price ticket on the individual food item is small—the vast majority under a dollar. Thus an unsatisfactory purchase is not a costly one.

3. The proportion of the family food bill that is open to wide-reaching experimentation is modest. Roughly two-thirds of the average family's food expenditures are confined to meat, dairy products, produce, and staples in which experimentation is less common. Thus only one-third is in a greater risk area, and for those, there are the avenues of redress noted above.

Consumer information that will contribute to good shopping is indeed important. But for a homemaker no amount of consumer information can replace shopping experience.[64] Nor can any amount of handholding by government serve as a substitute for experience. There will always be a group of new and inexperienced shoppers, and until they have experience, their job will be more complex. However, as expressed before, there has been no consumer cataclysm that demands any sizeable extension of government into teaching consumers how to shop the supermarket.[65]

REVIEW AND DISCUSSION QUESTIONS

1. Discuss the present and probable future status of telephone selling as a form of retail sales promotion.
2. Answer Question 1 with respect to mail-order selling by store retailers.
3. Summarize the information concerning telephone selling revealed by the survey of customers of department stores by students of the Harvard Business School. As a retailer, what use would you make of these data?
4. Account for the emphasis on packaging by retailers and manufacturers.

---

[64] Statistical evidence of consumer reliance on past buying experience and the experiences of acquaintances is available in J. G. Udell, "Prepurchase Behavior of Buyers of Small Electrical Appliances," *Journal of Marketing*, Vol. XXX, No. 4 (October, 1966), p. 51.

[65] *Food from Farmer to Consumer, op. cit.,* pp. 150–51.

5. Discuss the statement: "Packaging lags behind the economy in growth but its benefits to consumers continue to increase."

6. Based on observations in local stores, give four examples of labeling used to promote sales. In at least two of these examples, suggest how the labeling could be improved.

7. Explain the meaning and purposes of consumer premiums. How do you account for their present prominence?

8. Distinguish between the single-transaction type and the continuing-offer type of premium promotion and illustrate each one.

9. For a store to use trading stamps effectively as a sales promotional tool, what conditions and circumstances should prevail?

10. How do you account for the fact that some retail organizations have discontinued using trading stamps? In your opinion, does this development presage an overall decline in the use of this promotional device? Explain fully.

11. Visit three stores in your community using trading stamps and obtain the views of executives concerning their value and the problems connected with their use.

12. Explain briefly the six main factors responsible for the growth of premium merchandising.

13. Review the special forms of sales promotion (other than trading stamps) which have been used recently in your community. Appraise the results of these efforts.

14. What evidence, other than the work of the National Commission on Food Marketing, can you present to indicate the growing concern of the federal government regarding sales promotional practices?

15. Evaluate the recommendations contained in the final report of the National Commission on Food Marketing—*Food from Farmer to Consumer*—with respect to compulsory grading, labeling, packaging, and trading stamps.

SUPPLEMENTARY READINGS

A Blue Print for Telephone Selling and *Selling by Telephone* (New York: American Telephone and Telegraph Co., n.d.). These two pamphlets provide suggestions for improving selling efforts by those using the telephone.

BLUMENTHAL, L. A. "Scramble in the Market Place," *Dun's Review and Modern Industry,* December, 1965, Part II, pp. 86–87 ff. How the consumer is being wooed as never before by enterprising packagers is described in this article.

BROWN, S. H. "Sperry and Hutchinson's Very Successful Stagnation," *Fortune,* Vol. LXX, No. 5 (November, 1964), pp. 157–59 ff. The author reports on trends within the oldest and largest trading stamp company.

FULOP, CHRISTINA. *The Role of Trading Stamps in Retail Competition* (London: Institute of Economic Affairs Limited, 1964). This careful study of the economics of trading stamps adds much to our understanding of how stamps contribute to effective retail competition.

JOHNSON, T. A. *88 Ways to Make the Telephone Sell for You* (Englewood Cliffs, N.J.: Prentice-Hall, Inc., 1962). Although this volume treats selling in general, chapter xi is devoted to retailers specifically. A six-page bibliography is included.

MAYER, C. S. "Requiem for the Truth in Packaging Bill," *Journal of Marketing,* Vol. XXX, No. 2 (April, 1966), pp. 1–5. The author concludes that the proposed legislation would limit severely the freedom of the marketing manager in packaging and labeling.

Modern Packaging. Published monthly, this magazine covers all aspects of packaging, particularly from the manufacturer's point of view. The sections on "Profiles in Packaging" and "Packing Pacemakers" are of special interest.

NATIONAL COMMISSION ON FOOD MARKETING. *Food From Farmer to Consumer.* (Washington, D.C.: U.S. Government Printing Office, 1966). This controversial report reviews many aspects of retail food distribution. Of chief interest in connection with this chapter is the "overview and appraisal" chapter and the views of the minority members on pp. 125–89.

"Packaging: Yardsticks of Performance," *Forbes,* January 1, 1966, pp. 54 ff. Students interested in criteria for judging the value of packages should consult this article.

Premium Practice. A monthly publication, this trade journal covers current developments in the premium field, suggests the principal lines of merchandise suitable for use as premiums, and prepares an annual directory of suppliers.

RICH, S. U. *Shopping Behavior of Department Store Customers* (Boston: Harvard University, Graduate School of Business Administration, 1963). Part I of this study covers stores policies related to delivery service and telephone ordering; and Part II is devoted to customer shopping habits in the same service areas. It is probably the best analysis of telephone selling available.

The Role of Packaging in the American Economy (Cambridge, Mass.: Arthur D. Little, Inc., 1966). Prepared for the American Foundation for Management Research, this study emphasizes the increasing value of packaging to the consumer but points out that the amounts spent on packaging have failed to grow as fast as our economy.

Some Frequently-Asked Questions About S & H Green Stamps and the Trading Stamp Industry (New York: Sperry and Hutchinson Company, 1965). In this promotional brochure, the major trading stamp firm deals with all aspects of this promotional device.

VREDENBERG, H. L. AND FRISINGER, H. H. "The Value of Trading Stamps as Measured by Retail Prices," *Journal of Retailing,* Vol. XLI, No. 3 (Fall, 1965), pp. 28–32. Information on the retail value of collector's books in the Denver area is the subject of this study of trading stamps. Also cf. BUNN, V. A. *Trading Stamps and Retail Food Prices, 1960–1965* (Kansas City, Mo.: Midwest Research Institute, 1966).

20
CHAPTER

Personal Salesmanship

Except for self-service stores and purchases from vending machines or by mail, a customer-salesperson relationship is essential to consummate a retail sale. The importance of this relationship is evident when it is realized that the impression the customer receives from the salesperson often forms her opinion of the store. The attitude and actions of the salesperson in dealing with the customer can even nullify the sales-promotion efforts which are responsible for the latter's presence in the store. Stated positively, it is very important that the customer be treated in a manner that will please her, that will assist her to make purchases suited to her needs, and that will cause her to return to the store to make further purchases. These are the purposes of retail salesmanship; it should be the goal of every salesperson to aid in their accomplishment.[1]

SIGNIFICANCE OF PERSONAL SALESMANSHIP TODAY

Someone has defined salesmanship as "selling goods that won't come back to customers who will." If articles of merchandise sold to customers meet their needs adequately, if the prices paid represent good values, and if customers are satisfied with the services rendered by the store in connection with the sale of the goods, then these customers will continue to patronize the store. This continuous patronage, which is necessary for stores to operate successfully, is based upon good will—the disposition of a pleased customer to return to the store where she has been well treated. The importance attached to customer good will by one retail organization is indicated by

---

[1] All phases of personal selling are discussed in O. P. Robinson, W. R. Blackler, and W. B. Logan, *Store Salesmanship* (6th ed.; Englewood Cliffs, N.J.: Prentice-Hall, Inc., 1966).

these lines which are constantly reiterated to all store personnel: "Let no man and no woman leave this store at night without being able to say, 'I have done something today to preserve and increase the good will of Rich's.' "[2]

This Customer-is-King concept of salesmanship—to look at everything from the customer's point of view—is relatively new. For many years the doctrine of *caveat emptor* (let the buyer beware) prevailed. Under this doctrine the forces of persuasion and cunning were brought to bear upon the prospective customer, so that she would buy regardless of her intentions or the suitability of the goods for her requirements. Today, however, in marked contrast to the early concept of salesmanship, the idea is to help people to buy. The preference of satisfied customers for particular stores and particular salespeople is build upon the faith they have in the honesty and the sincere desire on the part of the stores and salespeople to serve the customers' interests.[3] Persuasion still has its place, but it is now directed toward explaining how needs and desires may be better satisfied through the purchase of particular goods and services.

Personal Salesmanship Still Necessary

Some observers believe that the era of informed, creative personal selling on the retail floor has passed and that we are now in the age of impersonal selling. Supporting this position is a discount house operator who stated within the hearing of one of the authors: "We don't want salesmen in our organization. Our people are educated order-takers. . . . Our clerks are trained to be courteous, to answer his (customer) questions and give him what he wants, but not to waste time trying to sell him anything. I believe this is the coming pattern of retailing—for every kind of merchandise—cars, motor-boats, everything. Selling has become an unnecessary vocation."

Those who take this "personal salesmanship is unnecessary" point of view are influenced by a number of developments, including the pre-selling of customers by national advertising; the growing part of the selling task which can be assigned to merchandise displays, packaging, and labeling; the rise of self-service and self-selection stores as illustrated by the supermarket and the discount house; and by the thought that the automated store lies just ahead. A few of them even see the end of the retail store as we know it, with the

---

[2] F. H. Neely, *Rich's: A Southern Institution since 1867* (New York: The Newcomen Society in North America, 1960), p. 14.

[3] "It is no exaggeration to appraise pleasing, cordial attention and service as being the prime factors in making people want to patronize a store." *Attracting and Holding Customers* (Dayton, Ohio: National Cash Register Company, 1963), p. 24.

customer "shopping" at home over a television set or ordering by telephone from a "warehouse with no floor traffic" establishment.

Although recognizing that the foregoing factors have lessened the importance of personal selling in *some* stores, most observers are of the opinion that personal salesmanship is still essential in the vast majority of retail stores and that, despite its numerous shortcomings, the great need is for improvement rather than curtailment.[4] As a matter of fact, executives in *service* stores of all types have already recognized the need for improvement in this direction, especially in view of the newer forms of competition among retailers and a greater variety and supply of merchandise on the market. Moreover, shorter hours and higher wages have forced retail store managers to devote more effort to the problem of increasing the productivity of employees.

Effectiveness of Retail Salesmanship Today

Undeniably, however, the quality of retail salesmanship today still leaves much to be desired. Too many salespeople are either uninformed about the merchandise they sell or too uninterested to pass along to the customer what they do know.[5] Discourteous treatment of customers is much too common. Slow service is *not* the exception. Chatting among salespeople while customers wait is so prevalent that ". . . even in full-service stores, customers are not approached by salespeople within a reasonable period of time in from 10 to 50 percent of the instances and . . . discourteous, uninformed, unintelligent floor selling is common . . ."[6]

For many years the Willmark Service System, Inc. of New York City has analyzed the selling efforts of salespeople in retail institutions of various types. Until quite recently it prepared a retail "selling quotient" for the United States: With 100 percent representing the ideal sales performance, its studies rated actual performance as about 75 percent—thus suggesting that retail selling is not in a healthy state. Moreover, the current situation has changed little from that described by the late Pierre Martineau almost a decade ago.

---

[4] Cf. David Gray, "The Future of Retail Salesmanship," *New York Retailer,* December, 1964, pp. 23–25.

[5] Cf. the series of articles on ineffective retail selling under the title "Sales Management Goes Shopping," *Sales Management,* February 19, 1965, pp. 85–92; March 19, 1965, pp. 73–74; and following issues.

[6] E. B. Weiss, quoted in Herbert Koshetz, "The Merchant's View," *New York Times,* November 11, 1965, p. F11. Of course slow service is also a result of too few salespeople in some stores. For a technique of determining the number needed cf. C. J. Stoker and Philip Mintz, "How Many Clerks on a Floor?" *Journal of Marketing Research,* Vol. II, No. 4 (November, 1965), pp. 388–93.

It is ironical that at the very time when a better educated and discriminating shopper expects more from the store and the clerk, management is dragging its feet in upgrading salespeople. The stores are more beautiful and interesting; they have escalators, air conditioning, and improved fixtures; they have buyers ranging far and wide to offer the broadest merchandising selection. But what about the salespeople?[7]

Improving Retail Salesmanship

What can management do to improve retail selling? One student of the subject recognized this problem some years ago and suggested these steps:

1. Place greater emphasis on self-selection and self-service. (This suggestion, of course, does not solve the problem. It merely dodges the problem by substituting impersonal sales methods for the salesperson.)
2. Pay salespeople more and thus attract better qualified personnel who can be taught the principles of salesmanship.
3. Adopt an "engineering approach" and provide better physical surroundings and equipment conducive to sales efficiency.
4. Develop and use a more effective program of training with emphasis on techniques of salesmanship.[8]
5. Outline a program of careful on-the-floor supervision, "the greatest single area for improving retail salesmanship." This program should include fixing departmental responsibility for such activities as (a) morning meetings on salesmanship techniques, (b) interviews with individual salespeople, (c) "listening in" on sales interviews, (d) answering salespeople's questions, (e) acting as a clearing house for sales ideas, and (f) emphasizing suggestion selling—"the phase of salesmanship where most retail salespeople are weakest"—and conducting suggestion-selling campaigns.[9]

All of these steps are applicable today. Only number 3 requires some explanation. Essentially, an engineering approach refers to the use of mechanical equipment, store layout improvements, and the better planning of the flow of work so that the salesperson has more time to devote to the selling task. Automation in its various forms has reduced substantially the time required for the performance of nonselling activities. The use of mechanical devices has speeded up the movement of merchandise from receiving areas and stock rooms to the selling floor; electronic equipment has decreased the time that sales personnel must give to the recording of sales transactions; and inventory-taking has been facilitated through the use of

---

[7] Cf. his "The Personality of the Retail Store," *Harvard Business Review,* Vol. XXXVI, No. 1 (January–February, 1958), pp. 52–53.

[8] This subject has been discussed in Chapter 8, pp. 231–42, above.

[9] R. H. Myers, "Retail Selling Can and Should Be Improved," *Journal of Retailing,* Vol. XXXIII, No. 1 (Spring, 1957), pp. 41–46.

tape recorders and other devices. But the adoption of such measures is only a good beginning; the future years will bring many more significant developments as the need for greater productivity on the part of salespeople and the necessity for reducing selling costs becomes more urgent.

Some manufacturers and trade associations are providing retailers with the means of evaluating the productiveness of their salespeople in relation to selling cost, as is indicated by Figure 20–1. In this figure,

. . . to determine how much a salesperson should sell, select the column headed with the weekly salary of the salesperson. Follow this column down to the salary cost percentage nearest that of your store. The dollar figures on the same line in the *Amount of Weekly Sales* column (extreme left or right) show what the salesperson should sell each week to earn his salary. Example: A salesperson receives $75.00 per week in a men's store having annual sales of $200,000. The salary cost percentage for stores in this classification is 11.5%, as shown by various studies. Under the column marked $75.00, locate this salary percentage or the one closest to it. The amount in the *Amount of Weekly Sales* column opposite is $650. . . [If the retailer is paying the salesperson] less than the table indicates he should be paid, he may be entitled to a raise. But if [he is being paid] more, the difference is coming directly out of . . . profit.[10]

In brief, retail management must recognize that the need for better salesmanship exists throughout the entire structure of retailing wherever salespeople are employed. Retailers must move quickly to meet this need if their profit margins are to be maintained.

ELEMENTS OF A RETAIL SALE

The major elements in any retail sale are (1) the store and its policies, (2) the customer, (3) the merchandise, and (4) the salesperson.

The Store and Its Policies

Policies of the store in which the sale takes place govern in a general way the selling methods pursued and the actions of the salesperson in relation to the customer. For example, in mass-selling stores, little individual attention is given the customer: one salesman may be serving three shoe customers at the same time. In contrast, many stores place so much emphasis on their standards of salesmanship that they prepare booklets for the detailed guidance of their salespeople. These standards usually cover the procedure to be followed in the selling process and the qualifications required of salespeople.

---

[10] The above excerpt is from National Cash Register Co., *Expenses in Retail Businesses* (Dayton, Ohio: The Company, n.d.), pp. 24–25.

In small stores, reliance is placed on verbal instructions from the proprietor.

The Customer

The customer is the very heart of the sale, a fact which the famous retailer, Marshall Field, recognized in his phrase, "Give the Lady What She Wants." And Jack I. Straus of R. H. Macy & Company states: "We are embarking on a major effort to demonstrate that we care that the customer finds what she wants, gets the help she desires, and derives satisfaction from every contact with Macy's."[11]

Unless the customer is pleased with her reception in the store, unless she is completely satisfied with the merchandise she purchases and the services rendered in connection with it, the sale has not been successful. The salesperson who is guided by this understanding, and consequently presents what he has to say from the customer's point of view, will be much more successful in retail selling than the person who allows his own interests or those of the store to dominate the transaction. In the long run the interests of the customer, the salesperson, and the store are identical, since successful operation is impossible without continuous satisfaction of customers.

Several types of information should be possessed by the salesperson who wishes to sell from the customer point of view. He should know something about consumer psychology and about buying motives—what pleases or irritates customers, what considerations motivate their buying, and their growing sophistication.[12] He should have a thorough knowledge of the merchandise he is selling and of the location of each item. He should know the fundamental principles of salesmanship—how to bring customers and merchandise together effectively. And he should recognize the importance of getting along with people—his customers, his associates, and his superiors.

The Merchandise

Merchandise Knowledge Required. The third important element in a retail sale is the merchandise. A thorough knowledge of the lines they

---

[11] Fred Eichelbaum, "Macy Sets All-Out Assault Against Offensive Service," *Women's Wear Daily,* November 11, 1965, p. 1.

[12] "To sell Mrs. Smith what Mrs. Smith buys, you must see what's seen through Mrs. Smith's eyes." Ralf Shockey, "Selling is a Science," Part IX, *Department Store Economist,* December, 1965, p. 88. Also cf. J. G. Udell, "A New Approach to Consumer Motivation," *Journal of Retailing,* Vol. XL, No. 4 (Winter, 1964–1965), pp. 6–10; and J. A. Belasco, "The Salesman's Role Revisited," *Journal of Marketing,* Vol. XXX, No. 2 (April, 1966), pp. 6–8.

WEEKLY SALARIES ➡		$40.00	$42.50	$45.00	$47.50	$50.00	$52.50	$55.00	$57.50	$60.00	$62.50	$65.00	$67.50	$70.00	$72.50	$75.00
SALARY COST PERCENTAGES																
	$ 150	26.7	28.3	30.0	31.7	33.3	35.0	36.7	38.3	40.0	41.7	43.3	45.0	46.7	48.3	50.0
	160	25.0	26.6	28.1	29.7	31.3	32.8	34.4	35.9	37.5	39.1	40.6	42.2	43.8	45.3	46.9
	170	23.5	25.0	26.5	27.9	29.4	30.9	32.4	33.8	35.3	36.8	38.2	39.7	41.2	42.6	44.1
	180	22.2	23.6	25.0	26.4	27.8	29.2	30.6	31.9	33.3	34.7	36.1	37.5	38.9	40.3	41.7
	190	21.1	22.4	23.7	25.0	26.3	27.6	28.9	30.3	31.6	32.9	34.2	35.5	36.8	38.1	39.5
	200	20.0	21.3	22.5	23.8	25.0	26.2	27.5	28.7	30.0	31.2	32.5	33.7	35.0	36.2	37.5
	210	19.0	20.2	21.4	22.6	23.8	25.0	26.2	27.4	28.6	29.8	31.0	32.1	33.3	34.5	35.7
	220	18.2	19.3	20.5	21.6	22.7	23.9	25.0	26.1	27.3	28.4	29.5	30.7	31.8	32.9	34.1
	230	17.4	18.5	19.6	20.7	21.7	22.8	23.9	25.0	26.1	27.2	28.3	29.3	30.4	31.5	32.6
	240	16.7	17.7	18.7	19.8	20.8	21.9	22.9	23.9	25.0	26.0	27.1	28.1	29.2	30.2	31.2
	250	16.0	17.0	18.0	19.0	20.0	21.0	22.0	23.0	24.0	25.0	26.0	27.0	28.0	29.0	30.0
	260	15.4	16.3	17.3	18.3	19.2	20.2	21.2	22.1	23.1	24.0	25.0	26.0	26.9	27.9	28.8
A	270	14.8	15.7	16.7	17.6	18.5	19.4	20.4	21.3	22.2	23.1	24.1	25.0	25.9	26.8	27.8
M	280	14.3	15.2	16.1	17.0	17.9	18.7	19.6	20.5	21.4	22.3	23.2	24.1	25.0	25.9	26.8
O	290	13.8	14.7	15.5	16.4	17.2	18.1	19.0	19.8	20.7	21.5	22.4	23.3	24.1	25.0	25.9
U	300	13.3	14.2	15.0	15.8	16.7	17.5	18.3	19.2	20.0	20.8	21.7	22.5	23.3	24.2	25.0
N	325	12.3	13.1	13.8	14.6	15.4	16.1	16.9	17.7	18.5	19.2	20.0	20.8	21.5	22.3	23.1
T	350	11.4	12.1	12.9	13.6	14.3	15.0	15.7	16.4	17.1	17.8	18.6	19.3	20.0	20.7	21.4
	375	10.7	11.3	12.0	12.7	13.3	14.0	14.7	15.3	16.0	16.7	17.3	18.0	18.7	19.3	20.0
O	400	10.0	10.6	11.3	11.9	12.5	13.1	13.8	14.4	15.0	15.6	16.3	16.9	17.5	18.1	18.8
F	425	9.4	10.0	10.6	11.2	11.8	12.3	12.9	13.5	14.1	14.7	15.3	15.9	16.5	17.0	17.6
W	450	8.9	9.4	10.0	10.6	11.1	11.7	12.2	12.8	13.3	13.9	14.4	15.0	15.6	16.1	16.7
E	475	8.4	8.9	9.5	10.0	10.5	11.0	11.6	12.1	12.6	13.1	13.7	14.2	14.7	15.3	15.8
E	500	8.0	8.5	9.0	9.5	10.0	10.5	11.0	11.5	12.0	12.5	13.0	13.5	14.0	14.5	15.0
K	525	7.6	8.1	8.6	9.0	9.5	10.0	10.5	10.9	11.4	11.9	12.4	12.8	13.3	13.8	14.3
L	550	7.3	7.7	8.2	8.6	9.1	9.5	10.0	10.4	10.9	11.4	11.8	12.3	12.7	13.2	13.6
Y	575	7.0	7.4	7.8	8.3	8.7	9.1	9.6	10.0	10.4	10.9	11.3	11.7	12.2	12.6	13.0
	600	6.7	7.1	7.5	7.9	8.3	8.7	9.2	9.6	10.0	10.4	10.8	11.2	11.7	12.1	12.5
S	625	6.4	6.8	7.2	7.6	8.0	8.4	8.8	9.2	9.6	10.0	10.4	10.8	11.2	11.6	12.0
A	650	6.2	6.5	6.9	7.3	7.7	8.1	8.5	8.8	9.2	9.6	10.0	10.4	10.8	11.1	11.5
L	675	5.9	6.3	6.7	7.0	7.4	7.8	8.1	8.5	8.9	9.2	9.6	10.0	10.4	10.7	11.1
E	700	5.7	6.1	6.4	6.8	7.1	7.5	7.9	8.2	8.6	8.9	9.3	9.6	10.0	10.4	10.7
S	725	5.5	5.9	6.2	6.5	6.9	7.2	7.6	7.9	8.3	8.6	9.0	9.3	9.6	10.0	10.3
	750	5.3	5.7	6.0	6.3	6.7	7.0	7.3	7.7	8.0	8.3	8.7	9.0	9.3	9.7	10.0
	775	5.2	5.5	5.8	6.1	6.4	6.8	7.1	7.4	7.7	8.1	8.4	8.7	9.0	9.3	9.7
	800	5.0	5.3	5.6	5.9	6.2	6.6	6.9	7.2	7.5	7.8	8.1	8.4	8.7	9.1	9.4
	825	4.8	5.1	5.4	5.7	6.1	6.4	6.7	7.0	7.3	7.6	7.9	8.2	8.5	8.8	9.1
	850	4.7	5.0	5.3	5.6	5.9	6.2	6.5	6.8	7.1	7.3	7.6	7.9	8.2	8.5	8.8
	875	4.6	4.8	5.1	5.4	5.7	6.0	6.3	6.6	6.8	7.1	7.4	7.7	8.0	8.3	8.6
	900	4.4	4.7	5.0	5.3	5.5	5.8	6.1	6.4	6.7	6.9	7.2	7.5	7.8	8.0	8.3
	925	4.3	4.6	4.9	5.1	5.4	5.7	5.9	6.2	6.5	6.7	7.0	7.3	7.6	7.8	8.1
	950	4.2	4.5	4.7	5.0	5.3	5.5	5.8	6.0	6.3	6.6	6.8	7.1	7.4	7.6	7.9
	975	4.1	4.3	4.6	4.9	5.1	5.4	5.6	5.9	6.1	6.4	6.7	6.9	7.2	7.4	7.7
	1000	4.0	4.2	4.5	4.7	5.0	5.2	5.5	5.7	6.0	6.2	6.5	6.7	7.0	7.2	7.5

Source: *Expenses in Retail Businesses* (Dayton, Ohio: National Cash Register Company, n.d.), pp. 24–25.

FIG. 20–1.   Form for evaluation of salespeople in retail stores.

$77.50	$80.00	$82.50	$85.00	$87.50
51.7	53.3	55.0	56.7	58.3
48.4	50.0	51.6	53.1	54.7
45.6	47.1	48.5	50.0	51.5
43.0	44.4	45.8	47.2	48.6
40.8	42.1	43.4	44.7	46.1
38.7	40.0	41.3	42.5	43.8
36.9	38.1	39.3	40.5	41.7
35.2	36.4	37.5	38.6	39.8
33.7	34.8	35.9	37.0	38.0
32.3	33.3	34.4	35.4	36.5
31.0	32.0	33.0	34.0	35.0
29.8	30.8	31.7	32.7	33.7
28.7	29.6	30.6	31.5	32.4
27.7	28.6	29.5	30.4	31.3
26.7	27.6	28.4	29.3	30.2
25.8	26.7	27.5	28.3	29.2
23.8	24.6	25.4	26.2	26.9
22.1	22.9	23.6	24.3	25.0
20.7	21.3	22.0	22.7	23.3
19.4	20.0	20.6	21.3	21.9
18.2	18.8	19.4	20.0	20.6
17.2	17.8	18.3	18.9	19.4
16.3	16.8	17.4	17.9	18.4
15.5	16.0	16.5	17.0	17.5
14.8	15.2	15.7	16.2	16.7
14.1	14.5	15.0	15.5	15.9
13.5	13.9	14.3	14.8	15.2
12.9	13.3	13.8	14.2	14.6
12.4	12.8	13.2	13.6	14.0
11.9	12.3	12.7	13.1	13.5
11.5	11.8	12.2	12.6	13.0
11.1	11.4	11.8	12.1	12.5
10.7	11.0	11.4	11.7	12.1
10.3	10.7	11.0	11.3	11.7
10.0	10.3	10.6	11.0	11.3
9.7	10.0	10.3	10.6	10.9
9.4	9.7	10.0	10.3	10.6
9.1	9.4	9.7	10.0	10.3
8.8	9.1	9.4	9.7	10.0
8.6	8.9	9.2	9.4	9.7
8.4	8.6	8.9	9.2	9.5
8.1	8.4	8.7	8.9	9.2
7.9	8.2	8.5	8.7	9.0
7.7	8.0	8.3	8.5	8.8

$145.00	$150.00	$155.00	$160.00	$165.00	$170.00	$175.00	$180.00	◄ WEEKLY SALARIES
96.7	100.0	103.3	106.7	110.0	113.3	116.7	120.0	$ 150
90.6	93.8	96.9	100.0	103.1	106.3	109.4	112.5	160
85.3	88.2	91.2	94.1	97.1	100.0	102.9	105.9	170
80.6	83.3	86.1	88.9	91.7	94.4	97.2	100.0	180
76.3	78.9	81.6	84.2	86.8	89.5	92.1	94.7	190
72.5	75.0	77.5	80.0	82.5	85.0	87.5	90.0	200
69.0	71.4	73.8	76.2	78.6	81.0	83.3	85.7	210
65.9	68.2	70.5	72.7	75.0	77.3	79.5	81.8	220
63.0	65.2	67.4	69.6	71.7	73.9	76.1	78.3	230
60.4	62.5	64.6	66.7	68.8	70.8	72.9	75.0	240
58.0	60.0	62.0	64.0	66.0	68.0	70.0	72.0	250
55.8	57.7	59.6	61.5	63.5	65.4	67.3	69.2	260
53.7	55.6	57.4	59.3	61.1	63.0	64.8	66.7	270
51.8	53.6	55.4	57.1	58.9	60.7	62.5	64.3	280
50.0	51.7	53.4	55.2	56.9	58.6	60.3	62.1	290
48.3	50.0	51.7	53.3	55.0	56.7	58.3	60.0	300
44.6	46.2	47.7	49.2	50.8	52.3	53.8	55.4	325
41.4	42.9	44.3	45.7	47.1	48.6	50.0	51.4	350
38.7	40.0	41.3	42.7	44.0	45.3	46.7	48.0	375
36.3	37.5	38.8	40.0	41.3	43.0	43.8	45.0	400
34.1	35.3	36.5	37.6	38.8	40.0	41.2	42.4	425
32.2	33.3	34.4	35.6	36.7	37.8	38.9	40.0	450
30.5	31.6	32.6	33.7	34.7	35.8	36.8	37.9	475
29.0	30.0	31.0	32.0	33.0	34.0	35.0	36.0	500
27.6	28.6	29.5	30.5	31.4	32.4	33.3	34.3	525
26.4	27.3	28.2	29.1	30.0	30.9	31.8	32.7	550
25.2	26.1	27.0	27.8	28.7	29.0	30.4	31.3	575
24.2	25.0	25.8	26.7	27.5	28.3	29.2	30.0	600
23.2	24.0	24.8	25.6	26.4	27.2	28.0	28.8	625
22.3	23.1	23.8	24.6	25.4	26.2	26.9	27.7	650
21.5	22.2	23.0	23.7	24.4	25.2	25.9	26.7	675
20.7	21.4	22.1	22.9	23.6	24.3	25.0	25.7	700
20.0	20.7	21.4	22.1	22.8	23.4	24.1	24.8	725
19.3	20.0	20.7	21.3	22.0	22.7	23.3	24.0	750
18.7	19.4	20.0	20.6	21.3	21.9	22.6	23.2	775
18.1	18.8	19.4	20.0	20.6	21.3	21.9	22.5	800
17.6	18.2	18.8	19.4	20.0	20.6	21.2	21.8	825
17.1	17.6	18.2	18.8	19.4	20.0	20.6	21.2	850
16.6	17.1	17.7	18.3	18.9	19.4	20.0	20.6	875
16.1	16.7	17.2	17.8	18.3	18.9	19.4	20.0	900
15.7	16.2	16.8	17.3	17.8	18.4	18.9	19.5	925
15.3	15.8	16.3	16.8	17.4	17.9	18.4	18.9	950
14.9	15.4	15.9	16.4	16.9	17.4	17.9	18.5	975
14.5	15.0	15.5	16.0	16.5	17.0	17.5	18.0	1000

(Right-hand vertical label: AMOUNT OF WEEKLY SALES)

Note: The figures in the top line of the table represent weekly salaries. Those in the extreme left and right columns are the weekly sales required to justify the salaries according to salary cost percentages.

offer is essential for salespeople to be successful in selling.[13] Although the amount of information needed will vary with the type of merchandise sold and the clientele served, in all stores the salesperson should be able to give a clear picture of the sizes, styles, designs, finishes, patterns, qualities, and colors of the merchandise. He should know, also, how to bring out points of superiority such as durability, utility, construction, economy, convenience, service, safety, cleanliness, taste, prestige, satisfaction, comfort, health, or beauty. And he should have the facts pertinent to a complete explanation of the uses of the merchandise, be familiar with its care, and be aware of the offerings of competing stores.

Sources of Merchandise Knowledge. The knowledge of merchandise required for effective selling may be obtained in many ways: experience; handling goods; asking others, including wholesale salesmen, the head of stock, and the buyer; learning from other salespeople and from customers; through manufacturers' representatives and printed material;[14] trade journals, home and fashion magazines, advertisements, newspapers, and books; and also by reading information on tags and labels that come on the product.[15] It is apparent from this list that the salesperson should be allowed no alibi in this regard.

It is unfortunate that many retail salespeople are sadly lacking in knowledge of the merchandise they are attempting to sell.[16] Responsibility for this condition is twofold: First, salespeople are to blame for their failure to prepare themselves adequately for successful selling. Second, store management—either through the proprietor in the case of the small store or the training division in the case of the large store—sometimes fails to impress employees sufficiently with the importance of knowing merchandise, neglects to provide instruction concerning it, and does not offer the supervision and follow-up necessary to determine how merchandise is being presented to customers.

The Salesperson

The final essential element in any retail sale is the salesperson. Good appearance, the right attitude, and his courteous treatment of the customer

[13] Cf. Bernard Groger, "War Against Walkouts—A Running Battle," *Women's Wear Daily,* February 4, 1966, pp. 1, 27.

[14] Cf. H. R. Kohn, "Salesgirls Let Hair Down on Maker's Product Poll," *Women's Wear Daily,* September 9, 1965, p. 14.

[15] Selling guides for 21 merchandise lines are given in A. E. Zimmer, *The Strategy of Successful Retail Salesmanship* (New York: McGraw-Hill Book Co., Inc., 1966), pp. 165–209.

[16] For evidence cf. the report of a shopping survey in four New York department stores by S. M. Rogers, "The Customer is Sometimes Right," *Women's Wear Daily,* November 15, 1966, pp. 1, 8.

are fundamental to success in selling.[17] The salesperson can easily nullify other forms of sales promotion, as well as his own knowledge of customer traits and merchandise, by failing to demonstrate a sincere interest in determining and filling satisfactorily the wants of the customer.

In general, the qualifications of a successful salesperson are much the same as those necessary for success in any line of business: hard work; confidence in oneself, one's company, and one's merchandise; courage to meet disappointment and defeat; judgment; discrimination and good sense; creative imagination or the capacity to develop ideas; a talent for getting along with one's associates and superiors; and knowledge of the job to be done.[18] If the salesperson also possesses or develops such qualities as a genuine interest in people, enthusiasm, the ability to instill confidence, and some flair for showmanship, his chances for success are enhanced.[19]

Since it is the salesperson's job to overcome natural causes for hesitation, he must be positive, active, creative, and self-confident. He must also be a good loser. It is not possible to close every sale attempted; but if the salesperson does his best and closes with a smile, there is much more likelihood that the customer will come back either after she has shopped around or the next time she is in the market for the type of merchandise in question.[20]

In summary, it is apparent that the responsibility of the salesperson is a vital one in retail selling. Much of this responsibility may be summed up in one word: *courtesy*. One of the most effective "courtesy platforms" which has come to the attention of the authors is that of Marshall Field & Company. Because of its comprehensiveness, and because it has proved so effective in building highly satisfactory customer-employee relationships, it is presented in full, as follows:

COURTESY PLATFORM—MARSHALL FIELD & COMPANY[21]

We, the members of the Marshall Field & Company organization, recognizing that courtesy is an essential part of every job in this business, endorse the following platform and pledge our united efforts to carry out the policies stated therein. We are convinced that true courtesy is important to the continued

---

[17] The importance of the salesperson's manner and attitude are emphasized in Ben Ashell, "Let's Make Retailing More Profitable," *Department Store Economist,* March, 1966, pp. 26–29.

[18] Cf. L. F. Barter, "The Sales Personality—Fact or Myth?", *Sales/Marketing Today,* April, 1965, pp. 21–23.

[19] Cf. Mendel Siegel, *How to Develop Your Personal Selling Power* (Chicago: Dartnell Corporation Press, 1966).

[20] Cf. J. E. Stafford and T. V. Greer, "Consumer Preference for Types of Salesmen: A Study of Independence-Dependence Characteristics," *Journal of Retailing,* Vol. XLI, No. 2, (Summer, 1965), pp. 27–33 ff.

[21] Reproduced by permission of Marshall Field & Company.

growth and success of Marshall Field & Company and to each of us as individuals. We subscribe to the proposition that courtesy is not only warmth and friendliness—not only seeing the other person's point of view—but also DOING THINGS RIGHT AND DOING THEM RIGHT THE FIRST TIME. Therefore, we pledge to work together to achieve our most important goal— 100% SERVICE TO 100% OF OUR CUSTOMERS AND 100% COURTESY TO EACH OTHER.

Bearing in mind that all of our relationships with other people—customers, fellow workers, and supervisors—should be based on co-operation and understanding:

we will—   I. Show a real interest in every customer through an attitude of friendliness and genuine helpfulness. Give every customer, no matter how small her purchase or how simple her request, the same courteous service we like to receive when we are customers;

we will—   II. Make certain that communications by telephone and letter reflect the same considerate and courteous service which we attempt to give in face-to-face contracts;

we will— III. Practice the principles of courtesy until courtesy becomes a habit;

we will— IV. Handle difficult situations (complaints, exchanges, emergencies), as willingly and pleasantly as we handle easy ones;

we will—   V. Make no promises which we cannot keep. Follow through on every promise we do make. When disappointments or unavoidable delays occur, let the person involved know where he stands;

we will— VI. Make a sincere effort to give accurate answers whenever information is requested. Remember that no question is so simple that it does not merit a helpful answer. Never hesitate to admit we don't KNOW, but always GET the answer;

we will— VII. Make a special effort to be helpful to all new employes—make them feel welcome and at home, take time to answer their questions and to give them the information they need. Show them our high standards by our own example;

we will—VIII. Remember that true courtesy extends to the employe across the aisle, to the fellow in the other department, to the person on the other end of the phone, to the person whose work we supervise, to the supervisor for whom we work. Giving consideration to the feelings and rights of the other person helps him in turn to understand our problems and respect our rights. Show our understanding in actions as well as in words;

we will— IX. Give every employe-customer the traditional Marshall Field & Company service;

we will—   X. Take a personal responsibility for maintaining an error-free record for ourselves and for our sections;

we will— XI. Make our own jobs and those of other people easier by proper care of equipment necessary to the performance of our jobs, and by respect for the property of others. Create a pleasant atmosphere for customers and employes by maintaining high standards of housekeeping;

we will— XII. Live up not only to the letter but to the spirit of all our policies and rules. By doing so, we make our business run more smoothly, our work easier and things more pleasant both for ourselves and the other person;

we will—XIII. Compliment a job well done. Make it a habit to recognize the good things people do;

we will—XIV. Never criticize or complain unless we have something constructive to offer about the thing of which we complain.

THE SELLING PROCESS[22]

Once the salesperson has an appreciation and understanding of the four major elements of a sale, he is in a position to proceed with the selling process. From an analytical point of view, this process can be thought of as involving seven steps, as follows: (1) approach and greeting, (2) determining the customer's needs, (3) presenting the merchandise effectively, (4) meeting objections, (5) closing the sale, (6) suggestive selling of additional items, and (7) developing good will after the sale.

In discussing the steps in the selling process, it is important to recognize certain qualifications at the outset. First, any classification of steps must be arbitrary. Second, some steps are unnecessary in consummating some sales. Third, the sequence of the steps performed will frequently vary and will depend upon the customer and upon the skill of the salesperson in defining the customer's wants. Fourth, the salesperson must not forget that his major task is to serve the customer in a courteous, intelligent manner. Devoting too much attention to the sequence of steps in bringing the sale to a successful conclusion often results in lost sales and dissatisfied customers. The successful salesperson must develop the ability to analyze each selling opportunity and to adapt his approach and his tactics to the particular situation.

Approaching and Greeting the Customer

A proper approach to the customer is a matter of skill and judgment. It requires friendly interest and a sincere desire to be of service, balanced by proper reserve and self-confidence. The customer must be welcomed with a genuine smile and a pleasant greeting; she must be made to realize that the opportunity to serve her is appreciated by the salesperson and by the store. If

---

[22] The persuasive and perceptive aspects of the selling process are discussed in R. M. Baker, Jr., and Gregg Phifer, *Salesmanship: Communication, Persuasion, Perception* (Boston: Allyn and Bacon, Inc., 1966), pp. 240–415.

this is done properly the sales transaction probably will prove to be a success.

In many stores customers are greeted by name and given a hearty welcome. Because most people like recognition and because they wish their patronage to be appreciated, they are pleased when these are evidenced as they enter the store. Although the number of customers waited upon by salespeople in large stores makes it difficult for them to remember names, this should nevertheless be encouraged.

Alertness and promptness on the part of the salesforce are essential to an effective approach. Despire the truth of this statement, salespeople sometimes gather in groups to converse and as a result neglect customers. Occasionally, salespersons deliberately avoid customers for fear of being held past their lunch hours or closing time. This condition can be corrected through proper instructions from superiors and through effective supervision.

Determining the Customer's Needs

After the customer has been properly greeted, her needs should be defined as quickly as possible. This task is easy for such staple items as groceries and toilet articles, since customers usually ask for a particular brand of merchandise. When women's ready-to-wear, gloves, hosiery, and other similar article are purchased, however, the task of determining the customer's needs is more difficult. Careful sizing up of the customer and a few well-phrased questions are very helpful in this connection. Her dress, speech, manner, and her reaction to the merchandise first shown, furnish valuable guides to the salesperson. By eliminating as quickly as possible those articles which do not meet her requirements, attention can then be concentrated on those that appear to suit her needs.

A common mistake made by salespeople in defining a customer's needs is to judge the desirability or suitability of the merchandise being shown by their own tastes and purchasing power. This mistake should be avoided since it serves to irritate and confuse the customer, with the result that sales are retarded rather than promoted.

Presenting the Merchandise Effectively

There is no sharp line of demarcation between determining the customer's needs and presenting merchandise, since proper demonstration often is necessary to ascertain her requirements. It is true, nevertheless, that effective presentation leading to purchase can be made only when the customer's needs are known.

Presenting merchandise to customers in a manner that will induce them to purchase involves the following: (1) knowledge of its location in the store or department, (2) wise selection of what is shown or demonstrated, (3) proper display of the merchandise, (4) careful selection of the chief selling points of the merchandise, and (5) effective presentation of these selling points. Since the importance of these factors should be obvious to the reader, further discussion of them is unnecessary.

Meeting Objections

Meeting objections satisfactorily probably constitutes the most difficult step in the selling process. Although they should be anticipated and answered as much as possible in the sales presentation, all of them cannot be foreseen.

Objections to purchase at retail may be divided into two groups: (1) genuine objections, constituting honest and sincere reasons for failure to buy; and (2) mere excuses, usually designed to conceal the real reason for failure to take action. Since genuine objections constitute definite obstacles to the consummation of the sale, they should be met squarely and without evasion. In contrast, excuses may often be ignored, although they may be recognized and answered by the salesperson. Sometimes excuses may be more difficult to handle than genuine objections, since they do not honestly reflect the opinions of the customer and, consequently, furnish no solid basis upon which the salesperson may work.

Some General Rules for Meeting Objections. Certain "proven" general rules are helpful to the salesperson in meeting objections, as follows:

1. Never argue with a customer. An argument may be won but a sale and a customer lost.
2. Learn to anticipate objections and incorporate answers to them in the presentation.
3. Deal with objections fairly and completely, making sure not to belittle the customer's opinions.
4. Inspire confidence on the part of the customer and contribute to her self-esteem by the tactful handling of her questions.
5. Avoid, if possible, mention of competitors and their merchandise. If the customer mentions them, speak well and briefly of them.

Knowledge of, and conformance to, these general rules, supplemented by the experience he gains in handling specific reasons customers give for failing to make purchases, will enable the salesperson to meet successfully the large majority of selling situations in his store.

Handling the Price Question. Because of the many and varied wants of *all* people and the limited incomes of *most* people, the fundamental objection to purchase for nearly all people is price. "I cannot afford it" and "I like it very much, but the price is too high," are common customer expressions with which salespeople are constantly faced.

In most cases, perhaps, price should not be mentioned until the suitability of the merchandise to the customers' needs has been demonstrated. When this has been done, the amount involved assumes less importance in the customer's mind. Many customers, however, will inquire about prices at the outset. In such instances, the salesperson should not hesitate in stating prices; but he should immediately pass on to stressing the values at these prices. It is sometimes advisable to show higher-priced merchandise of better quality, so that the difference between the various items may be demonstrated. Some firms have their salespeople follow a practice of "trading up"—of attempting to induce customers to buy better-quality merchandise at higher prices—a practice not difficult to follow in our present affluent society.

Closing the Sale[23]

If the salesperson has handled the transaction properly, closing the sale will come naturally and without particular attention being given to it by the customer. But many sales are not closed, and the best way for the salesperson to guard against such occurrences is to analyze each sale he loses, try to determine the mistakes he made in his presentation, and correct these errors in subsequent contacts with customers. Some of the more common avoidable errors are as follows:

1. Hurrying the customer; that is, attempting to rush her decision before she is ready to buy.
2. Failing to assist the customer in making a decision, perhaps by indifference or caustic comments.
3. Stumbling over obstacles without meeting objections squarely and confidently.
4. Stressing unimportant selling points as a result of poor preparation and failure to size up the customer properly.
5. Attempting to force action through high-pressure methods and because of irritation at the customer's delay in deciding on her purchase.

---

[23] Factors governing the close of a sale are explained and illustrated in C. A. Pederson and M. D. Wright, *Salesmanship, Principles and Methods* (4th ed.; Homewood, Ill.: Richard D. Irwin, Inc., 1966), pp. 481–516.

6. Acting discourteously when customers fail to purchase the merchandise shown. Resentment and disappointment overcome the salesperson's judgment.[24]

Knowledge of the reasons why sales are lost, however, is insufficient preparation on the salesperson's part. He must translate this knowledge into improved salesmanship and do all he can to minimize the mistakes that cause sales to be lost. In this connection, his own experiences should prove a valuable guide, since he will tend to use more frequently those methods he has found effective and to avoid using those he has found ineffective. In all instances, however, he should attempt to close the sale in a natural manner which will please the customer.

Suggestion Selling

Once the sale has been closed on the merchandise desired by the customer, the salesperson has an excellent opportunity further to serve the customer and promote his own interests by suggestion selling, such as:

1. Increasing the amount of the sale by suggesting better quality merchandise and pointing out the advantages of buying the better item, a form of the trading-up process referred to previously.
2. Increasing the amount of the sale by suggesting the larger sizes and explaining the saving they represent and by selling larger quantities or groups of the same item. For example, the $1.00 size of an item may contain three times the quantity of the 50-cent size, or three men's shirts may be sold at $11.50 instead of one at $3.95.
3. Suggesting related, associated, or companion items. To illustrate: The woman buying shoes may need hosiery, gloves, or a bag. Similarly, the man buying razor blades may need shaving cream or soap.
4. Suggesting seasonable, timely merchandise in demand by customers. During the winter season, cold remedies and vitamin tablets are required by many people. At Easter, millinery, spring clothing, and flowers are appropriate.
5. Suggesting special values or bargains being offered in the department or the store. These values may represent substantial reductions in the prices of regular goods for a limited period or may be caused by particularly advantageous purchases which permit lower-than-usual prices for such merchandise.
6. Suggesting new merchandise which has just arrived. Since some women (and men) like to be the first to wear or to exhibit something new, such a suggestion ordinarily arouses interest and may result in a sale if the goods appeal to the customer.

---

[24] This classification of avoidable errors by salespeople is based upon that presented by O. P. Robinson, C. H. Robinson, and G. H. Zeiss, *Successful Retail Salesmanship* (3d. ed.; Englewood Cliffs, N.J.: Prentice-Hall, Inc., 1961), pp. 408–10.

The current emphasis placed on suggestion selling by Edison Brothers Stores, Inc., a large retail footwear chain, is indicated by this recent statement by a company executive: "Edison does not believe in selling one pair of shoes. . . . A sale is not complete until two or three pairs are sold. [Other stores] now advocate this but Edison was the first to develop the principle and do a really scientific training job." The shopper also is invited "to look at matching handbags, hosiery, and other accessories that account for about one-fifth of [our] volume."[25] That these combined efforts, along with others, have been successful is shown by the facts that suggestion sales now constitute about 30 percent of the firm's total sales, and stock turnover and sales per store have increased sharply.

Since most retail salespeople dislike the additional mental and physical effort required, and since training and supervision are frequently lax in this direction, suggestion selling is practiced in only a small proportion of cases. Yet, although some customers resent suggestions and often emphasize this fact, others welcome them. The customer's attitude toward the suggestion depends upon the manner in which it is made, upon the merchandise involved, and upon the situation in which she finds herself. Suggestions are useless unless they are appropriate, definite, and helpful in the light of the customer's apparent and prospective needs. It is evident that they constitute a valuable method of increasing sales when used properly; but when used incorrectly, they may lose sales and customers.[26]

Developing Goodwill after the Sale

When the customer makes her original purchase or even when she has bought additional goods as a result of suggestions made by the salesperson, the selling process still has not been completed. "The customer must get *what* she ordered, *when* she expects it, properly wrapped and correctly billed."[27] She should also be satisfied with her purchase, and recall favorably the store and the department as a desirable place to trade. These goals call for effective action on the salesperson's part even after the customer has said, "I'll take it."

A cheerful and sincere expression of gratitude for the purchase will be remembered by the customer, and she will remember favorably her dealings with the salesperson and the store. For example: "Thank you very much, Miss Jones. I hope you will enjoy this article and that you will come in

---

[25] "New Shine for a Master Retailer," *Business Week,* April 16, 1966, p. 112.
[26] Cf. Ashell, *op. cit.,* pp. 26–29.
[27] Gray, *op. cit.,* p. 24.

again. It was a pleasure to serve you." The words used in greeting the customer are no more important than those used when she departs.

Even if no sale is made, the customer should be thanked for her interest. By doing so, the salesperson builds good will and makes friends for the store and for himself. By failing to do so, or by expressing resentment at the customer's inability to decide on a purchase at that time, he creates ill will and loses customers for the store.

In some small stores, salespeople are often responsible for seeing that the merchandise is placed on a delivery cart or truck as soon as possible, for wrapping the goods for mailing or for gifts, and for checking on the performance of articles such as washing machines or carpet sweepers after they have been used for several days. Interest evidenced in performing these responsibilities builds good will and is a mark of good salesmanship.

MANAGEMENT'S RESPONSIBILITY FOR PERSONAL SALESMANSHIP

Successful personal salesmanship in retail stores involves more than the development of proper attitudes, knowledge, and practices on the part of salespeople and other employees. It is the responsibility of management, through alert leadership and adequate supervision, to provide the direction and the type of selling atmosphere throughout the store which is conducive to effective selling. When this is done, customers will be pleased with the surroundings in which they shop; employees will be congenial in their relationships with each other and their supervisors, and happy with the conditions under which they work.

The proprietor of the small store and the supervisor in the large one have major responsibilities in the guidance, supervision, and energizing of the people who make up the sales force. These responsibilities consist—in addition to providing the proper selling atmosphere—of such factors as a fair distribution of work among employees, assignment of definite responsibility to each worker, and even-tempered supervision involving interest in and encouragement of the sales force. Management should also recognize that the maintenance of high standards in selling efforts necessitates rather close and constant observation of the selling process carried on in the particular store or department; that it requires detailed study of performance records; and that it demands correction of sales methods as a result of such observation and study. Moreover, skill and judgment should be shown in the conduct of meetings: an attitude of superiority should be avoided and employees should be encouraged to participate. When management meets these responsibilities, personal selling efforts will be improved and profit possibilities enhanced.

REVIEW AND DISCUSSION QUESTIONS

1. Define good will in your own words. Suggest five ways through which a salesperson in a drugstore can build good will for his company.
2. What is meant by the term *caveat emptor?* Illustrate this doctrine based on your own experience.
3. How do you explain the present general attitude that the quality of selling in retail stores has deteriorated in recent years?
4. Suggest ways in which the effectiveness of retail salesmanship may be improved. Be specific and give reasons.
5. Comment on the value of evaluation forms for salespeople as used in some retail stores. What uses should be made of Figure 20–1 showing "how much a salesperson should sell"?
6. Discuss some of the developments in automation that have reduced the time salespeople spend on nonselling activities.
7. What are the major elements in a sale? Indicate their interrelationships.
8. Visit a retail store in your community and observe the selling techniques employed. Describe three selling incidents and critically evaluate each.
9. Assume that you are a major executive of R. H. Macy & Company and you have been asked to outline a program designed "to demonstrate that we care that the customer finds what she wants, gets the help she desires, and derives satisfaction from every contact with Macy's." How would you proceed and what information would you develop in connection with this assignment?
10. From what sources may a prospective salesperson in a retail hardware store obtain merchandise knowledge?
11. Prepare a paper of about 1,000 words on "Courtesy as a Major Factor in the Selling Process."
12. Summarize the major steps in the "Selling Process." Of what value to a salesperson is knowledge of these steps? If possible, base your answer on your own selling experience.
13. "Meeting objections satisfactorily probably constitutes the most difficult step in the selling process." Discuss.
14. Define and illustrate suggestion selling. How do you account for the emphasis retail management places on this form of selling?
15. Discuss (1) the salesperson's responsibility for effective personal selling, and (2) management's obligations in connection with this activity.

SUPPLEMENTARY READINGS

ASHELL, BEN. "Let's Make Retailing More Profitable: A Salesperson's Guide to Better Selling." In a series of three articles under this title in the *Department Store Economist,* March, 1966, pp. 26–29; April, 1966, pp. 26–28; and May, 1966, pp. 32–33, the author discusses how to help salespeople improve themselves "at the place where it really counts—the selling floor."

BAKER, R. M., JR., AND PHIFER, GREGG. *Salesmanship: Communication, Persuasion, Perception* (Boston: Allyn and Bacon, Inc., 1966). A general text on salesmanship, this book treats "personal selling as a persuasive activity [based on] sound moral and ethical foundations."

DUNTON, LOREN. *How to Sell to Women* (New York: McGraw-Hill Book Co., Inc., 1965). The author points out differences in selling to men and women and suggests techniques for winning the confidence of women shoppers.

JOHNSON, H. W. *Creative Selling* (Cincinnati: South-Western Publishing Co., 1966). This practical treatment of selling, although containing no specific information on retailing applications, provides the reader with useful knowledge of selling techniques and selling aids.

KIRKPATRICK, C. A. *Salesmanship: Helping Prospects Buy* (4th ed.; Cincinnati: South-Western Publishing Co., 1966). Part C—The Selling Process, and Chapter XIX—"Selling in Retail Stores," are particularly pertinent to the discussion in this chapter.

PEDERSON, C. A., AND WRIGHT, M. D. *Salesmanship: Principles and Methods* (4th ed.; Homewood, Ill.: Richard D. Irwin, Inc., 1966). Although concerned mainly with outside selling, there is much in this general text of value to the retail salesman. The chapters on "Handling Objections," and "The Close" are especially helpful.

ROBINSON, O. P.; BLACKLER, W. R.; AND LOGAN, W. B. *Store Salesmanship* (6th ed.; Englewood Cliffs, N.J.: Prentice-Hall, Inc., 1966). An elementary treatment of retail selling, this volume provides suggestions for improving performance on the sales floor.

"Sales Management Goes Shopping," *Sales Management,* February 19, 1965, pp. 85–92; March 19, 1965, pp. 73–74 and following issues. Experiences of a shopper attempting to buy particular products in retail stores are recounted in these brief episodes.

SHOCKEY, RALF. "Selling is a Science," *Department Store Economist.* In a series of ten brief articles beginning in the April, 1965, issue and ending in January, 1966, the author treats all aspects of retail salesmanship. The last article, entitled "Department Store Selling Strictly Model T," suggests six important questions for top management to answer.

SLOM, S. H. *How to Sell Furniture* (New York: Fairchild Publications, Inc., 1965). A compact guide for furniture salesmen, this 64-page booklet discusses styles, woods, fabrics, and consumer shopping habits.

STAFFORD, J. E., AND GREER, T. V. "Consumer Preference for Types of Salesmen: A Study of Independence-Dependence Characteristics," *Journal of Retailing,* Vol. XLI, No. 2 (Summer, 1965), pp. 27–33. In this interesting study the authors relate consumer characteristics to the corresponding preferences for retail salespeople.

WEISS, E. B. "In Retailing Everybody Cares," *Advertising Age,* March 21, 1966, p. 90. The author, a confirmed and constructive critic of retailing practices, takes salespeople and management to task for the unrealistic images they are creating for retailing institutions.

WHITNEY, R. A.; HUBIN, THOMAS; AND MURPHY, J. D. *The New Psychology of Persuasion and Motivation in Selling* (Englewood Cliffs, N.J.: Prentice-Hall, Inc., 1965). Although applying to selling in general, the student of retailing will find this treatment of interest and value.

WINGATE, I. B.; GILLESPIE, K. R., AND ADDISON, B. G. *Know Your Merchandise* (3d ed.; New York: McGraw-Hill Book Co., Inc., 1965). Basic information chapters on leather, shoes, and plastics as well as other categories of textile and nontextile merchandise are provided by the authors in this helpful volume.

ZIMMER, A. E. *The Strategy of Successful Retail Salesmanship.* (New York: McGraw-Hill Book Co., Inc., 1966). In this practical discussion of retail selling the author also includes in appendix I selling guides for 21 merchandise lines.

21

CHAPTER

Customer Services

The retailer, who exists to serve his customers, needs to provide more than the proper assortments of merchandise at reasonable prices. Customers expect him to furnish various types of help in making purchases, to alter clothing, to deliver goods promptly, and to assure complete satisfaction with merchandise bought. Some of these "extra" services—those having to do with assistance rendered to the customer in connection with the sale and delivery of merchandise—have long been known as "customer services" and are discussed in this chapter. Often performed without charge to the customer and representing a form of nonprice competition, how well these services are carried out is very important in creating the store's image and in attracting customers to it.[1]

In addition to these traditional services, recent years have seen retailers adopt a long list of income-producing services to meet the changing demands of their customers, such as rental of tools and equipment by the hardware retailer. As a result, the term "customer services" should, in the judgment of the authors, be broadened to include these newer types. Used in this sense, the term reflects a growing awareness on the part of the modern retailer to break away from the traditional concept of customer services and furnish all of those he is expected to provide to meet the requirements of today's customers.

NATURE AND VARIETY OF CUSTOMER SERVICES

Specific Kinds of Customer Services

Among the more important traditional customer services are the altering of men's and women's clothing, wrapping merchandise, making deliveries,

---

[1] Cf. J. W. Wingate, "Revising the Store Image," *New York Retailer,* May, 1966, pp. 7–10.

handling complaints and making adjustments, accepting returns, and extending credit.[2] However, this category also includes such matters as a personal shopping service, aiding customers to find wanted goods, supplying merchandise information, accepting c.o.d. orders, establishing a branch post office, setting up a lost-and-found department, and furnishing rest rooms.

As already suggested, the foregoing services have been offered by retail stores for many years. Most quality-image stores are concentrating their efforts on improving their present customer services and are reluctant to add others for fear of harming their reputations. Many retailers, however, and particularly those catering to middle- and lower-income groups, are moving boldly to add such income-producing services as the following:

1. Automobile rentals (Alexander's, New York; Broadway Department Stores, Los Angeles).
2. Automobile and tire services (Goldblatt's, Chicago).
3. Charm school program (Montgomery Ward, Chicago).
4. Floral service (Bullock's, Los Angeles).
5. Health, accident, and hospitalization insurance (May Company, Los Angeles; Famous-Barr, St. Louis; J. C. Penney).
6. Sales and service on hair pieces, men's and women's (Gimbel's, New York).
7. "Consumer Advisory Service" (Hecht Company, Washington, D.C.).
8. All-accident group insurance (Carson Pirie Scott, Chicago).
9. Sports and theater tickets (J. L. Hudson, Detroit).
10. Mutual fund shares (Dayton Company, Minneapolis).
11. Rug and upholstery cleaning (Sears, Roebuck and Co.).

The expectation of customers regarding services is difficult to judge and, in many instances, only experimentation can provide the answer. Many customers, particularly those of smaller stores, expect a degree of personalized service not always possible among the large retailers. Consequently, some specialty stores have developed such service to a degree far exceeding the average department store and have been rewarded with greater increases in dollar volume and in unit sales than their larger competitors.[3] It is probable that the expansion of services will continue as management seeks additional profitable activities suited to the store's clientele and image.[4] One marketing executive refers to the improvement of customer service—"the

---

[2] Telephone and mail-order selling, often looked upon as customer services, are discussed in Chapter 19.

[3] Cf. Mort Sheinman, "Personal Service Paid Off in Specialty Store Sales," *Women's Wear Daily*, September 17, 1965, p. 21. Also cf. Milton Gussow, "Personal Service is Specialty of Suburb Specialty Shop," *ibid.*, November 10, 1965, p. 23.

[4] Cf. E. B. Weiss, "Coming: More Luxurious Retail Services," *Advertising Age*, July 13, 1964, p. 100.

need to give the customer tender, loving care in order to woo and win him"—as "the chief retailing trend of the Sixties."[5]

Establishing Customer Service Policies

Despite the necessity of providing customer services in some variety to meet the needs of the store's clientele, the retailer should move carefully in establishing the policies, procedures, and conditions under which these services will be offered. Fortunately, he has certain guides to assist him, as follows:

First, the policies and practices of competitors are important, since in most cases his customers also "shop" his competitors and he will be expected to meet their standards or to offer compensating advantages. Second, the type of merchandise he handles will influence the services he will render. Electric refrigerators, stoves, washing machines, and furniture, for example, usually cannot be transported by the purchaser and must be delivered by the seller. Moreover, since their unit value is high, some form of deferred payment is essential. In contrast, cosmetics, shoes, and hosiery can readily be carried by customers; and their comparatively low cost makes credit extension less essential. Third, the type of clientele—its income, location, and buying habits—served by the store influences the services that must be rendered. Generally speaking, the higher the income group appealed to, the greater the number of services expected and offered. Fourth, the store's pricing policy has a bearing on the nature and extent of the services rendered. To illustrate, when "bargains" are featured, attempts are made to restrict services and to shift some of them to customers. Fifth, the store's location also plays a role as suggested (1) by the downtown retailer who must offer delivery service while a similar retailer in a neighborhood area may rely on his customers to carry their purchases; and (2) by the retailer in a suburban area—where "do-it-yourself" is common—who is often expected to make available tools and equipment on a rental basis.

Customer Services and Customer Satisfaction. In the process of choosing the particular services he will offer to his customers, the retailer should bear in mind constantly his desired goal—keeping customers satisfied—especially after a sale has been made or the merchandise has been rented. This satisfaction, however, is a relative matter. The great majority of customers can and must be satisfied with their purchases and the store's service in connection therewith—a fact that is significant to the retailer, since he must rely on repeat purchases. But some customers present demands

---

[5] "Tender, Loving Care for the Masses," *Business Week,* March 5, 1966, p. 84.

that are impossible of fulfillment and dissatisfaction sometimes results. Although the retailer should take all reasonable steps to minimize these instances, he should not be discouraged when he loses an occasional customer. What is important, however, is his conviction that his policy is sound, after the conditions responsible for the dissatisfaction have been investigated.[6]

Scope of the Chapter

Within the scope of a single chapter, it is not possible to discuss each of the wide variety of "free" and income-producing customer services in detail. Credit services, for example, are so important in retail stores, and there have been so many significant changes in credit policies and practices in recent years, that a separate chapter is necessary to appraise them properly.[7]

In contrast, many services need only brief mention. To illustrate: attractive and well-equipped rest rooms for customers have become an essential in all stores, except in the very small, limited-line store. Air conditioning is being extended both to large and to small stores and even to those not appealing mainly to the upper-income groups; witness its use by the variety store chains and by low-priced restaurants. Some stores provide music to entertain shoppers. A few stores have gone so far as to establish children's playrooms, where children may be left during a shopping trip, or to provide auditoriums for use without charge by women's clubs. Beauty parlors may be operated at a loss to attract customers, and "free" educational classes may be conducted in knitting and sewing. The store may offer a check-cashing service or it may provide a branch post-office to accommodate its customers. Through a personal service bureau, theater and transportation tickets may be purchased. Or a lost-and-found department may be operated.

Brief mention must also suffice for the automobile parking problem and the service which retailers offer in connection with it. As parking has become more difficult, some retailers have provided their own facilities or made arrangements for their patrons to park in nearby garages or parking lots; others offer bus service at frequent intervals from parking lots to their stores; and still others have placed their stores in locations (1) where there is ample parking room in the streets, (2) where the store may operate its own

---

[6] States an executive of R. H. Macy & Company: "We are determined that there must be no deterioration in customer service, or in caring that the customer is pleased." Cf. "Macy Sets All-Out Assault Against Offensive Customer Service," *Women's Wear Daily,* November 11, 1965, p. 10. For a critical assessment of this pronouncement cf. E. B. Weiss, "In Retailing Everybody Cares—Yeah Yeah!", *Advertising Age,* March 21, 1966, p. 90.

[7] See Chapter 22.

parking lot, or (3) where several retailers may join together to offer parking facilities, as in a shopping center.[8] R. H. Macy & Company, in its new circular store in New York City, has gone one step farther with an arrangement that permits customers to drive their cars up a ramp and park adjacent to the department they wish to visit.[9] And another store provides conveyor belts to transport customers from the parking lot to the store.[10]

In this chapter our attention will be concentrated on the more important customer services, except the extension of credit, plus a few brief paragraphs dealing with six other customer services. Some consideration will also be given to the question of charging for these services.

ALTERATIONS

Alterations constitute a form of customer service which has become widely expected and without which it would be impossible to consummate many sales of clothing. Women's dresses often need to be shortened, made longer, or taken in at the hips. The coat sleeves of a man's suit need to be lengthened, while the waist of the trousers is too tight. Even children's garments usually require changes of some sort. The retailer should provide facilities for making these alterations.

Originally, most retailers offered a "free" altering service. During the last four decades, however, the situation has changed materially—although even now the charge may not be enough to cover the full cost of the alteration. At the present time, a charge is typically made for alterations on women's clothing, whereas minor adjustments (cuffing trousers, lengthening or shortening sleeves, altering waistlines) on men's clothing usually involve no extra charge. For such major alterations as recutting trousers or changing the degree of fullness across the back of a coat, however, an increasing number of retailers are now assessing the cost to the customer. Many small retailers strongly oppose this newer policy and state that they would prefer to raise their prices rather than begin to charge for alterations on men's and boys' clothing. It is quite common practice, nevertheless, to charge for any alterations on men's clothing during special sales events.

---

[8] Cf. R. C. Rich, "Parking Decks [with self-service] Solve New Problems for Cramped Shopping Centers," *Department Store Economist,* January, 1966, pp. 34–36; and *Parking Requirements for Shopping Centers* (Washington, D.C.: Urban Land Institute, Technical Bulletin No. 53, 1965).

[9] Cf. Figure 5–4, above, p. 127; and "Drive-Up Shopping Brings Cars to Circular Store's Doors," *Chain Store Age* (Executives Edition), January, 1966, p. 21.

[10] Cf. " 'Moving Sidewalk' to Serve Distant Cars, More Levels," *Modern Retailer,* April, 1966, p. 56.

WRAPPING MERCHANDISE

Wrapping of customers' purchases is a service provided by retailers of all sizes and types. In fact, it is seldom that any retailer escapes this obligation, although the amount and kind of wrapping service varies widely from store to store. The high-fashion store, for example, utilizes far different wrappings than does the drugstore or supermarket. In this connection the increasing use of shopping bags in attractive designs should be noted. Various sizes, shapes, and colors are available with store names printed thereon and there probably is no medium which so effectively keeps the store name circulating on streets, buses, and suburban trains at so slight a cost. Despite this development, the actual wrapping of goods purchased in the vast majority of retail stores is still necessary.

Wrapping Systems

There are three major types of wrapping systems in common use—clerk wrap, department or floor wrap, and central wrap.

Clerk Wrap. When a clerk-wrap system is employed, the salesperson waiting on the customer also does the wrapping. This system is usually preferred by the customer, since it enables her to carry out the whole transaction with one person. Not only is there a saving in time for the customer, but it gives her the feeling that she is really given service—a feeling she does not get if she has to go to a wrapping center and wait in line for her package. For small and medium-sized stores the clerk-wrap system has so much merit that it is the most widely used system in service stores (as distinguished from self-service stores). It is also used by large stores in departments carrying items for which no special packaging is needed, as for handkerchiefs, hosiery, and toilet goods.

Department Wrap. Under a department or floor-wrap system, a wrapping station is provided at a convenient spot where all merchandise sold in one or more related or adjacent departments is wrapped by employees specializing in this service. In some cases the station may employ one or several full-time wrappers, especially during busy seasons; in other cases the wrapping and cashier function may be combined in the same person. On "take-with" merchandise the salesperson may bring the goods to the wrapping desk, wait until they are wrapped, and return them to the customer; or she may excuse herself and leave the customer to wait for her package. In some stores the customer is expected to take her purchase to the wrapping desk. On "send" merchandise the goods are usually taken to the station by the salesperson.

Central Wrap. A central-wrap system localizes the wrapping service of a store in one or a few places, thereby achieving the advantages of greater specialization of labor. In addition, it makes possible the use of wrapping machines, which some retailers have found can wrap as much as 70 percent of all merchandise at substantial savings in both space and wages. Usually, the wrapping department will be placed in the basement of the store; but in the large store, where it may be deemed advisable to have two or three wrapping centers, these centers may be located on various floors adjacent to selling departments. In a sense, the check-out counter in the self-service store is a central-wrap system. In such cases, the "wrapping"—which involves placing the purchases in a large bag or in a box—typically takes place near the exit from the store. It is performed either by the cashier or a "bagger."

Prepacking

To assist the retailer with his wrapping problems, some manufacturers place goods in packages containing the number of units usually purchased by the customer. This practice is referred to as "prepacking" or "prepackaging." Used especially by manufacturers of lamps, china, glassware, and other breakable items, such packing reduces damage and handling costs.

Gift Wrapping

Gift wrapping is a service offered by a large number of stores throughout the year, but it is of most importance in the pre-Christmas period. When the volume is sufficient, it seems best to have special wrappers for this service, since customers want their gift packages to look especially well.

Although gift wrapping may be desired by the customer, the store must not overlook the fact that it is a fairly expensive service. Jewelry boxes of good quality given free with the purchase of merchandise may cost as little as a few cents or as much as $5.00 each; and the designing, lithographing, and varnishing of Christmas boxes amounts to a substantial sum.

Partly because of a fairly prevalent practice at Christmas time of buying goods in a low-grade store and having them wrapped in a higher-grade one, some stores make a charge for gift-wrapping service. Today, however, probably more than 50 percent of department and specialty stores still continue to provide free gift boxes and wrappings the year round.[11]

---

[11] One store furnishes prewrapped gift boxes at the point of sale to reduce wrapping expense and expedite service. Cf. "Instant Gift Wrapping, Instant Sales," *Department Store Economist,* March, 1966, p. 78. Others use ready-made gift boxes. Cf. "Ready-Made Gift Box Opening New Markets," *Printers' Ink,* February 25, 1966, p. 62.

DELIVERY SERVICE

Despite the growth of self-service stores with their "cash-and-carry" appeal and the increase in carrying of goods by customers, delivery of merchandise to the customer's home remains one of the most important services rendered by many retail stores. Although definite figures are not available, it seems reasonable to state that delivery service is rendered on at least one third of the goods sold at retail. Such service is practically universal for many "heavy" or "hard" goods—including furniture, stoves, refrigerators, washing machines, and television sets. The same holds true for items such as rugs, mattresses, and mirrors. Even in some of the supermarkets and chain organizations, where "cash and carry" is the *modus operandi,* delivery service can be arranged at a nominal charge. Moreover, the growth of telephone and mail-order selling and the unwillingness of more people to cope with the traffic problem in numerous metropolitan shopping areas have caused many people to have their purchases delivered to their homes.

Recent data on delivery expense indicate that it is quite costly and rising rapidly on a unit basis, largely because of increasing labor costs. Per-package cost for delivery now approximates 50 to 55 cents in the larger cities; and among department stores delivery costs probably range from 1.5 to 2.0 percent of net sales. Despite the cost involved, delivery service is usually performed on a "free" basis. However, some retailers require a minimum purchase of $2.00 for free delivery and levy a small charge (such as 50 to 75 cents) when the minimum is not reached. Likewise it is common practice to charge for deliveries by express or parcel post when made to an address outside the store's normal delivery area.

Delivery Systems

In general, retail delivery systems fall into a fivefold classification: (1) individual-store system, (2) mutual system, (3) consolidated system, (4) express, and (5) parcel post.

Individual-Store System. Under this system the individual store undertakes to provide delivery service by means of its own personnel and equipment. In the small store, such delivery may be performed in the car of the proprietor or in a small pushcart. If deliveries are of sufficient importance, a delivery boy may be employed full time to use his bicycle or to drive a delivery truck. No regular delivery routes are maintained; and, when necessary, deliveries may be made immediately. Otherwise, the employee making deliveries waits until a few orders have accumulated. No special system is set up for checking out goods to be delivered or checking in goods returned.

In medium-size and large stores, delivery service is often highly organized. The delivery department is made responsible for all goods as they leave the wrapping departments. Where clerk-wrap and floor-wrap systems are in use, the delivery department is usually responsible for picking up goods from the various selling floors. Once the merchandise is in the delivery department, it is sorted and delivered according to carefully laid-out routes.

The individual-store delivery system is the most flexible system which any store can use. Since it is under the control of the store, routes and delivery schedules can be arranged to meet the store's requirements. Furthermore, because the deliveryman is an employee of the store, he can be trained to serve the store's interest such as reporting to the proper store authorities all messages or complaints from customers. Moreover, when the system is store owned and the delivery trucks carry the name of the store, they serve as a medium of advertising. Finally, if the delivery service to be performed is sufficient to keep the delivery department busy, the cost of a store-owned system may be nearly as low as that of any other system.

Mutual Delivery System. In some cities the retailers have formed mutual or cooperative delivery systems. A delivery company, separate from the retail firms but owned by them, is set up. Expenses may be shared among the various stockholders according to some agreed basis. The delivery company picks up from each retailer all goods to be delivered, takes them to its own sorting station, sorts the merchandise, takes care of actual delivery, collects c.o.d. accounts, and returns goods that cannot be delivered or that customers do not want.

The advantages of the mutual delivery system, as compared with that of the individual store, are mainly two: (1) better delivery service to the customer through more frequent deliveries made possible by combining packages of all cooperating stores; and (2) lower cost to the store because of savings in space, personnel, equipment, and management supervision.

But certain problems are encountered when a mutual delivery system is used. These include the following: (1) building the necessary organization and providing the essential equipment to accomplish the objective; (2) determining an equitable basis upon which to allocate the expenses involved among the members of the group; and (3) maintaining effective control over the system to insure customer satisfaction. As a result of these factors, although mutual delivery systems have been very successful in some cities, they are not spreading rapidly at the present time.

Consolidated Delivery System. Consolidated delivery systems operate in a manner similar to that of the mutual systems, but they are not owned by the stores they serve. Instead, they are formed and operated by a group of individuals who are willing to perform the delivery service for retailers on a fee basis in the hope of making a profit. The United Parcel Service, with delivery facilities throughout the country, is an illustration of these systems. The rapid growth of this and similar organizations in recent years furnishes strong evidence of the need for such service.

The advantages of consolidated delivery systems are similar to those of mutual systems when compared with independent ones. When the consolidated system is used executives of individual stores are relieved of numerous management problems such as those associated with unionization activities. Experience reveals that unions often gain their first foothold with truck drivers. In view of such relief, it is likely that United Parcel Service and other similar organizations will continue to grow despite the preference of many retailers to operate and control their own delivery service.

Under consolidated delivery systems—just as under mutual systems—the difficult problem of allocating delivery charges remains. In both systems, three principal methods are followed: (1) a per-package charge (which may vary with either or both of the size or weight of the package) for each order sent out, (2) a flat weekly rate based roughly on the number or value of orders delivered for each merchant over a period of time, and (3) a combination of the flat weekly rate and a charge per order.

Delivery by Express and Parcel Post. The great bulk of retail deliveries is carried out by the types of delivery systems already discussed. All large stores and many small ones, however, use express companies and parcel-post service to some extent, especially in response to mail orders. Moreover, these methods are of value to the small store which may have few packages to be delivered and to the large store when its deliveries must be made over a very wide area. Even in these cases the packages must not be heavy or bulky, or the rates will prove excessive.

The cost problem for parcel post has become more acute by recent increases (1966) in the rates, which were accompanied by a broadening of weights and sizes of packages acceptable for mailing.[12] Although opportunity to mail larger packages was viewed with favor by retailers, their enthusiasm was tempered by the knowledge that costs would be greater. While the effects of these new rules on the use of parcel post by retailers cannot be fairly appraised at this time, it is noteworthy that past increases in rates had been accompanied by a decline in the volume of packages handled by the Post Office.

---

[12] For details on these changes cf. "Larger Parcel Post Packages," *Business Week*, September 3, 1966, p. 44.

CUSTOMER COMPLAINTS AND ADJUSTMENTS

No retailer, large or small, finds it possible to do business without receiving a number of complaints from customers. Although he should learn to take them in stride because of their inevitability,[13] a procedure or system should be established to handle complaints satisfactorily from the points of view of both the customer and the store. Even though the number of complaints has been reduced in recent years, most students of retailing agree that there are still far more than is necessary. By focusing attention on their fundamental causes, it would seem possible to reduce them substantially. Such a reduction would contribute significantly to lower retail expenses.

Major Causes of Complaints

In general, complaints may be traced to one or more of four factors:

Improper Buying. The purchase of goods unsuited to customers' needs is an important cause of complaints. Perhaps the store's buyers lack experience; perhaps they do not know what the customer wants; or perhaps they are simply careless in their buying. Whatever the reason, poor buying cannot help but result in customer complaints.[14]

Inefficient Store System. A weak store system results in many complaints by customers. The delivery order may fail to specify the number of packages, so that the driver may leave a certain address after having delivered one package instead of two. The result is a complaint that the delivery is "short."

Inadequately Trained and Careless Personnel. Salespeople who are unfamiliar with established procedures and practices governing the preparation of sales checks and credit slips, who do not dispatch "sends" to the delivery department promptly, and who fail to render courteous service to all customers, contribute to the number of complaints. Likewise, some retailers have inadequately trained repairmen to service the appliances and television sets which they sell.

Even in the store which has developed an adequate system and given careful and detailed training to its employees, complaints may develop from carelessness and mistakes. Incorrect addresses may be placed on "sends,"

---

[13] Cf. Isadore Barmash, "Complaints and Complaints—Retailers Take Them in Stride," *New York Times,* October 31, 1965, pp. F1, F12.

[14] Frequently it is unfair to place all blame for unsatisfactory merchandise upon the buyer. For example, variations in sizes of ready-to-wear among manufacturers are an important cause of complaints and returns.

wrong sizes may be delivered, and another account credited when goods are returned. Better supervision of employees can minimize much of this carelessness.

Habitual Complainers. Some customers are habitual complainers: they always seem to assume that even better merchandise should have been sold or better service given. If an automobile tire shows wear at the end of 20,000 miles, the customer feels that it should have gone 25,000 miles. The $4.00 shirt which begins to fray on the cuffs after repeated washings is brought back because it is defective. In brief, every store has a few customers who expect so much that, even though everything possible has been done to give satisfaction, complaints are still registered.

Point of View in Handling Complaints

Development of Good Will. To remain in business retailers must develop a large repeat business; and since this is not possible when customers feel that they have a just grievance against the store, complaints should be handled by personnel appearing friendly and sympathetic from the customer's point of view.[15] When such an attitude is evident, a major step has been taken toward maintaining the good will of the customer. Otherwise, she will turn to some other retailer. In addition, she may air her complaints to her friends, who may well follow her advice and give their business to a "more responsible" retailer. Reports one retailer, "Merchants spend millions of dollars on advertising each year to create public good will and then proceed to spill it down the drain by inadequate handling of customer complaints and adjustments."[16] Certainly the personnel in charge of complaints should recognize that they have an important part to play in building good will for the store.

In an effort to turn complaints into good will many retailers have very liberal adjustments policies.[17] Typical of these policies is that of Sears, Roebuck and Co.: "Liberal and prompt adjustments to our customers, *even if we may think they are wrong,* are desirable as a matter of policy. . . . The Sears motto, *Satisfaction guaranteed or your money back,* is a real policy, to be faithfully observed." In carrying out such a policy, some

---

[15] Cf. "The Customer is SO Right," *Time,* December 10, 1965, pp. 100, 102.

[16] Isidore Newman 2d, President, City Stores Company. Quoted by Isadore Barmash, "Complaints Mar Store-Ad Impact," *New York Times,* November 21, 1965, p. F1.

[17] Throughout the discussion that follows, an *adjustment* refers to the action taken by the retailer in an effort to satisfy the complainant. Sometimes the adjustment consists of making an *exchange,* that is, the merchandise returned by the customer is exchanged for other goods. Such exchanges may be even or uneven. Cf. the distinction between even and uneven exchanges in Chapter 26, p. 721, below.

retailers quite automatically make the adjustment requested by the customer. Others quickly make any adjustments called for by a failure on the part of the store; but, for other complaints, try to distinguish between (1) those made by customers who honestly feel they have a legitimate complaint, and (2) those who are merely taking advantage of the store's "the-customer-is-always-right" policy. While adjustments are made in the first case, they may be refused in the second instance.

Minimizing Complaints. In addition to building good will, the adjustment of complaints should provide the store with basic data which will enable it to reduce future complaints. If complaints are classified as to responsibility, for example, it may be found that many are arising because of delayed delivery or that salespeople lack adequate training in the handling of charge transactions. Careful analysis may also reveal that many complaints are originating because of defective merchandise being sold by a certain department. In such instances the information can be very valuable in the control of future complaints. All too often, however, executives fail to take prompt and effective action upon the basis of such data; therefore the complaints continue.

Procedures for Handling Complaints

In the small, one-man store, there is no question as to who shall handle complaints and make adjustments. In the store with several salespeople, the proprietor or manager usually takes this responsibility although minor matters may be handled directly by the salespeople. In medium-size and large stores, however, complaints usually are so numerous that the proprietor finds it impracticable to handle even the major complaints. In this situation, any one of three systems may be adopted: a centralized system, a decentralized system, or a combination of certain elements of both.

Centralized System. Under this plan the retailer establishes an adjustment department to which every complaint, regardless of its nature, is referred. This procedure has several advantages, both for the customer and for the store. For the customer (1) it permits her grievance to be handled by people trained to hear complaints and to make adjustments, and (2) it increases the probability that she will get an adjustment she considers satisfactory, since her complaint is heard by an impartial adjuster rather than by the salesperson involved in the transaction.

From the store's point of view the adjustment department offers the chance of using skilled adjusters who can handle difficult situations uniformly and build good will for the store. These adjusters are selected because of their patience, tact, and courtesy in meeting all types of individuals with complaints.[18] At the same time, salespeople and buyers are relieved of the duty of handling complaints, so that they have more time for their other responsibilities. Since the adjustment department provides a place where the complaint may be listened to and discussed in semiprivacy, the store does not "wash its dirty linen in public."[19] Finally, centralized adjustments make it easier to keep records of all complaints and to analyze them, so that the data may be used as a means of reducing future complaints.

Although the adjuster in a central department may give the customer a more satisfactory settlement than would a salesperson on the selling floor, most customers probably prefer to have their complaints handled on the sales floor. Not only does the customer consider the person who sold her the merchandise to be responsible for the situation; but she also feels that, by taking the matter to that person, she will avoid explaining the whole situation to a third party. Some customers object to the time consumed in locating the adjustment department, especially when they find that they have to wait in line for a "hearing." Such "red tape" is irritating to them. As a result, it often becomes difficult for the adjuster to handle the problem and leads to greater leniency than would otherwise be the case. Instead of accepting an exchange, as a particular customer might if her complaint were handled quickly by the salesperson, a long wait in line may lead her to demand and obtain a refund—and at once! Certainly, she is not in a frame of mind to be completely rational about the matter.

Decentralized System.   Under this procedure, authority to settle complaints is usually given to the department head or floorman. In some stores, especially in instances in which it is obvious that the store is at fault, head salespeople are authorized to make the adjustment. The refusal of adjustments, however, is reserved for executives.

Some of the benefits that accrue to the store from the decentralized system are as follows: It is more natural for the customer to bring her complaints to the selling department and to the salesperson whom she believes responsible. On the sales floor, where other merchandise may be shown to her, the customer is more willing to accept an adjustment in the form of an exchange of merchandise; whereas, in the adjustment department she may demand a refund. Although the decentralized system may avoid creating the unfavora-

---

[18] Cf. "Merchandise Adjuster's Life Called a Liberal Education," *Women's Wear Daily,* October 14, 1965, p. 9.

[19] There are exceptions to this statement, as in the case of one little old lady who entered a department store. Instantly a band began to play, an orchid was pinned on her dress, she was handed a $100 bill and found herself being photographed from all sides and taken before the TV cameras. "You are the one-millionth customer," the master of ceremonies beamed at her. "And now can you tell us what you came here for?" "Why, yes," the little old lady said, "I'm on my way to the complaint department."

ble impression which a complainant forms when she sees other persons also seeking settlements in the centralized department, it has the following limitations: salespeople and floormen often lack training in the handling of complaints; it takes time from their other duties; and salespeople are less willing to admit their error than an impartial adjustment bureau. Moreover, when variations in adjustments among salespeople and departments occur, customers are irritated.

Combination System. Many stores have tried to gain some of the advantages of both the centralized and the decentralized system by combining the two. The usual procedure is to use the decentralized plan for all complaints except (1) those that seem unreasonable to the department head or floorman and (2) those that involve a fairly substantial amount of money. Such a combination system enables the store to adjust the majority of complaints in a manner most satisfactory to the customer, that is, by the decentralized system. At the same time, it provides a skilled group of adjusters to handle all difficult cases. For the majority of medium-size and large retailers, some degree of combination of the decentralized and centralized systems seems desirable.

RETURNED GOODS

Closely connected with the problem of complaints and adjustments is the returned-goods problem. Few customer services are more widely used, and none is more abused since many customers consider the privilege of returns as part of their birthright. "In one large city, the merchants estimate that each day in customers' homes there is over one hundred thousand dollars' worth of merchandise that will ultimately be returned to the stores."[20] Returns for groceries, toilet articles, and books may not exceed 1 percent to 3 percent of sales; but returns of women's dresses,[21] furniture, and rugs normally range from 8 to 20 percent of sales; and radio returns may run as high as 25 percent. Among department stores of different size, returns and allowances to customers ranged from 3.94 to 8.54 percent of sales in 1965.[22] Certainly the problem of returned merchandise continues to plague many retailers, not only because of the quantities of goods returned but also because of the expense and managerial effort involved.

[20] O. P. Robinson, C. H. Robinson, and G. H. Zeiss, *Successful Retail Salesmanship* (3d ed.; Englewood Cliffs, N.J.: Prentice-Hall, Inc., 1961), p. 247.

[21] For statistics on returns of women's dresses, cf. Eric Mosbacher, "An Analysis of the Causes of Dress Returns to a Department Store in New York City," *New York Retailer*, May, 1966, p. 11.

[22] Sam Flanel, *Financial and Operating Results of Department and Specialty Stores in 1965* (New York: National Retail Merchants Association, 1966) pp. vii–viii.

Responsibility for Returns

Considerable merchandise is returned for which the customer or the store is only indirectly responsible. For example, lack of standard sizes among manufacturers results in some returns. Our chief interest, however, is how responsibility for returns may be divided between the store and its customers with the objective of minimizing the practice.

Store Responsibility. The store should probably be charged with responsibility for returns occasioned by the merchandise sold, the quality of service rendered to customers, and store policies. These factors are responsible for the great bulk of all returns. In regard to merchandise, stocks may be incomplete, quality of merchandise may be poor, designated size may be incorrect, merchandise may be overpriced (so that the customer will make a return as soon as she notes a lower price in another store), and merchandise may be inadequately described. Service returns are occasioned by delayed deliveries, incorrect alterations, goods damaged in delivery, and delivery of merchandise differing in size or color from that ordered.

Returns caused by store policies are many. The store may so encourage its salespeople to make sales that customers are "oversold." Or salespeople may suggest that the customer take home "on approval" one or more items in which she is somewhat interested, the hope being that she will decide to keep at least one; if she decides not to do so, she "can return the merchandise without any obligation." Too often, such a sales policy results in large returns. Easy credit policies encourage people to buy on credit, and returns are highest from credit customers.

The policy followed by many stores in accepting the great majority of returns without question also encourages returns. Some well-known companies, Marshall Field & Company, for instance, strongly favor a very liberal returns policy—recognizing that it encourages the customer to make purchases. Stores with such a policy, however, are few in number.

Customer Responsibility. Some customers "buy" merchandise for some special occasion, such as a wedding or a football weekend, and then return it afterwards. The blame for such returns is obvious. The customer is likewise responsible for returns occasioned by her change of mind as to price, color, quality, and style. To a large degree, she is also to blame for a significant part of the returns that stores experience on goods purchased as gifts for others. Such returns reach a peak in the days immediately following Christmas[23]—a peak which is accentuated by the practice of some retailers who, in an effort to build good will, advertise that they welcome exchanges.

[23] For evidence cf. Bernard Groger, "Stores Expect Many Returns After Best Yule," *Women's Wear Daily,* December 27, 1965, pp. 1, 36.

The Cost of Handling Returns

The cost of returned goods to the retailer may be suggested by examining certain expenses which are involved. In many cases, both deliveries and pickups are necessary. The goods have to be re-inspected, re-marked, and placed in stock again. Salespeople must devote additional time to resell returned merchandise. Markdowns are often required; a conservative estimate is that more than 50 percent of returned goods must be sold at a reduced price. Also, the store has a considerable sum invested in goods that are in the hands of customers but that will be returned to the store. Certainly, the interest on this investment should be considered as a cost of handling returned goods.

A study of one thousand typical returns made several years ago by George Plant of the National Retail Merchants Association revealed that the cost of handling each situation, including tracing, returning merchandise to stock, allowances given, and markdowns taken, was $1.08. With present-day high payroll costs and other operating expenses, the current cost would probably be double this amount. All in all, the total cost of handling returns is significant to the retailer.

Minimizing Returns of Merchandise

Returns Inevitable. Despite the high cost of retail returns, it is evident that they cannot be stopped. People will change their minds; and if one store refuses to accept returns, customers will shift to a store that is willing to extend this privilege. Floor coverings, furniture, and draperies cannot be judged so well by the customer in the retail store as they can in the home in which they are to be used. Many customers request that they be allowed to take such goods and return them if they are not suitable. Some delivery delays are inevitable. Hence, except for special events in which the retailer may specify that "all sales are final," he is not in a position to say simply, "No returns allowed."

Retailers are not too concerned when merchandise is returned within a three- to ten-day period, undamaged, with the price ticket intact, and accompanied by the sales check. Their main problems arise in connection with the return of merchandise that has been "out" for some time, that has to be remarked because the price ticket is gone, or for which there is no sales check. But even some returns of this nature are inevitable. The retailer's problem is to minimize returned goods and still keep the good will of his customers. How can this be done? Two approaches have been used: first, action by the individual store and, second, cooperative action by a group of retailers.

The Individual Store Approach.   Basically, the individual store program to minimize its returns must begin with the education of its own personnel. This program should set forth the steps necessary to reduce the internal causes of returns; and then proceed to acquaint the consuming public as to why these steps have been taken. If analysis reveals that returns are caused by merchandise defects and overpricing, the store should strive to improve its buying and selling. If unsatisfactory service causes returns, then steps should be taken to improve the service—to decrease delivery delays and merchandise damaged during delivery, to alter goods according to the customer's wants, and to equip salespeople to give accurate information concerning merchandise. Employees should be kept "return-conscious." If the store's policies of overselling and of "on-approval" sales are leading to a very high rate of returns, the logical thing to do is to modify these policies. A policy of making a charge for picking up returns may be used to replace a free pickup policy.

Saks Fifth Avenue, New York City, attempting to determine if a store with its quality appeal could limit returned-goods privileges, tried a new approach to the problem and started with its millinery department. After analyzing the returns carefully, it was decided to discontinue accepting them and the cooperation of buyers and salespeople was obtained. No formal announcement was made of the change in policy although signs were placed at fitting tables stating that millinery was not returnable. The same information was imprinted on sales checks by the charge plate device and customers were requested to sign the sales check as evidence of their knowledge of the policy. While some complaints were received from "chronic returners," net sales in the department showed no ill effects and returns dropped 80 percent and personnel was reduced 15 percent. Based on this success, a similar policy was adopted in other departments with satisfactory results.

Stores well intrenched in their communities may adopt policies which are not feasible for others. To illustrate: in such stores less than the full price may be refunded to cash customers or the refund may be made in merchandise certificates. This latter policy is used by some stores when merchandise is returned without sales checks but can be identified as actually having been purchased at the store. The use of merchandise certificates is based upon the theory that they will lead to the purchase of other merchandise in the store, whereas payment of cash will permit the customer to make purchases elsewhere. In some cases, as in the Saks Fifth Avenue illustration given above, retailers have attempted to make all sales final. It seems likely, however, that such a rigid rule will usually break down even when it has the support of other retailers in the area.

The Group Approach. Although the individual store can do much to reduce its returns, group action of the retailers within a given shopping area is often necessary for best results. The group can afford to do many things which the individual store cannot do. Also, some of the steps the individual retailer might take would merely drive his customers to competitors. To illustrate, many stores would like to reduce returns by making refunds on returned merchandise "a little harder to come by, but we don't dare. . . . Competition makes it impossible."[24] Group action, therefore, has the major advantages of making it easier to establish a sound educational program on the costliness of returns and of making it less difficult for individual stores to refuse returns because of the established "law" in the community governing such matters.

Realizing the advantages of group action, merchants in such cities as Dallas, Los Angeles, Kansas City, and Milwaukee have joined together to reduce returns. Such action usually involves agreement on one or more of the following points: establishing uniform time limits, setting up a standard policy of refusing to pick up certain merchandise for return, standardizing extra charges for return pickups, framing sanitary provisions and obtaining local ordinances involving sanitary considerations, activating educational campaigns and providing material for publicity drives, exchanging information about customers with records of excessive returns, and exchanging return-ratio data.

Despite the benefits that usually accrue from group action, two limitations of this method of reducing returns should be recognized. First, it is often difficult to reach an agreement on policies to be adopted. This problem is aggravated if the group is large and includes stores of different types offering a variety of services. Second, there is danger that suspicion will arise regarding the degree of compliance with the stated policies. Such suspicion can easily undermine the success of group efforts. Only when there is general compliance with the policies agreed upon among the cooperating stores can group action be made really effective in reducing returns.

SOME OTHER CUSTOMER SERVICES

In addition to the services we have already discussed, retailers furnish a wide variety of others, both income-producing and "free," designed to attract and hold customers. These customer services vary both among stores of different types and at different times. Briefly, a limited number of these services will now be considered.

---

[24] "Return Hangover Follows Christmas Buying Binge," *Women's Wear Daily*, December 30, 1965, p. 2.

Rentals

Renting of merchandise to customers is an example of an income-producing service that has grown rapidly among retailers during the past decade. In contrast to yesterday's renting of such items as formal wear, particularly for men, today the customer can rent power mowers, floor polishers, electric power tools, stapling guns, ladders, chain saws, and a host of other items. Many types of stores have established separate rental departments to meet the needs of their customers; while other retailers, such as those selling hardware, already believe that they have on their "shelves virtually every item that a prospective rental customer might ask for."[25]

Hardware retailers, and others who have entered the rental business, have been motivated by at least five basic factors: (1) the high profit potential when the operation is controlled effectively; (2) the absence of strong competition, since many chain and department stores continue to neglect the potential of renting;[26] (3) the additional sales produced by purchases of tools, both used and new; (4) the sales of related items—those designed to be used with the equipment rented; and (5) the overall store growth generated by new customers with needs for other merchandise and services.

Despite the growth of renting and the establishment of rental departments in many stores, the retailer's gains from offering a rental service are not automatically achieved. Before deciding to embark on the undertaking those operators considering a rental department should carefully weigh all the relevant factors including the following: (1) The size of the inventory investment required to provide a balanced stock of suitable merchandise; (2) the difficulty of displaying effectively a variety of used and unrelated items; (3) the setting of equitable rental rates; (4) the provision of adequate protection for the retailer, the customer, and the equipment or tools rented through proper insurance coverage; and (5) the establishment of proper controls over the issuance, care, and return of the rented items.

Personal Shopping Service[27]

Personal shopping service, one of the numerous "free" services, is illustrated by those retailers who advertise that they are equipped to give personal attention to all telephone or written communications. In some

---

[25] J. J. Sullivan, "Rentals Should Be Profitable—Not Just a Sideline," *Hardware Retailer*, May, 1966, p. 82. Also cf. F. A. Babione, "Retailer Adjustment to a Rental Economy," *Journal of Retailing*, Vol. XL, No. 3 (Fall, 1964), pp. 1–5, 48.

[26] Cf. "Sears Stops Rental Test," *Women's Wear Daily*, September 23, 1963, p. 23.

[27] Brief mention of personal shopping service as a form of sales promotion was made in Chapter 19, p. 561, above.

stores if the desired goods are not in stock, representatives of the shopping-service department will go out and find the merchandise. The service may be personalized by placing it under the name of an individual. To take a specific example, Marshall Field & Company has a large staff of shoppers to handle requests coming in by telephone and mail: Yet most of its personal shopping requests are addressed to "Pauline Shaw" (P for personal, S for shopping) and mail-order requests to "Mary Owen" (M for mail, O for order).[28] Many retailers, either on a year-around basis or just at such a peak selling period as before Christmas, also employ a number of especially well-trained salespeople who are available to customers upon request. These salespeople will accompany customers from department to department to assist in making selections. In some stores, these persons are called "escort shoppers" to distinguish them from "personal shoppers" who perform the shopping service as a result of written or telephone communications.

Personal shopping service is offered especially by large department and departmentalized specialty stores, but it is of growing importance in other stores. As a matter of fact, business conducted by the shopping-service division is increasing rapidly, and stores are competing seriously for it.

Helping Customers to Find Merchandise

The large majority of small retailers find it unnecessary to do more than provide salespeople to aid the customer in finding what she wants. But as the size of the store increases, the problem of helping customers to find what they want becomes more complicated. All of the merchandise may not be on one floor, or the sales floor may be so large—as in the modern supermarket and discount house—that all the merchandise cannot be seen from any one spot. Under these conditions, several steps may be taken to aid customers. The salespeople may be trained in answering customers' questions as to where certain goods are located; signs can be placed over each department or category of merchandise, as is done by most variety store retailers and supermarkets; store directories may be placed near the main entrance to the store or in and near the elevators; elevator operators may be trained so that they can direct customers to the various departments; and floormen and information booths may be provided to direct customers.

Supplying Merchandise Information

With customers demanding more and better information concerning merchandise than ever before, retailers are taking steps to provide improved

[28] Some firms also use fictitious names for handling complaints. Cf. Lee Berton, "Personal-But Phony: Some Firms Sign Fake Names to Their Letters," *Wall Street Journal,* August 10, 1966, p. 1.

data. Some large-scale operators have their own testing bureaus as a source of this information. Thus, R. H. Macy & Company has its Bureau of Standards and Sears, Roebuck and Co. has its merchandise laboratory.[29] Smaller retail organizations are making greater use of commercial testing firms; and both large and small retailers are asking their sources of supply to furnish them with more detailed information on such factors as fastness of color, shrinkage, and washability. When these data are received, they are passed on to salespeople for the purpose of improving selling efforts. In an increasing number of cases, at least part of this information is placed on labels attached to the merchandise.[30]

Accepting C.O.D. Orders

Many retailers sell some merchandise on a c.o.d. basis. Buying c.o.d. is especially convenient for the customer who places an order by mail or telephone and who does not have a charge account at the store. But because of the problems involved in handling such transactions many stores now add an extra fee for this service.

In addition to the expense of handling them, c.o.d.'s also result in a high percentage of returns—almost double that of cash and charge sales. Because of this fact some stores now refuse to accept c.o.d. orders unless a down payment is made or unless the total order is in excess of a specified amount.

Community Service Activities

Distinct from the kinds of customer services already discussed are the community-service activities engaged in by an increasing number of retailers. These services reflect the growing social consciousness that has developed during recent years among retailers in this country and, although in less degree, abroad.[31]

"Retailing Serves America" Awards. Convinced that community-service activities deserved encouragement and recognition, in 1961 the National Retail Merchants Association in cooperation with the *Reader's Digest* inaugurated the Retailing Serves America awards. The following year the same sponsors introduced the International Community Service competition.

The purpose of these awards is to provide public recognition of signifi-

---

[29] Cf. the previous discussion of these testing bureaus on pp. 331–32, above. For an institutional advertisement calling attention to the Quality Testing Laboratories of the Great Atlantic & Pacific Tea Co., cf. *New York Times,* March 21, 1966, p. 16.

[30] Cf. p. 554, above.

[31] On this subject cf. J. M. Patterson, "What are the Social and Ethical Responsibilities of Marketing Executives," *Journal of Marketing,* Vol. XXX, No. 3 (July, 1966), pp. 12–15.

cant contributions to community welfare by retailers of all types and sizes.[32] Awards are given in four different categories and the judges base their decisions primarily on the sincerity of purpose and the effectiveness of the community-service programs undertaken by the contestants. The categories include (1) stores with annual sales under $5 million, (2) retailers with sales of $5 to $25 million, (3) firms with sales over $25 million, and (4) stores outside the United States.

The kinds of community-service activities considered for awards are illustrated by the following: voter registration, community health programs, scholarships and charitable efforts in a Negro area, consumer education for home economics teachers, vocational training seminars, employment of the mentally retarded, fund raising for a working boys' home, and maintenance of a cultural center in the store for exhibitions of local talent in the arts.[33]

CHARGING FOR SERVICES

As we have noted,[34] many customer services are considered "free" because the retailer makes no separate charge for them and all customers pay the same prices whether or not they take advantage of the services. Other services, however, produce income (and profits) for the store: Thus it is common for retailers of women's clothing—and to an increasing extent men's clothing—to make a specific charge for alterations. A number of stores make a charge for delivery service, especially on small orders. Some merchants consider the store restaurant or tearoom as a customer service. Although a charge is made for the meals served, it may be made so low that the restaurant cannot possibly operate at a profit. These retailers are willing to continue the restaurant on such a basis because it attracts many people to the store; and while there, they purchase other goods. In fact, the restaurant service is partly "free," that is, paid for in the price of merchandise, and partly subject to a separate charge.

To Charge or Not to Charge

Probably one of the main reasons why some retailers have established rental departments is their desire to offset the increasing costs of the so-called "free" services and their inability to obtain the higher prices necessary to

---

[32] That community service yields important benefits is shown by the experience of a chain organization in Seattle. Cf. "Community Service Works Wonders for Seattle Chain," *Super Market Merchandising*, February, 1966, pp. 39–40.

[33] Samuel Feinberg, "Retailers' Social Consciousness at High Mark," *Women's Wear Daily*, November 9, 1965, p. 12. On the social responsibilities of business corporations in general cf. R. A. Wright, "Beyond the Profits: Business Reaches for a Social Role," *New York Times*, July 3, 1966, pp. F1, F16.

[34] Cf. p. 591, above.

offset these rising expenses because of competitive forces. Consequently, they have welcomed the opportunity to add additional services on a pricing basis that yield sufficient income to improve their profit picture.

Other retailers, however, reluctant to add income-producing services to their merchandising mix, have attempted to minimize the "free" services offered as one step in their cost-reduction programs. But they recognize that competition among retailers is a competition of services as well as merchandise. Consequently, they are weighing the value of such services rather carefully in the light of the higher prices they make necessary and the reactions of customers to these prices. The competition of the discount house and of self-service and self-selection stores with advertised savings to the customer has forced this reconsideration. It is likely, also, that retailers are increasingly aware of the fact that many customers are willing to pay directly for certain services they use. It is probable, therefore, that the current trends toward establishing income-producing service departments, charging (at least, in part) for some "free" services, and performing such services in less costly ways, will continue.

Certainly, the retailer should review with considerable caution the customer services he is furnishing and undertake additional ones only after scrutinizing several factors. What do customers expect in the way of service? What will the service cost? Can the store charge for the service, or offer it "free" and still retain its existing price policies? Are the store's customers of the type and income group which require the service? What are competitors doing? Is the service well adapted to the type of merchandise the store is selling? Even the retailer who is already offering services should evaluate each service in view of these same questions. Without doubt, a careful analysis along these lines will lead certain merchants to the conclusion that they are offering too many services, whereas others will decide to add still others.

REVIEW AND DISCUSSION QUESTIONS

1. Without reference to the textbook, define "customer services." In the light of your definition, explain what is meant by the expression "customer services are a form of nonprice competition."
2. Summarize the main guides available to the retailer in establishing his customer service policies.
3. How do you account for the wide variety of services offered by retailers? Why do some stores offer many services not provided by their competitors?
4. In your judgment, what factors are responsible for the growing interest of retailers in "income-producing" services? Explain.

5. How may the usual practice of charging for alterations in women's clothing and not charging for them in men's clothing be explained and defended?
6. Three major methods of wrapping merchandise are used in retail stores. Summarize the merits and limitations of each and indicate the conditions under which it should be used.
7. Distinguish among the major types of delivery systems and indicate the conditions under which each one might be used to advantage.
8. If you are in or near a city using the United Parcel System of delivery, visit the System's center of operations and ask one of its executives to explain the reasons for its growth.
9. Prepare a list of the chief causes of customer complaints in retail stores, classifying them into logical groups that will aid in finding solutions.
10. Discuss the relative merits of handling complaints in both small and large stores (a) by the salesperson and (b) in a central office.
11. Suggest several methods by which the percentage of returns may be reduced. Which methods do you believe have the best chances for success?
12. Some retailers believe that fixing specific responsibility for returns is one of the best ways of minimizing them. Suggest ways of assigning such responsibility to accomplish this goal.
13. Discuss the pros and cons of establishing a rental department in a hardware store.
14. How do you account for the growth in community service activities by retailers? Visit a few local retailers and ascertain their attitude toward this development.
15. Discuss the statement: "It is foolish to argue the wisdom of charging or not charging for customer services. In our present affluent society customers are able and willing to pay for the services they receive and expect to do so. The rapid growth of 'income-producing' services is evidence of this fact."

SUPPLEMENTARY READINGS

BABIONE, F. A. "Retailer Adjustment to a Rental Economy," *Journal of Retailing,* Vol. XL, No. 3 (Fall, 1964), pp. 1–5, 48. Although the author believes that "retailers should be able to adapt readily to rental business," he concludes they "have not (yet) ventured far" into this growing area of customer service.

COLE, H. G. *For Gracious Giving* (New York: Fairchild Publications, Inc., 1962). The author outlines the principles and practices for a gift-wrapping service in the store.

Hardware Retailer, May, 1966, pp. 82–99. In a related series of nine brief articles under the title "Rent It," important aspects of the rental problem are treated.

MOSBACKER, ERIC. "An Analysis of the Causes of Dress Returns to a Department Store in New York City," *New York Retailer,* May, 1966, pp. 11–18. This analysis is based on a careful study of a sample of returns. After determining the reasons for the returns, recommendations are presented to reduce them.

NATIONAL RETAIL MERCHANTS ASSOCIATION. *Customer Services Provided by Department and Specialty Stores* (New York: The Association, 1964). Summarizing 80 service practices in 340 stores classified according to annual sales, this study emphasizes the procedure involved in evaluating a service. Also cf. *Speeding Selling Service* (1962), which offers suggestions for improving service on the sales floor.

Parking Requirements for Shopping Centers (Washington, D.C.: Urban Land Institute, Technical Bulletin No. 53, 1965). Based on a study of 270 centers, this monograph suggests guide lines for determining the parking requirements of tenants.

"Tires, Batteries, Auto Accessories: One Example of How Chains Explore New Horizons," *Chain Store Age* (Executives Edition), January, 1964, pp. 13 ff. One form of expanding services to customers is detailed in this article.

VALDES, E. C. "Cash Refund Policies," *Retail Control,* April, 1962, pp. 31–36. Based on a questionnaire returned by 21 Los Angeles retailers, the author reports their policies on refunds for merchandise returns.

WEISS, E. B. "Does the Rising Demand for Services Cut Merchandise Sales?", *Advertising Age,* September 9, 1963, pp. 110 ff. This provocative discussion gives some of the reasons for the growth of services and their effect on sales volume.

22
CHAPTER

Retail Credit

As noted in the previous chapter, the granting of credit is a service demanded by an ever-growing number of customers. In fact, buying on credit has become such a well-established practice in American economic life that some observers use the phrase "credit economy." And with good reason: consumer credit is presently at the highest level in our history[1] and continues to grow despite actions by governmental agencies to limit its expansion.[2] Today millions of consumers buy from retail stores upon no other security than the confidence of the seller in their ability to meet their financial obligations when they become due. Retail stores promote credit sales through such measures as the active solicitation of "regular" and installment charge accounts; the development of such credit plans as "revolving credit" and "option terms"; better follow-up on inactive accounts; and improvements in methods of authorizing credit transactions. In brief, so important is retail credit to present-day retailing that it merits our careful study.

TYPES OF RETAIL CREDIT

Retail credit, also known as consumer credit, may be defined as present purchasing power based upon the confidence of the seller in the buyer's ability to pay his bills as they mature. For many years it commonly assumed two forms insofar as the retail store was concerned: open-account credit and installment credit. However, recent decades have witnessed the growth of

---

[1] Cf. the discussion in Chapter 1, pp. 13–14; and "I.O.U.," *Women's Wear Daily*, July 5, 1966, pp. 1, 30.

[2] Cf. B. A. Curran, *Trends in Consumer Credit Legislation* (Chicago: University of Chicago Press, 1965).

such additional forms as revolving credit, option-terms credit, and other variations in the original two basic types.

Open-Account Credit

When goods and services are sold on regular or open-account credit, they are turned over to the buyer before any payment is made and without requiring the buyer to pledge his purchases or any other assets as collateral. Although no definite payment date may be mentioned when the actual transaction takes place, it is generally understood that payment shall take place within ten days following the receipt of the bill. Bills are sent out monthly, often on a staggered or cycle basis. In practice, however, some payments are likely to be delayed; and this delay gives rise to the collection problem, to be discussed later in this chapter.

Although open-account credit involves some expenses which are avoided in cash sales, this service is quite typically offered "free" to the customer; that is, no separate charge is made for it. To an increasing extent, however, as noted in the discussion which follows, retailers are adding a "service" charge on past-due accounts to cover part of the cost involved and to encourage prompt payment of obligations.

Basis of Open-Account Credit. In stores of all sizes, open-account credit is usually extended on the basis of information as to a person's character, capacity, and capital. By his character is meant his willingness to pay his obligations. This willingness to pay is the most important factor in personal credit, and a good character rating will usually result in a person's obtaining credit even though his capacity and capital are limited. Character is indicated by such things as the number of years a person has lived in a rented house (the assumption being that he must be fairly regular in his rent payments to hold the house), his payment record with other retailers, and the community's judgment as to his honesty.

Whereas character indicates a person's willingness to pay, capacity refers to his ability to pay out of current income. In the case of a married woman who is not employed in some wage-earning job, the creditor checks on capacity by securing information about the husband: the husband's position, the number of years he has been in the same position, and his income—its size, stability, and rate of increase or decrease.

A second indication of ability to pay is offered by a person's capital, that is, his financial resources or assets. In judging capital, information is needed on ownership of physical property and securities. Such knowledge is of aid in setting credit limits, since it shows a store how far it can go in forcing payment if this should become necessary.

Installment Credit[3]

Among retailers installment credit is usually distinguished from open-account credit by the following: (1) a down payment is made upon purchase; (2) additional payments are made on a number of dates, which are specifically set at the time of purchase; (3) some security is required (typically, the goods purchased); (4) a separate charge is made for the credit extended; and (5) a written contract is used. However, in practice there are some exceptions to all these statements. Thus, the up-to-three-year "home modernizing" terms offered by many retailers typically require neither a down payment nor a pledging of the merchandise as security. Actually, the fundamental distinction between open-account and installment credit is that the latter involves a series of payments to be made on definitely set dates.

In contrast with open-account credit, which is usually considered as "free" so that the customer must rely on a comparison of prices between the credit and the cash store to discover what the credit service is costing, the cost to the customer of buying on installment credit can definitely be ascertained. One simple way of doing this is to inquire as to the total sums which must be paid, first, if cash is paid and, second, if the installment plan is used. For example, although variations exist among the kinds of goods bought and according to the amount purchased, the "payment table" of Sears, Roebuck and Co. shows that on purchases from $50.01 to $60.00 an additional $6.00 is charged for "easy payments" under the installment plan.[4]

Revolving Credit

During recent years "revolving credit" has been widely adopted by retail stores, particularly the larger ones.[5] Sears introduced this plan in 1953 and it now accounts for over 28 percent of the firm's total sales.[6] Montgomery Ward also does a significant percentage of its sales on this basis. Incorporating features of both open-account and installment credit, the objective of revolving credit is one flexible account covering all purchases except high-priced major appliances.

---

[3] For valuable information on this topic, cf. P. W. McCracken, *Consumer Installment Credit and Public Policy* (Ann Arbor, Mich.; University of Michigan, Bureau of Business Research, 1965).

[4] These terms were offered by the Company in its 1966 Spring and Summer Catalog, p. 425.

[5] Among multiunit groups in the hardware field, over 48 percent extend credit on this basis. "How Multiple Stores Buy and Sell," *Hardware Retailer,* June, 1966, p. 79.

[6] Sears, Roebuck and Co., *Annual Report,* for the year ended December 31, 1965, p. 6.

Specifically, revolving credit is an arrangement under which the retailer fixes the credit limit of the customer, permits her to make full use of this credit limit at all times, and gives the customer the choice of payment within thirty days or on an installment basis. Suppose, for example, that the credit limit is set at $200. The customer may purchase goods of this amount at one time and pay in full in thirty days or she may extend her payments for a longer period, typically six months but up to ten months is fairly common. If she elects to do the latter, a "service" charge of 1½ percent per month on the balance is added to her account. She may make additional purchases at any time up to her credit limit but, unless the bill is paid within the thirty-day period, the service charge is added.

The growth of revolving credit had a direct influence on the open-account terms offered by an increasing number of retailers. Some of them now add a similar service charge on all balances which remain unpaid after they are due; that is, they make a charge on past-due accounts. This practice, of course, is not new but it was little used prior to the development of revolving credit. Likewise, revolving credit has been used by some retailers to replace installment credit, that is, they will sell everything under the newer program.

The "Option-Terms" Plan

Another recent credit development is the so-called "option-terms" plan. Under this arrangement the "regular" or "open-account" customer has the option of paying her bill in full each month without a charge for credit service or of making a down payment (which is not required in the revolving-credit plan) followed by partial payments over a period of time. If she chooses to do the latter, then at least 25 percent of the amount of the purchases must be paid immediately and a carrying charge—commonly 1 or 1½ percent—is added to her account during each of the following months to compensate the store for this privilege. Many retailers consider this arrangement to be "ideal" and one which most retailers extending credit will ultimately adopt.

Other Types of Retail Credit

Without going into details, several other credit plans can be mentioned. The "90-day" or "3-pay" plan used for men's and women's clothing typically requires a one-third down payment with the balance split into three equal amounts payable over a period of three months. A service charge may or may not be added. "Ten-pay" and "twenty-pay" plans are also in use, but they are paid off in ten or twenty weeks, not months. Under "coupon book" plans the customer's credit limit is given to her in the form of a book of coupons which she spends as cash in the store. Advertised as providing "instant credit" to their users, these coupon books appeal chiefly to consumers who cannot qualify for other types of credit or who like the convenience of the coupon. Books are available in denominations of $25, $50, and $100, with individual coupons valued at 50 cents, $1, $2, and $5, and payments are made on a monthly basis.[7]

Consumer Credit Agencies

Although the present discussion is concerned mainly with credit and its problems from the point of view of the retail store, we should recognize that many goods are bought at retail on credit that is not extended by the retailer. To cite a few examples: Credit unions—cooperatives organized to extend small loans to members—have developed as an important source of funds for many persons who wish to buy on credit. Increasingly, banks are advertising their small-loan business, and many of these loans are arranged so that they can be repaid in small payments running over a period of some length. Some commercial banks even take over practically all of the credit-granting functions of the retailer—serving, in effect, as the "credit department" for a number of retailers in a community.[8] In a few cases, Morris Plan Banks have been established in the stores so that the stores' customers may borrow at the bank and use the funds for purchases rather than get credit from the store. The sales finance company, which is so important in the extension of credit for the sale of automobiles and other goods, is still another example of a nonretailer source of credit.

IMPORTANCE OF CREDIT SALES TO THE RETAILER

The importance of credit sales to the retailer is evidenced by three major factors: (1) the increasing volume of such sales; (2) the effectiveness of credit as a producer of sales; and (3) the usefulness of credit extension as a competitive weapon.

Increasing Volume of Retail Credit Sales

Total consumer credit outstanding has grown from $42 billion in 1956 to $88 billion in 1966.[9] Of this amount installment credit comprised $69

---

[7] "5 Newberry Units Offering Credit in Coupon Books, *"Women's Wear Daily,* April 13, 1966, p. 2.

[8] Cf. the discussion on pp. 641–43, below.

[9] Federal Reserve System data, *Economic Indicators,* May, 1966, p. 32.

billion ($29 billion of this was automobile paper) and noninstallment credit $19 billion. Widely used by all income groups and for the sale of all kinds of merchandise and services, consumer credit outstanding will probably continue to increase in the years ahead. So rapidly have people gone into debt that some of them have ended up in bankruptcy. Many retailers are concerned over the growing movement to offer charge accounts to teenagers and young adults, but others are finding that losses are not excessive and that the practice helps build sales volume.[10] However, all credit-conscious retailers share the belief that in our highly dynamic economy close control over all credit accounts is essential.[11]

Apparently about one out of every three retail firms offers to sell on credit. Of our entire retail volume, about one third is transacted on a credit basis, with installment sales accounting for about one third of the credit business and open-account credit (plus such modifications as revolving credit and option terms) making up the remaining two thirds.

Of course the importance of credit sales varies widely according to the type of merchandise handled by the retailer. Because of heavy sales on installment credit, over two thirds of all sales in furniture, household appliance, and jewelry stores are on credit. For department and specialty stores, credit accounts for 58 percent of total sales.[12] Among 95 multiunit hardware retailers operating 245 stores in 1965, 42 percent of the firms did 41 percent or more of their total sales volume on credit.[13] At the other extreme, practically all sales of variety stores and well over 80 percent of all food store sales are for cash.[14] Among discount firms, a preliminary study by a trade magazine revealed that 15 of the 32 reporting had credit sales averaging 13 percent of total sales.[15] Within fairly comparable fields, even competitors have different ratios of sales on credit to total sales. To illustrate, credit accounts for 47 percent of Montgomery Ward sales, while Sears, Roebuck has 58 percent on this basis.[16]

[10] Cf. "Sears Lowers Credit Barriers," *Women's Wear Daily,* November 20, 1965, p. 23; and "Teens Are Credit to Credit Scheme," *ibid.,* March 8, 1966, p. 16.

[11] Cf. "Is Credit Quality Getting Too Low?" *Business Week,* October 2, 1965, pp. 75–80.

[12] G. P. Samit, "1964 Credit Department Operating Results," in 1965–1966 *Credit Management Yearbook* (New York: National Retail Merchants Association, 1965), pp. 125.

[13] "How Multiple Stores Buy and Sell," *op. cit.,* p. 79.

[14] Cf., however, E. B. Weiss, "Food Must Be Sold On Credit," *Advertising Age,* January 4, 1965, p. 68; and "Groceries on the Cuff give Boost to Sales," *Business Week,* August 20, 1966, p. 134.

[15] "A Quick Look at Use of Credit Plans," *Discount Merchandiser,* February, 1966, pp. 54–56.

[16] Montgomery Ward & Co., Inc., *Annual Report* for year ended February 2, 1966, p. 18; and Sears, Roebuck and Co. *Annual Report* for year ended December 31, 1965, p. 6.

Retail Credit Increases Sales

Experience reveals, to quote one authority, that "charge accounts are one of the most powerful and profitable influences on sales in modern merchandising."[17] The rapid growth of some retailers—Aldens and Spiegel are well-known illustrations, but many communities have less widely-known retailers who likewise rely on credit promotions—is due largely to the emphasis which they have placed on easy credit terms. Invitations for credit purchases at such retail establishments are widely circulated by direct mail, over radio and television, through newspapers, and by periodic catalogs. Some of these firms rely so heavily on their earnings from credit accounts that they are often referred to as "finance companies which also have merchandise for sale."[18] But even retailers placing less emphasis on credit terms still find that credit builds business. This result may be attributed to the fact that customers usually expect and often demand credit service, that it affords the retailer a valuable contact with his customers, and that it aids him in building a current mailing list. In addition, the credit department itself acts as a sales agency.

Customers Expect and Demand Credit.[19] Customer demand for credit arises, in part, from the fact that it makes their buying more pleasant. Credit makes it unnecessary for customers to carry appreciable sums of money while on shopping trips. It frees patrons from limiting their purchases to those they had planned to make before they left home. Most stores are more willing to let credit customers take goods on approval. Buying on credit facilitates merchandise returns, since the store merely credits the customer's account. It aids buying by the telephone. Children or servants may be sent to the store to make purchases without the risk of entrusting money to their care.

The demand for credit service also arises because many people—for example, farmers with annual crops, teachers, government employees, and others with monthly checks—find it necessary to buy on credit during a part of the period between the dates on which their income is received. Many

---

[17] Ralf Shockey, "Selling is a Science! Part V: The Credit Bonanza," *Department Store Economist,* August, 1965, p. 30. The author suggests some practical ways of promoting credit sales.

[18] As a means of expanding their investments in consumer credit, some of the finance companies have bought into retail organizations. Thus Beneficial Finance Co. now controls Western Auto Supply Co.

[19] On this subject cf. R. D. Breth, "A Charge Account is a Many Splendored Thing," *Retail Control,* January, 1965, pp. 16–27; and R. M. Grinager, "What the Buyer Should Know About Credit," *The Buyer's Manual* (4th ed.; New York: National Retail Merchants Association, 1965), p. 372.

people who desire television sets, electric refrigerators, and expensive clothing find themselves without sufficient funds to make their purchases. If credit is not provided by a particular retailer, he merely drives potential customers to a competitor.

Affords a Contact with Customers. A customer who has a credit account with a store is likely to be a more steady customer and, hence, to buy a greater proportion of his goods from one source than the cash customer.[20] Although it is difficult to prove this statement satisfactorily, the experience of many retailers has convinced them that it is true. The case of a small hardware retailer in Dayton, Ohio, is illustrative. An analysis of his charge accounts revealed that the average credit customer spent with him $205 annually, far above the average for his cash customers.[21] On an annual basis, Aldens typical credit customer purchases three times as much as does the cash buyer.[22] Moreover, Aldens finds that the "drop outs" (those who cease regular buying) are four times as great among cash customers as compared with those buying on credit.

Aids in Building a Mailing List. Credit also acts as a producer of sales by providing the store with a selected mailing list. This list is significant for promotional purposes, since it is composed of persons who think well enough of the store to have taken the trouble to open a charge account. Having exact information as to the people trading at a store helps the retailer to get advertisements and announcements of special sales into their hands at a minimum of expense. By well-planned and consistent use of this list a retailer may increase his sales substantially.

The Credit Department as a Sales Agency. In addition to the general sales-increasing advantages of credit extension which have been discussed in the preceding paragraphs, the credit department itself is a valuable sales agency. The department's philosophy should be that of "how can credit be used to increase the store's sales." As one observer suggests, the credit department should be marketed just like the retailer's merchandise and other services.[23] Its effectiveness as a sales agency will reflect (1) the imagination and judgment exercised in the opening of new accounts, (2) the wisdom shown in the handling of active accounts, and (3) the ingenuity and skill demonstrated in the reopening of inactive accounts.

---

[20] Cash customers, of course, often resent the implications of this fact and make protests against the superior treatment in regard to special services accorded the credit customer.

[21] Cf. "How Much is a Credit Customer Worth?" *Hardware Retailer,* December, 1965, p. 48.

[22] *Aldens Annual Report* for the year ended January 31, 1964, p. 7.

[23] Robert Bartels, "Credit Management as a Marketing Function," *Credit and Financial Management,* May, 1965, pp. 14–15 ff. Also cf. T. V. Greer and C. G. Walters, "Credit Records: Information Tool for Planning," *Journal of Retailing,* Vol. XLII, No. 3 (Fall, 1966), pp. 11–18, 51.

Consider the charge accounts which have become inactive because former customers have transferred their purchases elsewhere. Telephone calls or letters showing an interest in them may be helpful in bringing them back to the store. Or they may be sent a regular monthly statement form with a "come-on" invitation where the itemized list would normally appear. Figure 22–1 illustrates this technique as used by one progressive retailer.

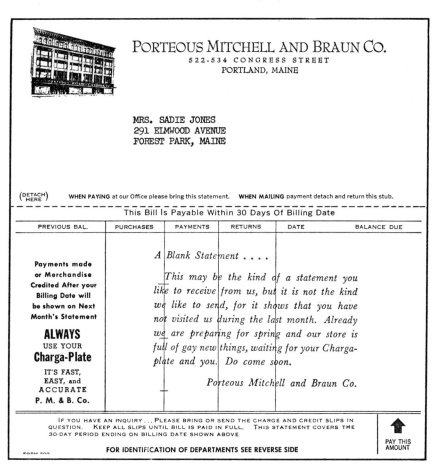

FIG. 22–1.   Use of credit department mailing list to stimulate sales.

Competitive Pressure to Extend Retail Credit

Another factor which demonstrates the importance of credit sales to the retailer is their value as a competitive weapon. In certain fields, such a large part of all sales volume is on a credit basis that customers have come to expect credit accommodation as a matter of course. In these fields, competition practically forces the retailer to extend credit or retire from business, as is true in the sale of furniture, household appliances, and television sets. Of particular interest in this connection, also, is the fact that certain well-known stores, famous for their "cash-and-carry" policies, are turning to credit selling. For example, in 1958 the J. C. Penney Company introduced selling on credit in a few of its stores; today credit is available in all Penney stores and accounts for over 33 percent of the firm's annual business.[24]

PROBLEMS OF SELLING ON CREDIT

Although selling on credit has its advantages, some major problems arise in connection with it. Three of these will be considered: (1) the costs connected therewith; (2) the influence of credit extension on prices and profits; and (3) the management problems involved.

Credit Costs

Selling on credit involves a store in certain costs which are avoided in sales for cash. These costs are made up mainly of three factors—the pay of the personnel involved, losses from bad debts, and the interest cost on the funds tied up. Although variations exist among different types of stores and among stores with different annual sales, the common cost figure for handling credit and accounts receivable in department stores in 1965 was 1.53 percent of sales.[25] Automation of some credit operations may eventually have some effect on this cost ratio but probably not enough to reduce it by any significant amount.[26]

Despite the care with which credit is extended, some losses are inevitable. In the smaller stores, where the personal relationship of proprietor and customer causes the proprietor to be less careful in granting credit and less willing to apply pressure in making collections, losses of from $\frac{1}{2}$ to 2 percent on credit sales are common. Representing the larger retailers, Sears' losses average about $\frac{3}{4}$ of 1 percent on credit sales, while Carson Pirie Scott's Chicago store experienced a comparable figure of one percent in

---

[24] *Annual Report* for the year ended January 31, 1966, p. 12. The Company presently is making a strong appeal to "young moderns" as users of its credit facilities. States an announcement by this firm: "In our present economy of abundance it is more important than ever for young people to learn thrift and sound money management. A good reputation for financial responsibility, established early, will be a valuable asset all their lives. . . ."

[25] Sam Flanel, *Financial and Operating Results of Department and Specialty Stores in 1965* (New York: National Retail Merchants Association, 1966), p. ix.

[26] Cf. the discussion on pp. 630–32, below.

1965.[27] Although it is not typical of retailers in general, an indication of the interest cost on funds is afforded by the fact that some retailers find themselves carrying accounts which are two or three times the value of the goods they have in stock.

There is some evidence that credit extension adds to operating cost by stimulating merchandise returns. This result is understandable since a customer is more willing to take out several items when he does not have to lay down the cash for them. Consequently, part of the cost of handling returns must be charged to the cost of extending credit.

The costs of installment credit are even larger than those for open-account credit. Since open-account customers are likely to keep their accounts active for several months or even years, one credit investigation may result in the opening of an account that produces a considerable volume of business. In contrast, installment credit customers shift more from store to store so that more money per dollar of sales must be spent in credit investigations. Bad debt losses on installments run even larger than for open-account credit. Moreover, the tracing of goods to be repossessed involves considerable expense, and the period over which payments are made is longer for installment sales, so that additional expense is involved in carrying the account.

Impact of Credit Extension on Prices and Profits

In view of the additional costs incurred when credit sales are made, one might conclude that, if credit stores are to make as large profits as cash stores, they require a larger markup to cover their higher costs. This conclusion is not necessarily true but is only one of several possible results from credit extension. For example, it is possible that, as a result of offering credit, the sales of a store will rise. The larger sales may enable the store to "spread" certain overhead costs so that the granting of credit may not increase its total cost-to-sales ratio. Hence, its former profit margin would be retained; and because of more business, greater total net profits would be achieved.[28]

Another possible result of credit extension is that the cost-to-sales ratio may rise somewhat so that, without increasing prices, the profit ratio will fall. However, the smaller net profit margin, when multiplied by the new total sales figure, may give a larger aggregate profit than was secured previously by a larger net profit margin and smaller sales.

---

[27] "Ask Prechecks on Credit Data," *Women's Wear Daily*, March 11, 1966, p. 22.

[28] Cf. Leonard Marks, Jr., "Six Steps to Profit Through Credit," *Credit and Financial Management*, August, 1965, pp. 10–13.

In spite of these other possibilities, however, it is probably true that credit selling is accompanied by somewhat higher cost ratios, higher prices, greater sales, smaller net profit margins, and larger total dollar profits.

Credit Management Problems

When a store sells on credit, accounts must be solicited; and someone must decide who is to get credit, in what amount it is to be granted, the time during which it is to be extended, and how collections shall be handled, including delinquent accounts and those involving customer bankruptcies. Credit extension also involves management in the problems of providing the additional working capital required, conforming to credit regulations established by the government, and deciding on the extent to which credit operations will be computerized. Briefly, let us examine some of these problems.

Promoting Credit Accounts. Since the cost of placing the average new charge account on the store's books is returned several times in profit, it is clear why retailers actively solicit charge accounts. Salespeople may be instructed to suggest to their cash customers the advantages of a charge account. By means of telephone or direct mail the retailer may solicit prospective credit customers chosen from membership lists of women's clubs, telephone directories, taxpayers' lists, and similar sources. Stores also make use of newspaper, radio, television, and direct-mail advertising to emphasize the conveniences of charge accounts and the ease with which such accounts may be secured.

Credit Standards. The person entrusted with the problems of deciding which customers shall be given credit and in what amounts—the proprietor in the small store, the bookkeeper or a head salesman in the somewhat larger store, and the credit manager in the medium-size and large organization—finds himself in a dilemma. If he sets low credit standards, a greater increase in sales may be secured than will result under more conservative extension of credit. Low standards, however, also entail greater debt losses, heavier collection expenses, and more personnel in the credit department. High credit standards reduce these cost elements but, as we have just noted, check the expansion of sales. The credit manager then faces the question: From the point of view of the store's total net profits, would it be better to liberalize our credit terms, thereby expanding sales but incurring a heavier credit cost; or should we be conservative and take smaller sales, thereby cutting our credit cost? Striking the balance so as to maximize the store's net profits is the job of the credit manager.

Credit Counselling Service. Motivated by their awareness of the need for improving consumers' knowledge of credit availability and the obligations it involves, but primarily concerned about the growing number of personal bankruptcies,[29] major retailers are joining with banks, finance companies, and chambers of commerce to set up and finance comprehensive educational programs through free credit counselling service bureaus. Twenty-three such bureaus are already in existence, most of them on a non-profit basis, and others are in the planning stage.

These counselling bureaus are providing valuable guidance to consumers through educational programs dealing with the economics of credit, and also in arranging prorating plans for the orderly settlement of debts in complicated situations where the individual needs assistance. They accept referrals by retailers for assistance in cases such as the following: "(1) When a check of the credit (or loan) application shows the person to be in, or heading for, financial trouble; (2) when a customer becomes seriously delinquent on an account or note; and (3) when employers receive garnishment notices on an employee."[30] As a step to reduce the number of consumer bankruptcies and to provide greater protection to the creditors when such emergencies develop, these bureaus have a significant role to play in a "credit economy."

Douglas Bill. Still additional credit management problems will be created for the retailer if the Douglas Bill is eventually passed. For several years Congress has been considering this proposal, sometimes referred to by its supporters as the "truth-in-lending" bill. If passed, it would require that all credit charges be stated both in dollars and as an annual interest rate in percentage terms. Most retailers object strenuously to the annual interest rate feature of the bill on the grounds that (1) the credit charge is not true interest on money but covers many other costs as well, (2) the rate is costly to compute for all items sold, and (3) the unscrupulous merchant could escape the impact of the bill by making no direct credit charge but raise his merchandise price to include credit cost.

With the Douglas Bill still before Congress, on November 1, 1966 Massachusetts became the first state to require full disclosure of simple interest rates on all installment credit agreements.[31] Considered by some to be even stronger than the Douglas proposal, the Massachusetts law came

---

[29] In 1965 bankruptcy petitions in the United States, 90 percent of them personal, reached an all-time high for the thirteenth consecutive year. In California alone, which has 8.8 percent of the nation's population and 11.4 percent of its disposable income, there were 30,197 personal bankruptcies in 1965, or 18.5 percent of the total for the United States. William McNeill, "Credit Aid Service Taking Wing in Southern California," *Women's Wear Daily,* April 6, 1966, p. 14. Also cf. "Chicago Bankruptcies Spawn Free Debt Management Group," *ibid.,* December 13, 1965, p. 6; and "I.O.U.," *op. cit.*

[30] McNeill, *op. cit.* Also cf. "Credit Management," *Stores,* March, 1966, pp. 45–47, for a discussion of retailers' contributions to these bureaus.

[31] Cf. "Some Victories for Truth-in-Lending," *Consumer Reports,* August, 1966, pp. 394–95.

under immediate attack from the Boston Retail Trade Board for the reasons mentioned in the preceding paragraph. As for other states, many of them place a ceiling on interest charges, while California requires retailers using revolving credit to report their credit charges to all applicants.

Automating the Credit Function. Another major credit management problem facing retailers today, particularly the larger ones, concerns the advisability of computerizing their credit operations. Together with the electronic processing of data to improve merchandise management responsibilities, the credit function provides abundant opportunities for the retailer to revolutionize his outdated and costly manual methods. While it is still true that today's retailers are "in the infant stage as far as computer applications to accounts receivable are concerned,"[32] tomorrow "computers may so alter the credit scene that billing, collection problems and written sales checks might be eliminated, new account applications be approved within hours, and credit scoring assume a vitally important role."[33] Or to quote the credit manager of the J. C. Penney Company: "Credit operations of 1970 and 1980 will be computer oriented. . . ."[34] And the benefits of the computer for credit operations will not be restricted to the large retailer. Computer service centers have been established to enable other retailers to have their data processed quickly and at a reasonable cost.

1. A Present-Day Computerized Credit System. Shifting from manual operations to EDP in the credit department of a large store is a problem of some magnitude, involving careful planning, the cooperation of many people, and the utmost detail in scheduling various activities. After a long trial and error period, designed to insure the adoption of "the most economical and practical approach to a computerized total credit operation," Lit Bros. of Philadelphia installed a system recommended by the National Cash Register Company which has been described as follows:

Ten cycles are used for handling accounts and related transactions, providing a balanced work load and convenient scheduling. All financial media is reference numbered in three parts.

On billing: The customer's statement shows a description of each transaction for the cycle month, as well as previous month's balance, total charges, total payments and credits, service charges and current month's balance. If an optional account is delinquent, the minimum is the current balance plus last month's payment.

Credit authorization is selective. Two lists are printed: An authorization list

---

[32] A. S. Robert of B. Altman & Company, New York City, in *Women's Wear Daily*, January 13, 1966, p. 50.

[33] G. P. Samit, quoted by Richard Rosenthal, "Retail Credit Men Warned to Keep Up with Changes," *ibid.*, November 18, 1965, p. 32.

[34] "Computer in Every Store Forecast by Credit Man," *ibid.*, May 5, 1966, p. 36.

and a ledger list. About 10 percent of all accounts are on the selective authorization list, updated every three days for all cycles. The ledger list is printed for each cycle after its billing.

It is possible to determine quickly the accounts for which credit sales could be authorized, further reviewed or referred to the credit department. On the manual system, an authorization averaged about three minutes: now it averages less than 30 seconds.[35]

The new system has provided faster service, improved the quality of floor authorization for credit sales, strengthened financial control, helped in collection follow-up, and provided useful sales information for soliciting credit accounts, reviewing inactive accounts, and analyzing departmental sales. In addition, it has permitted a substantial reduction in personnel expense through eliminating many manual operations.

2. Automation in the Future. The longerrun implications of computers on present-day techniques of extending credit are suggested by the following:

Though speculations about developments in the future are sometimes unrealistic, it now appears certain that by 1980 very few American shoppers will be carrying bulky checkbooks in their purses or large amounts of cash in their wallets. The present proliferation of credit cards of all sizes, shapes, and colors will also be largely a thing of the past. Money will still serve as a unit of accounts, a standard of value, and a store of wealth. However, money as we know it today (in terms of cash and checks and a variety of credit card charge accounts) will take on a new appearance when used as a medium of exchange involving most consumer transactions. . . .

Instead of paying for groceries at the supermarket check-out counter by cash (acquired by cashing a check at her bank or elsewhere), the housewife of the future will simply hand the store clerk a unique "funds identification card" which she alone can use. The clerk, before ringing up the amount of her purchase, will insert this identification card into an electronic apparatus which "reads" the card and establishes immediately and automatically an electronic communication to the customer's bank account. If sufficient funds are held in her account to cover this transaction or if the customer has an established line of credit with her bank large enough to cover the transaction, an indicator on the card-reading apparatus will inform the clerk accordingly. The clerk will then activate the device, causing the amount of the purchase to be automatically deducted from the customer's account and added to the account of the supermarket. . . .[36]

The authors of the foregoing statement go on to point out that for "the emergence of a checkless society," no major technological breakthroughs

---

[35] Trudy Prokop, "Lit Bros. 10 Philadelphia Units Finalizing Computer Systems," *ibid.,* April 5, 1966, p. 15.

[36] A. H. Anderson *et al., An Electronic Cash and Credit System* (New York: American Management Association, 1966), p. 15.

are required; rather, "only a refining of present knowledge" is necessary. They suggest further that these developments will increase the competitive ability of small retailers as compared with large-scale firms, and that retailers of all sizes will benefit as a result of a reduction in the cost of extending credit and through a reduction of their working capital requirements.

OPEN-ACCOUNT CREDIT PROCEDURE

Once the retailer has reviewed carefully the advantages and disadvantages of selling on credit and has decided to adopt such a policy, he must establish adequate procedures to implement it. These procedures, of course, vary with the kind and the size of the store and with the preferences of executives, although all conform to the same general principles. Broadly speaking, systemized routines are necessary for opening the account, maintaining credit information, identifying customers for whom accounts have been opened, authorizing purchases on credit, billing customers for purchases made, and collecting past-due accounts. The way these activities are handled will vary according to the basis or form of credit extended. In this section attention will be devoted to procedures for open-account credit.[37]

Opening Credit Accounts in the Medium-Size and Large Store

In general, the information needed by a retailer before he should open a charge account may be secured with the customer's cooperation or without his knowledge. The former method—which is the common one—is used when people, perhaps as a result of active solicitation, come to the store and ask for a charge account; the latter is used when a store, in its first contact with the customer, desires to notify her that an account has been set up in her name.

Opening an Account with the Customer's Aid. Five steps are commonly followed when an account is opened in this manner. These include an interview, obtaining outside information, approving the credit application, establishing the credit limit, and informing the customer.

1. *The Interview.* The credit interview with the customer is conducted by personnel from the credit department. Through questions and a credit application (Figure 22–2) information is secured about the applicant's character, capacity, and capital. The interview is also used to educate the customer in the proper use of the credit account which may be opened for her and to "sell the store" to her.

---

[37] In general, these procedures also apply to revolving-credit and option-terms plans.

2. *Obtaining Outside Information.* Some stores extend credit solely on the basis of information obtained during the interview—especially when the customer desires to make an immediate purchase. Most stores, however, gather additional information as well as check on that obtained during the interview before opening the account. In areas where such an organization

PLEASE DO NOT WRITE TO THE LEFT OF THIS LINE ——▶	IF MR. & MRS. PLEASE FILL OUT BOTH LINES			
	PLEASE PRINT FIRST NAME	MIDDLE NAME	LAST NAME	
ACCT. NO.	MR.			MAIL BILL TO
C/R P/H/V C YR M/C	MRS.			
LIMIT	MISS.			BUS. RES.
OPENING LETTER	RESIDENCE NUMBER & STREET	CITY	STATE	ZIP CODE
APPLICATION BY	LENGTH OF RESIDENCE YRS. MOS.	OWN RENT HOME PHONE NO.		
MO. DAY YEAR	FORMER NUMBER RESIDENCE	STREET CITY	STATE	LENGTH OF RESIDENCE YRS. MOS. OWN RENT
AMOUNT PENDING	EMPLOYED BY	BUSINESS ADDRESS		
PICKUP DATE	POSITION	BUSINESS PHONE NO.	HOW LONG YRS. MOS.	
AMOUNT RELEASED	FORMER EMPLOYER	BUSINESS ADDRESS	POSITION	HOW LONG
RELEASE OK'D BY	SPOUSES EMPLOYER HUSBAND WIFE	BUSINESS ADDRESS		
DOWN PAYMENT	POSITION	BUSINESS PHONE NO.	HOW LONG YRS. MOS.	
	AUTHORIZED BUYERS	PLEASE PRINT NAMES & RELATIONSHIP		
	NEAREST RELATIVE NOT LIVING WITH YOU	NAME	NUMBER & STREET CITY & STATE	RELATIONSHIP
	MY BANK	BRANCH	CITY	CK'ING SAVING
OTHER STORES WHERE I HAVE ACCOUNTS	FIRM	ACCOUNT NUMBER FIRM		ACCOUNT NUMBER
	FIRM	ACCOUNT NUMBER FIRM		ACCOUNT NUMBER

I UNDERSTAND MY ACCOUNT MAY BE PAID IN FULL AT ANY TIME AND THERE WILL BE NO SERVICE CHARGE ON ANY BALANCE PAID IN FULL BEFORE MY NEXT BILLING DATE. IF I CHOOSE TO PAY ACCORDING TO THE MONTHLY PAYMENT SCHEDULE I AGREE SERVICE CHARGES NOT IN EXCESS OF THOSE PERMITTED BY LAW WILL BE CHARGED ON THE OUT-STANDING BALANCES FROM MONTH TO MONTH. I UNDERSTAND THE MONTHLY SERVICE CHARGE WILL BE 1½ PER CENT ON THE BALANCE NOT EXCEEDING $1,000.00 AND 1 PER CENT ON ANY EXCESS; THAT SERVICE CHARGES WILL BE COMPUTED ON THE BEGINNING BALANCE; AND THAT MY ENTIRE BALANCE BECOMES DUE AND PAYABLE IMMEDIATELY IF ANY PAYMENT IS NOT MADE WHEN DUE. IF LEGAL ACTION IS NECESSARY TO AC-COMPLISH COLLECTION I AGREE TO PAY REASONABLE ATTORNEY'S FEES AND COURT COSTS.

REMARKS OR INSTRUCTIONS

CUSTOMER'S SIGNATURE(S) _____ SIGN YOUR NAME IN FULL AS YOU WILL SIGN YOUR SALES CHECKS

STORE WHERE OPENED

ROOS/ATKINS   CHARGE ACCOUNT APPLICATION

798 MARKET STREET, SAN FRANCISCO, CALIF. 94102   FORM 3030 7-65

Courtesy: Roos-Atkins, San Francisco, California

FIG. 22–2.   Application for charge account

exists, the local retail credit bureau is probably the retailer's most valuable source of outside information. The majority of these bureaus are owned by the stores that use and operate them on a nonprofit basis. Each participating store furnishes the bureau with detailed data on each of its credit customers, including the amount of credit extended and the promptness with which payments are made. When a member requests a report on a person, the complete data are given, but the sources are not disclosed. Hence, any store may make a full statement to the bureau without having its competitors become aware of its credit problems. An illustration of such a report is shown in Figure 22–3. When an individual moves to another area also served by a credit bureau, a copy of this record may go to the new location.

3. *Approving Credit Applications.* On the basis of the interview and

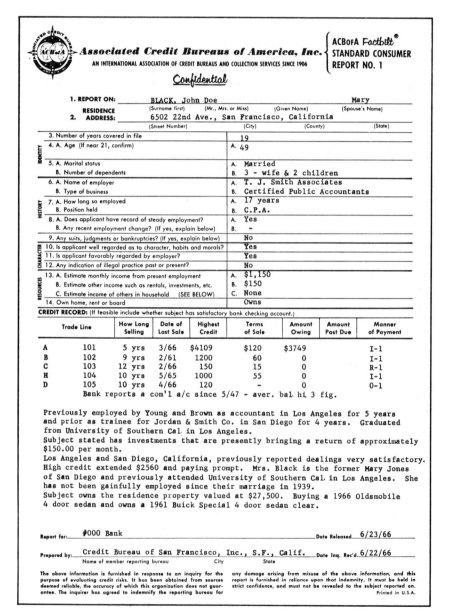

FIG. 22–3. Confidential credit report.

outside information, the credit manager decides whether or not to grant credit to the applicant. Usually, this decision is not difficult, since the majority of applicants easily meet the store's requirements. For a small percentage of the applicants the evidence may indicate that credit extension is clearly undesirable, and for another relatively small group the credit manager may find a decision difficult to make. In these latter cases, additional information may be sought, perhaps through a second interview with the applicant.

4. *Establishing the Credit Limit.* If the credit application is approved, the next step is to set a limit as to the amount of credit which will be granted. In fact, approval is commonly granted with a limit in mind. For a family with an annual income ranging from $3,000 to $5,000, perhaps $150–$200 is the maximum amount the store is willing to extend, whereas a $6,000 income may justify as high as $250 and more of credit. A fairly conservative rule is that the limit should be set at about twice the estimated weekly income of the customer. But income is not the only factor to be considered, since a person's capital, general business conditions, and the existing unemployment rate have an important bearing on the credit limit.

The credit limit set by the credit department is not a hard-and-fast limit which cannot be exceeded. Usually, it is set for control purposes: if a customer reaches her credit limit the facts of the case are reviewed. Under revolving credit, the use of partial payments and service charges make it possible to be quite flexible regarding the credit limit.

5. *Informing the Customer.* The customer should be informed promptly of the credit department's decision. When it is unfavorable, every effort should be made to avoid antagonizing the customer. Letters are useful devices in this connection since they avoid involving the credit manager in an argument. Probably no specific reason should be given for the refusal, since this also provides a point for controversy, but a brief paragraph stressing the advantages of trading at the store on a cash basis may prove helpful in retaining the customer's good will.

If the store has decided to extend credit, a letter still seems the best medium for informing the customer. Not only does it save time for both customer and credit manager, but it enables the store to provide the customer with a written statement of the store's credit rules. For example, information concerning billing dates and when payments are expected may be included as well as a description of the system used by the store to identify customers. The necessary coin, card, or "Charga-Plate" may also be enclosed in the envelope.[38] Some stores inform the customer of her credit limit, although this is not the usual practice.

---

[38] Cf. pp. 637–38, below.

Opening the Account without the Customer's Aid. When a retailer wishes to establish accounts in this manner, various ways are open to him for obtaining the names of potential credit customers, as we have noted previously. Some stores attempt to attract such customers by sending out letters (perhaps with a credit card or plate enclosed, a technique used by the J. C. Penney Company when credit selling was introduced in the 1958–62 period) to the effect that charge accounts have been opened in their names which can be used at will. This policy is justifiable when the store can gather sufficient outside information concerning the individual, perhaps from the files of the local credit bureau or through local banks.

Opening Credit Accounts in the Small Store

The close personal contact between the proprietor of the small store and his customers makes it quite easy for him to decide to whom he should extend credit. Having lived in the community for some time, he knows something about the character, capacity, and capital of the people; hence, he does not feel the need of the "red tape" through which the large stores go before extending credit. But this personal contact may work to his detriment if he permits his sympathies and emotions to influence his business judgment. It is difficult to refuse credit to friends, to impose a reasonable credit limit upon them, and even more difficult to pursue sound collection policies.

The large credit losses of many small stores indicate that their proprietors need to exercise better judgment in evaluating the credit qualifications of their customers. Although they do not require the formal credit-granting organization of the large store, they should make use of the same techniques. Data should be gathered from references and from the local credit bureau. When a credit bureau does not exist or is considered too expensive, the local banker may be a good source of information.

The small retailer will find it a good practice to adopt a credit limit even though it may be quite flexible. And, like his larger competitor, he should explain to each customer the general rules under which open-account credit is extended, when bills will be rendered, and when payment is expected.

Maintaining Current Credit Information

Unfortunately for the retailer, a person's credit standing is subject to rapid change. Financial reverses, death in the family, and sickness with its attending expenditures are only a few of the factors responsible for this change. As a result, retailers—both large and small—must take steps to keep up to date their information on credit customers.

For the small community or neighborhood store, where "everybody knows what everybody else is doing," the maintenance of current information seldom presents a serious problem. Most proprietors find that they gather sufficient information in informal conversations to enable them to estimate changes in credit ratings. The large store finds this problem more serious. One valuable source of information lies in its own records. If its accounts are given a periodic study, those that are gradually becoming slow-pay accounts can be discovered. In dealing with such accounts "revolving credit" and service charges may prove to be useful devices. Some stores find it desirable to subscribe to the annual rating books of local private credit bureaus to note changes in ratings. For information on day-to-day changes, local papers should be scrutinized for items on accidents, divorces, deaths, and bankruptcies.

Identifying Credit Customers

Personal Identification. Once an account has been opened, it is necessary that some means be provided by which the customer may be identified as the person having authority to make purchases against the account. In the small store, customer identification presents no problem. Even in the medium-size store, many customers become known by name to the salespeople, while others may identify themselves by means of a driver's license or a similar device. But in the large store the identification problem is a real one.

Identification Devices Carried by the Customer. Most large retailers rely on plastic cards and metal plates to identify their charge customers. The card usually contains the name, address, and account number of the customer. When the customer makes a credit purchase, she may hand the card to the salesperson, thereby both establishing identity and making it unnecessary for the clerk to ask the customer for her initials and the address to which the merchandise is to be sent. Many stores have mechanical devices which enable the salesperson to take the metal plate, called a "Charga-Plate" or "credit plate," and transfer the name and address recorded thereon directly to the sales slip by placing the plate and the sales slip in a small, hand-operated machine. Plastic cards may be handled in the same manner. In some cities, for example, New York, Boston, Chicago, and San Francisco, stores have cooperated in establishing a group "Charga-Plate" plan, under which only one plate need be carried for use in several stores.

The plan of having the customer carry some means of identification suffers two serious disadvantages. First, many customers do not carry the plate or card all the time, although the habit of carrying the identification device is growing steadily. Second, the device may be lost. Not only does this involve the store in the expense of replacing it, which expense is not too great; but unless the store is informed promptly when a credit token is lost, it may be found and used by an impostor.

Signature Identification. Another identification plan involves comparing the customer's signature with the signature obtained during the course of the credit interview. Under this plan, the clerk makes out the sales slip, asks the customer to sign it, and forwards it to the credit department. This method avoids the two main defects of the card or metal-plate method, although it may involve a short wait on the customer's part—perhaps a minute or two—to establish identification.

Authorizing Credit Purchases

"Charge-Take" Transactions. Credit customers often desire to take their purchases with them. Moreover, they do not like to wait for the credit department to check their credit standing. Consequently, it is common practice to allow a customer to take small purchases if she is recognized by the section manager or the store manager, particularly when she signs the sales slip. In these cases the steps of identification and authorization are identical. This procedure is also followed in practically all small stores, even when the purchase involves a substantial amount of money.

Large stores using a "Charga-Plate" or credit card usually permit customers to take purchases involving less than $25 without formal approval by the credit department. Sales of larger amounts, however, must be authorized by this department. One of two plans is commonly followed in this process: (1) sending the sales slip to the credit department by means of some form of conveyor or tube system or (2) calling the authorizer by telephone to get his approval.

Authorization by the credit department is usually carried out in a very short period. Perhaps thirty seconds may be sufficient, and seldom is more than three minutes necessary. If the store is large enough, there will be several authorizers, each of whom has the records of customers whose names fall in a certain part of the alphabet. When a case is referred to an authorizer, he turns to the customer's record. If it is clear, he gives his approval to the purchase at once. If the customer has exceeded her credit limit by a relatively large amount or some other irregularity is evident, the authorizer may request that the customer be referred to the office of the credit manager; or the authorization may be granted and the irregularity taken up with the customer by letter.

Currently, new mechanical systems are coming into use which decrease still further the time required for authorization. Illustrations are afforded by Carson Pirie Scott & Company of Chicago and R. H. Macy & Company of New York City, as follows:

At Carson Pirie Scott, a clerk steps to a touch-tone telephone and taps out the computer's extension, the customer's account number, and the amount of the purchase in question. In 30 seconds, an IBM 1440 tied to a 7770 audio response unit gives a spoken answer, either authorizing the sale or giving other instructions. The old personal credit check by phone took at least 45 seconds and could take several minutes.

Carson is starting with a hookup of 60 phones but plans to expand it to 1,000 phones in 11 stores. It could then handle 10,000 credit checks daily at a cost, according to an outsider's estimate, of perhaps $40,000 a year, not counting other uses of the computer.

Early in 1966, Macy's started using Ultronic Systems Corp.'s Validator, a desktop memory unit wired to 50 small keypunch units scattered through the store. When a credit card and sales slip are inserted in one of these units, the Validator draws on its memory of thousands of doubtful or "hold" accounts and flashes back instant word on whether or not to make the sale on credit. Macy's will rent the system from Ultronics for $15,000 a year.[39]

"Charge-Send" Transactions. The need for speed in authorizing these sales is not so great. All that is necessary is that the sale be authorized before the goods leave the store. Yet, although authorization may not take place immediately upon sale of the goods, the majority of stores use the same system for authorizing charge-sends as for charge-takes.

Billing the Customer

The final step in most credit sales is billing the customer for purchases made during the previous month. For many years, this was done by stores of all sizes at the end of each calendar month, although those with a large number of accounts adhered to a "cutoff" date near the end of the month to facilitate the preparation of bills for mailing on the first of the following month.

Cycle Billing. Today, although most small stores probably follow the practice of billing all of their customers on or near the first of the month, many large stores and some medium-size ones have adopted cycle billing. This form of billing, long used by gas and electric companies, refers to the practice under which the names in the credit files are divided systematically and statements are sent to a different group on a fixed billing date within the

---

[39] "Computer Memories Provide Quick Credit Check," *Business Week,* December 25, 1965, p. 49.

month. Thus, customers in the alphabetical group "A-B" may be billed on the second of the month; those in the group "C" on the fifth day; and so on throughout the month.

"Country Club" Billing. During the past two decades and more many retailers have adopted so-called "country club" billing, a laborsaving system

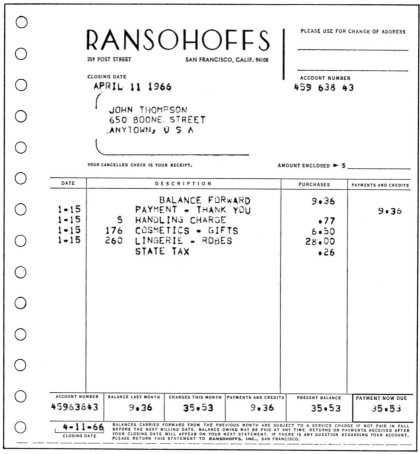

FIG. 22–4. Machine-produced monthly statement under descriptive billing system.

of maintaining customers' accounts and making out statements. Under the prior system (which is still used by many small retailers), each sales slip was recorded in the ledger as received by the accounting department; and an itemized statement was sent to the customer at the end of the month. "Country club" billing calls for no ledger entries; instead, the sales slips are filed and, on statement day, are sent to the customer together with a statement showing merely the addition of the slips. Prior to this day the store has satisfied its need for a record by a photographic copy of the sales slips, to which is added a copy of the statement with the dollar totals.

Descriptive Billing. While the majority of large stores still use "country club" billing, some have shifted to descriptive billing. This development is a direct result of the availability of electronic data-processing equipment for the handling of accounts receivable.[40] Sales slips are not sent to the customer; instead they are filed by the store and referred to only when a customer questions a particular charge. What the customer gets for a monthly bill is a machine-produced statement (see Figure 22–4) which may show (1) previous balance, (2) a dollar figure for each purchase together with a code number indicating the department in which each item was bought (if the customer wants to know the specific item covered by each figure she refers to her original copy of the sales slip), (3) total purchases and credits, (4) service charges, (5) amount due currently, and (6) the due date. Labor savings from this system of EDP billing have been substantial. In addition, many human errors are eliminated.

Sales Promotion and the Monthly Statement. Increasingly, monthly statements are being accompanied by sales promotional material. Among others, inserts announce dates for special sales, colorful pamphlets promote specific items, gift certificates are suggested, and customers using revolving credit are informed as to the dollar amounts which can be added to their accounts without an increase in the monthly payments. These steps again emphasize the opportunities for increasing sales that credit accounts provide.

Credit Cards

Recent years have witnessed a transfer of many of the steps involved in the granting and collection of open-account credit from retailers to commercial banks, independent retail credit organizations, and to the credit card companies.

Bank and Independent Retail Credit Plans. Although there are differences in the details of the various bank plans in use, essentially they operate as follows: A number of retailers in a community agree to let a bank serve them collectively as a "credit department." Customers may make their application for credit either at the bank or at one of the cooperating retailers. In either case, however, it is the bank—rather than the retailer—who passes on the merits of the application. Once approved, the customer gets a credit

---

[40] Cf. the earlier discussion of electronic data-processing equipment on pp. 138–41 above, and the later discussion on pp. 729–30.

card which serves to identify him and is valid at any of the cooperating stores. No special authorization is needed by the store on small purchases, but the bank may be called when significant amounts are involved and when the store has had no previous experience with a specific customer. The sales check for the item purchased on credit is forwarded to the bank, where the amount involved—less a charge which is usually 4 to 6 percent, depending on store volume—is entered to the retailer's account. Collection is handled by the bank, usually without recourse to the merchant, and the customers typically have the option of paying their bills in full monthly or shifting into a revolving-credit plan with a monthly service charge on the unpaid balance.

One close observer of the retail scene estimates that of the approximately "120 organizations throughout the country, [which] sponsor credit-card systems designed to permit retail merchants to concentrate on merchandising and leave consumer money-lending to the specialists," perhaps 100 are banks and the remainder independents.[41] The BankAmericard system, sponsored by the Bank of America, is the nation's largest, doing an annual business of over $200 million and having some 55,000 merchants and 1,765,000 card holders.[42] In the New York City area a similar service is offered by the Franklin National Bank, while five Chicago banks already serve 2,500 retailers.[43] Currently efforts are under way (1) to extend some of these bank-sponsored plans to banks in other geographic areas, the goal being a nationwide credit program; and (2) to achieve interchangeability among the credit plans of different banks.

Among the independent organizations the leader is the Uni-Serve Corporation, recently merged into the American Express Company as an autonomous subsidiary, which serves the Northeastern section of the country and does an annual volume of about $85 million. Next in size is the Central Charge Service in the Washington-Baltimore area with a credit volume around $50 million. Both firms are growth-minded and their credit volume will likely increase in the years ahead.

In some instances, independent shopping-centerwide retail credit card plans have come into existence, usually based on revolving credit. The retailers involved report that this plan is compatible with their own individual credit systems.[44]

---

[41] Samuel Feinberg, "From Where I Sit," *Women's Wear Daily,* December 28, 1965, p. 7.

[42] "Enlarging the Charge Card," *Business Week,* May 28, 1966, p. 42.

[43] "Chicago Banks Time Big Push for Charge Customers to Yule," *ibid.,* November 14, 1966, p. 20.

[44] Cf. "Centerwide Credit Cards," *Chain Store Age* (Executives Edition), April, 1966, p. E45.

Although there is current evidence of good profitability, many banks and independent plans have had a difficult struggle to get in the black. In fact, many banks have given up their programs because of such factors as insufficient volume, high expenses, unwillingness of large retailers to forego the advantages of their own credit systems, tendency for merchants to retain the "good" risk accounts and let the bank have the "poor" risks, and small size of the typical credit bill.

Credit Card Companies. Operating in a somewhat similar manner to the bank and independent plans mentioned, except that they cover a much wider geographic area and, in general, are usable for a greater variety of goods and services, are the credit card plans of such companies as American Express Company, Diners' Club, Inc., and Carte Blanche. While these firms originally experienced great difficulty in achieving satisfactory profits, they now seem to be doing much better as a result of improved operations and several increases in the annual charges to holders of their cards.[45] Increasingly, the credit cards issued by the major oil companies are also being used for the purchase of merchandise.[46]

Benefits and Limitations. The bank and independent credit card plans are especially advantageous to the small retailer, who normally finds it difficult to compete with the large retailer's credit service. All of the details of investigation at the time of opening an account, the subsequent maintenance of up-to-date credit information and of accounting records, the collection of accounts, and the credit risk itself are carried by others. The retailer's cash is not depleted by the growth of accounts receivable. Since the same credit card is valid in several stores, he may also gain business from the customers of other participating retailers.

The major limitations of the plans are found in the store's loss of "personal hold" on the customer, the charge for the credit service, and losses resulting from the fraudulent use of credit cards.[47] Since the customer's relationships on credit are largely with the organization giving the credit card and since his credit card may be valid at several competing retailers, his loyalty to any one retailer is reduced. Whether the usual 6 percent charge is excessive or not depends largely upon the individual retailer. Certainly there are retailers who are able to handle their credits costs, including losses, on a lower ratio to sales; but for others, even 6 percent would be an improvement over their current operations. Losses from the illegal use of stolen and lost

---

[45] "Credit Card Companies Come Into the Chips," *Business Week,* September 4, 1965, pp. 54–56.

[46] R. D. James, "Oil From Credit Cards Now Buy Other Goods; Rivals Aren't Upset," *Wall Street Journal,* August 22, 1966, pp. 1, 14.

[47] "Big Stores Resist Bank Credit Plans," *Women's Wear Daily,* August 23, 1966, pp. 1, 39.

credit cards are substantial: in Pittsburgh alone, a recent estimate by the Better Business Bureau placed such losses at $50,000 a month.[48] Although many retailers are attempting to institute closer checks to reduce unauthorized buying, the failure of salespeople to take the time necessary to check the cancellation lists on every credit card transaction, particularly during busy periods, has made such checks only partially effective.[49]

INSTALLMENT CREDIT PROCEDURE

Types of Installment Contracts

When sales are made on the basis of installment credit, the terms of the transaction are usually set forth in a contract.[50] Four major types of contracts are in common usage: the conditional sale contract, the chattel mortgage, the bailment lease, and general credit contracts.[51]

The Conditional Sale Contract. This type of contract accounts for at least half of all installment sales. Under it, although the goods are turned over to the buyer at once and the buyer becomes responsible for such factors as upkeep and taxes, title remains with the seller. The buyer agrees to make a series of stated payments. If he makes all these payments on the dates on which they are due,[52] title passes to the buyer when the last payment has been made. If payments are not made when they are due, however, the contract gives the seller the right to repossess the merchandise. But merely giving up the merchandise does not free the buyer from paying the unpaid balance; if the retailer does not get enough from the resale to cover the unpaid balance, he may sue the buyer for the balance.[53] Only when the whole unpaid balance has been liquidated is the buyer free from the contract.

The Chattel Mortgage. Under this type of contract, which is used mainly in those states where the conditional sale contract meets legal diffi-

---

[48] "Credit Card Frauds Up in Pittsburgh," *Women's Wear Daily,* December 1, 1965, p. 16.

[49] Cf. Leonard Sloane, "Frauds Plaguing Charge Accounts," *New York Times,* May 15, 1966, pp. F1, 9; and R. E. Dallos, "Cheating on the Cuff," *Wall Street Journal,* October 10, 1965, pp. 1, 18.

[50] There is an appreciable amount of state regulation of installment contract terms. Each retailer selling on installment should inform himself as to the laws of his state.

[51] Cf. National Association of Credit Management, *Credit Manual of Commercial Laws, 1966* (New York: The Association, 1966).

[52] In practice, there is usually some leniency shown in regard to payments on the exact dates stated in the contract.

[53] As a matter of fact, the seller does not have to repossess. Upon default, he may declare the whole unpaid balance due and sue the customer for this sum.

culties, title passes to the buyer at the time of sale and the seller takes a mortgage on the merchandise purchased. Repossession becomes possible if the buyer fails to fulfill any part of the contract. As with the conditional sale, if the repossessed property cannot be sold for a sum sufficient to liquidate the unpaid balance, the seller has the right of further legal action to collect the balance due him.

The Bailment Lease. This contract provides that the goods shall be merely rented to the buyer, the "rent" being the stipulated series of installment payments. Hence, title is held by the seller during the period of credit extension. When the rent payments have been completed, however, the seller agrees to turn over the title to the buyer for a nominal payment, such as $1.00.

General Credit Contracts. In contrast to the foregoing three kinds of contracts, general credit contracts do not give the retailer the right to repossess. Consequently, installment sales on such contracts demand just as thorough an investigation of the buyer's character, capacity, and capital as does open-account credit. In fact, if the buyer defaults on his payments, the recourse of the seller is the same as that under open-account credit, that is, the right to sue.

Repossession Not Sufficient Protection

Several factors have reduced the protection afforded the retailer by the right of repossession. First, and most obvious, is the extension of installment selling to soft goods which usually have limited repossession value. Second, even for durable goods, repossession value has become less certain. Fashion is becoming more important, and the market values of durable as well as soft goods are influenced by unpredictable changes in fashion. Third, competition on installment terms has weakened further the security afforded by repossession and increased the potential number of reclaiming actions.

In view of these trends the retailer feels the need of protection in addition to repossession. Actually, most retailers will make every effort to help the customer to complete the payments, even after default on a contract, rather than reclaim the goods. Merchants feel that they are better off to increase the length of the payment period, either by decreasing the size of each payment or by skipping a payment and adding it on at the end, rather than to take back the article. To minimize the number of defaulters, a charge is usually made when any such extension of payment is arranged.

Wage Assignments. The present-day use of a clause providing for a wage assignment in case of default was devised to provide some protection in addition to repossession. It may be used in connection with all four major types of installment contracts, but it is especially common with general credit contracts. When default occurs, the employer of the buyer is informed of the wage assignment contract. He is then required to pay part of the wages of the buyer directly to the seller, the percentage paid varying widely according to the laws of different states. As additional protection, wage assignment contracts may call for the signature of a third party to guarantee payments. When this protection is used, the usual procedure is to attach wages first; but if payment is uncertain from this source, as it would be if the buyer lost his job, payment is demanded of the guarantor.

Evaluating the Installment Credit Applicant

Evaluation of the installment credit applicant may be just as necessary as is the appraisal of the prospective open-account customer. However, if the merchandise is durable and is sold on terms giving an increasing excess of resale value over the unpaid balance as the payments are made, many retailers do not make a detailed credit investigation. The buyer may be interviewed briefly, his residence address checked, his employer contacted to inquire as to income, and the local credit bureau called for a rating. Most retailers, however, appraise the installment credit customer with much more care. The investigating technique is similar to that used in dealing with open-account customers and need not be repeated here.

Assistance from Finance Companies and Banks

Although retailers *originate* most of the installment credit extended to consumers for the purchase of goods, most of them do not hold such contracts to maturity but sell some or all of them to banks and finance companies. Through this step retailers get cash at once and may even be relieved of the collection problem. For this immediate cash payment, retailers accept something less than they would get if they carried the contract until all payments were made. In other words, the finance company takes over the retailers' "paper" at a discount.

COLLECTION OF PAST-DUE ACCOUNTS

The successful collection of past-due indebtedness requires that the retailer have a clear understanding of the collection function and of the merits and limitations of various collection policies. These are discussed in the following pages.

The Collection Function

The collection function includes more than just the final obtaining of cash from the negligent credit buyer. It begins with the making out of sales checks by the salesperson, such sales checks being necessary as the first record of the amount due the store; proceeds through the maintenance of records of the customer's debits and credits; includes all activities associated directly with trying to collect actual cash from the customer—sending statements, letters, and making telephone calls; and does not end until cash has been received and a receipt given or until the account has been deemed uncollectible.

Today the collection function "is being challenged anew with the imperative assignment of maximizing sales and minimizing losses, while retaining the highest possible factor of good will."[54] Some stores even refuse to designate collections as a nonselling function because of the continuous opportunities the collection department has "to retain good will and keep customers open to buy additional merchandise."[55] Accomplishment of this purpose, as in the handling of all other aspects of credit extension, requires sound policies and procedures.[56]

The Collection Problem and Credit Policies. The difficulties encountered in collecting overdue accounts are related directly to the policy followed by the store in extending credit. If a store gives credit to practically all applicants, it must expect to spend more money in trying to collect its accounts and also suffer more credit losses than the store that gives the credit privilege to a more carefully selected group. To a lesser degree the collection problem of a given store is also influenced by the credit policies of other stores. Even if one store tries to be fairly strict in its collection program, if other stores are lenient, a too exacting collection program will simply drive customers to competitors. It is this inability of a store to escape the consequences of policies followed by competing stores that, in part, is responsible for the attempt through credit bureaus to foster a uniform community credit program.

Advantages of Early Collections. The advantages of prompt follow-up on past-due accounts are readily apparent. Such action saves interest charges

---

[54] J. S. Robinson, quoted in "N.Y. Stores Eye Credit Ease When Strike is Over," *Women's Wear Daily,* January 13, 1966, p. 50.

[55] *Ibid.*

[56] Cf. "Improve Your Collection Procedures," *Hardware Retailer,* December, 1965, pp. 45–47.

on funds tied up in accounts, reduces payroll expenses for employees making out collection notices, and lowers the cost of stationery and postage. The longer an account is outstanding, the harder it becomes to collect. Once the person has used the merchandise so that enjoyment from it has begun to diminish, it becomes increasingly difficult to part with the money to pay for it. Early collections also lead to increased sales. Many customers hesitate to go near a store when their accounts are overdue; but, once the account is paid, they again become regular customers.

Granting the desirability of early collections, the retailer should handle collections with tact. In some cases, this means putting pressure on the debtor as soon as his account becomes overdue. But, in the majority of instances, accounts can be collected with less loss of customer good will if the store reserves its pressure until it has tried a few gentle reminders of the overdue account. Apparently, most credit customers mean to pay their obligations; but many of them seem to find that some delay is necessary. It should be the aim in making collections to reduce this delay as much as possible and yet retain the customer's patronage.

Collection Policies

Retailers differ as to the collection policies they follow. Unfortunately, many small retailers follow no carefully worked-out collection program; and this deficiency is responsible in no small measure for their low collection ratios.[57] Yet some small retailers have worked out effective collection programs. In general, when a collection policy has been formulated, whether by a large or a small retailer, it may be classified either as a uniform policy (that is, it is applied uniformly to all customers) or as a nonuniform policy (that is, it treats customers differently according to their past records and the facts of the present situation).

Uniform Collection Policy. Although it is difficult to generalize about the uniform collection policies of various retailers, the usual steps seem to be as follows: On or soon after the first of the month—or, if cycle billing is used, on a specified date during the month—each open-account debtor is usually sent a statement of his account at the store, together with a request for payment within ten days. On installment contracts the buyer has already been informed of the various payment dates and the exact sum due, so that a reminder is rarely used.

1. *Past-Due Statements.* If payment is not made and if the debtor

---

[57] A collection ratio expresses as a percentage the amount collected during a month to the uncollected amount at the end of the previous month.

makes no move to explain his situation to the collection manager, a second[58] statement (usually not itemized) is sent out. If the retailer follows a policy of placing an interest charge on past-due accounts, this action may be evidenced on the second statement—which is usually accompanied by an appropriate insert as illustrated in Figure 22–5. The time that elapses between the sending of the first statement and subsequent follow-ups will vary from retailer to retailer and from field to field; it also depends upon whether

PERHAPS ITS HAPPENED AGAIN...

NOW AND THEN WE SEND CUSTOMERS A REMINDER ABOUT THEIR OVER-
DUE ACCOUNT . . . ONLY TO RECEIVE A CHECK IN THE VERY NEXT MAIL. SO IF
YOUR PAYMENT IS ON ITS WAY, PLEASE DISREGARD THIS FRIENDLY NOTICE.
OTHERWISE, WON'T YOU SEND IT TO US . . . BEFORE IT SLIPS YOUR MIND.

J. C. PENNEY COMPANY, INC.

CUSTOMERS SAY THEY APPRECIATE...

BEING INFORMED WHEN THEIR ACCOUNTS BECOME PAST DUE. SO WE
HOPE YOU WILL ACCEPT THIS FRIENDLY REMINDER IN THE SAME SPIRIT. IF
YOU HAVE JUST SENT US YOUR CHECK, PLEASE DISREGARD THIS NOTICE
AND ACCEPT OUR THANKS.

J. C. PENNEY COMPANY, INC.

DID YOU FORGET US?

WE KNOW HOW BUSY ONE CAN GET THESE DAYS AND WE FEEL PERHAPS
THAT'S WHY YOU MAY HAVE FORGOTTEN THAT YOUR ACCOUNT IS NOW
OVERDUE. IF YOUR PAYMENT IS ALREADY ON THE WAY, PLEASE ACCEPT
OUR THANKS.

J. C. PENNEY COMPANY, INC.

Courtesy: J. C. Penney Company

FIG. 22–5. Effective inserts for use with statements on past-due accounts. These forms are used interchangeably.

the account is open-account or installment credit. In general, retailers selling goods consumed rapidly (for example, food) will mail reminders within a week after the account is past due; whereas department stores and furniture stores may wait from 30 to 60 days unless, of course, revolving credit is used. On installment contracts the notice will go out within 10 or 30 days following the due date.

2. *Letters and Telephone Calls.* When a customer has failed to respond to the reminders enclosed with their statements, the retailer may send a

---

[58] First, if an installment account.

letter that, although mild in tone, requests prompt action by the customer. As an illustration, the text of the letter used by the J. C. Penney Company for accounts overdue from 60 to 90 days is as follows:

To retain your good will . . .
is always of first consideration. That's why we have been so patient . . .
even though you haven't replied to any of our reminders that your account
is long over due.
Naturally, when customers don't get in touch with us, we can only
assume that they are no longer interested in this convenient way to shop.
And, obviously, that means it might be necessary to restrict future
purchases. Of course, you don't want this to happen . . . and neither
do we.
So won't you please mail us a check at once . . . or get in touch with
us within the next five days?

> Sincerely,
> Collection Department

AD:GW
Amount Due $_____
Account No. _____

If there is still no response, most credit men feel that the time has arrived to use pressure. Of course, the installment seller can repossess; but the open-account seller must use other tactics. Other more demanding letters may be sent. It may be pointed out that it is a matter of good business on the part of the customer to pay her bills; otherwise, she will lose her credit rating. Transfer of the account to a service-charge basis may be suggested. The self-interest of the customer may be appealed to by the threat of reporting the past-due account to the local credit bureau, where the information will become common knowledge of all the local credit managers. Legal proceedings may be threatened. Sometimes a telephone call to the debtor will bring a response when a letter fails, or the store may have a letter written by its attorney.

3. *Collectors.* If the store has been reasonably careful in extending credit, the preceding steps will collect most of the accounts. For those that are still outstanding, the personal collector is the next step. Depending upon the size of the store, the collector may be employed on a part-time or a full-time basis. Some stores use salesmen for collecting during periods when they are not needed in the store; or in the small store, the proprietor may make the necessary calls. Another plan is for several noncompeting stores to cooperate—usually through the local credit bureau—and employ a full-time collector. If personal collection fails, legal action is about all that remains, unless the store desires to turn the account over to a collection

agency.[59] If the account is small, legal action is too expensive, so that the account may be closed out as a bad debt.

Nonuniform Collection Policy. Some retailers believe that a collection program which treats all customers alike results in the loss of considerable customer good will. Although eventually they may go through steps similar to those just described, these retailers prefer to divide their negligent customers into groups, each group being made up of fairly comparable accounts. For example, some customers consistently pay their bills within 10 to 20 days of receipt of their first statement. These customers may be classified as "prompt-pay" customers. If a payment is missed by a customer who has been placed in this classification, the store will hesitate to put its collection machinery into operation. Rather, it feels that some situation has arisen which makes it necessary that the customer be allowed some delay. An immediate series of collection letters may cause her to think that the store does not appreciate the efforts she has made in the past to pay her bills promptly.

Another group of accounts may be classified as "sure pay, but slow." This group consists of a number of subgroups: one is composed of those people who "just forget" to pay or who have fallen into the habit of neglecting their bills; another is made up of those who will not pay unless pressure is exerted; and still another consists of those people who believe that the store has treated them badly—perhaps a salesgirl was discourteous, or perhaps on some occasion there was a considerable delay in authorizing a certain purchase.

Although other credit account groups might be added to complete the picture, perhaps the foregoing is sufficient to establish the point that there is no standard collection problem. While the large store cannot treat each account individually, it can classify accounts and submit comparable accounts to similar collection methods. The use of this technique does not imply that the store should be lax in its collections.[60] Rather, it means recognizing that differences do exist and that successful collections and the holding and building of customer good will demand that these differences be recognized. But once customers have been grouped according to their sim-

---

[59] Many credit bureaus also act as collection agents. Apparently, fees for this service equal 15–25 percent of the amount collected. An increasing number of stores are able to employ lawyers to perform this service at fees of 10–15 percent of the sums collected.

[60] "I have found it almost impossible to ruin the business by making people pay their bills. Once in a while I stir up a hornet's nest, of course, and wonder whether the gain was worth while. But usually the man who is forced to pay me the bill he owes gets over it. In the long run the results are either that I get rid of a bad customer for good, or he gets over it and forgets." R. E. Gould, *Yankee Storekeeper* (New York: McGraw-Hill Book Co., Inc., 1946), p. 91.

ilarities, the store should have a definite collection routine which operates quite automatically. Persistence and promptness are two great virtues in a sound collection system.

JUDGING THE EFFICIENCY OF THE CREDIT DEPARTMENT

All retailers, large or small, are vitally interested in the effectiveness with which credit and collection activities are being carried out. A variety of yardsticks are available for judging this effectiveness, including the following: (1) the number of new accounts opened in a given period; (2) the number of credit applications refused; (3) the number of delinquent accounts—usually obtained through a process of "aging" accounts; (4) the overall service rendered, as reflected in the number of complaints received and the time required for authorizing purchases on credit; (5) the percentage of delinquent accounts collected; (6) the writing off of uncollectible balances, i.e., losses from bad debts; and (7) the cost of operating the credit department in stores large enough to have such a department. In no other part of his business is it more necessary for the retailer to keep in touch with developments than in the credit department; and for the large retailer a well-trained and able credit manager or executive is a "must."

REVIEW AND DISCUSSION QUESTIONS

1. Point out the essential differences between open-account credit and installment credit.
2. Explain briefly the meaning of "revolving credit." Differentiate it from the "option-terms" credit plan.
3. Summarize the main points you would cover in explaining to a fellow student the importance of credit sales to retailers.
4. Since one observer notes that "charge accounts are one of the most powerful and profitable influences on sales in modern merchandising," how do you account for the fact that "many stores are still far from their potential in the use of credit?"
5. What factors are responsible for the development of Credit Counseling Services in several of our states?
6. How would you proceed in finding an answer to the question, "How much is a credit customer worth?"
7. "Credit selling inevitably raises the retailer's cost ratio and his prices." Evaluate this statement.
8. Examine the latest version of the Douglas Bill and report to the class your evaluation of it. What laws governing credit exist in your particular state?
9. "The automation of the credit function in retail stores constitutes the major problem of credit management today." Discuss.

10. What are the favorable and unfavorable factors of these two credit applications? Would you accept or reject them?
    a) An application is made by Mrs. A, age 50, in the name of her husband. Mr. A, age 55, has been selling encyclopedias, soliciting from door to door for the past 15 months. There is no bank account except a small inactive saving account. In 1965, Mr. A. bought furniture for $150, paying promptly in 18 monthly installments. He has had no charge accounts since. An account is desired so that a coat costing $29.50 may be charged.
    b) An application is made by Mr. B, age 30. He has been unemployed for 5 years. He has no bank account. His wife receives $300 per month from her brother. Mr. B wants to charge a man's wrist watch, valued at $50.
11. Visit a retail credit bureau in your community or in a nearby city and prepare a description of its organization and functions.
12. Explain (a) the methods employed in retail stores to identify credit customers and (b) the major methods of authorizing purchases on credit.
13. Distinguish among cycle billing, "country club" billing, and descriptive billing.
14. Discuss recent developments concerning credit cards sponsored by banks, independent organizations, and the general credit card companies.
15. Prepare a paper of some 1,200 words on the subject: "The Effects of Recent Developments in Retail Credit on Collection Policies and Procedures."

SUPPLEMENTARY READINGS

AMERICAN INSTITUTE OF BANKING. *Installment Credit* (New York: The Institute, 1964). This concise treatment of installment credit emphasizes establishing credit, obtaining and checking information, servicing loans, and collecting amounts due.

ANDERSON, A. H., *et al.* *An Electronic Cash and Credit System* (New York: American Management Association, 1966). The authors discuss the "tremendous problems and opportunities" which will result from the evolution of computer systems "linking banks, stores, and credit bureaus. . . ."

BRETH, R. D. "The Challenge of Charge Accounts to Discount Merchants," *Journal of Retailing,* Vol. XL, No. 4 (Winter, 1964–65), pp. 11–16, 58. The author discusses the growth and types of charge accounts used by discount houses. Also cf. "A Quick Look at the Use of Credit Plans [in 32 Discount Firms]," *Chain Store Age* (Executives Ed.), February, 1966, pp. E54–E56.

COLE, R. H., AND HANCOCK, R. S. *Consumer and Commercial Credit Management* (rev. ed.; Homewood, Ill.: Richard D. Irwin, Inc., 1964). This college textbook is written from the credit manager's point of view.

CREDIT RESEARCH FOUNDATION (ed.). *Credit Management Handbook* (rev. ed.; Homewood, Ill.: Richard D. Irwin, Inc., 1965). Designed to cover all phases of the subject, this collection of readings contains helpful information for the student of retailing.

HOCKER, W. G. (ed.). *Computerizing the Credit Accounts Receivable Operation* (New York: National Retail Merchants Association, 1965). Providing the credit manager with information needed to determine the equipment and systems necessary for efficient operation, this book is a "must" for this executive.

KNIFFIN, F. W. *Retail Credit and Collections* (Washington, D.C.: Small Business Administration, 1964). A bibliography, this publication covers both government and private publications.

LEWIS, L. L. (ed.). *Dartnell File of Credit and Collection Letters* (Chicago: The Dartnell Corporation, 1965). Although general in nature, the retailer will find many useful ideas in this portfolio of 250 field-tested letters designed to meet all collection and credit situations.

LURZ, J. J., AND TALKES, W. N. "Credit and Collection Problems," *Retail Control,* January, 1966, pp. 130–52. Reporting on the questions and answers during one session of the 1965 Controllers' Congress of the National Retail Merchants Association, current problems in credits and collections are brought into focus by this discussion.

MCALLISTER, E. R. *Retail Installment Credit: Growth and Legislation* (Columbus, Ohio: Ohio State University, Bureau of Business Research, Monograph No. 120, 1964). This study is an excellent treatment of its subject.

MORS, W. P. *Consumer Credit Finance Charges* (New York: Columbia University Press, 1966). A part of the current study of consumer credit by the National Bureau of Economic Research, the author sheds light on a subject of vital interest to consumers buying on credit.

NATIONAL RETAIL MERCHANTS ASSOCIATION. *Credit Currents.* Published monthly, this periodical treats timely topics and problems regarding credit of interest to retailers.

———. Credit Management Division. *Credit Management Yearbook* (New York: The Association, published annually). Also cf. *Facts You Should Know About Revolving Credit, Installment Credit and Credit Legislation* (n.d.), *Credit Department Operating Manual Outline* (n.d.), and *Credit in the Branch Store* (n.d.). These sources of information on various aspects of credit are among the best available.

———. *Effective Collection Methods and Control* (New York: The Association, n.d.). Students and retailers alike will find this manual of interest and help as a "how to" tool in collection matters.

PINGER, R. F. "The Role of the Computer in Credit Bureau Operations," *Retail Control,* November, 1965, pp. 153–160. This informative article discusses the problems involved in automatic credit checking, errors in identification, and related credit activities.

WEISS, E. B. "Consumer Credit Gets Dunked in a Goldfish Bowl," *Advertising Age,* July, 1965, pp. 95–96. The author reviews the social and retail trends "now dramatically reshaping consumer credit."

PART VII

Retail Control

23

CHAPTER

The Cost Method of Accounting Control

In previous chapters, attention has been given to important activities and problems with which the management of modern retail stores must deal. Unless these activities are coordinated properly and the problems encountered are solved, satisfactory profits cannot be realized.[1] But it is impossible to determine the results of operations unless complete, accurate records are kept of merchandise transactions, including purchases and sales, and of the expenses associated with the performance of these and related activities.

In this chapter, therefore, attention is devoted to the need for and purposes of financial records, to the determination of profits under the cost method of accounting, and to some of the fundamental types of records required for appraising results, including comparison of these results with similar stores. In the following chapter the retail inventory method of accounting and merchandise management accounting are described and illustrated. The aim of these two chapters is to develop basic principles of retail accounting:[2] they do not discuss the equipment used in performing accounting activities. It should be emphasized, however, that the newer electronic equipment is being employed in this area just as it is for other purposes.[3]

---

[1] Cf. Chapter 28, "Coordination and Retailing Management."

[2] For a review of certain general principles of accounting, cf. A. N. Lorig, "Some Basic Concepts of Accounting and Their Implications," *Accounting Review*, July, 1964, pp. 563–73; and T. D. Flynn, "Widening Interest in Accounting Principles," *Financial Executive*, March, 1965, pp. 18–19 ff.

[3] Cf., for example, E. J. Watson, "Computer Services for Small Business," *Management Accounting*, October, 1965, pp. 11–13; H. S. Garber, "Now: EDP Systems Every Store Can Afford," *Stores*, December, 1964, pp. 12–17; and W. W. Finke, "Computers: Yesterday, Today and Tomorrow," *Credit and Financial Management*, January, 1966, pp. 18–20.

ESSENTIALITY OF ACCOUNTING RECORDS

Some small merchants believe they know enough about their businesses through day-to-day contacts to make the keeping of formal books unnecessary. These retailers proceed on the theory that, if there is any money left over after bills are paid, they have made a profit. Unfortunately, however, court records are filled with cases of bankrupt retailers who "thought" they were making a profit until it was too late. Records of the United States Department of Commerce suggest that 84 percent of those who fail in retailing do not have adequate accounting and other records.[4] A retailer's accounting system should provide the facts required to judge the effectiveness of his various financial activities and to make logical decisions about future courses of action.[5] These facts, to be most useful, must be made available promptly to permit corrective action without delay.

During recent decades, accounting records have assumed increased importance because of frequent revisions in federal and state income taxes and changes in the social security law. Moreover, governmental regulations affecting the valuation of inventories and the extensive use of sales taxes have further emphasized the need for complete and accurate records. Since these conditions will undoubtedly prevail for some time to come the retailer must be prepared to meet them.

Although records are essential to successful operation, it should also be emphasized that a retailer can have too many records. In fact, some retailers maintain such elaborate systems of records that they neglect their major function—buying and selling merchandise. In other words, they become keepers of records rather than merchants.

Accounting Knowledge Required of Retailer

Although it is unnecessary, under normal circumstances, for the proprietor of the one-man store to have any extensive knowledge of bookkeeping methods, it is essential for him to know enough so that he can maintain a satisfactory accounting system and interpret properly the information the

---

[4] National Cash Register Co., *Profiting by Adequate Business Records* (Dayton, Ohio: National Cash Register Co., 1961), p. 2. And for business firms in general ". . . a study made at a leading eastern University found 78% of the unsuccessful companies did not have adequate cost and performance records." "Inadequate Records Pave the Road to Bankruptcy," *The Office,* June, 1965, p. 62.

[5] Cf. H. W. Cornish, "Systems in Small Business," *Management Accounting,* October, 1965, pp. 7–11.

system provides.[6] Large retailers require competent staffs to handle their accounting problems, but, like the small retailer, they should be able to appraise the results intelligently. Otherwise, sound management is impossible.

Purposes of Accounting Records

Accounting records serve six main purposes as follows:

To Determine Financial Results of Past Operations. Without adequate accounting records, it is impossible to determine the precise financial results of past operations. But keeping records does not insure the making of a profit; the records merely indicate the results of the operations—whether the risks inherent in the business have been recognized and met successfully. As was stated so well some years ago:

Profit and loss are inevitably associated with risk and uncertainty; there is no sure or guaranteed profit. Economists and statisticians may not always agree on theoretical definitions of profit, and their definitions may differ from the ordinary business usage. Among accountants and businessmen, however, there will be general agreement on the ordinary meaning of "net business profit" as a residual amount after the payment of all costs and expenses and after all taxes, and they will not be disturbed by the fact that such a figure from the point of view of the economist consists of a mixture of pure profit, interest, possibly some rent, and, on occasion, some wages of management. But whatever its theoretical content, profit essentially constitutes a reward for the successful management of business risks.[7]

Profits, of course, result from the maintenance of satisfactory relationship among sales, the cost of the goods sold, and total operating expenses. Losses occur when these relationships are not satisfactory. As we shall see, these are all important elements of the operating statement. But balance sheet accounts such as cash, accounts receivable, merchandise inventory, and accounts payable are likewise important. All of these are involved in the numerous risks which must be successfully undertaken by the retailer if profits are to be realized.

To Provide Information for Appraising Current Results and Making Future Plans. Not only do suitable accounting records furnish data on the results of past operations, but they also make possible the

---

[6] Organizations have been formed to assist small merchants in handling their accounting problems. The Accounting Corporation of America, for example, has developed extensive services along this line. Its bookkeeping-by-mail service, known as "Mail-Me-Monday," has received wide acceptance in recent years.

[7] M. P. McNair, E. A. Burnham, and A. C. Hersum, *Cases in Retail Management* (New York: McGraw-Hill Book Co., Inc., 1957), p. 37.

analysis of these results and comparison with previous periods. Studies of this nature, when supplemented with day-to-day information, provide data helpful in evaluating results of current operations and in making future plans.

To Furnish Information upon Which Credit Lines May Be Established. From time to time, most retailers must borrow money from banks to finance their operations. Before making loans, bankers require complete and up-to-date financial statements from applicants. Without records that supply this needed information in proper form, chances of favorable action upon the application are considerably reduced. Vendors, likewise, require ample evidence of financial soundness before credit will be granted. Since proper accounting records are evidence of good management, merchandise resources will be favorably inclined toward merchants who submit up-to-date and complete statements. Likewise, a prospective purchaser of a retail business looks for adequate accounting records as an aid to his appraisal of the worth of the firm.[8]

To Safeguard Company Assets. If accounting records are adequate, they are invaluable in protecting the retailer's assets. Through summarized statements and reports at frequent intervals, attention is centered on these assets; any changes are noted and investigated; and everything of value—tangible and intangible—is safeguarded.

To Meet Governmental Regulations. Frequent mention has been made throughout this book of the increasingly close relationship of government to the retail business. Today, more than ever before, detailed reports must be made by retailers to various local, state, and federal governmental agencies. Reports on taxable income; old-age pensions and unemployment insurance; withholdings of federal and state income taxes; and sales or retailers' occupational taxes collected are among those required.[9] Such reports, based on accurate and complete records, must be filed promptly to avoid penalties.

To Facilitate Comparisons with Standard Figures. An important function of accounting records is to provide information that may be used for comparing results against a standard and/or to exchange comparable information with other stores. To make possible comparisons against standard figures published by government agencies, university bureaus of business research, and retail trade associations, it is not necessary that ac-

---

[8] The significance of this statement can be illustrated by one instance. After Montgomery Ward & Company purchased a group of Chicago stores for $9 million, it discovered it had also assumed an unexpected liability of $3 million because of the group's unfunded pension plan. Cf. T. A. Wise, "Those Uncertain Actuaries," *Fortune,* Vol. LXXIII, No. 1 (January, 1966), p. 184.

[9] Cf. A. T. Samuelson, "Accounting vs. Federal Regulation; Is there an Emerging Discipline?", *Management Accounting,* October, 1965, pp. 14–21.

counting records be maintained according to the forms used by these organizations, but it is essential that the retailer make proper adjustments in his figures so that they are comparable to the standard figures. Similar precautions should be taken when operating and merchandising results are exchanged with other stores.

COMPUTING PROFITS AND LOSSES UNDER THE COST METHOD

To achieve the foregoing purposes of accounting records, the large majority of retail stores, including practically all small stores, use what is known as the cost method. In practice, this method requires that the retailer record the cost of all items entering the store, that frequently the unit cost be marked in code upon each item in addition to its retail price, and that the physical inventory be taken on a cost basis with adjustments so that it will conform to the axiom "cost or market, whichever is lower."[10]

Two important accounting statements, the operating statement and the balance sheet, are vital instruments in connection with determining the profits and the financial responsibility of the retailer. Since most students of retailing will have had at least one course in accounting, it is unnecessary to treat each of these statements in detail here.[11] Emphasis on a few of the major factors involved in each, however, together with an illustration of each, may prove helpful to the reader.

The Operating Statement[12]

Stated concisely, an operating statement (also known as an income statement and a profit and loss statement) is a summary of the results of operations carried on during a specific period of time, such as a month, six months, or a year. It shows the relationship that has prevailed for the period among sales, cost of goods sold, and expenses, and indicates the amount of the resulting profit or loss. As suggested by the highly simplified operating statement of Table 23-1, this relationship is as follows: net sales minus cost

---

[10] For a more precise statement of this rule cf. the discussion of inventory valuation, p. 663, below. Also cf. R. S. Lindbeck, "Conventional Retail—Lower than Cost or Market," *Accounting Review,* April, 1966, pp. 335–38; and M. A. Hartman, "A Simplified Solution to Cost or Market Problems," *ibid.,* January, 1966, pp. 127–29.

[11] Others not possessed with such knowledge should consult the section on "Basic Financial Statements" in *The Values of Total System Reports for Retailers* and its companion *Reference Supplement* (Dayton, Ohio: National Cash Register Co., 1966), pp. 3–10.

[12] For a detailed explanation of this subject cf. H. L. Margules, "Operating Statements," *The Buyer's Manual* (4th ed.; New York: National Retail Merchants Association, 1965), pp. 411–24.

of goods equals gross margin; gross margin minus operating expenses equals net profit before income taxes.

Net Sales. Taking a closer look at each element in the operating statement of Table 23–1, we note that the term *"net* sales" is used. This phraseology implies that there may be such a thing as "gross sales," and this is true. When a customer buys a $75.00 coat, the store records that a sale of

TABLE 23–1

OPERATING STATEMENT, JANUARY 1–JUNE 30, 1967
(Cost Method)

	Dollars	Ratio to Sales
Net sales.............................	$100,000	100.0
Cost of goods sold.....................	65,000	65.0
Gross margin.........................	$ 35,000	35.0
Operating expenses....................	30,000	30.0
Net profit before income taxes.........	$ 5,000	5.0

$75.00 has been made. However, if this coat is returned for full credit, the store's net sales will be $75.00 less than its gross sales. Likewise, if the customer, after taking the coat home, discovered the lining had a bad spot on it, but decided to keep the coat when the store returned $15.00 to her, gross and net sales would also be at a variance. Stated simply, the gross sales figure for a period is the total of all the prices on goods sold, regardless of whether sales are for cash or on some form of credit. The net sales figure for the same period is the gross sales figure minus any returns from and adjustments to customers. Consequently, the net sales figure of Table 23–1 was obtained as follows:

Gross sales.....................	$110,000
Returns and allowances..........	10,000
Net sales......................	100,000

Cost of Goods Sold. The $65,000 cost of goods sold figure in Table 23–1 represents what the retailer paid for the merchandise sold during the period covered by the operating statement.[13] When he inventoried his stock at the *close* of business on December 31, 1966, he discovered his cost for the merchandise on hand totaled $22,500.[14] During the January 1–June 30, 1967, period his purchases from various resources totaled $66,000. However, his cash and quantity discounts on these purchases came to $6,000 and he paid $950 to have the goods delivered to his store, so that his net cost of purchases was $60,950 ($66,000 − $6,000 + $950). When he inventoried the stock remaining in his store on June 30, 1967, he found it had a cost

---

[13] Also cf. discussion of "Cost of Merchandise" on p. 485, above.

[14] Cf. discussion in the next paragraph on the method of getting this inventory figure.

value of $18,450. From these figures we can see how the $65,000 figure of Table 23–1 was obtained, as follows:

```
Opening inventory at cost, January 1, 1967...$22,500
Purchases at cost (less discounts)..........  60,000
Freight and express.......................      950
Total cost of goods handled...............$83,450
Closing inventory at cost, June 30, 1967....  18,450
Cost of goods sold.....................$65,000
```

Earlier in this chapter mention was made of the need to adjust the closing and opening inventory figures so that they represent actual cost value at the time they are taken. Perhaps some items have become soiled or deteriorated or fashion changes have lowered the value of other goods in stock. Whatever the reason, whenever the typical retailer takes a physical inventory he discovers he would not then pay for some of it what he actually did at the time it was purchased. In recognition of this fact, he does *not* value his stock at the total of all his cost figures, but adjusts his cost figures so they reflect the current situation. In brief, he applies the rule: stock should be valued at actual cost or current replacement cost, whichever is lower—a rule which is usually shortened to "cost or market, whichever is lower." In the preceding paragraph this rule was applied to both the opening and closing inventory figures, so that they represented current cost at the time they were taken.

Operating Expenses. Chapter 25, "Expense Control," deals at some length with the elements included in the "operating expenses" item of Table 23–1. For our present purposes it is sufficient to point out that it includes all the costs of running the store, such as those involved in payroll, rent, advertising, insurance, supplies, and taxes (other than income taxes). When all these expenses are deducted from the dollar gross margin, the balance represents net profit before income taxes.

Preliminary Evaluation of Cost Method for Computing Profits and Losses

Although the merits and limitations of the cost method of computing profits will be more evident following the discussion of the retail inventory method in Chapter 24, a few words should be added at this point.[15] For relative simplicity of records and ease of understanding, there is much to be said for the cost method. However, since profits cannot be computed without a physical inventory[16] and since most retailers find it too time-consuming to "cost their stock" more than once or twice a year, the cost method does not

---

[15] Also cf. the discussion on pp. 678–82, below.

[16] This statement is not valid for retailers who can maintain a perpetual inventory figure. Cf. pp. 373–75, above.

provide a profit figure as often as desired by many retailers. Moreover, the cost method does not give the operator data on his stock shortages. Despite these limitations, and as already indicated, the great majority of retailers find the cost method of computing profits an eminently satisfactory one and continue to rely upon it.

THE RETAILER'S FINANCIAL POSITION: THE BALANCE SHEET

It is not sufficient for the retailer to know the outcome of his operations for a given period, as indicated by the operating statement. He should also know his financial position at the end of the period. This information is supplied by the balance sheet.[17] The retailer needs to know how much capital he has invested in the business and how this investment is distributed among such items as cash resources, accounts receivable, merchandise inventories, and fixtures and equipment. These are known as assets. In addition, he requires knowledge of his indebtedness—the nature and amount of claims against his assets. These claims are his liabilities. The amount of the retailer's net worth—the amount by which his total assets exceed his total liabilities—is especially important, as are the changes in the nature and amount of the assets and liabilities during the period.[18] Some of these elements are included in the simplified balance sheet of Table 23–2.

TABLE 23–2

BALANCE SHEET, DECEMBER 31, 1966 AND JUNE 30, 1967

ASSETS

	June 30, 1967	December 31, 1966
Cash	$ 6,000	$ 5,000
Customers' accounts receivable (less reserve for bad debts)	4,000	4,000
Inventory (at actual or current cost, whichever is lower)	21,000	19,250
Fixtures and equipment (after depreciation)	7,500	7,800
	$38,500	$36,050

LIABILITIES AND NET WORTH

Accounts payable	$14,000	$13,500
Loan from bank	3,500	3,000
Owner's net worth	21,000	19,550
	$38,500	$36,050

---

[17] Cf. E. G. Nelson, "The Relationship Between the Balance Sheet and the Profit-and-Loss Statement" in Maurice Moonitz and A. C. Littleton (eds.) *Significant Accounting Essays* (Englewood Cliffs, N.J.: Prentice-Hall, Inc., 1965), pp. 158–70.

[18] In 1966 many retailers were shocked by a ruling of the Securities and Exchange Commission under which any listed company with installment sales or other credit practices involving extension of customer's payments over more than one fiscal year, could no longer defer income taxes on such sales over the life of the contract. Stores classifying installment receivables as "current assets" in their balance sheets would be forced to show income taxes and other liabilities related to these sales as "current liabilities" for the same

In view of the reader's knowledge of accounting, it will not be necessary to explain further each of the elements in Table 23–2 and to discuss the desired relationships among them.[19] Instead we shall turn to an analysis of how, under the cost method, the operating statement and the balance sheet may be used by *small* retailers in the actual conduct of their businesses.

COST METHOD IN OPERATION

Daily Record

A basic principle of retail accounting is to record each day's transactions as they occur or to summarize them immediately at the close of the day. The retailer who waits a few days to make his entries will soon find that many significant transactions have already slipped his memory.

Figure 23–1 shows a simple, but adequate, form for the small retailer's daily record. Although designed specifically for operators of food stores, it can be readily changed to meet the needs of any small retail business. At the top of the form, spaces are provided for recording daily changes in cash (both that on hand and in the bank) and in credit accounts. The spaces under the heading "Cash Received Today" provide basic information on daily sales and collections on credit accounts, while the "Cash Paid Out Today" section gives a record of merchandise purchases and operating expenses. If, along with this daily summary, the small retailer maintains a check stub record showing the amount of each check, the person to whom the check was drawn, and items or services paid for by the check, he will have sufficient data upon which to prepare an operating statement and a balance sheet for any period or periods.

End-of-Month Statements

The daily record referred to above requires no great effort on the part of the small retailer and should provide all the information necessary until the end of the month, when it is customary to prepare summarized statements of the results of operations and financial position. Since it is easier for most retailers to close their books on Saturdays (the end of the week), months are frequently taken in periods of four or five weeks.

---

year. Since this change in practice, designed to make company financial statements more understandable to investors, would result in less favorable financial ratios and also reduce working capital, strong objections—but to no avail—were raised by retailers, especially the larger, publicly-owned ones. Cf. Isadore Barmash, "Merchants Irate Over S.E.C. Ruling," *New York Times,* February 13, 1966, pp. F1–14.

[19] For studies of balance sheet ratios for retailers of various types cf. "Ratios of Retailing," which appears each year in the September issue of *Dun's Review and Modern Industry.*

A simple form of monthly summary is shown in Figure 23–2. This form represents a combination of the operating or income statement and the balance sheet. The information called for on this form may be obtained from

Form A DAILY SUMMARY OF CASH AND CHARGE ACCOUNTS Date______

Cash on Hand		Cash in Bank		Due from Customers	
On hand last night (from line 7 yesterday)....	1	In bank last night (from line 17 yesterday)....	11	On books last night (from line 27 yesterday)....	21
Cash received today (from line 37 below).......	2	Deposited today (from line 6).............	12	Charge sales today (total of sales slips)........	22
Total (line 1 + line 2)........	3	Total (line 11 + line 12)........	13	Total (line 21 + line 22)........	23
Cash paid out today (from line 50 below).....	4	Checks written today (total from check book)....	14	Collected today (from line 35 below).......	24
Remainder (line 3 − line 4).........	5	Remainder (line 13 − line 14)........	15	Remainder (line 23 − line 24)........	25
Bank deposit today (to line 12)........	6	Charges by bank (from bank statement).....	16	Accounts written off	26
On hand tonight (line 5 − line 6)	7	In bank tonight (line 15 − line 16)........	17	On books tonight (line 25 − line 26)........	27

Cash Received Today			Cash Paid Out Today		
Cash sales (per cash register)			Merchandise purchased for cash		
Meats........		31	Meats {		38
Groceries........		32	Groceries { .... / .... / .... /		39
....		33			
Total cash sales........		34			
Collected on account			Other Merchandise........		40
....			Expenses paid in cash		
....			Wages to { .... / .... /		41
....			Rent........		42
....			Light, heat, power........		43
....			Ice........		44
....			Wrappings........		45
....			Gas, oil, truck repairs, etc........		46
....					
....					
....					
Total collected on account........		35	Advertising........		47
Other cash received (explain)			Other (........)		48
....		36	Owner's cash withdrawals........		49
Total all cash received (to line 2 above)........		37	Total all cash paid out (to line 4 above)........		50

© Institute of American Meat Packers

FIG. 23–1. A daily summary of cash and charge accounts.

the daily record sheet (Fig. 23–1) and from the check stubs. Although some clerical work is involved in this process, it may be done without difficulty by the proprietor or by someone designated by him.

Computing the Cost of Merchandise Sold. Perhaps the most difficult amount for the small retailer to calculate in his accounting work is the cost of the merchandise sold, to be entered on line B2 of Figure 23–2. As previously indicated, under the cost method of accounting the determination of this figure calls for: (1) a physical inventory to determine the value of

Form B — MONTHLY INCOME STATEMENT AND BALANCE SHEET — Month_____

Income Statement	Groceries	Meats		Entire Store	
Sales (totals from Form D or lines 31, 51, etc., of Form A).........					B1
Cost of merchandise sold (totals from Form C, "Merchandise Cost Summary," line C11)..					B2
Gross margin (line B1 less line B2)......					B3
Per cent of gross margin to sales.....					
Expenses (total from line B55 below).........					B4
Profit (Line B3 less line B4—carry to line B37 below)......					B5

Balance Sheet—End of Month

Assets			Detail of Expenses (from totals of lines 41 to 48, and 55 of Form A, or columns E41 to E48 of Form E, etc.)	
Cash on hand (from line 7—last day).....		B11	Wages.....	B41
Cash in bank (from line 17—last day).....		B12	Rent.....	B42
Due from customers (from line 27—last day).....		B13	Light, heat, power.....	B43
Merchandise inventory (from line C10 of Form C).....		B14	Ice.....	B44
Store equipment (from line B35 below).....		B15	Wrappings.....	B45
Auto trucks (from line B35 below).....		B16	Gas, oil, etc.....	B46
Building and land (from line B35 below).....		B17	Advertising.....	B47
Total assets.....		B18	.....	B48
Equities			.....	B49
Unpaid merchandise invoices (from line C4 of Form C).....		B21	Bad debts written off (from total of line 55 of Form A).....	B51
Borrowed money		B22	Depreciation taken (from line B34 below).....	B52
Other liabilities		B23		
Total liabilities.....		B24	Total of above items.....	B53
Owner's net worth (from line B40 below).....		B25	Less: Miscellaneous income (from line 48 of Form A).....	B54
Total equities.....		B26	Net total expense (to line B4 above).....	B55

Analysis of Fixed Assets	Store Equipment	Trucks	Building	Owner's Net Worth	
Valuation—end of last month (from balance sheet last month).......			B31	Net worth—end last month (from balance sheet last month)...	B36
Additional purchases this month (from cash summary and check book)....			B32	Add: Profit this month (from line B5 above)...	B37
Total (line B31 plus line B32)......			B33	Total (line B36 plus line B37)...	B38
Deduct: Depreciation taken (total to line B52 above).....				Deduct: Net withdrawals	B39
Valuation—end this month (to line B15, B16, B17).....			B35	Net worth—end this month (to line B25 above)...	B40

Institute of American Meat Packers

FIG. 23–2. Monthly income statement and balance sheet.

the stock on hand; (2) a list of the unpaid merchandise invoices; (3) the total paid out on merchandise account during the month; and (4) the opening inventory. Figure 23–3, monthly merchandise cost summary, provides a satisfactory form on which these data may be assembled and the cost of merchandise ascertained.

Form C   MONTHLY MERCHANDISE COST SUMMARY   Month_____

Inventory of Merchandise on Hand	Unpaid Merchandise Invoices
(total of each section to line C10 below; carry grand total to line B14 of balance sheet)	(total of each section to line C4 below; carry grand total to line B21 of balance sheet)
Meats (details on sheets attached)	**Meat Invoices**
....	....
....	....
....	....
....	....
....	....
Total meats.	Total meats..
Groceries (details on sheets attached)	**Grocery Invoices**
....	....
....	....
....	....
Total groceries...	Total groceries...........................
Other Items (details on sheets attached)	
....	....................invoices
....	....
Total other item '..........	Total_____........................
Grand total inventory	Grand total unpaid invoices
(to line C10 below)...........................	(to line C4 below)...........................

Calculation of Cost of Goods Sold	Meats	Groceries
C1 Merchandise paid for in cash (from cash payment record—totals of lines 38-39-40).............................		
C2 Merchandise paid for by check (from check book record—summarised same way).............................		
C3 Total merchandise paid for (line C1 plus line C2)		
C4 Add: Merchandise bills unpaid—end this month (total of list above).............................		
C5 Total (line C3 plus line C4).............................		
C6 Deduct: Merchandise bills unpaid—end last month (from list last month).............................		
C7 Remainder—cost of merchandise purchased this month (line C5 less line C6).............................		
C8 Add: Inventory of merchandise—end last month (from list last month).............................		
C9 Total (line C7 plus line C8).............................		
C10 Deduct: Inventory of merchandise—end this month (total of list above).............................		
C11 Remainder—cost of merchandise sold this month (line C9 less line C10—carry to line B2 in Form B).............................		
⊙ Institute of American Meat Packers		

FIG. 23–3. Monthly merchandise cost summary.

Returning to Figure 23–2, once the sales and cost of merchandise sold are known, the gross margin may be found. By deducting the total expense from the gross margin, the amount of profit (or loss) is obtained.

Comparing Results with Those of Similar Stores

Although the operating statement furnishes valuable information for the determination of profits—an absolute essential for income tax purposes—and although the balance sheet provides in summarized form a list of assets and liabilities and the retailer's net worth, their usefulness is not restricted to these values. In addition to making possible comparisons of significant figures and financial ratios with those of previous operating and financial periods, these important accounting statements permit comparison of such data with those of similar stores and thus offer a valuable guide to management.[20]

Operating Results.   So far as operating statement figures are concerned, comparisons with comparable stores cover such important matters as the over-all sales trend, average gross sales, gross margin, total expense, and pre-tax earnings. To illustrate the availability of such data for comparative purposes, note the information concerning each of these factors for department stores with annual sales from $5 to $10 million for the three-year period 1963–65 as shown in Table 23–3.[21]

TABLE 23–3

Selected Operating Results for Department Stores with Annual Sales of $5-10 Million in 1963-65

Item	1965	1964	1963
Net Total Store Sales—Percent change			
This Year/Last Year.................. 6.8		5.8	2.0
Average Gross Sale ($).................... 5.64		5.75	5.04
Gross Margin*..........................34.60		34.84	34.34
Net Operating Expenses*..................30.74		31.20	31.29
Pre-Tax Earnings*........................ 4.01		3.54	2.78

* Percent of sales. Pre-tax earnings represent income from merchandising operations adjusted for net other income or deductions but before federal income taxes.

Source: Sam Flanel, *Financial and Operating Results of Department and Specialty Stores in 1965* (New York: National Retail Merchants Association, Controllers' Congress, 1966), p. 23.

Balance Sheet Items.   Worthwhile comparisons are also possible from information supplied by the balance sheet. Some of the more common financial ratios used by retailers to determine how their financial positions at particular times compare with comparable businesses are the ratio of current assets to current debt, current debt to tangible net worth, and inventory to net working capital. Information concerning each of these for a variety of retail businesses is shown in Table 23–4, together with data for net profit on net sales and net profit on net working capital—these latter two comparisons also requiring information from the operating statement.

---

[20] Cf. Norman Bussel, "How to Increase Profits Through Figure Exchange," *Progressive Grocer,* September, 1965, pp. 161–65 ff.

[21] Similar but more detailed data for individual departments in department and specialty stores are published annually by the Controllers' Congress of the National Retail Merchants Association. For data covering retailers of many different types cf. *Expenses in Retail Businesses* (Dayton, Ohio: National Cash Register Co., n.d.).

TABLE 23-4

MEDIAN FINANCIAL RATIOS IN SELECTED LINES OF RETAIL TRADE, 1965

Lines of Retail Trade	Current Assets to Current Debt (Times)	Current Debt to Tangible Net Worth (Percent)	Inventory to Net Working Capital (Percent)	Net Profit on Net Sales (Percent)	Net Profit on Net Working Capital (Percent)
Clothing, Men's and Boys'. 2.51		59.8	97.7	2.63	9.71
Clothing, Men's and Women's. 3.00		47.0	95.8	2.18	6.74
Department Stores. 3.37		32.9	76.6	2.18	8.23
Discount Stores. 1.71		104.5	166.0	1.75	19.25
Dry Goods. 3.03		42.2	95.8	2.67	6.87
Furnishings, Men's. 3.35		37.3	108.9	1.87	9.06
Furniture. 3.19		44.5	56.1	2.39	6.74
Groceries and Meats. 1.97		46.8	118.4	1.30	22.38
Hardware. 3.62		30.0	85.6	2.16	7.17
Jewelers. .2.90		51.5	75.8	3.39	8.82
Lumber Yards. 3.72		32.9	66.4	1.89	7.08
Shoes, Family. 3.12		39.4	110.5	2.69	9.93
Women's Specialty Shops. 2.45		55.0	84.2	1.91	8.07

SOURCE: "The Ratios of Retailing," *Dun's Review and Modern Industry*, September, 1966, p. 53.

The Cost Method and Large Retailers

To some degree the discussion in the preceding paragraphs has been deliberately oversimplified to emphasize the point of view of the small retailer. The larger retailers operating under the cost method must maintain more detailed records. To illustrate: frequently their records are designed to provide data of the type described for each department and approximate gross margin figures are estimated monthly. Since physical inventories are not taken at such frequent intervals, book inventory figures are determined from the estimated gross margin. This procedure becomes more difficult as the number of departments within a store increases.

To secure current information not available under the cost method and obtain closer approximations to gross margin realized without the necessity of taking a physical inventory, almost all large stores and many medium-size stores use the retail inventory method of accounting. In the next chapter we turn to a discussion of this method and others now being evaluated by retailers.

REVIEW AND DISCUSSION QUESTIONS

1. Explain fully why today's retailer, regardless of whether he operates a "mom and pop" store or a nation-wide organization, must maintain adequate accounting records.

2. Comment on the following statement by an officer of the National Records Management Council: "Controls over the creation and processing of records are . . . only the beginning chapters. For a really satisfactory conclusion to your records story, try to make better use of the waste baskets in your establishment . . . Too many business men have the squirrel instinct. They hoard inactive or obsolete records."

3. "Recently, accounting records have assumed increased importance because of frequent revisions in federal and state laws." What state and/or federal laws have particular significance to the retailer from the accounting point of view and necessitate his continued familiarity with their provisions?

4. Summarize the chief purposes of accounting records in the retail business.

5. Comment on the meaning of the term "profit" from the point of view of the economist, the accountant, and the retail executive.

6. Visit a local banker and report on the kinds of information he requires from retailers before extending them credit. Has any particular type of information assumed special significance in recent months? If so, what is it and what are the reasons for this development?

7. As the proprietor of a small retail store describe the procedure you would follow in choosing the particular system of accounting you would employ. Be as specific as possible.

8. "Despite its limitations, the great majority of retailers find the cost method of computing profits eminently satisfactory and continue to use it." What are these limitations and what benefits does the method yield that offset them?

9. Distinguish between the operating statement and the balance sheet.

10. Explain and illustrate the meaning of the terms "gross sales," "net sales," "cost of merchandise sold," "gross margin," and "net profit."

11. Suggest three elements which might convince a retailer that his closing inventory is no longer worth as much as he originally paid for it. Could it ever be worth more than its cost?

12. After reviewing the information in footnote 18, p. 664, visit a large retailer in your community and determine his attitude toward the Securities and Exchange Commission regulation affecting accounting practice on credit sales. Report your findings to the class.

13. Explain the benefits which accrue to the executives of retail stores from comparing their operating results and financial ratios with those of similar stores.

14. Examine carefully the financial ratios for selected lines of retail trade in Table 23–4. Account for the most pronounced variations in "Current Assets to Current Debt" and in "Net Profit on Net Working Capital" among the different kinds of retailers.

15. Studies by the National Records Management Council indicate that "65 cents to 75 cents of every dollar spent on record keeping is wasted." Discuss the implications of this statement and suggest ways by which this waste may be reduced.

SUPPLEMENTARY READINGS

General accounting principles applicable to retail stores are covered in all standard textbooks on accounting. The following references are to specialized treatments of particular phases of this subject.

Accounting and Financial Data for Retail Stores: Primary Purposes and Uses (Norman, Oklahoma: University of Oklahoma, Bureau of Business Research, 1964). In this paperbound volume the reader will find elementary concepts of accounting treated in concise fashion.

ANDERSON, W. T., *et al. Accounting: Basic Financial, Cost, and Central Concepts* (New York: John Wiley and Sons, Inc., 1965). As the title indicates, this volume covers basic accounting concepts of interest to students of retailing.

BELL, H. F., AND MOSCARELLO, L. C. *Retail Merchandise Accounting* (3d ed.; New York: Ronald Press Co., 1961). Essentially a "how to do it" book, this volume explains the adaptations of accounting theory to methods and procedures in retail stores.

BRAND, E. A. *Modern Supermarket Operation* (rev. ed.; New York: Fairchild Publications, Inc., 1965). The sections of this volume dealing with financial ratios and operating results offer valuable supplementary reading in connection with this chapter.

FAIRCHILD PUBLICATIONS, INC. *Fairchild's Financial Manual of Retail Stores* (New York: published annually). Complete financial information covering more than 200 publicly owned retail organizations in about ten different types of businesses is given in this annual publication.

GOLDENTHAL, IRVING. *How to Benefit From Data On The Operating Statement* and *Retail and Cost Methods Compared* (Philadelphia: Chilton Co., 1959). Despite their age, these two pamphlets continue to provide a clear and practical approach to their subjects.

GORDON, M. J., AND SHILLINGLAW, GORDON. *Accounting: A Management Approach* (3d ed.; Homewood, Ill.: Richard D. Irwin, Inc., 1964). Chapters 1, 2, and 7—"Accounting and Business Enterprise," "Basic Elements of Accounting Method," and "Financial Statement Preparation"—respectively, are of special interest in connection with this chapter.

HELFERT, E. A.; MAY, E. G.; AND McNAIR, M. P. *Controllership in Department Stores* (Cambridge, Massachusetts: Harvard University Press, 1965). In this interesting volume of 154 pages, three careful students have analyzed the controller's job in detail and emphasized its relationship to the other major divisions in department stores.

NATIONAL CASH REGISTER COMPANY. *Expenses in Retail Businesses* (Dayton, Ohio: n.d.). This compilation of retailing data includes sales, gross margins, net profits, and other factors as well as operating expenses. Covering many types of retail businesses, the information is invaluable for comparative purposes.

———. *Profiting By Adequate Business Records* (Dayton, Ohio: 1961).

Written for the small retailer, this pamphlet emphasizes the accounting records and the equipment he needs to produce these records.

SCOTTON, D. W. *Operating Costs and Ratios: Retailing* (rev. ed.; Washington, D.C.: Small Business Administration, 1965). This compilation includes many retail financial ratios against which the merchant may compare his results.

SIMPSON, M. S. "How do Electronic Computers Affect Accounting and Auditing Techniques?" *Financial Executive,* February, 1966, pp. 38 ff. The reader of this valuable article should also review BOYLE, E. T., "What the Computer Means to the Accounting Profession," *Journal of Accountancy,* January, 1966, pp. 56–67.

WINGATE, J. W.; SCHALLER, E. O.; AND GOLDENTHAL, IRVING. *Problems in Retail Merchandising* (5th ed.; Englewood Cliffs, N.J.: Prentice-Hall, Inc., 1961). This paper-covered volume presents in Part I a clear and simple explanation of the retail operating statement.

24

CHAPTER

The Retail Inventory Method and Other
Accounting Concepts

Many retailers, particularly the large ones, using the cost method of accounting were dissatisfied with its shortcomings. They sought a method which would give a retail-price approach to their problems of inventory depreciation and inventory taking, and which would enable them to determine their profits at more frequent periods than at inventory-taking time. The retail inventory method of accounting provided the answer.

Just as the limitations of the cost method stimulated the growth of the retail inventory method of accounting, so has awareness of the shortcomings of the latter system encouraged the search for a new approach that will yield more positive benefits to the retailer under conditions existing today. Merchandise management accounting is one result of this search. In the present chapter attention is given to the retail inventory method of accounting, to inventory valuation under LIFO (last-in-first-out), and to merchandise management accounting. As in the preceding chapter, our interest is in basic principles and not in the equipment—such as the newer electronic data-processing machines[1]—used to perform accounting activities.

DEVELOPMENT AND BASIC PRINCIPLES OF THE
RETAIL INVENTORY METHOD

The retail inventory method, which derives its name from the fact that its procedures rely so heavily on records at retail (rather than cost) prices, is not new. There is evidence that accounting systems embodying the general

---

[1] Cf. the discussion on pp. 138–41, above.

principles of this method were in use in this country in the 1870's.[2] Widespread adoption of this method, however, did not come until it had won the qualified approval of the Bureau of Internal Revenue in 1920. While we do not know the exact number of stores now using this method of accounting, it clearly dominates in the department and departmentized specialty store fields. Furniture stores, men's clothing stores, jewelry stores, and chain food stores frequently use this method of accounting or various modifications of it. Many chain stores have found that better control over store managers is afforded when goods are charged to stores both at cost and retail prices. But what *is* this retail inventory method?

Fundamentals of the Retail Inventory Method

Costing a Retail Inventory. The essential ingredient of the retail inventory method of accounting is this: it provides a procedure for determining at any desired time the cost value of a closing inventory stated at retail value. For example, a retailer who knows that the closing value of his inventory at retail prices is $10,000 is able, through the retail inventory method, to ascertain a cost figure for his goods on hand.

Moreover, the cost value of the closing inventory can be computed regardless of whether the inventory figure is obtained by taking a physical inventory at retail prices, or by using the book record of the retail inventory. Actually, a major advantage of the retail inventory method is that it can be used with the book record of the inventory to determine operating results more often than is possible when a physical inventory is required. In practice, the retail inventory method is used to compute operating results several times a year based on book inventory figures. Physical inventories at retail prices are taken once or twice a year mainly to check the accuracy of the book inventory.

The retail inventory method, it should be emphasized, requires that both inventory and purchase figures be carried on the retailer's books at retail and at cost. The reasons for this will become clear in the paragraphs which follow. Since all physical inventories are taken at retail prices, however, it is not necessary to place cost information on the merchandise.

How can the closing inventory at retail be converted to a cost value? We begin with the case in which a physical inventory has been taken at retail prices and follow this with an illustration based on a book inventory figure.[3]

[2] Cf. M. P. McNair and A. C. Hersum, *The Retail Inventory Method and Lifo* (New York: McGraw-Hill Book Co., Inc., 1952), pp. 60–61.

[3] Both of these examples are taken from J. W. Wingate, E. O. Schaller, and Irving Goldenthal, *Problems in Retail Merchandising* (5th ed.; Englewood Cliffs, N.J.: Prentice-Hall, Inc., 1961), pp. 121–22.

1. *Conversion Based on Physical Inventory.* Based on the cost and retail records of his opening inventory and his purchases, and also on the figures for his closing physical inventory taken at retail prices, a retailer finds his position as indicated in Table 24–1. It is clear that the cost of the total

TABLE 24–1

FACTS NEEDED FOR CONVERTING PHYSICAL
RETAIL INVENTORY TO COST

	Cost	Retail
Opening inventory	$ 6,100	$10,000
Purchases	17,900	30,000
Total merchandise handled	$24,000	$40,000
Closing physical inventory at retail		$ 8,000

merchandise handled during this period is 60 percent of the retail for this merchandise, that is,

$$\frac{\$24,000}{\$40,000} \times 100\% = 60\%.$$

Assuming this same relationship in the closing retail inventory, its cost value may be calculated by multiplying its retail value by 60 percent (known as the cost percentage), as follows:

$$\$8,000 \times 60\% = \$4,800.$$

In brief, a closing physical inventory at retail may be converted to a cost figure by this formula:

Cost value of inventory = retail value of inventory × cost percentage.

2. *Conversion Based on Book Inventory.* The basic facts for this illustration are given in Table 24–2.

TABLE 24–2

FACTS NEEDED TO COMPUTE COST
VALUE OF BOOK RETAIL INVENTORY

	Cost	Retail
Opening inventory	$ 41,000	$ 65,000
Purchases	128,000	183,000
Total merchandise handled	$169,000	$248,000
Sales (from records)		$150,000
Markdowns (from records)		12,000
Shortages (estimated)		8,000
Total merchandise deductions		$170,000

The cost percentage is computed exactly as in the preceding illustration. Consequently, we find it as follows:

$$\frac{\$169,000}{\$248,000} \times 100\% = 68.1\%,$$

In this case, however, we do not have a physical retail inventory figure to which this cost percentage can be applied; so we must create one. We do this by subtracting from the total merchandise handled at retail everything which has decreased the value of this merchandise during the period covered by Table 24–2. Of major importance, of course, is the sales figure. From the retailer's record of daily sales, a total of $150,000 is obtained for the period. Markdowns also decrease the value of merchandise handled, and the retailer's record of these indicates a total of $12,000. In addition, all inventories shrink to some degree from shortages.[4] Based on his experiences in previous years, the retailer estimates these at $8,000. Deducting the total of these three items ($150,000 + $12,000 + $8,000 = $170,000) from the retail of all merchandise handled ($248,000) he obtains an estimated or book inventory figure of $78,000 at retail.

The final step of converting this $78,000 to cost is the same as if it were a physical inventory figure, that is, the standard formulae is used, as follows:

Cost value of inventory = retail value of inventory × cost percentage
= $78,000 × 68.1%
= $53,118

Basic Steps in Retail Inventory Method. In summary, the foregoing illustrations suggest that six basic steps are involved in the retail inventory method: (1) charging merchandise to a department or to an entire store at both cost and retail prices; (2) keeping complete and accurate records at retail prices of all additions to and deductions from this stock; (3) determining the markup percentage and through this the cost percentage on the total merchandise handled; (4) calculating from the records the closing retail book inventory, that is, the retail value of the merchandise at hand in the closing inventory; (5) applying the cost percentage to the retail book inventory; (6) taking a physical inventory at retail prices, usually semiannually or annually, to check the accuracy of the retail book inventory. If this check reveals that the retail book inventory exceeds the physical inventory, which is the usual situation, a stock shortage exists; if the physical inventory is larger than the book inventory, an overage exists.

Operating Statement under the Retail Inventory Method

Except for fairly obvious deviations, the remaining steps necessary to prepare an operating statement under the retail inventory method are similar

---

[4] Cf. discussion on pp. 393–95, above.

to those under the cost method. Continuing with the data of Table 24–2, sales are already given in the table. Cost of goods sold is $115,882, that is, the difference between total merchandise handled at cost ($169,000, as given in Table 24–2) and the computed cost value of the closing inventory ($53,118). Operating expenses for the period are taken directly from the appropriate records: in the present case they are assumed to total $26,618. Consequently, the operating statement will show

	Dollars	Ratio to Sales
Sales	$150,000	100.0
Cost of goods sold	115,882	77.3
Gross margin	$ 34,118	22.7
Operating expenses	26,618	17.7
Net profit before income taxes	$ 7,500	5.0

ADVANTAGES AND DISADVANTAGES OF THE RETAIL INVENTORY METHOD

With a knowledge of the fundamental concepts involved in the retail inventory method, let us appraise its usefulness to the retailer and review the reasons for its growth. These objectives may best be attained through summarizing the chief advantages and disadvantages of this method.

Advantages of the Retail Method

Provides Effective Control over Profit. Adequate retail management under the highly competitive conditions of today involves close and continuous review of the merchandising activities of the business. Assuming that expenses are known and controlled, profits depend upon the gross margin realized. Gross margin, in turn, depends upon the initial markup obtained and the markdowns taken. When full and accurate information is available at frequent intervals on these two factors, as it is under the retail method, prompt action may be taken to guard the planned or desired profit margin. Moreover, operating statements can be prepared frequently so that the profit trend can be observed and appropriate courses of action be determined.

Permits Valuation of Inventory on Conservative Basis. The retail inventory method permits conservative valuation of the closing inventory without the necessity of making a physical count of the merchandise. This result is achieved by applying the cost percentage to the book inventory at retail. But the question naturally arises: Why does this procedure yield an inventory valuation on a conservative or "cost or market, whichever is lower" basis? The general answer lies in the fact that the cost percentage is calculated *after* additional markups but *before* markdowns. Further explanation will clarify this point.

Assume that a retailer purchases a man's suit at $30 and marks it to sell for $50, the cost percentage being 60 percent. Assume, further, that the retail price is increased to $60 by taking an additional markup of $10, so that the cost percentage drops to 50 percent. It is evident that the new cost percentage, 50 percent, will have to be applied to the new retail price, $60, to obtain the actual cost of the suit, $30. If the old cost percentage, 60 percent, were applied to $60, the cost of the suit would be shown as $36, which is clearly in error.

Now let us make another assumption. Suppose that another suit costing $30 is marked to sell for $50 but fails to do so and a markdown of $5 is taken, the cost percentage advancing from 60 percent to 66⅔ percent with this change. While the new cost percentage of 66⅔ percent will reduce the suit marked down to $45 to its original cost of $30, the question aries: Does $30 represent a fair valuation of a suit which had to be marked down $5 to be sold? If the accounting maximum—anticipate losses but never profits—is adhered to, the loss caused by the markdown will be taken in the current period rather than in the following one. Consequently, the original cost percentage, 60 percent, will be applied to the reduced price of $45, yielding a book value of $27. Thus, the fundamental rule is that the cost percentage must always be calculated by including the additional markups but excluding the markdowns.[5]

Facilitates Taking the Physical Inventory. Because the physical inventory is taken at retail prices under the retail inventory method, it may be taken more easily and at less expense. There is less chance of error because no decoding is necessary, and entries on the inventory cards or sheets are made more rapidly. Moreover, it is possible to use personnel unfamiliar with the stock to list it and count it. Since it is easier to take inventories, they may be taken at more frequent intervals; thus, slow-moving items and irregularities in the stock may be detected more quickly. In addition, the retail method makes it possible to take inventories in different departments at various times—thus overcoming some of the problems connected with store-wide inventories—and to adjust them to the general fiscal closing. In this connection it should be mentioned that, in cases where stores operate branches merchandised by the parent store, inventory should be taken both in the parent store and the branches on the same day. Any other plan

---

[5] For a comparison of inventory valuation under the cost method and the retail method cf. *The Values of Total System Reports for Retailers* (Dayton, Ohio: National Cash Register Company, 1966), pp. 11–16

necessitates careful cut-offs of interstore transfers and is complicated and costly.

Aids in Controlling Stock Shortages. By providing a book inventory figure, the retail inventory method makes possible the determination of stock shortages. Once determined, their causes may be ascertained and corrective measures adopted to minimize them. Stock shortages constitute an ever-recurring problem in most retail stores.

Furnishes Equitable Foundation upon Which to Base Insurance Coverage and Adjust Claims. When accurate and reliable records are kept, it is comparatively easy for retailers to establish proper insurance coverage and to obtain satisfactory adjustments on their insurance claims more quickly. These records, since they consist of irrefutable evidence, provide a sound and equitable basis for settling arguments.

Reveals Weaknesses in Procedures and Brings Improved Results. One of the important advantages of the retail inventory method is the benefit that accrues to the retailer through his careful follow-up of procedures and methods. This follow-up—including marking and remarking of goods, proper recording of markdowns, and the like—is essential to insure the accuracy of the figures upon which the retail method depends. Procedures are carefully appraised in the light of changing conditions, and revisions may be made when needed.

Furnishes Basis for Dollar Control. A final significant advantage of the retail inventory method is the valuable aid it provides in the control of merchandise on a dollar basis.[6] By placing continued emphasis on the fundamentals of the retail method and by concentrating the attention of department managers and others on their accountability for merchandise in terms of dollars, a merchandise consciousness is developed which results in better stock control and better profits. As pointed out before, the value of the retail inventory method as a means of merchandise control is one of the chief causes for its widespread use.

Disadvantages of the Retail Method

Despite its numerous advantages, the retail inventory method has certain important limitations which the retailer must recognize.

An Averaging Method. Probably the major disadvantage of the retail inventory method can be traced to the fact that it is an averaging method. By "averaging method" is meant that, in obtaining the cost percentage, the total *cost* of the merchandise handled and its total *retail* value are

---

[6] Cf. discussion of dollar control on pp. 371–74, above.

used (Table 24–2). Since low-markup merchandise tends to sell faster than high-markup goods, the former is represented in the total dollar purchases to a greater degree than it is at any time in the stock on hand. Consequently, when the closing book inventory at retail is reduced to cost by applying the cost percentage, the resulting valuation is higher than would be obtained by tabulating the specific costs of the items on hand. This disadvantage is particularly significant for stores and departments having (1) wide variations in markups and (2) many special sales events featuring merchandise at lower-than-usual markups.

Accurate Recording of Price Changes Required. Since the heart of the retail method consists of the maintenance of a book inventory figure which may be reduced to a cost or market basis at desired intervals, it is essential that this figure be accurate. Such accuracy depends upon the care exercised in recording all charges for merchandise delivered to the department, price changes such as markdowns and additional markups, transfers of goods to and from the department, and sales. Some unscrupulous buyers, however, may manipulate records—for example, markdowns—to their own advantage, with the result that the final figures are inaccurate.[7] Such manipulation, of course, will show up in the stock shortage figures if the buyer does not have the opportunity to alter the physical inventory figures. Only close supervision by management can overcome this danger.

Unsuited to Certain Stores and Departments. Retailers who desire to operate under a single, storewide accounting system may find it inadvisable to use the retail inventory method. The method is not suitable for certain merchandise—such as bakery goods, soda fountain sales, and prescriptions—where composition or manufacturing takes place. It is evident that for such merchandise incoming goods may be charged at retail prices; but because of changes in form before the merchandise is sold or because of difficulties in measuring ingredients accurately when small quantities are purchased, it is practically impossible to account for the goods on a retail basis. Moreover, drapery and furniture workrooms, devoted to preparing merchandise for use by customers, should be operated on a cost, rather than a retail, basis. Since many retailers have encountered little difficulty in operating the large majority of their departments on a retail basis and the remainder on a cost basis, however, this disadvantage is not serious.

Costly to Operate. A final limitation of the retail inventory method is the cost involved to operate it satisfactorily. The expense is greater than

---

[7] "Buying manipulation of inventory figures is the rule, not the exception, in the nation's large department stores." Cf. "Juggling: Buyers Stock in Trade," *Women's Wear Daily,* December 13, 1965, p. 1. Also cf. Richard Rosenthal, "Shortages Demand Scratch, So Buyers Build Up Kitties," *ibid.,* November 2, 1965, p. 14.

for the cost method because of the numerous records required to maintain complete and accurate book inventories for departments and the store as a whole. In the final analysis, of course, the costs involved in maintaining this system must be more than offset by the benefits it yields. That this is the case is evidenced by the large number of retailers using this method of accounting.

INVENTORY VALUATION UNDER LIFO

One of the main reasons for the growth of the retail inventory method of accounting is that it enables retailers to determine the lower of cost or market value on their closing inventories without facing the difficult problem of arriving at a reasonable and acceptable (to the government) depreciation figure on their merchandise inventories. Moreover, as most retailers and informed students know, it is customary in the retail business to attempt to sell "old" stocks first and "new" stocks last. Consequently, the established practice was FIFO (first-in, first-out), with the inventory accounting following the physical movement of goods.

Following 1939, however, many retailers, led by the control executives of department stores who recalled their experiences in previous war periods, sought methods of minimizing the effects of inflation on their profits. Under the FIFO method of inventory valuation, larger profits result during periods of rising prices because higher values are placed on ending inventories than on the goods on hand at the beginning of the year and the difference is added to profits, often termed "paper profits," upon which taxes must be paid. To remedy this situation, the LIFO (last-in, first-out) system was proposed and after much debate was approved by the Bureau of Internal Revenue in 1947.

LIFO Illustrated

The following illustration, showing how LIFO works, has been reproduced from *Fortune.*

Rising Prices. Suppose a retailer of mechanical pencils buys 5,000 pencils at 50 cents each in January of a given year; by the latter part of the year his inventory is running low and he buys 5,000 more pencils, but the price has risen to 75 cents each. During the complete year he sold 5,000 pencils, 3,000 of them at $1 each and 2,000 of them at $1.50 each (the latter price being established when he learned that the price to him was going up). In order to simplify this example, assume he has no other costs of doing business. Here's how it works out:

	FIFO		LIFO
	(First in, first out)		(Last in, first out)
Sales...	$6,000		$6,000
Cost of goods sold (5,000 @ 50¢)..........	2,500	(5,000 @ 75¢)	3,750
Reported profits before taxes..............	$3,500		$2,250
Federal income taxes (assumed arbitrarily			
at 50%)............................	1,750		1,125
Net profit............................	$1,750		$1,125
Ending inventory valuation (5,000 @			
75¢)...............................	$3,750	(5,000 @ 50¢)	$2,500

The obvious results of going to LIFO in a period of rising prices are pretty clearly shown—(1) lower federal income taxes, (2) lower reported net profit, and (3) lower ending inventory valuation. . . .

Falling Prices. Suppose the retailer finds that the cost of pencils goes back down to 50 cents each early in the following year. He then sells at $1 apiece again. Then later in the year he reorders and finds the cost 40 cents each. At that time he cuts his selling price to 80 cents. Assuming

Purchases.......................	3,000 @ 50¢	$1,500
	2,000 @ 40¢	800
Sales...........................	3,000 @ $1	3,000
	2,000 @ 80¢	1,600

his profit and loss statement might look like this:

	FIFO		LIFO
Sales...	$4,600		$4,600
Cost of goods sold (5,000 @ 75¢ = $3,750; reduction of		(2,000 @ 40¢)	
inventory to market—3,000 from 50¢ to 40¢ = $300)...	4,050	(3,000 @ 50¢)	2,300
Reported profits before taxes.........................	$ 550		$2,300
Federal income taxes................................	275		1,150
Net profit...	$ 275		$1,150
Ending inventory valuation (5,000 @ 40¢—result of re-			
duction to market price).........................	$2,000	(5,000 @ 50¢)	$2,500

The results of being on LIFO in a period of declining prices are clearly shown: (1) higher federal income-tax payments, (2) higher net profit, and (3) higher ending inventory valuation. . . .

Steady Prices. If costs are constant over a long period, it makes no difference whether you are on FIFO or LIFO.[8]

The Future of LIFO

Although LIFO has made substantial progress as a method of inventory valuation among large retailers and professional accounting firms in the past twenty years, it has not been adopted by the smaller firms and even the majority of large retailers have continued with more traditional methods of

---

[8] "The Facts of LIFO," *Fortune,* December, 1951, p. 198.

inventory valuation. As to the future, the continued upward trend of retail prices we have experienced for over three decades is certainly a strong incentive toward the eventual acceptance of LIFO by more retailers. On the other side are (1) the added complications which LIFO introduces into the accounting system and (2) the fact that, when a retailer adopts this valuation procedure, he must continue it even if the price level turns down.[9] After weighing the advantages and disadvantages, two careful students of this subject conclude:

> Although any final assessment of virtues and demerits will have to wait on a longer accumulation of experience, it is reasonable to conceive that Lifo inventory accounting will have a substantial future in retailing. That Lifo will ever fully supplant Fifo-cost-or-market for retail business seems doubtful, however, unless indeed the two concepts are some day amalgamated. . . .[10]

MERCHANDISE MANAGEMENT ACCOUNTING

Strictly speaking, merchandise management accounting is more a method of merchandising and pricing than it is a form of accounting.[11] Since it relies so heavily on accounting records and demands some accounting information not required for other purposes, however, a few paragraphs concerning it may appropriately be included in this chapter.

Objectives of Merchandise Management Accounting

Merchandise management accounting seeks, among other objectives, to improve *dollar* profit (rather than *percentage* profit) through better determination and interpretation of costs by individual items. Those who helped develop it felt that the retail inventory method of accounting places too much emphasis on department or store-wide gross margin percentages and they deplored "the fixed habit of looking at departmental expenses, both direct and allocated, as applying across the board to all the goods sold in the department."[12] It was pointed out that this traditional approach discouraged retailers from purchasing merchandise which might move in great quantity if priced with a lower-than-normal markup.

---

[9] Cf. Maurice Moonitz, "The Case Against LIFO as an Inventory-Pricing Formula," in Maurice Moonitz and A. C. Littleton (eds.), *Significant Accounting Essays* (Englewood Cliffs, N.J.: Prentice-Hall, Inc., 1965), pp. 439–49.

[10] McNair and Hersum, *op. cit.,* p. 379.

[11] Cf. the earlier discussion of "Individual Item Pricing," in Chapter 16, above.

[12] M. P. McNair and E. G. May, "Pricing for Profit: A Revolutionary Approach to Retail Accounting," *Harvard Business Review,* Vol. XXXV, No. 3 (May–June, 1957), p. 111.

Need for Merchandise Management Accounting. One writer has presented these five "significant observations" showing the need for merchandise management accounting.

1. The important decision-making level for retailers is necessarily the individual item and all managerial decisions must be reduced to this level. Consequently, financial and accounting data should be supplied on an individual item basis if that basis will best serve management's needs.

2. There is "practically a vacuum" of financial and accounting information at the individual item level since it has been centered around the organizational level of responsibility.

3. In view of the situation described in (2) above, retailers have been forced to rely upon the financial information available, that is, percentage relationships of initial markup and expenses to sales price is yardsticks in measuring the results of their merchandising operation. This practice, of course, serves to obscure the variations in cost and profit of individual items and to mislead management.

4. Rate of stockturn, although recognized as important by retailers, has never been properly integrated into their financial thinking but instead viewed traditionally in relationship to sales price alone. Since real profit, from an economic point of view, may be properly measured only in terms of earning power on invested capital, the profitability in relation to sales price must be combined with the turnover factor to accomplish this objective.

5. Retailers, particularly department stores, have only limited operating expense data with respect to the goods sold and therefore have generated a concept of "cost" limited to the cost of the goods obtained from the manufacturer. This concept, of course, excludes from "cost" those costs which are incurred in providing essential customer services which are a definite part of the economic value of the ultimate product acquired by the consumer.[13]

Some Concepts of Merchandise Management Accounting

The Concept of Cost Patterns. Merchandise management accounting recognizes that the variable (or direct) cost involved in retailing the many items sold in a department or in an entire store varies widely from item to item. While one item may be received and marked with a minimum of effort, sold without special advertising and with little of the salesperson's time, another item has the reverse characteristics. To use figures, the total variable cost to handle the first item may be 15 cents, while to handle the second 60 cents may be required. However, within a given department or store there are typically many items which involve comparable variable costs. Thus there emerges the concept of cost patterns—the grouping of

---

[13] The authors are indebted to R. I. Jones for these "significant observations." Cf. his pamphlet *Merchandise Management Accounting in Practice* (Chicago: Arthur Andersen & Co., 1957), pp. 2–9.

items with similar variable costs.[14] Such grouping is essential, since to figure variable costs on each item in stock would be too costly for the typical retailer. Thus group A items may fall in a 15-cent variable cost pattern; group B, 30 cents; group C, 60 cents; and so on.

The Concept of Contribution to Overhead. Once the variable cost of handling an item is determined, it is not difficult to compute its contribution to overhead and profit, or what is often referred to as its controllable profit. Continuing with the figures developed in the preceding paragraph, when a group A item sells to yield a gross margin of 25 cents, its contribution to overhead is 10 cents. In contrast, a group C item must carry a gross margin of 70 cents to yield a controllable profit of 10 cents.

It should be emphasized that a retail store should not avoid all products which fail to make some contribution to controllable profit. Stores carry many items which do not meet this requirement for such reasons as building traffic, matching competitors' offerings, and broadening assortments. But awareness of an item's contribution (or lack of it) to fixed expenses and profit is a guide of some importance to management.

The Concept of Turnover. Finally, the importance of turnover is emphasized under merchandise management accounting. While the importance of a satisfactory rate of stockturn has long been recognized by retailers, it has never been fully integrated into their pricing of individual items. To illustrate, because of the extremely low markup, many retailers have long considered cigarettes as nonprofit merchandise. More recent studies, which take into account the low selling expenses involved and the extremely high turnover, disclose that cigarettes are highly profitable.[15] The importance of turnover is also evident from the fact that "many merchandise lines having comparable profit experience at the controllable profit level have significant different experience after reflecting the turnover factor. . . ."[16]

In brief, then, merchandise management accounting attempts to—

1. Determine the total dollar cost which is quite closely associated with the handling and sale of each item in stock. This step is made easier by the development of cost patterns.

2. So price each item of merchandise that, after taking turnover into consideration, it yields the maximum dollar contribution to overhead. To emphasize

---

[14] Throughout this discussion the term "variable cost" is used in a very broad manner since, in practice, some of the costs assigned by merchandise management accounting to specific items does not vary directly with the specific item. In fact, the only costs not allocated to specific items are these: real estate; furniture, fixtures, and equipment; control and accounting; superintendency and building operations; personnel and employee benefits; and other fixed and policy expenses. Cf. McNair and May, *op. cit.*, p. 117.

[15] J. P. DeLuca, "Space Yield Findings on Cigarettes," *Chain Store Age* (Supermarket Executives Ed.), January, 1965, pp. 85–88.

[16] Jones, *op. cit.*, p. 13.

the significance of this "dollar variable cost-price-turnover" relationship, consider the case of a Group A item which is currently priced to yield a gross margin of 25 cents and a contribution to overhead of 10 cents. Assume that sales per week are 1,000. Under these conditions, this item makes a weekly contribution to overhead of $100. Now assume the price is reduced by 5 cents so the gross margin falls to 20 cents and the contribution to overhead to 5 cents, but that weekly sales advance to 3,000 units. The net results is a $150 weekly contribution to overhead.

Present and Probable Future of Merchandise Management Accounting

Although the most enthusiastic proponents of merchandise management accounting—primarily academicians and at least one public accounting firm—envisioned the system as the answer to many of the retailer's problems, few of the executives of even our most progressive stores share this opinion. Only a relatively few have adopted the system and, in general, even they have been dissatisfied with it.[17]

Failure of more retailers to adopt merchandise management accounting is due to a number of factors. So long as stores are merchandised departmentally, they will continue to emphasize departmental results. Tradition, resistance to change, unavailability of cost data and unwillingness to provide it, lack of understanding, and similar factors have caused many retailers to stay with the *status quo*. Moreover, since comparisons of data among similar stores are common today, it would seem that a considerable number of stores would have to adopt the system at a particular time to make possible the continuance of such comparisons.

Dissatisfaction with merchandise management accounting on the part of retailers who have adopted it has resulted from its failure to meet the expectations of its users and because of the unforeseen difficulties involved in its operation. As a pricing tool stressing the cost-retail price relationships of individual items on a current basis, the system tends to neglect the longer run problems of cost patterns, changes in the "promotional mix," and the activities of competitors. For example, the emphasis merchandise management accounting places on short-run and marginal factors "generally tends to lower prices if the buyer is a profit maximizer and is given no other guidance."[18]

---

[17] Cf. Roger Dickinson, "Marginalism in Retailing: The Lessons of a Failure," *Journal of Business,* Vol. XXXIX, No. 3 (July, 1966), pp. 353–58. Also cf. Peggy Heim, "Merchandise Management Accounting: A Retailing Experiment in Explicit Marginal Calculation," *Quarterly Journal of Economics,* Vol. LXXVII, No. 4 (November, 1963), pp. 671–75; and D. J. Dalrymple, *Measuring Merchandise Performance in Department Stores* (New York: National Retail Merchants Association, 1964).

[18] Dickinson, *op. cit.,* p. 355. This source also discusses other deficiencies of merchandise management accounting which cannot be treated here.

In view of the difficulties discussed and others, it is unlikely that merchandise management accounting will gain wide acceptance in the foreseeable future, despite the growing need for marginal analysis in the solution of retailing problems.[19] It seems certain, however, that the wide scope of technological developments having application to retail operations; the increasing competition of retailers for consumer patronage in our affluent society; the growing pressure of personnel for higher wages and better working conditions; and the necessity of controlling prices and costs to insure a reasonable level of profit, will result in the continued critical evaluation of present accounting systems and the search for improved methods and devices.

REVIEW AND DISCUSSION QUESTIONS

1. Explain the meaning of the term "retail inventory method" in your own words and describe the fundamental concepts on which this method of accounting is based.
2. In your opinion, what factors are responsible for the growth and widespread use of the retail inventory method?
3. Precisely, why does the use of the retail inventory method require that both inventory and purchase figures be maintained in terms of cost and retail prices?
4. Explain and illustrate how a closing physical inventory at retail can be converted to a cost basis.
5. Specifically, what information of importance to management does the "retail method" provide that is not available under the "cost method"?
6. Explain and evaluate at least three of the chief limitations on the retail inventory method.
7. Visit a store in your community using the "retail method" and ascertain from the controller or chief accountant the reasons why they do so. Check these reasons against the advantages of the method given in the textbook.
8. Despite the growth of the retail inventory method, it is not practicable to use this system of accounting in some departments. Name three of these departments and explain why it is not feasible to use the retail method in them.
9. What is meant by a "stock shortage"? A "stock overage"? Which is most common in retail stores? Why?
10. Prepare a short presentation of the essential features of FIFO and LIFO for delivery before your retailing class.
11. Illustrate with the use of hypothetical figures the effects on profits of adopting the LIFO system of inventory valuation during (a) a period of rising prices and (b) a period of declining prices.

---

[19] This need is emphasized by Dickinson, cf. *ibid*. pp. 357–58.

12. Explain concisely what is meant by "merchandise management accounting" and the factors responsible for the emergence of the concept.

13. In view of the factors mentioned in question 12, how do you account for the limited adoption of "merchandise management accounting" by retail stores?

14. Visit the accounting officer in a leading retail store in your community and prepare a brief summary of his opinion concerning the merits and limitations of merchandise management accounting.

15. Prepare a paper of some 1,500 words on the topic "Retail Accounting: Retrospect and Prospect."

SUPPLEMENTARY READINGS

The annual reports of retailing firms offer one of the more valuable sources of material on retail accounting practices. Be sure to read the fine print (usually referred to as "Notes to Financial Statements") in the rear of these reports. Changes in accounting procedures are frequently relegated to this section.

BELL, H. F., AND MOSCARELLO, L. C. *Retail Merchandise Accounting* (3d ed.; New York: Ronald Press Co., 1961). The authors present a careful analysis of the entire subject. They use a "how-to-do-it" approach.

DICKINSON, ROGER. "Marginalism in Retailing: The Lessons of a Failure," *Journal of Business,* Vol. XXXIX, No. 3 (July 1966), pp. 353–58. Also cf. HEIN, PEGGY, "Merchandise Management Accounting: A Retailing Experiment in Explicit Marginal Calculation," *Quarterly Journal of Economics,* Vol. LXXVII, No. 4 (November 1963), pp. 671–75. In these articles the authors discuss the reasons why merchandise management accounting has not been more widely accepted.

McNAIR, M. P., AND HERSUM, A. C. *The Retail Inventory Method and Lifo* (New York: McGraw-Hill Book Co., Inc., 1952). Initially undertaken as a revision of McNair's *The Retail Method of Inventory,* the authors have so improved and enlarged on the former treatment that the current volume is really a new book. It covers the retail inventory method and LIFO in excellent fashion and is unquestionably the outstanding book in these fields.

McNAIR, M. P., AND MAY, E. G. "Pricing for Profit: A Revolutionary Approach to Retail Accounting," *Harvard Business Review,* Vol. XXXV, No. 3 (May–June 1957), pp. 105–22. A strong and long-time advocate and student of the "retail method," emphasizes in this article, with the capable assistance of Miss May, the need for "a new method of approach, with a new framework, new concepts, and some new terminology" in retail accounting. Also cf. their "A Practical Approach to Merchandise Management Accounting," *Stores,* May, 1958, pp. 39–50.

MOONITZ, MAURICE, AND LITTLETON, A. C. (eds.). *Significant Accounting Essays* (Englewood Cliffs, N.J.: Prentice-Hall, Inc., 1965). Professor Moonitz discusses "The Case Against LIFO as an Inventory-Pricing Formula," in Part VI of this collection.

NATIONAL RETAIL MERCHANTS ASSOCIATION. *The Retail Inventory Method in Practical Operation* (New York: The Association, n.d.). This small volume contains a concise explanation of the retail inventory method and furnishes helpful illustrative forms and examples. Also cf. the *Stock Shortage Control Manual,* which contains recommended procedures for minimizing inventory shrinkage.

————. *The Buyer's Manual* (4th ed.; New York: The Association, 1965). Chapter 41, MARGULES, H. L., "Operating Statements"; and Chapter 42, AUS, E. R., "Merchandising Arithmetic," are pertinent to the present chapter.

WINGATE, J. W., AND FRIEDLANDER, J. S. *The Management of Retail Buying* (Englewood Cliffs, N.J.: Prentice-Hall, Inc., 1963). In the technical appendix to this textbook, Merchandise Management Accounting as a pricing concept is analyzed.

WINGATE, J. W., SCHALLER, E. O., AND GOLDENTHAL, IRVING. *Problems in Retail Merchandising* (5th ed.; Englewood Cliffs, N.J.: Prentice-Hall, Inc., 1961). Problems involving the retail inventory method are included in Chaps. xiv–xv and Appendix B; LIFO and FIFO in Appendix C; and merchandise management accounting in Appendix D.

YOUNG, E. R. *Introduction to Merchandise Management Accounting for Small Retail Outlets* (Salt Lake City, Utah: University of Utah, 1964). The author states the basic principles and outlines the procedures of MMA for the small retailer.

25
CHAPTER

Expense Control

No problem facing the retailer today is more urgent, more continuous, and more vital to his existence than effective control of his expenses. This statement is true because of two rather obvious facts: (1) expense permeates the structure of every retail enterprise and (2) proper control of all expense items is essential if reasonable profits are to be realized, particularly today with a profit squeeze existing in many types of retail stores.[1] Expressed as a percentage of net sales, expenses of retail stores vary with such factors as the type of store, i.e., grocery, jewelry, or department store; with the annual volume of sales; with the size of city in which the store is located; and during the course of a business cycle. Consideration of each of these factors is outside the scope of this volume.[2] In the present chapter attention is centered chiefly on the methods by which expenses may be controlled in all types of stores.

THE NATURE OF EXPENSE CONTROL

As emphasized in the two previous chapters, profits are the result of a satisfactory relationship among sales, gross margin, and total expenses. And achieving such a relationship is not easy with conditions changing constantly. Profits may be improved, for example, by increasing the gross margin dollars without a proportionate rise in expenses, by reducing expenses without a commensurate reduction in gross margin; and by a combination of

---

[1] Cf. "Stores Eye Sharp Tools to Cut Costs," *Women's Wear Daily,* January 12, 1966, pp. 1, 32.

[2] Cf. the discussion in C. F. Phillips and D. J. Duncan, *Marketing: Principles and Methods* (5th ed.; Homewood, Ill.: Richard D. Irwin, Inc., 1964) pp. 141–44 and the statistics assembled in *Expenses in Retail Businesses* (rev. ed.; Dayton, Ohio: National Cash Register Co., n.d.).

these two methods. Since competitive influences often make it difficult to widen the gap between net sales and cost of goods sold—thus increasing the gross margin—it is the universal practice among successful retailers to maintain constant vigilance over their expenses.

In the process of reducing expenses, however, it is significant to note that instances are rare in which sizable savings are effected through major economies in one phase of operation. However, cases are rather numerous in which small savings have been realized in a variety of store activities, with the aggregate of such savings being substantial. This situation demonstrates the value of and the need for continuous and close examination of all expenses to the end that they will be minimized and profit possibilities enhanced. When this is done, expenses are "controlled."

At the very beginning of this discussion, it should also be recognized that expense control does not always mean expense reduction. On the contrary, the retailer may well find that, by increasing certain expenses, he can so increase his sales that he adds to his profit in spite of higher costs. Certainly this is the aim of all advertising expenditures and of customer services. Hence, expense control should be thought of as deciding upon and limiting actual expenses to those that are necessary for the maximization of profit.

Effective expense control involves (1) the appropriate classification of expenses, with a definition of each item of expense; (2) the distribution or allocation of expenses to departments and to functions; (3) the close scrutiny and comparison of expenses, including the analysis made possible through the use of an expense budget; and (4) the corrective action necessary to effect the changes suggested by the analysis of expenses. Let us first consider the classification of expenses.

EXPENSE CLASSIFICATION

Expense classification divides all the expenses of retailing into a number of clearly defined groups, such as rent, advertising, and salaries. One of its aims is to provide a detailed breakdown that the retailer can use year after year, thus allowing him to note expense trends for each classification. A second purpose is to provide bases permitting comparisons with other stores for the same period and over a span of time. Through such intra- and interstore comparisons, expenses that are out of line may be identified and proper remedial action may be taken.

Expenses are classified in various ways among different types and sizes of stores, both multi- and single unit. These variations may be made clear if we examine the expense classifications used in different types of stores.

Expense Classification in Single-Unit Hardware Stores

Although the majority of small independent retailers employ a simpler expense classification, the one used by the National Retail Hardware Association in a report to its member stores classifies the items of expense as indicated in Table 25–1.

TABLE 25–1

CLASSIFICATION OF EXPENSES IN RETAIL HARDWARE STORES

  I. Paid out in salaries
      1. To owners and managers
      2. To salespeople, office and others
 II. Other costs of doing business
      1. Office supplies and postage
      2. Advertising
      3. Donations
      4. Telephone and telegraph
      5. Losses on notes and accounts
      6. Delivery expense (other than wages)
      7. Depreciation—Delivery equipment
                      —Furniture, fixtures and tools
      8. Rent
      9. Repairs to building
     10. Heat, light, water, power
     11. Insurance*
     12. Taxes* (excluding federal income tax)
     13. Interest on borrowed money*
     14. Unclassified—including store supplies
III. Total expense (not including interest on investment)

*Not including amounts paid in connection with real estate ownership.

SOURCE: "Profits Up Substantially in 1965," *Hardware Retailer*, July, 1966, p. 67.

Expense Classification in Chain-Store Organizations

Expense classifications in chain-store organizations may be illustrated by that used in food stores as shown in Table 25–2.

This classification, which is based on *The Standard Manual of Accounts for the Food Chain Industry,* is quite similar to that used by hardware stores, although there are some differences in terminology. In practice, a number of subgroups may be used to identify further the nature of the expense.

Expense Classification in Department Stores

Natural Classification. The National Retail Merchants Association suggests for smaller department stores a sixteen-point natural classification

TABLE 25–2

CLASSIFICATION OF EXPENSES
IN FOOD CHAINS

Payroll
Supplies
Utilities
Communications
Travel
Services purchased
Promotional giveaways
Professional services
Donations
Insurance
Taxes and licenses (except on income)
Property rentals
Depreciation and amortization
Repairs
Unclassified
Interest

SOURCE: Wendell Earle and John Shee-
han, *Operating Results of Food Chains*, 1964–
65 (Ithaca, N.Y.: Cornell University, 1965).

of operating costs. Along with these basic, natural divisions of expense, four additional category groups are provided for redistribution and offset purposes. Together, they constitute "the backbone of the system of expense classification" recommended by NRMA.[3] This grouping, which is given in Table 25–3, is referred to as a natural classification because it assigns expenses on a simple, understandable basis that most retailers have used for many years.

Expense Centers. For the larger stores, the Association recommends that the natural division of expenses be assigned to 23 so-called expense centers, with each center designating a particular activity or service essential to the operation of the store such as management, sales promotion, and delivery. These 23 centers are shown in Table 25–4 with the natural divisions of expense applicable to each one. For example, divisions for the management expense center are these: payroll, taxes, supplies, services purchased, unclassified, traveling, insurance, professional services, and donations. Each natural subdivision, of course, will bear the number of the expense center of which it is a part in addition to the expense item which it designates. Thus, general management payroll would be designated 110–01.[4] Stores using the expense center classification can study their cost

---

[3] *Retail Accounting Manual* (New York: National Retail Merchants Association, Controllers' Congress, 1962), p. III–1.

[4] In this volume it is not practicable to discuss all aspects of expense classification covered in the *Retail Accounting Manual, ibid.* Readers interested in a more comprehensive treatment should consult that source, especially Chapter VI, "Elements of Reports and Statistics."

TABLE 25-3

NATIONAL RETAIL MERCHANTS ASSOCIATION
NATURAL DIVISION OF EXPENSES

	Expense Division	Illustration of Costs Included
01	Payroll	Salaries, wages, commissions, bonuses, prizes for contests, etc., received by all employees.
02	Fringe benefits	Not in itself a pure natural division, but provided to permit optional redistribution of fringe benefits from expense center 630 to other expense centers.
03	Advertising	Space costs in newspapers, radio and television time, direct mail, and other media.
04	Taxes	Federal (excluding income taxes), state, county, city, unemployment, social security, disability, etc.
06	Supplies	All items consumed in operation of business such as stationery and wrapping, packing, and cleaning materials.
07	Services purchased	Nonprofessional services rendered by outsiders—delivery, repairs, armoured cars, collection agencies, etc.
08	Unclassified	All expenses not included in other natural divisions—net cash shortages, policy adjustments, want ads., etc.
09	Traveling	Out-of-town travel expenses for all employees.
10	Communications	General postage, telegrams and cables, telephone service and rental of communications equipment.
11	Pensions	All payments to retired employees in nature of pensions, retirement allowances, and contributions to pension funds.
12	Insurance	All types of insurance coverages—fire, liability, and others.
13	Depreciation	Depreciation of book value of buildings, furniture, fixtures and equipment, rolling stock, etc.
14	Professional services	Services of a highly specialized and professional nature such as legal fees, public accountants' fees, and appraisal fees.
15	Donations	Contributions to welfare, charitable, and educational institutions.
16	Bad debts	Bad debts, bad checks, and fraudulent purchases less recoveries.
17	Equipment costs	Costs of all equipment rented or leased (except communications equipment)
20	Real property rentals	Expenses incurred or rent paid for real estate used in the business, less any income received from sub-rentals.
91	Expense transfers	Expenses transferred from one expense center to another to reflect actual operating costs of each center.
92	Outside revenue and other credits	Transactions involving credits related to such items as advertising and cost of merchandise in workroom departments as well as outside revenue not classified as gross or other income.
93	Multiple-store distribution	Designed to provide a vehicle for redistribution of accumulated central organization expenses to individual selling units.

SOURCE: *Retail Accounting Manual* (New York: National Retail Merchants Association, Controllers' Congress, 1962), pp. III–1 to III–5. The reader is referred to this source for additional information.

trends and also make comparative analyses with other firms for each center and each expense item within a center.

DISTRIBUTION (ALLOCATION) OF EXPENSES

Once a suitable classification of expenses has been adopted by the retailer, he is in a position to distribute or allocate these expenses to selling depart-

TABLE 25-4

NATURAL DIVISIONS BY EXPENSE CENTER

	Payroll	Fringe Benefits*	Advertising	Taxes	Supplies	Services Purchased	Unclassified	Traveling	Communications	Pensions	Insurance	Depreciation	Professional Services	Donations	Bad Debts	Equipment Costs	Real Property Rentals	Expense Transfers	Outside Revenue & Other Credits	Multi-Store Distribution
110 Management	01			04	06	07	08	09			12		14	15						99
120 Property and Equipment				04							12	13				17	20	91	92	99
210 Accounting and Data Processing	01				06	07	08	09	10				14			17		91	92	99
310 Accounts Receivable	01				06	07	08	09	10							17		91		99
320 Credit and Collections	01				06	07	08	09							16	17		91	92	99
410 Sales Promotion	01		03		06	07	08	09	10									91	92	99
510 Service and Operations	01				06	07	08	09					14							99
550 Telephone and Other Utilities	01				06		08		10									91		99
570 Cleaning	01				06	07	08									17			92	99

Code	Account	01	48	04	06	07	08	09	10	11	12	13	14	17	91	92	99
580	Maintenance and Repairs	01			06	07	08								91	92	99
610	Personnel	01			06	07	08	09					14				99
630	Supplementary Benefits	01		04	06	07	08			11	12		14		91	92	99
720	Maintenance of Reserve Stock	01			06		08							17			99
740	Receiving and Marketing	01			06	07	08							17			99
750	Shuttle Service	01			06	07	08							17			99
810	Selling Supervision	01	48		06		08										
820	Direct Selling	01			06		08	09							91	92	
830	Customer Services	01			06	07	08	09	10					17	91	92	99
860	Wrapping and Packing	01			06		08									92	99
880	Delivery	01		04	06	07	08	09			12	13		17	91	92	99
910	Merchandising	01			06	07	08	09					14				99
920	Buying	01			06		08	09									99
930	Merchandise Control	01			06		08								91		99

* See special explanation for Expense Division 02 in Table 25–3, p. 695, above.

SOURCE: *Retail Accounting Manual, op. cit.*, p. IV-1.

ments within a store or to the several stores in a chain organization—an essential second step in expense control. This task is a difficult one because not all retail expenses can be clearly traced to specific departments of a store or to the individual units of a multiunit organization.[5]

Direct and Indirect Expenses

To permit a sound allocation of expenses, most retailers classify their cost items into two broad groups—direct and indirect. Generally speaking, direct expenses are those occasioned by the existence of a particular department, and which would disappear if the department were dropped. Such costs are illustrated by a department's payroll, the supplies it uses, and the newspaper space bought for advertising the products sold in the department. In contrast, indirect expenses are those not occasioned solely by a particular department, so that they would not disappear even if a particular department were dropped. Such costs are the rent paid by the store; heat, light, and power; and office overhead. Although it is generally agreed that all direct expenses should be carried by the department causing them, there is a considerable difference of opinion as to how indirect expenses should be allocated.[6] Three methods are used to distribute retail expenses.

Methods of Allocating Expenses

The Net Profit Plan. Under this plan of expense distribution all expenses, both direct and indirect, are divided among the departments of the store. When those assigned to a specific department are deducted from the departmental gross margin, the net profit for the department is determined. In brief, each department is considered as a separate profit-making entity and is judged on its ability to produce profit.

Under the net profit plan, all direct expenses are assigned directly to the selling departments causing them; and all indirect expenses are distributed among the selling departments according to as logical a method as can be devised. For example, general management expense may be divided up in ratio to the net sales of the various departments, accounts payable cost may be assigned in ratio to the number of invoices involved, while the most

---

[5] The discussion which follows refers to distribution of costs among selling departments, but the reader can easily transfer the basic ideas to the units of a chain or branch organization.

[6] Some of these variations of opinion are set forth in a discussion of the problems involved in allocating office expenses in R. G. Baker, "Allocating Corporate Expenses," *Retail Control*, May, 1965, pp. 33–47. Mr. Baker also covers the advantages and disadvantages of allocation.

logical base of allocating checking and marking expense may be the number of pieces marked. In general, net sales are used as the base for indirect cost distribution only when some other logical base cannot be found.

The chief merits of allocating all expenses, thus making it possible to show a net profit (or loss) figure for each selling department, are that it furnishes a basis for judging the merchandising capacity of the department head, fixes responsibility for the over-all performance of the department, provides a basis for rewarding exceptional performance through salary increases or bonuses, makes the department head conscious of the need to control indirect costs as well as the direct ones, and corresponds to top management thinking on this subject. Its major limitations center around the fact that department heads are judged on the basis of many expenses over which they have no control, that the allocation of many indirect expenses to their departments is arbitrary at best, that such allocation is time-consuming and costly, and that the final figures do not reveal the true "profit" of the selling department.

The widespread dissatisfaction with the net profit plan, particularly the allocation of indirect expenses, has been responsible for the development of the contribution plan.

The Contribution Plan. This plan of expense distribution was probably first enunciated by the late Carlos B. Clark of the J. L. Hudson Company in 1933 under the title "Reservoir Concept."[7] Working on the assumption that any allocation of indirect expenses is arbitrary and may be unfair to certain departments, he suggested that only the escapable or direct expenses be distributed to the various departments. That is, each department would be charged for the expenses which were directly incurred by the department and which would disappear if the department were discontinued;[8] all other expenses would be placed in a general bracket with no attempt at departmental distribution. When this procedure is followed, the department expense budget shows the estimates for various direct expenses and a balance that it can contribute toward the store's indirect expenses and profit.

In addition to its simplicity the contribution plan's major advantage is that it forces people throughout the entire store to concentrate just on those expenses over which they have some control, and this applies to the heads of such services as credit, delivery, and accounting as well as to the selling department managers. Among the major disadvantages are these: (1) it does not provide a total expense figure for the department so it is of little aid

[7] " 'Reservoir Concept' is Keynote of Future Profits," *Retail Ledger*, December, 1933, p. 13.
[8] For example, selling, delivery, and newspaper and direct mail advertising expenses.

in pricing; and (2) selling department heads may make inordinate demands for credit, delivery, and other services for which they are not assigned a share in the cost.

Following Clark's proposals, some department and specialty stores, as well as some chain organizations, adopted the plan. But it was not until the 1950's, when certain other ideas regarding retail accounting were given prominence, that deserving recognition of the merits of the "reservoir concept" became evident. Today the "contribution plan," as it is now known, is used in many of the larger retail organizations.

Combined Net Profit and Contribution Plan. The third plan of expense distribution is designed to combine the best features of the other two. Some retailers desire more detailed information than gross margin, controllable expenses, and "contribution" in weighing the results and value of various selling departments. Although interested in such facts, they want additional data on departmental expenses so that they can improve their control and increase profits. Consequently, they prepare reports for their selling department heads which show both a department's "contribution" and its "net profit." From the department's dollar gross margin all direct expenses are deducted to give a "contribution" figure which can be compared with comparable figures for other departments and other stores. The analysis then goes on to apply the principles of the net profit plan under which the "contribution" is decreased by the deduction of the indirect expenses allocated to the department.[9] These steps may be illustrated as follows:

Net sales..	$60,000
Cost of merchandise sold..........................	40,000
Department gross margin.........................	$20,000
Direct expense of the department................	9,000
Contribution of the department..................	$11,000
Indirect expenses distributed to the department[10]..	8,400
Department net profit............................	$ 2,600

Recommendations by the Controllers' Congress. The Controllers' Congress of the National Retail Merchants Association has prepared a statement of basic principles and recommendations concerning expense allocation or distribution, as follows:

1. In expense distribution the requirements of cost finding and expense control within the individual store are of prime importance. Thus, policies should be adopted in the light of conditions prevailing in the individual store,

---

[9] For suggestions of a desirable procedure to be followed in establishing a combination plan, cf. *Retail Accounting Manual, op. cit.,* p. VIII–4.

[10] In some cases, these indirect expenses would be classified into two groups: (1) those assigned to departments in ratio to net sales and (2) those assigned on other bases.

rather than in accordance with uniform requirements needed for comparability.

2. The direct expenses involving no element of judgment in allocation or proration should be charged direct to selling departments and the difference between these direct expenses and the gross merchandise margin should be shown at frequent intervals as the direct contribution.

3. In general, there should be no double distribution of indirect expenses, but the allocation in practically all instances should be direct to the selling departments.

4. In the allocation of indirect expenses the best and most practical bases should be used to reflect true costs and for this purpose the units of productivity measurement proposed in this manual should be used when possible.

5. It is not necessary that the allocation of indirect expenses be made more often than semi-annually. At such times the deduction of these allocated indirect charges from the contribution should be made in order to show the controllable profit.

6. Proration of indirect expenses on the basis of net sales should be used sparingly and only in the absence of good and practical bases for more accurate cost allocation. If desired, the indirect expenses prorated on the basis of net sales, may be deducted semiannually from the controllable profit to show a departmental net operating profit, but the carrying of departmental cost finding to this final stage may be regarded as optional.[11]

EXPENSE COMPARISONS AND ANALYSES

When a retailer's expenses have been classified into groups comparable with those of similar retailers and have been properly allocated to assure comparability both over time and with other firms, the important task of analyzing them may begin. This analysis usually involves three steps: (1) a review of the retailer's own expense trends over a period of time; (2) a comparison of his expenses with those of other retailers; [12] and (3) the analysis of expenses through an expense budget.

Review of Expense Trends and Comparisons with Similar Firms

Dollar and Percentage-of-Sales Reports on Expenses. One of the most effective ways for the retailer to review the long-run trends in his costs is through a five- or ten-year expense table. Consisting of dollar figures for each item in the retailer's expense classification together with these figures expressed as a percentage of sales, this table serves as a constant reminder of

---

[11] *Retail Accounting Manual, op. cit.,* pp. VIII–5, 6.

[12] As one example cf. "Compare Your Labor Costs Under the Minimum Wage Law," *Super Market Merchandising,* January, 1966, p. 27. Figures are given for sixteen companies.

expense trends. Through it the retailer is aware, for example, that his delivery cost ratio is steadily rising, his fixtures and equipment ratio is falling, or his advertising ratio is moving upwards. These trends call for study on his part. What are the reasons for them? Are more of his customers demanding delivery service or are his salespeople failing to encourage customers to carry their purchases? Has he failed to spend enough in an effort to keep his store fixtures and equipment up to date? Is he using more advertising, more expensive media, or are advertising rates rising? By answering these and many other questions the retailer decides on the steps he should take to control his expenses.

Our emphasis on long-run expense trends does not imply that a retailer should analyze his expenses only once each year. Many large retailers provide their executives with a flow of daily, weekly, and monthly expense reports. Such reports call for careful, continuous analysis.

Comparisons of a retailer's expenses with those of similar firms is also made possible through reports expressing each cost as a percentage of sales. Table 28–1 on page 767 provides such data for the "most profitable one third" of a group of hardware stores. By placing his own figures alongside those in this table, a hardware store operator can learn much about the areas in which his expenses are "out of line." Data similar to that of Table 28–1 are now available for practically all retail fields.[13]

Production Unit Accounting. Some department and specialty stores as well as chain-store organizations use production unit accounting as a means of reviewing their own long-run expense trends and of making expense comparisons with other firms. Production unit accounting differs from expense center accounting in that it involves making *use* of the data accumulated in the various expense centers to improve operations and enhance profits. Essentially, the goal of production unit accounting is to secure a unit cost figure for as many of the store's activities as possible. It seeks answers to such questions as: What is the trend in the productivity of labor in our accounts payable office? What is our cost per unit of merchandise delivered? What is our payroll unit cost for cleaning the store? Is our productivity of labor increasing or decreasing in the performance of this activity? While, for reasons indicated below, not all expense centers can be subjected to production unit accounting, perhaps this technique can be used for one third to one half of them.

1. *Elements Considered in Production Unit Accounting.* Production unit accounting defines three chief elements involved in any activity: (1) the "work load" or amount of work to be done; (2) the speed or rate at

---

[13] Cf. *Expenses in Retail Businesses, op. cit.,* and "How Do You Compare on Store Expenses?", *Super Market Merchandising,* March, 1966, p. 38.

which it can be done, termed "productivity"; and (3) the labor cost per hour of performing the job, called the "effective pay rate." These elements or factors are applied to each expense center where feasible, i.e., where there is a payroll account and where the job can be measured. Their relationships may be expressed in a simple formula as follows:

Work load (units) ÷ Productivity = Hours used × Pay rate = Payroll Expense.

An illustration will emphasize these relationships.

2. *Example of Production Unit Accounting.* Let us assume that in the cleaning (of the store) expense center, where the measuring unit is "selling area times selling days," the data shown in Table 25–5 are available. The

TABLE 25–5

COMPUTATIONS FOR PRODUCTION UNIT ACCOUNTING

Period	Work Load (Units)	÷ Productivity	=	Hours Worked	×	Effective Pay Rate	=	Payroll Expense	Payroll Cost per Work Unit
1.........4,800		1.0		4,800		1.40		$6,720	$1.40
2.........6,000		1.0		6,000		1.40		$8,400	1.40
3.........4,800		1.2		4,000		1.40		$5,600	1.17
4.........4,800		1.2		4,000		1.45		$5,800	1.21

SOURCE: Adapted from *Retail Accounting Manual, op. cit.,* p. XII–4.

"Period" column refers to four consecutive periods of 4, 5, 4, and 4 weeks, respectively. The "Work Load (Units)" column shows the time used by the cleaning staff to do the job in each of the periods. Since the work load is determined by the size of the space and the frequency of the cleaning, these facts must be known. In this instance there were 200,000 square feet of selling space and it was cleaned six days each week. Reducing the area to units of 1,000 square feet, during the four-week periods there were 200 units cleaned 24 times or 4,800 work units. Then, if we divide the work load of 4,800 hours by the hours used—4,800, we obtain a productivity unit of 1.0. That is, each unit of 1,000 square feet of selling area was cleaned each hour. Now, assuming that the total payroll for the cleaning staff was $6,720, and knowing that the hours worked were 4,800, simple division reveals that the effective pay rate was $1.40 per hour. The payroll cost of doing each unit of the cleaning was also $1.40.[14]

The effect of each of the variables involved in the expense of the cleaning center—work load, productivity, and pay rate—is shown for the other three periods. Note that in period (3), an increase in productivity, i.e., the rate at

---

[14] Payroll cost per unit = payroll ÷ work units = $\dfrac{\$6,720}{4,800}$ = $1.40

which the work was performed, to 1.2 units per hour with the same work load of 4,800 units and the same pay rate resulted in a decrease in expense of $1,120 ($6,720 — $5,600) and the payroll cost per unit of work fell to $1.17. In period (4), an advance in the payroll expenses resulted in a rise in the payroll cost per unit of work.

In brief, an analysis of the data of Table 25–5 enables a retailer to tell whether an advance (or decline) in his payroll cost per work unit is a result of changes in productivity or in pay rate. Thus he is aided in determining why his unit cost is changing, and knowing why is essential to corrective action. Also by comparing his figures with those of comparable retailers he is made aware of how his experience departs from (or conforms to) their results.

Production unit accounting is not as simple as our brief treatment may lead the reader to believe. Our purposes in including some of its elementary aspects here have been to emphasize its value as a method of analyzing certain expenses and to indicate that constant study is being made to develop improved methods of cost reduction in retail stores. The interested reader will find it advisable to consult the more detailed literature which is available in this area.[15]

The Expense Budget

No management tool is as effective for the purpose of analyzing and controlling the costs involved in retailing as the expense budget. Its importance, therefore, warrants a somewhat detailed examination of the basic principles involved in preparing and using this management aid.

Nature and Purposes. An expense budget is simply a series of estimates or a forecast in dollars of the various expenses a store will incur in a budgeted period. This period, as is true with the merchandise budget, normally consists of one season or six months; but it is usually broken down into months, or even weeks or days, depending on the needs of the store. The primary purpose of the budget is to make a careful forecast of expenses of all kinds, so that adequate provision can be made to meet them and the store's profits can be safeguarded.[16] Besides providing a definite goal and fixing responsibility on certain individuals in the store for attaining this goal, the procedure involved in developing the budget gives the store's executives a better understanding of the necessity of coordinating all of the store's

---

[15] Especially recommended is chapter xii in the *Retail Accounting Manual, op. cit.,* on which our discussion is primarily based.

[16] The expense budget, together with the merchandise budget, is incorporated into an over-all store financial budget.

activities. In addition, at the close of the budget period, the retailer is able to analyze the extent of and reasons for any variations between planned and actual expense figures. Put another way, the expense budget provides a means of analyzing each expense classification both *before* and *after* the actual expenditure takes place.

Desirable Requisites. To accomplish its purposes, an expense budget should be planned carefully, constructed with discrimination and judgment, and judiciously administered. It should be simple and still provide the necessary information to permit effective control. To maximize its benefits, each executive should understand the purposes and uses of the expense budget and participate in its formation.

The budget should be flexible. If business conditions change suddenly and sales fall or rise more rapidly than was expected when the budget was constructed, changes should be made in the budget so that it can still serve its purpose as an effective instrument of control. Those responsible for budgetary control, however, must be sure that conditions really have changed and that the unfavorable results being shown are not due merely to poor management. After all, the budget is a mechanism for control; it points to a goal (a definite amount of profit) and permits measurement of the degree of progress toward this goal. If the goal is changed too frequently and if there is disagreement regarding the necessity of such changes, confidence in the budget is lost. If the original estimates are drawn up with care and take into consideration actual foreseeable conditions, some changes in detail will have to be made; but significant revisions should be few.

The budget should be an effective device for localizing responsibility and authority. In most large stores, the general manager is responsible for the entire budget, although he will rely heavily upon the controller both for preparing it and for using it as a control device. Moreover, he will delegate responsibility to others—for example, to each department manager to hold the expenses within the figures set for his department. But upon one person's shoulders should rest the responsibility of seeing that the store remains within its budget. Along with this responsibility must go authority—the ability to allow or disallow any particular expenditure. Otherwise, it is impossible to give credit or to fix blame when actual results are compared with those planned.

Some Objections to Expense Budgets. Despite the foregoing commendable purposes of the expense budget, some retail executives object to its use. They claim that the drawing up of the budget may make the organization so penny-conscious that outlays sufficient for its growth and development will not be made; that a budget is based upon overoptimistic sales estimates, with resulting large totals for operating expenses, and that these sums are spent even if the estimated sales fail to materialize; and, finally, that a budget lacks sufficient flexibility because of the difficulty of acting quickly when conditions change.

The foregoing contentions have some validity. In general, however, they are directed more at misuse of a budget than at the expense budget itself. If the aim of the budget—to serve as a tool for maximizing profits from a long-run point of view—is understood by all executives, there is no reason why they should become too penny-conscious. Likewise, if those responsible for the budget consistently overestimate sales, the moral seems to be to let someone else do the estimating, not to throw out the budget. Moreover, if an adequate check is maintained during the budget period, there is no reason why all budgeted funds should be spent if sales do not meet expectations. After all, a budget sets reasonable expenditures, not minimum ones. It is a guide, not a control; and it is an aid to the judgment of management, not a substitute for it.

Budgeting Procedure. In setting up an expense budget, at least three important steps are involved:

1. Setting control figures or estimates based on all pertinent, available information. Basic data of two kinds are required for this purpose:
   a) An over-all total expense figure.
   b) A control figure for each major expense account. These figures should be adjusted to the overall control figure. Small stores do not need a budget that is more detailed than that provided by these control figures. Such estimates, however, should be broken down by months.
2. Setting departmental budgets (or individual store budgets in the case of a chain). This step necessitates the following actions:
   a) Each department head is asked to prepare a budget for his department. Unless the contribution plan is used, indirect cost must be prorated to the departments before this budget can be built up. Under the expense center concept, of course, attention is focused on each center and budgeting relates to selling departments only insofar as the planning of direct expenses is concerned.
   b) Department budgets are adjusted so as to conform to the control figures. These adjustments are made by the merchandise manager, by the controller, or by the budget committee, often working closely with department buyers.
3. Breaking down the control and department budgets into monthly, or even shorter-period budgets.

Let us discuss these steps in more detail.

Store-Wide Control Figures. Although variations are found among stores of different types and sizes, the majority of retailers using an expense budget arrive at their overall expense figure by combining these two methods: (1) through estimating planned sales for the budget period and (2) by accumulating it on the basis of various expenses incurred during the previous year with adjustments for changes anticipated during the budget period.

1. *Based on Estimate of Sales.* When the first method is used, the retailer must also estimate his cost of merchandise, thus securing a dollar figure for gross margin.[17] By taking from this gross margin figure his desired net profit, he secures an overall expense figure. Then this amount is adjusted according to previous expense experiences in the store and the retailer's judgment of conditions that will prevail during the forthcoming budget period.

2. *Based on Past Expenses.* When overall expense figure planning is based on past experience, adequate records are required. Despite recent improvement in the record-keeping activities of small retailers, thousands of them still do not have adequate accounting systems: They could not prepare accurate budgets by this method even if they wished to do so. But where records are available, they may be used as the basis for estimating each expense item. In this process, many stores begin with the expenses that are relatively fixed in nature—in other words, those that do not vary much with total sales, such as taxes, property rentals, and insurance. By giving first consideration to these costs, over which the store has less control but which it must meet, the store management obtains a figure to which the "controllable" accounts can be adjusted.

Actually, such fixed costs as taxes, property rentals and insurance are not so predetermined as they may seem at first glance. Take property rentals, as an example. Perhaps the size of the store should be expanded, thus increasing the total charge for the period. Or perhaps a part of the building may be sublet to some other operator, thus reducing the total amount to be charged against the store. Again, it may be possible to reduce this amount by negotiating with the landlord.

Turning to the expense items over which the retailer has relatively more control, each of these should also be reviewed regarding a possible increase or decrease over the preceding comparable six-month period. Perhaps some full-time employees may be replaced by part-time help. Or perhaps a new method of compensating employees will result in increased productivity, thus allowing the use of fewer clerks and decreasing total payroll cost. On the contrary, due consideration may convince the retailer that he has been operating his store with too few employees and that the better service made possible by more employees would increase his sales.

It should be evident that considerable care is essential in building the estimates for each expense center. Methods of cutting all costs and the

---

[17] How the retailer obtains his planned sales figure has already been discussed, cf. "Planned Sales," pp. 406–8, above.

consequences of such cutting, as well as the possible advantages to be secured from expanding expenses in certain areas, need study. The net result of such action is a well-considered estimated figure for each kind of expense. When these expenses are totaled, an overall expense figure is obtained.

Despite the care exercised in developing overall and major account expense control figures by the build-up method, adjustments are often necessary to accommodate developments that could not be foreseen. Since the budget must be realistic, prompt adjustments should be made in the figures as such developments occur.

Departmental and Chain-Unit Budgets. For the large store which is departmentized or for the chain organization, the control figures previously set up should be broken down by departments or by individual stores.[18] The best approach, probably, is to have department heads or individual store executives participate actively in the formulation of the budget figures.[19] These individuals may even prepare preliminary budget estimates of their own based on a careful study of previous experience and the conditions under which they expect to operate during the budget period.[20]

As an aid to setting up the departmental budget, however, the firm's budgetary officer or committee must see to it that the department head is provided with all available, pertinent information. Since no budget is better than the information upon which it is based, and since intelligent estimates cannot be made without reliable and adequate data, the importance of such action is obvious. In addition to the information needed from within the store, similar data for comparable departments in other stores are also necessary, as well as information concerning the outlook for general business, price trends, competition, and contemplated changes in store policy. The total number of transactions in relationship to number of employees is likewise important. And, where feasible, the department head should be told how much of the general overhead of the store is to be charged against his department and the bases upon which these expenses will be allocated.

Possessed of the detailed data suggested, the department executive is in a position to make estimates of the direct expenses for his section for the six-month period. This process requires that the exact needs of his department during the budget period be reviewed carefully in consultation with his assistant and others in whose judgment he has confidence. Since wages and

---

[18] In chain organizations the manager may break them down further by departments.

[19] Although the practice of budgeting probably is more highly developed among industrial firms than among retailers, a lower level of management in making up and using the budget is included by retailers as compared with industrial firms.

[20] To facilitate the discussion, the following analysis is expressed in terms of department budgets. However, the same analysis applies to the individual store in the chain-store system, with the store manager building the budget rather than the department buyer.

salaries typically constitute one half or more of the total operating cost, particular care should be exercised in budgeting the payroll figure.[21] Let us look briefly at the procedure involved in arriving at such a figure, as well as for advertising costs.

1. *Constructing a Department Payroll Figure.* In performing this task the best approach seems to be (1) to set a control figure, (2) to consider the work to be done, (3) to estimate the number of employees needed to perform this work, (4) to arrive at the total payroll needed, and finally, (5) to adjust this "total-payroll-needed" figure to the control figure.

In a selling department, the payroll control figure may be obtained by taking the payroll-to-sales ratio of previous years. For example, the records may show that it has cost a particular department 7 percent of sales for salespersons. But such a figure should be scrutinized with care. It is advisable to compare it with the payroll ratio of comparable departments in other stores, as well as to adjust it to the overall payroll figure for the whole store.

The work to be done in the department may be expressed in terms of the number of transactions expected during various weeks of the budget period. To illustrate: assume that the estimated sales for the first week of the period are $4,000. Based on past sales data, the average sale may be estimated at $2.50. Dividing this average sale into the total estimated sales, we arrive at 1,600—the number of transactions expected during that week. The number of transactions to be expected in the other weeks of the whole period covered by the budget may be estimated in a similar manner.

These estimates of weekly transactions must now be put in terms of employees. Again, we turn to past experience and find that, in comparable periods of past years, each employee has been able to handle about 400 transactions. By dividing this figure into the number of transactions anticipated in the week under consideration, i.e. 1,600, we find that 4 employees will be needed to handle sales in the department. If wages per salesperson average $80 per week, the total weekly payroll will be $320. In making these estimates, however, it should be held in mind that there is a minimum number of employees each department must retain. Irrespective of the number of expected transactions during a certain period, it takes some employees to prevent shoplifting and to keep merchandise arranged, as well as to provide prompt service to customers.

It now remains to adjust the built-up payroll figure to the control figure. As has been suggested, the control figure was put at 7 percent of sales ($4,000); consequently, the payroll for this week must not exceed $280.

---

[21] Cf. Fred Eichelbaum, "Stores Labor to Overcome Suffocating Payroll Costs," *Women's Wear Daily*, January 13, 1966, p. 52; and Dowell Bates, "Selling Cost Control," *Retail Control*, January, 1966, pp. 55–68.

Our built-up payroll results in a total cost of $320. Necessary adjustments may be made by increasing the total sales without increasing the number of employees; by increasing the transactions per employee-hour, thus handling the estimated sales with fewer employee-hours; and by shifting employees among departments.

2. *Constructing a Department (or Individual Chain Unit) Advertising Figure.* Like the budgeted figure for payroll, building a useful estimate of advertising expense involves considerable care. The benefits a well-conceived advertising budget yields, however, affords adequate compensation for the efforts expended. When the department (or store) manager undertakes the budgetary task it causes him to review past results and to consider the expense before it occurs. In this analysis he seeks to obtain sufficient advertising at a lower total cost as well as a better integrated advertising program. Moreover, careful preplanning affords assurance that the funds available are spent in such a way as to give the department steady representation and provide for all special sales events.

The actual building up of the advertising budget is quite comparable to the steps in preparing the budget for other expense accounts: first, setting a control figure; second, building up expenses on the basis of the work to be performed; third, adjusting the built-up figure to the control figure; and, fourth, breaking down the final expense figure into monthly, then weekly, and then daily figures.

The general control figure will be based on past records, adjusted to present conditions. Thus, records may show that 3 percent of sales has been spent on advertising in a particular department. If this figure is in line with what is being spent by comparable departments in other stores, if the competitive situation has not changed significantly from previous years, and if no major changes have been made in objectives, this figure may be accepted as the control figure for the new budget.

The work to be performed by advertising will vary widely from department to department and from store to store. Location, kind of goods carried, degree of newness, merchandising policy, the policies and practices of comparable departments in other stores, and business conditions—all are important considerations. Through study of these factors an estimate of the total amount to be spent for advertising during the budget period can be determined.

3. *Adjusting Department or Store Budgets to Control Figures.* After each department or chain-store manager has prepared *his* budget, it is reviewed with the merchandise manager, the controller, or the budget committee (if one exists) and checked against the control figures. If particular expenses are found to exceed those provided for in the control budget for

the whole store, adjustments must be made. These adjustments may involve a reduction in estimates or a revision of the control figure for the store as a whole, or both. Changing the figures for the store as a whole, however, should be a matter of last resort and only after all means of reducing the various department expense budgets have been exhausted.

Breaking Down the Budget Period into Smaller Divisions. The third major step in setting up an expense budget is to divide the six-month budget into monthly budgets or even shorter ones. This breakdown applies to departmental and individual chain-store budgets as well as to the overall control figures. Through this procedure, every person responsible for holding expenses within the limits of the six-month budget has a means of following his success from month to month or from week to week, as the case may be. Such a breakdown is not very difficult if the store has records of past expenditures. Although the total expenditures may change from year to year, there is usually less change in the timing of the various expenditures. Delivery expenses, for example, will show little variation among similar months over a period of years.

Analyzing Expenses through the Budget. At the beginning of our discussion of the expense budget it was emphasized that this budget permits analysis of each expense classification *before* and *after* the expenditure of funds. The ensuing discussion has included the kind of analysis of expenses necessary in building an adequate budget. To complete the picture, however, a few comments should be added regarding the importance of reviewing the results at the close of the budget period.

A well-planned expense budget form, regardless of the period it covers, provides space for entering both planned and actual figures for each expense item in the budget. At the close of each budget period, these planned and actual figures should be carefully studied to determine the reasons for any variations. Why did actual advertising cost fall below the planned figure?[22] Did we use too many full-time people rather than relying on part-time personnel at peak selling hours, or was the budget figure too low? It is through this kind of analysis that the retailer secures the information he needs for corrective action.

CORRECTIVE ACTION

Classifying, distributing, and analyzing expenses—while essential actions looking toward the control of expenses—are just means to an end: the

---

[22] Roos-Atkins, San Francisco, subjects its advertising cost to a break-even-point analysis. Cf. E. H. Gauer, "The Mathematics of Advertising for Profits," *Men's Wear,* February 19, 1966, pp. 158–59.

corrective action to which they give rise. Put another way, expense control does not actually take place until someone does something about the expenses which the analyses shows are out of line.

Records: A Step to Control, Not Control

Some retailers, in the mistaken belief that records alone will give them control of expenses, have piled form on top of form and analysis on top of analysis. For one English retailer this situation reached such an absurd height that he found it necessary to junk 80 tons of record-keeping forms, saving an estimated $14 million in the cost of filling them out and substantially adding to his net profits.[23] While many small retailers still need additional data as a basis of taking corrective action, many large retailers need fewer forms and more executive action.

Expense Budget Facilitates Control

One of the main advantages of using an expense budget is that it allows early remedial action. Even in small stores where budget preparation may be restricted to a few major expenses, the proprietor or his assistant finds it avisable to prepare monthly reports comparing actual expenditures with those budgeted. Such a report enables the proprietor to keep in close touch with the store's progress in remaining within its budget. If expenses are exceeding the budget, this fact is brought to his attention in ample time for corrective steps to be taken.

In the medium-sized and large store, where expenses are under the control of a large number of individuals, it is necessary to keep a tighter rein over actual expenses. Consequently, more attention is given to budget figures and, particularly, to deviations from them. Some retailers require that, *before* any significant item of expense is undertaken, even if it is within the limits of the budget, the executive authorizing the expense must get it approved by an expense controller. Suppose that a department manager wants some needed supplies and submits a requisition to the expense controller. If the latter finds that the expense budget for this department can stand the additional expense, he authorizes the expenditure. Otherwise, he refers it to the controller or some other major executive for approval. In this way, all expenses are controlled before they are made. Of course, not all expenses should be

[23] Cf. the action taken by Sir Simon Marks, head of Marks & Spencer, as related in Christina Fulop, *Competition for Consumers* (London: The Institute of Economic Affairs, 1964), p. 186; and "The English Unorthodoxy of Marks & Spencer," *Dun's Review and Modern Industry,* October, 1966, p. 128.

handled by requisitions, since some are indirect costs over which the department executives have little control. But it is advisable that all important direct expenses be subject to this kind of control.

REVIEW AND DISCUSSION QUESTIONS

1. "No problem facing the retailer today is more urgent, more continuous, and more vital to his existence than effective control of his expenses." Discuss.
2. Explain and illustrate the meaning of the following statement: "Expense control does not always mean expense reduction."
3. Discuss the two main goals or aims of expense classification.
4. How do you account for the fact that different kinds or types of stores classify their expenses in different ways?
5. Consult in your library the latest copies of *Financial and Operating Results of Department and Specialty Stores* and *Departmental Merchandising and Operating Results of Department and Specialty Stores,* published annually by the Controllers' Congress of the National Retail Merchants Association. Compare and contrast the type of information provided and the form in which the data are presented.
6. Based on the information you obtain from the sources in question 5, explain the reasons for the variation in the expense ratios of different departments.
7. Summarize the chief differences between the natural classification of expenses for department stores and the expense center concept.
8. Explain briefly the purposes of expense allocation and the three major methods of accomplishing these purposes.
9. In your judgment what would be the most logical bases upon which to allocate the following expenses to selling departments in a department or large specialty store? (a) General management; (b) customers' returns of merchandise; (c) credit and billing; (d) checking and marking; and (e) personal shopping service. State your reasons in each case.
10. Discuss the methods and advantages of expense comparisons in retail stores.
11. What is meant by "production unit accounting" and what are the main objectives it is designed to accomplish?
12. Discuss the expense budget from the point of view of (a) purposes, (b) requisites, and (c) the steps involved in establishing one in small and medium-sized stores.
13. In view of the benefits derived by retailers through expense budgeting, how do you explain the opposition to it on the part of some executives?
14. Assume that you are the operator of a small hardware store. Explain how you would set up an expense budget. Answer the same question assuming that you operate (a) a food chain and (b) a men's clothing department in a department store.
15. Describe the process by which a budget figure covering a specific period is constructed for payroll or for advertising in a departmentized store. Use illustrations to make your meaning clear.

SUPPLEMENTARY READINGS

LeKashman, Raymond and Stolle, J. F. "The Total Cost Approach to Distribution," *Business Horizons,* Vol. VIII, No. 4 (Winter, 1965), pp. 33–46. Reviewing distribution costs from warehousing to customer services, the authors suggest methods of controlling these costs.

"Margins: Why Are They Rising?" *Progressive Grocer,* April, 1966, pp. 218–221. Between 1955 and 1965, gross margins in food stores increased 24 percent, suggesting the significance of expense control in this field.

Martin, R. J. "The Supermarket: A Study of Size, Profits, and Concentration," *Journal of Retailing,* Vol. XL, No. 4 (Winter, 1964–1965), pp. 23–26. The author's discussion of trends in supermarket profits is of special interest in relation to this chapter.

National Association of Retail Clothiers and Furnishers. *Annual Survey of Operating Expenses for Men's Wear Stores* (Washington, D.C.: The Association, published annually). These expense figures are classified according to the annual sales of each store.

National Cash Register Company. *Expenses in Retail Businesses* (rev. ed.; Dayton, Ohio, n.d.). This small volume stresses the importance of expense control and provides expense data for a variety of retail stores.

National Retail Furniture Association. *Operating Results of Furniture Stores* (Chicago: The Association, annual reports). These reports are of much value to all retailers of home furnishings.

National Retail Merchants Association, Controllers' Congress. *Departmental Merchandising and Operating Results of Department Stores and Specialty Stores* (New York: The Association, annual reports). The outstanding characteristic of these reports, known as MOR, is the departmental breakdown of the data presented.

————. *Financial and Operating Results of Department and Specialty Stores* New York: The Association, annual reports). Known as FOR, these reports provide the basis of evaluating one store's results with other comparable establishments.

————. *Retail Accounting Manual* (New York: The Association, 1962). The official NRMA accounting manual for retail stores, this volume details the expense accounts in retail stores including expense centers. A recent addition is the grouping of accounts for single-store companies and those operating branches.

National Retail Merchants Association, Store Management Division. *400 Ways to Reduce Expenses* (New York: The Association, 1964). Containing ideas used in 28 store-operating areas, this collection should prove a useful source of help to retailers.

Operating Results of Food Chains (Ithaca, N.Y.: New York State College of Agriculture, Cornell University, published annually). This summary of expenses provides valuable information on chains of various sales volumes.

RADOLF, HERMAN. "Retail Operating Ratios," *Journal of Retailing,* Vol. XLI, No. 4 (Winter, 1965–66), pp. 50–51, 61; and *ibid.,* Vol. XLII, No. 3 (Fall, 1966), pp. 70–71. The author reveals that although improvements in 1964 and 1965 operating results took place in various types of stores, certain control problems still remain.

Variety Store Merchandiser. (New York: Merchandise Publishing Company.) This monthly publication makes annual surveys of merchandising and operating ratios of variety-general merchandise chain stores. In the June issue "Operating Ratios Contrasted for Variety—General Merchandise and Selected Companies" is presented and in the November issue will be found a "Profit Engineering Study of Variety—General Merchandise Chains."

26
CHAPTER

Control of Sales Transactions

All retail stores, regardless of type or size, must perform a number of activities related to the actual sale of merchandise to the customer, such as presenting the customer with a sales check or a sales register receipt, receiving and safeguarding money, and recording the transaction in such a way as to provide the information desired. To insure proper performance, suitable equipment must be secured and procedures or routines must be planned carefully, carried out smoothly, and revised when conditions change. When these steps have been taken, the retailer will have adequate control over his sales transactions. Depending upon the size of the organization, the establishment of this control system may be the direct responsibility of the proprietor, the controller, a systems committee or department, or the research department.

THE NATURE OF SALES TRANSACTIONS SYSTEMS

A sales transactions system consists of the procedures, methods, and devices established to handle various types of sales. Basic to its determination is a decision on the kinds of sales a specific retailer will make, and the kinds of equipment available for implementing the procedures to provide the type of service the retailer wishes to give his customers.

Goals of Sales Transactions Systems

The main goal or purpose of a sales transactions system is to insure smooth functioning of this aspect of the business through procedures and routines adapted to the firm's particular needs. Other purposes include the provision of accurate information of the type desired in a form suitable for use and at the proper intervals, the reduction of errors by making their causes more obvious, and the minimizing of losses from employee dishonesty. And, it should be emphasized, an adequate and efficient sales transactions system is the foundation stone of automation in the field of retailing.

Even in a small "family" store a sales transactions system yields valuable benefits. Once it has been established, information flows smoothly and regularly to the places designated, with the result that less time is required for direction and supervision. Consequently, efficiency is increased because additional work can be turned out with less effort in the same period of time. Furthermore, a good system for handling sales transactions provides a record of activities in the precise form desired, thus eliminating needless checking and worry by the store manager, except when the system indicates that something is wrong.

Careful Planning Essential. The importance of carefully planned sales transactions systems is greater today than ever before. Not only are various types of sales transactions being subjected to close scrutiny but developments in electronics and automation have brought far-reaching changes in methods, devices, and equipment. An essential task for the new retailer as well as for the established store under present competitive conditions, therefore, is to provide for a thorough study of the alternative methods of handling sales transactions now available to him. Adequate planning may lead to a system that is simpler, easier and less expensive to operate, and with less duplication of steps. Moreover, it may provide a system through which more of the essential and less of the nonessential information will be supplied than in one that is patched together to meet needs and desires as they develop in day-to-day operation.

Requirements of an Effective System for Sales Transactions

Simplicity. Simplicity is essential in a sales transactions system to insure understanding and conformance. The problem of instructing employees, both old and new, in new procedures is difficult at best and a relatively simple system will minimize this task.

Adapted to Needs of the Particular Business. Too often, retail executives, impressed with the success of a prominent store, attribute a considerable part of its achievements to its system. Although a suitable system does influence a store's success, no retailer is justified in adopting and installing another store's system without a survey of his needs and without recognition of possible essential differences between the two stores. Not only is thorough analysis of the needs of the business essential to the establishment of an effective sales transactions system, but revisions in procedures and routines should be made when conditions change. In other words, procedural review and revision are continuous tasks.

Reasonable Cost of Installation and Maintenance. The cost of a sales transactions system should be reasonable in the light of the benefits to be derived from its use. In other words, no system should be adopted unless (1) it provides the necessary information and (2) it results in savings greater than the cost of installation and maintenance.

Provides Prompt Customer Service. Customer service is of special importance to the retailer. Consequently, regardless of the adaptability of the sales transactions system to the store's other requirements and regardless of its simplicity, its adoption is unwise unless it gives proper customer service. Customers want and expect prompt, courteous attention and rapid completion of sales transactions once their decisions to buy have been made.[1]

Furnishes Desired Information Quickly and Accurately. The retailer is well aware of the importance of having needed information in the form desired furnished quickly and accurately. For example, the value of data on sales frequently depends upon the speed with which the data are made available.

Permits Adequate Protection of Assets. Providing adequate safeguards for the company's assets, particularly cash and merchandise, is an essential requisite of all sales transactions systems. Such safeguards are necessary to afford protection from both outsiders (customers and others) and insiders (employees). Some unscrupulous customers attempt to take advantage of stores in all ways possible, especially in regard to refunds, exchanges, and adjustments. Employees, also, sometimes appropriate cash and merchandise for their own benefit and for the benefit of relatives and friends in the role of customers.[2] Obviously, the system used should minimize these temptations.

TYPES OF SALES TRANSACTIONS

As already mentioned, basic to any planning of a sales transaction system is a decision on the kinds of sales which the retailer will make. Ideally this decision should be made even before a store is opened, since it will govern largely the kinds of sales-handling equipment which will be required. This equipment, in turn, may involve making physical changes in the store

---

[1] For discussions of ways to speed up the sales transaction cf. *Attracting and Holding Customers* (Dayton: National Cash Register Company, 1963), especially sections II and VI, and *Speeding Selling Service* (New York: National Retail Merchants Association, 1962).

[2] A common statement in retail stores is that "employees are 99 percent honest—the system must be designed to protect the store from the 1 percent."

necessary to permit its full utilization. In fact, a consideration of some importance in the selection of a particular site for locating a store is the suitability of the building for the activities contemplated and for the types of equipment that will be required. It is much easier and less expensive to install the necessary equipment as the store is being built or remodeled than at a later date.

In about half of all retail stores, sales transactions are of two basic types—cash and credit. The remaining half of the stores sell for cash only. There are many variations of the two basic types, however, and knowledge of these variations is necessary to understand their influence on the procedures established to handle them.

Cash Sale

A cash sale is the type of sales transaction in which the customer pays for the merchandise at the time of purchase. Payment may be made by cash, check, or merchandise certificates. There are two main forms of cash sale: the *cash-take* (*"take-transaction"* or *"take-with"*) and the *cash-send* (or *"send-transaction"*). In the former the customer carries her purchase; and in the latter the goods are sent to her home or to some other address she may specify.

C.O.D. Sale

In this type of sales transaction, which is usually treated as a form of cash sale—but a relatively unimportant one for most retailers—the customer pays for the merchandise when it is delivered to her home by the store or by common carrier. The amount collected may be either the full amount of the sale or the balance that remains after partial payment has previously been made at the store. The latter type of transaction is frequently referred to as "part-pay c.o.d." Some stores make an extra charge for c.o.d. service.

Charge Sale

A charge sale is a sales transaction in which the amount of the purchase is charged to the customer's account, to be paid for usually by the tenth or the fifteenth of the following month. Wide adoption of cycle billing, however, has brought variations in payment dates; while the revolving credit plan permits payment over a longer period than the normal thirty days.[3] As with

---

[3] On cycle billing, cf. pp. 639–40, above; on revolving credit, cf. pp. 619–20, above.

cash sales, there are two kinds of charge transactions, the *charge-take* and the *charge-send.*

Budget, On-Contract, or Installment Sale

This type of sales transaction was originally limited to sales of high-value items, but in more recent years has been extended to many other types of merchandise. In such a sale the customer signs a conditional sales contract or chattel mortgage form, promising to make weekly or monthly payments of a specified amount until the total amount of the sale, plus a carrying charge, is paid. The store retains title to the merchandise, although the goods are in the possession of the customer; and the retailer may repossess the goods in case payments are discontinued.

Will-Call Sale

Also known as a *layaway* and a *deposit sale,* this kind of sales transaction has been discontinued by many stores in recent years. When used, the customer pays a definite percentage of the selling price of an article, usually 10–20 percent, to reserve it for an indefinite period—during which time payments are continued until the merchandise is fully paid for and released. Once deposits have been made on items of merchandise purchased under this plan, the goods are held in the department or moved to a "will-call" office, where they are always available on customers' calls. The will-call sale is really a variation of installment selling with one important exception—the store holds the merchandise until payments are completed.

Discount Sale

A discount sale takes place when a discount or reduction from the regular price is granted the purchaser. Such reductions are given store employees and certain types of customers such as clergymen, dressmakers, medical doctors, and dentists, depending on the type of store. Some stores classify sales to employees as E.D. (employee discount) transactions. Although employees may pay cash for their purchases and still receive the discount, it is common to charge the goods to their accounts and to deduct the amounts from their wages at monthly or more frequent intervals.

Budget-Book Sale

This kind of transaction, resembling both a cash sale and a budget or on-contract sale, is one in which merchandise certificates, purchased upon a definite contractual basis, are used as cash when goods are bought. These certificates are often bound together in a "budget book." The budget book contains certificates of various denominations, such as $0.25, $0.50, and $1.00, which can be exchanged for merchandise items anywhere in the store. A book may contain tickets aggregating $10, $15, or $25 in value. The customer must ordinarily pay a small carrying charge, as in the case of budget or on-contract sales; and she agrees to make payments for the book or books on specified dates, usually over a period of three months or less.

Exchange Sales

Exchange sales transactions occur when the customer returns merchandise to the store and then purchases additional items. In departmentized stores, an exchange sale applies only to one department. That is, if goods are returned to one department and a purchase is made in another, then the transaction is a refund or credit in the "receiving" department and a new sale in the "selling" department. Exchange sales are of two types—even and uneven. An even exchange is one in which the retail price of the goods returned is the same as that of the new selection. An uneven exchange is one in which the retail price of the goods returned is different from that of the new merchandise selection. It is apparent that this difference may be in favor of the customer when the merchandise returned is higher in price than the new purchase or that it may be in favor of the store when the goods returned cost less than the new selection.

RECORDING SALES

When policy decisions have been made regarding the types of sales transactions to use, the retailer should proceed to develop methods and devices to record and control these transactions properly. Recording is achieved typically by (1) handwritten sales checks or sales slips, as they are also called, and (2) sales register receipts and tapes.[4] Many small stores rely solely upon sales (cash) registers, although those selling on credit make some use of sales checks. Medium and large-sized stores use sales registers in some departments and sales checks in others, but recent years have witnessed a large increase in the former recording method. Many stores, including the typical supermarket, drugstore, and variety store—regardless of its size—rely entirely on the sales register. In some stores, however, both registers and sales checks are required in all departments; the sales check providing a "shipper" for delivery purposes and also information for controlling merchandise.

---

[4] Recording by the newer types of electronic equipment is discussed in pp. 729–30. below.

Trend toward Sales Register Receipts

The increasing use of sales register receipts and away from the handwritten sales check is quite understandable. On the one hand, the mechanism of the sales register has been improved so much that the sales register receipt can fulfill more of the functions formerly assigned to the sales check. In fact, current equipment provides for the recording of such a variety of information regardless of the type of transaction that the term "cash register" is being increasingly superseded by the term "sales register."[5] Even when charge-send transactions are involved, the sales register permits the recording of necessary information by inserting the sales slip in the slot provided on the register.[6] On the other hand, rising retail wages have encouraged many retailers to forgo some of the additional information which could be provided by the more expensive sales check.

In view of the foregoing, and even though the current rapid development of electronic equipment may make both the handwritten sales check and the sales register receipt less necessary in future years, it is advisable to examine the purposes and uses of sales checks under present conditions.

The Sales Check

Functions of the Sales Check. The major purposes of the sales check are: to provide a definite record of sales transactions; to make it possible to analyze sales and to allocate them among departments, salespeople, and classifications of merchandise; to furnish a receipt to the customer as well as a record of monies turned in to the cashier by the salespeople; to provide a "shipper" to accompany merchandise delivered to the customer's home; and to furnish a record upon which merchandise returns and adjustments may be adjudicated.

Using the Sales Check. The foregoing functions are accomplished by having the salesperson write upon each check the necessary data. In large stores, this information commonly includes the date; salesperson's number; department number; the kind of sale—cash, charge, or c.o.d.—for example; name and address of the customer and/or name and address of the person to whom the goods are to be sent in the case of all goods to be delivered; and a brief description of the merchandise sold. For transactions other than "cash," additional data such as disposition of the merchandise, i.e., whether "taken" or "sent," and the purchaser's signature are required. In smaller stores the information called for on the sales check is much more limited. To facilitate

[5] The National Cash Register Company has adopted this new terminology.
[6] Cf. the discussion on pp. 726–27, below.

sales auditing, adjustments, and similar matters, sales books are numbered serially; and sales checks are numbered 1–50 inclusive. A sales check used by one large retailer is shown in Figure 26–1.

The customary practice is to make out sales checks in triplicate. The original copy, known as the control copy, constitutes the store's record of the sale and in many stores continues to be used for analyzing and classifying sales, for preparing reports, and for similar purposes. The duplicate copy is the customer's copy and accompanies the merchandise, regardless of its disposition. The triplicate copy is a tissue-paper record of transaction, which remains in the sales book. Sales books containing tissue copies are filed carefully and are of much value to the adjusting office in tracing and investigating inquiries and complaints. Some stores have specially designed sales checks for such purposes as recording sales of "warehouse" merchandise and telephone orders.

In most stores a close control is maintained over sales books. A record is kept of the serial number of each book issued to departments and to salespeople, and all sales checks must be accounted for

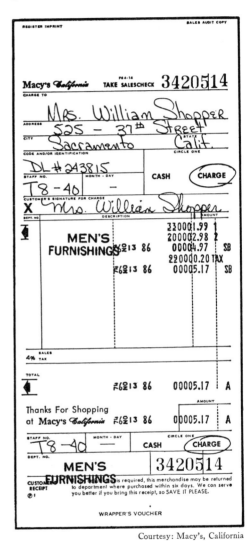

Courtesy: Macy's, California

FIG. 26–1. "Take" sales check.

when the original copies of the sales checks pass through the sales audit department.

Changes in Sales Checks. Recent years have witnessed many changes in the forms of sales checks to accommodate the developments in sales registering equipment which furnish pertinent information quickly and eliminate the necessity of salespeople entering details on the sales check. One firm has devised a punch card form for all charge-take sales—and these account for over 80 percent of its total sales. Consisting of but a single check with a perforated customer receipt stub, it can be completed in four steps in contrast to the eleven operations required for the tri-part sales check used previously.

Other firms are employing new automatic equipment which permits the recording of all basic sales data on the sales register in a single "pass" across the keyboard by the salesperson. Automation also permits the economical use of separate sales checks for major types of sales transaction. Thus, Macy's of California has different sales checks for these kinds of transactions: "take" and "send" for both cash and charge sales, "c.o.d.," and "returned merchandise vouchers" covering cash refunds and credits to accounts. The "take" and "send" sales checks are used both for customers' and employees' transactions and also, with appropriate notations, for "even" and "uneven" transactions.

SELECTING SALES-HANDLING EQUIPMENT

Two major types of sales-handling equipment are widely used at the present time: sales (or cash) registers and carrier systems, the latter including the overhead-conveyer type and the pneumatic-tube type. In addition, certain kinds of electronic equipment are being developed. As already noted, sales registers of various kinds are universally used in retail stores, both small and large, and significant improvements in them have been made in recent years. Overhead conveyors, such as baskets and small carriages are still used in some stores in smaller communities. In view of the improvements in sales registers to meet increasing demands for accurate, complete data at a moment's notice, manufacturers of pneumatic-tube systems have attempted to meet the challenge by making improvements of their own.

In the retail trade, it is common to apply the term "decentralization" to that method of handling sales transactions in which sales are consummated locally in departments by means of sales registers. Frequently, also, the term is applied to those instances in which floor cashiers or inspector-cashiers are used. The term "centralization" is used to refer to that method under which all sales—cash, charge, and others—are handled in a central location or locations (1) by means of a conveyor or tube system or (2) when the customer brings all her packages to one point as under a check-out system in self-service operation.

Steps Involved

In choosing equipment, the first step is to determine the data desired. Much of this information will be dictated by accounting requirements, some by the type of store and type of clientele, and some by the desires of the owner or executives. The next step is to inquire how the characteristics of the specific store or department will affect the system and the equipment: Will there be a great volume of small transactions, in each of which the customer is in a hurry; or will there be a more leisurely atmosphere, with a comparatively small number of large sales? Will the business be mostly cash or largely charge? Will the number of salespeople be fairly constant, or will a great number of "extras" be required on certain days of the week or in certain months of the year? Will close supervision of salespeople be required?

Original cost and economy in operation are likewise important considerations in choosing the type of equipment to be installed. In some cases, two types of equipment may provide the same information, the same control, and approximately the same customer service; but one will cost more than the other. Although cost alone should not be the decisive factor, it should certainly not be neglected.

With an understanding of his needs, the retailer is ready to examine the merits and the limitations of the equipment available. As has been indicated previously, significant developments are now taking place in sales registering equipment and, to a lesser degree, among carrier systems; and electronic equipment is increasing in importance. The retailer should review these developments carefully as he proceeds with his selection.

Advantages of Sales Registers

The major arguments favoring the use of sales registers in retail stores are as follows:

1. Sales registers provide a fast and efficient method of serving customers who enter the store. Customers expect and demand prompt courteous service; and sales registers make this possible by allowing the salesperson to give the customer a receipt and change without a delay.

2. Sales registers are sufficiently flexible to permit handling peak periods of the day, week, or month without confusion. Since the retail business is characterized by wide variations in sales volume, this advantage of the sales register is a significant one.

3. Sales registers are flexible in location. The mobility of most types of sales registers makes them particularly well suited for use in departments that have peak periods and seasonal changes in their fixtures and general layout (for example, beach shops, riding shops, and toy sections). This flexibility of position, when properly carried out, reduces the fatigue of salespeople and increases productiveness.

4. Sales registers are economical in the use of supplies. As compared with the use of sales checks for cash transactions, for example, a department store which

has about five million sales register transactions a year and pays 15 cents and more for each for its sales books will save approximately $13,000 annually through the use of sales registers.

5. The use of sales registers tends to reduce the number of packages delivered. Experience has shown that when the salesperson takes the customer's money, "rings" it on the sales register, and wraps the merchandise, the customer will in most instances take the package with her, especially small-bulk items.

6. The newer sales registers furnish a record of sales which may be audited quickly and economically, and provide other kinds of information required for improving departmental operations. The sales register shown in Figure 26–2, while it offers the customary receipt and validates sales checks in the conventional manner, also records on tape all basic sales data using computer language. Among other facts, these sales data include the department, class of merchandise and unit control number as shown on the price ticket, amount of the transaction, and the salesperson's code. If the transaction is a charge sale, the customer's credit card is inserted in the credit-card reader on the sales register. As the register operates, the account number shown on the card in punchhole code is automatically recorded on the register's tape in optical-type font that can be read electronically.

7. Sales registers provide a speedy and effective method for handling "cash-send" transactions as well as "cash-take" sales. When the sales check has been completed by the salesperson, it may be placed in a slot of the sales register before the amount of the sale is registered. Then, through the use of a special key on the register, the sales check is stamped or authorized; the sales register receipt is thus eliminated. It is unnecessary, therefore, for floor or central cashiers to be used; in this way, important savings are effected.

The Sales Register and the Self-Service Store Check-Out.   In Chapter 6 the rise and present-day significance of self-service in retailing was noted, together with the reasons for this development.[7] From the point of view of the present chapter, the importance of self-service is that it involves a centralized system of handling sales transactions with the sales register playing an important role. In contrast with the centralized system used in some stores, however, in which the sales slip may be transported to a central desk by a conveyor or pneumatic tube, under self-service the customer brings her packages to the check-out stand. Here the checker "rings up" each item on a sales register, collects the money or prepares the appropriate credit record, places the purchases in a bag or box (a task which is frequently assigned to a "bagger"), and drops in the bag the sales register receipt as the customer's record of the transaction. In some types of stores, such as the supermarket and the variety store, a single check-out area—with a varying number of check-out stands—is used; but in a large discount house, for example, there may be a check-out operation for the "fenced-off" food area and perhaps still another for the drug area, with the remaining departments

[7] Cf. pp. 166–72, above.

FIG. 26-2. National Cash Register Company Model 53 optical font sales register with credit card reader.

having their own sales registers. Regardless of the exact arrangement, sales registers are used for the reasons given in the previous section of this chapter.

[Three decades ago, when the self-service idea was new,] . . . the check-out operation was little more than a cash register on a table. Today . . . [it is] a complex engineering challenge . . . [which] involves: (1) getting [the] customer through the check-out with minimum waiting time; (2) check-out losses . . . the undercharge errors in extensive tests . . . in one [supermarket] chain . . . [reaching] .70 percent of sales; (3) the problem of training and supervising check-out employees; (4) the selection and maintenance of equipment . . . which continues to take an increasingly large share of new store investment; [and] (5) the challenge to develop techniques for scheduling check-out employees.[8]

In addition, there are the control problems which result from using the checker as the one who gives out trading stamps.

---

[8] "Checkout Management," *Chain Store Age* (Grocery Executives Edition), March, 1962, p. 66.

To meet some of the foregoing problems of check-out operations, various sales-register systems, some incorporating devices for issuing the right number of trading stamps where these are given, have been devised to simplify and speed up the check-out procedure. Other developments in check-out fixtures and equipment are taking place almost continuously, but the basic emphasis continues to be on the training and supervision of the checker.[9]

Advantages of Pneumatic Tubes

Despite the numerous improvements in sales-registering equipment, most of them correlated with increasing automation of retail operations, and despite the growth of self-service and the use of check-outs in supermarkets and other stores, some retail establishments find advantages in carrier systems for handling sales transactions. When pneumatic-tube systems—which we shall use to illustrate the general classification of carrier systems—are employed, sales checks are commonly made out to record the sale and are dispatched to a central cashier. The chief arguments in favor of the use of tube systems are as follows:

1. Tube systems provide a maximum form of control. This control is effected by requiring the making out of sales checks for each transaction; the centralization of cash handling by those qualified to make change promptly; and, where cashier-inspectors are used, the checking of the goods wrapped against those listed on the sales check. Furthermore, the location of cashiers in central tube rooms minimizes the possibility of armed robbery or of thefts by employees.

2. Tube systems are particularly suited to the handling of peak sales periods since they can absorb a large number of carriers simultaneously. They also enable salespeople to do interdepartmental selling in rush periods and permit the use of mobile groups which may be shifted from department to department.

3. Tube systems provide greater opportunity for suggestion selling, thus tending to increase the average sale. The time that elapses between the dispatch of the carrier to the central station for change and its return may be used for this purpose. In rush periods, of course, this time may be spent in waiting on other customers.

4. Tube systems relieve the necessity of technical training for salespeople in the use of sales registers. Likewise, the mental strain of having salespersons "balance out" each day and other problems connected with the handling of cash are avoided.

5. Since tube systems require the use of sales checks, the duplicate copy of this check provides the customer with an itemized receipt covering her pur-

---

[9] On all aspects of check-out operation cf. E. M. Harwell, *Checkout Management* (New York: Chain Store Publishing Corporation, 1963) and *Department Store Check Out* (Dayton, Ohio: National Cash Register Company, n.d.). How one supermarket chain "dresses up" the check-out procedure is related in "Checkers Wear Paris Original: Charm Course and Fashionable Dress for Super Valu Woman Checkers," *Progressive Grocer*, January, 1966, pp. 178–79.

chases. Many customers, particularly those of large stores, dislike sales register receipts because they are not itemized. They have found that a duplicate sales check saves many disputes when merchandise is returned for exchange or refund.

6. Tube systems facilitate the authorization of charge sales. This advantage is made possible because of the ease and speed with which sales checks may be dispatched to the credit authorizer and the customer's signature compared with that on file before the goods are released.

7. Tube systems provide rapid service as mechanical messengers in the distribution of reports, requests, and messages among various departments of the store.

Electronic Sales-Recording Equipment

Previous reference has been made to the increase of automated devices in retailing operations, particularly merchandise control, credit authorization, and the registering of sales.[10] Judging by current trends, as evidenced by the equipment illustrated in Figure 26–2 and discussed on page 726, even more of tomorrow's sales-handling equipment will be electronic in nature.[11] Although the description and use of this newer equipment must be restricted here because of its great complexity and variety, there are two electronic machines in particular which have contributed so much to the handling of sales transactions that the retailer should be familiar with them—the counter device or point-of-sales recorder and the optical scanner.

Counter Device. The counter device or "point-of-sale recorder" is operated by the salesperson. In response to the pressing of keys or the insertion of prepunched price tickets, the device prints a sales slip with all the pertinent information—such as type of sale, salesperson, and price. It also performs the necessary arithmetic computations, such as total amount of the sale and the sales tax due. The sales slip prepared by the salesperson in this manner requires about half the time of the manual sales check. In addition to providing a sales slip, the point-of-sale recorder can be used to develop basic inventory control data, including that necessary for the operation of model stocks and unit control. Our interest at this point, however, is the sales-handling aspect of electronic devices.

---

[10] Cf. pp. 138–41, 380–82, and 630–32, above.

[11] The newer forms of electronic data processing equipment available from such firms as IBM, National Cash Register Company, Burroughs Corporation, Monroe/Sweda, Olivetti-Underwood, and Farrington Manufacturing Company and used in recording and analyzing sales transactions are described in Bert Berger, "Accelerating Retail Velocity with EDP," *Chain Store Age* (Executives Ed.), May, 1966, pp. E28–E32. Also Cf. W. A. Kleinschrod, "Finding the 'IR' System for You," *Administrative Management,* Vol. XXVI, No. 4 (April, 1965), pp. 62–68 ff. The author gives a summary review of techniques and equipment for information retrieval ranging from manual systems to the most complex ones.

Some types of counter devices contain perforated or sensitized tape on which all the desired data are recorded. Periodically, perhaps at the close of business each day or more frequently if desired, these tapes are removed and "fed" into a computer maintained at a central point within the store or mailed to the headquarters of the chain system. It is hoped that this type of counter device will also be of value to the medium-sized retailer, since his investment could be limited to the device itself, relying upon computing centers available on a fee basis to process the tapes for him. Other counter devices are connected directly with the central computer. Obviously, use of this latter type of equipment is limited to operators of large retail establishments.

Optical Scanner. The optical scanner or reader, like the counter device, is another means of activating the computer. It moves rapidly across typed or handwritten letters and numbers, translating them into "machine language" or electrical impulses.[12] So far as sales transactions are concerned, the speedy and accurate "reading" of sales register slips and sales checks by the optical scanner permits prompt forwarding of data to the computer with resultant savings in both time and money.

Equipment Should Be Fitted to Needs

In considering the different types of equipment it should be remembered that all types are in use by many different stores and are providing satisfactory service. Many complaints and arguments for or against a particular type of equipment are based on prejudice, on personal preference and belief not based on facts, and on experience with poorly operated equipment. Frequently, the equipment is blamed for poor service when the particular model or type does not meet the store's needs. Sometimes equipment is blamed when the layout is at fault. There may not be enough tube stations or sales registers, for example, with the result that the salesperson takes many unnecessary steps, wastes his time at an overloaded wrapping desk, and has to go so far away from his selling station that he cannot start helping other customers until the carrier returns.

Poor service blamed on equipment often is caused by a management attitude of cost-consciousness rather than an attitude of customer-consciousness. Consequently, the management either provides an insufficient number of cashiers or credit authorizers to handle promptly the volume of

---

[12] Cf. *Perspectives in Optical Scanning* (Chicago: Standard Register Company, 1965); *Meet the NCR 420–2 Optical Reader* (Dayton, Ohio: National Cash Register Company, 1966), and "Data Acquisition and Display," *Dun's Review and Modern Industry,* September, 1966, Part II, pp. 143–44 ff.

business or sets up an inadequate system of training for both the salespeople and the nonselling employees. No type of equipment, including that which is electronically operated, can be expected to provide satisfactory service unless it is properly selected and is adapted to the situation existing in the particular store or department.

Finally, it should not be forgotten that the equipment comprises but one part of the sales transactions system designed to provide fast and courteous customer service at the lowest cost to the store; to afford protection to management; and to furnish the data required to control merchandise, permit auditing of sales, and prepare the necessary statistical reports. Moreover, the sales transactions system should be related to other systems of the store to provide overall operating efficiency.

REVIEW AND DISCUSSION QUESTIONS

1. Explain the meaning and purposes of a "sales-transactions system."
2. In the light of the purposes referred to in Question 1, what do you consider to be the essential requisites of a system designed to meet these objectives?
3. Discuss the statement: "An adequate and efficient sales-transactions system is the foundation stone of automation in the field of retailing."
4. Why is it important for the proprietor of a new store to decide on the types of sales transactions he will provide and the methods he will employ to record them even before the store is opened?
5. Distinguish among these types of sales transactions: cash, C.O.D., budget, budget book.
6. Account for the increasing use of sales (cash) registers and the decline in the use of the handwritten sales check.
7. What recent changes have taken place in the form and use of handwritten sales checks?
8. Assume that you are the owner and operator of a small store in a farm community and do a considerable business on credit. Would you use sales checks or depend solely on a sales register? State your reasons.
9. What is meant by "centralization" and by "decentralization" in the handling of sales transactions?
10. Explain briefly the main factors to be considered in selecting suitable sales-handling equipment.
11. "Today's check-out operation is complex and involves at least five problems or challenges." What are they?
12. Survey the retail stores in your community or a nearby one to determine the extent to which carrier systems are being used and the reasons for doing so.
13. Make a survey similar to that mentioned in Question 12 to determine the

use of automation in the handling of sales transactions. Try to learn the major problems that have been encountered and also the benefits derived from automation.

14. Explain the meaning, method of operation, and purposes of the counter device or point-of-sale recorder and the optical scanner. What is their relation to the computer?

15. Review the latest developments in the recording of sales transactions in the business periodical literature in your library. Based on this review, what are likely to be the most significant improvements in the next ten years? Explain your reasons.

SUPPLEMENTARY READINGS

AUTHORS' NOTE: Only a limited amount of information is available on sales transactions systems as such in current literature. Probably the best data on equipment for handling sales transactions are those prepared by the manufacturers of such equipment. These include, among many others, the Lamson Corporation, Syracuse, New York; The Burroughs Corporation, Second Avenue at Burroughs, Detroit, Michigan; Diebold, Inc., 818 Mulberry, S. E., Canton, Ohio; Farrington Manufacturing Company, 850 Third Avenue, New York, N.Y.; International Business Machines, Armonk, New York; Litton Industries, Inc., 9370 Santa Monica Blvd., Beverly Hills, California; National Cash Register Company, Main and K Streets, Dayton, Ohio; and Olivetti-Underwood Corporation, 1 Park Avenue, New York, N.Y. These firms serve retailers of all kinds and sizes.

Representative of the kinds of information in this general area of value to the retailer are the following:

GARBER, HAROLD, AND HELFANT, SEYMOUR. *Retail Merchandising and Management with Electronic Data Processing* (New York: National Retail Merchants Association, 1966). Of special interest in connection with this chapter is the authors' discussion of instore equipment needs.

HARWELL, E. M. *Checkout Management* (New York: Chain Store Age Publishing Corporation, 1963). Looking at the checkout in the self-service store as "a huge transmission belt which processes tonnage into consumer transactions," the author covers checker accuracy, scheduling and training of checkout employees, checkout supervision, and equipment for the checkout operation.

JONES, W. F. "Automating the Retailer," *Retail Control,* May, 1966, pp. 46–52. The Assistant Controller of Joseph Horne Co., Pittsburgh, describes the details of planning and conversion involved in the company's adoption of an automated system.

NATIONAL RETAIL MERCHANTS ASSOCIATION, RETAIL RESEARCH INSTITUTE. *Proceedings of Annual Electronic Data Processing Conference* (New York: The Association, annual reports). Beginning in 1959, the Institute has published annually the papers delivered at this conference.

"So You Want to Go into Computers?" *Super Market Merchandising,* February,

1966, pp. 43–44. Emphasizing that "profitable computer installations among retailers are 'few and far between,' " the controller of the Jewel Companies, Inc. offers advice to potential users.

TIPPER, HARRY, JR. *Controlling Overhead.* (New York: American Management Association, 1966). After reviewing problems of managing overhead, the author suggests a positive approach to solving them. The discussion of systems and procedures has particular relevance to the topics in this chapter.

TRIPPETT, B. L. "The Automation of Retail Transactions," *Retail Control,* January, 1965, pp. 35–46. An informative article in which the author describes, with emphasis on sales transactions, the "Total System" of the National Cash Register Company.

27
CHAPTER

Retail Insurance

THE RISKS OF RETAILING

The retail organization, whether large or small, is constantly subject to many risks. For example, the operator of a neighborhood drugstore has certain risks concerning his merchandise. Some of it is perishable and must be moved quickly to avoid losses, and the same speed of movement is essential for seasonal items of merchandise. His whole stock is subject to the risks of price changes, shifts in customer demand, fire, robbery, water and smoke damage, and the like. His investment in his building and equipment is also in danger of being destroyed by fire, wind, explosion, floods, or even riots.[1] Furthermore, the retailer always finds that he is liable to many persons—to the customer who falls because an employee carelessly leaves a small packing box in the aisle, to the customer who claims his prescription is incorrectly compounded, and to the employee who wrenches his shoulder while lifting a box.

The foregoing list is by no means complete, but it is perhaps sufficient to prove the contention that the retailer assumes a large number of risks. And it should be emphasized that, from the retailer's point of view, these risks are significant. A tornado or a disastrous fire in an uninsured building which he owns may wipe out the results of many years of successful retailing; and even a tornado or a fire that does not completely destroy the building may

---

[1] The concern of retailers and insurance companies over rioting in racially disturbed areas with damage losses estimated at $45 million in July, 1966, is outlined in "Insurance Policies Hit in Riot Toll," *Women's Wear Daily*, July 22, 1966, pp. 1, 26. Also cf. L. N. Conroy, "Store Protection and the Watts Area Riots," *Retail Control*, May, 1966, pp. 7–17.

force him into bankruptcy.[2] If his sprinkler system breaks, the damage to his merchandise may total many thousands of dollars. A single suit brought by the customer who fell over the packing box and injured his leg may result in a court award under which the small retailer may struggle for years to regain his previous financial position.

Dealing with Retail Risks

The retailer has three main methods of dealing with the risks that are inherent in retailing: (1) reducing or minimizing these risks, (2) transferring them to others, or (3) assuming them.

Minimizing Risks. The first method may be illustrated by considering the fire hazard. To reduce the risk of loss from fire, the retailer may install an automatic sprinkler system in his store or provide a number of chemical fire estinguishers. He may construct a fireproof building or place fireproof doors between various sections of the building to slow up the spread of a fire. Metal fixtures may be used. He may have his electrical wiring checked from time to time, and he may make sure that rubbish does not accumulate in his stock or receiving room. Other specific suggestions for minimizing risks will be found in reports of the insurance inspector and in the loss prevention programs of the insurance company.

Transferring Risks. Transferring risks to others is well illustrated by the practice of many retailers of hand-to-mouth buying. By following such a policy, the retailer throws back onto the manufacturer or wholesaler much of the risk of shifts in fashion, perishability, and price change. In this chapter, however, we are interested mainly in transferring risks through insurance.

Insurance is a social device whereby one person is enabled to make a contract with another or with others, the second party agreeing to assume certain definite risks of the first party upon payment by the later of a compensation called the "premium." From the retailer's point of view, it allows him to exchange a possible loss of unknown amount for a known premium. To the insurance company, it contemplates the combining of many risks into a group so that the law of averages may apply. The larger the number of separate risks of a similar character combined into one group, the less the uncertainty as to the amount of loss that will occur. Insurance

---

[2] Tornado damage in an area quickly reaches large figures. Cf. "Betsy Adjustments Saw Business Meet Its Toughest Test," *National Underwriter,* February 11, 1966, pp. 1 ff.; and R. L. Hendrick and D. G. Friedman, "Potential Impacts of Storm Modification on Insurance," *ibid.,* December 17, 1965, pp. 1 ff.

does not prevent loss aside from the results of its prevention activities, but it indemnifies for loss that does occur.

Assuming Risks. The retailer finds that, in spite of all he may do to minimize risks and to transfer them to others, there are a large number of risks that he must assume, at least in part. Assumption of risk on his part is necessary even in regard to the fire hazard, since the merchant usually finds that a serious fire results in losses not entirely covered by insurance. Although a hand-to-mouth buying policy may shift certain risks to wholesalers and manufacturers, the retailer must assume various risks on at least a minimum of stock. For many retailers the cost of certain insurance policies seems prohibitive, so they would rather assume the risk than pay the required insurance premium.

Variations in Retail Practice. There are wide variations in the ways in which different retailers make use of the three methods of dealing with risks. This statement applies to fairly comparable merchants, but even more so to those of different types. By way of illustration, whereas one grocery retailer will try to shift risk to others by hand-to-mouth buying, another will try to add to his net income by "outguessing the market." Or again, one shoe store operator will take out insurance against breakage of his plate-glass windows; another will take a chance that nothing will happen to his windows. A retailer operating from a single establishment will consider fire insurance for his building, equipment, and stock as an essential; in contrast, a chain organization with scattered units may prefer to assume all or part of its own fire risks.

Although it is not surprising that there is a difference of opinion among retailers as to how to deal with retailing risks, a considerable part of these differences may be traced to the retailers' failure to consider carefully the relative merits of insurance. Especially is this statement true of many small retailers. Far too many of them go on the assumption that "it won't happen to me," or they conclude that the premium looks too large, or they lack knowledge of the available insurance policies, or they simply get so busy with other matters that they fail to buy proper insurance. The end result is that they are totally unprepared for the emergency created by a fire in their store, the collision of their delivery truck with another vehicle, and the customer who falls and injuries his leg.

Still another reason for a wide divergence in current practices of retailers in regard to insurance is found in the rapid rise of the price level over the past three decades. What was an adequate amount of fire insurance even ten years ago is completely inadequate today. Many retailers have adjusted their coverage accordingly, but some have not.

Types of Insurance. In the following paragraphs several forms of insurance for retailers are described. Owing to the extraordinary expense which would be involved, no retailer would carry all of these forms. Yet all of them and perhaps others are considered from time to time by the managements of retail concerns. Thus the purpose of this chapter is not to suggest that the retailer must be an insurance expert; rather it is to provide sufficient background for him to determine whether or not to buy a particular insurance contract recommended by someone who specializes in the insurance field. Each proposed policy requires a careful analysis of the various hazards, the insurance coverages obtainable, and the particular needs of the business.

At least eight types of insurance are available to the retailer and deserve his thorough consideration:

1. Tangible property insurance
2. Business interruption or
       loss-of-use insurance
3. Liability insurance
4. Crime hazards insurance

5. Surety bonds
6. Life, group, and
       disability insurance
7. Credit insurance
8. Unemployment insurance

TANGIBLE PROPERTY INSURANCE

The bulk of the typical retailer's investment is in buildings, fixtures and equipment, and merchandise which are exposed to numerous hazards such as fire, windstorm, explosion, riot and civil commotion, sprinkler leakage, water damage, earthquake, and aircraft damage. Consequently, the adequate coverage of tangible property is one of his major insurance problems. To illustrate the importance of such coverage, in 1964 store fire losses in the United States reached a high of $181 million with 40,600 stores suffering damage.[3] These figures represent substantial increases over 1960's $104 million of losses in 39,700 stores.

Fire Insurance

Policy Provisions. The traditional fire insurance policy of the past stated that, in consideration of a certain premium, the insurance company agreed to indemnify the policyholder for the actual cash value, ascertained with proper deductions for depreciation, of the property lost or damaged as a result of fire. In recent years, however, this provision has been changed so

---

[3] Reprint from *Fire Journal*, September, 1965. Page numbers not given. For 1965 the two largest fire losses among retailers were Spencer Gifts, an Atlantic City, New Jersey, mail order house—$5.2 million, and a shopping center in Columbia Heights, Minneapolis —$3.0 million. Cf. "U.S. Fire Loss Damage in 1965 Flares Past '64 by $1 Million," *Women's Wear Daily,* January 5, 1966, p. 34.

that the indemnity now covers replacement value, i.e., the actual cost of replacing the property exclusive of depreciation. The new basis is important to the retailer since his working capital (and in some cases his borrowing capacity as well) often is being utilized completely and assumption of the depreciation might force him to restrict his growth. Some farsighted retailers have arranged their insurance against catastrophic risks so as to combine their physical damage coverage and their business interruption coverage.[4] This arrangement permits replacement of the business premises without a serious drain on working capital and, at the same time, provides for reimbursement of the continuing expenses and profit in the same amounts that would have been experienced had the catastrophe not occurred.

With respect to coverage against fire loss, usually the retailer will want such insurance to include his building (if he owns it), equipment and fixtures, and merchandise. The policy covers fire loss, even though the fire does not originate in the premises of the assured. Damage caused by lightning is also covered under the standard policy, whether fire ensues or not.[5] In addition, damage caused by smoke and water as a result of fire is also covered; and if property endangered by fire is removed to a place of safety, such property is automatically covered at the new location for five days.

The policy does not cover accounts, bills, currency, deeds, evidences of debt, money, notes, or securities; and unless it is specifically agreed in writing, it does not cover bullion or manuscripts. It also provides that the insurance company shall not be liable for loss or damage caused directly or indirectly by invasion, insurrection, riot, civil war or commotion, military or unsurped power, order of any civil authority, theft, or neglect of the insured to use all reasonable means to save the property during and after the fire.

Determining Value of the Property.   As noted previously, the fire insurance company now commonly agrees to indemnify the policy holder for the actual replacement value of the property lost or damaged as a result of fire. Such value may be ascertained by an outside appraisal company, by means of the retailer's records, or by estimate. In regard to merchandise, its value for insurance purposes includes not only its cost in the market but also the expense of transporting, receiving, marking, and similar activities.[6] To maintain adequate protection at all times on a merchandise stock which fluctuates in value some retailers report approximate merchandise values to

---

[4] Cf. the discussion of business interruption insurance on pp. 743–45, below.

[5] Control over insurance policies is exercised by the individual states, with the result that standard policies differ from state to state. The retailer should read his own individual contracts to find out exactly what is and what is not covered by these contracts.

[6] For an explanation of how insurance men determine cash value at the time of loss of the merchandise, cf. J. L. Sybrant, "Sybrant of GAB Gives Retail Men Facts on Actual Cash Value," *National Underwriter,* February 4, 1966, pp. 1, 20.

the insurance company each month and have their policies so written that they cover the amount reported. Such policies are known as "reporting form policies."

The Coinsurance, Reduced Rate, or Contribution Clause. When a coinsurance clause is attached to a fire insurance policy, the policyholder, in consideration of a reduced rate, agrees to carry insurance equal to a certain percentage of the actual value of the property insured (usually 80 percent, or even more); failing to do that, he becomes a coinsurer and collects only that proportion of his loss which the amount he carries bears to the amount required.[7] For example, if the value of the property insured is $50,000 and the policyholder agrees to carry at least 80 percent insurance, the amount required to comply with the coinsurance clause would be $40,000. If, however, the policyholder carries only $30,000 insurance and has a loss that is partial, he can collect only three fourths of the loss because he is carrying only three fourths of the amount required to comply with the clause. If the loss is $10,000, he will collect $7,500 and will have to stand $2,500 himself.[8] If the policyholder carries the required amount of insurance, however, he collects the full amount of his loss up to the amount of the policy.

Nearly all large retail firms carry insurance with the coinsurance clause incorporated in the policy, since they wish to take advantage of the considerable reduction in the rate and, at the same time, to be fully protected. Moreover, the principle of coinsurance does not apply to fire insurance only but to many other types of insurance. Very material reductions from the published rates are granted on windstorm, sprinkler leakage, explosion, riot and civil commotion, and many other forms of insurance, for the incorporation of certain percentages of coinsurance.

Sprinkler Systems. Another way for the retailer to reduce the cost of his fire insurance is to place a sprinkler system in his store. Since such a system automatically reduces the fire hazard, the insurance company will grant a lower rate. Even if the retailer has to borrow the money to install the system, he may still find it worthwhile.

Smoke Damage

Since the fire insurance policy covers smoke damage only as a direct result of fire, smoke damage caused by faulty operation of heating devices without

---

[7] Cf. R. H. Butz, "How the Coinsurance Clause Works in Your Fire Insurance Policy," *Air Conditioning, Heating & Refrigeration News,* January 17, 1966, p. 16.

[8] If the insured does not carry the required amount, the liability of the insurance company may be determined as follows:

$$\frac{\text{Amount of insurance carried}}{\text{Amount required under coinsurance clause}} \times \text{Loss} = \text{Insurance company's liability.}$$

fire occurring outside of the device is a hazard to be considered. In consideration of a small additional premium, many fire insurance policies may be
extended to cover smoke damage not resulting directly from fire; or a
separate policy may be issued.

Cyclone, Tornado, Windstorm, and Hail Insurance

Several studies in connection with windstorms make it evident that almost
without exception every portion of the United States is subject to this risk.
Since severe windstorms cause great property loss without reaching the
intensity of tornadoes or cyclones, windstorm policies are drawn to cover all
such direct loss and damage even though an actual tornado or cyclone does
not occur. They can also be endorsed to cover hail and damage to awnings,
signs, and temporary additions.

The windstorm insurance policy is closely related to the fire insurance
policy. If a building covered by fire insurance should be blown down,
windstorm insurance is needed to pick up where the fire insurance leaves off.
To avoid complications under such circumstances, it is wise to carry both
kinds of insurance with the same company and in equal amounts.

Explosion and Riot and Civil Commotion Insurance

The fire insurance policy does not cover damage by explosion unless fire
ensues and then only for damage by fire. Since the hazard of explosion is
serious for many retailers, especially as a result of the introduction of natural
gas, refrigerating gas, paint spraying, fuel oil, synthetic liquids, and a myriad
of mechanical appliances, the explosion policy is important. It covers all
direct loss or damage by explosion, excluding explosions originating within
steam boilers, pipes, flywheels, engines, and machinery connected therewith.
Some retailers prefer the riot and civil commotion policy which gives
protection against all losses covered by the simple explosion policy and, in
addition, direct loss caused by riot, riot attending a strike, insurrection, civil
commotion, and explosion directly caused by any of the foregoing.

Aircraft and Motor Vehicle Property Damage Insurance

With the exception of damage caused by sonic booms, this policy covers
all direct loss and damage by airplanes and other aerial craft, or objects falling therefrom, and by automobiles or other motor vehicles, including fire
ensuing from such accidents. The motor vehicle property damage clause is
limited to damage done by vehicles other than those owned or operated by

the person taking the insurance. For example, it would afford protection against a loss occasioned by an automobile that "jumped" the curb and penetrated into the interior of a store; it would not protect the retailer if his own deliveryman had the identical accident.

The Extended Coverage Endorsement

The tendency for property owners to insist upon coverage for an increasing number of hazards has led insurance companies to offer an endorsement to the fire insurance policy, known as the extended coverage endorsement. This endorsement gives protection against loss occasioned by the factors already discussed, that is, loss or damage from windstorm, hail, explosion, riot, aircraft, motor vehicles, and smoke. It is attached to the fire insurance policy at a much lower cost than if the coverages were written under separate policies. Moreover, it is more convenient than employing individual policies to secure the desired coverage.

Sprinkler Leakage Insurance

Since many retail stores are protected by sprinkler systems and since the stock carried is particularly susceptible to damage by water, sprinkler leakage insurance is practically a necessity for them. The policy covers against all direct loss and damage caused by leakage—or by bursting of sprinkler pipes—not resulting from fire, whether the leakage originates in the building or not.

Water Damage

Closely related to the damage caused by sprinkler leakage but entirely separate from an insurance point of view is the hazard of water damage. A water damage policy covers loss or damage caused by the accidental leakage of water from the plumbing system, bursting water mains or pipes, and the like, regardless of where it originates, as well as damage caused by water from roofs or coming through open windows and skylights, and floods.

Fire, Theft, Collision, and Comprehensive Automobile Coverages

The ordinary policy covering fire and theft of the motor vehicle insures against loss or damage to the automobile caused by fire, including lightning; the risk of transportation while being transported by rail or water; and theft, robbery, vandalism, breakage of glass and equipment excluding tools and repair equipment unless the entire automobile is stolen. For a small additional cost the policy can be extended to include tornado, windstorm, hail, earthquake, and water damage. Such a policy may be written with or without collision coverage. Most automobiles may be insured under the comprehensive form of policy which covers any loss or damage, with a few unimportant exceptions. Deductible provisions, of course, may be included. Five or more vehicles under one ownership, used for business purposes, are eligible for fleet rates.

Goods in Transit

The very nature of retailing causes the majority of merchants to have merchandise in transit practically at all times. For those retailers who desire it, there is a form of shippers' policy which covers almost all goods and merchandise owned by the store or held by it in trust, on commission or consignment, or on which it has made advances, or sold but not delivered, while the goods are in transit to and from the store on nearly every form of transportation. It provides protection against such hazards as fire, lightning, cyclone, tornado, flood, and transportation during the entire time the merchandise is in transit. The policy is usually written at a deposit premium based on the estimated gross annual sales and an adjustment is made at the end of the policy term on the basis of the actual gross sales.

For retailers who do not wish to insure all goods in transit under the form just described but who may wish to carry insurance against the usual motor truck cargo hazard on cargoes carried by specific trucks or automobiles, other policies are available. Rates on these more limited policies are based upon the type of equipment, the territory covered, and the types of merchandise carried. For retailers making some use of parcel post in delivering merchandise, an insurance policy is available to cover the safe arrival of the property, subject to a few exceptions.

Some Other Kinds of Tangible Property Insurance

Space limitations make it impossible to discuss each of the many other kinds of tangible property insurance. Some West Coast retailers, and a relatively few elsewhere, despite rates which seem high in relation to the rates for other hazards, deem it desirable to carry insurance against damage caused by earthquakes. Plate-glass insurance, under which the insurance company agrees to replace or pay for plate glass broken by practically any cause except fire, is fairly widespread among retailers of all sizes. Some merchants will desire power-plant insurance to provide protection against loss occasioned by steam-boiler explosion, flywheel explosion, engine breakage, and electrical machinery breakdown. Concerns that sell goods on the installment plan usually have relatively large outstanding balances. To protect the retailer against loss on such goods before full payment has been received, there is a form of insurance known as deferred payment insurance, which covers the merchandise while it is in the possession of the purchaser.

The growing use of high-cost computers and related equipment has produced an insurance problem for many large retailers. Careful consideration must be given to adequate insurance covering such contingencies as (1 the physical loss of the equipment used, (2) the effect that the loss of tape, punched cards, and other memory devices would have, and (3) the extra expense involved should the computer or input data be lost.

The Commercial Property Floater

To meet the needs of an increasing number of retailers some insurance companies now issue a commercial property floater policy. Such a policy, which is applicable to merchandise, equipment, and fixtures, covers property on an all-risk basis regardless of its location. Specific exemptions are losses resulting from floods, earthquakes, war, employee dishonesty, and some other similar claims. This type of policy, of course, is designed to replace the need for a large number of separate policies and still provide the desired protection.

BUSINESS INTERRUPTION OR LOSS-OF-USE INSURANCE

So far, our discussion has dealt principally with the insurance of property. We have seen that coverage under the fire insurance policy is against direct loss or damage by fire without compensation for business interruption. The same fact applies to other types of property insurance policies as well. For that reason the further loss occasioned by business interruption or loss of *use* of property, which is frequently as great as or greater than the actual property damage, should be anticipated.

Business Interruption Insurance

A retail firm depends upon its earnings to pay interest on its debt, if it has one; to fulfill contracts; and to pay expenses, taxes, and dividends to stockholders. If business should be interrupted by fire or windstorm, for instance, earnings will cease. Business interruption insurance, also known as use and occupancy insurance, protects against the loss of earnings in the face of certain disasters. Stated positively, it seeks to provide for the net profit and for meeting continuing expenses as if there had been no business interrup-

TABLE 27–1

QUARTERLY PROFIT AND LOSS STATEMENT OF A RETAILER SHOWING
INFLUENCE OF BUSINESS INTERRUPTION INSURANCE

Statement Items	Results without Business Interruption Insurance	Results with Business Interruption Insurance
Gross sales.......................................	$ 000.00	$ 000.00
Less: Sales allowance and returns.....................	000.00	000.00
Net sales...	000.00	000.00
Less: Cost of merchandise sold......................	000.00	000.00
Gross margin...................................	000.00	81,493.23
Salaries—official...............................	23,374.22	$23,374.22
Salaries—sales.................................	8,472.69	8,472.69
Salaries—office................................	6,234.37	6,234.37
Advertising....................................	1,924.36	1,924.36
Traveling expense...............................	1,426.19	1,426.19
Stationery and postage...........................	897.00	897.00
Office supplies.................................	623.27	623.27
Telephone and telegraph.........................	227.92	227.92
Legal expense..................................	250.00	250.00
Audits..	375.00	375.00
Subscriptions and donations.......................	200.00	200.00
Light, heat, and water...........................	2,726.94	2,726.94
Taxes...	4,250.00	4,250.00
Insurance......................................	1,236.00	1,236.00
Rent..	9,000.00	9,000.00
Interest.......................................	3,010.20	3,010.20
Miscellaneous..................................	472.99	472.99
Total operating expense.........................	$64,701.15	$64,701.15
Net operating loss..............................	$64,701.15	$16,792.08*

* Net operating profit

tion. Although it rarely achieves these goals completely, it is of great aid to the retailer whose business is interrupted for a period.[9]

The data of Table 27–1 give some indication of business interruption insurance in action. For retail organizations which do not desire such complete coverage, policies are available that enable the firm to meet only certain of its fixed expenses during a business interruption—for example, its rent.

Rain Insurance

Although it is not ordinarily carried by retailers, there is a form of insurance known as rain insurance which covers loss on expense incurred or

---

[9] Cf. "New Concept in U and O Loss Adjustment in Chicago Decision," *National Underwriter,* June 4, 1965, p. 11.

loss of income on events that are dependent upon favorable weather for success, when such loss is caused by rain, hail, snow, or sleet. Such insurance may be considered in the case of special sales events, in preparation for which considerable expense has been incurred. The rates vary with the area, the time of year, the time of day, and the number of hours of exposure, as well as the amount of rainfall required before the policy pays.

LIABILITY INSURANCE

Liability insurance seeks to provide protection against a financial loss from the liability imposed by law for bodily injuries or damage to property resulting from accidents of one kind or another.

General or Public Liability of the Retailer

In the eyes of the law, every man is his brother's keeper. He must do certain things which a reasonably prudent person would do and must not do anything which a reasonably prudent person would not do. Should this principle be violated, he is guilty of negligence. In view of the thousands of customers who may visit a store in a single year—where they may slip on a wet spot, be injured in elevators or on escalators, trip over a box in the aisle or a rug, or bump into a counter or "merchandise island"—the retailer needs protection.[10] He is also legally liable for the negligent acts of his employees. In addition, there is always the danger that a customer will bring suit because of injury sustained from a product which she has purchased in the store. To protect himself, therefore, against such claims—even if these claims are groundless—public liability insurance is necessary. As a matter of fact, in view of the courts' trend toward larger awards for personal injuries,[11] such protection is more essential to today's retailer than it was to his counterpart fifty years ago.[12]

Owners', Landlords', and Tenants' Public Liability Policy

The usual policy covering general liability for accidents occurring on or about the premises is known as the owners', landlords', and tenants' public

---

[10] Cf. the excellent discussion by E. W. Fowler, Manager, Engineering and Safety Department, American Insurance Association, in "My Client While She Was in Your Store . . . ," *Retail Control,* March, 1966, pp. 18–31.

[11] A. F. Southwick, Jr., "Mass Marketing and Warranty Liability," *Journal of Marketing,* Vol. XXVII, No. 2 (April, 1963), pp. 6–12; and, by the same author, "Products Liability: A Broadening Concept," *Management Review,* March, 1966, pp. 21–25.

[12] Friedricka Kessler, "The Protection of the Consumer Under Modern Sales Law," *Yale Law Journal,* December, 1964, pp. 262–85.

liability policy. It provides indemnity for loss from claims made upon the retailer as a result of an accident causing bodily injury (including death at any time resulting therefrom) suffered or alleged to have been suffered by any person not employed by the retailer while such persons are on the insured premises, sidewalks, and other adjacent ways. It may also be extended to cover such injuries occurring elsewhere if caused by the use, maintenance, or existence of the insured premises or of the business conducted on the premises or by the employees of the insured who are required to leave the premises in the course of their duties.

The insurance company agrees (1) to defend in the name of the retailer all such suits—even if false—brought against the insured; (2) to pay— irrespective of the limits of insurance—all court costs levied against the insured in any such litigation, all interest accruing up to the date of settlement by the insurer upon the insurer's share of the judgment rendered in such suit, and all expenses incurrd by the company for investigation, negotiations, and defense; and (3) to reimburse the retailer for such immediate surgical and medical relief as is necessary at the time of the accident.

Except for very small retailers, the cost of public liability insurance is on a retrospective basis, that is, it is based on the previous loss experience of the store. To minimize costs, of course, continuous attention must be given to the causes and prevention of injuries to customers and employees.[13]

Elevator and Escalator Public Liability Insurance

Elevator and escalator public liability coverage may be secured in a separate policy or, typically, in connection with owners', landlords', and tenants' public liability policies by properly designating and describing the elevators and escalators and paying the required additional premium. The inspection service of the insurance company carrying the policy is extremely valuable as a preventive measure and in many states replaces the state inspection.

Products Liability Insurance

Increasingly, suits involving injury from products are finding their way into our courts. Such suits are illustrated by the person who found or claimed to have found a tack or small nail in a pie, broken glass in a frankfurter, or a button in an ice-cream sundae; the person who claimed he became ill

---

[13] In this connection cf. "Is Safety First?", *Women's Wear Daily,* June 27, 1966, pp. 1, 9.

through the use of a certain product; and the man who claimed the steering wheel of his new car failed to function so that an accident resulted. Although exact figures are lacking, it is estimated that product cases reaching the courts now total at least 10,000 each year. Even more important, perhaps four times this number are settled out of court. In addition, as in other injury suits, the dollar settlements being granted by the courts are climbing with each passing decade.[14]

Since (1) the injured person can sue the retailer of the product and is not required to sue the manufacturer (in fact, so far as foods are concerned, the law in most states holds the retailer primarily responsible for the sale of products unfit for human consumption) and since (2) it is often quite difficult to pass the liability back to the manufacturer, the retailer frequently considers the purchase of products liability insurance. This policy provides indemnity against claims for injury (including death at any time resulting therefrom) to persons not employed by the insured, for which the assured may be liable as a result of accidents arising from consumption, handling, or use away from the premises of the insured, resulting from any products manufactured, handled, or distributed by the merchant. The insurance company agrees in such a policy to defend all suits, whether groundless or not, brought because of such occurrences, or to settle for them, and to pay all costs, interest, and expenses incurred, including the cost of any immediate surgical relief necessary at the time of any such accidents.

For stores that handle drugs a similar policy, called a druggist's liability policy, may be obtained; or this risk may be included with other products in an "all-risk" policy. Stores dispensing liquor may obtain a special policy to cover the liability thereby incurred. This policy may be broad enough to cover liability for death or injury attributable to intoxication resulting from consumption of liquor purchased in the store.

Comprehensive General Liability

When a retailer wishes to buy liability protection of the three types just discussed, he will usually do so in a single comprehensive general liability policy. Thus, one transaction assures him of protection against claims arising from customers because of accidents in the store or the use of products.[15]

---

[14] Cf. "Court Views Extent of Liability Coverage in Products Policy," *National Underwriter,* January 14, 1966, p. 15; "Products Liability Rule Continues to be Broadened: Key Cases Cited," *ibid.,* February 18, 1966, pp. 16–17; and "Products Litigation Booms: Defense Questions Burgeon," *ibid.,* May 13, 1966, pp. 1, 42.

[15] On "package policies" cf. R. H. Elliott, "New Comprehensive General Liability Policy," *Best's Insurance News,* February, 1966, pp. 32 ff.

Automobile Public Liability and Property Damage Insurance

The increasing use of motor vehicles has been accompanied by an ever-increasing death and accident list. Since the owner of an automobile may be held liable for injuries to other persons caused by the negligent operation or maintenance of the automobile, it is imperative that the owners of motor vehicles provide themselves with protection against such claims.

The automobile public liability policy protects the retailer on account of loss or expense from his legal liability resulting from accidental automobile injuries (or death at any time resulting therefrom) suffered or alleged to have been suffered by any persons. The property damage liability insurance policy is of a similar nature, except that it protects the owner of the automobile against his legal liability for damage to the property of others, including liability for loss of use of the damaged property. Public liability and property damage insurance may also be written to cover automobiles under a single ownership as a fleet, under conditions similar to the requirements for fleet rating for fire insurance.

Some retailers find it desirable to include an "automobile nonownership" clause in their automobile policies. Such a clause gives protection in case an accident occurs when an employee is using his own car on the retailer's business—making an emergency delivery or going to pick up another employee.

Workmen's Compensation

Since some injuries are unavoidable in producing and marketing goods and services, it is believed that the consumers of these goods and services should bear the cost of such injuries. Consequently, employers are now required by law either to buy workmen's compensation insurance from an insurance company or to carry their own insurance. If the retailer adopts the latter alternative (which does not exist in all states), he is required to post a bond with the state. This latter step is usually taken only by the larger firms.

Workmen's compensation insurance provides benefits to employees according to definite schedules of benefits set forth in the compensation acts of the various states for any injury sustained in the course of their employment. Benefits are usually paid without regard to negligence and cover temporary and permanent disablement; loss of or loss of use of arms, legs, and the like; and death. In addition, the insurance company agrees to pay necessary medical, surgical, and hospital fees as required in the statutes. In case of fatal injury, funeral expenses are covered.

CRIME HAZARDS INSURANCE

Insurance coverages offered against crime hazards are generally written by the casualty insurance companies and are often issued to protect money as well as merchandise. One of the important forms of insurance of this type for the retailer is the so-called "mercantile open-stock burglary insurance." This policy protects the assured against direct loss by burglary of merchandise and fixtures and equipment, if the burglary occurs outside of store hours and entry into the store is gained by force—and such losses may be substantial.[16] It should be noted that this insurance does not cover losses from shoplifting or inventory shortages, but only against actual burglary. The basic premium may be subject to discount for alarm systems and watchmen.

Other coverages for crime hazards are also available. The interior robbery policy offers protection against robbery of property from within the insured premises during business hours. If money, securities, and valuable merchandise are kept in safes or vaults, insurance against burglary of the contents and damage to such property is available through the mercantile-safe burglary insurance policy. Some stores which pay employees in cash may carry a paymaster robbery insurance policy. Retailers wishing to protect themselves from dishonest acts of their own employees may purchase a fidelity schedule bond or a blanket bond. These bonds cover loss by fraud, forgery, misapplication, misappropriation, and other dishonesty. They cover not only loss of money but loss of merchandise and other property.

Closely related to the insurance coverage requirements mentioned in the preceding paragraphs is that needed for protection against vandalism and malicious mischief. These risks have assumed greater importance in recent years.

SURETY BONDS

There are other forms of bonds sometimes required in a retail business which are not connected with the crime hazard, as are fidelity bonds. Such bonds are certain license or permit bonds and custom bonds, usually required by law or ordinance. License and permit bonds may be required, for example, before placing a swinging sign over a sidewalk, to install a sidewalk elevator, or to handle certain commodities. Importers may be required to give bond in connection with the entry at customhouses of merchandise received from foreign countries.

---

[16] Cf. T. M. Patton, "Crime Aspects of Special Multi-Peril Policies," *Best's Insurance News,* February, 1966, pp. 25 ff.

LIFE, GROUP, AND DISABILITY INSURANCE

Life insurance for business protection is a comparatively recent development. Formerly, life insurance was considered only as a family matter; today however, many retailers consider such protection essential. The death of the head of an organization, of an important merchandise executive, or even of a financial backer may cause the company to go through a period of readjustment when additional funds may be required to keep the business going: so-called "key-man" insurance may be desirable in these situations. Another reason for carrying business life insurance is that it provides a way of retiring the estate of the deceased from the business. In the closely held corporation there is always the danger that the estate may sell its interest to the disadvantage of the living stockholders. When a partner's death occurs in connection with a partnership, it is obvious that the advantage of having sufficient cash to purchase the dead partner's interest is important and may be necessary to the continuance of the business. Life insurance may also be used as a method of hedging against the possible failure to pay a bond issue at maturity because of the death of the managing head of a business.

In Chapter 9, "Retail Personnel Management," we mentioned group life insurance as a personnel policy. Typically a single policy is issued to the employer, with individual certificates being provided for each insured employee. The premium may be paid by the employer or jointly by employer and employee. This type of insurance may be issued only to firms with more than 10 employees; and when the workers contribute, it is frequently required that least 75 percent of the employees to whom the insurance is offered be insured.

The amount of insurance for each employee may be fixed by any one of several different plans. The group insurance plan may provide for a flat amount of insurance for all employees; for varying amounts for different classes of employees, determined by wage or occupation; or for increasing amounts, based upon length of service. All employees actually at work are insured, regardless of age or physical condition, no medical examination being required except when employees do not elect to come under the plan within a certain time period. When an employee's insurance is canceled by termination of employment, he has a period of thirty-one days during which he may apply for a regular life insurance policy in the same company without medical examination. Under paid-up group plans the insurance is not canceled by retirement or termination of employment, but continues for a reduced amount depending upon such factors as age, length of service, and salary bracket.

Similar group insurance may be issued covering disability caused by sickness or accident, and we often find that firms are supplementing their group life insurance with group disability insurance.[17]

CREDIT INSURANCE

With the tremendous increase in consumer credit outstanding in recent years,[18] more and more retailers are giving consideration to credit insurance. At a nominal charge, they sell the credit customer a policy which, upon his death, pays the outstanding balance of his account. This policy eliminates the debt burden from falling upon the debtor's family and guarantees the store prompt payment.[19]

UNEMPLOYMENT INSURANCE[20]

In contrast to most of the kinds of insurance discussed above, which are optional with the retailer, so-called "unemployment insurance" is obligatory for many retailers. The Social Security Act, passed in August, 1935, provided, among other things, for what amounts to a national system of unemployment insurance.[21] Under the Act, as amended, retailers and many other businessmen employing four or more persons[22] are required by law to turn

---

[17] In 1965 the Social Security Act was amended to liberalize the definition of disability by deleting the requirement that it be of "long-continued and indefinite duration." The law now reads that disability is "the inability to engage in any substantial gainful activity by reason of any medically determinable physical or mental impairment which can be expected to last for a continued period of not less than six months." Cf. J. F. Follmann, "Medicare and Disability Income Insurance," *Best's Insurance News*, January, 1966, p. 40.

[18] Cf. pp. 13–14, above.

[19] A credit problem of some concern to many retailers relates to the possible loss or destruction of their records of customers' indebtedness. Because these records constitute an asset of considerable value to many retailers, their protection through accounts receivable insurance is highly desirable.

[20] Many retailers think of unemployment insurance as a tax rather than an insurance item.

[21] For a historical review and analysis of unemployment insurance cf. William Haber and M. G. Murray, *Unemployment Insurance in the American Economy* (Homewood, Ill.: Richard D. Irwin, Inc., 1966).

[22] In June, 1966, the House of Representatives passed a bill (H.R. 15119) to become effective January, 1969, expanding coverage to those employed by firms having one or more workers, including outside salesmen and agent-drivers not considered workers under common law rules. It increased, also, the existing federal tax paid by employers effective January 1, 1967 and the yearly workers' taxable wage base, on which the tax is figured, from $3,000 to $3,900 on January 1, 1969 and to $4,200 on January 1, 1972. Although prospects for passage of this bill by the Senate appeared very good, the 89th Congress, 2d Session, adjourned without enacting such legislation. On the background events of this bill cf. "The Looming Fight Over Jobless Pay," *Business Week*, April 30, 1966, pp. 76, 78.

over to the federal government a payroll tax equal to about 3 percent of total payrolls. To encourage states to take over the function of providing the machinery for unemployment insurance, however, the law provides that states establishing an approved system of unemployment insurance may collect up to 90 percent of the tax, which would otherwise go to the federal government and be of no direct benefit to the inhabitants of the state. At present, all states have approved plans; some of these include provisions under which the actual cost to the employer may be reduced by "experience rating," i.e., the store's success in minimizing unemployment among its regular employees.

Although there is much variation in detail among the laws of the various states, most of the laws provide for a waiting period before unemployment insurance payments begin, after which the unemployed person is paid a weekly benefit. The maximum benefits, exclusive of dependents' allowance, vary from state to state, from a low of $30 in Iowa and Mississippi, to a high of $55 in California. Most benefits, however, fall in the $40 to $50 range. The period during which the benefit is paid varies from 22 weeks in South Carolina to 39 weeks in California, Connecticut, Illinois and Hawaii.[23] In 40 states the maximum period for payment of benefits is 26 weeks but in 9 states additional weeks of benefits may be paid when special unemployment conditions exist as specified by law. Recent years have witnessed an increasing liberalization of unemployment insurance, particularly with respect to a shortening of the waiting period before payments begin, an increase in the amounts paid, and a lengthening of the period during which payments are made.

BUYING INSURANCE

Essential Kinds of Insurance

There are two basic types of insurance which practically all retailers will agree are essential, as follows:

1. Fire—covering buildings, fixtures and equipment, and merchandise
2. Liability—including general public, automobile, elevator (if there is one in use), and workmen's compensation

In addition, all retailers with eight or more employees are required by law to contribute to unemployment insurance. But, as already mentioned, beyond these basic policies retailers disagree as to what kinds of insurance are essen-

---

[23] *Unemployment Insurance: State Laws and Experience* (Rev. ed.; Washington, D.C.: U.S. Department of Labor, Manpower Administration, 1965), charts 5 and 8.

tial. Actually, whether a certain kind of insurance is or is not essential for a particular retailer frequently depends upon such factors as the retailer's financial position, his size, the field of operation, and the type of operation (for example, chain or independent).

Need for Careful Buying. It should be emphasized that the mere purchase of an insurance policy does not necessarily mean that the retailer is properly insured. To buy insurance that is not required or that does not adequately fit the needs may be just as wasteful and unwise as if no insurance were carried. A careful analysis of the protection required and the hazards existing or possible, together with a broad survey of the insurance contracts available, is necessary before the retailer can feel that his insurance problems have been well handled. Moreover, rapid changes in modern economic life make it imperative that the retailer's insurance program be subjected to frequent and careful review. The new retailer will soon discover what the experienced retailer already knows: that to determine the insurable value of a property and to keep it up to date requires a considerable amount of work.

Because of the technical nature of insurance, the small retailer must rely largely upon the services of insurance agents and brokers. Since these agents and brokers vary widely in ability, the merchant needs to use considerable care in selecting one to aid him. On occasion, even the large retail organization, which may have an executive who spends considerable time working upon the firm's insurance needs, will find valuable the services of the agent or the broker.

Reducing Insurance Cost through Deductibles. One way to reduce the cost of an insurance policy is for the retailer to assume part of the risk, that is, to engage in a degree of self-insurance.[24] Based on his past experience and the advice of a broker or insurance agent, he decides how much risk he is willing to assume on merchandise, fixtures and equipment, and crime losses, and then purchases insurance to cover losses in excess of the deductible amounts. To illustrate, a few years ago one of the leading women's ready-to-wear chains decided that its annual fire insurance premium of $50,000 a year was larger than necessary. After study, a decision was reached that the corporation could afford to self-insure up to $15,000 per store; so it sought an insurance company which would write a policy with a $15,000 deductible clause. At that time no United States company would write the policy, but Lloyd's of London did. Incidentally, the corporation estimated its total savings in a few years at from $175,000 to $200,000.

Where self-insurance through deductibles is used, the retailer's accounting records should reflect this fact. Specifically, the retailer should gradually

---

[24] Cf. O. E. Futter, "Three Ways to Save Money on Insurance," *Super Market Merchandising,* January, 1965, pp. 40–42.

build up a reserve for "Uninsured Risk" by expensing part of the additional premium he would otherwise be paying an insurance company. Such a reserve is available for unusually large self-insurance losses suffered in any one year.

From Whom to Buy Insurance

Kinds of Insurance Organizations. Typically the retailer will purchase his insurance from a stock or mutual company; but in a few instances he may join a reciprocal exchange.

1. *Stock Insurance Companies.* These corporations are in business to make a profit for their stockholders by assuming risks for a compensation, called a "premium." They charge a definite amount for insurance; and if losses exceed the premium income, the stock companies bear the loss alone without any further payment by the retailer. These companies, like all other kinds of insurance organizations, are examined by the insurance departments of the various states and regulated by statute. They handle by far the largest share of the insurance business, doing about 85 percent of all the fire insurance business of the country and the larger part of the casualty insurance business.

2. *Mutual Organizations.* Such organizations seek to provide insurance on a nonprofit basis. They require the payment of a cash premium—usually at the full stock-company rate—with an agreement among the insurers that, should losses and expenses exceed the premium income, the deficit is to be paid out of reserves. If the reserves are exhausted, payments are made prorata. In practice, well-organized mutuals find that the regular premium income more than meets their needs, and the excess is returned to the policyholders as dividends or set aside as a reserve.

3. *Reciprocal Exchanges.* Used by a few retailers, especially department stores, the reciprocal exchanges are not corporations but private, voluntary associations of businessmen, each member agreeing to insure every other member. A retailer in a reciprocal exchange actually goes into the insurance business, although the affairs of the exchange are operated by an attorney-in-fact, who is given very wide powers. The exchange differs from the mutual in that it is not incorporated and in that all funds placed by a member in the association remain his property unless it is necessary to use them to meet losses or expenses. If he retires from the exchange, all funds which he has deposited and which have not been paid out are returned to him. The exchange gives him insurance on a cost basis, which, in the case of sound reciprocal exchanges, frequently results in a considerable saving for the retailer.

Selecting the Insurance Carrier. Since the reason for buying insurance is to minimize or eliminate risk, the organization providing the insurance should be so strong and reliable that indemnity for loss will be certain. An apparent saving in insurance premiums may prove to be a poor investment if there is any question as to such indemnity. The carrier should be selected only after a careful investigation of the financial positions and past records of a number of carriers.

HANDLING INSURANCE CLAIMS

When a loss does occur, it immediately becomes necessary for the policyholder to take certain steps in conformity with the provisions of the contract. The policy will ordinarily require that immediate notice of loss be given to the insurance company; and in the case of policies covering crime hazards, notice to the police may also be required. But the requirements usually do not end there. The standard fire policy, for instance, provides that:

The insured shall give immediate notice, in writing, to this Company, of any loss or damage, protect the property from further damage, forthwith separate the damaged and undamaged personal property, put it in the best possible order, furnish a complete inventory of the destroyed, damaged and undamaged property, stating the quantity and cost of each article and the amount claimed thereon, and the insured shall, within sixty days after the fire, unless such time is extended by this Company, render to this Company a proof of loss . . . [such proof of loss to give certain definite detailed information regarding the loss and the property involved].

The insured is also required to exhibit the remains of any property involved, submit to examination under oath, and produce for examination books of account and other papers.

It is evident that the insured has certain definite obligations which come into being with the occurrence of the loss. The settlement of claims, therefore, will be greatly facilitated if the insured is prepared to act as required by the contract and if he has maintained adequate, up-to-date records to comply with the requirements.

REVIEW AND DISCUSSION QUESTIONS

1. Differentiate, using illustrations, among the three main methods of dealing with the risks of retailing.
2. Name five major risks in retailing and explain briefly the method or methods for dealing with each.
3. How do you explain the wide variations in the ways with which different retailers deal with the risks of retailing?

4. Assume that you have been asked to explain the benefits of carrying adequate insurance to a small retailer. What points would you mention to emphasize the importance of such coverage?

5. One supplementary reading listed at the close of the chapter is Bert Berger, "Guidelines for An Effective Chain Insurance Program." Prepare some guidelines of your own before reading that discussion and then compare your list with the seven principles given by Mr. Berger. What major principles did you omit?

6. Describe how you would deal with each of the risks listed below if you were (a) a small grocer retailer, (b) the general manager of a large free-standing discount store, (c) the general manager of a mail-order company operating out of one establishment, and (d) the general manager of a large variety chain:

   (1) Fire   (5) Products liability
   (2) Smoke damage   (6) Open-stock burglary
   (3) Business interruption   (7) Employee dishonesty
   (4) Liability to public   (8) Possible death of
           because of automobile   major executive

7. If you were the chief executive, what types of property insurance would you deem it advisable to carry in each of these cases: (a) the operator of a small shop selling women's dresses, (b) a small drugstore operator, (c) a national food chain, and (d) a moderate-sized department store? Give your reasons.

8. Among the various types of potential losses incurred by the retailer, in what area (fire, public liability, etc.) do the greatest losses occur? How do you explain this situation?

9. In your judgment, what factors are responsible for the change in provisions of the fire insurance policy under which the policyholder now is indemnified in case of loss for the *replacement value* of the property rather than for its *actual cost* after *proper deductions* for depreciation?

10. What is meant by coinsurance? Explain the insurance company's liability in this situation: The value of the property, completely destroyed by fire, was $100,000; the coinsurance clause called for 80 percent insurance; insurance carried was $50,000; the loss from the fire was $10,000.

11. Discuss the merits and limitations of an "all-risk" policy for retail stores. Include consideration of the advisability of monthly payments of premiums if such a policy were to be adopted.

12. Assume that you are the proprietor of a supermarket and are considering taking out a business interruption policy. How would you proceed in arriving at a decision?

13. How do you account for the fact that the products liability rule continues to be broadened? As a food retailer would you carry products liability insurance? Why or why not?

14. Argue the case for and against this subject: "Unemployment Compensation Benefits Have Been So Liberalized That They Unduly Penalize the Employer."

15. Explain briefly how a retailer should appraise an organization from which he should purchase his insurance.

SUPPLEMENTARY READINGS

BERGER, BERT. "Guidelines for an Effective Chain Insurance Program," *Chain Store Age* (Executives Edition), January, 1966, pp. 18–20. Seven basic principles of a sound program, with emphasis on casualty and liability coverage, comprise the treatment in this article.

DENENBERG, H. S., *et al. Risk and Insurance* (Englewood Cliffs, N.J.: Prentice-Hall, Inc., 1964). The nature of risks and their treatment are emphasized in this introductory textbook.

EILERS, R. D., AND CROWE, R. M. *Group Insurance Handbook* (Homewood, Ill.: Richard D. Irwin, Inc., 1965). This volume is a valuable primary source of information on all phases of group insurance.

"Georgia Field Men Study Bowling Alley, Supermarket Hazards," *National Underwriter,* May 6, 1966, pp. 1, 42. About one half of this article covers such hazards as fire, defective wiring, heating, and equipment in supermarkets.

GREENE, M. C. *Insurance and Risk Management for Small Business* (Washington, D.C.: Small Business Administration, 1963). Emphasizing that losses could mean the difference between growth and failure, the author discusses the importance of insurance to the small firm. Also cf. from the same source WATSON, D. A., and HOMAN, A. G. *Insurance Management in Small Firms* (1962).

GREGG, D. W. (ed.). *Life and Health Insurance Handbook.* (2d ed.; Homewood, Ill.: Richard D. Irwin, Inc., 1964). Many of the topics covered in this comprehensive volume apply to retailing.

JACKSON, P. H. *Developments in Group Insurance* (Bryn Mawr, Pa.: *Journal of the American Society of Life Underwriters,* 1965). This 35-page reprint reviews the new developments in group coverages and is of particular interest to retailers.

KOVAC, JOHN. "How to Lower Your Insurance Costs," *Progressive Grocer,* March, 1966, pp. 119–29. A study of 5,000 food stores by a leading supermarket insurer, the author pin-points ways to spot accident-prone areas and to reduce accidents through analysis of their causes.

LONG, J. D., AND GREGG, D. W. (eds.). *Property and Liability Insurance Handbook* (Homewood, Ill.: Richard D. Irwin, Inc., 1965). This valuable reference for the retailer covers all aspects of property and liability insurance.

MEHR, R. I., AND CAMMACK, EMERSON. *Principles of Insurance* (4th ed.; Homewood, Ill.: Richard D. Irwin, Inc., 1966). In this widely used textbook all aspects of the field are considered.

MEHR, R. I., AND HEDGES, B. A. *Risk Management in the Business Enterprise* (Homewood, Ill.: Richard D. Irwin, Inc., 1963). The authors review the risks of business in this volume and suggest ways of handling them.

NATIONAL RETAIL MERCHANTS ASSOCIATION, CONTROLLERS' CONGRESS. *Insurance Savings Through Loss Prevention* (New York: The Association, n.d.). Designed to suggest savings in premium costs, this book is a comprehensive guide to the prevention of property loss and to liability claims.

SOUTHWICK, A. F., JR. "Mass Marketing and Warranty Liability," *Journal of Marketing,* Vol. XXVII, No. 2 (April, 1963), pp. 6–12. The tendency for courts to assign increased responsibility to sellers in damage cases is emphasized by the author. Also cf. his "Products Liability: A Broadening Concept," *Management Review,* March, 1966, pp. 21–25.

WALKER, P. "A Casualty Insurance Survey for the Smaller Client," *Journal of Accountancy,* Vol. CXX, No. 1 (July, 1965), pp. 30–33. The author suggests methods by which the CPA can help the small businessman secure needed insurance protection.

WILLIAMS, C. A., JR., AND HEINS, R. M. *Risk Management and Insurance* (New York: McGraw-Hill Book Co., Inc., 1964). Various phases of business risks and how to handle them are covered in this general textbook.

28
CHAPTER

Coordination and Retailing Management

COORDINATION ESSENTIAL TO PROFITABLE OPERATIONS

It cannot be overemphasized that management's prime responsibility is to operate profitably. It is the retailer who operates at a profit who can provide jobs at competitive wages and on a continuing basis. He is the one who can afford to engage in research activities designed to develop more effective ways of performing the retail functions. Without a profitable business he cannot support community projects, nor adapt his policies and practices to a changing environment. Thus, everything he does to insure a profitable operation is important to him and to the community or communities in which he does business.

Coordination of all store activities is one essential step to profitable operation. Every retail firm needs some individual, or a very small group of individuals, to keep the various departments or divisions functioning as well-integrated units. Someone must be in a position from which he can look out over the whole organization and come to a conclusion as to whether it is (1) well adjusted to present conditions, and (2) flexible enough to meet conditions which may exist in the future.[1] The purposes of this chapter are to discuss the factors involved in this process of coordination, explain some of the methods employed in adjusting to current and future conditions, and indicate some of the problems that arise in connection therewith.

---

[1] Cf., for example, C. G. Adamy, "Evolutionary Changes Produce Revolutions in Food Chain Retailing," *Progressive Grocer,* April, 1966, pp. 324–26. The president of the National Association of Food Chains stresses "the need for the development and use of more sophisticated management techniques."

Adjustment to Present Conditions

To discover the adjustments called for by current conditions the retailer should possess an inquiring, critical mind and consult associates continuously to find answers to such questions as the following: Are we spending enough for advertising to hold our place in the community or communities in which we operate? Would it be better, considering the competition of a nearby discount house, to "trade up" in services and merchandise or to reduce prices? Do we have enough salespeople on the floor to give the degree of service expected by our clientele? Is it desirable to appoint a fashion coordinator for wearing apparel and one for home furnishings to insure greater uniformity of quality and prices in the offerings of the various selling departments? Are there new techniques and equipment which might help us improve our customer service and increase annual sales? What innovations have been adopted recently by our chief competitors? Are we conducting sufficient research to provide information upon which to base management decisions?

Adjustment to Changing Conditions

The coordinator must also be responsible for the adjustment of his organization to changing conditions—and this task is great because the rate of change today is constantly accelerating. In fact, possibly no period of comparable length in the history of retailing has called for as many adjustments as have the years since 1950. As suggested in the first chapter of this book, the outpouring of consumer's goods, the rise in population and in consumer purchasing power, shifts in consumption patterns, and the suburban movement have caused progressive retailers to make many adjustments in location, size of store, hours of operation, merchandise lines, services rendered, promotional methods, and equipment used, to mention but a few. There is no reason to expect that the decade ahead will call for fewer adjustments than have the past fifteen years, so tomorrow's retailer should be prepared for further changes. To quote one close observer of the retail scene: "The future has had a way recently of sweeping down upon us and becoming part of today—or tomorrow, at the latest. It is not enough to discern the dimension of change the future will bring, we must also be able to appreciate when that future, as fashioned by change, will arrive."[2]

---

[2] Robert Beyer, "Top Management in the 1970's and Beyond," *Retail Control*, March, 1966, p. 56. Also cf. *A View to 1970* (Chicago: Super Market Institute, 1965), and J. B. Werner, "What's Ahead in Management?" *Dun's Review and Modern Industry*, January, 1965, pp. 32–33 ff.

In brief, only by a continuous adaptation to changing conditions can retail organizations render satisfactory customer service and achieve maximum profits. Indeed, unless the retailer looks ahead, notes the trends, plans *his* adjustments carefully, utilizes the newer management tools available to him, and coordinates his entire organization to effect the necessary adjustments, he may find that *he* is no longer in business. Retailing history is filled with examples of retailers, both large and small, who have failed at this task.

RESPONSIBILITY FOR COORDINATION

Since the function of coordination, or the harmonious adjustment of parts, is necessary and, in view of constantly changing conditions, is a continual process, we should next ask: Who in the retail organization should be responsible for this function? The answer is clear, and it is one concerning which there is little dispute among students of retailing: Coordination is a function of the general manager of the organization or of a small executive committee of two or three men. In practice, one-man responsibility for coordination seems desirable; and in the majority of retail organizations the general manager bears such responsibility.

In the large retail organization the general manager finds that day-to-day contact even with the more important activities of the business is impractical; consequently, he must rely upon numerous individuals to whom authority and responsibility are delegated. The personnel manager, for example, must coordinate all activities relating to the employment, training, compensation, and welfare of employees. The merchandise manager, likewise, must assume responsibility for the maintenance of well-balanced stocks of goods in all selling departments. These individuals and others should report to the general manager either orally or in writing as frequently as warranted by the importance of the particular function or combination of tasks over which they exercise control. After all the facts are in, however, it makes for speed of action and centralizes responsibility if one man "has the final word."

Executive Leadership in Coordination

In the retail organization, where the human element is so important, it is difficult to overstate the need of executive leadership in achieving coordination.[3] Unless the personnel of the store is convinced of the ability of its leader or leaders and unless the leader becomes the driving force of the whole organization, success will be limited at best. It is not an overstatement

---

[3] Cf. "The Retail Executive's Personal Qualities," pp. 35–42, above.

that the quality of a store's leadership determines what the store is or is not. The type of executive who issues orders without explanation, commanding execution from a "scared-to-death" staff, and who strong-arms his way to results without consideration of his employees is being less frequently placed in positions of ultimate responsibility. At the same time, the achievement of effective coordination requires a "driving" type of person who understands the determinants of job satisfaction.[4]

Major Tools of Coordination

The job of coordination in retail stores is a difficult one. Consideration and understanding of the problems associated with human relationships and a willingness to assume authority and meet issues as they arise are essential to success in this area. Likewise, the retailer needs an objective and inquiring mind.

Some retailers, in facing the problems of coordination, rely heavily on what they term their "instinct." Said a chain-store executive to one of the authors: "I believe I run my business by the feel. I instinctively know when a thing is wrong and realize its value when it is good, but to sit down and enumerate these things is rather difficult to do." By no means are all those who follow this procedure failures in business; in fact, the executive just quoted built a food chain which was a financial success. Based on many years of daily contact with his growing organization, he could sense trends and make adjustments without being conscious of the thought processes through which he went.

Typically, however, the retailer needs more than "instinct" and, fortunately, there are a number of aids or tools available to him in carrying out the coordination function.[5] Four of these tools are especially important— internal standards, comparisons of operating and merchandising results with those of other retailers, the budget, and research.

INTERNAL STANDARDS

Standards may be defined as "criteria of satisfactory performance under existing conditions and circumstances. They are not to represent an ideal which can seldom be attained nor should they be considered as marks to shoot at; but, rather, as fair measures of immediate attainable perfor-

---

[4] Cf. V. H. Vroom, *Work and Motivation* (New York: John Wiley & Sons, Inc., 1964), pp. 99–174.

[5] Cf. "Retailing: Yardsticks of Performance," *Forbes,* January 1, 1966, pp. 111–13.

mance . . ."[6] Viewed in this light, a standard is an important tool of co-ordination. It should be stressed, however, that setting standards or goals is not enough. Some form of "control" is needed by which management can discover promptly the quality of performance in terms of these standards.

Types of Internal Standards

Three types of internal standards are commonly used in retail stores: physical standards, operating and merchandising cost-ratio standards, and unit-cost standards. Each type has its place in coordinating *every* retail organization, although the degree to which each will be used varies from one firm to another.

Physical Standards. Physical standards are those that serve as yard-sticks for quantity factors. The stock turnover ratio is a good example. A certain retail jewelry store operator may conclude that he operates satisfacto-rily if his average stock on hand does not exceed annual sales; a gift shop operator may find that his average stock should be about one third of sales; and for a gasoline service station operator the corresponding figure may be one twentieth of sales. These stock turnover figures of 1, 3, and 20 are physical standards, relating one physical factor (average stock on hand) to another (goods sold in the course of a year).

Some organizations devise standards for the division of their business among various departments. Such standards, although they involve physical elements, are usually expressed in terms of sales. Thus, a food chain may decide that 55 percent of its business should be in dry groceries and dairy products; 12 percent in fruits and vegetables; 28 percent in meats, and 5 percent in nonfood items. Or a small department store may find that its main floor should account for 60 percent of its business, with the basement and second floor accounting for 20 percent each. Whenever the main floor's percentage of sales falls below this figure of 60 percent, the management is given warning that some department or several departments on that floor are not operating as they should.

Many other physical standards are in everyday use. Some large depart-ment stores have standards covering the number of packages a wrapper should handle per hour or per day, the number of prospective employees interviewed per hour by interviewers in the personnel department, the number of sales per day per salesperson (these figures varying from depart-ment to department), and the number of letters types per hour or per day by stenographers in the mail-order department. Department stores and variety

---

[6] J. B. Heckert and R. B. Miner, *Distribution Costs* (2d. ed.; New York: Ronald Press Co., 1953), p. 209.

organizations sometimes set standards as to the number of people entering a store in relationship to those who pass by and the percentage of those who make purchases after having entered the store.

Operating and Merchandising Cost-Ratio Standards.   Operating and merchandising cost ratios are in wider use than either of the other kinds of standards. These standards merely relate particular costs of retailing— rent, wages, advertising, taxes, and insurance—and the merchandising re- sults achieved in a given period to total retail sales. For example, in chain- store operations a standard relating rent to expected sales is of the utmost importance in locating a new store. Knowing that in towns comparable in size to the one under consideration rent does not exceed 5 (or 2, or 4, depending upon the kind of business) percent of sales, estimates of sales for each of several possible locations can be made and the corresponding rents asked can be expressed as a percentage of the estimated dollar sales. If it does not seem possible in any of the locations to achieve a ratio as low as 5 percent, there must be some compensating advantage in having a location in this town, or a lease will not be considered. One food chain has classified all towns in its operating area according to population, using 500 people intervals, and set up rent standards for each population class. These stand- ards are religiously applied in deciding where to establish new stores; the end result is that the firm has experienced exceptionally good results in its store expansion campaign.

As another example of the use of operating cost-ratio standards, it is common practice for retail stores to compare their results with those of "typical" stores operating under comparable conditions. These typical figures are available from a variety of retail trade associations and from such publications as the *Progressive Grocer* and the *Hardware Retailer.*

Unit-Cost Standards.   Some operators make considerable use of unit- cost standards, that is, standards which set forth the cost of performing a specific act. In fact, production unit accounting—referred to in Chapter 25—is designed to provide this type of information. Frequently the standard for wrapping is of this variety, the department store calculating that its cost of gift wrapping during the Christmas season should be $0.25 per package. It may also calculate that its wage cost per average sale should be $0.40; its delivery cost per package, $1.00; and its cost per prospective employee interviewed, $4.00.

Using Internal Standards

Establishing Standards.   Most retail organizations use standards based on their past experience. The variety chain which adopted a standard of 5 percent of sales for rent did so because its past operations had proved profitable when this 5 percent figure was obtained. This procedure was also used by the firm in deciding that its wage cost for salespeople should not exceed 12 percent of sales: a study of company records revealed that a 12 percent figure was both obtainable and profitable.

Unfortunately, many retailers establish standards merely on the information which they carry in their heads. If a standard is to serve its real purposes, however, considerable care must be exercised in adopting it. To illustrate: two authorities have suggested five steps in setting effective cost standards, as follows:

1. Classify the costs according to functions and activities expressive of individual responsibility.
2. Select units or bases of measurement through which the standards can be expressed.
3. Analyze past experience relative to the cost of the functions and specific activities involved with a view to selecting the best experience and indications as to the best procedure.
4. Consider the effect on costs of expected changes in internal conditions and of the sales program as planned.
5. Summarize the judgment of those . . . whose experience and training qualify them to judge the measures of satisfactory performance.[7]

Standards Not Applicable In All Areas. It is not possible, of course, to set up objective standards for all areas in which the retailer is interested. For such matters as the courtesy with which his salespeople treat customers, the quality of wrapping done by the personnel performing this task, and the honesty of his employees, the retailer has to rely on such devices as his own observation, complaints of customers, and reports of hired shoppers. Yet standards can be devised for so many important matters that they become an essential device in the successful coordination of retail activities.

Written Standards Advisable. Too many merchants (especially small retailers), even after they have decided on satisfactory standards, do not put them in writing. As a result, these standards are thought about only in odd moments and no comparisons of actual results are made against them. Without a close examination on paper, the retailer may minimize the effects on profitable operation if his wage ratio exceeds his standard. In other words, if standards are to fulfill the purposes for which they are intended, they should be in written form, compared with actual results, and prompt action initiated when significant differences are revealed.

---

[7] *Ibid.,* pp. 210–12.

COMPARISON OF RESULTS WITH THOSE OF OTHER RETAILERS

The second major tool of coordination for the retailer is the comparison of his operating and merchandising results with those of comparable retailers. Perhaps he is trying to run his store with poorly-trained employees, a fact that would be reflected in comparatively low sales per salesperson, a high returned goods ratio, and a low ratio of actual buyers to the number of people entering the store. Perhaps he is not advertising enough; this situation might be reflected in a low advertising ratio and stationary or declining sales as compared with other retailers. Without some direct comparisons, unfavorable trends may exist for a considerable period before they are recognized by management and measures adopted to correct them.

Among hardware retailers, for example, the average net profit before taxes in 1965 was but 2.20 percent of sales; yet one third of those reporting had earnings of 6.75 percent.[8] If the hardware retailer compares his own experience with that of stores in the "most profitable one third" and in the "remaining two thirds" (Table 28–1) he will obtain valuable information concerning points of strength and weakness in his operations.

Some Sources of Comparative Data

Data for comparative purposes are made available to the retailer by a number of sources, only a few of which can be mentioned here. The United States Department of Commerce releases data on such matters as credit collections and monthly sales for several types of stores. Dun & Bradstreet, Inc., issues several detailed comparisons of operating cost ratios for retailers in all common fields of operation.[9] The National Cash Register Company has published several compilations of expenses and other operating results based on various sources.[10] The annual *Fairchild's Financial Manual of Retail Stores* reports, among other things, capital, surplus, assets, liabilities, and ten-year comparisons of sales and profits for over 200 publicly owned retail organizations.[11] Even more detailed data on a limited number of fields will be found in the reports released by the bureaus of business research of such institutions as the University of Michigan and Cornell University. The Cornell data, for example, covers the operating and merchandising aspects

---

[8] *Management Report—A Report of Retail Hardware Store Experience—1965* (Indianapolis: National Retail Hardware Association, 1966), pp. 2, 8.

[9] Cf., for example, "The Ratios of Retailing" *Dun's Review and Modern Industry,* September, 1966, pp. 52–53.

[10] Cf. *Expenses in Retail Businesses* (Dayton, Ohio: National Cash Register Co., n.d.).

[11] Fairchild Publications, Inc., 7 E. 12th St., New York, 10003.

TABLE 28–1

OPERATING AND MERCHANDISING RESULTS OF MOST PROFITABLE AND
OTHER RETAIL HARDWARE STORES IN 1965

Description	Most Profitable One Third	Remaining Two Thirds
Stores	293	586
Stores offering installment sales	36%	39%
Current year's sales vs. previous year	106.18	103.57
Average sale per customer	$ 2.93	$ 3.11
Average sales per Store	100.00%	100.00%
Cost of goods sold	67.55	68.95
Margin	32.45	31.05
Paid out in Salaries		
To owners and managers	7.00%	7.70%
To salespeople, office and other	8.70	10.85
Total paid out in Salaries	15.70	18.55
Other Costs of Doing Business		
Office supplies and postage	0.35%	0.45%
Advertising	1.50	1.70
Donations	0.05	0.05
Telephone and telegraph	0.30	0.40
Losses on notes and accounts	0.20	0.15
Delivery expense (other than wages)	0.50	0.65
Depreciation:		
Delivery equipment	0.25	0.30
Furniture, fixtures and tools	0.40	0.45
Rent	2.55	3.05
Repairs to building	0.05	0.05
Heat, light, water, power	0.90	0.95
Insurance*	0.80	0.95
Taxes* (excluding federal income tax)	1.10	1.35
Interest on borrowed money*	0.05	0.30
Unclassified, including store supplies	1.00	1.30
Total Expense (not including interest on investment)	25.70	30.65
Net Profit	+ 6.75%	+ .40%
Cash Discount and Other Earnings	1.35	1.35
Total Earnings (before Federal Income Tax)	+ 8.10	+ 1.75
Profit on Investment (Not Including R. E.)	+16.95	+ 4.50
Active Owner's Return on Investment (not including R. E.)	+31.55	+24.30
Salary per year per owner or manager	$ 5,595	$ 6,575
Salary per year per salesperson	3,765	4,095
Salary per year per office employee	3,125	3,160
Salary per year per other employee	3,225	3,410
Salary per year per employee (not owners or managers)	3,660	3,870
Sales per year per person employed	30,040	26,420
Merchandise inventory per $10,000 of sales	3,010	3,080
Average stock turn times	2.20	2.30
Credit sales	40%	45%
Average accounts receivable collection	73.9 days	70.0 days
Average capital turn times	2.15	2.70
Current asset ratio	11.34	5.78
Total debt to tangible net worth	12.45%	27.61%
Quick Asset Ratio	4.65	1.89
Turns of Working Capital	2.31	2.70

* Not including amounts paid in connection with real estate ownership

SOURCE: *Management Report—a Report of Retail Hardware Experience—1965* (Indianapolis: National Retail Hardware Association, 1966), p. 9.

of food chains. The Controllers' Congress of the National Retail Merchants Association prepares annual reports on merchandising and operating results of department and specialty stores, classified according to annual sales and by departments within stores. From time to time, the *Journal of Retailing* publishes compilations of operating ratios, retail sales, and profits.[12] For certain purposes—such as determining whether a store is holding its percentage of business in a community—the releases of the Bureau of the Census are of interest. In addition to the National Retail Merchants Association, already mentioned, valuable data are also released by such trade associations as the National Retail Furniture Association, the National Retail Hardware Association, and the National Association of Retail Druggists. *Discount Store News, Chain Store Age, Women's Wear Daily,* and other trade papers are still other sources of information.[13]

In some cases, especially in ownership and chain groups of department stores, it is possible for a retailer to work out a system whereby operating results of various stores are exchanged directly among the operators involved. Thus the representatives of the various stores in groups such as Federated Department Stores and Associated Merchandising Corporation, organizations such as Allied Stores Corporation and Gimbel's, and buying offices such as Frederick Atkins, Inc., have periodic meetings at which cost and other comparisons are made. This exchange of information is of special value to the retailer because he may be sure that he is comparing his results with those of quite similar retailers.

BUDGET

The budget provides a third major tool used by the retailer to achieve an effective degree of coordination of activities.[14] As previously indicated, the steps involved in setting up the budget force the various executives of the store to plan and to coordinate their activities, even before effort is expended in the actual buying and selling of merchandise.[15] Each official in the organization is given a goal in very specific terms—some in terms of goods to be handled, others in terms of sales to be achieved, and still others in

---

[12] Cf. Herman Radolf, "Retail Operating Ratios," *Journal of Retailing,* XLI, No. 4 (Winter, 1965–66), pp. 50–51 ff; and R. J. Robichaud, "Retail Profit Rise—What Does It Mean?" *ibid.,* Vol. XLII, No. 3 (Fall, 1966), pp. 52–67.

[13] To illustrate the point: *Discount Store News* publishes annually, usually in August, a broad study of the discount industry; in June (in 1966, it was the June 1 issue) *Women's Wear Daily* tabulates sales, net profits, and net worth for nearly 100 retail organizations.

[14] Cf. E. I. Hanson, "The Budgetary Control Function," *Accounting Review,* April, 1966, pp. 239–43.

[15] Cf. pp. 704–5, above.

terms of advertisements to be written and placed—and a definite amount of money is allocated for the attainment of these goals. Day by day, week by week, and month by month, reports on actual operations should be checked against the planned goals.[16] This checking demands a constant stream of reports covering all aspects of the organization's operations: monthly profit and loss statements; daily, weekly, and monthly sales; gross margin data; expense figures; reports on purchases, stocks on hand, and goods in transit; original markups and markdowns by various departments; turnover data; and the like. Deviations from the main goals at which the firm is aiming are recognized by the general manager, and explanations are sought for such deviations with a minimum of delay. Only through prompt action on his part can the full benefits of the checking process be realized.

Because of detailed discussions of the budget in previous chapters,[17] it is unnecessary to devote more attention to it here. Its importance as a coordinating device, however, cannot be overemphasized and it is advisable for the reader to restudy these sections from this point of view.

RETAIL RESEARCH

Retail research may be defined as the organized search for, and the analysis of, facts related to problems in the field of retailing. It includes, also, recommendations by the researcher designed to solve the problem being investigated and the essential follow-up to determine the results of their adoption.

Research is the fourth important tool used to an increasing extent by the retailer to coordinate his activities. Yet its actual use at the present time can easily be exaggerated. In fact, it is the authors' opinion that all too many retailers are failing to make sufficient use of this valuable instrument; an opinion shared with one retailer who believes that research in retailing "is still in a very primitive stage . . . retailing compared to industry, gives research a second-class status."[18] This situation is especially acute in the small and medium-sized independent store. One might go so far as to say that one

---

[16] "In the modern, progressive business of today, the budget provides the target—and yardstick—for business to measure the efficiency of . . . operations against desired results. Budgeting has been described as precise planning—committing a plan of operations to quantitative terms." L. P. Neely, "Trends in Budgeting and Budgeting Techniques," *Budgeting,* March, 1965, p. 1. Also cf. R. L. Jones and H. G. Trentin, *Budgeting: Key to Planning and Control—Practical Guidelines for Managers* (New York: American Management Association, 1966).

[17] Chapter 14, "Merchandise Management through the Budget," and Chapter 25, "Expense Control."

[18] H. S. Landsman, Federated Department Stores, quoted in Samuel Feinberg, "From Where I Sit," *Women's Wear Daily,* February 9, 1966, p. 12.

of the dominant reasons for the slow progress of many small stores lies in the fact that their proprietors lack the time (or, at least, refuse to take the time) and ability to undertake research.[19] Clearly, it is an important advantage—and, as already suggested, one by no means yet used to its full possibilities—of the large retail organization that it can employ qualified personnel to carry on necessary research activities.[20]

Main Steps in Retail Research

Assuming that the problem upon which information is desired has already been recognized and defined, there are four steps involved in retail research. These steps may be stated briefly as follows:

1. Gathering and summarizing the data
2. Analyzing and interpreting the data
3. Preparing a report containing recommendations for improvement
4. Following up to see that the adopted suggestions are actually put into effect and noting the results of their adoption.

Some large retailers perform all four of these steps in a research department or research bureau; in other stores, only the first two or three steps are handled there, with the general manager taking care of the fourth step. Among smaller firms the proprietor or general manager is usually closely associated with all four steps.

Some Requisites of Effective Research. Retail research cannot be carried on effectively unless two broad conditions are present. First, management must be research-minded. Specifically, it (1) must recognize the importance of developing information to serve as an aid in making decisions; (2) should not be so impatient for results that studies are hurried and conclusions are based upon inadequate data; and (3) should recognize and appreciate the costs involved in productive research.

The second requisite of effective retail research is that it should be conducted by persons thoroughly familiar with scientific research techniques and directed by an individual whose experience and knowledge justify management's confidence in his recommendations. But research should do more than provide recommendations for solving short- and long-term prob-

---

[19] Of course, this research does not have to be of the formal type, nor does it even have to be thought of as research by the executive. A good manager can recognize many problems and sense their solution through day-by-day contact with his business.

[20] That some of the larger organizations are research minded is evidenced by S. O. Kaylin, "Research and Development Program: Key to Ward's Dynamic Leap," *Chain Store Age* (Executives Ed.), December, 1964, pp. 11–40; and "National Association of Food Chains Puts Research Foot Forward," *Super Market Merchandising,* December, 1964, pp. 37–43.

lems. Just as essential is the obligation to raise provocative questions for consideration by top management. And these questions cannot be raised by incompetent personnel! The qualifications of a good research director are reviewed in a later section of this chapter.[21]

Nature and Scope of Retail Research

An understanding of the nature and scope of retail research can best be provided by a brief examination of some of the areas to which research is currently being applied.[22] From this discussion we shall omit that research in retailing which is concerned with such matters as a study of interstore memorandum forms, revision of welcome booklets, and a check of employee and public restrooms. These activities, of course, may be considered necessary and useful, but they are tactical, not strategic, applied not basic, and "not likely to lead to any major new breakthroughs in retailing."[23]

Customer Research. In recent years no subject in the field of marketing, perhaps, has received more attention from social scientists and practitioners than consumer motivation and behavior. Retailers need information regarding consumers as a means of improving their decisions on the goods and services to provide. More and more they are thinking in terms of creating favorable images of their stores and products as inducements to continuous patronage.

Broadly speaking, customer research refers to studies that are focused on customer attitudes, beliefs, buying habits, and motives.[24] It is designed to build up favorable public relationships, first, by providing customers with opportunities to express their views with respect to such matters as merchandise carried, prices charged, and services rendered and, second, by bringing about changes in these matters so that they better fulfill the customers' wants. The actual research is usually carried out by telephone calls, mail inquiries, and personal and group interviews, although a few retailers make use of consumer panels.

A good illustration of consumer research is a recent study conducted by Federated Department Stores. For a specific division of the firm, answers were sought to two main questions: (1) What is the present customer mix

---

[21] See p. 778, below.

[22] Some of the illustrations were prepared by Robert Arkell and are used here with his permission. For another classification of areas where research is important cf. Frank Mayans, "Research in Retailing," *Retail Control,* May, 1966, pp. 33–44.

[23] Landsman, *op. cit.*

[24] Cf. H. I. Isaacson, "Why Not Research the Consumer?" *New York Retailer,* December, 1965, pp. 2–6; and "The Image Builders," *Women's Wear Daily,* May 31, 1966, pp. 1, 45.

(income, age, occupation) and what should this mix be in ten years? (2) If the division wants to increase its share of the market among important market segments (such as women working downtown, higher price-line customers, blue-collar customers) what does it need to do? Among other matters, the study revealed that the division had its strongest appeal to upper-middle income families, a "group expected to grow tremendously in the next decade." Furthermore, the research made it possible "to compute how much added business the store would have simply on the basis of the customer mix of the future as people's income rose."[25]

Sales Projections. In our discussion of the merchandise budget in Chapter 14 it was pointed out that "the first step . . . is to plan sales."[26] While some retailers do their sales planning "by guess and by gosh," others base their forecasts on a considerable amount of research. Such a firm as Sears, Roebuck and Co. estimates its sales five years in advance, correcting those forecasts from time to time as conditions warrant. About six to nine months prior to a specific selling season (for example, in January for the following fall season), this forecast is "firmed up" for that season. With such a forecast, a retailer can proceed to the planning of his other activities with a greater degree of assurance.

Product and Assortment Research. Research concerning the products and assortments to handle in the light of expected sales and available floor space involves both customer studies as well as information from other areas. In view of the increasing variety of products offered by resources,[27] such research becomes more essential for profitable operation with each passing day. Moreover, as the Retail Marketing Manager of E. I. duPont de Nemours & Company, stated recently: "The retailer can play an important part in working toward new products that mean increased consumer satisfaction if he is . . . willing to look beyond today's sales and make an investment in the long term."[28]

A recent development of some significance in product and assortment research is the formation of marketing research organizations which purchase information related to product movement "from food chains and wholesalers, process it into usable form, and resell it in regular reports to manufacturers."[29] Through scientific sampling techniques that yield a rea-

[25] Mayans, *op. cit.,* p. 36.

[26] P. 406, above.

[27] The number of items handled in supermarkets, for example, has grown from 3,750 in 1950 to 7,100 in 1965. Cf. "High Lights of U.S. Food Retailing—1965," *Progressive Grocer,* April, 1966, p. 56.

[28] "Research Needed at Retail Level, Stores are Told," *Women's Wear Daily,* March 3, 1966, p. 32.

[29] "Researchers Snap Up Supermarket 'Secrets'," *Business Week,* March 5, 1966, p. 83. Also cf. "MRCA Gets Rich Supermarket Data," *ibid.,* April 30, 1966, p. 134.

sonably accurate national picture, computer analysis makes it possible to issue reports to clients just one week after the information is collected. The research organizations engaged in this work, including, among others, the Market Research Corporation of America, Selling-Areas-Marketing, Inc., and Speedata Corp., are challenging the long-established store audits conducted by A. C. Nielsen Company and Audits and Surveys, Inc.

Management Research. Research having to do with the overall management of a retail organization is illustrated by a study of the responsibility and authority of all key management positions. Such a project may involve a comparison of the organization structure of the firm in the light of defined goals with that of its competitors. Another example is a study of the various reports flowing to top management for its guidance. One study of this type recommended that some reports be dropped or consolidated, that others be added, and that the timing and methods of preparation for others be changed.

Merchandising Research. This type of research, which is concerned primarily with the problem of gathering, summarizing, and interpreting merchandising statistics, is steadily assuming greater significance. At least three main factors are responsible for this development: (1) the tremendous volume of merchandising data becoming available, (2) the mounting complexity of the information retail management must understand to make valid merchandising decisions, and (3) the "speed virtually beyond comprehension by which this volume of data can be collected, transported, stored, retrieved, and processed."[30]

As a specific illustration of merchandising research, one store was on the verge of notifying a prominent manufacturer of men's clothing that his line would be discontinued because it carried a lower markup than competing brands. When the research department found that alteration costs, markdowns, and other cost aspects were lower on the brand in question than on directly competitive lines, however, it was concluded that the lower markup was more than offset by these savings. Consequently, a profitable item was retained rather than discarded.[31]

Advertising and Display Research. A few illustrations will indicate the nature of such research. In one store the jewelry department was showing unsatisfactory results. Investigation revealed (1) that sales volume had declined; (2) that unimpressive unit displays were used with most of the stock in drawers behind the counter; and (3) that a competitor, whose volume was rising, had extensive displays of jewelry on the counter with

---

[30] Cf. Robert Beyer, *op. cit.*, pp. 57–58.

[31] For specific studies of product profitability, cf. R. D. Buzzell, *Product Profitability Measurement and Merchandising Decisions* (Boston, Mass.: Harvard Graduate School of Business Administration, 1965).

spotlights to focus attention on them. Steps to improve displays were taken; volume gained 15–20 percent immediately and remained at a satisfactory level. In another store, a specific study of direct-mail pieces was undertaken to be sure the recipients were not those already being reached by the firm's newspaper advertisement. A food chain has used advertising and display research to test the effectiveness of special displays in the sale of specific food products, to determine how best to group products on the shelves of a self-service operation, to analyze a number of special promotions, and to measure the sales effectiveness of various labels.

Personnel Research. Today the significance of the human factor in the success of a business is widely recognized. Yet,

No part of the productive resources of industry operates at lower efficiency than the human resources. The few enterprises that have been able to tap this unused reservoir of human ability and attitude have achieved spectacular increases . . . management of men should be the first and foremost concern of operating management rather than the management of things.[32]

It is in view of the foregoing situation that the importance of personnel research comes into focus.

Personnel research covers human relations problems involving rank-and-file employees and also executives. It is a broad and constantly expanding area of study embodying activities associated with selection, training, compensation, and evaluation of employees at all levels. Research projects are now being conducted in many stores to obtain answers to such questions as the following: Are aptitude tests desirable in the selection of employees? What is the degree of correlation between results of aptitude tests and the demonstrated ability of employees under actual working conditions? Is our store competitive in training methods, salaries, and promotional schedules with other stores in the city? How effective is our follow-up when transfers and separations are involved?

Operating Research. This type of research involves the investigation of problems related to operating activities of the store.[33] It includes such matters as store layout; maintenance of the building; all forms of customer service; and receiving, marking, and warehouse operations. High service standards may be set by top management, but careful follow-up through research studies is essential to determine whether they are being maintained. For example, one establishment, concerned over its high marking room

---

[32] Peter Drucker in *The New Society,* quoted by Matt Wigginton, "Responsibility in Decentralized Multi-Unit Operations," *Retail Control,* April, 1966, p. 38.

[33] Increasingly, the term "operations research" is being applied to all forms of scientific research in retailing, particularly operational problems and customer studies. We shall use the term in its more limited sense as defined in the text.

costs, investigated the problem and found that checkers were opening each box of hosiery to determine the total quantity in the shipment. By changing to an outside-of-box count only, and relying upon markers' tickets and the number of price tickets attached to goods to reveal the total figure, costs were reduced and goods moved through the marking room more rapidly.

Systems Research. The increasing complexity of business, accompanied by the growing demand for prompt and accurate data upon which to base decisions, has generated the need for improved information systems based on such technological advances as the vastly improved sales registers and EDP. And the role of systems in store management is certain to expand still more in the future as advances in equipment technology continue.

The need for research in the systems area is emphasized by an existing paradox. In the words of a public accounting executive: "While the time available for reaction in business [to the urgent need for systems work] is being shortened, the preparation time required in the systems area is being lengthened significantly. With today's methods and . . . level of systems training . . . we can look forward to years of preparation. . . ."[34]

Despite this paradox, the "information revolution" will generate an accelerating search for better retailing methods. Systems research will render valuable assistance in this search through developing data useful in providing greater knowledge about customer behavior patterns and preferences regarding styles and prices. It will aid also in evaluating alternative advertising programs and relieve buyers of the trouble of making repetitive and routine decisions regarding staple items. These and other benefits will likely be accomplished, at least among the larger organizations, through a centralized "Information Management Facility."[35]

Correspondence Research. Research of this type involves studies of a store's correspondence with its customers and merchandise resources. Such studies are designed to enhance sales through greater customer good will and improved relationships with vendors. By setting up tests and applying results to the store's correspondence, research may increase the store's reputation and prestige in the community.

Basic Retail Research. As indicated by the foregoing paragraphs, most of the current retail research deals with day-by-day operating problems. Such research draws "upon a reservoir of existing ideas and techniques—psychological, managerial, and technological. It is directed at meeting current competition, but not through innovation; it strives to increase sales, but

---

[34] Robert Beyer, *op. cit.,* p. 64. This source presents nine basic steps in applying systems planning to the retail organization.

[35] *Ibid.,* pp. 61–63.

only through customary inducements; it looks to more efficient customer services, but only within the framework of traditional procedures."[36]

Research on day-by-day operating problems is of great importance and needs to be expanded. At the same time, there is a growing opinion that more basic research, which might lead to significant innovations in retailing, must be undertaken.[37] It has been suggested that this type of research might study such problems as:

1. What are the predictable changes in consumer tastes, wants, and satisfactions deriving from the single fact that twice as many youngsters are going to college now as did a decade ago?

2. Are our stores properly organized to capture more and more consumer dollars? Do traditional department and classification breakdowns we have lived with for years parallel what the consumer thinks of when she comes in to buy? How can these classifications be flexible?

3. How much do we really know about the potentials of after-hours, Saturday night, and Sunday selling, of merchandising geared to convenience?

4. Have we really thought through the automobile revolution that General Wood (retired head, Sears, Roebuck) foresaw? Are we even now meeting more than a fraction of the customer's needs centering around the auto?

5. Have we given adequate thought to the tremendous field of services of all kinds—insurance, travel, gift shopping, perhaps using our mailing lists effectively to sell the services of other businesses?

6. Have we really learned the full lesson that the discount house taught us about how appliances can be sold more cheaply if one sells them according to clearly defined services or the lack of them?

7. Are we right in assuming that the millions of dollars we spend year after year in taking markdowns is really the only way to move slow merchandise? Would premiums, such as the soap people use, perhaps move them faster?

8. Are we keeping close watch on the fact that children are getting bigger in planning our stocks to predictably "popular" sizes? Or are we losing a lot of sales because we do not have big enough sizes—or big enough shoes, for example? Who really knows?

9. What sort of systems and equipment, designed especially for our needs, are we developing to reduce the delays, errors and monumental foul-ups in our so-called customer services, merchandise handling methods, and office procedures?

10. What are we doing to develop simpler, more effective, less costly information and communications systems, to replace the frightful ones we have to live with simply because we have failed to demonstrate how unproductive, misleading and expensive they really are?

11. Who has started an experimental store simply to try out and pilot new ideas? If not, why not?[38]

---

[36] H. F. Clark and H. S. Sloan, quoted by Samuel Feinberg, "From Where I Sit," *Women's Wear Daily*, February 14, 1962, p. 4.

[37] Cf. J. V. Petrof, "The Need for More Abstract Thinking in Retailing," *Journal of Retailing*, Vol. XLI, No. 2 (Summer, 1965), pp. 16–18.

[38] Landsman, *op. cit.* For other suggestions by Professor R. D. Entenberg, cf. Samuel Feinberg, "From Where I Sit," *Women's Wear Daily*, February 11, 1966, p. 11.

While some basic research may be carried out by the research departments of individual firms, in university bureaus of research, and through trade associations, further joint efforts by many retailers may offer the best approach. Perhaps the retail field needs a Retailing Science Institute organized along the lines of the Marketing Science Institute established in 1960 to develop fundamental knowledge in the marketing field, including retailing, and to make its findings widely available.

Conducting Retail Research

As has been indicated previously, effective research activities necessitate proper management attitudes and, in large retail organizations at least, a research staff qualified to conduct them. The latter point requires amplification.

An Independent or a Salaried Research Department? In facing this question it is easy to conclude that the employment of an independent man to conduct research should be resorted to only by the small retail organization which cannot afford to maintain its own full-time, salaried research department. In practice, however, this conclusion does not receive wide support. Certain large retail organizations maintain that the use of independent research men reduces their cost, since even the large company may not want to carry on research at all times. It allows the firm to employ a research counselor who is especially well equipped to handle the particular problem to be investigated, and who has a completely objective point of view. Lacking close personal friends in the company, he can be thorough in his investigation and make the recommendations he considers advisable without fearing that a friend will lose his job.[39]

At the same time, it can be argued with validity that a large retail organization should be conducting research at all times, and doing so through independent agencies is too expensive. Also, a full-time department can acquire a vast amount of information about the firm for which it is working—information on policies, clientele, and competitors—which enables it to do its work in a shorter period of time and with less trouble to the executives of the firm.

The advantages of continuous research are so great that in the large retail organization it seems advisable to employ a full-time research director on a

---

[39] One very successful retail organization reports to the authors that a shift from a company owned to an independent research organization resulted in uncovering many facts not previously known. Of course, much depends on the quality of the outside researcher; some companies have discovered to their sorrow that the methods of some market researchers leave much to be desired. Cf. T. J. Murray, "The Muddle in Marketing Research," *Dun's Review and Modern Industry,* January, 1965, pp. 50–56.

salary basis. This step has been taken by several leading concerns in the department store, chain, and mail-order fields. For special research jobs requiring skills that the director might not possess, or for investigations that directly touch the security of the positions of certain close friends of the director, however, it is probably wise to make use of an independent investigator.[40]

Qualifications of the Research Director. Irrespective of whether the research director is independent or a full-time employee of the retailer, he should possess certain qualifications.[41] He needs to be well trained in the principles and methods of research and to have a considerable background of actual experience both in research and, preferably, also in retailing. Without this experience in retailing, his recommendations are likely to be looked upon by some of the firm's executives as "theoretical"; and they probably will be less sound than those a more experienced man would make. In addition, the director should be able to gain the confidence of the firm's executives so that they will cooperate with him in gathering data. In drawing conclusions, he should be objective and show a keen analytical sense. Moreover, he should be familiar with current subjects requiring practical research in his company and have the capacity to raise pertinent questions regarding future plans. Finally, the abilities to write and to present orally short, convincing reports are important. Unfortunately, there exists today a glaring shortage of research professionals who posses these qualifications.

The Research Report. The research report made to management should be concise and yet complete enough to provide the essential data required to interpret properly the findings. Clearly it should avoid terminology unfamiliar to its readers. Effective organization and presentation are necessary to bring into focus the important conclusions. Since many executives are not "figure-minded," they dislike detailed statistics. They are concerned primarily with the results of studies made, their significance in connection with the problem at hand, and the reasons for and recommendations concerning future action. These facts should guide the report writer.

Research Assignments. The research director in the large store should both report to and be considered an "arm" of the general manager, by

---

[40] Some firms follow the policy of assigning particular problems demanding study to young men in their organizations, especially to young college men. Such a plan enables the employee to acquire a vast amount of information about the company in a short time, gives the company an objective analysis of the problem, and provides an opportunity for the employee to demonstrate his ability to organize and present his findings effectively.

[41] How the research director for a manufacturer actually spends his time is detailed in Richard Osk, "A Day in the Life of a Marketing Research Director," *Sales Management,* April 15, 1966, pp. 33–38. A "Survey of Marketing Research Directors of *Fortune* 500 Firms," will be found in an article with this title by J. R. Krum in the *Journal of Marketing Research,* Vol. III, No. 3 (August, 1966), pp. 313–17.

assisting the latter to coordinate the activities for which he is responsible. Thus, a large number of the projects handled by the research department will originate with the general manager. But this is by no means the sole source. As a matter of fact, if the research director is capable and succeeds in winning the confidence of the various department executives, he will find these executives constantly coming to him with problems. The merchandise manager needs assistance in evaluating the type of sales recording equipment that will be most helpful in controlling inventories in various departments. The operating manager is concerned with the causes of an increase in customers' returns of merchandise. The sales manager of the automotive accessory chain wants to know how to get the store managers to cooperate in carrying out suggestions from headquarters.

In some organizations, all assignments originate in the two ways suggested by the foregoing paragraph, that is, either from the general manager or from another executive. In contrast, although the approval of the general manager is usually necessary before the actual investigation can begin, some firms allow the research director to originate many projects of his own. There is some evidence that this is being done to an increasing degree. Firms following this policy find it especially necessary that their research director be a man of broad background in retailing, and familiar with current developments in the field.

KEEPING "CURRENT"

As suggested early in this chapter, all retailers, regardless of size, should keep abreast of changing conditions and adapt their policies and practices to these changes. In the highly dynamic era in which they operate at present this two-fold obligation is difficult to fulfill. How, then, does the retailer learn about the developments in our dynamic economy so that he may adjust his internal operations to them?

Among small retailers, this knowledge of changing conditions, insofar as an effort is made to obtain it, is secured through the efforts of the proprietor. A vast amount of information can be acquired by watching competitive developments in the immediate vicinity; reading trade papers; traveling; attending conventions; and talking with salesmen, manufacturers, and competitors.

Even among large firms the general manager relies heavily upon these same sources, although in a minority of concerns they are supplemented in various ways. The director of research may investigate and report on all changes which come to his attention. Perhaps the firm subscribes to some advisory services which provide forecasts as to inventories of manufacturers, the business situation, and wholesale and retail prices. Or it may employ an economist who keeps executives informed regarding external changes and suggests what might be done in the light of these conditions. Whenever the organization is large enough, the use of an economist seems highly advisable since he is not so close to day-by-day operations that he "cannot see the forest because of the trees."

It should be emphasized that, whether it is formally recognized or not, making adjustments to changing conditions always involves forecasting or projecting operations into the future. Such forecasts are made in the various budgets—merchandise, expense, and financial. Prompt action is required, of course, when experience or observation reveals a deviation from planned or anticipated conditions.

Looking Ahead on Automation

In concluding this section on keeping abreast of changing conditions, stress should again be placed on the area of automation. Since retailing tomorrow may be affected so much by this factor, management has a special responsibility to be informed about it.[42] One authority suggests this responsibility includes the following:

1. Management should become familiar with all the latest developments in the mechanization and automation of retailing operations, including the current status of electronic data processing.[43]
2. It should make a careful evaluation of the company's needs and requirements and the suitability of the available equipment or processes in the light of the firm's needs.
3. Assuming that investigation reveals the need and value of mechanization, make plans for installation of system and anticipate the problems likely to arise. At least two major areas will require study: (a) choosing the activities to be covered such as classification control, control at the item level, accounts receivable, and promotion; and (b) making the organizational changes necessary to carry out the installations.
4. Scheduling the conversions involved in the application of the new system to the various activities to be included.

---

[42] This responsibility rests on the small retailer as well as the large one. For suggestions on evaluating the potential benefits of computers to small retailers, cf. D. H. Sanders, *Introducing Computers to Small Business* (Park Ridge, Ill.: Data Processing Management Association, 1966).

[43] Cf. W. F. Jones, "Automating the Retailer," *Retail Control,* May, 1966, pp. 46–52; and Arthur Voight and Richard Benson, "Status of Data Processing Today," *ibid.,* April, 1966, pp. 54–64. By no means are all retailers advocates of EDP. Although growing in use and yielding benefits to many, its glamour and pretentious promise are losing their luster for some stores. Cf. reports of experience with it in various cities in *Women's Wear Daily,* June 20, 1966, pp. 14–22.

5. Review the new installations continuously to discover unanticipated developments in operation and to improve their usefulness as tools of management.

6. Look to the future, seeking constantly to be prepared to meet the challenges and the opportunities our growing economy will provide. "The stores of the 1970s and beyond are taking shape today."[44]

THE FOLLOW-THROUGH IN COORDINATION

Once again, we need to stress the fact that effective coordination of retail activities is impossible without constant attention and follow-through by top management. Far too many retailers, for example, have established research departments which have turned out recommendations; but these recommendations, after acceptance, have not actually been put into operation or have been put into operation in a very half-hearted manner. Unless top management is actively interested in following through on the recommendations of its research department, or has good reasons for not doing so at the time, the department should be abolished, no matter how good it may be. Otherwise, it is just "going through the motions," and needless costs are being incurred.

As noted previously, one of the duties of the research department is to make a follow-up report on all of its adopted recommendations. In the smaller store this follow-up becomes the direct obligation of the proprietor. But regardless of the size of the firm, this report is so important that it should be made the definite responsibility of someone in the organization.

Communication Essential

The "follow-through" so essential to effective coordination requires a well-developed system of communication within the retail organization, since the desired adjustments cannot be made unless the personnel is fully informed as to what is expected of them. In the small store it is not difficult for the proprietor to inform his employees of the plans he has in mind to adjust to present or future conditions. He has ample opportunity to chat with them either individually or in a group as to his plans. As the store grows larger, however, and as contact between proprietor and employee becomes less frequent, communication should be placed on a more formal basis. Meetings should be scheduled; and written statements of plans and the reasons for them should be disseminated at the appropriate time.

The task of communication is especially difficult for the chain-store organization with widely scattered units. Although also relying heavily upon

---

[44] Robert Beyer, *op. cit.,* p. 65.

written material, such firms as J. C. Penney Company still like to have their people "talk things over." To this end, planned meetings are held throughout the organization: the headquarters operating committee of seven key executives meeting twice a week; all zone managers as a group coming to the New York headquarters several times a year and for a period of a week once a year, together with all district managers; district managers gathering each week with their zone manager; store managers being visited in their stores periodically by their district manager and meeting once a quarter with him in a group; and, finally, each store manager consulting daily with his staff. The easy communication made possible by these meetings and similar ones in other companies is an important factor in explaining the coordination evident to the observer of the J. C. Penney Company and other well-managed companies.

REVIEW AND DISCUSSION QUESTIONS

1. State the case for the statement: "The first duty of management is to operate profitably." Can you think of any valid arguments against this statement?
2. In your own words, define the term "coordination" as applied to the retail organization.
3. Who in the retail organization should be responsible for the coordination function? Differentiate between this responsibility in the large store and the small one.
4. Explain briefly the major tools of coordination for the retailer. Do you consider any one most important? Why or why not?
5. How do you account for the fact that operating and merchandising cost standards are in much wider use than other types of internal standards?
6. What steps are involved in setting cost standards for a particular retailer? Illustrate.
7. Obtain copies of the annual surveys of merchandising and operating results for department and specialty stores issued by the Controllers' Congress, National Retail Merchants Association in the FOR and MOR reports. Compare and contrast the types of information presented in each report.
8. Examine recent copies of *Fairchild's Financial Manual of Retail Stores* and the Annual Report on Food Retailing published by the *Progressive Grocer*. Report to the class on the kinds and usefulness of the information contained in each publication.
9. Explain precisely how the budget can be used as a coordinating tool by management.
10. Assume that you have been asked to explain the importance of research in retailing to one of your associates. What points would you cover and in what sequence would you arrange them?
11. Under present conditions, in what areas of retailing do you believe research would prove most fruitful? State your reasons.

12. Differentiate between applied research and basic research in the field of retailing. Give illustrations of each type.

13. "Retail research should do more than provide recommendations for solving short- and long-term problems. Just as essential is the obligation to raise provocative questions for consideration by top management." Discuss!

14. What is meant by the "business information revolution?" What factors are responsible for this development and what problems has it created for retailing management?

15. Discuss briefly the specific areas of management responsibility in connection with the growth of automation in retailing.

SUPPLEMENTARY READINGS

BLANKENSHIP, A. B., AND DOYLE, J. B. *Marketing Research Management* (New York: American Management Association, 1965). In this well-organized volume, the authors offer "organization and functional clues on how to run an efficient research operation."

CARPENTER, R. N. *Guidelist for Marketing Research and Economic Forecasting* (New York: American Management Association, 1966). This volume provides an outline of publications and other sources of data related to all phases of marketing, including retailing.

FEINBERG, SAMUEL. *How Do You Manage?* (New York: Fairchild Publications, Inc., 1965). Business leadership and its effectiveness in relation to the main functions of management are discussed by a long observer of the retail scene in this volume.

GUTTMAN, A. H. "The Function of Retail Research," in National Retail Merchants Association, *The Buyer's Manual* (4th ed.; New York: The Association, 1965), pp. 388–99. Written by the director of research, Bloomingdale's, New York City, this article summarizes the need for and uses of research in retail stores.

KAUFMAN, FELIX. "Data Systems that Cross Company Boundaries," *Harvard Business Review,* Vol. XLIV, No. 1 (January–February, 1966), pp. 141–55. The author examines the impact of automation on business organization and policies and describes the nature and operation of a computer network.

KEPNER, C. H., AND TREGOR, B. B. *The Rational Manager: A Systematic Approach to Problem Solving and Decision Making* (New York: McGraw-Hill Book Co., Inc., 1965). This practical book is concerned mainly with a sound approach to business-problem solving and taking corrective action to improve future prospects.

LINOWES, D. F. "The Top Executive's New Look," *Management Services,* May–June, 1966, pp. 15–25. The author suggests a set of general duty outlines for the job of the chief executive under present conditions.

"Marketing Through Retailers," *Department Store Economist,* April, 1966, pp. 20–25. This report on a national forum of the American Management Association provides an excellent summary of the obligations and opportunities of retailing as viewed by executives of leading firms in the field.

MAYANS, FRANK. "Research in Retailing," *Retail Control,* May, 1966, pp. 33–34. The operating vice president for marketing research of Federated Department Stores presents a comprehensive picture of the functions and uses of research by retailers.

MCNEAL, J. U. *Dimensions of Consumer Behavior* (New York: Appleton-Century-Crofts, 1965). This book of readings covers three aspects of consumer behavior: psychological, sociological, and research techniques.

MESSNER, JOHANNES. *The Executive: His Key Position in Contemporary Society* (St. Louis: B. Herder Book Co., 1965). How the executive's role is affected by sociological and other forces in our economy is reviewed in this treatment.

MITCHELL, W. N. *The Business Executive in a Changing World* (New York: American Management Association, 1965). This volume analyzes the major executive functions and tells how they may be performed best in our dynamic economy.

NATIONAL RETAIL MERCHANTS ASSOCIATION, RETAIL RESEARCH INSTITUTE. *Operations Research in Retailing—Case Studies* and *Electronic Data Processing for Retailers* (New York: The Association, n.d.). These two publications furnish basic information on various applications of operations research to retailing functions. An updating service is also available to keep retailers abreast of the latest developments in this rapidly growing field.

NEWMAN, W. H., AND LOGAN, J. P. *Business Policies and Central Management* (5th ed.; Cincinnati, Ohio: Southwestern Publishing Co., 1965). One of the better combination text and case books in the field, this volume integrates recent concepts into a sound analytical framework.

OLIVE, B. A. *Management: A Selected List of Books, Pamphlets, and Journals* (Ithaca, N.Y.: Cornell University, Graduate School of Business and Public Administration, 1965). This comprehensive, interdisciplinary bibliography on the administrative sciences is a valuable reference for students and practitioners alike.

PERHAM, JOHN. "Where are Tomorrow's Executives?" *Dun's Review and Modern Industry,* June, 1966, pp. 36, 91–93. In this article a presidents' panel "discusses the causes and cure of a growing problem."

"Prediction Reporting," *Chain Store Age* (Executives Edition), March, 1966, pp. E32–E34. "Crystal ball gazing [has developed] into a respectable and valuable management function, a useful tool in fashioning vital decisions affecting the future." The publisher terms this process "Prediction Reporting."

REILLY, P. J. *Old Masters of Retailing* (New York: Fairchild Publications, Inc., 1966). Reviewing the founding and present status of 35 prominent stores in this country, Canada, and England, this treatment provides valuable insights to the managerial problems and tactics of retail executives.

SAMPSON, R. C. *Managing the Managers.* (New York: McGraw-Hill Book Company, 1965). The chief value of this volume to the retailer is the application of behavioral sciences to the day-to-day problems confronting him.

SUPER MARKET INSTITUTE. *The Personal Problems of Management* (Chicago: The Institute, 1966). This collection of nine essays takes "a searching look at the life of an executive and the ways his business responsibilities involve his personal life."

VALENTINE, R. F. *Performance Objectives for Managers* (New York: American Management Association, 1966). "This handbook sets forth . . . the new dynamic concept of managing by objectives and demonstrates how managerial efficiency can be increased by following logical techniques."

WASSON, C. R. *Research Analysis for Marketing Decision* (New York: Appleton-Century-Crofts, 1965). In eleven chapters of 278 pages, all aspects of distribution research are discussed. Emphasis is placed on the significant management questions for which research can offer aid.

WOLFE, H. D. *Business Forecasting Methods* (New York: Holt, Rinehart and Winston, Inc., 1966). Emphasizing that good forecasting requires good tools, the author presents the "measured and methodical steps" for making forecasts.

INDEX

Index

*This book has been set in 11 point Garamond
#3, leaded 2 points and 10 point Garamond
#3, leaded 1 point. Chapter numbers are 36
point Jefferson Gothic and part numbers are
24 point Garamond Bold. Chapter titles and
part titles are 18 point Garamond Bold. The
size of the type page is 27 by 46½ picas.*